PROPERTIES OF LAW

Essays in Honour of Jim Harris

Properties of Law

Essays in Honour of Jim Harris

Edited by
TIMOTHY ENDICOTT
JOSHUA GETZLER
and
EDWIN PEEL

OXFORD
UNIVERSITY PRESS

OXFORD
UNIVERSITY PRESS

Great Clarendon Street, Oxford OX2 6DP

Oxford University Press is a department of the University of Oxford.
It furthers the University's objective of excellence in research, scholarship,
and education by publishing worldwide in

Oxford New York

Auckland Cape Town Dar es Salaam Hong Kong Karachi
Kuala Lumpur Madrid Melbourne Mexico City Nairobi
New Delhi Shanghai Taipei Toronto

With offices in

Argentina Austria Brazil Chile Czech Republic France Greece
Guatemala Hungary Italy Japan Poland Portugal Singapore
South Korea Switzerland Thailand Turkey Ukraine Vietnam

Oxford is a registered trade mark of Oxford University Press
in the UK and in certain other countries

Published in the United States
by Oxford University Press Inc., New York

First published 2006

British Library Cataloguing in Publication Data
Data available

Library of Congress Cataloging in Publication Data
Data available

Typeset by Newgen Imaging Systems (P) Ltd., Chennai, India
Printed in Great Britain
on acid-free paper by
Biddles Ltd., King's Lynn, Norfolk

ISBN 0–19–929096–2 978–0–19–929096–3

1 3 5 7 9 10 8 6 4 2

Foreword

It was my privilege to be taught by Jim Harris, to whose memory this volume is dedicated. I changed late from classics to law, and the accommodation he effected for me meant that for a term I had tutorials alone with him. The experience was austere, bleak, riveting, exhilarating. Those lessons are the foundation of my thinking even now. A lapse into loose thought, a failure to 'find out what the cases say, first', a superfluity or obscurantism, a lapse into pedantry, an error of system or method, finds rebuke in the memory of his intellectual power, his dedication to clean, productive thought, and his capacity for creative synthesis in law. Above all, there is the memory of his rigour, exacted always of himself but demanded also of his students: rigour that, properly applied, is rewarded with creative insight.

The congeniality and humour—occasionally in tutorials, and lavishly on feast occasions—came after. For that was Jim's path—vision as a product of stern application. It led to a life of bounteous professional creativity, detailed, dissected, and honoured in the pages that follow. The essays that Timothy Endicott, Joshua Getzler, and Edwin Peel have collected and edited are a fitting tribute to Jim's written work, for they span his creative sweep and reflect the complexity of his legacy. They also honour the power and grace of his person, for he engendered respect, trust, admiration, and loyalty in those privileged to know him.

There is an aching poignancy in the fact that this is not a *Festschrift*, garlanded by colleagues and pupils and presented during Jim's lifetime, but a volume in his memory. He died sooner than he ought. The world has need of him, for his engagement with the human rights concepts that in many jurisdictions now shape legal thought and practice held high promise of practically significant innovation. In his last major paper, he claimed to have established the different existence-conditions for different kinds of rights. This was to be the start of a longer and important journey of conceptual discovery. That task his death now leaves his successors to fulfil. This volume in his memory is a start. The rest remains with us.

Edwin Cameron

Johannesburg, South Africa
2 July 2005

Preface

Jim Harris was one of the giants of academic law of the late twentieth century. He was also a remarkable man, possessed of deep faith, quiet courage, and a lively, liberal mind. The chapters of this book, which address the major themes of Jim Harris's work, reflect the admiration and affection the contributors feel for him, tempered with sadness that we cannot present the volume to him as we had planned.

To the contributors we offer thanks for all they have done to celebrate Jim Harris. The essays demonstrate the breadth of Jim's influence, both as a teacher and as a writer, on generations of legal scholars. The range of subject matter reflects the formidable breadth of Jim's own work. Important themes run through that work; for convenience, we have grouped the essays in sections dealing with the philosophy of law, the theory of property, the use of precedent in the common law, and the theory of human rights.

We conclude this collection of essays on Jim's work with a note on the life of a man who influenced and inspired the contributors. When Jim was told in 2003 that a *Festschrift* was planned for him, his radiant smile spoke of his pleasure. The contributors knew that he was gravely ill and that time might be short, but such was Jim's steadfast optimism that we felt some hope that he might see the completed book. Now, after his death, we present this book as a tribute to a much-loved man who used his great gifts to enrich the legal and academic community and whose life lit up everyone around him.

Timothy Endicott, Joshua Getzler,
and Edwin Peel

Oxford
21 July 2005

Acknowledgments

The editors are grateful to Professor José Harris, who offered warm encouragement from the start. Our colleague Michael Spence helped us to conceive the volume. We are indebted to our anonymous referees who supplied many valuable suggestions, to Emily Coates for her excellent research assistance, and to the publishers who were highly professional at every stage.

Contents

III. PRECEDENT

IV. HUMAN RIGHTS

List of Contributors

Brian Bix is Frederick W. Thomas Professor of Law and Philosophy, University of Minnesota.

Jes Bjarup is Professor of Jurisprudence in the Juridiska Institutionen, University of Stockholm.

The Honourable Justice Edwin Cameron is a Judge of Appeal in the Supreme Court of Appeal of South Africa.

Hugh Corder is Professor of Public Law and Dean of the Faculty of Law in the University of Cape Town.

Julie Dickson is a Fellow and Tutor in Law, Somerville College, Oxford.

John Eekelaar is a Fellow of Pembroke College, Oxford, and a Reader in Law in the University of Oxford.

Timothy Endicott is a Fellow and Tutor in Law, Balliol College, Oxford.

Richard A. Epstein is the James Parker Hall Distinguished Professor of Law in the University of Chicago, and Peter and Kirsten Bedford Senior Fellow in the Hoover Institution.

Joshua Getzler is a Fellow and Tutor in Law, St. Hugh's College, Oxford.

Tony Honoré is the Regius Professor of Civil Law, Emeritus, at All Souls College, Oxford.

Jeremy Horder is a Fellow of Worcester College, Oxford, and a Reader in Criminal Law in the University of Oxford, and has been a Law Commissioner since January, 2005.

David Lametti is an Associate Professor of Law in the Faculty of Law and Institute of Comparative Law, McGill University.

Stephen R. Munzer is Professor of Law in the School of Law, University of California at Los Angeles.

Stanley L. Paulson is the William Gardner Hammond Professor of Law, Washington University in St. Louis.

Edwin Peel is a Fellow and Tutor in Law, Keble College, Oxford.

James Penner is Professor at the School of Law, King's College London.

Isabelle Rorive is Professor in the Law Faculty and a Fellow in the Centre for Comparative Law and History of Law, University of Brussels (Université Libre de Bruxelles).

Bernard Rudden is the Professor of Comparative Law, Emeritus, in the University of Oxford, and a Fellow of Brasenose College.

Lionel Smith is the James McGill Professor of Law in the Faculty of Law and Institute of Comparative Law, McGill University.

Table of Cases

England and Wales

Scotland

European Court of Justice

European Court of Human Rights

South Africa

Australia

Belgium

Botswana

Canada

Germany

Micronesia

New Zealand

United States

Zambia

Zimbabwe

Table of Legislation

PART I
LEGAL THEORY

1

J.W. Harris's Kelsen

*Stanley L. Paulson**

(i) Introduction

In Britain, just as elsewhere, Hans Kelsen has been recognized by leading figures in the field as the foremost legal philosopher of the twentieth century.[1] At the same time, Kelsen remains outside the mainstream in British legal thought. Four exceptions establish the rule. That is, Kelsen's legal theory has played a genuinely significant role in the work of J.W. Harris, H.L.A. Hart,[2] Sir Hersch Lauterpacht,[3] and Joseph Raz,[4] and their work has, in turn, contributed to a better understanding of Kelsen's legal theory. In Harris's case, I have in mind his monograph on

* I wish to express my gratitude to the Alexander von Humboldt Foundation (Bonn–Bad Godesberg), which supported, *inter alia*, this work through the conferral of the Humboldt Research Prize (2003–4). As awardee, it was my good fortune to be able to spend 19 months in residence at the University of Kiel, and I remain grateful to my host there, Robert Alexy, for his gracious hospitality. I also wish to thank the editors' anonymous referee as well as Bonnie Litschewski Paulson and Torben Spaak, all of whom gave me good advice on the text.

1 HLA Hart, for example, described Kelsen as 'the most stimulating writer on analytical jurisprudence of our day': HLA Hart, 'Kelsen Visited' (1962–3) 10 *UCLA Law Review* 709, 728, reprinted in SL Paulson and BL Paulson (eds.), *Normativity and Norms. Critical Perspectives on Kelsenian Themes* (Clarendon Press, 1998), 69, 87.

2 See HLA Hart, *The Concept of Law* (2nd edn., Clarendon Press, 1994), along with Hart, 'Kelsen Visited', n.1 above, and HLA Hart, 'Kelsen's Doctrine of the Unity of Law', in HE Kiefer and MK Munitz (eds.), *Ethics and Social Justice* (SUNY Press, 1968), 171, reprinted in Paulson and Paulson, n.1 above, 553. See also N Lacey, *A Life of H.L.A. Hart* (OUP, 2004), 249–53 *et passim.*

3 See H Lauterpacht, 'The Nature of International Law and General Jurisprudence' (1932) 12 *Economica* 301, and H Lauterpacht, 'Kelsen's Pure Science of Law', in *Modern Theories of Law* (Preface by WI Jennings, OUP, 1933), 105. See also H Lauterpacht, *The Function of Law in the International Community* (Clarendon Press, 1933), 383–438, and H Lauterpacht, 'Règles générales du droit de la paix' (1937) 62 *Recueil des Cours* 95, paras. 12–13. On Lauterpacht, see M Koskenniemi, 'Hersch Lauterpacht (1897–1974)', in J Beatson and R Zimmermann (eds.), *Jurists Uprooted. German-speaking Émigré Lawyers in Twentieth-century Britain* (OUP, 2004), 601; H Kelsen, 'Hersch Lauterpacht' (1961) 10 *ICLQ* 2.

4 See J Raz, *The Concept of a Legal System* (2nd edn., Clarendon Press, 1980), chs. 3–6, along with J Raz, 'Kelsen's Theory of the Basic Norm' (1974) 19 *American Journal of Jurisprudence* 94, and J Raz, 'The Purity of the Pure Theory' (1981) 35 *Revue Internationale de Philosophie* 441, both reprinted in Paulson and Paulson, n.1 above, 47 and 237 respectively.

Law and Legal Science[5] in particular, but I also draw on some of his other work, both on Kelsen and in a Kelsenian vein.[6]

Three foci stand out in the Kelsenian dimension of Harris's work. First, there is the question of the nature and structure of the legal norm.[7] On the *nature* of the legal norm, Kelsen and Harris appear on first glance to have very similar positions. Harris's nomenclature—the legal norm *qua* 'semantic entity', the legal norm *qua* 'normative meaning-content', and the like[8]—is Kelsenian through and through. I return to the issue in section (ii). On the *structure* of the legal norm, there are readily apparent differences. In Kelsen's mature statements on the matter,[9] the 'independent legal norm' is an empowering norm addressed to the legal official, while 'dependent legal norms'—obligation-imposing and permissory norms addressed to the legal subject—are understood as conditions built into the independent legal norm or, more precisely, into the antecedent clause of its hypothetical formulation. For Harris, it is the obligation-imposing and permissory modalities that capture the structure of the legal norm, which, not incidentally, is addressed to the legal subject, not to the legal official. The difference between the respective views of Kelsen and Harris on the structure of the legal norm reflects the very different criteria they employ in ordering the 'raw materials' of the law.[10]

Both Kelsen and Harris have defensible grounds for the criteria they employ, grounds rooted in their respective assumptions about the goals of legal philosophy. To be sure, Harris criticizes Kelsen's doctrine of empowerment, arguing that it leads to an indefensible doctrine of 'normative alternatives'.[11] The criticism is well-taken, for Kelsen's doctrine of 'normative alternatives' is indeed indefensible. It can—and should—be excised from Kelsen's theory, but doing so would in no way affect Kelsen's doctrine of empowerment. I return to this issue, too, in section (ii).

A second focus is Harris's 'basic legal science *fiat*'.[12] Its fundamental principles—exclusion, subsumption, derogation, and non-contradiction—address a central task of legal science, Harris argues, the systematization of legal norms.[13] Harris

[5] JW Harris, *Law and Legal Science* (Clarendon Press, 1979) (hereafter *LLS*).

[6] JW Harris, 'When and Why does the Grundnorm Change?' (1971) 29 *CLJ* 103; JW Harris, 'Kelsen's Concept of Authority' (1977) 36 *CLJ* 353; JW Harris, 'Kelsen's Pure Theory of Law', in JW Harris, *Legal Philosophies* (Butterworths, 1980), 59; JW Harris, 'Kelsen and Normative Consistency', in R Tur and W Twining (eds.), *Essays on Kelsen* (Clarendon Press, 1986), 201; JW Harris, 'Kelsen, Revolutions and Normativity', in E Attwooll (ed.), *Shaping Revolution* (Aberdeen UP, 1991), 1; JW Harris, 'The Basic Norm and the Basic Law' (1994) 24 *Hong Kong Law Journal* 207; JW Harris, 'Kelsen's Pallid Normativity' (1996) 9 *Ratio Juris* 94.

[7] Throughout the text, I use 'legal norm' rather than the conventional 'legal rule' simply to preserve Kelsen's nomenclature. Joseph Raz has invited attention to the only difference between legal norms and legal rules, namely, that the former but not the latter can be either particular or general. See J Raz, 'Voluntary Obligations and Normative Powers' (1972) 46 *Proceedings of the Aristotelian Society. Supplementary Volume* 79, 79, reprinted in Paulson and Paulson, n. 1 above, 451, 451. See also Harris, *LLS*, n.5 above, 35–6.

[8] Ibid. 11, 13.

[9] See text in section (ii), below.

[10] I draw the phrase from R Pound, 'Law and the Science of Law in Recent Theories' (1933–4) 43 *Yale Law Journal* 525, 526.

[11] See Harris, *LLS*, n.5 above, 87–8.

[12] See ibid. 34, 62, 70–92, 125 (emphasis in original).

[13] See ibid. 10, 12, *et passim*.

rightly remarks that logic as employed in the law—in particular, in the judicial decision—is not peculiarly legal in character, but is, rather, a species of practical reasoning.[14] By contrast, the basic legal science *fiat* does exhibit a 'rule-systematizing logic' peculiar to the law, and this important doctrine lies at the very core of Harris's legal philosophy as sketched in *Law and Legal Science*.

Harris writes that the basic legal science *fiat* is 'derived from Kelsen's concept of the basic norm',[15] and this may be true as an autobiographical statement. The more interesting question, however, is whether the basic legal science *fiat* is an accurate reflection of the basic norm. Here I am sceptical. I argue in section (iii) that Harris's basic legal science *fiat* reflects, instead, the doctrine of hierarchical structure (*Stufenbaulehre*) as understood in the Vienna School of Legal Theory.

A third focus in the Kelsenian dimension of Harris's work is the 'normativity problematic' in the law. Many have argued that Kelsen addresses the problem of normativity, although different writers have attributed to Kelsen very different views in the name of normativity. Harris dismisses Kelsen's 'theory' or 'conception' of normativity as 'narrow, eccentric and etiolated—pallid normativity',[16] but it is not clear that Harris's view captures the import of 'normative' in Kelsen's legal theory. Whereas Kelsen, from the beginning, went to great lengths to challenge those defending naturalism in legal science, developing a normative or non-naturalistic theory of legal science as his alternative, Harris criticizes Kelsen's 'theory of normativity' on the ground that its force in explicating the legal 'ought' is so weak as to make hash of the notion.

There is an irony in Harris's position here. His aim, especially in *Law and Legal Science*, has been to show that Kelsen's project is best understood as the development of a theory of legal science,[17] and this is a noteworthy thesis. But then, at what is arguably the single most important juncture in Kelsen's work on a theory of legal science, namely, his idea that a normative theory of legal science is the only viable alternative to naturalism in legal science, Harris resorts to brusque dismissal of Kelsen on normativity. I speculate, in section (iv), on how things came to this.

My general thesis is twofold. On the one hand, Harris's work on the structure of the legal norm and, in particular, on the basic legal science *fiat* is both a significant contribution to our understanding of Kelsen and a contribution to legal philosophy as a whole. In particular, the basic legal science *fiat* underscores Harris's illuminating view that Kelsen's theory was, above all, a theory of legal science. On the other hand, I argue that Harris's dismissal of Kelsen on normativity counts as a failure to come to terms with Kelsen's project.

[14] See generally R Alexy, *A Theory of Legal Argumentation* (trans. R Adler and N MacCormick, Clarendon Press, 1989).

[15] Harris, *LLS*, n.5 above, 78.

[16] Harris, 'Kelsen's Pallid Normativity', n.6 above, 95, and see 99; beginning at 102, one or another of these adjectives turns up on nearly every page. See also Harris, 'Kelsen, Revolutions and Normativity', n.6 above, 4, 6, 13; Harris, 'The Basic Norm and the Basic Law', n.6 above, 228.

[17] See Harris, *LLS*, n.5 above, 18–22, 78–83, 105–6, *et passim*.

(ii) On the Nature and Structure of the Legal Norm

As noted above, Kelsen and Harris appear to be saying much the same thing when they address the question of the *nature* of the legal norm. Harris speaks of the legal norm *qua* 'semantic entity', the legal norm *qua* 'normative meaning-content', the legal norm *qua* 'unit of meaning' and *qua* 'unit of meaning-content', and he speaks of the legal system as 'a *field of normative meaning*'.[18] What is more, Harris expressly endorses these distinctly Kelsenian formulations of the nature of the legal norm:

> Despite fluctuations in his views on many other points, Kelsen maintained for half a century the theory that law is pure norm. One of his leading themes was the demonstration that legal rules are abstract entities identifiable neither with the events which give rise to them (their legislative history), nor with the events which constitute their application (judicial or administrative enforcement); and that the sort of abstract entity which they constitute is normative meaning-content.[19]

As I have suggested, Harris endorses Kelsen's formulations of the nature of the legal norm, but he appears to go further than that, endorsing Kelsen on the nature of the legal norm generally. Speaking of Kelsen's thesis in the quoted passage, namely, that law is pure norm, Harris goes on to say: 'On this major point, it will be argued, Kelsen was right.'[20]

Can this ringing endorsement of Kelsen's position be taken at face value? I have my doubts, notwithstanding the fact that Harris's talk of the legal norm as a 'semantic entity', as an 'abstract entity', and the like is indeed Kelsenian. First, Harris does not subscribe to anything remotely like the ontology underlying Kelsen's 'pure norm' thesis. Kelsen had argued that the legal norm *qua* objective sense-content (*Sinngehalt*) is found in a second world[21] not unlike Heinrich Rickert's second world of the sense-content of judgments (*Urteilsgehalt*)[22] or Gottlob Frege's third world of 'thoughts' (*Gedanken*).[23]

[18] Harris, *LLS*, n.5 above, 11, 13, 34, 35 (emphasis in original), and see generally 34–41.

[19] Ibid. 34 (footnote omitted); in support of this interpretation, Harris quotes from H Kelsen, *Pure Theory of Law* (2nd edn., trans. M Knight, U California Press, 1967) (hereafter *PTL*), para. 26, Harris, *LLS*, n.5 above, 35.

[20] Ibid. 34.

[21] On the legal norm *qua* objective sense-content (*Sinngehalt*), see e.g. H Kelsen, *Reine Rechtslehre* (1st edn., Deuticke, 1934), paras. 5, 7, *et passim*. On Kelsen's two-worlds doctrine, see e.g. H Kelsen, *Allgemeine Staatslehre* (Julius Springer, 1925), paras. 5(c), 13(b).

[22] See H Rickert, *Der Gegenstand der Erkenntnis* (6th edn., JCB Mohr, 1928) (hereafter *GE 6*), 248. On the extent to which the ontology of the Baden neo-Kantians is reflected in Kelsen's work, see SL Paulson, 'Faktum/Wert-Distinktion, Zwei-Welten-Lehre und immanenter Sinn. Hans Kelsen als Neukantianer', in R Alexy *et al.* (eds.), *Neukantianismus und Rechtsphilosophie* (Nomos, 2002), 223.

[23] See G Frege, 'Der Gedanke' (1918–19) 1 *Beiträge zur Philosophie des deutschen Idealismus* 58. For the English-language text, 'Thoughts' (trans. P Geach and RH Stoothoff), see G Frege, *Collected Papers on Mathematics, Logic, and Philosophy* (ed. B McGuinness, Blackwell, 1984), 351. On Frege's difficult notion, see the illuminating discussion by T Burge, 'Frege on Knowing the Third Realm' (1992) 101 *Mind* 633.

Secondly, Harris explicates his own notion of 'pure norm' in terms of the practice of legal scientists and legal officials:

> Unfortunately, Kelsen failed to make it clear that laws are pure norms simply because it is the practice of legal scientists (including legal officials) to treat them as such. In other words, the pure-norm theory of law is not about 'law', but about that pervasive institutional discipline, the practice of legal science.[24]

It is not obvious, however, that the practice of legal scientists and legal officials can shed light on the ontology of legal norms, and it is not obvious that Harris's reading of Kelsen in terms of 'legal practice'[25] sheds any light on the matter either. In any case, Harris does not argue the point. As for Kelsen, the ontology that he developed, or at any rate adumbrated, is a direct response to naturalism in legal science. I return to this theme in section (iv).

When Harris turns to the *structure* of the legal norm, he appeals to a doctrine of norm-individuation, following the example of Kelsen and, long before Kelsen, that of Jeremy Bentham.[26] That is, answering the question of structure by turning to criteria of individuation is familiar from Bentham's legal theory—or, more accurately, from the work of those in the latter part of the last century, Hart[27] and Raz[28] in particular, who have drawn on and written about this aspect of Bentham's legal theory. Bentham wrote:

> What is a law? What are the parts of a law? The subject of these questions, it is to be observed, is the *logical*, the *ideal*, the *intellectual* whole, not the *physical* one: the *law* and not the *statute*. An inquiry directed to the latter sort of object, could neither admit of difficulty nor afford instruction.[29]

Bentham answers the question of the structure of the legal norm by appealing to the command. As he is quick to add, however, the command is but one of four aspects of the expression of the legislator's will.[30] To spell out the 'aspects' of legislation is to develop a deontic quadrat, Bentham's remarkable discovery long before the flowering of deontic logic in the twentieth century.

Early in his work, Kelsen introduced a doctrine of individuation that is comparable to Bentham's in some respects, though not in the answer Kelsen gives to the question of structure.

[24] Harris, *LLS*, n.5 above, 35.

[25] See ibid. 34–41 *et passim*; Harris, 'The Basic Norm and the Basic Law', n.6 above, 208–9; Harris, 'Kelsen's Pallid Normativity', n.6 above, 96–7.

[26] For Harris's discussion of Bentham, including Bentham's doctrine of individuation, see Harris, *LLS*, n.5 above, 25–34, 93–4, 117, 147–8.

[27] As Hart neatly puts it, 'to settle the individuation of a law it is necessary to ask not, or not merely, "what is law?" but "what is *a* law?"': HLA Hart, 'Bentham's *Of Laws in General*' (1971) 2 *Rechtstheorie* 55, 57 (emphasis in original).

[28] See Raz, *The Concept of a Legal System*, n.4 above, 50–9, 70–8, 85–92, 140, 146, *et passim*.

[29] J Bentham, *An Introduction to the Principles of Morals and Legislation* (1789), (ed. JH Burns and HLA Hart, Athlone Press, 1970), 301 (emphasis in original).

[30] J Bentham, *Of Laws in General* (ed. HLA Hart, Athlone Press, 1970), ch. 10, esp. 95–8.

The question of whether the legal norm is to be understood as an imperative or as a hypothetical judgment is the question of the *ideal* linguistic form of the legal norm or, indeed, the question of the essence of the objective law. The practical wording used in concrete legal systems is irrelevant to the solution of the problem. The legal norm (in its ideal form) must be constructed from the content of statutes, and the components necessary to this construction are often not present in one and the same statute but must be assembled from several.[31]

Fundamental to individuation, as Kelsen understood it, was the possibility it afforded of distinguishing legal norms from moral norms on the basis of form alone. As he argues in *Main Problems in the Theory of Public Law*[32] and later in his major treatise on constitutional law,[33] the command as an answer to the question of the structure of the legal norm is not a live option, for moral norms, too, are characteristically formulated as commands.[34]

In writings from the late 1930s up to and including the second edition of the *Pure Theory of Law*, which first appeared in 1960, Kelsen's predominant position on individuation is that the legal norm in its 'ideal' or reconstructed form is an empowering norm. Of special interest is Kelsen's examination of Georges Scelle's legal theory.[35] Here Kelsen defines empowerment as 'the capacity to bring about certain legal changes by means of one's behaviour',[36] and he confirms the wide scope of empowerment, from public and private law to public international law. What is more, he introduces the hypothetically formulated sanction-norm *as an empowerment* and characterizes legal obligation in its terms, namely, as one function of the competence to impose sanctions. There is the possibility, Kelsen writes,

of basing the concept of legal obligation ... on that of competence, of tracing legal obligation back to competence. If, namely, the legal obligation of an individual to behave in a certain way is acknowledged as given only if, in the event of the opposite behaviour, another individual is empowered by the legal system to impose a sanction on the first individual, and, furthermore, if the empowerment to impose a sanction counts as 'competence', then the legal obligation of one individual is based on the sanction-competence of the other.[37]

Then, in later works, beginning with *General Theory of Law and State* (1945), Kelsen reinterprets the modal auxiliary 'ought', no longer taking it to be linked directly to legal obligation. Rather, 'ought' is akin to a variable, a placeholder,[38]

[31] H Kelsen, *Hauptprobleme der Staatsrechtslehre* (JCB Mohr, 1911) (hereafter *HP*), 237 (emphasis in original).

[32] See ibid. 36, 40, 42–3, 49–50, 53, 70, 189–245, *et passim*.

[33] See H Kelsen, *Allgemeine Staatslehre* (Julius Springer, 1925), paras. 10–12.

[34] See Kelsen, *HP*, n.31 above, 33–57, 203, *et passim*. For a statement of the entire programme in brief compass, see H Kelsen, *An Introduction to the Problems of Legal Theory* (a translation of the First Edition of the *Reine Rechtslehre*) (trans. BL Paulson and SL Paulson, Clarendon Press, 1992), paras. 10–12.

[35] H Kelsen, 'Recht und Kompetenz. Kritische Bemerkungen zur Völkerrechtstheorie Georges Scelles', in H Kelsen, *Auseinandersetzung zur Reinen Rechtslehre* (ed. K Ringhofer and R Walter, Springer-Verlag, 1987), 1 (the manuscript dates from the late 1930s).

[36] Ibid. 72.

[37] Kelsen, n.35 above, 75.

[38] See H Kelsen, *General Theory of Law and State* (Harvard UP, 1945) (hereafter *GTLS*), 61 (immediately following title of sect. D). To be sure, Kelsen does not state *expressis verbis* in this treatise

designating, *inter alia*, that under certain conditions a sanction *can* be imposed—that is, an official is *empowered* to impose a sanction—while leaving open the question whether there is also an obligation to impose it. Moreover, on Kelsen's new interpretation, if it is clear from the positive law that official *A* is indeed obligated to impose the sanction, this says that a higher official *B* is empowered to impose a sanction on *A* if *A*, under the designated conditions, fails to impose the sanction on the subject. Thus, 'obligation' is simply shorthand for a pair of empowerments found at adjacent levels in the hierarchical structure of the legal system. There is no independent, deontic characterization of legal obligation.

Coming full circle, back to the programme Kelsen announced in *Main Problems in the Theory of Public Law*, the result is this: the legal norm in its ideal or reconstructed form is an empowering norm. This development speaks directly to Kelsen's stated goal, namely, his wish to distinguish the legal norm by means of its '*ideal* linguistic form' as sharply as possible from its counterpart in morality.

In Harris's case, too, the structure of the legal norm reflects the application of a doctrine of norm-individuation. As he neatly puts it:

> The law does not announce, on its face, into what units it can most usefully be split up. There is no *given* structure. We may dip into the well of legislative source-materials with conceptually-shaped buckets of many kinds, and we will then bring up rules, standards, laws of any favoured pattern. One of the tasks of legal theory is to give reasons for preferring one bucket-shape to others.[39]

What then are Harris's criteria for individuation? On first glance, he appears to be appealing to the 'values of legality and constitutionality':[40]

> There are . . . good reasons why [the] normative field should primarily be divided into units called 'positive legal rules'. It is in terms of such units that the values of legality and constitutionality are expressed. . . .[41]

The values of legality and constitutionality cannot, however, serve as Harris's criteria for individuation, for he spells out these values entirely in terms of officials' conformity to law,[42] whereas, as we shall see, his individuated legal norm is addressed to the legal subject.

In fact, Harris draws his criteria for individuation directly from the basic legal science *fiat*.[43] Early in *Law and Legal Science*, he sets out his most complete

the doctrine of 'ought' *qua* placeholder. As I read him, however, the doctrine is understood when the present text is coupled with that of 'Recht und Kompetenz'; see quotation in the text at n.37. The doctrine of 'ought' *qua* placeholder is stated explicitly in later texts. See Kelsen, *PTL*, n.19 above, paras. 4(b), 18, 28(b). HLA Hart, J Raz, and JW Harris have all invited attention to this shift in Kelsen's doctrine of 'ought'. See Hart, 'Kelsen's Doctrine of the Unity of Law', n.2 above, 186, reprinted in Paulson and Paulson, n.1 above, 569–70; Raz, *The Concept of a Legal System*, n.4 above, 47; Harris, *LLS*, n.5 above, 40–1; Harris, 'Kelsen's Pallid Normativity', n.6 above, 100–1.

39 Harris, *LLS*, n.5 above, 92 (emphasis in original).

40 See ibid. 20, 95.

41 Ibid. 20.

42 See ibid. 11–12, 50, 74, *et passim*.

43 See ibid. 20–1, 70–1, 92–106.

statement on the structure of the legal norm:

The internal structural elements of each positive legal rule, it will be argued, are three in number[:] the act-situation which is the subject of the duty or exception from duty, an *ought* or *may* deontic operator, and the specification of the conditions under which the duty or exception from duty exists.[44]

Harris argues, first, that the basic legal science *fiat* describes 'individual legal rules imposing duties or granting exceptions to duties',[45] secondly, that 'different parts of legislative material originating in the same source, and different materials originating in different sources, will often have to be read together to yield the content of a single rule',[46] and, thirdly, that other, more complex units are reducible to the basic units.[47] If I understand him correctly here, he is saying, reasonably enough, that the task is to strike the optimal balance in the relation between the structure of the legal norm and the basic legal science *fiat*.

There is nothing in the nature of things that dictates either the priority of empowering norms addressed to legal officials, as in Kelsen's legal theory, or the priority of obligation-imposing norms addressed to legal subjects, as in Harris's.[48] As both theorists correctly argue, these decisions reflect criteria for individuation, which, in turn, reflect more fundamental decisions on the part of the legal theorist about the goals of legal philosophy.

Although not ascribing to Kelsen the priority of empowering norms, as I do, Harris goes on, in *Law and Legal Science*, to argue that Kelsen is led astray by his doctrine of empowerment:

Theorists have sometimes inferred, as Kelsen did, that rules have a deontic function of 'authorize' [or 'empower'] distinct from command or permit. This led Kelsen to bizarre conclusions: that an unconstitutional statute (not subjected to judicial annulment) must be regarded as impliedly authorized by the constitution; and that laws enacted inconsistently with treaties must be regarded as authorized by international law, even though their enactment constitutes a delict by international law.[49]

Harris's criticism of Kelsen's doctrine of 'normative alternatives' is exactly right.[50] As Harris writes, the doctrine is indeed bizarre. Kelsen develops it with an eye to explaining how the law deals with legal *errata*, but his explanation goes off the track. Here is his statement of the doctrine in the legislative context:

If a statute enacted by the legislative organ is considered to be valid although it has been created in another way or has another content than [that] prescribed by the constitution,

44 Harris, *LLS*, n.5 above, 20–1 (emphasis in original), see also 40.

45 Ibid. 70, see also 93.

46 Ibid. 94.

47 Ibid. 21.

48 Harris says as much; see text at n.39 above. I am indebted to JR Sieckmann for helpful discussion on this point.

49 Harris, *LLS*, n.5 above, 86 (footnotes omitted). Kelsen's expression for 'to authorize' is '*ermächtigen*', literally, 'to empower'. See e.g. H Kelsen, *Reine Rechtslehre* (2nd edn., Franz Deuticke, 1960), paras. 6(d)(e), 18, 28(b), 29(f), 30(a), 41(b).

50 See Harris, *LLS*, n.5 above, 87–8, and see, too, the discussion in Harris, 'Kelsen's Concept of Authority', n.6 above, 358–9, and in Harris, 'Kelsen and Normative Consistency', n.6 above, 214–20. See also G Maher, 'Customs and Constitutions' (1981) 1 *Oxford Journal of Legal Studies* 167, 172–5.

we must assume that the prescriptions of the constitution concerning legislation have an *alternative character*. The legislator is entitled by the constitution either to apply the norms laid down directly in the constitution or to apply other norms which he himself may decide upon. Otherwise, a statute whose creation or contents did not conform with the prescriptions directly laid down in the constitution could not be regarded as valid.[51]

To illustrate Kelsen's concern here, suppose that the applicable constitutional norm covers legislation up to point *n*, but not beyond. Then a statute is enacted with a provision that reaches to point $n + 1$. Suppose, too, that there is no likelihood that the constitutional norm, as a matter of unwritten or 'common' constitutional law, will be read as reaching to $n + 1$. Such a reading of the constitutional norm—so the supposition—would lead to anomalies elsewhere in the legal system, anomalies that officials are aware of, and want to avoid. Kelsen argues that the statute, which *ex hypothesi* falls outside the scope of the constitutional norm, is valid thanks to a second normative path, the 'normative alternative':

The provisions of the constitution concerning the procedure of legislation and the contents of future statutes do not mean that laws can be created only in the way decreed and only with the import prescribed by the constitution. The constitution entitles the legislator to create statutes also in another way and also with another content.[52]

As far as I can tell, Kelsen never recognized the disastrous consequences that stem from his doctrine of 'normative alternatives', namely, that its adoption would lead straight away to the collapse of his rule-based legal system. If the second path is recognized as a 'normative alternative' to the legal rule, then legal rules no longer impose constraints. The only point that needs to be emphasized here, however, is that Kelsen's doctrine of 'normative alternatives' does not follow from his defence of the empowering norm and its priority.

(iii) On the Basic Legal Science *Fiat*

Harris's basic legal science *fiat* gives expression to four principles: (1) exclusion, (2) subsumption, (3) derogation, and (4) non-contradiction:

The Basic Legal Science *Fiat*: 'Legal duties exist only if imposed (and not excepted) [1] by rules originating in the following sources: ... or [2] by rules subsumable under such rules. Provided that [3] any contradiction between rules originating in different sources shall be resolved according to the following ranking amongst the sources: ... and provided that [4] no other contradiction shall be admitted to exist.'[53]

Taken together, the four principles provide a 'rule-systematizing logic of legal science',[54] with machinery for identifying the legal system along with its rules and for resolving conflicts between legal rules.

51 Kelsen, *GTLS*, n.38 above, 156 (my emphasis). 52 Ibid.
53 Harris, *LLS*, n.5 above, 70 (emphasis, quotation marks, and ellipses in original).
54 Ibid. 10.

The principle of exclusion specifies the various independent sources of law in the legal system. As Harris writes, these sources in the United Kingdom would include parliamentary statutes, judicial precedents, 'and (within very narrow limits) custom'. Each of the independent legal sources is expressed in a 'constitutional source-rule', and the set of constitutional source-rules identifies the legal system. For this reason, Harris calls the principle of exclusion, specifying the constitutional source-rules, 'the most basic of all the logical principles of legal science'.[55]

The second principle is subsumption. For Harris, subsumption means simply 'falling within the scope of' a presupposed, appropriate higher-order or subsuming rule. Following the principle of subsumption, one traces the legal decision through the hierarchy of sources, up to the point of the constitutional source-rule, where the principle of exclusion comes into play. In short, as Harris puts it, a 'rule "originates in" a source when it is directly subsumable under a constitutional source-rule describing that source'.[56]

Harris's third principle is derogation. It serves to invalidate a legal norm found in a lower-ranked source that conflicts with a legal norm found in a higher-ranked source. A point not fully developed by Harris, but understood in his principle of derogation, is that the principle calls not only for a ranking of the sources of law according to the derogation canon *lex superior derogat legi inferiori*, but also for the incorporation into the basic legal science *fiat* of those derogation canons that address conflicts between norms within a given source of law. Here I have in mind the canons *lex posterior derogat legi priori*[57] and *lex specialis derogat legi generali*.

Harris's fourth principle is non-contradiction. Although conflicts between legal norms are ordinarily resolved by means of the principle of derogation, none of the derogation canons is applicable to the 'express norm conflict', in which, theoretically, the conflicting norms were issued by the same source at the same time and at the same level of generality.[58] What is more, in one context at least, the express norm conflict is not merely a theoretical possibility. I have in mind the conflict between provisions of a single statute. To be sure, as both Kelsen and Harris are quick to point out, the fact that a conflict appears to have arisen between two provisions of a single statute would be 'a ground for advocating another interpretation of at least one of the provisions'.[59]

Harris suggests that '[t]he basic legal science *fiat* is derived from Kelsen's concept of the basic norm'.[60] In this connection he quotes a passage from Kelsen's *General*

[55] Harris, *LLS*, n.5 above, 71. [56] Ibid. [57] Ibid. 72.

[58] For the issues that arise here, see generally B Celano, 'Norm Conflicts: Kelsen's View in the Late Period and a Rejoinder', in Paulson and Paulson, n.1 above, 343.

[59] Harris, *LLS*, n.5 above, 81, and see Kelsen, *PTL*, n.19 above, para. 34(e). See also ibid. paras. 16, 35(j), and 45(c)(d)(e), where Kelsen purports to solve norm conflicts by means of an 'indirect' application of the principle of non-contradiction. See also, however, ibid. para. 5(a), where the result of introducing the reconstructed legal norm into this context, to be sure *en passant*, is to 'dissolve' the problem of norm conflicts. Understandably, Kelsen, in the bulk of his writings, addresses the problem of norm conflicts apart from the reconstructed legal norm.

[60] Harris, *LLS*, n.5 above, 78.

Theory of Law and State:

> By formulating the basic norm, we do not introduce into the science of law any new method. We merely make explicit what all jurists, mostly unconsciously, assume when they consider positive law as a system of valid norms and not only as a complex of facts . . . That the basic norm really exists in the juristic consciousness is the result of a simple analysis of actual juristic statements. The basic norm is the answer to the question: how—and that means under what conditions—are all these juristic statements concerning legal norms, legal duties, legal rights, and so on, possible?[61]

The connection between the basic legal science *fiat* and Kelsen's basic norm, Harris writes, is that the basic legal science *fiat*, in 'making explicit the logical procedures of legal science', has precisely the same function as Kelsen's basic norm.[62]

I do not find this comparison convincing, for two reasons. First, Harris's basic legal science *fiat* is directed above all to hierarchical orderings of the sources of law. As we have seen, Harris calls the principle of exclusion 'the most basic of all the logical principles of legal science'.[63] And he does so because the principle of exclusion specifies both the sources of law and their hierarchy, all with an eye to norm issuance. The principle of derogation provides for a second ordering of the sources of law, this time with an eye to resolving norm conflicts. In the Vienna School of Legal Theory, these principles are given expression not in the basic norm[64] but in the doctrine of hierarchical structure (*Stufenbaulehre*), as this doctrine was developed by Adolf Julius Merkl of the Vienna School and, following him, Hans Kelsen.[65] Their doctrine emphasizes the hierarchy of the sources of law *vis-à-vis* norm issuance and—just as in Harris's basic legal science *fiat*—provides for a distinct hierarchical ordering of sources of law *vis-à-vis* derogation.[66]

There is a second reason for scepticism about Harris's comparison of his basic legal science *fiat* with Kelsen's basic norm, namely, the thoroughly neo-Kantian character of the statement on the basic norm that Harris quotes from Kelsen's text. In a standard neo-Kantian move, Kelsen takes the fact of legal science (*das Faktum*

61 Ibid. (the ellipsis is found in Harris's quotation). Quoted from Kelsen, *GTLS*, n.38 above, 116–17. See also Kelsen, *An Introduction to the Problems of Legal Theory*, n.34 above, para. 29; Kelsen, *PTL*, n.19 above, para. 34(d).

62 Harris, *LLS*, n.5 above, 78.

63 Ibid.

64 To be sure, there is an exception to the rule. In his monograph of 1928, *The Philosophical Foundations of Natural Law Theory and Legal Positivism* (trans. WH Kraus as an appendix to *GTLS*, n.38 above, 389 (trans. of title altered)), Kelsen builds the principle of non-contradiction into the 'sense of the basic norm', see ibid. 406–7.

65 Merkl was already busy at work on the *Stufenbaulehre* during the War. See e.g. AJ Merkl, 'Das doppelte Rechtsantlitz' (1918) 47 *Juristische Blätter* 425–7, 444–7, 463–5. For Kelsen's reception of Merkl's doctrine, see H Kelsen, ' "Foreword" to the Second Printing of *Main Problems in the Theory of Public Law*', in Paulson and Paulson, n.1 above, 3, 13–14. On the *Stufenbaulehre* generally, see M Borowski, 'Die Lehre vom Stufenbau des Rechts nach Adolf Julius Merkl', in SL Paulson and M Stolleis (eds.), *Hans Kelsen—Staatsrechtslehrer und Rechtstheoretiker des 20. Jahrhunderts* (Mohr-Siebeck, 2005), 122.

66 See R Walter, *Der Aufbau der Rechtsordnung* (Leykam, 1964), 55; R Walter, 'Der Stufenbau nach der derogatorischen Kraft im österreichischen Recht' (1965) 20 *Österreichische Juristen-Zeitung* 169.

der Rechtswissenschaft) as his point of departure[67] and then asks: what conditions must obtain without which legal science would not be possible? The basic norm, on this reading, stands in for these neo-Kantian conditions. There is, however, no Kantian or neo-Kantian component in Harris's work at all.

These critical remarks do not aim to undermine the value of Harris's basic legal science *fiat*. On the contrary, Harris's *fiat* proves to be enormously instructive, for it invites attention to Kelsen's legal theory as primarily a theory of legal science. And this is a fundamental contribution to our understanding of Kelsen.[68] What is more, as I argue in section (iv), it is within the framework of legal science that Kelsen speaks of the normativity of the law in a rich and suggestive way.

(iv) On the Normativity Problematic

Kelsen refers in one of his papers to the origins of 'norm' in the Latin *norma*.[69] The twists and turns in philosophy that record the development of the concept of normativity, from its beginnings in Vitruvius's *De Architectura*,[70] need not occupy us here.[71] Suffice it to say that where reconstructions of Kelsen's own legal theory are concerned, the 'normativity problematic' divides into three parts. First (not generally familiar), there is Kelsen's lengthy and sustained reply, from the beginning, to naturalism in legal science. I take up this development in part (a) of the present section. Then (also less than familiar), there is Kelsen's normative or—better—non-naturalistic theory of legal science. This theory is my focus in part (b) of the present section. Finally, turning to the familiar reading of 'normativity' in legal philosophy, namely, as marking a range of views on both the nature of the legal 'ought' and the reasons for complying with it,[72] there is Kelsen's thoroughly positivistic doctrine of normativity. This I take up—with attention to Harris's criticism of Kelsen—in part (c) of the present section. What I have to say in part (c)

[67] See e.g. H Kelsen, 'Rechtswissenschaft und Recht' (1922) 3 *Zeitschrift für öffentliches Recht* 103, 128.

[68] For references to *Law and Legal Science*, n.5 above, in this connection, see n.17 above, and see also Harris, 'Kelsen and Normative Consistency', n.6 above, 203–5.

[69] H Kelsen, 'On the Concept of Norm' (trans. P Heath) in H Kelsen, *Essays in Moral and Legal Philosophy* (ed. O Weinberger, D Reidel, 1973), 216, 216 (the article was first published in 1965).

[70] See Vitruvius, *De Architectura*, (trans. MH Morgan, Harvard UP, 1926), bk. 9, Introduction, at para. 6 (Vitruvius's treatise is dated *circa* 27 BC).

[71] For a variety of perspectives in recent philosophy that underscore the richness of the concept, see e.g. RB Brandom, *Making it Explicit* (Harvard UP, 1994); J Dancy (ed.), *Normativity* (Blackwell, 2000); CM Korsgaard, *The Sources of Normativity* (CUP, 1996). See, too, the perspicuous statement on the central role of normativity in the Kantian tradition—that is, categories of the understanding as *rules* for combining representations in judgements—in T Pinkard, *German Philosophy 1760–1860. The Legacy of Idealism* (CUP, 2002), 26–36, 46–7, 67, *et passim*.

[72] For a helpful and wide-ranging discussion, see T Spaak, 'Legal Positivism, Law's Normativity, and the Normative Force of Legal Justification' (2003) 16 *Ratio Juris* 469. See also the discussion, drawing on Raz's work, in the text beginning at n.89 below.

builds on the first two parts, for, as I have suggested, everything of interest offered by Kelsen on the normativity problematic is found in the theory of legal science that he develops as an alternative to naturalism in legal science, and this point bears on attributions to Kelsen of other views about normativity, too.

(a) Kelsen's Reply to Naturalism in Legal Science

In the latter part of the nineteenth century, in a paper entitled 'Norms and Laws of Nature', Wilhelm Windelband gave expression to the concept of normativity as Kelsen came to understand it, adumbrating a basic distinction between the normative disciplines and the natural sciences:

With its laws, psychology explains how we actually think, feel, want, and act. By contrast, the 'laws' found in our logical, ethical, aesthetic conscience have nothing to do with theoretically explaining the facts associated with them. They simply say what the qualities of these facts ought to be if the facts are to meet with universal approbation as true, good, and beautiful. These 'laws' are, therefore, not laws according to which something must objectively take place or can be subjectively comprehended. Rather, they are ideal norms according to which the value of what comes about of natural necessity is judged. These norms are, therefore, rules of judgment.[73]

Drawing on Windelband's distinction, Kelsen, at the outset of *Main Problems in the Theory of Public Law* (1911), lists the normative disciplines and includes not only ethics, aesthetics, logic, and philology, but also legal science.[74] He had, from the beginning, condemned as utterly wrongheaded the very real inroads made by naturalism into the legal science of the day,[75] and Windelband's distinction was grist for the young legal theorist's mill. Legal science was a normative science, that is, a non-naturalistic science, and the task Kelsen set for himself was to demonstrate that this was indeed so.

To be sure, that demonstration, to the extent it can be regarded as successful, came later. In *Main Problems* and, a decade later, in *The Sociological and Legal Concept of the State* (1922),[76] Kelsen concentrated on arguments designed to show

[73] W Windelband, *Präludien* (JCB Mohr, 1884), 211, 219, and in the 9th edn., 2 vols. (JCB Mohr, 1924), ii, 59, 67. To be sure, neither Frege nor Husserl follows Windelband here. Addressing, in particular, the laws of logic, both argue that these laws are descriptive in nature. The prescriptive counterparts of these laws are constructions to the effect that one ought to follow the descriptive law. See G Frege, *Grundgesetze der Arithmetik* (Hermann Pohle, 1893/1903), i, Preface, pp. v–xxxvii, xv; E Husserl, *Logical Investigations* (trans. JN Findlay, Routledge & Kegan Paul, 1970), i, para. 41 (Husserl's treatise was first published in 1900–1).

[74] See Kelsen, *HP*, n.31 above, 4–6.

[75] The most prominent example is Georg Jellinek, whom I take up immediately below. On naturalism in legal science in this period, see generally P Goller, 'Leo Geller und der naturalistische Rechtsrealismus jenseits von Rechtsidealismus und positivistischer Rechtsdogmatik' (2001) 23 *Zeitschrift für Neuere Rechtsgeschichte* 81, and for a detailed statement on the entire period, see M Stolleis, *Public Law in Germany, 1800–1914* (trans. P Biel, Berghahn Books, 2001), 419; M Stolleis, *A History of Public Law in Germany 1914–1945* (trans. T Dunlap, OUP, 2004), 1–105 *et passim*. I have reviewed the latter of the Stolleis volumes under the title 'The Theory of Public Law in Germany. 1914–1945' (2005) 25 *Oxford Journal of Legal Studies* 525.

[76] H Kelsen, *Der soziologische und der juristische Staatsbegriff* (JCB Mohr, 1922), para. 20.

that naturalism in legal science was mistaken. As an illustration, it is instructive to consider his criticism of Georg Jellinek's legal theory.[77] Jellinek's 'two-sides' theory of law seemed to reflect a normative or non-naturalistic dimension, namely, a 'juridico-normative' side that appeared not to be reducible to anything factual, along with a 'social' or 'historico-social' side that was supposed to represent the factual dimension of the law. Kelsen, however, argues correctly that, on Jellinek's view, legal norms cannot be 'anything other than "is"-rules, with the "ought" reflected—psychologically—in one's subjective consciousness of rule-governed action'. On the basis of 'this thoroughly psychologistic orientation' toward legal norms,[78] Jellinek's legal theory is revealed for what it is, a species of naturalism.[79]

It is no accident that Kelsen speaks here of Jellinek's psychologistic orientation. The anti-naturalism of Kelsen's legal theory is a reflection of other anti-naturalistic programmes developed in philosophy at the same time, including the campaign against psychologism in logic and in the theory of knowledge, that is to say, against attempts to 'reduce' these fields to psychology.[80] Among the critics of psychologically inclined—or, the pejorative expression, 'psychologistically inclined'—logicians of the later nineteenth century were, above all, the philosophically inclined mathematician Gottlob Frege and the mathematician-turned-philosopher Edmund Husserl, and Kelsen was aware of Husserl's role here.[81] Frege and Husserl were only the most prominent of a host of *fin de siècle* philosophers who campaigned against naturalism. The naturalistic turn in psychology serves as an illustration. The young turks in experimental psychology—most prominently, Oswald Külpe and Edward Bradford Titchener—broke at the end of the nineteenth century with the master, Wilhelm Wundt, in order to reconstitute psychology on a purely empirical basis. Among their anti-naturalistic critics were the neo-Kantian philosophers Heinrich Rickert and Hugo Münsterberg. While endorsing the young turks' naturalistic position in the case of psychology, both Rickert and Münsterberg sought to preserve the autonomy of the *Geisteswissenschaften* or humanistic fields. Reflecting Wundt's influence, these disciplines had earlier been thought to be based on psychology, and they were therefore seen as threatened by the reconstitution of psychology in naturalistic terms.

In short, Kelsen was engaged in a common enterprise with others in philosophy, doing battle against naturalism with an eye to preserving the autonomy

[77] See G Jellinek, *Allgemeine Staatslehre* (2nd edn., O Häring, 1905), 11–12, 61–2, 71–2, 120, 130–4, 267, *et passim*, and in the 3rd edn. (O Häring, 1914), 11–12, 63, 74, 125, 136–40, 274, *et passim*.

[78] Kelsen, *Der soziologische und der juristische Staatsbegriff*, n.76 above, para. 20.

[79] There is a consensus on the point that Jellinek's legal theory is naturalistic, with Kelsen himself having adduced the most powerful arguments. In the recent literature, see Stolleis, *Public Law in Germany, 1800–1914*, n.75 above, 440–4; W Ott, *Der Rechtspositivismus* (2nd edn., Duncker & Humblot, 1992), 67–9; C Möllers, *Staat als Argument* (CH Beck, 2000), 12–35.

[80] There is a large literature on psychologism. See the broad-ranging statements with close attention to primary sources in M Rath, *Der Psychologismusstreit in der deutschen Philosophie* (Karl Alber, 1994), and in M Kusch, *Psychologism. A Case Study in the Sociology of Philosophical Knowledge* (Routledge, 1995).

[81] See Kelsen, *HP*, n.31 above, 67 n.1, and ' "Foreword" to the Second Printing of *Main Problems in the Theory of Public Law*', n.65 above, 7–8.

(*Eigengesetzlichkeit*)[82] of the discipline in question—be it logic, be it one or another of the *Geisteswissenschaften*, be it legal science. When, at a later point in his work, Kelsen does provide the rudiments of a normative or non-naturalistic theory of legal science, he draws on the work of the Baden neo-Kantians. Of special interest here is the doctrine of methodological form, which, in legal science, serves as Kelsen's 'law of normativity'.

(b) Kelsen's Normative or Non-Naturalistic Theory of Legal Science

In the last chapter of his treatise, *The Object of Knowledge*,[83] Heinrich Rickert, erstwhile student of Windelband's and the leading figure in the Baden School of Neo-Kantianism after Windelband's death in 1915, distinguished 'constitutive categories' of objective reality—for example, the category of permanence—from the 'methodological forms' that are part and parcel of the various standing disciplines. Rickert's basic idea is that objective reality, constituted transcendentally, must be sharply distinguished from the processing (*Bearbeitung*) of the material given in objective reality. Objective reality is constituted by means of the categories of reality, while the processing of the material of objective reality is the work of the methodological forms found in the standing disciplines. Rickert offers lawfulness (*Gesetzlichkeit*) as an example of a methodological form in the natural sciences.[84] In fact, the example has to be taken as the *genus* of methodological forms in the natural sciences generally, for it has application to all of them.

Rickert begins with the constitutive categories of reality:

> The unique significance of ... the forms that have been discussed in terms of the examples of causality and permanence requires that they be given a special name, one that distinguishes them as original forms, in contrast to methodological forms. Building on the expression 'objective reality', we could speak ... of 'objective forms of reality'. But we prefer ... the term 'constitutive'. In that these particular forms constitute what is presupposed as finished product or as real material of cognition, 'constitutive' designates exactly what we mean. Thus, the categories that shape the objective, real world from what is in fact given should be called the *constitutive categories of reality*.[85]

The respective methodological forms—Rickert alludes to them in the quotation above—are peculiar to the various standing disciplines. Referring in the treatise to Cartesian dualism, Rickert writes:

> This *other* species of dualism, according to which the world is supposed to consist of two types of reality, each excluding the other—the world of *extensio* and the world of *cogitatio*—is created by physics, and by psychology, each with its respective methodological form.[86]

[82] See ibid. 6.

[83] See H Rickert, *Der Gegenstand der Erkenntnis* (2nd edn., JCB Mohr, 1904), 205–28, Rickert, *GE 6*, n.22 above, 401–32.

[84] See ibid. 409–10.

[85] Ibid. 406–7 (emphasis in original), cf. Rickert, *Der Gegenstand der Erkenntnis* (2nd edn.), n.83 above, 211.

[86] Rickert, *GE 6*, n.22 above, 424 (emphasis in original); see also 404, 410, 411, 424, 426, *et passim*, and cf. Rickert, *Der Gegenstand der Erkenntnis* (2nd ed.), n.83 above, 208, 210, 217, 221, *et passim*.

Physics has its own methodological form, and so does psychology.

Legal science, too, has its own methodological form, namely, imputation (*Zurechnung*) or, as Kelsen sometimes puts it, the 'law of normativity' (*Rechtsgesetz*)[87] As he explains:

Just as the law of nature links a certain material fact as cause with another as effect, so the law of normativity links legal condition with legal consequence (the consequence of a so-called unlawful act). If the mode of linking material facts is causality in the one case, it is imputation in the other, and imputation is recognized in the *Pure Theory of Law* as the particular lawfulness, the autonomy, of the law.[88]

Where the legal condition in the reconstructed, hypothetically formulated legal norm obtains, the methodological form of legal science—the imputation relation—marks the legal position of *liability* on the part of the legal subject to the imposition of a sanction. By the same token, the satisfaction of the antecedent condition marks the legal position of *empowerment* on the part of the legal official, namely, to impose the sanction in question. Kelsen's recasting of the legal modalities in terms of the scheme of liability and power, immunity and disability, marks the point at which the entire system is governed by the peculiarly juridical methodological form, imputation.

The 'normative' or non-naturalistic import of Kelsen's enterprise, the force of his 'law of normativity', plays itself out in the context of normative legal science, understood as Kelsen's alternative to naturalism in legal science. As he argued, the *modalities* of the reconstructed legal norm resist the naturalist's effort to account for them in factual terms. In particular, the underlying law-like character of imputation, Kelsen's methodological form, serves to explain *non-causal change*. If individual *A* is subject to an exercise of legal power by *B*, and *B* exercises this power, the legal position of *A* is thereby changed, and the change, Kelsen insists, is not a causal change. It is, rather, a 'normative' change.

Coming full circle, Kelsen, as a part of his sustained reply to naturalism in legal science, understood normativity in these terms. It goes without saying, however, that normativity in the literature, including the literature on Kelsen, has not been understood in these terms, and I turn now to 'normativity' on the more familiar reading.

(c) Kelsen's Positivistic Doctrine of Normativity

In a rewarding study of Kelsen's legal theory, Joseph Raz attributes to Kelsen the concept of 'justified normativity', that is to say, the view that 'to judge the law as normative is to judge it to be just and to admit that it ought to be obeyed'. On this view, Raz continues, '[t]he concepts of the normativity of the law and of the

87 On imputation, see Kelsen, *HP*, n.31 above, 121–88; SL Paulson, 'Hans Kelsen's Earliest Legal Theory: Critical Constructivism' (1996) 59 *Modern Law Review* 797, reprinted in Paulson and Paulson, n.1 above, 23. On the mature 'law of normativity', see SL Paulson, 'Zwei radikale Objektivierungsprogramme in der Rechtslehre Hans Kelsens', in Paulson and Stolleis, n.65 above, 191.

88 Kelsen, *An Introduction to the Problems of Legal Theory*, n.34 above, para. 11(b) (trans. altered).

obligation to obey it are analytically tied together'.[89] Similarly for Harris, in so far as he suggests at some points in his writings that Kelsen appears to be endorsing something very much like the concept of 'justified normativity':

Kelsen repeatedly insists that it is of the essence of a norm that it is valid, that it is binding, that the conduct it stipulates 'ought' to be performed. These synonymous characterizations apply to all norms, whether moral or legal. In that sense, the same conception of normativity applies to morality and the law.[90]

Given this standard of 'justified normativity' or something like it, Harris's conclusion seems clearly right: what Kelsen in fact offers in the name of normativity is 'narrow, eccentric and etiolated'.

The correct rejoinder, however, is to reject the standard. As applied to Kelsen, it cannot be right. At the very juncture at which Raz introduces the notion of 'justified normativity',[91] Kelsen has a fully developed position, namely, his sanction theory. Kelsen explicates the import of the legal 'ought' not in terms of justifying reasons but by appeal to the sanction.

More precisely, Kelsen's explication of what he understands by 'normativity' can be spelled out in terms of two closely related theses: first, a thesis focused on the legal 'ought' and, secondly, a thesis focused on the legal 'can'. Kelsen explicates the legal 'ought', the binding quality of the law, by appeal to the sanction that can be imposed if the subject fails to comply. As we have already seen, 'ought' in Kelsen's later writings is a placemarker,[92] and for the legally operative 'ought' in the present context, Kelsen directs us away from the legal subject, focusing on the legal organ:

That somebody is legally obligated to [perform act *a*] means that [a legal] organ 'ought' to apply a sanction to him [in the event that *a* is not forthcoming].[93]

[89] Raz, 'Kelsen's Theory of the Basic Norm', n.4 above, 105, reprinted in Paulson and Paulson, n.1 above, 60.

[90] Harris, 'Kelsen's Pallid Normativity', n.6 above, 102, see also 99, 101, 106, 110. In the text quoted here, Harris refers to Kelsen, *GTLS*, n.38 above, 30; H Kelsen, 'Value Judgments in the Science of Law' (1942) 7 *Journal of Social Philosophy and Jurisprudence* 312, 323–4; Kelsen, *PTL*, n.19 above, para. 4(c); H Kelsen, 'Law and Logic' (trans. P Heath), in Kelsen, *Essays in Moral and Legal Philosophy*, n.69 above, 228, 230 (the article was first published in 1965); H Kelsen, *General Theory of Norms* (trans. M Hartney, Clarendon Press, 1991), 2–3, 27–8. To be sure, at other points in 'Kelsen's Pallid Normativity', n.6 above, Harris points to the distance between Kelsen's view of normativity and 'justified normativity', see e.g. ibid. 110, 114. The ambivalence reflected in what Harris attributes to Kelsen in the name of normativity is, I believe, significant. Had there been no occasion to attribute to Kelsen something like 'justified normativity', there would have been no occasion to criticize it as 'pallid' either.

[91] Raz's attribution makes sense only if one assumes, with him, that the ordinary legal subject has been supplanted by 'the legal man'. The moral beliefs of the legal man are 'identical with the law' and can therefore be mapped isomorphically onto the corresponding legal norms: see J Raz, 'The Purity of the Pure Theory', n.4 above, 451–2, reprinted in Paulson and Paulson, n.1 above, 246. However ingenious Raz's construction may be, it is contrived; the legal man has no practical application. For criticism directed to Raz's legal man, see R Alexy, 'Hans Kelsens Begriff des relativen Apriori', in Alexy *et al.*, n.22 above, 179, 198; U Bindreiter, *Why* Grundnorm? *A Treatise on the Implications of Kelsen's Doctrine* (Kluwer, 2002), 92–5, 113–14; Harris, 'Kelsen's Pallid Normativity', n. 6 above, 112–13.

[92] See text at n.38 in section (ii), above.

[93] Kelsen, *GTLS*, n.38 above, 60. As Kelsen put it in an article of 1928: 'I ought or am obligated not to steal or I ought or am obligated to repay a loan received means in *positive* law *nothing other* than if I steal, I ought to be punished, if I fail to repay a loan received, then a sanction ought to be imposed

Secondly, the value that the variable 'ought' takes in this context is the legal 'can', that is, the legal organ is *empowered* to impose the sanction. By the same token, the legal subject is *liable* to the imposition of the sanction—the subject is not, in other words, immune thereto. Liability, thus understood, is a direct reflection of the application of the methodological form peculiar to legal science, that of imputation. And since empowerment—in Hohfeldian parlance—is the legal 'correlative' of liability, it, too, reflects directly the role of imputation *qua* methodological form.

This is to say that Kelsen, far from defending a concept of 'justified normativity', defends something closer to what Raz has termed the concept of 'social normativity', which Raz attributes to Hart. As Raz puts it:

> To anyone regarding the law as socially normative, the question 'why should the law be obeyed?' cannot be answered by pointing out that it is normative. The law is normative [on this view] because of certain social facts. It should be obeyed, if at all, for moral reasons. The normativity of the law and the obligation to obey it are distinct notions.[94]

Thus, whereas the normativity of the law and the obligation to obey it are necessarily linked in the case of 'justified normativity', they are altogether distinct notions in the case of 'social normativity', which is to say that 'social normativity' stands for a thesis of legal positivism. The legal positivist answers the question of bindingness in non-moral terms, the most prominent example being Kelsen's appeal to the sanction. The legal positivist leaves to morality the other reading of 'bindingness' in the law, a reading that triggers the classical question of normativity in political philosophy, namely, why one ought to obey the law.[95]

That Kelsen defends a thoroughly positivistic concept of normativity cannot come as a surprise. After all, beginning in *Main Problems*, he embarked on an elaborate reconstruction, arriving at the '*ideal* linguistic form' of the legal norm in order to distinguish the legal norm as sharply as possible from the moral norm.[96] Part and parcel of this distinction was the sanction theory, and the legal 'ought' is to be understood in its terms.

A normativity thesis is of course present in Kelsen's theory, but it is derivative,[97] and that will come as a disappointment to those looking for something closer to 'justified normativity'.

on me': H Kelsen, 'The Idea of Natural Law' (trans. P Heath), in Kelsen, *Essays in Moral and Legal Philosophy*, n.69 above, 27, 32–3 (emphasis in original) (trans. altered). Thirty years later, in the 2nd edn. of the *Pure Theory of Law*, Kelsen is defending the same view: see *PTL*, n.19 above, paras. 5(a), 6(b)(d), 9, 28(a)(b), *et passim*; see also SL Paulson, 'Zwei Wiener Welten und ein Anknüpfungspunkt: Carnaps *Aufbau*, Kelsens Reine Rechtslehre und das Streben nach Objektivität', in C Jabloner and F Stadler (eds.), *Logischer Empirismus und Reine Rechtslehre* (Springer, 2001), 137, 169–74.

94 Raz, 'Kelsen's Theory of the Basic Norm', n.4 above, 105, reprinted in Paulson and Paulson, n.1 above, 60.

95 See, in a vast literature, R Dworkin, *Law's Empire* (Harvard UP, 1986), 190–5; J Raz, 'The Obligation to Obey: Revision and Tradition', in J Raz, *Ethics in the Public Domain* (Clarendon Press, 1994), 325–38.

96 See text in section (ii), above.

97 For Kelsen's case, see text at nn. 92–3 above. To be sure, a full statement of Kelsen's normativity thesis—'normativity' on the more familiar reading—would go well beyond what I offer here, taking into account, *inter alia*, his doctrine of 'dependant legal norms'. See Kelsen, *PTL*, n.19 above, para. 6(e).

(v) Concluding Remark

Thanks to Harris, we have the central insight that Kelsen worked first and foremost to develop a theory of legal science. Harris also makes it clear that, from the standpoint of normativity as he and others understand it, Kelsen's writings are unsatisfactory, offering merely a 'pallid normativity'. Harris is correct on both counts, but the latter does not reach far enough. The correct move, as I have argued, is to reject the notion that Kelsen's enterprise reflects in any way whatever the concept of 'justified normativity'. Far more fruitful—and far more faithful to the texts—is to understand the peculiarly Kelsenian notion of normativity as a part of the theory of legal science that he developed as an alternative to naturalism in legal science. Although Harris fails to come to terms with Kelsen's normativity thus understood, his highly instructive emphasis on legal science as the *leitmotif* of Kelsen's legal theory remains an outstanding contribution to our understanding of Kelsen.

2

Interpreting Normativity

*Julie Dickson**

(i) Introduction

Interpreting the views of Hans Kelsen was one of Jim Harris's long-standing academic interests. In a series of articles and book chapters from the early 1970s onwards, Harris developed a distinctive and sometimes critical take on several important aspects of Kelsen's thinking. In this essay, I will focus on Harris's interpretation and critical analysis of Kelsen's account of the normativity of law. The search for an adequate understanding of legal normativity has generated a series of enduring puzzles for analytical jurisprudence. Is 'ought' to be understood in the same way in legal and moral contexts, or is there a specifically legal sense of 'ought'? Do legal 'oughts' provide reasons for action? If we say that something ought to be done according to law, are we thereby committing ourselves to law's (moral?) justifiability? One of Harris's distinctive contributions to this debate was his contention, especially in work in the 1990s, that Kelsen espoused a 'pallid' or 'etiolated' normativity in his theoretical understanding of law.[1] My main tasks in this article will be to discuss what Harris meant by this, to examine whether he was justified in interpreting Kelsen's views in this way, and to consider the relevance of this issue for understanding law.

My approach will be comparative in part: in order to understand and critically analyse Harris's distinctive interpretation of Kelsen on the normativity of law, I will contrast Harris's account with that offered by Joseph Raz on the same topic. Raz is an interesting comparator in this regard for several reasons. Both theorists exhibit considerable interest in Kelsen's account of the normativity of law, but, in pursuing that interest, they offer significantly different interpretations of Kelsen's views. Moreover, Harris engaged directly with and attempted to refute Raz's rival interpretation of Kelsen's views in some of his more recent work on this topic.

* Fellow and Tutor in Law, Somerville College, Oxford.

[1] See JW Harris, 'Kelsen, Revolutions and Normativity', in E Attwooll (ed.), *Shaping Revolution* (Aberdeen University Press, 1991), 1; JW Harris, 'Kelsen's Pallid Normativity' (1996) 9 *Ratio Juris* 94.

Finally, Raz believes that Kelsen succeeds precisely where Harris regarded him as failing, namely in making a useful contribution to explaining the normativity of law.

(ii) Interpreting Normativity?

This essay discusses rival interpretations of Kelsen's account of the normativity of law. But what exactly is meant by an account of the normativity of law? For some legal theorists, the question of law's normativity is the question of how law can create reasons for action which we would not have but for the presence of law, or of how, and under what conditions, law's prescriptions can have the normative force that they purport to have.[2] Harris's interest in examining Kelsen's views on the normativity of law, however, does not appear to be driven by these issues. Rather, he is concerned with Kelsen's preoccupation with analysing the character of normative discourse in legal contexts, i.e. analysing the 'ought' statements frequently used to provide legal information about what one ought to do according to law. On this way of understanding the question, legal theorists attempting to explain the normativity of law are seeking a correct interpretation of normative or ought statements in legal contexts, especially in contexts where information is given about what law requires, i.e. they are seeking to understand what it means to say, or what we are committed to in saying, 'according to law, one ought to φ'.[3]

Throughout his legal philosophical career, Harris emphasized the importance of an adequate understanding of legal statements giving information about what law requires. For example, in *Law and Legal Science*, Harris declares his theoretical ambitions as follows:

> It is one of the principle aims of this book to investigate the primary descriptive activity of legal science. We shall accordingly be concerned to inquire into the logical status of statements made by legal scientists when they purport to describe the present law on a topic, that is, when they convey information about part of the 'legal system' in the sense of a momentary system of valid rules.[4]

[2] e.g. SR Perry, 'Hart's Methodological Positivism' (1998) 4 *Legal Theory* 427, especially sections IV and V. Although many legal theorists have been interested in such questions, I cite Perry here because he provides a recent example of a theorist who refers to these questions specifically as questions of law's normativity.

[3] I am not claiming that the two lines of inquiry outlined above may not be linked (for example, the line of inquiry which I attribute to Harris may be an essential precursor to the first line of inquiry mentioned above), nor indeed that they may not both be viewed as parts of the same overall enterprise of providing an explanation of law's normativity. Rather, I am merely attempting to bring better into focus the specific philosophical concerns which motivate Harris in his work interpreting Kelsenian normativity.

[4] JW Harris, *Law and Legal Science, An Inquiry into the Concepts Legal Rule and Legal System* (Clarendon Press, 1979), 20.

In those aspects of his work which concern us here, Harris notes that understanding the character of statements used to convey legal information was also one of Kelsen's central and lifelong intellectual preoccupations:

> Everywhere where there is law there are people who, on a daily basis, purport to give information about the currently valid law. On innumerable occasions they make statements of the form: Such and such is illegal; persons in circumstances X have a legal duty to do Y, or a legal right to claim Z; conduct of a certain kind constitutes a criminal offence, or a civil wrong. Kelsen, from first to last throughout his writings, maintains that his theory makes explicit what is implied by such statements... For Kelsen, pride of place is accorded to legal information-giving.[5]

Harris also notes that Kelsen's approach to this issue is anti-reductivist: Kelsen rejected the idea that a statement of what ought to be done according to law could be reduced to a statement of facts concerning, for example, the actions of certain legal officials, or predictions of what those actions would be if certain conduct occurred.[6] However, Harris claims, nor can Kelsen explain legal oughts as statements of value, or as statements of what there is good reason to do, because of his relativism as regards moral values:

> Such statements should not be understood as referring to moral values. As a relativist, Kelsen denied that there could be objective assertions about morals.[7]

and because of the self-imposed methodological limitations of Kelsen's pure theory of law:

> It is, said Kelsen, not the business of the science of law 'to approve or disapprove its subject'. Let lawyers stick to their last. If asked for information about the law, they can, scientifically, only describe norms.... Whether conduct is, by any other criterion, right or wrong is a private and wholly subjective value judgement...[8]

If, according to Kelsen, legal ought statements cannot be reduced to statements of fact, nor interpreted as statements of value, how are we to understand them? This is Harris's central concern in interpreting Kelsen on the normativity of law. Before considering Harris's views in more detail, however, it is valuable to pause for thought, to ask why the question is important at all.

Harris notes that, for Kelsen, the sheer ubiquity of the practice of legal information-giving provides one central reason why a proper understanding of legal ought statements is important.[9] Moreover, for Harris, a particularly interesting puzzle

[5] Harris, 'Kelsen's Pallid Normativity', n. 1 above, 96.

[6] JW Harris, *Legal Philosophies*, (2nd edn., LexisNexis UK, 1997), 65; 'Kelsen's Pallid Normativity', n. 1 above, 97. In this article I am concerned, to a large extent, with Harris's interpretation of Kelsen, and so many references are to articles and book chapters in which Harris interprets Kelsen, rather than directly to the relevant parts of Kelsen's works themselves. Detailed references to parts of Kelsen's work which Harris regards as justifying his interpretation can be found in those of Harris's works which I cite here. My own views on aspects of Kelsen's work are discussed later in this article.

[7] Harris, *Legal Philosophies*, n. 6 above, 65.

[8] Ibid., 67.

[9] Harris, 'Kelsen's Pallid Normativity', n. 1 above, 96.

arises in interpreting Kelsen's views on the normativity of law, namely how to understand legal oughts if they are neither reducible to statements about past, present, or future facts, nor to statements of value. In his writings on the normativity of law in general, and in work interpreting Kelsen's view of legal normativity, Joseph Raz also places importance on the need for legal theory to find a solution to a particular aspect of this puzzle.[10] Raz claims that normative language can be used to make statements about what ought to be done according to the norms of a given legal system even by those who believe that those norms neither are justified nor provide reasons for action.[11] We could, for example, use normative language to give information about what is required according to the norms of a radically racist legal system, or one which was in force thousands of years ago, in whose goals and values we do not believe. Raz claims that this practice of using normative terminology and making normative statements about what ought to be done, whilst not oneself being committed to the normative force of those statements, i.e. while not believing that there are good reasons to do that which is stated, is common in legal contexts, and is also more ubiquitous than is sometimes thought in other normative contexts.[12] Raz views the ubiquity of this practice as both an encouragement and a challenge for a theory like Kelsen's which seeks a non-reductive and yet value-free theoretical explanation of the normativity of law: an encouragement, because the sheer prevalence of such statements, and of people's ability to make them, lends support to the thesis that we can make normative statements about what is required according to law, without being committed to the normative force of those statements; a challenge, because it is no easy matter to explain the sense of 'ought' at work in contexts where it seems it is not being used to state what there is good reason to do because the speaker is not committed to the normative force of the ought statement he is making.[13]

Harris and Raz thus share a commitment to explaining Kelsen's view of statements about what ought to be done according to law, where such statements cannot be reduced to statements of fact and are not readily interpreted as statements of value, or as statements of what there is good reason to do. They both believe that the ubiquity of such statements in legal contexts, and the kind of puzzles to which they give rise, renders them an important feature of law which legal theorists should seek to explain. However, Harris and Raz part company as

[10] See, e.g., J Raz, *Practical Reason and Norms* (2nd edn., Princeton University Press, 1990), ch. 5, especially 154–5, 170–7; J Raz, *The Authority of Law* (Clarendon Press, 1979), 140–5, ch. 8, especially 153–7.

[11] Raz, *Practical Reason and Norms*, n. 10 above, 170–1; Raz, *The Authority of Law*, n. 10, above, 153–7.

[12] Raz, *Practical Reason and Norms*, n. 10 above, 175; *The Authority of Law*, n. 10 above, 156. In these works, Raz gives as examples of non-committed normative statements outside the legal context the advice regarding what not to eat given by a non-vegetarian to his vegetarian friend, and the advice regarding what ought to be done according to Rabbinical law given by a Roman Catholic expert on Rabbinical law to a less well-informed orthodox Jewish friend.

[13] Raz, *The Authority of Law*, n. 10 above, 153–4.

regards their respective interpretations of Kelsen's views on this issue, adopting significantly different stances on Kelsen's understanding of legal oughts.

(iii) Interpreting Kelsen: Harris vs. Raz

According to Harris, Kelsen is using 'ought' in a 'special' and 'eccentrically narrow'[14] way in his theory of law. In one telling passage Harris characterizes Kelsen's use of 'ought' as follows:

> Kelsen's normativity is etiolated because, for him, 'ought to do' carries no implications of 'there is real value in doing' or 'there are reasons for doing.' He is ferociously relativistic. There are no values 'out there,' not even provisionally 'out there,' upon which oughtness might build.... The ground of the 'ought' contained in genuine assertoric normative sentences is not, logically, any emotive commitment which the speaker may happen to experience towards the merits of the norm-authority. It is, ultimately, a purely formal basic norm of whose technically fictitious character the well-informed user of normative language should be aware.... The 'ought' of norms, then, both legal and moral, is exclusively relative to the will of norm-authorities, ultimately, to the will of those who are taken to have been empowered, by the basic norm, to lay down the top tier of a legal or moral order.'[15]

On this interpretation, 'ought' is used in a special sense by Kelsen because it does not carry with it the implication that if we state that we ought to do something, we are stating what there is good reason to do, or what there is value in doing. Elsewhere in his writings on this topic, Harris refers to Kelsenian normativity as, 'merely a formal top-dressing added to the system of prescriptions which are, as a matter of fact, by and large obeyed and enforced'.[16] Ultimately, this 'top-dressing' of normativity is supplied by the presupposition of the basic norm, i.e. the assumption, on the part of those making normative statements about what ought to be done according to law, that those who created the historically first constitution were authorized to do so, and that hence coercive acts ought to be performed according to the conditions laid down in the historically first constitution and the norms validated by it.[17] As the passage quoted above indicates, however, according to Harris the presupposition of the basic norm does not result in law-makers' prescriptions being regarded as reasons for action; it merely results in their being regarded as oughts in some pallid sense, in which 'ought to do' does not connote 'there are good reasons to do' or 'there is real value in doing'.

[14] Harris, 'Kelsen, Revolutions and Normativity', n. 1 above, 4.

[15] Harris, 'Kelsen's Pallid Normativity', n. 1 above, 102–3. Internal page references to works by Kelsen omitted.

[16] Ibid., 103.

[17] Harris, *Legal Philosophies*, n. 6 above, 66, 75–6, 78; Harris, 'Kelsen, Revolutions and Normativity', n. 1 above, 6; Harris, 'Kelsen's Pallid Normativity', n. 1 above, 103. For a useful summary of Kelsen's views on the function of the basic norm, see H Kelsen, 'The Function of a Constitution', in R Tur and W Twining (eds.), *Essays on Kelsen* (Clarendon Press, 1986). The role which the basic norm plays in Kelsen's theory will be discussed further in sections (iv) and (v).

This, then, forms the core of Harris's solution to the puzzle of how, according to Kelsen, it is possible for individuals in legal contexts to make ought statements which are not reducible to facts, but which do not seem to be readily interpreted as statements of value, or as statements of what there is good reason to do. As was noted in section (ii), for Joseph Raz, one important aspect of this puzzle is to explain how individuals who are not committed to the normative force of the statements which they make can, nonetheless, use normative terminology to talk about what ought to be done according to law.[18] In a sense, on Harris's interpretation of Kelsenian oughts, this aspect of the puzzle does not arise: when we encounter a Kelsenian ought, we should not interpret it as a statement of what there is reason to do, and then wonder how, in legal contexts, such statements can frequently be made by individuals who do not believe that there *is* reason to do the act(s) in question. Rather, as the ought statement does not purport to state what there is reason to do, or what there is value in doing, in the first place, it can be used without concern by those who do not believe that there are good reasons to do that which law requires.[19] To make use of an example of Kelsen's: 'even an anarchist, if he were a professor of law, could describe positive law as a system of valid norms, without having to approve of this law'.[20] According to Harris's interpretation of Kelsen, the anarchist professor can do this, and indeed has no dilemma to face in so doing, for in making statements about what ought to be done according to law, he is not making statements about what there is good reason to do which would conflict with his anarchist beliefs about what there is good reason to do:

If legal normativity is merely Kelsenian pallid normativity, the professor is no hypocrite just because he makes use of legal terminology . . . Normativity of so formal and exiguous a kind need not worry them or their addressees.[21]

Harris's solution to the puzzle of how Kelsen views normative statements which seem neither to be reducible to statements of fact, nor to be statements of value, is thus to postulate a special 'etiolated' sense of normativity which is employed by Kelsen throughout his work. Joseph Raz, however, is committed to a more full-blooded conception of normativity, believing that normative statements are best understood as statements of reasons for action, and that Kelsen is best interpreted as sharing his view on this point. This results in Raz needing a different kind of answer to the puzzle of the possibility of normative statements which are neither reducible to statements of fact, nor plausibly interpreted as value judgements on the part of those making them concerning what there is good reason to do. The answer in question is supplied by an explanation of what Raz refers to as 'detached normative statements'.

[18] See the discussion at the end of section (ii).

[19] See Harris, 'Kelsen's Pallid Normativity', n. 1 above, 105.

[20] H Kelsen, *The Pure Theory of Law* (2nd edn., trans. M. Knight, University of California Press, 1967), 218.

[21] Harris, 'Kelsen's Pallid Normativity', n. 1 above, 106.

Building from his own work in *Practical Reason and Norms*,[22] and from a textual analysis of aspects of Kelsen's work,[23] Raz contends that Kelsen views the normativity of law as justified normativity, wherein to regard a legal prescription as normative is to accept it as justified, i.e. to accept that there is good reason to do that which it requires. According to this view, only those who accept the prescriptions of a legal system as justified, and as providing reasons for action, can presuppose the basic norm, and hence regard law as normative/interpret the legal system as consisting of valid norms.[24] As was noted earlier, however, Raz also maintains that in many contexts people sometimes use normative terminology and make normative statements whilst not being committed to the normative force of those statements, i.e. whilst not themselves believing that there is good reason to do that which, according to the statement they are making, ought to be done: anarchist law professors can inform their students about what is required according to a legal system they regard as unjustified; Roman Catholic experts on Rabbinical law can advise Jewish friends on what ought to be done according to the norms of orthodox Judaism, and so on.[25] How are these two ideas to be reconciled? The answer is supplied by the idea of statements from a point of view. On Raz's interpretation of Kelsen, law is normative only for someone who regards the norms of a legal system, and the basic norm grounding those norms, as justified, and as providing reasons for action. Raz thus asks us to imagine a hypothetical point of view—which he terms the point of view of the legal man—from which all, and only, those norms of a given legal system are regarded as justified. Legal scientists, whose job it is to give a theoretical exposition of valid law, as well as law teachers and legal practitioners giving theoretical or practical advice about what is required according to law, are then characterized as making statements about what ought to be done from the point of view of the legal man, although they themselves do not endorse his point of view.[26] According to Raz, these 'detached normative statements'[27] about what is required according to a given normative system can be made by those who do not believe in the justification of the system in question, as is the case when a Roman Catholic makes statements about what ought to be done according to Rabbinical law. The Roman Catholic is not making statements of what there is reason to do, *tout court*, because he does not believe that Rabbinical law provides reasons for action. Nonetheless, according to Raz, he is stating what there is reason to do from the point of view of orthodox Judaism, and his statements are fully normative in that sense, although the speaker in his personal capacity is not committed to the normative force of those statements. Likewise, the legal scientist, practitioner, or law teacher making statements about what is required according to law adopts a point of view, and, in Kelsen's terminology, presupposes the basic norm (i.e. presupposes that one ought to act according to

[22] See especially J Raz, *Practical Reason and Norms*, n. 10 above, ch. 5, and especially 170–7.
[23] See Raz, *The Authority of Law*, n. 10 above, chs. 7 and 8, especially 134–45 and 153–9.
[24] Raz's interpretation of Kelsen's views will be discussed further in section (v).
[25] Raz, *The Authority of Law*, n. 10 above, 156–7. [26] Ibid., 140–3. [27] Ibid., 153.

the terms of the historically first constitution, and the norms laid down by that constitution), but does so in a 'special professional and uncommitted sense'.[28] That is to say, while acting in their professional capacity, they adopt the point of view of the legal man, and they make statements from that point of view in giving advice and information about valid law. This, then, is Raz's solution to what Kelsen's anarchist law professor is up to in his day job of making statements about what ought to be done according to the norms of a given legal system to his students: he is making normative statements from a point of view, the point of view of legal science, or of the legal man, to which he is not committed.

For Harris, then, the apparent puzzle which arises in interpreting Kelsen's work, concerning how it is possible to make normative statements which are neither reducible to statements of fact nor plausibly interpreted as value judgements about what there is reason to do on the part of those making them, is avoided by postulating that Kelsen employs a 'pallid' conception of normativity, in which 'ought to do' does not connote 'there are good reasons for doing'. For Raz, however, there is no etiolated or pallid conception of normativity at work in Kelsen's position, and to interpret law as normative is to regard it as providing reasons for action. But, in legal and other contexts, it is possible to make what Raz refers to as detached normative statements, i.e. statements about what there is reason to do from a point of view to which one is not committed. For Raz, Kelsenian normativity is full-blooded normativity, but those giving legal information about what ought to be done according to law need not adopt a full-blooded or committed attitude towards the normative statements which they make.

(iv) A Closer Look at 'Pallid' Normativity

As was discussed above, Harris contends that Kelsen's conception of normativity is 'special' and 'eccentrically narrow.'[29] Thus far, the narrowness in question has been characterized in negative terms: that, for Kelsen, stating that we ought to do something does not imply that we have good reason to do, or that there is value in doing, the thing in question. This, however, does not provide us with a positive account of what—according to Harris—legal normativity *is* for Kelsen. If legal oughts are not to be understood by reference to reasons for action, then how are they to be understood? At several points in his work on this topic, Harris claims that Kelsenian oughts are 'will-relative'.[30] By this, he means that, in order for such oughts to exist, there has to have been an act of will on the part of some authority resulting in a conduct-guiding norm being laid down:

> if I am using such normative terminology appropriately, then I must be saying that the conduct is stipulated by some norm which, as a historical fact, some norm-authority has enacted.[31]

[28] Raz, *The Authority of Law,* 143.

[29] Harris, 'Kelsen's Pallid Normativity', n. 1 above, 99.

[30] e.g., Harris, 'Kelsen, Revolutions and Normativity', n. 1 above, 6, 11, 13; Harris, 'Kelsen's Pallid Normativity', n. 1 above, 103, 106, 112.

[31] Harris, 'Kelsen's Pallid Normativity', n. 1 above, 101.

For Kelsen, the authority of all the norms of a legal system can be traced back to the basic norm, i.e. to the assumption that one ought to conduct oneself according to the terms of the historically first constitution of that legal system, and the norms created according to that constitution.[32] According to Harris's 'will-relative' interpretation of Kelsenian normativity, the practice of legal information-giving, of making legal ought statements characterizing someone's position according to law, is thus ultimately a matter of reporting the content of what has been willed by the makers of the historically first constitution, and of the norms created according to that constitution:

Genuine assertoric sentences can only be uttered, according to Kelsen, when they repeat the content of what some norm-authority, legal or moral, has prescribed.[33]

[Kelsenian oughts] are no more than relative-to-constitution-makers-will oughts.[34]

According to Harris, this is the conception of normativity which is employed by Kelsen throughout his work,[35] and, as the quotations above indicate, he regards it as applying equally to legal and moral normative contexts. Genuine normative discourse about what ought to be done according to morality must also consist in a report of what has been willed by some moral authority.[36] This raises an interesting point in terms of Harris's use of the terms 'pallid' and 'etiolated' in characterizing Kelsen's conception of normativity. These terms suggest that Kelsenian normativity is to be contrasted with, and understood as pale in relation to, some other, more full-blooded, conception of normativity. However, clearly Kelsenian legal normativity is not a pallid version of Kelsenian moral normativity, because, on Harris's interpretation of Kelsen, the same 'will-relative' conception of normativity applies to both.[37] Kelsenian legal normativity must be pallid in relation to something else. For Harris, the something else in question appears to be the way in which he thinks legal normativity is commonly understood:

Kelsen's normativity is misleading because oughtness in law is commonly supposed to be something much more than pallid will-relativity—amounting to either *prima facie* or conclusive reasons for action.[38]

32 See, e.g., Kelsen, *The Pure Theory of Law*, n. 20 above, 200–1; Kelsen, 'The Function of a Constitution', in Tur and Twining, n. 17 above, *et passim*.

33 Harris, 'Kelsen's Pallid Normativity', n. 1 above, 101.

34 Ibid., 106.

35 Although in 'Kelsen's Pallid Normativity', n. 1, above, 95, Harris claims that Kelsen occasionally 'strayed, unwittingly, into a more full-blooded version of normativity', Harris discusses what he means by this claim in the same article at 114–5. Harris mentions this point only very briefly in passing, and in the rest of his work on this topic he discusses and criticizes Kelsen's espousal of a pallid, will-relative normativity. It is this latter interpretation which I focus on in this article.

36 See also Harris, 'Kelsen's Pallid Normativity', n. 1 above, at 102: 'Kelsen . . . repeatedly insists that it is of the essence of a norm that it is valid, that it is binding, that the conduct it stipulates "ought" to be performed. These synonymous characterisations apply to all norms, whether moral or legal.'

37 Of course, this is not to say that, for Kelsen, there are no other differences between legal norms and moral norms. As Harris notes in *Law and Legal Science*, n. 4 above, at 103, one important such difference is that Kelsen claims legal norms are distinctive in stipulating that a coercive act be performed by officials when certain conditions are met.

38 Harris, 'Kelsen, Revolutions and Normativity', n. 1 above, 13.

It seems, therefore, that it is in relation to this common supposition that Kelsen's 'will-relative' conception of normativity is viewed by Harris as pallid and etiolated.[39]

How successful is Harris's interpretation of Kelsenian normativity? Does it do adequate justice to the way in which Kelsen himself characterizes his views? On an examination of certain points which Kelsen was at pains to emphasize in his writings, some doubts emerge. In explaining the relationship between acts of will and norms, Kelsen draws an important distinction which seems to be under-attended to in Harris's interpretation, namely the distinction between subjective and objective oughts.

As Harris notes, throughout his writings Kelsen draws a fundamental distinction between the categories of 'is' and 'ought'.[40] According to Kelsen, an act of will directed towards the behaviour of another—an 'is'—can be given a normative interpretation, i.e. can be interpreted as an 'ought', and, if it is so interpreted, then we can express this by saying that the 'ought' is the meaning of, or is the interpretation given to, the act of will.[41] However, in explaining this idea of an ought as the meaning of an act of will, Kelsen then draws another vital distinction between an ought which is the subjective meaning of an act of will (for ease of reference, I will refer to this as a subjective ought), and an ought which is the objective meaning of an act of will (an objective ought):

> 'Ought' is the subjective meaning of every act of will directed at the behaviour of another. But not every such act has also objectively this meaning; and only if the act of will also has the objective meaning of an 'ought,' is this 'ought' called a 'norm.' If the 'ought' is also the objective meaning of the act, the behaviour at which the act is directed is regarded as something that *ought* to be not only from the point of view of the individual who has performed the act, but also from the point of view of the individual at whose behaviour the act is directed, and of a third individual not involved in the relation between the two.[42]

Kelsen gives as an example to illustrate his point two 'oughts' whose content is that someone should hand over some money: one is the 'ought' of a tax official, and one the 'ought' of a gangster. According to Kelsen, both of these oughts have the same subjective meaning, i.e. from the (subjective) point of view of the gangster or tax official respectively, another individual ought to hand over some money to them. However, only the ought of the tax official can be interpreted not merely as a subjective ought, but as an objective ought or as a valid norm, because only in the case of the tax official is the ought in question authorized by a higher norm, i.e. the tax law empowering him to collect particular sums of money from particular individuals when certain conditions are met. The tax official's ought is, we might

[39] I return to this point in section (vi).

[40] Harris, 'Kelsen's Pallid Normativity', n. 1 above, 100. For Kelsen's views on this point, see Kelsen, *The Pure Theory of Law*, n. 20 above, 2–7.

[41] Ibid., 3–9.

[42] Ibid., 7 (emphasis in original).

say, an ought against the whole world, it is an ought which is objectively valid, and has the meaning that the money ought to be handed over, not merely from the point of view of the tax official, but from the point of view of the individual from whom the money is being demanded, and indeed from the point of view of anyone seeking to understand what the normative situation is in the scenario in question. The existence of a higher authorizing norm, then, is what allows subjective oughts to be interpreted as objective oughts, i.e. as valid norms. This same explanation is applied by Kelsen all the way up the hierarchy of norms. If we ask why we are to interpret the act of will of the legislature in passing the tax statute—which is, thus far, merely a subjective ought, an ought from the point of view of the legislature—as having an objective meaning, i.e. as a valid norm, then we are referred to the existence of the higher authorizing norms of the constitution, and authorizing those, some historically prior constitution. Finally, we are brought to the historical act of will of the framers of the historically first constitution. This, too, can be interpreted as creating merely a subjective ought, i.e. an ought only from the point of view of those framers, unless there is a higher norm which authorized the creation of that constitution, and which hence allows us to interpret their acts of will as creating objectively valid norms. Kelsen answers the question of how there can be a norm authorizing the oughts of the framers of the historically first constitution by postulating the idea of the *Grundnorm* or basic norm, which is 'not a positive norm, posited by a real act of will, but a norm presupposed in juristic thinking'.[43] To presuppose the basic norm is to presuppose that one ought to conduct oneself according to the terms of the historically first constitution and the norms validated by that constitution. It is the presupposition of the basic norm which enables us to interpret the subjective oughts of the framers of the historically first constitution as having an objective meaning, and as creating valid norms which state what ought to be done, not merely from the point of view of those framers, but from the point of view of those who are subject to those norms, and also from the point of view of anyone seeking to understand law in normative terms.

I have lingered over an explanation of these familiar features of Kelsen's theory of law in order to emphasize the distinction he draws between subjective and objective oughts, and the role of higher authorizing norms, and, ultimately, of the basic norm, in allowing subjective oughts to be interpreted as objective ones. As I am primarily interested in matters of interpretation for the moment, I do not wish to examine directly the success of, or difficulties with, this account as an explanation of law's normativity. Rather I want to emphasize two important points which Kelsen is attempting to establish with this account, and which must be adequately explained in interpreting his position: (1) in order for something to be a valid norm, for Kelsen, it must amount to something more than the subjective ought which is the subjective meaning of an act of will, and (2) it is the function of

[43] Kelsen, 'The Function of a Constitution', in Tur and Twining, n. 17 above, 115.

higher authorizing norms, and, ultimately, it is the function of the basic norm to provide this 'something more'. The presupposition in juristic thinking of the basic norm allows the subjective oughts of the framers of the historically first constitution to be interpreted as objective oughts stating what ought to be done, not merely from the point of view of those framers, but from the point of view of those at whose behaviour the oughts are directed, and from the point of view of anyone seeking to understand the legal system in question in normative terms.

One difficulty with Harris's interpretation of Kelsen on the normativity of law is that it does not appear to take adequate account of these two points, or to do adequate justice to Kelsen's distinction between subjective and objective oughts. Harris's claim that Kelsenian ought statements are not statements of reasons for action and are merely 'will-relative', in the sense of merely being reports of those oughts laid down by the acts of will of those who frame constitutions and legislate thereunder, appears to characterize legal normativity in the way that Kelsen characterizes subjective oughts. If oughts are understood as being merely 'relative-to-constitution-makers-will oughts'[44] then it would seem that, in Kelsen's terminology, they remain merely the subjective meanings of acts of will, which are oughts only from the point of view of those willing them. Harris's account does not appear to leave room for the distinction between subjective and objective oughts, because the 'will-relative' interpretation of legal ought statements which Harris offers appears to be indistinguishable from the way that Kelsen characterizes subjective oughts.

Faced with this charge, I suspect that Harris would heartily have denied it, especially as the distinction between subjective and objective oughts is mentioned in his characterization of Kelsen's position:

> In the case of law, to say that conduct is 'illegal' is to do no more than to interpret the 'subjective meaning' (the subjective 'ought') of the norm-authority's will as its 'objective meaning' (an objective 'ought', a valid norm).[45]

The problem is, however, that despite mentioning this distinction, it is difficult to see how Harris actually accounts for and does adequate justice to it in his characterization of Kelsenian normativity. Even at those points in his work where Harris mentions the distinction, the characterization of Kelsen's position offered by him appears to reduce legal norms to subjective oughts, i.e. oughts which are oughts only from the point of view of those willing them: in the case of law, from the point of view of the framers of the historically first constitution:

> The professor of law, the textbook writer, the travel agent and the well-informed revolutionary may speak of 'legal duties' without compromising their politics. According to Kelsen, they do thereby embue conduct with objective 'oughts,' but they are no more than relative-to-constitution-makers-will oughts.[46]

[44] Harris, 'Kelsen's Pallid Normativity', n. 1 above, 106.
[45] Ibid., 101 (internal footnote references to Kelsen's work omitted).
[46] Ibid., 106.

One way of focussing more precisely on the problem which I am attempting to explain here is to ask what is the difference, on Harris's interpretation, between Kelsen's categories of subjective and objective oughts? If Harris characterizes objective oughts as 'relative-to-constitution-makers-will oughts',[47] as he does in the passage quoted above, then how do these differ from, and how is there room on his account for them to differ from, subjective oughts which, according to Kelsen, are oughts only from the point of view of those willing them? As was noted above, the difference, for Kelsen, lies in the existence of a higher authorizing norm, and, ultimately, in the presupposition of the basic norm, which allows the subjective meaning of an act of will to be interpreted as an objectively valid norm. Harris acknowledges that Kelsen views the presupposition of the basic norm as adding something to the subjective prescriptions of law-makers, but he characterizes what is added as:

> merely a formal top-dressing added to the system of prescriptions which are, as a matter of fact, by and large obeyed and enforced.[48]

and characterizes the basic norm itself as:

> ... a formal device for turning supposed prescriptions into so-called 'oughts'.[49]

The problem is, however, that it is difficult to see how, on Harris's interpretation of Kelsen, *anything* is added by the presupposition of the basic norm, and it is difficult to see that the basic norm has any turning to do, or any function to perform. Subjective oughts, according to Kelsen, are oughts only from the point of view of those willing them. This being so, a report of a subjective ought is merely a report of the content of an act of will of another and does not amount to a statement of what ought to be done from the point of view of those on the receiving end of the ought in the question. This seems to tally exactly with Harris's understanding of Kelsenian pallid normativity as 'will-relative' normativity.[50]

For Kelsen, however, the existence of higher authorizing norms, and, ultimately, the presupposition of the basic norm, operates so as to alter the situation, turning subjective oughts into objective ones, and transforming them from being mere reports of the subjective prescriptions of others into objectively valid norms which state what ought to be done, not merely from the point of view of those willing them, but also from the point of view of those at whose behaviour the ought is directed, and indeed from the point of view of anyone seeking to understand the passing scene in normative terms. Kelsen may be accused of not fully explaining exactly what it is to presuppose the basic norm, or how so doing turns oughts from subjective prescriptions into objective norms, but he is striving to explain an alteration in the normative situation which occurs when a subjective ought is interpreted as an objective one by virtue of the presupposition of the basic norm. The 'pallid normativity' which Harris attributes to Kelsen, however, appears to

[47] Harris, 'Kelsen's Pallid Normativity', 106. [48] Ibid., 103. [49] Ibid., 6.
[50] Ibid., 101, 106.

amount to no more than Kelsen's subjective ought, and it is not clear from Harris's writings that anything is added by the presupposition of the basic norm, or that it alters anything in the normative situation, allowing subjective oughts to be interpreted as objective ones. In Harris's account, although he speaks of Kelsenian normativity adding a 'top-dressing' to subjective prescriptions, his 'will-relative' characterization of Kelsenian norms appears to leave those norms meeting only the conditions which need to be met for something to be a subjective ought according to Kelsen. It is very difficult, therefore, to see what the distinction between the subjective and the objective ought is on Harris's interpretation of Kelsen's position, and it is difficult to see what function the basic norm is performing on this interpretation, because, according to Harris, even when the basic norm is presupposed oughts remain will-relative.

(v) Raz and the Hypothetical Point of View of the Legal Man

I have argued above that in emphasizing the distinction between subjective and objective oughts Kelsen is attempting to establish that: (1) in order for something to be a valid norm it must amount to something more than an ought which is the subjective meaning of an act of will, and (2) that it is the function of higher authorizing norms, and, ultimately, it is the function of the basic norm, to provide this 'something more'. The presupposition of the basic norm allows the subjective oughts of the framers of the historically first constitution to be interpreted as objectively valid norms which prescribe what ought to be done, not merely from the point of view of those framers, but from the point of view of those at whose behaviour the oughts are directed, and also from the point of view of anyone seeking to understand law in normative terms. Harris's interpretation of Kelsen does not appear to take adequate account of, or sufficiently explain, these points, which Kelsen himself views as central to his account of legal normativity.

In my view, Joseph Raz's alternative interpretation of Kelsenian normativity does a better job of taking into account and attempting to explain these aspects of Kelsen's position.[51] As was already noted in section (iii), Raz contends that Kelsen views legal normativity as justified normativity, wherein to regard a legal prescription as normative is to accept it as justified, and to accept that there is good reason to do that which it requires. He reaches this conclusion *via* the claim that there are two possible understandings of the normativity of the law: social normativity and

[51] My aim in this article is primarily to explain and illuminate Harris's interpretation of Kelsen by contrasting it with Raz's, and I do not attempt to argue conclusively in favour of Raz's interpretation here. My point is merely that Raz appears to take into account, and to attempt to explain, Kelsen's distinction between subjective and objective oughts, and that, in my view, Harris's interpretation fails to do this adequately. For Raz's views on this point, see *The Authority of Law*, n. 10 above, 134–45, 150, 153–9; J Raz, 'The Purity of the Pure Theory' [1983] *Revue Internationale de Philosophie*, 442, especially sections IV–VI.

justified normativity. According to Raz, Kelsen's 'subjective ought' is a species of social normativity, wherein prescriptions can be considered as norms if they are socially upheld as binding standards.[52] Raz claims that Kelsen rejects social normativity, and that such a rejection is evidenced by the fact that Kelsen claims that someone interpreting the law as consisting merely of subjective oughts does not view it as normative, i.e. as consisting of objectively valid norms. According to Raz's interpretation of Kelsen, therefore, we need to understand legal prescriptions as something more than reports of the socially upheld oughts emanating from the acts of will of others in order to view law as normative:

> Describing the law as commands of a sovereign is, on this theory, describing them as subjective 'ought'. If one does not presuppose the basic norm, then judgements about the lawfulness of action, understood as judgements about their conformity to the commands of a sovereign, are merely subjective value judgements. Kelsen acknowledges that the law can consistently be interpreted in this way, but in this case it is not regarded as normative.[53]

Having rejected a social normativity interpretation of Kelsen on this point, Raz goes on to claim that Kelsen's distinction between subjective and objective oughts can only be made sense of if Kelsen is understood as espousing a concept of justified normativity according to which legal prescriptions are considered as norms only by those who regard them as justified.[54] On this view, only those who accept the prescriptions of a legal system as providing reasons for action can presuppose the basic norm, and hence interpret the legal order as consisting of objectively valid norms. This, therefore, amounts to the 'something more' mentioned in point (1) above: in order for a legal prescription to be interpreted as a valid norm, it must amount to more than an ought which is the subjective meaning of an act of will, in the sense that it must be regarded as providing reasons for action. In defending his rejection of a social normativity interpretation of Kelsen on this point, and in supporting his contention that Kelsen is employing a concept of justified normativity, Raz thus makes use of, and thereby gives an important explanatory role to, Kelsen's distinction between subjective and objective oughts.

As was discussed in section (iii), although Raz contends that, for Kelsen, law is regarded as normative only by those who consider legal norms as justified, he is well aware and believes that an adequate legal theory must explain the phenomenon of individuals who are not committed to the justifiability of legal norms—like the anarchist law professor—making normative statements about what ought to be done according to law.[55] Raz's way out of the puzzle posed by such individuals' use of normative statements lies with his claim that such individuals—including legal theorists, law teachers, and legal practitioners—can make normative statements from the hypothetical point of view of the 'legal man', i.e. a point of view from which all, and only, those norms of a given legal system are regarded as justified, without themselves being committed to that point of view. Such statements

52 Raz, *The Authority of Law*, n. 10 above, 134–5. 53 Ibid., 135. 54 Ibid., 136–7.
55 Ibid., 153–4.

are termed 'detached normative statements', and although the normativity with which they are imbued is a justified normativity wherein 'ought to do' connotes 'there is good reason to do', the attitude towards that normativity on the part of those legal theorists, law teachers, and legal practitioners making the statements in question is detached and uncommitted.[56]

Harris considers, and rejects, the rival interpretation of Kelsenian normativity offered by Raz. In so doing, he expresses some doubts concerning the usefulness of Raz's 'legal man' device in explaining how it is possible for those who are not committed to the force of normative statements nonetheless to make them.[57] Harris disputes the analogy which Raz draws between a Roman Catholic making normative statements about what ought to be done from the point of view of orthodox Judaism, whilst not being committed to the tenets of that religion, and the legal theorist or legal practitioner making normative statements about what ought to be done according to law whilst not being committed to the justifiability of the law.[58] It is worth quoting Harris's view on this point at some length in order to try to understand his objection:

> The problem with this analogy is that, in the case of the non-believing adviser, there is a real point of view which he can adopt, whereas the 'legal man' does not exist. The believer subscribes to a religious value-system from which, from his point of view, genuine substantive 'oughts' can be derived. The hypothetical legal man has, by assumption, no extra-legal moral system on which he bases the normativity of the law . . . He merely assumes that law and moral truth are one. He is not in the position of one who believes that there are good moral reasons why the law should be obeyed, for that would suppose that there can be extra-legal grounds for moral obligations. The 'legal man' supposes that there are none. For this curious creature law is all the morality there can be, and morality is understood, reflexively, as all that is required by law.
>
> So far as substantive moral grounding is concerned, the hypothetical 'legal man' stands in the air.[59]

That the 'legal man' is a curious character need not be denied by anyone, Raz included. As Harris notes, he and his point of view are hypothetical—there is no actual individual who regards as morally justified all, and only those, norms of a given legal system—and Raz offers no explanation of how he could have acquired, or whether he could be justified in, his view. Although all this can be granted, I am puzzled as to why Harris thinks it matters. Raz himself clearly views the point of view of the legal man as a hypothetical point of view of someone who cannot be assumed actually to exist.[60] The legal man's worth turns on his usefulness as an explanatory device in capturing the character, and explaining the possibility, of the kind of statements which Raz terms detached normative statements, not on

[56] Raz, *The Authority of Law*, 142–5, 153–9.

[57] Harris, 'Kelsen, Revolutions and Normativity', n. 1 above, 7; Harris, 'Kelsen's Pallid Normativity', n. 1 above, 112–3.

[58] See Raz, *The Authority of Law*, n. 10 above, 153–9.

[59] Harris, 'Kelsen's Pallid Normativity', n. 1 above, 113.

[60] Raz, *The Authority of Law*, n. 10 above, 140–1.

whether such persons exist in reality, or on whether their beliefs would be plausible or justifiable if they did. In the passage quoted above, Harris also appears to present the example of the non-believing 'religious adviser' as having some plausibility and explanatory power which is lacking in the example of someone (e.g. the anarchist law professor) making statements from the point of view of the legal man, because in the case of the non-believing religious adviser, there are actual believers with actual beliefs whose point of view the non-believer can adopt. This, however, may be missing Raz's point somewhat:

> It is important not to confuse such statements from a point of view with statements about other people's beliefs. One reason is that there may be no one who has such a belief. The friend in our example may be expressing a very uncommon view on an obscure point of Rabbinical law. Indeed Rabbinical law may never have been endorsed or practised by anybody, not even the inquiring Jew.[61]

In this passage, Raz is keen to emphasize that statements about what ought to be done from a certain point of view should not be interpreted as statements about other people's beliefs.[62] He claims that statements can be made about what ought to be done according to a given normative system, even when few people have, or, in extreme cases, no one has, beliefs about certain of those norms. The issue, then, is not whether the legal man or the believer in the norms of Rabbinical law exists, or whether they believe in all the norms of their respective normative systems, but how best to characterise statements about what ought to be done according to a normative system made by those who do not regard the norms of the system in question as justified. Raz's hypothetical legal man is a thinking aid in this regard; an explanatory device which illustrates the point of view of a particular normative system from which detached normative statements can be made. *Contra* Harris, the anarchist law professor making statements from the hypothetical point of view of the legal man and the Roman Catholic making statements from the point of view of orthodox Judaism are not in disanalogous situations: neither is making statements about the beliefs of others; both are making statements about what there is reason to do from the point of view of a normative system to which they are not committed.

(vi) From Legal Theory to Law: Interpreting Normativity

The discussion of Harris's and Raz's respective positions in the last two sections focussed squarely on how best to interpret aspects of Kelsen's views on the normativity of law. While I believe that the significance of Kelsen's contribution to

[61] Raz, *The Authority of Law*, n. 10 above, 156–7.

[62] See also Raz, *The Authority of Law*, n. 10 above, at 153: 'A detached legal statement is a statement of law, of what legal rights and duties people have, not a statement about people's beliefs, attitudes, or actions, not even about their beliefs, attitudes, or actions about the law.'

twentieth century legal philosophy, and Harris's long-standing interest in understanding and analysing Kelsen's views, justifies scholars paying close attention to these points of interpretation, Harris himself was quick to note the dangers of becoming embroiled solely in interpreting what Kelsen was trying to say, without also considering whether what he had to say provides an accurate and adequate characterization of aspects of law itself. As Harris puts it:

> [Kelsen] may have been mistaken in all his claims, but he deserves that at least they be tested by reference to what actually does, or might, go on in social life.[63]

As was discussed at the outset of this article, legal statements—such as those made by the legal practitioner, law teacher, or legal scientist—giving information about what is required according to law are taken by Harris, Raz, and Kelsen to be a ubiquitous and important feature of the social practice of law. An analysis of the character of such statements is thus taken by all three theorists to be an important task of jurisprudence. Raz's work interpreting Kelsen on the normativity of law combines an exegetical analysis of what Kelsen was saying on this topic with a claim that Kelsen offers important insights into the character of different kinds of normative statements encountered within legal contexts.[64] Raz's interpretation of Kelsenian normativity attempts to explain the normative claims of a given system of prescriptions in a way which does justice to how those claims should be understood from, as it were, the system's own point of view. From the point of view of orthodox Judaism, normative statements concerning what ought to be done according to Rabbinical law are not reducible to the beliefs of orthodox Jews, nor to the content of the historical acts of will which laid down the founding tenets of Rabbinical law. Rather, they are statements of what there is reason to do, of what there is value in doing, according to orthodox Judaism. This point of view—what the system itself means by its claim that something ought to be done—is what Raz is eager to do adequate justice to, in adopting a justified conception of normativity both in his own work and in his work interpreting Kelsen. At the same time, however, Raz wants to account for the common phenomenon of people making statements about what ought to be done according to normative systems, while not being committed to the normative force of those statements. Raz contends that Kelsen's account of normativity is particularly helpful in drawing attention to the possibility and character of these detached normative statements, and Raz's explanatory device of the hypothetical point of view of the legal man, and his account of the possibility of making detached normative statements from that point of view, attempts to provide an explanation of them. Ultimately, the success or otherwise of Raz's account of the normativity of law, and of his interpretation of Kelsen's views on this issue, is to be assessed by how well the account explains the character of the

[63] Harris, 'Kelsen's Pallid Normativity', n. 10 above, 95.

[64] Raz, *The Authority of Law*, n. 10 above, 144–5, 157.

claims of normative systems, and the variety of types of normative statement which can be made regarding such systems in legal contexts.

For Harris, too, the ultimate goal is an adequate explanation of the place of normativity in law, and of the character of legal statements giving information about what is required according to law. However, whereas for Raz, Kelsen's views provide valuable insights into these issues, for Harris, Kelsen's work on this topic amounts to a cautionary tale of how not to offer an adequate explanation of the normativity of law. Having developed and defended his interpretation of Kelsen as espousing a 'pallid', 'will-relative' conception of normativity, Harris finds such an account woefully inadequate and incapable of explaining the character of legal statements which give information about what is required according to law. In my view, it is not an easy matter to pinpoint exactly why Harris regards Kelsen's account of normativity as inadequate. At various points in his writings he refers to it as 'contrived and artificial',[65] and 'unsatisfactory and misleading'.[66] On one occasion, Harris characterizes the sense in which the account is unsatisfactory as follows:

> It is unsatisfactory to proclaim that law entails 'ought' only in the sense that, if we put it beyond argument that the constitution-makers had authority to do what they did, then you 'ought' to fulfill the law's demands.[67]

Is it the fact that the account puts the authority of constitution-makers beyond argument which Harris finds unsatisfactory here? That is to say, is his objection that Kelsen's approach does not allow debate on the conditions under which constitution-makers' authority is justified, and that this renders his theory unsatisfactory and 'unilluminating',[68] as an explanation of some centrally important features of legal practice? Other remarks which Harris makes regarding Kelsenian oughts, for example, '[f]or the purpose of any significant moral or political controversy, this is no ought at all'[69] suggest that this may be the case.

Harris's contention that Kelsen's conception of legal normativity is 'misleading' is also of interest here. As was already noted in section (iv), according to Harris, Kelsen's conception of normativity is misleading in relation to the fact that oughtness in law 'is commonly supposed to be something much more than pallid will-relativity—amounting to either *prima facie* or conclusive reasons for action'.[70] It is not entirely clear to whom Harris attributes this common supposition. On some occasions in his writings, he talks of there being 'a widely shared view',[71] without qualification as to who might share it, which seems to suggest that the view is one held by people generally, including those who create, administer, and are subject to law. At other points, however, he seems to have in mind a widely shared view of the legal philosophical community.[72] In either case, it is curious that Harris terms

[65] Harris, 'Kelsen's Pallid Normativity', n. 1 above, 115.

[66] Harris, 'Kelsen, Revolutions and Normativity', n. 1 above, 13. [67] Ibid., 13.

[68] Ibid., 11. [69] Ibid., 13.

[70] Harris, 'Kelsen, Revolutions and Normativity', n. 1 above, 13.

[71] Harris, 'Kelsen's Pallid Normativity', n. 1 above, 110. [72] Ibid., 113.

Kelsen's conception of normativity 'misleading'[73] in relation to this common supposition, for Harris himself finds the common supposition misleading in rather a dramatic way. Far from agreeing with the alleged supposition that oughtness in law amounts to either *prima facie* or conclusive reasons for action, Harris rejects this view of law's normativity root and branch by rejecting the thesis that law is intrinsically normative at all:

> Should we not consider the possibility that, contrary to a widely shared consensus between modern positivist and anti-positivist legal philosophers, the law is not intrinsically normative: That to assert the existence of a legal duty is not necessarily to claim that something ought to be done?[74]

Harris thus adopts an understanding of the character of legal statements giving information about what is legally required which departs radically from the 'common supposition' that oughtness in law amounts to 'either *prima facie* or conclusive reasons for action.'[75] Although he regards such statements as statements of legal duties, he contends that they are not to be understood as statements of what ought to be done at all:

> Propositions of law assert the existence (or absence) of duties prescribed by the law presently in force in some jurisdiction. They do not, in and of themselves, assert that anything, from any point of view, ought to be done.[76]

Given his criticism of Kelsen's conception of normativity as 'pallid' and 'misleading' in relation to a commonly supposed and more full-blooded conception of normativity, wherein legal ought-statements are statements of reasons for action, this is an intriguing turn of events. One might have thought that, as Harris views Kelsenian normativity as pallid and as being too 'thin',[77] to allow legal theorists to debate matters of significant moral and political controversy, such as whether and under what conditions legal authority is justified, then he would instead embrace a more full-blooded, reasons-for-action-based view of legal normativity instead. However, although some of his remarks in discussing Raz's work indicate that Harris understands the attraction of such a view,[78] it is an attraction which he vigorously resists, and he adopts instead an understanding of legal duties wherein not only do they not amount to reasons for action, but they do not state, from any point of view, what ought to be done at all. Harris's interpretation of Kelsenian normativity as pallid does not lead him to embrace a more full-blooded conception of the normativity of the law, but rather sends him off in a dramatically different direction, to reject the idea that law is intrinsically normative.

73 Harris, 'Kelsen, Revolutions and Normativity', n. 1 above, 13.
74 Harris, 'Kelsen's Pallid Normativity', n. 1 above, 113.
75 Harris, 'Kelsen, Revolutions and Normativity', n. 1 above, 13.
76 Harris, 'Kelsen's Pallid Normativity', n. 1 above, 115.
77 Ibid., 110.
78 Ibid., 112, where Harris states that Raz's interpretation of Kelsenian normativity, 'would have the advantage of viewing law and critical morality as sharing the same normativity whilst adhering to legal positivist premises . . .'.

(vii) Conclusion

Although Harris contends that we should consider and explore the possibility that, although there are many ways in which normativity 'hovers above'[79] the law, law is not intrinsically normative, he did not develop or defend this idea extensively in his later work interpreting Kelsen which has been under consideration here. In this context, the few remarks which he makes in support of his view that normativity is not intrinsic to law draw on the way in which people subject to law think about and talk about legal prescriptions and their consequences in their everyday lives.[80] In making these remarks, Harris reveals his methodological colours, i.e. that he believed that the final court of appeal on this issue is the ability of legal theories adequately and accurately to explain the way in which law is experienced, used, and talked about by those who create, administer, and are subject to it. As Harris himself noted, his views on this topic demonstrate that he was not afraid to swim against the legal philosophical tide on the issue of the normativity of law.[81] His trend-bucking views were sparked by his long-standing interest in interpreting Kelsen, and by his frustrations with the pallid conception of normativity which he attributed to Kelsen. Harris's work interpreting Kelsenian normativity was thus a fruitful springboard for his own thoughts on the relationship between normativity and law, as well as a source of thought-provoking commentary for many students of jurisprudence, myself included, trying better to understand Kelsen's work. I have disagreed with some aspects of his views in this article, but it is beyond dispute that a scholarly and distinctive interpretation of Kelsen, and a willingness to buck legal philosophical trends are the hallmarks of Jim Harris's work interpreting legal normativity.

[79] Harris, 'Kelsen's Pallid Normativity', n. 1 above., 113.
[80] Ibid., 113, 115.
[81] Ibid., 113.

3

Reductionism and Explanation in Legal Theory

*Brian Bix**

My direct interactions with Professor J.W. Harris were not that many—and certainly not as many as I would have wanted. I sat in on one of his courses when I was a doctoral student at Oxford, and occasionally sought his advice on jurisprudential matters, both during my time at Oxford and later. Though I always learned a great deal from our contacts, it is not here that he had his most significant impact on me. From long before I met him, I have benefited enormously from his writings—in particular his general work in legal theory and his excellent writings on Hans Kelsen[1]—and I am confident that the learning process will continue for as long as I have the good judgement to consult Harris's work.

One of Harris's most provocative ideas was his reworking of a basically Kelsenian approach to legal theory in his book *Law and Legal Science* (a work which derived from his LSE doctoral thesis).[2] In that text, in the course of an

* Frederick W. Thomas Professor of Law and Philosophy, University of Minnesota. I am grateful to Torben Spaak and an anonymous reader for comments on earlier drafts of this article.

[1] On Kelsen, see, e.g., JW Harris 'When and Why Does the Grundnorm Change?' (1971) 29 *CLJ* 103; JW Harris, 'Kelsen's Concept of Authority' (1977) 36 *CLJ* 353; JW Harris 'Kelsen and Normative Consistency', in R Tur and W Twining (eds.), *Essays on Kelsen* (Clarendon Press, 1986), 201; JW Harris 'Kelsen's Pallid Normativity' (1996) 9 *Ratio Juris* 94. For roughly a generation in Anglo-American legal theory, it seemed that only Harris and Stanley L Paulson (another contributor to this collection) were doing serious and sustained work on Hans Kelsen. Kelsen studies lose a great deal with Harris's passing, and the only small consolation is that English-language legal theorists now have access to more writings from Continental European and South American scholars in the field—through translation or those theorists' willingness to write in English. See, e.g., SL Paulson and BL Paulson (eds.), *Normativity and Norms: Critical Perspectives on Kelsenian Themes* (Clarendon Press, 1998), collecting many Kelsenian works.

On Harris's contribution to legal theory generally, see, e.g., JW Harris, *Law and Legal Science* (Clarendon Press, 1979); JW Harris, 'Unger's Critique of Formalism in Legal Reasoning: Hero, Hercules and Humdrum' (1989) 52 *MLR* 42; and JW Harris, *Legal Philosophies* (2nd edn., Butterworths, 1997). The last, *Legal Philosophies*, is a 'student text', but that label distracts from its eminent value, both in making difficult material accessible to those new to a subject, and in the original scholarship that pervades that work.

[2] JW Harris, *Law and Legal Science* (Clarendon Press, 1979). On the similarities in spirit between Kelsen's work and Harris's book, see SL Paulson, 'Subsumption, Derogation, and Noncontradiction in "Legal Science"' (1981) 48 *U Chicago LR* 802, 802–4, 818.

ambitious and meticulous rethinking of legal theory, Harris offers an expressly reductionist theory of law. In particular, he developed an approach to law that portrays law entirely in terms of the imposition of duties, or exceptions from them.[3] It is important to note that this view of law was not offered as part of a conventional view of what legal theory is or does. While most legal theorists speak broadly about offering theories about 'the "nature" of law'[4] or 'the concept of law',[5] Harris referred more narrowly (or, perhaps, more precisely) to 'the practices and values of legal science',[6] where 'legal science' was understood as 'that activity, widespread in countries with developed legal institutions, whose necessary objective is the systematic exposition of some corpus of legislative materials'.[7] Whether the difference in focus (between 'the nature of law' and 'legal science') is significant for our purposes is a matter that will be revisited below.

Harris referred to his own approach as 'reductionist'.[8] He argued that such reductionism 'is a necessary consequence of the logic and values of legal science.'[9] In constructing a theory about law that reduced[10] law or legal rules to essentially one type of norm, Harris is in good company: John Austin and Hans Kelsen were also reductionists. Austin argued that all law could be understood in terms of orders backed by threats—commands of a sovereign[11] (and similar views can be found in the works of Thomas Hobbes and Jeremy Bentham[12]). Kelsen argued

[3] For example: 'the legal system described by legal science is comprised of individual legal rules imposing duties or granting exceptions to duties': Harris, n. 2 above, 70. See also ibid. 20–1, 81, 84, 92–106, 167.

[4] See, e.g., J Raz, 'Two Views of the Nature of the Theory of Law: A Partial Comparison' (1998) 4 *Legal Theory* 249, 251 ('At its most fundamental, legal philosophy is an inquiry into the nature of law.').

[5] HLA Hart, *The Concept of Law* (2nd edn., Clarendon Press, 1994) (hereafter Hart, *Concept*).

[6] Harris, n. 2 above, 13. [7] Ibid., 2.

[8] Ibid., 21: 'The view here suggested of the basic units of which legal systems are comprised is reductionist in nature. It means that descriptive statements in legal science which are not descriptive of duty-imposing or duty-excepting rules are reducible to statements about the conditions under which the duties imposed by various rules exist.' See also ibid., 93, 98–102.

[9] Ibid., 21.

[10] In the jurisprudential literature, 'reductionism' sometimes refers to a different kind of reduction: trying to restate normative phenomena in purely empirical terms. While Harris and Kelsen were reductionists in the monism/pluralism terms discussed in this article, they were not reductionists in the normative/empirical sense. John Austin was arguably a reductionist in both senses; HLA Hart strongly opposed both types of reductionism.

[11] e.g., J Austin, *The Province of Jurisprudence Determined* (1832) (ed. Wilfrid E Rumble, CUP, 1995), Lecture I.

[12] For Hobbes, see T Hobbes, *Leviathan* (1651) (ed. Richard Tuck, CUP, 1996), ch. 26, 183: 'I define civil law in this manner. Civil law is to every subject those rules which the Commonwealth hath commanded him, by word, writing, or other sufficient sign of the will, to make use of for the distinction of right and wrong; that is to say, of what is contrary and what is not contrary to the rule.' For Bentham, see J Bentham, *Of Laws in General* (1782) (ed. HLA Hart, Athlone, 1970), 1: 'A law may be defined as an assemblage of signs declarative of a volition conceived or adopted by the *sovereign* in a state, concerning the conduct to be observed in a certain *case* by a certain person or class of persons, who in the case in question are or are supposed to be subject to his power: such volition trusting for its accomplishment to the expectation of certain events which it is intended such declaration should upon occasion be a means of bringing to pass, and the prospect of which it is intended should act as a motive upon those whose conduct is in question.'

that all legal norms should be understood as authorizations to officials to impose sanctions.[13]

Of course, as there have been prominent advocates of reductionism, like Austin and Kelsen, there have also been prominent opponents, of whom the best-known example may be H.L.A. Hart. Hart's argument had been that theories that reduce law to a single type of rule hide important facts about the plurality of objectives of legal rules, and the variety in the ways that different kinds of rules are experienced by legal subjects. Reductionist or monistic portrayals of law are thus claimed to be inferior to theories that, by their pluralistic description, capture the full richness of legal regulation.[14]

Given this standard objection to reductionism ('social life is complex, so theories that purport to describe social institutions do better when they disclose more of this complexity'), why would theorists even consider a reductionist/monistic approach?[15] Here is one possible line of response: to be able to say 'law is basically X'—where 'X' might be 'duty' or 'a command from the sovereign' or 'an authorization to an official to impose sanctions'—seems a basic instance of what analytical legal philosophy hopes to do: to give us some insight into law that we did not have (or, at least, could not articulate) earlier.

Reductionism in legal theory raises standard questions regarding theorizing generally about social practices and institutions: in particular, the costs and benefits of simplification in the construction of models and theories.[16] There is an obvious and interesting comparison with debates within and about economics. Neo-classical economics is built around a simplified model of human behaviour, in which people are assumed to be the rational maximizers of their preferences. This model of human behaviour has been attacked as inaccurate, misleading, and distorting, both by non-economists and by some economists who have chosen to incorporate a more complex model of human behaviour in their work (this has included the 'behavioural economists' who have incorporated Herbert Simon's work on bounded rationality and the empirical findings relating to cognitive biases[17]). Additionally, economists sometimes add other simplifying (and concededly

[13] e.g., H Kelsen, *General Theory of Law and State* (Russell & Russell, 1945), 58–61, 143–4; H Kelsen, *Pure Theory of Law* (trans. Max Knight, California, 1967), 114–19. See generally SL Paulson, 'Kelsen and Harris on the Legal Norm, the Basic Legal Science *Fiat,* and the "Normativity Problematic" ' (this volume), Part I. There are, however, complications in Kelsen's work—especially viewed over time—which may raise questions for the characterization of his theory as being clearly 'reductionist' in this way. See, e.g., SL Paulson, n. 2 above, 808–9.

[14] Hart, *Concept,* n. 5 above, 26–42.

[15] Harris's actual response to Hart was along a different line: that types of rules do not correspond neatly to purposes. Harris, n. 2 above, 99–100.

[16] Compare, e.g., John Finnis's argument that it is better to build a legal theory around the 'ideal type' of law rather than around a 'lowest common denominator' shared by all legal systems: J Finnis, *Natural Law and Natural Rights* (Clarendon Press, 1980), 3–11. Other thoughtful meta-theory discussions in recent jurisprudential texts include W Lucy, *Understanding and Explaining Adjudication* (OUP, 1999), 17–41; and WJ Waluchow, *Inclusive Legal Positivism* (Clarendon Press, 1994), 9–30.

[17] For 'bounded rationality', see, e.g., HA Simon, 'A Behavioral Model of Rationality' (1955) 69 *Quarterly J Econ* 99; for cognitive biases, see, e.g., D Kahneman, P Slovic, and A Tversky (eds.),

unrealistic) assumptions, e.g., sometimes assuming that the parties have full information, that transactions are costless, and the like.[18] Economists offer a number of defences of their simplified models: primarily, that a more complicated (more realistic) set of assumptions would, on one hand, create a model so flexible that empirical observations would be unable to support or refute it; and, on the other hand, create too many factors to allow for useful predictions.[19]

By contrast, what are we to say about (descriptive or conceptual[20]) theories about the nature of law? To evaluate theories about the nature of law—either at the level of particular theories, or at the level of generalized advice about such theories (e.g., whether to have reductive or complex theories)—one must start with a distinct sense of the purpose of such theories. To ask that theories about the nature of law offer useful predictions is to misunderstand what they are about. Theories about the nature of law are not—or not, primarily—empirical claims about current or future behaviours, but rather efforts to offer explanations and insights regarding the nature of a particular social institution (that is also a reason-giving practice).[21]

As to how to judge the value of a theory or conception of law, commentators' views diverge sharply. For example, Joseph Raz argued that the usual principles of theory construction should not be used in choosing among possible alternatives, as 'law' is not (merely) an arbitrary concept we produce to help understand our world; rather, it is an existing concept we are trying to understand, 'a concept entrenched in our society's self-understanding' that we are trying to clarify.[22] Thus, for Raz at least, one should not prefer a simpler, more coherent, and more monistic theory of the nature of law (as one might do in constructing a theory elsewhere in the study of social action), if the view of law we are trying to capture and articulate is not itself simple, coherent, or monistic in this way. (Raz's approach will be discussed in greater detail below.)

Judgment under Uncertainty: Heuristics and Biases (Cambridge, 1982). On the application of these ideas to economic and legal work, see CR Sunstein (ed.), *Behavioral Law & Economics* (CUP, 2000).

[18] Game theory can be seen as an effort to build a predictive economic theory that alters some, but not all, of the assumptions of neo-classical economics, e.g., by allowing that parties' knowledge is often imperfect and asymmetric, and that there are often significant transaction costs. See generally E Rasmusen, *Games and Information: An Introduction to Game Theory* (3rd edn., Basil Blackwell, 2001), 280.

[19] See, e.g., RA Posner, *Economic Analysis of Law* (6th edn., Aspen, 2003), 17–18.

[20] This phrase is intended to be both broad and somewhat precise: precise in capturing the range of claims offered on behalf of theories of the nature of law, but simultaneously broad, in that the difference between 'descriptive theories' and 'conceptual theories' (and analytical legal theorists have claimed, at various times, to be offering one or the other or both) are substantial. On these points, see, e.g., B Bix, 'On Description and Legal Reasoning', in L Meyer (ed.), *Rules and Reasoning* (Hart, 1999), 7; B Bix, 'Raz on Necessity' (2003) 22 *Law and Philosophy* 537.

[21] On why this dual nature—social institution and reason-giving practice—can cause difficulty for theories of law, see J Finnis, 'On the Incoherence of Legal Positivism' (2000) 75 *Notre Dame LR* 1597, at 1603–5; BH Bix, 'Legal Positivism', in MP Golding and WA Edmundson (eds.), *The Blackwell Guide to the Philosophy of Law and Legal Theory* (Basil Blackwell, 2005), 29, 44–5.

[22] J Raz, 'Can There Be A Theory of Law?', in Golding and Edmundson, n. 21 above, 324, 331 (hereafter Raz, 'Theory of Law'); J Raz, *Ethics in the Public Domain* (Clarendon Press, 1994), 221 (hereafter Raz, *Ethics*).

Those sceptical about Platonist or conceptual analyses of law (like Brian Leiter, who prefers a naturalistic approach to legal philosophy[23]) are inclined to test theories of law by how 'fruitful' they will be in our other (more empirical, perhaps sociological) studies of law.[24] From this perspective, if our choice among theories about the nature of law is not grounded in some pre-existing Platonic Form/Idea of law (and if a single precise concept is not picked out simply by linguistic usage), then we should select theories on the basis of usefulness (and we may discover that different theories are the most useful for different purposes—e.g., the best theory of law for the purpose of sociological investigations might be different from the best theory for historical research).

Other theorists hold more tightly to the idea that theories of law are attempts to understand something independent of us, and that we can judge that some theories will do better at this than others. For Joseph Raz, such theories should capture the 'essential' attributes of law. Under this approach, our concept of law (not '*the*' concept of law, not some unchanging Idea we are 'discovering') is a matter about which we can be right or wrong in our theories, and which we cannot simply re-invent for our own purposes.[25] Similarly, Raz rejects the notion that we (as theorists) can choose a concept of law[26] based, say, on its fruitfulness for further research, or even according to its simplicity or elegance; rather, it is a concept already present, already part of our self-understanding.[27]

Even for those of us initially sympathetic to Raz's position, there are some obvious difficulties that must be overcome. First, one must clarify the idea of a society's self-understanding: for example, in this case, what are the parameters of 'this society' in space and time? Are we talking about 'Western' nations for the past three centuries, or a particular state within the United States at the present (give or take a month or two)? The broader the definition of 'us', the more likely it seems that any view(s) about law will be either highly disputed or (to the extent agreed upon) vague to the point of being uninteresting. This is connected with the second point: that a number of commentators (e.g., Stephen Perry[28]) have argued that views about law are contested, and that any choice among such views involves a moral or political choice.

A different sort of problem is raised by the idea of 'understanding' or 'explanation'. To the extent that we reject evaluating theories about law (solely or primarily) based on fit with linguistic practices or 'usefulness' in social scientific work, in

[23] See B Leiter, 'Naturalism in Legal Philosophy', in E N Zalta (ed.), *The Stanford Encyclopedia of Philosophy* (Fall 2002 edn.), http://plato.stanford.edu/archives/fall2002/entries/lawphil-naturalism/ (hereafter Leiter, 'Naturalism in Legal Philosophy').

[24] B Leiter, 'Realism, Positivism, and Conceptual Analysis' (1998) 4 *Legal Theory* 533, at 546–7.

[25] Raz, 'Theory of Law', n. 22 above, 331; J Raz, 'On the Nature of Law' (1996) 82 *Archiv für Rechts- und Sozialphilosophie* 1.

[26] On the connection between concepts and knowledge, see Raz, 'Theory of Law', n. 22 above, 324–8.

[27] Raz, *Ethics*, n. 22 above, 221; Raz, 'Theory of Law', n. 22 above, 331.

[28] e.g., SR Perry, 'Hart's Methodological Positivism' (1998) 4 *Legal Theory* 427. For one response to Perry, by a conceptual legal theorist, see J Coleman, *The Practice of Principle* (OUP, 2001), 197–210.

favour of evaluating the extent to which the theory 'explains' or helps us better to 'understand' the law, then we need to be concerned about the mushiness of those concepts. Of course, it may be that we can do no better than to live with these imprecise—and, to some extent intuitive—notions, for they may be resistant to further clarification. Examples may be better than analysis here: those who find the work of John Austin persuasive believe that they now 'understand' the nature of law better through Austin's claim that law is basically the command of a sovereign;[29] and similarly for H.L.A. Hart's view that legal rights are best understood as legally protected choices.[30] And in both cases these are theories that purport to offer insights about a social practice, though at the cost of a less than perfect fit with practices and participant perceptions.[31] Equally important, insight is no longer insight if its distortion of the subject of explanation is too significant. Hart's critique of Austin's theory of law[32] is grounded on the view that Austin's theory distorts our understanding of law more than it enhances it (because Austin's command theory fails to account fully for the variety of legal rules, cannot distinguish legitimate legal systems from pure impositions of force, and so on).

A more recent version of the basic trade-off of legal theories—'insight' as against 'fit'—is the debate between 'inclusive legal positivism' and 'exclusive legal positivism'.[33] These are alternative interpretations of the legal positivist idea that there is no necessary connection between law and morality. Inclusive legal positivists state that there can be moral criteria for legal validity, but where this occurs it is a contingent matter, grounded in a conventional source (while there is still no *necessary* moral content to legal systems or to valid legal rules). This reading of legal positivism has the advantage of being able to incorporate smoothly the way that constitutional provisions in many countries seem to set moral standards as necessary criteria of legal validity, and the way that common law decision-making in some countries seems to make moral standards sufficient in limited circumstances for legal validity. By contrast, exclusive legal positivists argue that it is part of the nature of law (and thus true for all legal systems) that the content of legal rules can be ascertained without recourse to moral evaluation. In this debate, one might conclude, roughly, that inclusive legal positivism seems more compatible with the way most commentators and participants think about law (in particular, constitutional law), while exclusive legal positivism, at some cost in 'fit', does a better job of saying something interesting about the nature of law (that law is tied

[29] See Austin, n. 11 above. For a largely receptive treatment of Austin's work, see Roger Cotterrell, *The Politics of Jurisprudence* (2nd edn., LexisNexis, 2003), 49–77.

[30] See HLA Hart, *Essays on Bentham* (Clarendon Press, 1982), 163–93 (hereafter Hart, *Essays*).

[31] As Hart, for example, expressly concedes. See ibid., 188–93.

[32] See Hart, *Concept*, n. 5 above, 18–49.

[33] There are useful article-overviews of exclusive legal positivism (by Marmor, at 104–24) and inclusive legal positivism (by KE Himma, at 125–65) in J Coleman and S Shapiro (eds.), *The Oxford Handbook of Jurisprudence and Philosophy of Law* (OUP, 2002).

in distinctive ways to the nature of authority and practical reasoning).[34] Of course, some observers might feel about exclusive legal positivism the way Hartian legal positivists feel about John Austin's legal theory: that it offers not so much an insight into law, as a distortion of it.

One additional point: one might inquire of Raz if the objective of legal theory is the proper explanation of a collective self-understanding (or that part of self-understanding that deals with institutional rule-guidance and dispute resolution), why is that task not best done by sociologists or opinion polls? This challenge is related to the argument Brian Leiter has raised from philosophical naturalism,[35] that there is neither need nor justification for 'armchair' conceptual analysis; rather, we should all turn to empirical work. This is not the place to consider the challenge of philosophical naturalism at length,[36] but it is a view that must be taken into account (whether one's theory of law is monistic/reduced or pluralistic/complex).

Within the context of how theories of law should be constructed, Harris creates distinct problems—or, perhaps, to the contrary, offers a distinct solution—in *Law and Legal Science*, when he portrays his approach *not* as a theory of law, but as a theory about the view of legal science. For Harris, 'legal science' summarizes what judges and legal commentators do: creating a coherent field of meaning—a consistent set of duties—from past official actions. If one were to be uncharitable,[37] one would say that this seems to beg the most important question: whether law is *in fact* the way it is portrayed by legal commentators and judges. Commentators, from the logical-positivist-like scepticism of the Scandinavian legal realists to the modern-Left critique of schools like critical legal studies, feminist legal theory, and critical race theory, have all raised significant questions about the way law is portrayed by judges and conventional 'legal scientists'. The proper response to this challenge is, first, to concede that there is value in discussing, in a searching and inquiring way, 'what law is', and including in that discussion a willingness to consider ontological issues and sceptical responses. However, one should also (1) agree with Harris that it is beneficial to consider the perspective of the judge or the legal counsellor giving advice, perspectives that assume the validity of

[34] See B Bix, 'Patrolling the Boundaries: Inclusive Legal Positivism and the Nature of Jurisprudential Debate' (1999) 12 *Canadian J Law & Jurisprudence* 17.

[35] See Leiter, 'Naturalism in Legal Philosophy', n. 23 above.

[36] A response might go along the following lines: that a naturalist approach might work well with judicial reasoning (analogous to the naturalist turn in epistemology), where one can substitute for armchair conceptual debates about judicial reasoning empirical investigations of how judges in fact reason and what the consequences are for different approaches to judicial reasoning. When the conceptual question is about how to divide 'law' from non-law, it is not clear how empirical work should, or could, supplant conceptual work. For recent discussion on the relative merits of naturalist and conceptual legal theories, see, e.g., B Leiter, 'Beyond the Hart/Dworkin Debate: The Methodology Problem in Jurisprudence' (2003) 48 *American J Jurisprudence* 17, 43–51; and J Coleman, n. 28 above, 210–7 (criticizing Leiter's argument).

[37] As one commentator was: M Davies, 'Review' (1981) 44 *MLR* 605.

the legal system and the values of legality and constitutionality, even if taking this perspective involves (temporarily) bracketing foundational or ontological questions; and (2) agree with Harris[38] (and H.L.A. Hart and others[39]) that there is often too much temptation to be distracted and misled when one chases metaphysical questions (*e.g.*, where and when a norm 'exists'). As Harris pointed out, to put forward an analysis of 'legal science' is not to exclude or preempt other social or philosophical approaches to law.[40] If nothing else, Harris reminds us that the perspective of 'legal science' (whether in the mouth of a judge, legal counsellor, or textbook writer) is distinctive: seeking order (system—hierarchy and non-contradiction) from the chaos of official actions.

Harris's 'legal science' does capture a distinctive and significant aspect of how the legal system operates and how it is experienced: both by Holmes's 'bad man'[41] trying to figure out how far he can go and still be safe from civil or criminal sanction, and by the Hartian subject who takes the 'internal point of view' on law[42] and who wants to be clear on what the law (accepted as creating reasons for action) asks of her. However, it is important to realize that there are other aspects of law for which 'legal science' fits poorly. In particular, to repeat Hart's point against Austin,[43] at least some citizens some of the time experience legal rights and powers in a way different from, and not easily reduced to, some condition on a future duty.

Conclusion

One cannot judge reductionism in social theory and legal theory as good or bad, without saying much more about the objectives with which the theory—in this case, theories about the nature of law or about 'legal science'—have been, or can be, proposed. Additionally, any such analysis must bring forward the trade-offs that can and should be made in constructing such theories. In a sense, reduction is the basic process of theorizing: for descriptive and conceptual theories, simplifying the complexities of history or of daily life to show a basic underlying truth. However, at some point, the 'simplifications' become distortions muddying any purported insights that the theory might offer.[44]

In Harris's wonderful and wonderfully provocative work, *Law and Legal Science*, the reductionist view of law serves to display clearly a certain way of

[38] See Harris, n. 2 above, 36 (discussing 'Kelsen's increasing preoccupation with the reification . . . of norms').

[39] See Hart, *Concept*, n. 5 above, ch. 1; see generally B Bix, 'Questions in Legal Interpretation', in A Marmor (ed.), *Law and Interpretation* (Clarendon Press, 1995), 137–54.

[40] Harris, n. 2 above, 165.

[41] OW Holmes, Jr., 'The Path of the Law' (1897) 10 *Harvard LR* 457, 460–1.

[42] Hart, *Concept*, n. 5 above, 88–91.

[43] Ibid., 26–44.

[44] For predictive models (e.g., the models in economics), the distortions work differently, creating a danger that the predictions may be corrupted (that is, false).

talking within and about law: judges and citizens using legal norms as reasons for action, and citizens seeking legal advice on how to avoid legal sanctions. The value of similar reductionism within more broadly focused (descriptive or conceptual) theories about the nature of law remains more doubtful. Law as practised and experienced seems too broad and nuanced to be portrayed so narrowly.

4

Scepticism and Scandinavian Legal Realists

*Jes Bjarup**

(i) Introduction

It was my good fortune to get a British Council Fellowship to study jurisprudence at the University of Edinburgh. During my stay in Edinburgh, from 1978 to 1980, I also had the good fortune to meet Jim Harris and we became friends, sharing a common interest in jurisprudential questions as well as smoking a pipe and sipping a whisky whilst exchanging views on life in general. It was with great sorrow that I heard of his illness, followed by his premature death. Sadly, Jim is no longer among us, but he is still present in his book, *Legal Philosophies*.[1]

This paper is written as a tribute to Jim, and I wish to consider his account of the Scandinavian realists. When moving from Denmark to Sweden in 1995, I introduced *Legal Philosophies* as a textbook in the jurisprudence course at Stockholm University, since he presents an account of the Swedes Hägerström and his pupil Olivecrona, and the Dane Ross. Jim mentions Lundstedt only in the bibliography, perhaps because he endorses Rawls's view that Lundstedt 'expresses Hägerström's leading ideas in a dogmatic and unilluminating way'.[2] The Scandinavians have had an impact upon legal thinking in their own countries and, as Jim remarks, also aroused interest among English lawyers, in contrast to those in the United States by whom they are largely ignored.[3] As Frederick Schauer and Virginia J. Wise put it, the Scandinavians survive 'only in the museums of jurisprudential archaeology'.[4] The rejoinder is that it may be possible to learn something by visiting museums, especially since Jim is right that the Scandinavians are concerned with the law as a condition of culture. He also holds that 'the so-called "legal realists", both in Scandinavia and in America, are better

* Author's address: Jes Bjarup, Bygholm Soepark 19A, DK8700 Horsens, Denmark, jes.bjarup@stofanet.dk.

[1] JW Harris, *Legal Philosophies* (2nd edn., Butterworths, 1997).

[2] J Rawls, 'Review of A. Vilhelm Lundstedt, *Legal Thinking Revised*' (1958–9) 44 *Cornell Law Quarterly* 169–171, at 169.

[3] Harris, n. 1 above, 98.

[4] F Schauer and VJ Wise, 'Legal Positivism as Legal Information' (1996–7) 82 *Cornell L Rev* 1080–1100, at 1081.

termed "legal sceptics" '.[5] In this paper, I wish to consider what the sceptical position that Jim attributes to the Scandinavian authors is about, in relation to knowledge (section (ii)), to morality (section (iii)), and to law and legal science (section (iv)).

(ii) Knowledge

The term 'scepticism' may be used to refer to an inquiry reflecting upon the proper way to follow in order to arrive at truth. The ancient Greek sceptics are engaged in such inquiries, leading them to adopt the sceptical position that any inquiry into any subject matter leads to the result of suspension of belief and judgement. Thus, their sceptical approach is a global scepticism, since it is always possible to present conflicting and convincing judgements with respect to where truth lies. Conflicting judgements cannot both be true, and the sceptic needs a criterion of truth in order to determine which he should accept, but there is no satisfactory criterion of truth to be found. As such, there is no way of deciding between conflicting judgements. It follows that the sceptic is left with no reason for preferring one to another, and is therefore bound to treat them as of equal strength of acceptance. He cannot accept them all because they conflict. He cannot accept any of them for lack of a criterion. It follows that the only sensible attitude is the suspension of judgement. This is not an attitude of despair, but, on the contrary, an attitude of detachment that will lead to the goal of living a flourishing life in terms of intellectual quietude and peace of mind.[6]

Scepticism is also a matter of concern for the Scandinavians, in the sense of an inquiry reflecting upon the proper way of knowing what there is. But the scepticism they advance differs from the ancient scepticism, since it is a local scepticism about morality and law, based upon the belief that there is scientific knowledge of the world. In this respect, they do not appeal to the suspension of belief as the proper attitude to adopt, but adopt the dogmatic attitude that does not doubt that the world in time and space is there for human beings to know. But then they differ, since the Swedish lawyers Olivecrona and Lundstedt appeal to Hägerström's philosophy which provides the sure path of scientific inquiries into the nature of morality and law, whereas the scientific approach pursued by the Dane Ross is grounded in logical positivism, as Harris duly notes.[7] I would like to consider this, since Hägerström is committed to a version of realism that makes the label 'realism' appropriate for his understanding of reality, in contrast to Ross who only uses the label as a catchword in his battle against jurisprudential idealism.[8]

[5] JW Harris, 'Olivecrona on Law and Language—The Search for Legal Culture' (1981) 94 *Tidskrift for Rettsvitenskap* 625–646, at 626.

[6] J Annas, 'Doing without Objective Values: Ancient and Modern Strategies', in M Schofield and Gstriker (eds.) *The Norms of Nature* (CUP, 1986).

[7] Harris, n. 1 above, 107.

[8] A Ross, *On Law and Justice* (Stevens and Sons, 1958), 64.

Hägerström held the prestigious chair of practical philosophy at the University of Uppsala from 1911 until his retirement in 1933, and claimed that philosophy is the supreme science dedicated to demonstrating the property of knowing not only what there ought to be, but also what is. One way is the subjective view that takes its starting point in the consciousness of the knowing subject. That leads to the epistemological position that the subject can know nothing but itself and the contents of its consciousness, which is related to the ontological position that nothing exists except one's own consciousness.[9] The subjective view is a version of idealism that Hägerström has endorsed, but it leads to a global scepticism that destroys the possibility of any knowledge of the world. However, it does not lead Hägerström to adopt the sceptical stance of suspension of belief, but rather produces a state of anxiety that leads him to look for the proper way to find the truth. His solution is found in the distinction between the act of judgement and the object that is thought about which G.E. Moore applies in his rejection of idealism. Within Sweden, Hägerström is well known for his rejection of idealism, and it seems to me that he is familiar with Moore's argument.[10]

According to Hägerström, consciousness is characterized by being an intentional consciousness of objects that exist apart from consciousness and which determine the content of consciousness, rather than the other way round. This leads him to reject the subjective view that is held, not only by ordinary people, but also within science, adopting the Cartesian or modern view of knowing things inside out, as opposed to the Medieval view of knowing things outside in, to use A. Mark Smith's phrases.[11] Thus, Hägerström returns to the Medieval view of knowing things outside in that is grounded upon the impact of what there is upon consciousness. This is the objective view that takes its starting point in reality and explains Hägerström's concern with metaphysics. But the metaphysics he rejects is the existence of a super-natural or super-sensible world beyond the natural or sensible world in time and space. In this respect, Hägerström adopts the dogmatic position that there can be no knowledge of the super-natural world since it does not exist, and to talk about it is nothing but a more or less ingenious play with words without any meaning.

Although Hägerström rejects metaphysics, it is often overlooked that he proceeds upon a metaphysical or ontological view that 'maintains the completely logical character of sensible reality'.[12] By this phrase, Hägerström does not refer to the idealist doctrine that reality is mental or spiritual, but rather that reality has a cognitive structure, since concepts are embedded in objects. This implies that Hägerström subscribes to realism in the sense that universals are found in objects

[9] A Hägerström, 'A Summary of my philosophy' (1929), in A Hägerström, Philosophy and Religion (trans. RT Sandin, George Allen & Unwin, 1964), 36.

[10] J Bjarup, 'Ought and Reality. Hägerström's Inaugural Lecture Re-considered' (2000) *Scandinavian Studies in Law*, Peter Wahlgren ed., *Legal Theory* 11.

[11] A M Smith, 'Knowing Things Inside Out: The Scientific Revolution from a Medieval Perspective' (1990) 95 *The American Historical Review* 726–744.

[12] Hägerström, n. 9 above, 37.

and their properties that exist apart from human beings within the world in time and space. It follows that knowledge is confined within the bounds of possible experience of objects or concepts, since human beings are part of the world in time and space and are in touch with objects that make an impact upon them. This raises the philosophical question: what is the principle of knowledge that accounts for the expression of knowledge in terms of true judgements. Knowledge within the various sciences is grounded upon assumptions about what there is, whereas the philosophical approach makes no assumptions since, in philosophical thinking, the mind does nothing, but is simply a passive spectator of what there is.

Hägerström adopts the position of the judicious spectator whose philosophical thinking mirrors what there is, since there are causal chains leading from objects to the sensations of objects by the epistemic knower. Since concepts are embedded in the things themselves, it follows that sensory experience has a conceptual content that can be expressed in meaningful words related to concepts, or in sentences expressing judgements or propositions having truth-value, as opposed to words as mere noises or utterances devoid of meaning. The fact that there are causal chains between objects and their impact upon the minds of human beings raises the question of how to account for the fact that errors exist. Hägerström's answer is that human error is due to confused ideas about the world, based upon the impact of feelings. What matters then is to purify the human mind in general from the impact of feelings upon thinking that leads to wishful thinking, which is a common trait among people. It may be noticed that Hägerström has a low opinion of ordinary people and their common sense. He also has a low opinion of the scientific mind and rejects the realist position advanced by Plato and his rationalist followers, locating concepts in a super-sensible world apart from the sensible world in time and space. This is Harris's understanding of the term 'realism'.[13] But Hägerström is committed to another version of realism that locates concepts in the sensible world in time and space that explains his rejection of the nominalist position held by empiricists that concepts are abstractions from sensory experience of objects and their properties, serving as tools to describe and explain what there is.

Hägerström also rejects Kant's view that the human mind approaches nature with pure intuitions of space and time, and categories of its own making, in order to find the truth within the bounds of experience. That view leads Kant to hold that human understanding 'is itself the lawgiver of nature'.[14] This is tantamount to the subjective view that Hägerström rejects, holding that nature itself is an intelligible order of necessitating causes and their effects. Thus, the world in time and space is formed of concepts as the only objects of knowledge. This view is supported by the belief that God ordains the course of nature, in terms of laws of nature, as advanced by Descartes, and related to the belief that Man is created in

[13] Harris, n. 1 above, 98.

[14] I Kant, *Critique of Pure Reason* (trans. N Kemp Smith, Macmillan, 1976), A 127.

God's image and thus has the capacity to arrive at knowledge of the world. Hegel holds a similar view, claiming that human beings participate in the divine thoughts. For Hägerström, this is another example of the subjective view that must be discarded since there is no God. Hägerström sides with David Hume, holding that human beings are solely intelligent animals, alongside other animals within the natural world. This leads Hume to claim that there are no necessary relations between events and that reasoning concerning causes and effects is only a matter of regularities among events, based upon the influence of custom. By contrast, Hägerström appeals to reason and locates the causal principles—that every event has a cause, that every cause has a particular effect, and that similar causes produce similar effects—within the natural world of things and events. It follows that there is an objective order of things, determined by necessary causal relations that is there for science to discover. Hägerström calls his philosophical approach 'rational naturalism', in order to distinguish it from the prevailing view of rational idealism committed to the subjective view. Hägerström's naturalism is the foundation for the objective view that maintains that scientific inquiries must be based on experience of facts, in order to arrive at knowledge. Hägerström is adamant that 'modern science in general, and therefore modern legal science, seeks to use only such notions as corresponds to facts'.[15] This implies that scientific inquiries must account for what there is in terms of qualitative descriptions of sensible objects and causal laws between events, as opposed to the view that nature can be described in quantitative concepts and explained by using mathematical reasoning. This is manifested in the modern view of physics, presenting an account of moving bodies in terms of mathematical laws, that Hägerström holds to be a version of the subjective view, explaining his concern to reject Einstein's theory of relativity.

Hägerström's rational naturalism is not accepted by scientists or philosophers in Sweden but he is the cognitive sovereign for the lawyers Lundstedt and Olivecrona, who recognize it as the proper foundation for their inquiries into the nature of law and legal science.[16] This is not the case for Ross's appeal to logical positivism as the epistemological foundation for his jurisprudential approach.[17] Hägerström rejects logical positivism as another version of the subjective view that grounds knowledge in sense-data as the foundation for the construction of concepts. This leads to a split among the Scandinavians, Lundstedt and Olivecrona siding with Hägerström against Ross. This is in turn important, since it leads to crucial differences among the Scandinavian realists, manifested in their different conceptions of what jurisprudence is about; the Swedes holding that it is about the proper theory of law related to a conceptual analysis of legal concepts, in

[15] A Hägerström, 'Der römische Obligationsbegriff im Lichte der allgemeinen römischen Rechtsanschauung. I, Einleitung, in K Olivecrona (ed.), *Inquiries into the Nature of Law and Morals* (trans. CD Broad, Almqvist & Wiksell, 1927), 1.

[16] AV Lundstedt, *Legal Thinking Revised* (Almqvist & Wiksell, 1956); K Olivecrona, *Law as Fact* (Humphrey Milford, 1939).

[17] Ross, n. 8 above, 67.

terms of an inquiry into their historical origin. By contrast, Ross holds that philosophy 'is not a theory at all, but a method. This method is logical analysis. Philosophy is the logic of science, and its subject the language of science'.[18] It follows that jurisprudence is concerned with the logical analysis of the language used within legal science, in order to clarify the fundamental concepts used to account for the law.

(iii) Morality

The Scandinavians agree, however, that there can be no moral knowledge, since there are no moral facts to be known. Thus, they are moral sceptics, but their scepticism is a local scepticism that only questions the existence of moral facts and not the existence of natural facts. However, it is impossible to derive moral facts or an 'ought' from natural facts or an 'is'. This is the Humean is/ought cleavage that only states a logical point, as Harris notes, since a conclusion containing an 'ought' cannot be derived from premises that do not include an 'ought'. The question is, rather, whether values are part of the world, and this is denied by the Scandinavians. The starting point for their moral scepticism is not Hume's, but Kant's view:

> The understanding can know in nature only what is, what has been, or what will be. We cannot say that anything in nature *ought to be* other than what in all these time-relations it actually is. When we have the course of nature alone in view, *'ought'* has no meaning whatsoever. It is just as absurd to ask what ought to happen in the natural world as to ask what properties a circle ought to have. All that we are justified in asking is: what happens in nature? What are the properties of the circle?[19]

For Hägerström, nature is devoid of any meaning or value, since the rational mind of the philosopher has no conceptual experience of any inherent values in things themselves. It follows that moral realism that holds the ontological or metaphysical view that there are moral facts and which is related to the epistemological or cognitive view that these facts can be known by means of experience or reason is false, if not meaningless. This is also Ross's position, based on his adherence to logical positivism. However, Kant makes room for moral facts and moral truths, based upon the use of the will or practical reason. The understanding or the use of theoretical reason is responsible for the intelligibility of the natural world as an intelligible world within the natural sciences. The use of practical reason is responsible for the intelligibility of the moral world, since the meaning of 'ought' is brought about by the use of the will or practical reason having the capacity to set ends, by means of rational choices, through which objective values enter the world. This makes room for moral knowledge, in terms of duties to respect the

[18] Ibid., 25. [19] Kant, n. 14 above, A 547/B575 (his italics).

dignity of human beings as autonomous persons and responsible agents. Hägerström and Ross restrict the concept of reason to theoretical reason, to the exclusion of the will or practical reason. For Hägerström and Ross, the will is not reason with respect to action, but rather any impulse to behave which is grounded in feelings.

This leads the Scandinavians to advance the nihilist view that there are no moral duties with corresponding rights. It is also the case that 'nothing is either good or bad, but feeling makes it so', to paraphrase a line from Hamlet. Hägerström's moral nihilism holds that moral concepts are not embedded in persons, actions, and states of affairs and this is related to his non-cognitive view that moral judgements are, properly speaking, not judgements expressing moral beliefs, but rather utterances expressing feelings. In the case of scientific judgements, the mind is faced with the existence of concepts or real ideas, related to the features inherent in objects to be recorded by means of using concepts to express beliefs. In the case of moral judgements, the human mind is not faced with any moral concepts at all, but only with imaginary ideas as expressions of various feelings or volitions that are expressed in empty words. This implies that Hägerström subscribes to a version of nominalism that holds that the moral vocabulary is not a natural language of concepts, but a super-natural or meta-physical language of words devoid of any cognitive meaning. The moral vocabulary has, however, an emotive meaning, since it is used to express and evoke feelings and volitions in relation to various states of affairs that are important for human existence.

Hägerström's moral nihilism is a philosophical doctrine that has practical consequences, since it implies that moral language cannot be used to convey any moral beliefs concerning what is right or wrong, or what is good or bad. It does not follow that people should act immorally, and Hägerström's nihilism is not advanced to destroy ordinary moral values, but rather to save them, by curing people of their illusions. Hägerström subscribes to Auguste Comte's philosophy, holding that humanity is progressing from the theological state, characterized by superstitious beliefs in the existence of God as the source of values, through the metaphysical stage, characterized by the magical belief that human beings have natural rights related to their selfish interests, to the positive stage of scientific knowledge, based on facts and the cultivation of benevolent, or altruistic, feelings among people. Hägerström's philosophy addresses the burning political issue of his day, between the socialist class and the capitalist class, since 'one fights the better if one believes that one has right on one's side'.[20] Thus, if the capitalist belief that an action is right can be shown to be illusory, it follows that the opposite socialist belief that the action is wrong is also illusory. Hägerström regards people who believe that actions are right or wrong as misguided and in need of instruction. The instruction cannot be to offer any moral advice, since there is no moral knowledge, and the task is rather to put people into a position whereby they lose their moral beliefs.

[20] Hägerström, n. 15 above, 5.

Hägerström's conceptual analysis demonstrates to his own satisfaction that there are no moral duties with corresponding rights. If this is so, then political conflict can be neutralized, since people will realize that there is no reason to evoke any moral rights and to engage in any violent attack on the existing social and cultural institutions. As he puts it, 'only barbarians make an assault on them by casting stones'.[21] Hägerström's philosophy turns morality into a purely private matter, in terms of an autonomous morality dedicated to the pursuit of realizing one's supreme values. This is a non-cognitive activity that makes one's values immune from any scientific criticism, based on the cognitive activity to find the truth. To be sure, one's values may be informed by scientific truths to promote a detached or tolerant view of people and their behaviour. This is, however, a moral position that lacks any scientific standing according to Hägerström's conceptual analysis. For Hägerström, the supreme value is peace, and this can be achieved by means of the law of the land to regulate human behaviour in order to fulfil human needs and desires.

Ross's conceptual analysis of moral language is not based upon Hägerström's philosophy, but upon Charles Stevenson's theory of ethics.[22] Thus, Ross proceeds upon a distinction between the cognitive use of language to express beliefs and the non-cognitive use of language to express attitudes and exercise influence. The cognitive use of language is found within science and philosophy of science. The distinction between science and philosophy of science corresponds to the distinction between substantive ethics and meta-ethics. Meta-ethics is concerned with the conceptual analysis of the moral vocabulary leading Ross to hold that moral propositions do not express beliefs that can be verified, but are only sentences used to express feelings. It follows that substantive ethics cannot use the moral language as a cognitive language, but solely as a non-cognitive language. This does not rule out that Ross uses it to express his moral commitments. Thus, it is possible both to reject the existence of values and to be as serious as ever about one's own moral commitments, as Ross illustrates by writing that 'while I may classify a certain order as a "legal order", it is possible for me at the same time to consider it my highest moral duty to overthrow that order'.[23] However, according to Ross's conceptual analysis, there can be no moral duties at all, and his commitment cannot be a matter of belief, but solely a matter of the feelings with which he happens to be stuck.

Ross also considers the use of the principles of justice and of social welfare in relation to the legal order as a just or good legal order. The principles of justice are related to the idea of natural rights that Ross rejects as a metaphysical ideal. This is also the position held by Hägerström and Lundstedt. However, Lundstedt appeals to his method of social welfare as the scientific method to be used in relation to the making, and application, of the law. Ross takes issue with Lundstedt, holding that

[21] A Hägerström, 'On the Truth of Moral Propositions' (1911), in Hägerström, n. 9 above, 77–96, at 94.

[22] Ross, n. 8 above, 297 ff.

[23] Ibid., 32.

the method of social welfare is just another version of utilitarianism that cannot be sustained from a scientific point of view. This is contested by Lundstedt, who claims that his method of social welfare is not a version of utilitarianism, but a scientific method, appealing to Hägerström's authority for support. This does not impress Ross, since the method of social welfare assumes that there can be moral knowledge and, yet, as Hägerström has shown, this is not the case. This is also the position of Olivecrona who refrains from engaging in any moral evaluation of the law on the basis that this is not a scientific question concerning facts, but a political question concerning values. For Ross, the question of what the law ought to be is the concern of what he calls 'legal politics' that cannot be conceived to be a matter of moral knowledge, as claimed within theories of natural law or natural right on the one hand, and utilitarian theories on the other. Legal politics, he claims, concerns evaluations based on sociological knowledge of the functions of the law. As he puts it, 'so far as legal politics is determined by rational insight it is applied sociology of law. For the rest, it is based in evaluations outside the realm of rational cognition'.[24] Legal politics is important for the role of lawyers as rational technologists, putting their knowledge and skill into the service of those holding the political power within a state. This is the important message which he advances in his book.

It may be noticed that the American realists make room for the moral evaluation of the law. In his book, Harris refers to Karl Llewellyn and Jerome Frank as legal sceptics. But Llewellyn is 'ready to do open penance for any part I may have played in giving occasion for the feeling that modern jurisprudes or any of them had ever lost sight of this', that is to say 'with zeal of justice, and with zeal for improving the *legal* techniques for doing the law's business'.[25] Frank writes in his preface that: 'I do not understand how any decent man today can refuse to adopt, as the basis of modern civilization, the fundamental principles of Natural Law, relative to human conduct, as stated by Thomas Aquinas'.[26] The Scandinavians would reject the appeal to justice as meaningless and, for the Swedes, this is also the case with Thomistic natural law. Ross is more sympathetic when the metaphysics is discarded: 'there is plenty of scope for a sociological-realistic form of legal politics' within Thomism of today.[27]

(iv) Legal Science

The law is important for the Scandinavians. As Hägerström puts it, 'the law is undeniably a condition of culture itself. Without it, as the Sophist Protagoras

[24] Ross, n. 8 above, 24.

[25] K Llewellyn, 'On reading and using the newer Jurisprudence' (1940) 40 *Columbia LR* 581, reprinted in K Llewellyn, *Jurisprudence* (u Chicago Press, 1962), 128. (his italics).

[26] J Frank, *Law and the Modern Mind* (Stevens & Sons, 6th Impression 1949), xvii.

[27] Ross, n. 8 above, 245.

already saw, we should never have been able to win the lordship over other species'.[28] Protagoras is a strong believer in organized society, based on the value of law against all attempts to appeal to nature for guidance. Hägerström shares this view, but this claim calls for a philosophical analysis into the nature of the law and fundamental legal concepts. Hägerström's philosophical analysis proceeds on his ontological or metaphysical view that concepts are embedded in things or facts, and this corresponds with his epistemological view that legal science can only use concepts that correspond to facts. This is manifested in his elaborate inquiry into the language of Roman law, in terms of fundamental legal concepts of right and duties, in order to find the facts that correspond with these concepts. The reason for the inquiry into Roman law is that it is the origin of legal concepts, not only in the historical sense, but also in the logical sense. In Roman law, as he puts it, 'we may expect to find the concepts presenting themselves in a more naive form. But we may also expect to find them free from that confusion of thought which inevitably arises, when, egged on by the general critical tendency of modern science, jurists attempt to reduce to actual facts the content of the mystical concepts which they employ'.[29] Hägerström's inquiry demonstrates that there is no inherent feature of right or duty in persons and their actions, and this implies that these words do not express concepts, but are used to express mystical or imaginary ideas that human beings have the natural right to freedom or that human beings have the capacity to put themselves under duties and be their own makers of laws.

Applying Comte's law of the three stages, Hägerström argues that legal thinking has not yet reached the positive stage of scientific knowledge based upon experience and using concepts corresponding to facts. Legal thinking is still held captive within the theological stage, as manifested in the appeal to the will of God, or the will of the sovereign to account for the authority of the law, and the metaphysical stage, as manifested in the appeal to natural rights as the foundation for the state and its legal order. For Hägerström, the law is neither an expression of reason, as held by theories of natural right or theories of natural law, nor is the law an expression of the will of the sovereign or the will of the state, as held by theories of legal positivism. What is common to these different theories is the view that the legal language is a normative language, using concepts to inform people about what is right and wrong, in terms of reasons for action. Ordinary citizens and lawyers believe that they are saying something important when they use legal rules and legal concepts like 'right', 'duty', 'wrong', and 'property' to regulate human conduct and make legal decisions. As a matter of fact, this is an illusion, since there are no legal rules or legal concepts. It is, of course, an illusion that has a profound effect on the behaviour of human beings who suffer from it. For Hägerström, and his disciples Lundstedt and Olivecrona, it has no effect, since they would not suppose they were talking sense when they were, in fact, talking nonsense.

[28] A Hägerström, 'Review of Hans Kelsen, *Allgemeine Rechtslehre*' (1928), in Hägerström, n. 15 above, 257–298, at 262.

[29] Hägerström, n. 15 above, 16.

Hägerström's legal scepticism rejects the existence of a normative reality, since this is nothing but a super-sensible reality of metaphysical ideas in terms of the world of 'ought'. There is but one world—the world in time and space—in terms of the sensible reality that is there to be known by experience and expressed in terms of empirical concepts. The implication is that the language of the law is a magical or non-cognitive language that is devoid of any conceptual meaning, but the language can be used to cause people to behave as an effect, if necessary by means of using force. Thus, the Scandinavians subscribe to the positivist view that the law is concerned with the use of sanctions, in terms of organized force. They also admit that the law is a human artefact that is brought about by human beings. As Olivecrona puts it, 'it is obvious that every rule of law is a creation of men'.[30] But they are adamant that legal rules do not express the personal will of any commanding authority. The law is rather an impersonal instrument that can be used to regulate the behaviour of people within a state. This is important, since people have conflicting moral feelings and volitions with respect to what proper behaviour is, in relation to other people and to things, and the appeal to their personal feelings may lead to conflicts. The remedy is to introduce the law, but this requires that the law be independent from any personal will in order to be followed. Thus, Olivecrona conceptualizes the law as 'independent imperatives', that is to say, the impersonal and imperative use of words that make an impact upon the minds of people, thereby producing the appropriate behaviour.

Olivecrona holds that the cause of legal rules is found in the will of the legislator, in response to human needs. This presents him with the difficulty that the effect that a law is passed by the legislator must contain his will, applying the causal principle that a cause produces a similar effect.

Hans Kelsen also deals with this question, appealing to the *Grundnorm* that authorizes persons to legislate and turn their subjective will into the objective meaning of the law, in terms of the ought of legal norms. For Olivecrona, this is pure nonsense since: 'it is impossible to explain rationally how facts in the actual world can produce effects in the wholly different "world of ought" '.[31] The rejoinder is that Kelsen does not subscribe to Hägerström's division between the supersensible world of ought and the sensible world of is. For Kelsen, there is but one world—the world in time and space—that includes the normative perspective of the ought, using the principle of imputation to relate grounds or sanctions with consequences or delicts, on the one hand, and the empirical perspective of the is, using the causal principle to relate causes with their effects, on the other. From the normative perspective, Kelsen holds that the law is a hierarchical system of norms, having a conceptual or normative meaning about the proper use of force. The law is a coercive order that is solely addressed to public authorities, informing them about the making and application of valid legal norms that is the subject-matter of legal science to describe in terms of propositions having truth-value. The law can

[30] Olivecrona, n. 16 above, 16.
[31] Ibid., 21.

also be studied from the empirical perspective that is pursued within the social sciences, e.g., sociological or psychological inquiries into the causal relations between norms and human behaviour. Olivecrona endorses Kelsen's view that the law is a coercive order consisting of rules about the use of force and used as a social technique to regulate the behaviour of human beings. But he rejects Kelsen's view that legal rules can be conceptualized as norms having a normative meaning in terms of ought. Legal rules must be conceptualized as independent imperatives that are devoid of any conceptual meaning, but they have an emotional impact upon the minds of people to produce the appropriate behaviour. This is realized through upbringing and education and also through the fact that the law can be enforced, if necessary by means of sanctions. These are social facts and the concern for legal science to study from the empirical perspective as the only scientific perspective dedicated to describe and explain the use of empty words. The function of the law 'is to work on the minds of people, directing them to do this or that or to refrain from something else—not to communicate knowledge about the state of things'.[32] Olivecrona takes John Austin to task for holding that legal rules communicate knowledge, as opposed to the truth that they only have 'a suggestive function' since the use of the legal language has an impact upon the mind of people.[33] Ross sides with Olivecrona, but prefers to conceptualize legal rules as 'directives', that is to say 'utterances with no representative meaning but with intent to exert influence'.[34] As he puts it, 'the law is not written to impart theoretical truths, but to direct people—judges and private citizens alike—to act in a certain desired manner. A Parliament is not an information bureau, but a central organ for social direction.'[35]

The rejoinder is that using the law as a means of social suggestion presupposes that the law has a cognitive meaning, referring to the states of affairs or action which people are directed to bring about or perform. Olivecrona refers to J.L. Austin's account of speech acts, and R.M. Hare's account of the moral language to hold that it is a fallacy to reduce imperatives to indicatives. To be sure, legal rules cannot be conceptualized as indicatives or empirical propositions. But neither can the rules be conceptualized as imperative sentences devoid of conceptual meaning, since this is false. The Scandinavians make the capital error of ignoring the fact that the law is brought about by human beings as normative precepts to serve as guidance for the conduct of human beings as responsible persons and rational agents. And using J.L. Austin's classification of speech-acts, Olivecrona and Ross commit the fallacy of confusing the illocutionary act of passing a valid law as reason for belief and action with the perlocutionary force of the law in terms of its causal impact upon human beings.

For the Scandinavians, the important fact about the law as independent imperatives or directives is that the meaning of the law is constituted by its social

[32] Ibid., 21. [33] K Olivecrona, *Law as Fact* (2nd edn., Stevens & Sons, 1971), 126.
[34] Ross, n. 8 above, 8. [35] Ibid., 8.

function as the causal element producing the appropriate behaviour as effect. In this way the law is firmly placed within the natural world in terms of an instrument of social and psychological conditioning that can be used to produce a partnership between people with respect to their behaviour and relations to things, and thus sustain and improve the social and cultural conditions for human beings to live a flourishing life. The implication is that 'the legal order is throughout nothing but a social machine, in which the cogs are men'.[36]

In this respect, there is an important distinction between being an intelligent cog and a mere cog. The latter category comprises ordinary people and ordinary lawyers who merely follow the rules laid down as causes for their behaviour. The intelligent cogs are Hägerström and his disciples, in possession of knowledge of how to operate the machinery by means of using legal magic to further the interests of society. But even the intelligent cogs are nothing but social animals who behave according to their knowledge of causes. This makes room for the fact that there are other intelligent animals who realize that the use of legal magic is a device to suppress them, and who may also have the capacity to resist the impact of social suggestion. As an intelligent animal, Hägerström has anticipated this objection, holding that if human beings are not under the sway of the magical words of the law then they are abnormal beings. This is false, since it is neither a conceptual nor an empirical truth. Hägerström faces the problem that his philosophical approach cannot conceptualize human beings as responsible persons and rational agents having the capacity to act for reason, as opposed to be acted upon by external factors.

The use of the appropriate language is a problem for the Scandinavians. Hägerström has demonstrated to his own satisfaction that nothing in reality corresponds to the legal concepts. His philosophical analysis implies that the language of the law is a magical language, and this raises the question whether the magical vocabulary of words should be replaced with a scientific vocabulary of concepts. Hägerström's analysis presents his legal disciples Lundstedt and Olivecrona with the question of what to do. The answer is that there is no need to replace the magical language of the law. Once its magical nature is understood, it can be used as a tool of persuasion to regulate human movements in relation to other human beings with respect to things, and Lundstedt uses his method of social welfare as the foundation for his support to further the democratic socialism of the Swedish welfare state.

It is quite otherwise in relation to the scientific knowledge of reality, since this requires the use of concepts that correspond to facts. According to Hägerström, 'legal science has become one of the special sciences. Like physics and chemistry, e.g., its function is merely to establish the facts within a certain region, to reach general principles by induction, and to make deductive inferences from the inductively established results'.[37] Hägerström's rational naturalism is committed to the

[36] A Hägerström, 'On Fundamental Problems of Law' (1939), in Hägerström, n. 15 above, 348–366, at 354.

[37] A Hägerström, 'The Concept of Declaration of Intention in the Sphere of Private Law' (1935), in Hägerström, n. 15 above, 299–347, at 299.

positivist view that experience of fact is the only way to ensure scientific knowledge. Legal science is concerned with establishing the facts, and the facts cannot be normative, but only empirical facts. It follows that Hägerström rejects Kelsen's view of legal science that provides information about the law as a normative fact in terms of reasons for belief and action. What Hägerström's legal science is about is accounting for the empirical facts, or the causal relations between legal rules and human behaviour, in order to arrive at empirical laws in terms of regularities between one event, that is to say legal rules, and another event, that is to say the impact of legal rules upon human behaviour. This is surely important, but requires the use of empirical concepts, as opposed to the magical words used in the law according to Hägerström's conception of science. Hägerström's philosophy provides the framework for the empirical study of the law, but this is not pursued by him. It is left to his disciples Lundstedt and Olivecrona.

In this respect, Lundstedt considers the possibility of replacing the magical vocabulary of the law, in terms of rights and duties, with scientific concepts, but admits that 'it will be impossible in the common practice of law (be it outside or before the courts) to eradicate them. If legal writers use such a term and if they are afraid thereby to be misunderstood they may place the term in question between quotations marks'.[38] Thus, Lundstedt continues to use the terms with quotation marks to indicate that, when he talks about 'rights', he is talking sense, whereas other people talking about rights are talking nonsense. Lundstedt's claim that this furthers the mutual understanding among writers is simply false. For his part, Olivecrona cannot see any need to replace the received legal vocabulary with a new scientific vocabulary. Once the metaphysical nature of the legal vocabulary is duly recognized, it can be used to convey information about the working of the law. This is important since Olivecrona holds the sceptical position that the law in terms of independent imperatives does not contain any information. Hence, the importance of legal science, but the information cannot be information about the conceptual meaning of the law, since it has none. It can only be information about the causal impact of independent imperatives upon the minds of people, but this depends upon an empirical inquiry in order to provide reliable information. I agree with Harris that Olivecrona raises some interesting questions for legal sociology which he then fails to address. Thus, Olivecrona may be seen to be inconsistent, failing to engage in sociological inquiries, and I shall return to this below.

Ross also makes a valiant effort to establish the scientific status of legal science as an empirical social science, but, in the end, he also fails. Ross is committed to logical positivism and is not concerned with the conceptual analysis of the law, in contrast to the analysis of the sentences used with legal science. The law is expressed in directives lacking representative or conceptual meaning, in contrast to the scientific account that is expressed in empirical propositions with representative or cognitive meaning that require verification in order to establish whether

[38] Lundstedt, n. 16 above, 17.

they are true or false. He proceeds upon the principle of verification according to which the meaning of a proposition is its method of verification.[39] It follows that legal science cannot use the directive or emotive language used in the law, since it is devoid of cognitive meaning. It also follows that propositions within legal science or legal propositions require verification. This leads Ross to hold that legal propositions are concerned with the predictions of legal decisions made by the courts under certain conditions, that is to say 'if an action should be brought on which the particular rule of law has bearing, and if in the meantime there has been no alteration in the state of law (that is to say, in the circumstances which condition our assertion that the rule is a valid law), the rule will be applied by the courts'.[40]

Ross follows Kelsen in holding that valid laws are only addressed to legal officials. The reason is not that the application of the law by the courts is decisive for the validity of legal rules. The reason is rather that the application of the law by the courts is decisive for the verification of legal propositions, and the reference to the courts, rather than people, makes the method of verification easier to carry out. However, this raises the question concerning the way in which judges decide cases. Ross mentions the traditional view that the legal decision is a syllogism, whereby the reasoning contains the premises leading to the judgement as the conclusion. This view is also known as 'formalism' and is vigorously rejected by the so-called 'free-law movement' in Germany and by American legal realists in favour of the view that a judge arrives at his decision by emotional intuitions or hunches and then presents his reasoning as 'a façade designed to support belief in the objectivity of the decision'.[41]

Harris refers to the fact that: 'Ross, like the American realists but unlike other Scandinavian realists, is specifically court-centred'.[42] I beg to differ. To be sure, Ross is court-centred, but the reason for this is that it is required in order to decide whether legal propositions are true or false. Lundstedt and Olivecrona are also court-centred, yet reject Ross's method of verification and account of legal propositions in terms of predictions about what judges will do. For the Swedes, the task of legal science is to provide information to the public in general, and to the courts in particular, about what to do when faced with legal questions. They face the problem that the information cannot be legal information about the meaning of the legal rules, since such rules are devoid of meaning. The information cannot be empirical information since they are not engaged in any sociological inquiries about the working of the law. As noted above, this may suggest that they are inconsistent in confusing their legal information with sociological information. It seems to me that they know what they are doing, since they use the inherited vocabulary as a re-enforcement of its impact upon the minds of people. According to Olivecrona, rules exist only as ideas in the minds of people. This position

[39] Ross, n. 8 above, 40. [40] Ibid., 41. [41] Ibid., 44.
[42] Harris, n. 1 above, 108.

commits him to the idealist view that people must constantly have ideas in mind in order for the permanent existence of rules. He also claims that 'it is impossible to ascribe a permanent existence to a rule of law or to any other rule'.[43] If this is so, the task of legal science is to serve as a reminder to keep the rules in existence.

Ross departs from Olivecrona's position, claiming that rules do have a permanent existence apart from the minds of people. For Ross, like the American realists, the task of legal science is to offer empirical information about these rules, whereas Harris continues to write that 'Ross differs from the American realists precisely by insisting that decisions which concur with the pre-existing rules do show that rules effectively control decisions'. Again, I beg to differ. The American realists are concerned with the impact of what Ross calls 'pragmatic considerations' that lead them to inquire into the way in which judges, as a matter of fact, do arrive at decisions, and also how judges should arrive at decisions through attention to the social sciences. Ross stresses the importance of the pragmatic considerations, but fails to present any empirical evidence for their impact upon judicial decision-making. This seems to me to put him apart from the American realists.

Ross stresses the importance of the verification of legal propositions, in order to decide whether they are true or false, on the one hand, and scientific or non-scientific propositions, on the other. Concerning verification, Ross draws attention to the formalist and anti-formalist theories, and it is a matter of surprise to read that he 'shall not attempt here to assess the merits of these conflicting theories, but merely point out the relevance they have to the question of the practical value of the doctrinal study of law'.[44] If formalism is correct, then scholarly legal knowledge of the law makes it possible to predict the outcome of legal decisions. By contrast, if anti-formalism is true, then scholarly knowledge is not sufficient to predict the outcomes of legal decisions, since they depend upon non-legal factors. Ross proceeds upon the assumption that formalism is correct, since this makes it possible to verify legal propositions and thus present reliable information that explains and predicts judicial behaviour. But in a later section concerning the judicial method or legal interpretation, he rejects formalism in favour of anti-formalism, holding that judges are motivated by pragmatic considerations in favour of a decision, and 'then a façade of justification is constructed, often differing from that which in reality made him decide the way he did'.[45] If this is true, then Ross's method of verification will be of no use to verify legal propositions, and this is surely important for legal science since it implies that legal science contains no reliable information about whether legal rules control decisions. It also implies that legal propositions cannot be classified as scientific propositions as opposed to non-scientific utterances. Ross claims that there is a crucial distinction between the cognitive expression of beliefs and the non-cognitive expression of evaluations within his understanding of legal politics, but he also admits that the distinction cannot be

[43] Olivecrona, n. 16 above, 47. [44] Ross, n. 8 above, 44. [45] Ibid., 152.

maintained within the social sciences.[46] This ruins Ross's scientific approach, which turns out to be an expression of his attitude towards exercising an influence in relation to the making, and application, of the law. Ross may be criticized for being inconsistent, but it seems to me that he knows what he is doing as a rational technologist.

(v) Conclusion

The Scandinavian realists are committed to the sceptical position that there can be no knowledge of the law as a normative fact in terms of reasons for belief and action, but this position is held in a dogmatic way as the only possible scientific stance. They are also committed to the view that the language of the law is a magical language, devoid of any normative or cognitive content, but that there is no reason to abandon the use of legal magic if it is informed by science as opposed to morality. This makes the scientific approach all-important and they acknowledge that there can be knowledge about the law as an empirical fact. However, they fail to engage in any sociological or psychological inquiries into the causal impact of legal rules upon the minds of people and their behaviour. The Scandinavians suggest that if their view of law and legal science is accepted and carried through, then there is no need for any violent revolutions to establish the conditions that make it possible for human beings to live a flourishing life in peace, security, and productivity, within a legal culture. This result can be achieved by peaceful means by purifying the minds of people from the magical belief that moral ideas are important for the making and application of the law, to the enlightened belief that what matters is only scientific knowledge. The Scandinavian realists proceed upon the belief that the law must be informed by scientific knowledge, and they conceive lawyers as rational technologists who transform scientific knowledge into the law. This is a global view that is advanced by the Scandinavian realists and their contributions to maintaining a legal culture deserve to be taken seriously. They face the challenge that their belief in science may be seen as a magical belief that can be questioned, in order to make room for moral inquiries into the making and application of the law as a human artefact; not in terms of rules as a means of social suggestion, but in terms of rules that are concerned with the respect for the dignity and freedom of human beings.

[46] Ross, n. 8 above, 48.

5

Judges' Use of Moral Arguments in Interpreting Statutes

*Jeremy Horder**

(i) Introduction

My focus in this Chapter will be the judicial use of merit-based and, in particular, moral argument to determine the legal scope or effect of a statute. Can such argument appropriately be used to this end, even if substantially unsupported by argument that is (as we shall see) more properly called 'legal'? If merit-based and, in particular, moral argument can be so deployed, what restrictions, if any, are there on the way in which it ought to be deployed? My argument will be that it can be legitimate for judges to rely on moral arguments to determine the legal scope or effect of statutes. They should rely on such arguments, however, only when the way in which they are used meets certain 'modesty' conditions. My concern is largely, although not solely, with two such conditions. First, the higher courts should not try to bolster the legitimacy of using moral argument by seeking to give it an 'expert' or a 'consultative' basis (as explained below).[1] Such a basis for using moral argument to underpin legal authority can rarely be established adequately when it is limited to, and driven by, the obligation retrospectively to resolve an individual dispute. It can usually only be established, in a way that confers greater legitimacy to a law based on it, when it is established through some form of investigative executive action, on behalf of the legislature, detached from the exigencies of the *lis inter partes*. Secondly, unless otherwise instructed by the legislature,[2] courts should not use moral argument to determine the scope and

* Law Commissioner for England and Wales; Worcester College and Faculty of Law, Oxford.
I am very grateful for the help of Julie Dickson, John Gardner, Timothy Endicott, and the anonymous referee in writing this Chapter: 'patient tutors to a dense pupil', to use Ronald Dworkin's phrase.

[1] This modesty condition does not apply when the court is set up specifically to function as an expert or consultative tribunal: See H Collins, 'Democracy and Adjudication', in N McCormick and P Birks (eds.), *The Legal Mind: Essays for Tony Honoré* (Clarendon Press, 1986), ch. 4.

[2] See section 6 below.

effect of statutes in a way that is meant to establish or to exemplify a corpus of values specially prized by the judiciary, values partly independent of those that the legislature intended should exercise a decisive influence in context.

(ii) Harris's Concept of Legal Obligation and the Judicial Role

For Jim Harris, whilst laws can be clearly valid or invalid, a finding that a law is valid carries with it no necessary implication for the citizen of 'normativity', no implication that the law ought to be obeyed by the citizen, whether or not the 'ought' in the claimed implication is understood as formal or as substantive.[3] The domain of posited law is simply the domain of what is 'required by... legal prescription'.[4] For Harris, from the citizen's point of view, the idea of legal obligation 'hovers over rather than being intrinsic to, ascriptions of legality'.[5] Nonetheless, a legal system provides an institutional setting in which legal officials themselves must, as a matter of professional ethics and obligation, be concerned with the obligatoriness of law, at least in a formal sense:

> All legal-information-giving takes place against a background assumption that legality and constitutionality are among the political role-values of officials of modern states. Such officials characteristically purport to direct organised coercion in accordance only with a closed set of rules which originate in a listed and ranked hierarchy of sources. To assert that a legal duty exists is not the same thing as predicting any particular outcome, but it typically has point because avowed official role-values exclude public statements of the form: 'This court has no concern with what our law requires!'[6]

The key here is the part played by what Harris calls 'role-values' in the process of law application, what—where judges are concerned—John Gardner calls 'the professional obligation... not to refuse to decide any case that is brought before them and that lies within their jurisdiction'.[7] Judges ought to regard valid laws within their jurisdiction as legally obligatory. That a rule is legally valid, then, places an obligation on judges, by virtue of the nature of their role, to regard it as legally obligatory (even though they may, of course, see such laws as devoid of intrinsic merit) and to give judgment accordingly. In a way, this might seem obvious, but not so obvious is the scope of this legal obligation in the interpretation of statutes. Judges can, as a matter of *fact*, be legally obliged to interpret a statute in a particular way, even when it cannot be said that the case in question involves straightforward law application. I will consider such cases in section (iii), before going on in later sections to consider the nature of judicial obligation in more

[3] J W Harris, 'Kelsen's Pallid Normativity' (1996) 9 *Ratio Juris* 94, 110. Harris is especially severe on Joseph Raz's view that there is something in the idea of a formal sense in which, legally speaking, one 'ought' to obey a law: J Raz, *The Authority of Law* (Clarendon Press, 1979), chs. 7 and 8. See also J W Harris, *Law and Legal Science* (Clarendon Press, 1979).

[4] Harris, 'Kelsen's Pallid Normativity', n. 3 above, 110. [5] Ibid., 114. [6] Ibid.

[7] J Gardner, 'Legal Positivim: 5½ Myths' (2001) 46 *American Journal of Jurisprudence* 199, 211.

controversial cases, where judges must exercise discretion, and hence—perhaps—moral argument, to determine the scope and effect of a statute.

(iii) Legal Obligation and Statutory Interpretation

Courts will be 'interpreting' legislation, rather then simply applying it to the facts, in at least some cases in which they are seeking to give effect to the 'utterance meaning' of a statute. Utterance meaning is to be distinguished from bare sentence meaning (a semantic issue) or (more or less private) speaker's meaning. Harris expressed this distinction as being one between what he called the 'will' model, which 'appeals to historical information about the motives or intentions of those who created a legal rule', and what he called the 'natural-meaning' model, which 'invokes the acontextual import of the words employed in the canonical formulations of a rule'.[8] The basic idea is sound, but the way in which Harris presents it would now be rejected by many theorists. What should be contrasted with the natural-meaning model is not a historical search for the intentions—for the 'will'—of those who enacted the legislation in question. That is a model best left behind as associated with the rule of an un-commanded commander. It cannot realistically be expected to reflect the complex character and practices of multi-party, bi-cameral legislatures.[9] The natural-meaning model, with its acontextual connotations, should instead be contrasted with what Jeffrey Goldsworthy calls 'utterance meaning', the meaning of words in their legislative context.[10] What matters, according to an 'utterance meaning' account of interpretation, is not so much what the legislature actually intended to achieve through legislating, but how the legislature supposed that judges would understand the words the legislature used in seeking to achieve their aims. For, as Gardner puts it, [s]o long as one can work out how the relevant others [i.e. the judges] will read what one says or does, one can also adapt what one says or does to anticipate their readings. . . . By this feedback route, one has the power intentionally to determine what law one makes even though the norm for interpreting that law does not refer to one's intentions . . .'.[11]

Goldsworthy, perhaps not without a hint of wavering between the 'will' model and the 'utterance meaning' model, explains the latter thus:

> Utterance meaning is what evidence, readily available to the intended audience, suggests that the speaker intended to communicate in making the utterance. That evidence includes not only sentence meaning—the literal meaning of the words uttered—but

[8] J W Harris, 'Unger's Critique of Formalism in Legal Reasoning: Hero, Hercules and Humdrum' (1989) 52 *MLR* 42, 46.

[9] See J Waldron, 'Legislators' Intentions and Unintentional Legislation', in A Marmor (ed.), *Law and Interpretation* (Clarendon Press, 1995), 330–31.

[10] J Goldsworthy, 'Marmor on Meaning, Interpretation, and Legislative Intention' (1995) 1 *Legal Theory* 439, 442.

[11] N. 7 above, n.219. As Cumming-Bruce LJ once put it (*Davis v Johnson* [1979] AC 264, 316): 'An Act means what the words and phrases selected by the parliamentary draftsmen actually mean, and not what individual members of the two Houses of Parliament think they mean.'

also . . . contextual factors . . . factors which can indicate the speaker's intention to convey by his or her utterance something in addition to, or different from, its sentence meaning [such as] the circumstances when the statute was passed, and its purpose, in so far as these are, or were at the time, common knowledge.[12]

The search for the utterance meaning of a statute is predominantly a factual enquiry, what Goldsworthy describes as 'the cognitive process of understanding the meaning genuinely possessed by the statute'.[13] That being so, when judges look beyond mere sentence meaning in search of utterance meaning, they are still fulfilling their primary function as 'norm-applying' institutions, and have not switched roles to become norm-creating institutions.[14] It is the fact that they are still the legislature's norm appliers, not partly independent norm creators, when they determine the content of the utterance meaning of a statute, that explains the English legal system's acceptance that courts can set down their determinations as exclusionary rules which bind future courts irrespective of the merits. Some examples may help to illustrate the more general point.

In *Whiteley v Chappell*,[15] the defendant personated a dead man in order to cast a vote in the latter's name. The Poor Law (Amendment) Act 1851 prohibited the personation, at any election, of 'any person entitled to vote'. The defendant was found not guilty. A dead man cannot by any reasonable stretch of the imagination be a 'person entitled to vote', and so the defendant did not personate such a person. Perhaps, by Ronald's Dworkin's test of whether an interpretation of a statute 'shows the political history including and surrounding that statute in the better light',[16] the court's interpretation of the 1851 Act was a bad one, since it is personation, in general, that is the evil or mischief struck at by the Act. The fact remains, however, that the dead are not persons 'entitled to vote'. *Whiteley v Chappell* thus illustrates the essentially factual nature of the enquiry into utterance meaning that the court, as a norm-applying institution, saw itself as bound to conduct, irrespective of what Parliament might 'really' have wanted. As Lord Reid famously put it, some 100 years later:

We often say that we are looking for the intention of Parliament, but that is not quite accurate. We are seeking the meaning of the words which Parliament used. We are seeking not what Parliament meant but the true meaning of what they said.[17]

[12] N.10 above, 442 and 451. As Bennion puts it, 'the express words of every Act have the shadowy accompaniment of a host of implicit statements': F Bennion, *The Interpretation of Statutes* (2nd edn., Butterworths, 1992), 3. The English courts have endorsed the idea that the search for 'utterance meaning' is what it means to be giving effect to Parliamentary intention: see *Royal College of Nursing of the UK v Dept of Health and Social Security* [1981] 1 All ER 545 (HL), 564–5 (*per* Lord Wilberforce).

[13] N.10 above, 45.

[14] Raz's phrases: see J Raz, *Practical Reason and Norms* (2nd edn., OUP, 1990), 132–41. So, I would reject, as far too hasty, Aileen Kavanagh's conclusion that once one moves beyond the literal meaning of legislation and finds oneself searching for 'deep meaning', the legislation in question must be indeterminate, with the result that there is no particular solution that is right (although there may be solutions that are clearly wrong): see A Kavanagh, 'The Elusive Divide between Interpretation and Legislation under the Human Rights Act 1998' (2004) 24 *OJLS* 259, 263–4. Utterance meaning may be 'deep' but also determinate.

[15] (1868) LR 4 QB 147.

[16] R M Dworkin, *Law's Empire* (Fontana, 1986), 313.

[17] *Black-Clawson International Ltd v Papeirwerke Waldhof-Aschaffenberg* [1975] AC 591, 613.

Here are two more examples where the courts have regarded themselves as bound by utterance meaning, albeit examples more consonant with, in a broader sense, 'what Parliament meant' or really wanted. In English law, bigamy (contrary to section 57 of the Offences Against the Person Act 1861) takes place when 'whosoever, being married, *shall marry* any other person during the life of the former husband or wife...' (my emphasis). In *R v Allen*,[18] the Court for Crown Cases Reserved had to decide whether the defendant was guilty of bigamy when, being already lawfully married, he then 'married' someone falling within the prohibited degrees of affinity (a former wife's niece). Given the degree of affinity between them, this was someone to whom he could not validly be married in law, even had he been free to marry. The court held that the phrase: 'whosoever, being married, shall marry...', meant, 'whosoever, being married, 'shall *go through a marriage ceremony*...'. So, Allen was found guilty, because he had gone through such a ceremony.[19] A similar kind of example, under a different statute, is *Alder v George*.[20] The defendant was charged, under section 3 of the Official Secrets Act 1920, with obstructing a member of His Majesty's forces engaged in security duty 'in the vicinity of' a prohibited place (in this case, a Royal Air Force station). The defendant was actually inside the station when the obstruction took place, and hence claimed that his act fell outside the scope of the statute, because it took place 'in' and not 'in the vicinity of' a prohibited place. It was held that the words 'in the vicinity of' meant, in context, 'in or in the vicinity of', and so the defendant was guilty. As Viscount Simon put it, in *Barnard v Gorman*:[21]

> We must not give the statutory words a wider meaning merely because on a narrower construction the words might leave a loophole.... If, on the proper construction of the section, that is the result, it is not for the judges to attempt to cure it. That is the business of Parliament. Our duty is to take the words as they stand, [but] to give them their true construction... always preferring the natural meaning of the word involved, but nonetheless always giving the word its appropriate construction in context.

These are two cases in which the court prefers utterance meaning to sentence meaning, in order to give effect to the 'true meaning of what [Parliament] said', to use Lord Reid's words, even though to do this involves interpreting one set of words ('shall marry'; 'in the vicinity of') as if they were a different set of words ('shall go through a ceremony of marriage'; 'in or in the vicinity of'). So, once again, it is not that the courts' rulings show 'the political history including and surrounding that statute in the better light' (although that is certainly true) which makes them rulings the courts are bound in law to give. It is that, as a matter of

[18] (1872) LR 1 CCR 367.

[19] The case would perhaps now be treated as one in which Allen attempted to commit bigamy, it being irrelevant in law that he could not commit bigamy: see ss. 1(2) and 1(3) of the Criminal Attempts Act 1981. At the time *Allen* was decided, this option would not have been regarded as soundly based in law.

[20] [1964] 2 QB 7.

[21] [1941] AC 378.

fact, the rulings correctly interpreted what Parliament meant by the words employed.[22]

That the courts are giving effect to the utterance meaning of a statute, in such cases, and are hence applying already existing legislative norms, rather than creating fresh norms before applying them, is what gives special importance to the binding character of such cases as precedents. In *Re Schweppes Ltd's Agreement*,[23] two judges in the Court of Appeal decided a point of statutory interpretation (an interpretation of the Restrictive Trade Practices Act 1956) in a particular way, and Wilmer J dissented. Later that very day, the same three judges confronted the identical point of law in *Re Automatic Telephone and Electric Co Ltd's Agreement*.[24] This time, Wilmer J did not dissent, deciding that he was bound to follow the decision in *Re Schweppes*. Punctilious though this approach might seem, it is fully justified. An essentially factual interpretation of Parliament's utterance meaning cannot be as infinitely revisable as the evaluative question, to recall Dworkin's words, of 'which story of the legislative event is overall the best story'.[25] So, it might be argued, Wilmer J's approach would only be unduly punctilious if the question at issue had been one more purely of merit-based or moral judgement. It is to such cases that I now turn.

(iv) Two Justifications for Judicial Use of Moral Reasoning

Should courts ever engage in law-creation, when it is open to them to do so, to resolve a dispute arising under statute? My argument will be that they can and should. Goldsworthy has put the argument this way:

> If a statute is insufficiently determinate to resolve a dispute, then out of sheer necessity judges must add something to it; they cannot wash their hands of a dispute and leave the parties to take up arms. But this power is strictly limited to *supplementing* the existing meaning of a statute. A judicial power to *alter* that meaning, not out of necessity, but because it requires or permits something absurd, is incompatible with orthodox constitutional norms.[26]

[22] Things are sometimes not quite as simple as this. Complexity comes in when the question is whether a statute is 'always speaking', namely whether the words used were meant by Parliament to have their contemporary meaning, whatever that might be (perhaps many years later), rather than to retain the meaning they had at the time of enactment: see *Fitzpatrick v Stirling Housing Association* [1999] 4 All ER 705 (HL). The question in this case was whether a same-sex partner could inherit a protected tenancy, on the death of his partner (the tenant), as a 'member of the tenant's family residing with the tenant at death'. The House of Lords divided on the question whether Parliament intended the words 'member of the tenant's family' to be given their contemporary meaning, whatever that might be (which was thought to include some same-sex partners) or their original meaning (which did not encompass such partnerships). It seems likely that, in this case, the Law Lords divided not so much over the utterance meaning of the statute, but because they had rival views of, to use Dworkin's phrase (n. 16 above, 346), 'which story of the legislative event is overall the best story'.

[23] [1965] 1 All ER 195. [24] [1965] 1 All ER 206. [25] See n. 22 above.

[26] N.10 above, 458 (Goldsworthy's emphasis).

Goldsworthy's claim at the end cannot now be accepted in Britain in quite this simple form, because Parliament has, through section 3 of the Human Rights Act 1998, itself instructed the courts to depart from the statutory (utterance) meanings of statutes passed before that Act, in so far as is consistent with bare sentence meaning, if the utterance meanings would otherwise produce one kind of moral 'absurdity', namely breaches of human rights.[27] So, for example, in *Ghaidan v Godin-Mendoza*,[28] the House of Lords held that the surviving homosexual partner of a deceased tenant could inherit a protected tenancy under the Rent Act 1977, not merely as a 'member of the family', but as a surviving 'spouse' (for the purposes of paragraph 2 of Schedule 1 to the 1977 Act). The House so held, even though it was accepted that Parliament in 1977 intended that the term 'spouse' should have a relatively fixed meaning that excluded same-sex partners. This approach involved the House of Lords altering the statute's meaning, through a creative understanding of the lexical meaning of the term 'spouse'. The House adopted this approach, though, simply in order to avoid a breach of the surviving partner's human rights (rights protected by Articles 8 and 14 of the European Convention on Human Rights), protection of which by the English judiciary, through its enactment of the Human Rights Act 1998, Parliament itself intended that the partner should enjoy.[29]

A further complexity is raised by the way Goldsworthy makes his perfectly sensible claim at the beginning of this passage. It may be widely accepted that when, to use Goldsworthy's words, 'a statute is insufficiently determinate to resolve a dispute', a court may have to use merit-based argument to supplement the meaning to ensure that the dispute is resolved. The House of Lords did this, for example, when interpreting what it would mean for a Local Authority to discharge a statutory obligation to run transport facilities in an 'efficient and economic' way.[30] What, though, of cases in which the wording of a statute is in itself sufficiently determinate to resolve the dispute, but only by reading further words into the statute can judges ensure that serious injustice—moral absurdity—is avoided in the resolution of the dispute? An example is provided by *R v K*.[31] In this case, the defendant was charged with indecent assault on a woman, contrary to

[27] See the discussion below, text at n. 96. Where legislation passed after the Act is in issue, it could be said that the 'utterance meaning' will presumptively carry with it an implication that the statute in question complies with the Human Rights Act 1998; but it is still open to the court to decide that a post-1998 statute cannot be made compliant with that Act without abandoning utterance meaning in favour of (a twisting of) bare sentence meaning, short of a declaration of incompatibility.

[28] [2004] 2 AC 557.

[29] For criticism of the Privy Council's failure to take this kind of human rights-focused approach to statutory and constitutional interpretation in death penalty appeals, see E W Thomas, 'The Privy Council and the Death Penalty' (2005) 121 *LQR* 175, criticizing *Lennox Ricardo Boyce and Jeffrey Joseph v The Queen* [2004] 3 WLR 786, and *Charles Matthew v State of Trinidad and Tobago* [2004] 3 WLR 812.

[30] *Bromley London Borough Council v Greater London Council* [1983] 1 AC 768. The House of Lords took this to mean that the transport system should be run on 'ordinary business principles'.

[31] [2002] 1 AC 462 (HL).

section 14(1) of the then Sexual Offences Act 1956. At the relevant time, the victim consented to the defendant's acts, but the victim was aged 14. By section 14(2) the consent of a girl aged under 16 was no defence to the offence under section 14(1). The defendant nonetheless claimed that he should be acquitted because the victim had told him she was aged 16, and he had no reason to disbelieve her. This claim—in effect, a denial of any *mens rea* in relation to the victim's age and hence, as to her capacity validly to consent—was met by the Prosecution's argument that neither section 14(1) nor section 14(2) contained a mental element to which the defendant's claim could be related in law. The Prosecution bolstered this argument by pointing out that just such a mental element, to which a claim of this type could be related, *was* provided for in adjoining sub-sections dealing with different instances in which consent was not valid. So, for example, section 14(4) analogously provided that, although a woman who was mentally defective could not give her consent to what would otherwise be an indecent assault, there could be no conviction unless the defendant 'knew or had reason to suspect her to be a defective'. The Prosecution argued that the implication must inevitably be, thus, that no such mental element is to be 'read in' to section 14(2), because it would have been expressly provided for, as in the other sub-sections, if that had been thought appropriate.

Far from accepting such arguments, however, the House of Lords implied an even more generous mental element into section 14(2), holding that the defendant could not be convicted unless the prosecution proved that he did not honestly believe that the girl was aged over 16 (whether or not such a belief was soundly based). On similar facts, under earlier legislation, the Court of Appeal had upheld a conviction in *R v Forde*[32] in such circumstances, stating:

> The words of a statute cannot be construed, contrary to their meaning, as embracing cases merely because no good reason appears why those cases should be excluded. It is not the duty of the court to make the law reasonable, but to expound it as it stands, according to the real sense of the words.[33]

In *R v K*, however, the majority held that there was a 'compellingly clear' case for the implication of a subjective mental element into section 14(2),[34] an implication justified by the presumption that a mental element is required in the case of all statutory crimes. Further, the majority regarded the 1956 Act as purely a consolidation statute. Hence, no significance was to be attached to the juxtaposition of sub-sections with, and sub-sections without, express provision for mental element. Developing this approach, Lord Bingham said: 'there is nothing in the language of this statute which justifies, as a matter of necessary implication, the conclusion that Parliament must have intended to exclude . . . *mens rea*.'[35] The approach of the majority, represented by Lord Bingham, involves the use of merit-based

[32] [1923] 2 KB 400 (CA). [33] Ibid., 404 *per* Avory J.
[34] The words 'compellingly clear' come from the speech of Lord Steyn, [2002] 1 AC 462, 477.
[35] [2002] 1 AC 462, 474.

reasoning (the application of the presumption of *mens rea*) to reach a result contrary to that which would be determined by the statute, if it were left unsupplemented by the extra wording which the application of the presumption entails. Such use by courts of merit-based argument is controversial. Yet, I will defend the practice in section (v), subject to some important limitations, observed by the majority. These limitations centre on the fact that the majority's approach seeks to keep faith with the ideals of the supremacy of Parliament, and of the limited law-creating role of the courts, by treating the interpretive dilemma as one brought about by legislative oversight. As Lord Bingham put it, '[s]ince the 1956 Act was a consolidation Act, there was no opportunity to correct this apparent absurdity'.[36]

Lord Millett, though, took a different approach in *R v K*, that was not subject to such limitations. He agreed with the result: 'with some misgiving, for I have little doubt that we shall be failing to give effect to the intention of Parliament and will reduce section 14 of the Sexual Offences Act 1956 to incoherence'.[37] He justified reaching the result on the quite different basis that:

> Parliament has signally failed to discharge its responsibility for keeping the criminal law in touch with the needs of society... the persistent failure of Parliament to rationalise this branch of the law even to the extent of removing absurdities which the courts have identified, means that we ought not to strain after internal coherence even in a single offence. Injustice is too high a price to pay for consistency.[38]

Here, then, is an example in which purely merit-based argument is being employed to justify supplementing the words of a statute, to avoid what is thought to be a morally intolerable result, even though to do this is considered to be, as it was suggested to be in *Forde*, contrary to the utterance meaning of the legislation. This approach is far more controversial than that of the majority. In section (vi), I shall argue that it should not be followed (except in the most extreme cases).

Putting aside the special case of methods of argument dictated by the Human Rights Act 1998 (addressed in section (vii) below), courts should not employ merit-based argument to supplement statutory wording where the result produced is believed to be contrary to the utterance meaning of the Act, however neglectful Parliament may have been when it comes to rationalizing an area of law, or to keeping it 'in touch with the needs of society'. Why? First, only the legislature has the time, opportunity, and resources at its disposal to investigate fully the demands of 'rationalization', and of the 'needs of society' (the 'expertise' reason for judicial restraint). As Lord Lowry put it, in justifying the House of Lords' refusal to abolish the presumption that a child defendant aged between 10 and 14 years of age did not know that what he did was seriously wrong:

> [I]t should be within the exclusive remit of Parliament. There is a need to study other systems... a task for which the courts are not equipped. Whatever change is made, it

36 [2002] 1 AC 462, 470. 37 Ibid., 479. 38 Ibid., 480.

should come only after collating and considering the evidence and after taking account of the effect which a change would have on the whole of the law.[39]

Secondly, only the legislature is in a position fully to consult on, to explain, and to justify law-creation, where persons or groups interested in or affected by it other than the parties to the dispute are concerned, in a way that can give the law creation a measure of moral, as well as legal, authority, even in the eyes of its opponents (the 'reciprocity' reason).[40]

(v) Legal and Moral Reasoning

No one doubts that judges should not act in a biased, corrupt, arbitrary, indiscreet, lazy, or self-interested way, something commonly highlighted in the oath which must be sworn upon taking up office as a judge.[41] Is this, largely negative, set of obligations coupled with an obligation positively to act on some kinds of reasons, rather than others, when exercising law-creating powers?[42] It is convenient to start by setting out the views of a theorist who thinks that judges are under such a positive obligation. For Raz, perhaps to emphasize the difference in his thinking between the norms judges are bound to apply and norms they are free to create, the positive obligation on judges when creating legal norms is to use moral reasoning:

Given that the courts are manned by people who will act only in ways they perceive to be valuable, principles of adjudication will not be viable, will not be followed by the courts, unless they can reasonably be thought to be morally acceptable, even though the thought may be misguided.... [Q]uite commonly courts have the discretion to modify legal rules, or to make exceptions to their applications, and where they have such discretion they ought to resort to moral reasoning to decide whether to use it and how. It follows that legal expertise and moral understanding and sensitivity are thoroughly intermeshed in legal reasoning.[43]

I shall come back in due course to the important point right at the end here (a point that is, rightly, loosely expressed) about the 'intermeshing' of legal expertise and moral understanding. There is, though, an ambiguity in this passage concerning what Raz believes to be viable principles of adjudication. In the penultimate sentence, it seems clear that he thinks judges are under a positive obligation to employ moral reasoning, as such, when they have a discretion to modify legal

[39] *C (A Minor) v DPP* [1996] 1 AC 1, 40.

[40] For something like this account of moral and legal authority, see, e.g., M Sellers, 'Republican Impartiality' (1991) 11 *OJLS* 273; S Hershovitz, 'Legitimacy, Democracy, and Razian Authority' (2003) 9 *Legal Theory* 201, 214.

[41] So, a nominee for the European Court of Justice must swear that: 'I will perform my duties impartially and conscientiously. I swear that I will preserve the secrecy of the deliberations of the court': *Rules of Procedure of the Court of Justice* (May 2004), Title I, chap. 1, Art. 3(i).

[42] See J Raz, *The Morality of Freedom* (Clarendon Press, 1986), 47.

[43] J Raz, *Ethics in the Public Domain* (Clarendon Press, 1994), 333–4, 335.

rules, to create exceptions, fill gaps, and so forth. In the early part of the passage, however, he makes what looks like a weaker claim that principles of adjudication must 'reasonably be thought to be morally acceptable, even though the thought may be misguided'. This claim is not the same as the claim at the end, because a court might reasonably think it morally acceptable, for example, to do as other judges have always done, to decide as efficiency or as prudence dictates, and so on, without supposing that to rely on such justifications for a decision is, *ipso facto*, positively to engage in 'moral reasoning'. If a court reasons in this way, then its decision will have authority as a piece of official dispute-resolution, because the court has complied with its negative obligations, even though many may think that the decision itself is poorly reasoned.[44] If this sounds like too weak a statement of what it means authoritatively to reason to a conclusion, *qua* judge, then let me modify it. Principled adjudication involves the use of reasoning that, morally speaking, may be employed in a particular context, even though such reasoning may not itself be moral reasoning (it could, for example, be economic or prudential reasoning). Few would doubt, though, that Raz is right to suggest that the use of judicial discretion ought to be adequately supported by moral reasoning, whatever other reasons may also be called on to support the decision.[45] Is it ever, though, a sufficient justification for the use of judicial discretion that it is supported by moral reasoning? So long as such reasoning is of a kind appropriately relied on in resolving a *lis inter partes*, I believe that it can be sufficient; but how we answer the question may depend on the political make-up of the court structure in the jurisdiction under discussion. Let me take this point further.

The main responsibility for judicial law-making lies with appeal courts. On an orthodox or traditional view, the main function of a domestic appeal court is to correct errors of law that were crucial to a lower court's decision.[46] It is in the correcting of such errors, of course, that judicial law-making may occur. On the orthodox or traditional ('British') view, this, error-correcting, view of the function of appellate courts is tied to an understanding of legal reasoning—even when innovative—as a form of expert opinion or thought that is relatively autonomous from purely moral or political opinion or thought. Harris himself sought to explain this sense that reasoning is 'legal' when it has this expert character.

[44] As Hart puts it, speaking of gap-filling: '[h]e [the judge] must not do this arbitrarily: that is he must always have some general reasons justifying his decision and he must act as a conscientious legislator would by deciding according to his own beliefs and values ...', in HLA Hart, *The Concept of Law* (Clarendon Press, 1961), 273.

[45] In putting the matter in this way, I leave open the question whether it is enough that a decision of a court is support*able* by sound moral reasoning, i.e. that there are 'guiding' reasons favouring the decision, even if they are not reasons that explain the decision itself ('explanatory' reasons). In making law, must courts make what they take to be moral reasons part of the explanatory justification for the decision? For the distinction between guiding and explanatory reasons see Raz, n. 14 above, 15–19.

[46] But see *Practice Direction* [1988] 2 All ER 831, in which it is said that, even though there is no legal restriction along these lines, leave to appeal to the House of Lords will not be given in civil cases, in practice, unless a point of law raised is one of general public importance.

For him, the demands of the rule of law and the separation of institutional powers mean that legal reasoning ought to be relatively isolated from 'open-ended ideological disputation',[47] even though legal rules 'may incorporate standards or values whose implementation calls for political judgment'.[48] The relative isolation from pure ideological disputation is brought about by the way in which reasons already to be found in a body of law may be understood by lawyers to restrict the range of available alternative solutions open to the judge, though they do not determine the solution reached itself.[49] The restrictions will restrict, on an exclusionary basis, even if they are self-imposed, in the sense that they are simply constituent parts of 'the common values and shared practices of a legal culture' (to use Raz's phrase) accepted in practice as 'ultimate' constraints by all lawyers.[50] Even when there is a range of alternative solutions, judges may follow what Harris calls the 'doctrine' model of legal reasoning. This 'prays in aid of a proposition, claimed to constitute part of the present law, some maxim belonging to an official tradition'.[51] This is the kind of doctrinal reasoning, distinguished by Max Weber as 'conceptual casuistry', the use of analogical argument founded on the meaning of concepts ('shall marry', as compared with 'shall go through a marriage ceremony'),[52] and is what gives reasoning commonly employed by lawyers its expert character. One can gain expertise and renown as an exponent of casuistical reasoning in much the same way (although they involve different skills) that one can become an accomplished debater or rhetorician. As in the case of the skilled political debater, the great exponent of conceptual casuistry relies, in part, on the moral force of arguments. His or her special skill or expertise lies, though, in filtering the light shed by these arguments through the prism made up of the set of 'constitutive' conventions that is the practice of legal reasoning, conventions that are partly autonomous in the sense that (to use Andrei Marmor's words): 'the point of engaging in them is not fully determined by any particular purpose or value that is external to the conventions constituting the practice'.[53]

When employing reasoning, in this sense, judges are not resting the authority of their decisions *solely* on an implicit claim, for example, about the quality—and

[47] N. 8 above, 62. [48] Ibid., 56.

[49] Ibid., See further, JM Finnis, 'Reason and Authority in Law's Empire' (1987) 6 *Law and Philosophy* 357, esp. 370–6.

[50] The constraints are 'ultimate' in that they are not authorized by any higher norm.

[51] Harris, *Law and Legal Science*, n. 3 above, 46.

[52] Ibid. For the marriage example, see text to n. 19 above. Conceptual casuistry has been well exemplified, in Harris' own area of expertise, by Ben McFarlane's ingenious attempt to group together for expository purposes 'secret' trusts, set up by will, and a *congeries* of *inter vivos* dispositions made subject to a constructive trust, because an undertaking was given by the purchaser to confer a right on someone in relation to property purchased, by the giving of which an advantage accrued to the purchaser in relation to the acquisition of the property: B McFarlane, 'Constructive Trusts Arising on a Receipt of Property *Sub Conditione*' (2004) 120 *LQR* 667.

[53] A Marmor, 'Legal Conventionalism' (1998) 4 *Legal Theory* 509. Marmor goes on to point out that constitutive conventions are, naturally, prone to change through practice, and this is as true of legal practice as of any kind of conventionalism. Marmor uses the idea of constitutive conventions to shed light on the acceptance by judges of the rule of recognition, not on legal reasoning more generally. So, he is not responsible for the use to which I have put his theory.

hence authority—of their moral insight. They are relying, in part, on the quality of the decision as an exemplar of conceptual casuistry, as an example of what Raz refers to as lawyers' 'knowledge of the law and their skills in interpreting laws and in arguing in ways that show their legal experience and expertise'. They are doing this even if, in cases that break new ground, such reasoning also relies, for much of its persuasive force on arguments distilled from lawyers' 'wisdom and understanding of human nature . . . moral sensibility . . . enlightened approach etc'.[54] So, such reasoning is capable of providing a somewhat more legitimate basis for the authoritative creation of rule-like norms binding on future courts than purely moral reasoning can do. Indeed, in that regard, John Gardner has gone further by arguing that judges—perhaps, especially appeal court judges—*must* reason in something like this manner (he seeks to give it more conceptual clarity) when engaged in law-creation. For him, judges:

> have a professional obligation to reach their decisions by legal reasoning . . . simply to reason morally or economically or aesthetically . . . would admittedly be a violation of a judge's professional obligations. For judges admittedly have a professional obligation to reach their decisions by legal reasoning. [Only a legislature] 'is entitled to make new legal norms on entirely nonlegal grounds. . . . A legislature is entitled to think about a problem purely on its merits. . . . But not so a judge. Barring special circumstances, a judge may only create [a] new legal norm on legal grounds, *i.e.* by relying on already valid legal norms in creating new ones.[55]

Gardner does not rule out entirely the possibility that judges may (have to) employ modes of reasoning other than 'legal' reasoning in this sense—i.e., reasoning through partial reliance on already valid legal norms—when they create law in deciding a case; but he thinks they should not employ other modes of reasoning at an 'early stage in the game'.[56] For him, it is only when the resources on which legal reasoning in his sense is based run out that judges become entitled to discharge their professional obligation to decide cases within their jurisdiction by reliance on, say, moral or prudential reasoning alone. That may be absolutely right when one is confronted by a legal system that reflects the orthodox or traditional, 'British' view of the function of appeal courts; but it may be too restrictive as an

[54] Raz, n. 3 above, 48.

[55] N. 7 above, 215 and 217. In conversation, Gardner has expressed to me the view that the requirement that judges rely, in part, on 'already valid' legal norms, when engaged in law-creation, is satisfied in cases where such reliance takes the simple form of reliance on an overruled case or dissenting judgment (coupled with supporting moral or economic etc. arguments), even though it would not be natural to describe such sources as 'already valid' legal norms. I have my doubts about how satisfactory an understanding of his thesis this is, because the case for reliance on overruled cases and dissenting judgments seems to be merit-based, not source-based; and, so, it is unclear how much difference there really is between reliance on such 'legal' sources and reliance on moral arguments deployed, say, by a famous philosopher. Tentatively, one might suggest his thesis would look less artificially restrictive if it insisted only that, to be truly 'legal', reasoning must involve reliance, in part, on what might be called 'existing legal materials' (which, of course, include dissenting judgments and overruled cases), rather than on the narrower notion of already valid legal norms.

[56] N. 7 above, 215.

account, for example, of the practice of some Supreme Courts or trans-national appeal courts, which can be entitled to determine for themselves, at least to some extent, the criteria that are to count as having 'legal' relevance (as is the case with the European Court of Justice[57]). In that context, Gardner's understanding of distinctively 'legal' reasoning seems too restrictive, in that it insists, at least presumptively, that such reasoning be founded, in part, on already existing legal materials, if the reasoning is to be legal but not legislative in character. It may be, however, that the way in which a jurisdiction (or a group of legally connected jurisdictions, acting collectively) shapes the powers and membership criteria for a trans-national or Supreme Court, frees judicial decision-makers in that Court from the duty to observe this kind of constraint, even presumptively.

A Supreme Court, for example, can usually pick and choose the issues on which to rule, on the grounds of their public importance, and, like a trans-national court, it is not necessarily tied to functioning as the highest legal authority to which one can appeal in search of 'error correction' across the whole field of public and private law. So, for example, a Supreme Court might seize on a case in which a doctor has been charged with murder through euthanasia, and—without reliance on previous doctrine governing criminal law defences—create a wholly new defence to intentional killing of having acted 'in the best interests of the patient', with an eye solely to protecting at least some doctors from such prosecutions in the future. Whatever one thinks of the intrinsic merits of such a step, the Supreme Court might be fully authorized to do this, in that it is one of its acknowledged functions to create and develop criminal defences, whether or not such a step is taken by reliance, in part, on already-valid legal norms. Naturally, there will be a 'retrospective' element to the Court's reasoning, even in such an instance, in so far as the character of all moral arguments is shaped by and draws on, for its force, past and present practices, the use of variations on familiar examples, and, in general, what Sabina Lovibond calls '[a] common evaluative culture';[58] but that retrospective element will not be the same as reliance on an 'already valid' legal norm.

In that regard, of course, membership of a trans-national or Supreme Court may not necessarily be confined to—and may not even include—practising lawyers or those with previous judicial experience,[59] cutting away the necessarily 'expert' input into decision-making assumed by the orthodox or traditional view of appeal courts' functions. For example, not a single one of the nine Justices who

57 The European Court of Justice has the power to develop its jurisdiction, in order to ensure the adequate legal protection of persons subject to European law: see the discussion in KPE Lasok, *The European Court of Justice* (2nd edn., Butterworths, 1994), 8–9.

58 S Lovibond, *Ethical Formation* (Harvard University Press, 2002), 43. As she says, at 45: 'we can think of particular moral judgments—when they are true rather than false—not just as bringing us into harmony with a certain consensus of feeling or opinion, but as disclosing to us the "layout" of a certain domain of reality, namely, the moral domain.'

59 See the discussion in R Stevens, *The English Judges: their Role in the Changing Constitution* (Hart Publishing, 2002), 152, and in H Corder, 'Judicial Authority in a Changing South Africa' (2004) 24 *Legal Studies* 253.

decided *Brown v Board of Education*[60] had judicial experience before becoming a member of the Supreme Court. Even in England and Wales, as Sir Sydney Kentridge has reminded us,[61] until the end of the nineteenth century (and for some time afterwards), high judicial appointment was a generally recognized reward for those who had performed political services, such persons forming the great majority of judges appointed between 1832 and 1906. My point is not that those judges were appointed by virtue of some special merit that they possessed (although some of them proved to be outstanding judges). My point is that, so long as such judges comply with their 'negative' obligations to remain free from bias, indiscretion, idleness, and so forth, there is no special reason why non-lawyer members of appeal courts—especially Supreme or trans-national courts—should feel bound by the 'positive' obligation to reason in accordance with the constraints of conceptual casuistry familiar to their legally trained colleagues.

In particular, the widely accepted obligation on a constitutional court to sustain the view that a constitution is a 'living' instrument relevant to present-day conditions is commonly recognized as freeing judges from the obligation to adopt the more accustomed 'expert' perspective on decision-making appropriate for error-correction, as I have described it. As Aguda JA has put it, 'the primary duty of the judges is to make the constitution grow and develop in order to meet the just demands and aspirations of an ever developing society which is part of the wider and larger human society governed by some acceptable concepts of human dignity'.[62] As indicated at the end of section (iii), however, it is strongly arguable that this 'primary' duty must be discharged within the limitations imposed by judicial recognition of (in many states) the supremacy of legislatures, and (more generally) of the inherent limitations of the *lis inter partes* as a means of seeking to meet 'the just demands and aspirations of an ever developing society'. Before discussing an approach to statutory interpretation that respects these limitations, however, let me turn my attention to one that does not.

(vi) Judges as Moral Authorities (*Sed Quis Custodes Custodiet?*)

In section (iv) above, we saw that, in *R v K*, Lord Millet justified the reading of words into a statute to reach a result he acknowledged to be contrary to its utterance meaning, as justifiably done by judges because (in his words) 'Parliament has signally failed to discharge its responsibility for keeping the criminal law in touch

[60] 347 US 483 (1955).

[61] Sir Sydney Kentridge, 'The Highest Court: Selecting the Judges' (2003) 62 *CLJ* 55, 64. Kentridge does not himself regard this model for judicial appointment as appropriate.

[62] *Dow v Attorney-General* [1992] LRC (Const) 623, 668 (Supr Ct of Botswana). See also *Ministry of Home Affairs v Fisher* [1980] AC 319 (PC), and the discussion in N Jayawickrama, *The Judicial Application of Human Rights Law* (CUP, 2002), ch. 5; A Barak, 'Foreword: A Judge on Judging: The Role of a Supreme Court in a Democracy' (2002) 116 *Harvard LR* 19, 28–9.

with the needs of society.... Injustice is too high a price to pay for consistency.'[63] A former judge of the Court of Appeal of New Zealand has likewise argued that, where fundamental human rights are involved in constitutional interpretation:

> [T]he judicial compunction to search for the legislature's intention in the wording of the statute when the lives of people and their fundamental rights are at stake is deficient... [the issue is] whether [judges] adopt a 'meaning' which, while it may not accord with Parliament's intention... will safeguard the fundamental rights and freedoms enshrined in the constitution.[64]

Whilst such an approach may be defensible if Parliament *has itself* instructed judges to interpret legislation in accordance with the demands of human rights jurisprudence, it is much more controversial as a stand-alone claim about the interpretation of legislation in general. It represents what might be called the 'substantive' objection to placing complete faith in the ability of legislated law to 'get it right'.[65] Can legislatures be trusted never to act arbitrarily, wickedly, or neglectfully? If not, in the eyes of some judges and theorists, there is a role for judges in modifying the impact of legislation that is the product of such actions. This is achieved through judicial law-making, inspired by what is taken to be a more congenial or appropriate set of values.

Ronald Dworkin has, of course, argued most forcefully for such a role for judges, one in which they interpret legislation in accordance with what they take to be the soundest view of a jurisdiction's political culture, but, if possible, and if need be, go on to annul it if it is inconsistent with that view.[66] The modern positivist who does most to develop the substantive objection to placing complete trust in legislated law is, however, one of Dworkin's best-known critics, Joseph Raz. Raz says:

> The courts are, or at least they should be, above the rough-and-tumble of everyday political pressures. They should be relatively immune to passing fashions. In constitutional matters they may succeed in representing a lasting consensus, even at times when prevailing trends disguise its existence from the majority of the public, and even in the face of a government whose reforming zeal blinds it to the need to preserve the fabric of the political culture.[67]

For Raz, this substantive objection to placing complete faith in legislated law is to a degree limited, because judges must recognize that 'only democratic politics can be sufficiently sensitive to the results of change, and only democratic politics can respond adequately to the different interests and different perspectives of different subcultures'.[68] Nonetheless, the courts are charged by him with the responsibility

[63] *R v K* [2002] 1 AC 462, 480.

[64] Thomas, n. 29 above, 179–80.

[65] In the next section, I will contrast it with what will be called the (more justifiable) 'technocratic' objection that underpins the approach to interpretation ushered in by the Human Rights Act 1998.

[66] R Dworkin, *Freedom's Law* (OUP, 1996), ch. 1.

[67] N. 42 above, 260.

[68] N. 43 above, 374.

for maintaining 'a common understanding of the legal culture of the country [in accordance with] the common values and shared practices of the legal culture'.[69] What are we to make of this staunch defence of a (small 'p') political role for judges in deciding cases?

The fact that the need to use moral reasoning is often encountered by the highest courts may lead them to give a commitment, as in *R v K*, to an interpretive preference for respecting individual rights, when these are finely balanced (in the resolution of an interpretive difficulty) against the value of, say, efficiency in the pursuit of state policy.[70] However, as we will see in the next section, the giving of this kind of commitment must be made perfectly consistent with acknowledging the supremacy of Parliament and the limited role of judicial law-making (what I will call part of a 'technocratic' approach to interpretation). It should involve nothing so ambitious as the free-ranging use of moral argument in dispute-resolution to engage in what Raz describes as the pursuit of a 'lasting consensus', or in what Lord Millett describes as 'keeping the criminal law in touch with the needs of society'. Indeed, Raz's articulation of the substantive objection, and of the role for judges that he envisages as part of it, bristles with difficulties. Certainly, judges should be above the rough-and-tumble of everyday political pressures, but that is true of elected politicians *qua* legislators as well.[71] Moreover, how plausible is it that, in constitutional cases, judges should seek to, '[represent] a lasting consensus'? As Raz himself notes,[72] issues commonly fall for judicial determination in a haphazard and unsystematic way, depending on the vagaries of litigation and the peculiar nature of individual disputes. A century or more could separate judicial consideration of two adjoining sections in a statute (and the later court might be bound to follow the now out-of-date decision of the earlier one), making the reaching of 'lasting consensus' in an area of law a wholly unrealistic goal. In the same era, different judges, in interpreting or extending (or, in some jurisdictions, annulling) different pieces of legislation, will inevitably construe the idea of the 'lasting consensus' which they are meant to represent in very different ways, even at different stages of an appeal in the same case. That fact about appellate litigation is what long ago led Simpson to claim that what Raz calls the 'common values and shared practice of a legal culture' cannot, in practice, easily be distinguished from the values and practices of lawyers themselves, period.[73] Cynical though it might seem, Simpson's claim gains force when one considers that, in Raz's account, given that the consensus is meant to stand opposed to the 'reforming zeal' of legislators, and to the 'prevailing trends' that hide the nature of true consensus from most of

[69] N. 43 above, 374 and 375.

[70] See further, *Patel v Attorney-General* [1968] Zambia LR 99; *Commissioner of Taxes v CW Ltd* [1990] LRC Const 544 (Sup Ct of Zimbabwe).

[71] See, more broadly, J Waldron, *The Dignity of Legislation* (CUP, 1999).

[72] N. 2, above, 194–201.

[73] See AWB Simpson, 'The Common Law and Legal Theory', in AWB Simpson (ed.), *Oxford Essays in Jurisprudence* (2nd Series. Clarendon Press, 1973), 77.

the public, judges themselves can presumably be the only arbiters of what it means to achieve lasting consensus. Worse still, the goal of reaching a 'lasting consensus' through a creative approach to understanding the scope of (or *a fortiori* through a decision to annul) legislation that, *ex hypothesi*, blunts the force of that legislation, seems to be a classic example of what Dworkin rightly identified as a 'policy' goal unfit for judges to pursue.[74] This is not because judges should be concerned only with 'principles' that are supposedly distinct from 'policies' (the Achilles' heel in Dworkin's development of his point). It is because judicial decision-making arising out of a *lis inter partes* is a wholly inadequate means by which to investigate what might constitute such a consensus, or to determine whether deciding one way rather than another will do something to achieve it.[75]

(vii) Using Moral Reasoning Whilst Maintaining Due Deference

There cannot be a distinctively 'positivist' answer to the question of how judges should strike a balance between using moral reasoning to resolve cases they are duty-bound to resolve and (where this is constitutionally appropriate) showing proper regard for legislative supremacy and for the limited role of courts in law-making.[76] What is perceived to be the right balance will understandably vary very considerably from one legal and political tradition to the next, depending on a host of factors that have nothing to do with the (in)validity, as such, of law. Yet, all positivists have become familiar with what Gardner vividly describes as 'the pincer movement against legal positivists as a group. Either legal positivists agree that judges should not decide cases on their merits (absurd!), or they become committed to the view that judges are part-time legislators (intolerable!)'.[77] Why do positivists find themselves facing the 'pincer movement'?

One side to the 'pincer movement', that concerned with decrying the role of judges as part-time legislators, draws inspiration from what is (misleadingly, as it happens) thought to be a stark contrast in positivist thinking between the authority of laws which judges are duty bound to uphold, an authority supposedly

[74] R Dworkin, *Taking Rights Seriously* (Duckworth, 1977), 22–8. I do not mean to suggest that Dworkin would himself regard the attempt to reach such a consensus as inappropriate for judicial determination.

[75] These are not unfamiliar kinds of criticisms of attempts by theorists to articulate and invest great significance in a grandiose, substantive role for judges in controversial cases: see J Waldron, 'A Rights-Based Critique of Constitutional Rights' (1993) 13 *OJLS* 18, for a development of some of these points. See further, CJ Peters, 'Participation, Representation, and Principled Adjudication' (2002) 8 *Legal Theory* 185. English appeal cases are so driven by *lis inter partes* considerations, that it is not even clear that a court can rely on a case not cited by the parties in argument, let alone rely on a whole line of policy argument, without finding itself guilty of procedural irregularity in reaching judgment: D Dabbs, 'Fairness and the Magician's Hat' [2003] *New Law Journal* 1436.

[76] Gardner, n. 7 above, 210 and 213. As Gardner explains at 213, one could, in theory, perfectly well be a positivist who believed that all the positing should be done *ex post facto* and *ad hoc* by judges in individual cases.

[77] N. 7 above, 215.

wholly independent of merit-based considerations, and the authority of moral reasoning which is employed to justify law-making, an authority that is by its nature merit-based. Other than in special situations, as when those in question are bound by religious faith so to regard their relative positions, no one can claim an 'expertise' basis for authority over how the balance of moral reasons must tip, substantively, for any individual fully capable of deciding how the balance tips for themselves.[78] One does not, *ipso facto*, do better substantively to follow someone else's assessment of the way the balance tips without oneself having regard to the merits.[79] That does not mean that there can never be a basis for authority over how the balance of moral reasons tips, and hence no basis for binding others in that regard. In flourishing democracies, for example, it could be that citizens are all bound by a collective decision on a moral matter, even though many disagree with it, because at some point they all had an adequate chance to influence the outcome. This is, though, a procedural, as opposed to a substantive, basis for authority. In that regard, though, it is a kind of authority that can be possessed readily enough by a legislature, but it is almost inconceivable that it could be possessed by a court.[80] Legislatures are clearly in a far better position than the courts to give 'deliberative' authority to moral decision-making, the authority that comes from having a procedure which ensures that as many minds as possible are brought to bear on how to fashion appropriate solutions. Five heads may be better than three, and three better than one, in the higher courts; but that hardly compares with the deliberative authority that a democratic system of representative government, involving the work of hundreds of members of Parliament, can give to difficult, but fully debated, decisions.[81] That is, then, one argument for the sovereignty of Parliament over the use of moral justifications for law-making.

More subtly, though, someone may be an expert on the content and relative importance of a set of moral obligations in the balance (as when someone is an expert on Jewish law), or an expert on the nature and range of reasons that are in the balance (as when someone has made a broad and deep study of factors relevant to, say, the ethics of assisted suicide). Sometimes, courts try to clothe their decisions with this kind of 'expert' basis for authority on moral matters, as by making the decision of a doctor-turned-judge crucial to the outcome of a disputed question with a medical dimension, such as whether someone who has had a sex change can marry another person of the 'same' sex.[82] Laudable though such efforts by courts are, however, they are doomed to failure.[83] No doctor-turned-judge

[78] See Hershovitz, n. 40 above, 214.

[79] So, the so-called 'service' conception of authority has no application to moral reasoning, pure and simple: Raz, n. 42 above, 53: 'the alleged subject is likely better to comply with the reasons which apply to him . . . if he accepts the directives of the alleged authority as authoritatively binding and tries to follow them, rather than by trying to follow the reasons which apply to him directly.'

[80] See Hershovitz, n. 40 above, 213–19.

[81] See Waldron, n. 9 above; Hershovitz, n. 40 above.

[82] See *Corbett v Corbett* [1971] P 83.

[83] I am speaking here of the higher courts. In specialist tribunals, the expertise of the tribunal can lend an expert basis to its authority. There is a good discussion in Collins, n. 1 above.

can speak on such a matter with the authority of (say) a national Medical Association and, in the context of a *lis inter partes*, no court can properly account for the views of all those whose expertise might be germane to the decision. As suggested above, it is the legislature and (at its behest) the executive that are in the best position to account for all such views, in virtue of the time and resources at their disposal, and because they are not bound by *lis inter partes* constraints. Moreover, when decisions on moral matters must be made, and given binding status, the legislature is in a far better position than the courts to give its decision a 'reciprocity' basis for authority, for much the same kinds of reasons. This is an authority derived from the more-or-less exhaustive efforts made to consult interested parties and account for their views, to explain the decision fully, and (if possible) to mitigate its impact on those made worse off by the decision, and so on. Courts sometimes try to give their decisions authority on a 'reciprocity' basis, by hearing briefs prepared by at least some interested bodies not party to the dispute; but, once again, their efforts are doomed to failure, because their consultation processes will inevitably be crude, and very incomplete.[84] Where does that leave the case for the use of moral argument in law-making by judges set out in section (v)?

Both within and outwith positivist theory, there has always been what one might call a 'technocratic' objection to reposing complete faith and confidence in legislated law (which can be contrasted with the substantive objection to doing so, discussed in section (vi)). Famously, for Bentham, in an ideal world, at the end of a codification process there ought to be:

> no *terrae incognitae*, no blank spaces: nothing is at least omitted, nothing unprovided for [because] so long as there remains any, the smallest scrap, of unwritten law unextirpated, it suffices to taint with its own corruption—its own inbred and incurable corruption—whatsoever portion of *statute* law has ever been, or ever can be, applied to it.[85]

Bentham was, however, perfectly well aware that legislatures tended to fall far short of the ideal of crafting legislation in the way he commended. As he himself memorably put it:

> The country squire who has his turnips stolen, goes to work and gets a bloody law against stealing turnips. It exceeds the utmost stretch of his comprehension to conceive that the next year the same catastrophe may happen to his potatoes. For two general rules . . . in

[84] See, e.g., *R (on the application of S) v Chief Constable of South Yorkshire* [2004] 4 All ER 193, where, when considering the lawfulness of retaining DNA samples from unconvicted persons, the House of Lords encountered procedural difficulties when considering written evidence from the pressure group, 'Liberty': see the speech of Lord Steyn, ibid., 203. Evidence from other pressure groups, perhaps those opposed to the stance taken by 'Liberty', appears not to have been considered.

[85] Bentham's emphasis. Cited in P Schofield and J Harris, *'Legislator of the World': Writings on Codification, Law and Education, The Collected Works of Jeremy Bentham* (OUP, 1998), 20–1. For more detailed analysis, see A Perreau-Saussine, 'Bentham and the Boot-Strappers of Jurisprudence: The Moral Commitments of a Rationalist Jurisprudence' (2004) 63 *CLJ* 346.

modern British legislation are: never to move a finger till your passions are inflamed, nor ever to look further than your nose.[86]

One does not have to be quite this cynical about legislative processes to see how the technocratic objection to placing complete faith in legislated law arises. Hart laid considerable emphasis on it (albeit not by that name) in his attempt to rehabilitate the judicial role.[87] The objection comes in the form of an argument in two stages: (1) a legislature will never so perfect its legislative technique that it can avoid the need for future revision of the law, in the light of unanticipated circumstances, and (2) law-making by the judges themselves is warranted when the need for such revision has been revealed by a case in which great injustice would be done were judges seised of the case not to engage in some (necessarily) *ex post facto* law-making. The first stage is clearly easier to accept than the second. Legislatures are not omniscient, and the Parliamentary time spent on individual pieces of legislation must necessarily be limited.[88] Once enacted, though, statutes usually have an indefinite 'shelf-life', meaning that anomalies and gaps with the potential to work injustice are bound to appear over time. A legislature may be understandably reluctant to address these anomalies and gaps until the case for a comprehensive overhaul of the law has become pressing, a process that might be a century or more in the making. What, then, of the more controversial second stage?

For Bentham, of course, '[no] degree of wisdom . . . can render it expedient for a judge . . . to depart from pre-established rules',[89] and when the utterance meaning of a rule, correctly interpreted, covers a case, no doubt he is right. It is, though, quite conceivable that a legislature may have reasons to tolerate judicial gap-filling and exception-creation, to protect litigants from great injustice, pending a more comprehensive review of a statutory scheme. These reasons may be at least as compelling as the rule-of-law reasons the legislature has to give departments of government the ongoing task of identifying gaps and anomalies following executive monitoring of the impact of legislation (the two processes are hardly mutually exclusive).[90] The existence of such justice-based reasons is part of the moral and political background that underpins the willingness of most legal theorists to tolerate, or even to encourage, the limited use of judicial discretion to create law.[91] After all, as Hart suggested,[92] whatever the obvious jurisprudential differences,

[86] Bentham MSS, in the library of University College, London, cxl 92, cited by G Postema, *Bentham and the Common Law Tradition* (Clarendon Press, 1986), 264. For a modern expression of this view, see P Robinson, MT Cahill, and U Mohammed, 'The Five Worst (and Five Best) American Criminal Codes' (2000) 95 *Northwestern Univ. LR* 1, 64: 'The very immediacy and import of criminal law render it all the more susceptible to mere politicking rather than deliberate craftsmanship'.

[87] See Hart, n. 44 above, 130–6.

[88] See ibid., 126–31.

[89] Cited by Postema, n. 86 above, 197.

[90] See further Lord Devlin, *Samples of Law-Making* (Clarendon Press, 1962), 71.

[91] It follows, of course, that in different political circumstances, theorists are likely to be, and should be, much less supportive of a judicial discretion to make law, as when judges tend to be incompetent, biased, or corrupt, or all three (as they often were in Bentham's time).

[92] N. 44 above, 130–6.

there is hardly that much practical political difference between, on the one hand, a minor law-making role for judges and, on the other hand, the role that they fulfil when the legislature has given them a broad-ranging discretion to judge conduct against open-textured standards such as 'reasonableness'. The employment of such standards is often meant to avoid the very situation in which, confronted by a failed legislative effort to capture in a statutory formulation all the particular instances of conduct that ought to be provided for, courts find themselves needing to extend the law to fill in gaps or to correct anomalies. As Gardner puts it (impliedly agreeing with Goldsworthy):

> No closure rule, however ingenious, can guarantee to eliminate . . . gaps. They are endemic to law, in all legal systems, thanks to the positivity of law. This makes it inevitable that if judges are to decide all cases validly brought before them, they will sometimes have to go beyond the mere application of posited (including legal) norms. And once they have exhausted all the normative resources of posited norms, what else is there for them to rely on but the merits of the case and hence the various norms that might now be posited in order to resolve it?[93]

One could speculate at length about what the constitutional position would be of Bentham's postulated 'Contested Interpretation Committee', a committee that would have the power to resolve interpretive doubts without creating or being bound by precedents.[94] Judges, however, unlike agents of the executive monitoring the effect of legislation, have what Gardner calls 'the professional obligation . . . not to refuse to decide any case that is brought before them and that lies within their jurisdiction'.[95] Such cases may, of course, involve the imposition of criminal and/or civil liability, setting back the autonomy of individuals. So, morally speaking, permitting particularistic and pressing considerations of justice—a concern for avoiding gross injustice in particular circumstances—to carry weight when the stages (1) and (2) above have been passed is, as a matter of conscience (if nothing else), unavoidable for judges *qua* decision-makers. That is the lesson of cases such as *R v K*; but the 'technocratic' justification for law-making by judges need not necessarily itself be a piece of judge-crafted principle. It can be explicitly adopted by the legislature.

In that regard, the Human Rights Act 1998 is a classic case of a piece of legislation shaped with the technocratic objection very much in mind, when it comes to dealing with legislative failures to account for rights protected by the European Convention for the Protection of Human Rights of 1950. Section 3 provides that, 'so far as it is possible to do so, primary legislation and subordinate legislation must be read and given effect to in a way which is compatible with the Convention rights'.[96] The section clearly anticipates that there may be instances

[93] N. 7 above, 212.

[94] See further JR Dunwiddy, 'Adjudication under Bentham's Pannomion' (1989) 1 *Utilitas* 283, cited by Perreau-Saussine, n. 85 above, 356.

[95] N. 7 above.

[96] The Human Rights Act 1998 is not unique in taking such an approach: see, e.g., s.5(1) of the Constitution of the Republic of Trinidad and Tobago Act 1976, which provides that existing laws

after, not just before, the passing of the Act in which the statutory wording could be construed, contrary to the 1998 legislature's intention, in a way incompatible with Convention rights, something the courts are now charged with avoiding, through creative interpretation of the sentence meaning of that wording.[97] In cases where it is impossible to read and give effect to legislation in a way compatible with Convention rights, although the courts must then give effect to the legislation, under section 4 a higher court may issue a 'declaration of incompatibility', triggering a permission granted by section 10 to change the law through subordinate legislation to bring it in line with Convention rights. The technocratic objection is evident here too, when post-1998 statutes are in issue. Such declarations of incompatibility may be made, and subordinate legislation then passed to bring the law into line with Convention rights, even though—following the Human Rights Act 1998—in passing the original statute the relevant Minister of State must formally have declared in Parliament that the legislation is consistent with Convention rights.[98] The point, then, is not that legislation cannot be permitted to cut across the demands of human rights considerations, and the courts are there to make sure that the legislature does not cut across them. The point is that, except where a contrary meaning has been made crystal clear, the legislature now does not intend its enactments—past or present—to cut across those demands. The technocratic objection suggests that it may be quite appropriate for a court to be granted the task, in so far as it cannot twist the wording to fit with human rights demands, of pointing out when the legislature has, contrary to its intention, done just that.

(viii) Conclusion

I draw the following conclusions from the argument:

(a) When a statute needs interpretation because it cannot straightforwardly be applied, judges have an obligation to interpret in accordance with the statute's utterance meaning.

(b) When courts interpret statutes in that way, they are still giving effect to the (utterance) meaning of enactments.

governing those islands 'shall be construed with such modification, qualifications, adaptations, and exceptions as may be necessary to bring them into conformity with this Act' (the Act brought into effect the constitution itself). S. 5 seems to go considerably further than s. 3 of the Human Rights Act 1998, however, in allowing for 'modifications [and] adaptations' by the courts to legislation, something that seems inevitably to draw the courts into re-drafting.

[97] See, e.g., J Coppel, *The Human Rights Act 1998* (John Wiley & Sons, 1999), 32–3, and the discussion of *Ghaidain* in the text at n. 28 above.

[98] Underlining the technocratic orientation of the Human Rights Act 1998, by s. 5, the Crown is entitled to notice that a declaration of incompatibility is under consideration, and may be joined as a party to the proceedings, upon giving notice, making it possible for the Government to make representations on the issue of compatibility, and to seek to appeal any decision to make such a declaration.

(c) Sometimes, judges may have to resolve disputes arising under statute by creating rather than merely interpreting the law, if great injustice is to be avoided.

(d) When judges do create law to avoid great injustice, by reading words into a statute, the spirit in which they do so should be technocratic (providing for the unintended or unforeseen), rather than substantive (acting as guardians of a set of judicially endorsed values).

It would be pointless to deny that sometimes it will be hard to distinguish technocratic from substantive arguments in favour of judicial law-making. It has not been my intention to suggest that the two can always be kept entirely distinct. An example is provided by instances (as in *R v K*) in which judges imply *mens rea* elements into criminal offences created by statute, when the statute is silent on the matter. Are they doing this because, as Lord Devlin once put it, '[t]he fact is that Parliament has no intention whatever of troubling itself about *mens rea*',[99] a technocratic justification for judicial activism? Or are they doing it because, as Lord Kenyon once put it, '[one should] adopt any construction of the statute that the words will bear, in order to avoid such monstrous consequences as would manifestly ensure from a construction [favouring strict liability]', a substantive justification?[100] One may well find the technocratic and the substantive arguments being deployed in a mutually reinforcing way, and not kept distinct because one argument—the technocratic argument—is perceived to be in some sense more legitimate than the other. As Sir Rupert Cross argued, in this context, presumptions, like the presumption of a *mens rea* requirement, may simply 'supplement the text', but may equally 'operate at a higher level as expressions of fundamental principles governing both civil liberties and the relations between Parliament, the executive and the courts'.[101]

In acknowledging this, however, one should not be led to exaggerate the glimmer of truth in Bentham's famous claim that precedent is, 'in the hands of the judge, power everywhere arbitrary, with the semblance of a set of rules to serve as a screen for it'.[102] Judges can themselves devise self-denying ordinances that take effect at a second-order level of legal principle, 'ultimate' rules of discretion,[103] to guard against just such a development through use of the power of interpretation. In the criminal law context, for example, Lord Lowry has indicated that:

> [W]hen discussing the propriety of judicial law-making... I believe, however, that one can find in the authorities some aids to navigation across an uncertainly charted sea. (1) If the solution is doubtful, the judges should beware of imposing their own remedy. (2) Caution should prevail if Parliament has rejected opportunities of clearing up a known difficulty or has legislated, while leaving the difficulty untouched. (3) Disputed matters of social policy

[99] Devlin, n. 90 above. [100] *Fowler v Pagett* (1798) 7 TR 509.

[101] J Bell and Sir George Engel, *Cross on Statutory Interpretation* (3rd edn., Butterworths, 1995), 165–6. [102] In Scofield and Harris, n. 85 above, 20.

[103] Raz, n. 3 above, 96–7.

are less suitable areas for judicial intervention than purely legal problems. (4) Fundamental legal doctrines should not be lightly set aside. (5) Judges should not make a change unless they can achieve finality and certainty.[104]

These 'modesty' conditions for the use of merit-based (including moral) argument in statutory interpretation are intended only to guide and have, perhaps, been honoured as much in the breach as in the observance.[105] Nonetheless, the conditions express in a decisive and clear-sighted way the obligations of judges not only to respect the law-making primacy of Parliament, but also to acknowledge the limits of the *lis inter partes* as a means of developing the law. They are well up to the task of ensuring that a piece of statutory interpretation subsequently putting them into practice will satisfy Dworkin's famous test for the adequacy of an interpretation, namely that it:

show[s] a piece of social history—the story of a democratically elected legislature enacting a particular text in particular circumstances—in the best light overall [being] sensitive... to... convictions about the ideals of political integrity and fairness and procedural due process as these apply specifically to legislation in a democracy.[106]

104 *C (A Minor) v DPP* [1996] AC 1, 28.

105 Surely, for example, the decision in *R v K* (discussed in the text at n. 31 above) does not meet conditions 1–3, even if it meets conditions 4 and 5?

106 Dworkin, n. 16 above, 338. Dworkin defines 'fairness' at 165 as 'political procedures... that distribute political power in the right way'.

PART II

PROPERTY

6

Weak and Strong Conceptions of Property: An Essay in Memory of Jim Harris

*Richard A. Epstein**

By no stretch of the imagination would I count myself as a close friend of Jim Harris. Until May of 2003, I only knew of his work from afar. But when I came to Oxford to deliver the Hart Lecture, he graciously invited me and my wife to Keble College for lunch, where on one occasion I got the full flavour of the man. Undeterred by his blindness, he was at once courteous, lively, and insistent. He cared deeply about the field to which he made such a major contribution, and seemed primed to take on new intellectual challenges in the years to come, before his life was so tragically cut short.

On this occasion, I hope to honour the memory of this splendid gentleman by critiquing his general views of property. In so doing, I shall concentrate first and foremost on his comprehensive contribution to the theory of property law, his magisterial *Property and Justice*,[1] which energetically puts forth his general theory in great detail. I shall add to that discussion analysis of particular portions of his work in his various articles, including his Maccabaean Lecture for 2001, 'Reason or Mumbo Jumbo: The Common Law's Approach to Property',[2] in which he takes me to task for the strong positions of property rights that I took—and continue to hold—in my 1985 book *Takings*.[3] There is much at stake in this debate, for the vision that one takes of property is important not only in the way in which individuals organize their relationships with each other, but also in the way in which individuals organize their relationship to the state.

The dispute that I am about to address, moreover, is not one that originates with Harris or myself, but has a distinct lineage that can be traced back to the

* James Parker Hall Distinguished Professor of Law, The University of Chicago; Peter and Kirsten Bedford Senior Fellow, The Hoover Institution. I should like to thank Stephen Munzer, Lior Strahilevitz, Joshua Getzler, and an anonymous referee for raising sharp criticism to the positions I have taken here. Eric Murphy, The University of Chicago, Class of 2005, provided his usual excellent research assistance.

1 JW Harris, *Property and Justice* (Clarendon Press, 1996) (hereinafter, Harris, *P & J*).

2 JW Harris, 'Reason or Mumbo Jumbo: The Common Law's Approach to Property' (2002) 117 *Proceedings of the British Academy* 445 (hereinafter, Harris, 'Mumbo Jumbo').

3 RA Epstein, *Takings: Private Property and the Power of Eminent Domain* (Harvard. UP, 1985).

earliest times. Indeed, this dispute covers two debates going on side by side, the one with rights to *property*, as some resource tangible or intangible, external to the self, and the *liberty* interest that people have in the way in which they lead and conduct their own lives. For these purposes, I shall think of the two positions as the *weak* and *strong* positions respectively. The weak position on liberty treats it as covering the right to bodily integrity and freedom of motion, but refuses to give automatic protection to claims for the use and disposition of labour. The weak position on property follows similar lines, and accepts and defends the rights of exclusion and possession, but does not accord similar heft to the rights of use and disposition. The strong position places the rights of use and disposition on a par with those of exclusion, both for liberty and property. Jim Harris was a distinguished defender, perhaps the most distinguished defender, of the weak side of the debate. With a sensible pragmatic streak, he disdained grand theories that treated liberty and property as the central conceptions of the modern state. I have long fallen prey to that temptation and have unhesitatingly backed the strong position, which I will once again do here. In order to do so, however, I shall point to matters on which Harris and I are in strong agreement, as well as those on which we differ.

Part (i) of this Chapter begins by setting out a short summary of the Harris position. Because of its necessary brevity, this part ignores much of the subtlety and erudition that he brought to its defence. In dealing with these issues, Harris, in the tradition of British academic lawyers, was suspicious of the generalizations that count as the stock in trade of political theorists. In consequence, he tended to avoid claims of two sorts. First, he rejected arguments that property rights were in some logical way necessary to and inherent in the human condition. Rather, they were to be understood as part of the social context in which they arrived. The second is the intellectual converse of the first: he distrusted universalist demonstrations that purport, usually erroneously, to show the internal contradictions of the traditional common law synthesis of property law, which synthesis he judged to be just about the right approach. It is a pleasure to respond to someone who thinks that you are wrong on the merits, as opposed to those who regard your position as so incoherent that it does not deserve mention in the first place.

Part (ii) of this chapter contains the exposition of the alternative view of liberty and property and their relationship to other key elements within the law. I hope to show that the weak account leaves too much running room for government discretion, which in turn results in the adoption of legal rules that have strong negative consequences for overall social welfare. In addressing this issue, it is worth noting that Harris showed a lively interest in economic theory, and had a good eye for some of its excessive pretensions to govern the world.[4] But at the

[4] See Harris, *P&J*, n. 1 above, 145–9, in which he makes the very sensible point that anyone who deals with the theories of the evolution of property rights, as articulated by Y Barzel, *Economic Analysis of Property Rights* (CUP, 1989), and Harold Demsetz's immensely influential 'Toward a Theory of Property Rights' (1967) 57 *Am Econ R* 347, does not have to redefine traditional conceptions of

same time, his engagement with economics was largely defensive. He did not use it to explain, for example, the relationship between private and common property rights, even though he did talk in places about that connection.[5] And, as an Englishman, even with broad comparative interests, he spent relatively little time in dealing with the constitutional aspects of the subject in light of the American experience,[6] with which I have been intimately engaged for a long time. Yet the combination of those two fields makes a stronger case for the more strong view of property protection, even though the current state of American law cuts much in Harris's defence of the weak view.

Part (iii) of this chapter carries the common law analysis forward into the constitutional domain. In it, I argue that much of the weakness of American constitutional law relies on its systematic adherence to the weak conception of property and liberty.

(i) Harris and the Weak Conception of Property

(a) The Central Thesis: Strong Exclusion and a Spectrum of Use Rights

In dealing with conceptions of property generally, Harris displays the great virtue of a sturdy consistency in setting out his basic position, which runs as follows. Harris staunchly defends the proposition that our notions of both liberty and property allow individuals exclusive rights, with respect both to their own persons and the external things which are subject to ownership. He is also a strong believer that the right to exclude, although paramount, is by no means the only element that is contained in the set of rights associated with both liberty and property. Rather, his position is that there is a continuum or spectrum of uses that extend from those that are relatively limited to those that are full-blooded. Thus, ultimately it is an exercise of political judgement, heavily dependent on context, as to which packet of these indefinite use rights should be afforded to an owner in particular situations. Harris is uneasy with the traditional metaphor that treats property as though it were a bundle of rights because he thinks that this approach makes it appear, falsely in his view, as though one could *list* with precision the use and disposition rights associated with the concept of property.[7] Instead, Harris prefers

property rights, but need only stress that they offer a theory on their evolution from one form (e.g., a rule of first possession for beavers) to another (e.g., a rule of territories). Indeed, one weakness of the Demsetz position is that it understates the conflict that takes place during these transitional periods, which is all too apparent to students of the English Enclosure movement.

[5] See Harris, *P&J*, n. 1 above, 15–16, 31, 109–10, 114–15.

[6] See ibid., 151–4.

[7] See ibid., 65. But in specific contexts, he does use the phrase, and to no ill effect. 'The doctrine of estates in land permits various bundles of rights to be allocated to different persons over the same resource as do trusts, corporate holdings, and non-ownership proprietary interests': ibid., 132, and see also ibid., 147.

broader definitions of property that speak not just of the right of exclusion but also of 'amalgams of open-ended *prima facie* use-privileges, control-powers and powers of transmission'.[8] 'The content of ownership interests, anywhere along the spectrum from mere property to full-blooded ownership, is an imprecise and fluctuating product of cultural assumptions and, as such, is presupposed by legal regulation'.[9]

In fleshing out this system, Harris first notes the class of 'property-independent prohibitions', which limit the use of property wholly without regard to the rules of ownership as such.[10] To those limitations are added the rules that operate internally to the property system, which include property-limitation rules. These rules, including nuisance, planning, and environmental protection, adjudicate both the boundaries between neighbours, and also broader disputes about conflicting land use.[11] The expropriation rules, in turn, deal with such matters as the execution of judgments, the forfeiture of property in bankruptcy, and takings and taxation. That is, these rules deal with the full range of coercive transactions in which the state imposes its will by force, with or without compensation on a property owner.[12] Lastly, there are rules of appropriation (or, as is sometimes said, acquisition), which detail how property interests are acquired: whether by purchase, succession, state grant, or, to be complete, original acquisition from the state of nature.[13] The same kinds of rules fit in well with other classifications. For example, at the heart of the common law treatment of property rights are those rules that speak of the acquisition, protection, and transfer of property, which are subsequently subject to common law rules that govern the coercive use of government force against private ownership.

In juggling these multiple balls in the air, Harris's basic attitude demands patient examination of particular contexts, to see how property works in conjunction with other conceptions so as to give us a fuller picture of the overall legal position. In so doing, he rejects the effort to use the ideas of liberty and property so capaciously that they organize virtually all of our political and social lives. To him, property is (in the best, non-combative, sense of that term) a pragmatic conception, which is an indispensable component of any political order. But it is not transformed into an all-inclusive notion that forecloses all political debate over the proper structure of our governing institutions.

(b) The Coherence of Property

In the course of his writings, Harris carefully avoids the cynical position that liberty and property mean exactly what we want them to, neither more nor less.[14] Nor

[8] Harris, 'Mumbo Jumbo', n. 2 above, 466. [9] Harris, *P&J*, n. 1 above, 64.

[10] JW Harris, 'Who Owns My Body' (1996) 16 *OJLS* 55, 60 (with property-independent prohibitions, '[i]t is criminal to commit assault or homicide with a weapon, but it is completely irrelevant whether the accused owned the weapon or not'.) (hereinafter, Harris, 'My Body').

[11] Ibid., 60. [12] Ibid. [13] Ibid., 60–1.

[14] See ibid., 58, for a particularly lucid statement of these ideas.

does he think that they are vacuous add-ons to a public discourse that is better conducted by using a different set of terms. That simple and sensible proposition allows him effectively to take on many important writers on property. For example, Harris rightly chides Bruce Ackerman for insisting in one breath that even 'the dimmest law student' soon learns that nobody 'owns' anything,[15] when Ackerman promptly chastizes sophisticated judges for falling into that trap in the next.[16] In a similar vein, he rightly takes some pointed jabs at Thomas Grey's well-known essay, 'The Disintegration of Property',[17] with its theme 'that the specialists who design and manipulate legal structures of the advanced capitalist economies could easily do without using the term "property" at all'.[18] In Harris's view, it will not do to say that the idea of ownership is without content, simply because we might be able to persuade our students that it has no meaning. Rather, the confident and common usage of the term indicates that property still has resonance in multiple arenas, even if we can lose our way in applying property ideas in difficult contexts.

More generally, Harris avoids the regrettable tendency today on the part of political theorists of all persuasions to take the view that contentions with which they disagree should be regarded as 'incoherent', and hence be rejected without a more detailed examination of how they play themselves out in practice.[19] Harris never falls prey to that tendency, and, consequently, consistently avoids grand conceptual arguments in a futile effort to win particular disputes. His sensible method is well illustrated by his critique of Charles Donahue for taking the position that 'full-blooded ownership' carries with it two 'inherent contradictions' on matters of both alienation and use.[20] First, Donahue claims that the purportedly unlimited rights of transmission conferred by law allow the present owner to place limitations on the transmission rights of subsequent owners, in violation of the original proposition. And, secondly, Donahue notes that any full-blooded conception of ownership carries with it unlimited use rights of the owned thing.

It is a pleasure to watch Harris swing into action. Harris rightly says that full ownership at time T1 allows that owner to impose restrictions on the rights of disposition of a subsequent owner Y at T2. The explanation for this, I would add, is that the full rights of transmission by owners are not compromised so long as X, the original owner, and Y, the alienee, at time T2 may combine their interests in order once again to re-establish full title in Z at time T3. At this point, divided ownership *by contract* is simply an exercise of basic ownership rights and not a

[15] See BA Ackerman, *Private Property and the Constitution* (Yale UP, 1977), 26–7. See also Harris, 'Mumbo Jumbo', n. 2 above, 456.

[16] Ibid., 456.

[17] TC Grey, 'The Disintegration of Property', in JR Pennock and JW Chapman (eds.), *Property* (Nomos XXII, NYUP, 1980), 73, 74 (quoted in Harris, 'Mumbo Jumbo', n. 2 above, 454).

[18] Grey n. 17 above, 73.

[19] For one such example, see L Murphy and T Nagel, *The Myth of Ownership: Taxes and Justice* (OUP, 2002), which derides the coherence to undermine the view that we should all be taxed as if he owned our pre-tax income.

[20] Harris, *P & J*, n. 1 above, 248 (criticizing C Donahue Jr., 'The Future of the Concept of Property Predicted from its Past', in Pennock and Chapman (eds.), n. 17 above, 28, 33–4).

contradiction of them. Division through successive interest is no more a contradiction than the various forms of concurrent ownership, such as joint tenancy or tenancy by the entirety. What really matters is the question whether the state may *by law* limit the rights of transmission of property. For example, it does just that with the rule against perpetuities on the one hand—wholly inconsequential in the grand scheme of things[21]—and with a system of transfer (gift and death) that cannot be avoided by clever draftsmanship on the other—having powerful implications regarding the way in which various resources are owned and held.

Harris is equally adamant and persuasive on his second point, dealing with property use. While legal systems have been quick to accord the owner *exclusive* use of his property, subject to narrow exceptions that deal with cases of necessity,[22] they have never accorded owners the *unlimited* right to use their property in whatever fashion they see fit. As Harris never tires of pointing out, no conception of property rights is so absolute, expansive, and, I will add, insane, as to allow a person to defend himself against charges of aggression by proving that he committed an offence against another's person or property solely with things that he owned. 'If deliberate homicide is prohibited, it would never be even a *prima facie* defence that the murderer was using his own dagger.'[23] Indeed, the situation could hardly be otherwise. The key role that rights to exclude play in a system of property is necessarily correlative. If one person has a right to exclude, then it necessarily follows that some limitations have to be placed on the use rights of other individuals.

The same tough-minded attitude can be extended to other authors whose work Harris did not discuss. Thus, his approach goes far to discredit the efforts of Robert Lee Hale to undermine any system of property rights by showing that it is incoherent to draw any distinction between consent and coercion.[24] That argument rests on the odd view that every refusal to deal could well be counted as an exercise in coercion that might in principle be regulated by the state. Harris would have recoiled, I am confident, against any effort to equate the rare instances of force (or the threat of force) with the ability to say no, on which the entire system of trade and commerce necessarily rests. And his own work reflects just that terminological confidence, for Harris consistently uses terms like consent and permission in ordinary ways, to capture the common sense views of most people.

[21] For discussion of the point, see RA Epstein, 'Past and Future: The Temporal Dimension in the Law of Property' (1986) 64 *Wash ULQ* 667, 710–13.

[22] See, e.g., *Ploof v Putnam*, 81 Vt 471, 474–6 (Vt. 1908).

[23] Harris, *P & J*, n. 1 above, 32. See also Harris, 'Mumbo Jumbo', n. 2 above, 457, and Harris, 'My Body', n. 10 above, 60, for similar sentiments.

[24] See RL Hale, 'Coercion and Redistribution in a Supposedly Non-Coercive State' (1923) 38 *Pol Sci Quart* 470. That theme is pursued in BH Fried, *The Progressive Assault on Laissez Faire: Robert Hale and the First Law and Economics Movement* (Harvard UP, 1998). For my criticism of this misguided adventure, see RA Epstein, 'The Assault that Failed: The Progressive Critique of Laissez Faire' (1999) 97 *Mich LR* 1697, and RA Epstein, *Skepticism and Freedom: A Modern Case for Classical Liberalism* (U of Chicago Press, 2003), 110–14.

For example, he writes in speaking of the proposition that X (that is, any person) 'owns' R (any resource), that 'the implication may be that for anyone else to meddle with R without X's consent would be wrongful. X is protected by trespassory rules, usually embodied in law in the form of civil or criminal prohibitions'.[25] The word 'consent' is used without the slightest philosophical self-consciousness. The contrast between Harris and Ackerman on this could not be more pointed. Harris understands the motivations of ordinary people, and does not take them to task for their inability to see that property is a relationship between individuals *over* things as opposed to a relationship between individuals *and* things.

(ii) The Strong Position: Welfare and Restraint of the State

The difficulties that I find in Harris's work are associated with the positive portion of his general programme. To be sure, Harris is certainly correct to note the heavily culture-dependent reasons for any particular choice of property arrangements. But it is not sufficient to rest on that general proposition because it is possible to specify with some degree of particularity *which* system of ownership rights is appropriate in *which* context and why. It is here where Harris's gritty pragmatism leads him away from constructive generalizations, which allow for the sensible sorting out of private and common property.[26] For the moment, however, I shall concentrate my focus on land and chattels: much is to be gained by setting a strong presumption in favour of what Harris terms the full-blooded system of ownership—which creates the incentives to invest and develop property—and then allowing deviations from that system only upon a clear showing that these result in a general social improvement from the previous state of affairs. These deviations should be gauged, at least in theory, by either of the two familiar efficiency measures of social welfare. The stronger, and more ideal, standard is the Paretian one, which demands of each deviation from the system of (full-blooded) ownership rights a new state of affairs in which at least one person is better off than he was in the earlier state of affairs, and no one is left worse off.

Frequently, this Paretian standard is criticized on the ground that its exacting nature is too restrictive, because it cuts off changes in the legal rules that are beneficial overall, but which leave at least one person worse off than before. The chief obstacle lies in the impossibility—because of transaction costs—of tendering compensation that would move all the losers from the change to the same level of personal utility that they had in the previous state of affairs. Hence, a weaker standard is often proposed, namely that of Kaldor-Hicks efficiency, whereby the possibility that such compensation could be tendered (while leaving the payer better off than before) suffices, even if it is not in fact paid.

[25] Harris, 'Mumbo Jumbo', n. 2 above, 461.
[26] For discussion, see text to nn. 57–64 below.

There are, without doubt, cases in which the latter standard allows for general changes that the former would block, but as we are dealing with the general structures of legal institutions, and not isolated transactions, the differences between these two positions turn out to be less significant than their similarities. The key point is that *neither* standard allows for transactions in which the losers could not be compensated for their losses out of the gains to the winners. Stopping bad social changes (e.g., many zoning laws) can be done without choosing between these two standards. That is, these unsound changes fail *both* tests. Indeed in many cases, the proper approach for the articulation of general rules is, if anything, still more stringent, for in principle it requires not only that there be a gain, but that that gain be divided, to the extent that human institutions can achieve it, pro rata among all individuals.

This argument quite simply suggests that by any sensible measure of social welfare, the creation of strong discretion in political institutions results, in general, in substantial social welfare losses. These losses could have been avoided if the set of state options was more constrained (whether by constitutional rules or social practice) than it is at present, which adopts an approach far more congenial to Harris's way of thinking than to mine. The difference between Harris and myself on this point stems in part from the different constitutional cultures in which we were raised. The English system, which starts with the postulate of parliamentary supremacy, has little place for any restriction on sovereign decisions about the definition or regulation of property rights. Rather, the only limitations arise from strong political conventions, fully observed in Great Britain, against wiping out the interests in question by arbitrary forms of expropriation, for which Harris shows, sensibly, little or no patience, unless justified, as in cases of bankruptcy and the like.[27] In contrast, the American system, which operates with some constitutional restraints at both the federal and the state level, must make peace with a very broad prohibition on state action that reads: 'nor shall private property be taken for public use, without just compensation'.[28] There is also the closely analogous constitutional development under the due process clause that provides: 'nor shall any state deprive any person of life, liberty, or property, without due process of law'.[29]

[27] Harris, *P & J*, n. 1 above, 37–8,

[28] US Const. amend. V. There are analogous provisions in all state constitutions. Needless to say, it is easy to find cases where the state interpretations differ from the federal ones. Compare *Hawaiian Housing Authority v Midkiff*, 467 US 229 (1984), where virtually any 'conceivable' public purpose will allow the state to take property upon payment of just compensation, with *County of Wayne v Hathcock*, 684 NW2d 765 (Mich 2004), denying that takings for economic development are permissible takings for public use. Note that *Hathcock* accepted the constitutional challenge to the Michigan scheme under state law. That decision remains good law in Michigan even though the Supreme Court rejected similar arguments by a close 5-to-4 vote in *Kelo v City of New London*, 545 US__, 125 S.Ct. 2655 (2005).

[29] US Const. amend. XIV. The interpretive move, hotly debated, is whether the phrase 'without due process of law' could be rendered as 'without just compensation'. That move was taken with little discussion in *Chicago, Burlington & Quincy Railroad Co v Chicago*, 166 US 226 (1897), rejecting the view that due process covers only procedural rights to hearing and notice:

The legislature may prescribe a form of procedure to be observed in the taking of private property for public use, but it is not due process of law if provision be not made for compensation. Notice to the

At this point, courts necessarily have to decide the scope of the rights to possess, exclude, use, or dispose of property in question. In practice, the modern US Supreme Court veers quite close for constitutional purposes to the minimum definition of property rights that Harris favours, so that his work has, perhaps, an unintended international appeal.[30] But while he would regard the American Supreme Court as commendably cautious in a world of intense variety, I regard its persistent performance as a giant missed opportunity to stabilize a wide range of liberty and property interests against unprincipled and disruptive forms of government intrusion.

The full project, as I see it, requires that we work on two dimensions. The first is an account of property rights that deserve protection from the political order, and the second is the set of reasons why the state might limit the use and exercise of that power. One piece of evidence that Harris has not put forward a complete theory of property rights is that he does not offer any account of the 'police power'. This power, within the framework of American constitutional law, offered the compendium of independent reasons that could be used to limit rights of either liberty or property in order to advance 'the safety, health, morals or general welfare' of the public at large.[31] Many of the concerns that Harris raises are, as he rightly notes, not simply questions of the definition or meaning of property, but rather social questions about the justification for property rights when faced with various competing concerns, each of which has to be analysed systematically in its own terms.[32] That same observation applies to matters of personal liberty, to which

> owner to appear in some judicial tribunal and show cause why his property shall not be taken for public use without compensation would be a mockery of justice. Due process of law as applied to judicial proceedings instituted for the taking of private property for public use means, therefore, such process as recognizes the right of the owner to be compensated if his property be wrested from him and transferred to the public.

Ibid., 236 (Harlan J).

30 For discussion, see text to nn. 82–89 below.

31 For an early account see E Freund, *The Police Power: Public Policy and Constitutional Rights* (Callaghan & Company, 1904), p. iii (defining the police power 'as meaning the power of promoting the public welfare by restraining and regulating the use of liberty and property'). For a judicial definition, see *Lochner v New York*, 198 US 45, 53 (1905):

> The right to purchase or to sell labor is part of the liberty protected by this amendment, unless there are circumstances which exclude the right. There are, however, certain powers, existing in the sovereignty of each State in the Union, somewhat vaguely termed police powers, the exact description and limitation of which have not been attempted by the courts. Those powers, broadly stated and without, at present, any attempt at a more specific limitation, relate to the safety, health, morals and general welfare of the public. Both property and liberty are held on such reasonable conditions as may be imposed by the governing power of the State in the exercise of those powers, and with such conditions the Fourteenth Amendment was not designed to interfere.

32 On this point, he is not alone. Indeed, his arguments here parallel in instructive ways those which were first developed by HLA Hart on the question of defeasibility in law and morals. See HLA Hart, 'The Ascription of Responsibility and Rights' (1949) XLIX *Proceedings of the Aristotelian Society (New Series)* 171–94, reprinted in A Flew (ed.), *Logic and Language (First Series)* (B Blackwell, 1952), 145–66. Hart himself abandoned this essay: H.L.A. Hart, *Punishment and Responsibility* (Clarendon Press, 1968), preface, citing PT Geach, 'Ascriptivism' (1960) 69 *Philosophical R* 221; G Pitcher, 'Hart on Action and Responsibility' (1960) 69 *Philosophical R* 226. The great mistake of this position is that it treats defeasibility as a property of the meaning of (some) words, when its proper

Harris also directs his attention, and it is instructive to see how the differences in view play out between us. Let me start with liberty and turn to property.

(a) The Strong Conception of Liberty

On several occasions, Harris offers a long critique of what he regards as the facile, and possibly dangerous, effort to use the concept of individual self-ownership, which has its most famous articulation in the work of John Locke,[33] as the basis of judgements about difficult personal matters such as personal health and medical treatment, sexual freedom for adults, and sexual abuse of minors.[34] Yet here, I think that he overstates the dangers of the terminological use of the 'self-ownership' language, and misses the real source of difficulty that sometimes attends its use. Let it be supposed that individuals do have self-ownership of their bodies, and that this does entail the exclusive right to use and dispose of it as they see fit. Just where do we go wrong? The three issues are exclusion, use and disposition, which I take up in that order.

1. Exclusion

As Harris recognizes, this position carries with it an immediate dividend, in that it makes clear that individuals cannot be owned and possessed by other persons, or otherwise trifled with at the will of others.[35] To put the point in Harris's terms, one great advantage of this approach to the subject matter is that it stoutly affirms, in the context of bodily integrity, the 'keep off' sign, or the exclusive right to possession that Harris regards as so critical to property rights. I can think of no

role is to show the relationship in a system of legal presumptions between certain descriptive propositions (he hit me) and certain legal conclusions (he is liable), which may be overridden for any number of reasons. This is captured in ordinary language by the obvious difference between killing and murder, where the former is the prima facie case of the latter, which by definition admits of no excuse or justification. For my elaboration of this theme, see my Hart Lecture, RA Epstein, 'The Not So Minimum Content of Natural Law' (2005) 25 *OJLS* 219.

[33] The much celebrated, and mooted, passage reads:

> Though the earth, and all inferior creatures, be common to all men, yet every man has a property in his own person: this nobody has any right to but himself. The labour of his body, and the work of his hands, we may say, are properly his. Whatsover then he removes out of the state that nature hath provided, and left it in, he hath mixed his labour with, and joined to it something that is his own, and thereby makes it his property.

J Locke, *Second Treatise of Government* (GW Gough (ed.), Basil Blackwell, 1976), ch. 5, para 27. Note too that Locke had a strong religious component in his position, treating it as God's gift 'to Adam, and his posterity in common'.This component differs from the traditional Roman law position that treats property in the intial position as a *re nullius*. See Gaius, Inst., 2.66. Locke also did not treat individuals as wholly autonomous, but viewed them as 'servants' of God, and indeed as his 'property'. All this accounts for his opposition to suicide. For one reconciliation of the religious and secular strands in Locke, see SR Munzer, *A Theory of Property* (CUP, 1990), 41, n. 2. See also J Waldron, *God, Locke, and Equality: Christian Foundations of John Locke's Political Thought* (CUP, 2002).

[34] Harris, *P & J*, n. 1 above, 184–8. See also Harris, 'My Body', n. 10 above, 55–84, for a more extended version of the same point.

[35] Ibid., 62.

reason why we would want to avoid the use of any language, whether of autonomy or self-ownership, that works to preserve the bodily integrity of each and every person against the depredation of everyone else. This position makes sense not only because of some deontological belief in the independence of all persons, but also because it has manifest advantages under any consequentialist theory that one could devise.[36] The need for property rights in the first place stems from the manifest inability of people, even if endowed with full contractual capacity, to purchase the rights from all of the myriad individuals on the face of the globe. The institution of personal liberty from physical invasion thus counts as the sensible *first* step in the overall improvement of human welfare by allowing us to achieve through law an end—the mutual renunciation of force—that could not be obtained through voluntary exchange. The use of the term self-ownership adds a social punch behind this basic conviction: you can't meddle with me, which is exactly why the term private property *was* used to help children learn not to allow adults 'to interfere with you privately'.[37]

2. *Use*

Now suppose that we take the argument one step further forward, and assume that individuals in virtue of their self-ownership have the right to use and dispose of their persons in such manner as they see fit. The claim with respect to use cannot be unlimited, given that we have to respect the like liberty and bodily integrity of other individuals under the various property-limitation rules. So just as ownership of the dagger does not give us the right to kill other individuals, so too ownership of our hands does not allow us to strangle whomsoever we please. At this point, the recognition of limited ownership rights forces us to develop rules which determine which of our actions count as aggression against the exclusive rights of self-ownership that other persons have in their own bodies. That is, rules should develop that illustrate that we can use our own bodies only to the extent that this use does not harm other people's use of their bodies.

The upshot of this discussion is the need to develop, as part of the province of the tort law, a detailed set of rules as to what counts as the use of force in this invasive sense. In this regard, I still prefer the Roman law approach that starts from those causes of action that work *corpore corpori* and then reach out to cover more indirect forms of conduct that should be treated in the same way.[38] Thus, to give only one example, if an individual cannot kill another person by his own hand, then he cannot set a carefully concealed trap into which that person will fall to his own death. The idea of self-ownership thus invites us to work out the rules

[36] For further discussion of these issues, see R Nozick, *Anarchy, State and Utopia* (Basic Books, 1974), especially ch. 7, 'Distributive Justice', which has in turned been criticized in GA Cohen, *Self-Ownership, Freedom and Equality* (CUP, 1995). For my response to Cohen, see RA Epstein, *Skepticism and Freedom*, n. 24 above, 129–38.

[37] Harris, 'My Body', n. 10 above, 55.

[38] See Justinian's Dig. 9.2 (the *Lex Aquilia*), which tracks the progression from cases of *occidere* to *causam mortis praestare*.

of proximate cause and affords us an important signal that they should be the same in dealing with persons as with property. Although inquiry into invasions is the first step in any comprehensive system of tort law, it is far from being the whole field. When some invasions do take place, issues of justification (self-defence) or excuse (insanity) have to be coped with as well.[39] But once again the seamless integration of liberty and property work themselves into the fabric of our law. I see no danger in the use of the self-ownership concept so long as we are aware that the definition of the boundaries around a person is not the only task that faces a well articulated system of law.

Harris responds to this line of argument by claiming that it proves too much because it contains the implicit concession that individuals are allowed to engage in massive acts of self-destruction, which are typically not allowed by any legal system, given the strong prohibitions against suicide, bodily immolation, and sales into slavery.[40] Harris is absolutely right to insist that absolute propositions about self-ownership are often embarrassed by the extreme cases advanced to test them. But, that said, there are at least two responses to his position.

First, in at least some cases, we can identify situations where mental imbalances and impairments lead people to take actions that they would not do if fully sane. Here it is exceedingly hard to prove these personal weaknesses in the individual case.[41] The advantage of a blanket prohibition is that it reduces the costs of making the determinations and eliminates the false positives, i.e., those cases where a person might be found sane, when in fact he is not. I think that reasons of this sort account for much of the objection to suicide and to selling one's self into slavery. That position, however, is itself subject to qualifications, for while it is one thing to doubt the rationality of a person in perfect health who wants to commit suicide at the age of 29, the same arguments do not apply with equal force to a person who for years has been bedridden and in great pain towards the end of his or her life, and seeks either to kill himself or herself, or get the assistance of someone else to finish the job. The dominant rule in the legal system is to deny that right, even though the error costs are far higher, but to allow people the privilege of slow starvation and dehydration if they so choose. The overlapping issues of rationality, consent, and competence are difficult to disentangle. But I do not think that the use of the self-ownership language frustrates or complicates this inquiry. Quite the opposite, that term (or individual autonomy) offers a baseline against which we can measure the various efforts at individual self-realization, which is the goal in many informed-consent situations, involving the various choices in medical care.

Secondly, it is critical to note that the same issue can arise in connection with the right to destroy tangible property, which is limited in many cases for reasons

[39] Indeed, I think that here the pleas can rotate sequentially until joinder of issue. See Epstein, 'The Not So Minimum Content of Natural Law', n. 32 above.

[40] Harris, 'My Body', n. 10 above, 63.

[41] For a more complete statement of my views on euthanasia, see RA Epstein, *Mortal Peril: Our Inalienable Right to Health Care* (Addison-Wesley, 1997), 299–358.

that track those which develop with respect to self-inflicted harm to the person.[42] There is a serious question whether people are in their right minds when they choose to destroy the old homestead, some valuable work of art, and more controversially, unpublished manuscripts of great intellectual and historical interest. There is a further debate whether destruction after death should be governed by different rules from destruction in life, given that the latter involves the cooperation of another person, under blessing of the state, while the former does not. In sorting through these permutations, the scattered body of case law zigs and zags through the hidden shoals, with at most middling success. The content of these rules is not to the point here. What does matter for our purposes is that the use of 'ownership' language is important to create the presumption against limiting the right to destroy. But so long as we can eschew the perils of a dogmatic absolutism, I don't think that the use of the self-ownership language leads us into trouble on the uses that individuals may make of their personal liberty.

3. *Disposition*

After use comes disposition, with a fresh set of problems. Do the strong views of self-ownership have the tendency to lead us astray here? In dealing with that issue, the proper starting point is, as Harris agrees, that in most ordinary cases, such as those which deal with contracts of sale, hire, lease, or employment between ordinary individuals, the full-blooded right of disposition works fairly well. As long as these people have better information about their own preferences than anyone else, as they usually do, the presumption is justified. Indeed, Harris was quite perceptive to note that one advantage of the conventional rules of ownership is that it allows these garden-variety transactions to go forward on a non-problematic basis. He writes, 'We get by in daily life with a range of conventional property talk which has no problems in "knowing" who owns a particular book or a car or a house or a ten pound note. Otherwise we could not borrow or lend or sell, or use things without consulting other people's preferences'.[43] And that last task would inevitably mean consulting them as well, but to an uncertain effect as to whether they (or which of them) should just have a say or an absolute veto power over what it is that we (by which he means, each of us individually) shall do with what we own.

The stakes here are quite profound, for we could easily imagine a regime in which no person was allowed to take a job unless he first secured the permission of a majority of people who worked at a competitive firm, or of a government agency that was charged with the task of deciding which sector of the economy could benefit most from an additional infusion of labour. It is a very short walk down the land from a state in which the preferences of other individuals are taken into account to a major administrative state, where the preferences of the individuals

[42] For the most comprehensive recent account of this subject, see L Strahilevitz, 'The Right To Destroy' (2005) 114 *Yale LJ* 781.

[43] Harris, 'My Body', n. 10 above, 58.

to the transaction are not. Along that path are the full range of rules that limit the disposition of labour, either to protect the individual against himself, as in cases of selling one's self into slavery, or, more frequently, to protect others from his competition. On Harris's view if the use rights of things are to be arrayed along a spectrum, then the same could well be said with respect to liberty interests as well. Yet I can see little or no benefit that has come from the huge surge in employment law restrictions, for example, which set the minimum wages that can be paid, the maximum hours that can be worked, the set of vacations and benefits that can be provided, *ad infinitum*.

The explanation for my enduring scepticism depends on a set of considerations that in general fall outside Harris's scope of interest, precisely because of his marginal interest in economic theory as an explanatory tool. But in dealing with employment contracts, three propositions ought to hold centre stage. The first of these is that exchanges motivated by self-interest work for the mutual benefit of both parties. Hence, they presumptively meet the stringent Paretian standard of making somebody (at least two) better off, without making anyone worse off. The proposition takes into account all benefits and costs, in both the short and the long run, because these all come back to the same person. Who would enter a voluntary contract in order to become worse off?

Obviously, this presumption of benefit is sound in the great majority of contracts, especially when we recall that the test of mutual benefit is in expectation, which will not be fulfilled in all cases. It is easy to conjure up hypothetical examples of workers who accept a pittance to work in stifling conditions that shorten their lives. It is much more difficult to find standard practices that comport with this model. In practice, left to their own devices workers experience wage gains with increased productivity. The common account of the nineteenth century employment contracts writes as though workmen were routinely left bereft of compensation when injured in risky employments. In fact, as early as the 1860s, workers' compensation schemes were introduced voluntarily in the mines and on the rails.[44] And real wages in the United States moved up even during the pre-New Deal Period when there were sharp constitutional limitations on wage and hour laws.[45] What then are the ways that it can be overcome? Two come to mind.

First, there could be some defect in the contracting process whereby one person takes advantage of the ignorance or weakness of another, as by duress or fraud, or even undue influence. Dealing with this critical issue in individual cases simply counts as an effort to police the disposition of labour and thus falls generally into

[44] For one such scheme, see *Griffiths v Earl of Dudley* (1882) 9 QB 357; for discussion, see RA Epstein, 'The Historical Origins and Economic Structure of Workers' Compensation Laws' (1982) 16 *Ga LR* 775.

[45] For those limitations, see, e.g., *Lochner v New York*, 198 US 45 (1905). For evidence of the increase in wages, see, e.g., US Bureau of the Census, *Historical Statistics of the United States: Colonial Times to 1957* (US Dept. of Commerce, Bureau of the Census, 1960) 72 (Series D 36–45) (decline in child labour); ibid., at 91 (Series D 589–602) (decline in average work week for unskilled labour); ibid., at 25 (Series B 92–100) (increase in wages).

a regime of contract law that builds on property law, and is wholly consistent with it. That is, holding a gun to my head to get me to dispose of my property is treated the same as using such coercion to get me to contract for labour. As with every branch of law, the harder one pushes on difficult cases, the more difficult the inquiry runs. Thus if we allow people to plead mistake too easily, then many useful transactions could be undone by the opportunistic repudiation of a contract that was fully solid from its inception. Yet, at the same time, I think that we would be loathe to enforce contracts for slavery, in part because we have no confidence that these would take place in the absence of duress or misinformation. Thus, the case looks somewhat like that of the suicide of a healthy person. It follows that we can be too lax in enforcing contracts, or perhaps too rigid. But none of this makes self ownership a poisoned concept. Problems of the scope and proof of the conditions that undermine contract are a big deal, but they are an offshoot of the initial rules of personal liberty, and not a contradiction of them.

Secondly, there are the rules that deal with externalities on third persons. No one thinks that contracts to murder third persons should be enforced, and contracts to create slavery do have the unfortunate consequence of consigning the hapless offspring to a status determined by their parents. But it would be a mistake to dwell on the negative externalities from some prohibited transactions. Instead, the key point to note is that any successful transaction will always have at least some *positive* externalities on some people. Greater wealth in A and B increases the opportunities for exchange for other people. But, it will be said, what about direct competitors who lose out in particular cases? Well, what of it? To allow their preferences to control is the end of a competitive industry, with its promise of allocating labour to its highest marginal value. Although the cases and academic literature are replete with references to 'ruinous' or 'destructive' competition, there is no *systematic* loss from these activities, such as occurs with that subset of contracts (itself difficult to identify) that operate 'in restraint of trade' where the formation of monopoly practices leads to allocative distortions. Hence, the fixation on the right of disposition in labour cases does not in general lead to any real mistakes of policy. Quite the opposite; it leads us away from the meddlesome influences of the strangulation of labour markets that can arise through excessive regulation with its economic decay and inefficiency. This dislocation takes place precisely because these rights of disposition are treated as contingent, and thus subject to extensive state regulation, under either the British system of parliamentary supremacy or the American constitutional order.

Most of Harris's concerns do not deal with these comprehensive schemes of state regulation. Rather, they deal with cases where the system of freedom of contract may not work well, and for the same reasons of competence that dog any regime that celebrates freedom of use with respect to one's own body under any and all circumstances. Thus, Harris notes that if the property language allows a child or woman to say 'keep off', it also allows her to say with equal fervour, 'please enter', at which point the door is open to widespread forms of sexual abuse.

But even if the self-ownership language is given full sway, everyone should pause for cases involving infants, sick people, and persons under great personal anxiety or distress. In these situations, duress or the like might counter the initial presumption of Paretian efficiency through contract. The use of self-ownership language should not determine whether people can sell themselves into slavery or take their own lives on a whim. Shaky people can be easily exploited in ways that factory workers cannot, so the inescapable competence issues loom large indeed. It marks the soul of good sense to look with suspicion on certain transactions, especially those which to ordinary understanding appear to disadvantage the person who is labouring under these disabilities. For just that reason, we justify certain arrangements that ease the task of disposition. Hence, the reliance on living wills, powers of attorney, and family consent that rises up in all cases of serious illnesses of the very young, old, feeble, or sick.

The point here is that the protection of the right to dispose of one's own body or labour does not preclude any particular examination of the context in which these transactions take place. To the contrary, it works to improve it, by again focusing on the ultimate interests that this complex array of procedural devices is intended to protect. In all the years that I have dealt with medical matters, I have never once met anyone conversant with bioethics who swept competence issues under the rug because of an excessive devotion to the principle of autonomy or self-ownership. But I have encountered many settings where an unwillingness to allow the rights of disposition has placed serious impediments on needed efforts at co-operation.

Most notable are the strict restrictions on organ transfers, where gifts are permissible but sales are not. That one major restraint has created long queues of desperate donees.[46] Many individuals defend the current system on the ground that it controls for corruption and influence. But this view is doubtless incorrect. The huge value associated with an organ suggests that political strings will be used to acquire them, and recent evidence suggests that just this is the case.[47] It is just wishful thinking to believe that the introduction of cash is the only source of potential corruption. Instead, the ability to pay cash on the barrel to organ providers (donors is now the wrong word) would probably do much to neutralize the corruption by easing the present acute shortages. At the present time, there is much sentiment in favour of the use of presumed consent statutes, whereby those

[46] See, for easy verification, http://www.unos.org/, where a one second search revealed this data summary:

Waiting list candidates: 87,115, as of Sept. 2004 at 10:42 pm.
Transplants (Jan.–Sept. 2004): 20,305, as of 12 Mar. 2004.
Donors (Jan.–Sept. 2004): 10,598, as of 12 Mar. 2004.

For a more complete breakdown, see http://www.unos.org/data/default.asp? displayType=usData.

[47] See, e.g., Sh Zink *et al.*, 'Examining the Potential Exploitation of UNOS Policies' (2005) 5(4) *Amer J of Bioethics* 1: 'The policies addressed in this paper enable those on the list with the proper resources to gain an advantage over other less fortunate members, creating a system that benefits not the individual most in medical need, but the one with the best resources'.

who do not explicitly decline to donate their organs are presumed to consent. But why do we go through this rigmarole when there is evidence that even small cash payments will induce people to sign up as organ donors when they renew their driver's licences.[48]

There is no reason to think that incentives will not work in other contexts, even with live donors whose organs are more valuable than cadavaric ones. By keeping the transactions above board, it would allow for the use of third party advisors and brokers to help structure the transactions. The numbers cry out for voluntary exchange. Assume that any live organ transplant holds out a 1 per cent risk of death or serious injury to the donor, but a 60 per cent chance of a five- or ten-year respite for the donee. The gains from trade are obvious, but what 'donor' would take that risk for a stranger without some compensation, if only in the form of life and disability insurance, for himself? The prohibition against any compensation for risk and loss of time stops transactions that might save lives or otherwise go through. Yet the medical risks to a donor are no greater if he is paid than unpaid, and unpaid transfers within families are today a prominent source of transplanted organs. In fact, over 25 per cent of the organs transplanted in the first nine months of 2004 were intra-family transplants.[49] It is not surprising to see this large number of transactions within a family when sales are prohibited, because in this context there is a type of in kind compensation such that, although technically a gift, the donor does receive compensation back in the form of continued interactions and the like with the donee.

This system deserves to fall of its own weight, and, at the margins, that decay is happening today, as resourceful individuals who chafe under the restrictions do what they can to avoid them. We have recent stories in the United States of folks advertising for organs and receiving 'directed donations' that put themselves to the head of the queue. More recent are the reports of organ swaps in which A, a relative of B, transfers an organ to C, a relative of D, while D in turn transfers an organ to B—in of course simultaneous exchanges, lest one side back out of an unenforceable deal.[50] If we followed a framework that set its initial presumption in favour of the disposition of labour or body parts, then I doubt that we could ever justify a state of the world in which the total shut-down of this market would occur. The arguments about coercion and misinformation are rarely strong enough to justify a total ban. Indeed in some family situations, the ability to offer cash or benefits in kind *reduces* the risk of coercion because it is no longer necessary to brow beat reluctant relatives.

[48] A $7 discount on a driver's licence fee appears to make people 40% more likely to sign up as organ donors, relative to those, such as veterans, who can sign up for free. My thanks to Dave Undis of Lifesharers for the information. For the story, see a link to the *Savannah Morning News*: http://www.savannahnow.com/stories/040505/2934088.shtml

[49] The precise number is 5,276 out of 20,205. Note that this figure understates the level of live transfers. Heart transfers are necessarily cadaveric, for example.

[50] J Graham, 'Perfect fit: 2 couples exchange gift of life; Transplant swaps gaining popularity', *Chicago Tribune*, 5 Dec. 2004, C1.

Thus far, I have spoken about the issues of incompetence for adults, but, thinking globally, the rules on infancy follow a similar pattern. The overwhelming risk of social dysfunction means that we block sexual contact with minors, with or without their consent. Our hope is to keep them together in body and spirit so that they can exercise responsible choices when they are of full age. The consensus against child abuse is shared by everyone on all sides of the political spectrum. The self-ownership talk that Harris recognizes[51] is common in many circles, and has done, and can do, nothing to derail this consensus.

In sum, the need to include a right of disposition in the conception of liberty sets the stage for a robust law of contract. It does not, however, determine its precise content of the contractual rules. Rather, the full scorecard is this: for most cases, where competence is not an issue, the language of self-ownership helps to strengthen rights of exclusion, use, and disposition. In the smaller, but critical, set of transactions where competence is in issue, no one is lulled into inaction by use of self-ownership to capture what is served by protecting a liberty interest, or figuring out how it should be protected. Thus, it provides the best of both worlds.

(b) Strong Property and Possession

A similar critique may be brought to bear against Harris's view on property, with its emphasis on strong exclusion rights and relatively weak use rights. In order to show why this is the case, I shall start with his treatment of the rules of occupation, which under traditional Roman and common law doctrines were the *only* way in which something, unowned in the state of nature, could be reduced to ownership. I will then move on to question his use and expropriation rights in connection with the takings problem.

1. Initial Occupation

The rules of occupation, which allow an individual to claim ownership of an external thing by taking possession, have long been subject to detailed scrutiny and criticism from within the academy.[52] Scholarly criticism of these rules stands in odd contrast to the continued powerful influence that they exert over the day-to-day affairs within legal systems. Harris's own writing on the subject is designed to demonstrate that this rule is fundamentally misguided, when the language of self-ownership is used to link liberty with property, by claiming that an individual is entitled to the fruits of his or her labour.[53] Harris rightly points out that the fundamental difficulty of this argument is its failure to explain in sufficient fullness why the unilateral action of one individual is sufficient to create in him a right that is good against all the world. Clearly that deficit must be addressed.

[51] See text to n. 35 above.

[52] See, e.g., LC Becker, *Property Rights: Philosophical Foundations* (Routledge and Kegan Paul, 1977); R Schlatter, *Private Property: The History of an Idea* (George Allen & Unwin, 1975); J Waldron, *The Right to Private Property* (Clarendon Press, 1988).

[53] Harris, 'My Body', n. 10 above, 65–75.

In his answering, Harris is correct to note that the Lockean metaphor whereby an individual is said to claim ownership of a thing by virtue of 'mixing' his labour with it does not advance the ball. Why, he asks, must the payment for this effort take the form of outright ownership of the thing, as opposed to some lesser interest or some side payment?[54] Harris is also correct to reject the common argument that no one can object to the taking that causes harm to no one else. All transactions that take something out of the commons necessarily reduce that amount that is left for everyone else, so that the condition could only be satisfied when resources are infinite, which they never are. Thus, under this logic everyone could always object because each person is always harmed. And, as Harris perceptively notes, the very fact that patent rights are always subject to limitations, even if they take nothing from the commons, shows that the general claim is overstated.[55]

Harris helps resurrect the case for the first possession rule by offering an excellent summary of the instrumental arguments in its favour. But, at the end of the day, I think that he is too dismissive of it.[56] As he notes, the strong positive of that rule is that it works to assign discrete pieces of property to single owners so as to set the stage for a set of market transactions. These transactions allow for the improvement of overall social welfare through voluntary exchange, which is why the right of disposition is generally regarded as a key element of private property, just as it is for ordinary liberty of the person. One reason why we tolerate the loss of items from the common is that, as Locke noted, those who do not take are compensated, at least in part, by the increased opportunities that they have to buy from others, which in turn adds value to their own labour.[57] The decentralized structure thus works to counteract the concentration of government power. It is no accident that Locke, who is the champion of private property, is also the champion of popular government from below, which in extreme cases embraces the right of revolution.[58]

Why then does Harris so badly underestimate the positive, if empirical, arguments for the occupancy rules? The chief defect in his position lies in his philosophical critique of the instrumental position. Having acknowledged its positive strength, his approach is then to attack it from within by undercutting its initial premise that individuals own their own bodies and *therefore* must own all the resources or improvements that they produce.[59] But so long as the self-ownership principle, modestly understood, makes sense, this frontal attack is too broad for its own good. What is needed instead is an account of those situations where the instrumental justifications for the first possession rule break down, followed by proposals to set the situation right. Let me mention a couple of the considerations that show the limitations of the first possession rule, without dethroning it entirely. It is a good

[54] Ibid., 67. [55] Ibid., 68. [56] Ibid., 66.

[57] J Locke, *Second Treatise of Government* (ed. GW Gough, Basil Blackwell, 1976), ch. 5, paras. 47–51. [58] Ibid., ch. 19.

[59] Harris, 'My Body', n. 10 above, 67–8.

rule because it works well in 95 per cent of the possible scenarios, and the unique 5 per cent should not lead to total abandonment but only a modification in those cases.

First, any comprehensive theory of property rights must address the critical question whether all resources should be privatized in the first place. This is not a new inquiry; indeed the opening passages of Justinian's Institutes deal with various forms of common property which include the air, water, and 'in consequence' the beach.[60] Historically then, the first possession rule coexists with the exact opposite rule for some resources—privatization by occupation is necessarily forbidden. Any adequate theory of property rights, instrumental or otherwise, has to explain this duality. The answer does not lie in some deep psychological affection for, or aversion to, private property by ordinary people. Most individuals, even with strong libertarian orientation, can move from a public street to a private home with great aplomb.

Yet Harris's work does not address the considerations—dare one say trade-offs—needed to explain why both forms of property survive. The right answer generally boils down to a trade-off between two problems: hold-outs and externalities. Common property left open to all prevents blockades but raises co-ordination difficulties among the various owners. Conversely, private property minimizes governance disputes but creates negative externalities.[61] The one problem cannot be reduced unless the other is aggravated. Include more people in the group and the co-ordination problems increase. Exclude more people from the group, and the costs that do not have to be taken into account in making a decision rise. A more articulated response to the efficiency challenge becomes clearly imperative. One clue to the overall situation is that a wide range of voluntary institutions combine private with common elements: co-operative housing contains private units and common halls. Historically, the open-field system in medieval times, a commons with limited access, involved property being held privately for growing and in common for grazing.[62] The efficiency explanation for this dual system is that the optimal plot size for cattle is larger than that for growing. In addition, the scattering of private plots prevented various forms of strategic behaviour among various members of this commons. Aboriginal systems

[60] Justinian's Inst., 2.1.1.

[61] For a more complete elaboration of this theme, see RA Epstein, 'On the Optimal Mix of Common and Private Property' (1994) 11 *Soc Phil & Pol* 17.

[62] For discussion, see HE Smith, 'Semicommon Property Rights and Scattering in the Open Fields' (2000) 29 *J Legal Stud* 131. The phenomenon is not limited to England. Note that Smith speaks of a 'closed commons', which is created by voluntary arrangement among multiple owners, and excludes all outsiders. The beach is ordinarily an open commons, available to all. There is no reason to think that all commons have to be of the same sort, and good reasons to think that this need not be the case. With water for example, generally only riparians may remove water from a navigable river, but anyone may have access to that river for transportation. Generally speaking, the more resources that must be consumed for the property to be used, the more closed the arrangement, which is why cattle work on the closed commons and rivers on the open model.

show the same duality.[63] Likewise the pooling arrangements for oil and gas are often driven by the simple fact that the size of the underground field is larger than that of the surface farms, leading to the rise of various sharing schemes.

In dealing with these observed dualities, it is important not to treat an efficient form of dual ownership as though it is an automatic sign that the *processes* that were used to reach any given allocation of rights were necessarily efficient as well. There is no doubt that the pooling arrangements in oil and gas, for example, often shifted wealth from out-of-state to in-state producers in ways that eluded the judges who passed on these schemes.[64] In my own work on parking on public streets, some combination of private and public uses is clearly necessary to maximize the value of public highways.[65] But it hardly follows from that general proposition that any particular scheme of space allocation is necessarily efficient. It is commonplace to find that spaces are allocated through political processes to people who have little or no legitimate claims to them, as when the parking spaces in a given neighbourhood are reserved to local residents to the exclusion of everyone else. Indeed, one of the weaknesses of Demsetz's famous thesis on the evolution of property rights—the rights evolve in fashion to minimize harmful externalities—shows just this weakness.[66] It tacitly assumes that the movement to any new regime of property rights necessarily gives fair shares to all holders under the previous regime, when political pressures frequently skew the distribution of the gains in favour of the politically connected. Just this combination of efficient redefinition and political redistribution may be the defining feature of the English enclosure movement.[67] There the transformation of land from the commons may have resulted in an efficient form of property holdings, but that would hardly justify wiping out customary titles without compensation.[68] The efficiency analysis developed by Henry Smith should not be understood to exclude the operation of other political factors.

The heavy presence of political influences in property rights, however, need not be directed toward the creation of an inefficient form of property holdings. The rational political actor, no matter how selfish, would prefer some end state with the best form of ownership, which allows him to satisfy the weak claims of the

[63] For similar discussion, see MJ Bailey, 'Approximate Optimality of Aboriginal Property Rights' (1992) 35 *JL & Econ* 183; for a discussion of the management rules for commons generally, see E Ostrom, *Governing the Commons: The Evolution of Institutions for Collective Action* (CUP, 1990).

[64] See *Ohio Oil Co. v Indiana (No. 1)*, 177 US 190 (1900). For a discussion of how the scam worked, see RA Epstein, 'The Modern Uses of Ancient Law' (1997) 48 S *Carolina LR* 243, 254–8.

[65] See RA Epstein, 'The Allocation of the Commons: Parking on Public Roads' (2002) 31 *J Legal Stud* 515 (hereinafter Epstein, 'Parking').

[66] H Demsetz, 'Toward a Theory of Property Rights' (1967) 57 *Am Econ Rev* 347, criticized on those grounds in Epstein, 'Parking', n. 65 above, 518–21.

[67] See, e.g., RC Allen, *Enclosure and the Yeoman: The Agricultural Development of the South Midlands, 1450–1850* (OUP, 1992). See also J Getzler, 'Judges and Hunters: Law and Economic Conflict in the English Countryside, 1800–60', in C Brooks and M Lobban (eds.), *Communities and Courts in Britain 1150–1900* (Hambledon Press, 1997), 199–228.

[68] G Clark and A Clark, 'Common Rights to Land in England, 1475–1839' (2001) 61 *J Econ Hist* 1009.

vanquished while gobbling up as much as he can for himself. Within the framework it is clear that in the end the mix of common and private ownership survives only because, as an empirical matter, each works better in some contexts than in others. Here is a first cut as to why. Common property is successful when the variety of uses is relatively limited, as on a river, when the need for movement is critical. The legal solution that allows all to have access to the resource, and none to exclude others, works, as a first approximation, to maximize the value of the resource in question. The nightmare to be avoided is of toll booths along the river, which in rapid succession dissipate the going value of the resource, by creating blockades in what is now called, fashionably, an anti-commons.[69] But in those cases where intensive development of property is required for effective use, only private property rights allow individuals to recoup the gain from their investment. It was for just this reason that Adam Smith rightly noted that a dominant switch in the ownership structure of land, from a commons to private property, took place with the rise of agriculture under, of course, the banner, 'he who sows should reap'.[70] I know of no theory of Hegelian self-realization that can begin to explain the richness and variety of property arrangements.[71] Harris pays passing attention to the commons, but he does not treat it as an indispensable data point for the overall analysis.[72] And it is instructive that the index to *Property and Justice* contains no entries that discuss water law, oil and gas, the spectrum, or mining, all of which have elements of common property that require close analysis.

Secondly, for those forms of property that should be privatized, serious obstacles still remain. Let me mention two. The first goes to timing. The first possession rule is in reality a specialized case of the more general rule that holds, prior in time is higher in right. That rule is *ordinal* in form in that the gap between successive claimants does nothing to alter the strict priority of the first taker. If the gaps between claimants are large, the rule works quite well. Hence, it was used along the frontier, with the slow movements of populations across open territories, where everyone wants to have a friendly neighbour or two. But if the gaps become too small, the rule becomes unworkable. In this context, an auction system, whereby potential owners can bid for various parcels, works better. It would be inconceivable, for example, to allocate large chunks of the spectrum to the first user, when any telecommunications company could in some sense occupy the entire spectrum within seconds.[73] But it hardly follows from that point that we

[69] See MA Heller, 'The Tragedy of the Anticommons: Property in the Transition from Marx to Markets' (1998) 111 *Harvard LR* 621.

[70] A Smith, *Lectures on Jurisprudence* (ed. RL Meek, DD Raphael and PG Stein, Clarendon Press, 1978) 149 ff.

[71] See GWF Hegel, *Elements of the Philosophy of Right* (ed. Allen W Wood, CUP, 1991), whereby property becomes the means in which the will projects itself into the world, but which becomes in general subject to the higher will of the state.

[72] See Harris, *P & J*, n.1 above, 15–16, 31, 109–10, 114–15.

[73] See text to nn. 76–81 below.

should be indifferent to the system of spectrum allocation, or embrace the administrative state, whose failings I shall discuss presently.[74]

The second problem with privatization and the first possession rule is the standard tragedy of the commons whereby each person will use an asset, such as capturing wild animals or removing oil and gas from the commons, in ways that jeopardize the long-term stability of it. The perverse private incentives are clear and have been well understood for a long time.[75] Any individual who takes from a common pool resource obtains *all* the gains from what he takes, but bears only a fraction of the costs. Standard self-interested actions will lead to the premature exhaustion of the pool, relative to the sustainable level of exploitation undertaken by a single owner. The decisive inequality is that private costs are less than private benefits, that are in turn less than social costs. The self-interested individual compares the first two elements, while the correct social judgement requires a comparison of the last two elements (since private benefits equal social benefits in these situations). The need for state abrogation of the first possession rule stems from this persistent disjunction of private and social costs. The form of regulation, as with the spectrum, is absolutely critical, but beyond the scope of the discussion here.[76] What does matter is that the strongest criticisms and stoutest defence of the first possession rule both come from a fuller appreciation of the instrumental constraints at work in designing a property system. Harris, who has a cautious, but considerable, respect for the market system does not develop the instrumental arguments that limit the scope of the first possession rule. But, taken at their best, these limits undo the advantages of the rule in only a small class of cases, and even with these cases, as with hunting, the proper strategy is not to abandon the rule, but to place some independent limits on the size of the catch.

2. *The Consequences of First Possession*

The second issue in dealing with the nexus of liberty and property concerns the consequences of taking possession, assuming that it confers some property rights. Harris expresses his bottom line in his succinct and forcible way:

> To the extent that a first occupant has a right correlating with a duty imposed by some trespassory rule, nothing follows as to the use privileges and control-powers which the occupant ought to be conceded over the thing occupied.[77]

The illustration that he gives refers to the famous passage in Blackstone which notes that in prehistoric times possession of any thing gave only a usufructuary interest during the period of occupation, 'but the instant that he quitted the use

[74] See, for an early demonstration, RH Coase, 'The Federal Communications Commission' (1959) 2 *JL & Econ* 1.

[75] See, e.g., HS Gordon, 'The Economic Theory of a Common-Property Resource: The Fishery' (1954) 62 *J Pol Econ* 124.

[76] See generally RQ Grafton, D Squires and K J Fox, 'Private Property and Economic Efficiency: A Study of a Common Pool Resource' (2000) 43 *JL & Econ* 679.

[77] Harris, *P & J*, n.1 above, 215.

or occupation of it, another might seise it without injustice'.[78] Similarly, the fruits from the trees could be gathered by anyone who chose, even though the trees themselves were held in common. In commenting on the distribution of private and common rights, Blackstone then concludes by noting how Cicero 'compares the world to a great theatre, which is common to the public, and yet, the place which any man has taken is for the time his own'.[79]

How does one evaluate this state of affairs, a point on which Blackstone had the key fundamental insight? The situation in which people had mere usufructuary interests is cheap to administer. But, as applied to natural resources, that image of short-term claims precludes any form of investment that might improve the overall situation. Much of the history of property law, therefore, involves the movement to a system in which the initial occupation of property gives one ownership in fee simple. Thus, as Blackstone continues his tale of nature, he does not push the analogy of the theatre licence, but stresses that the incentives to provide shelter and safety are created once the person who invests in the future could capture the positive return his efforts generate. The reach of the term 'possession', therefore, had to be expanded, both in ordinary use and legal convention. The term had to allow a party to keep, or be regarded as keeping, possession of his home when he ventured out into the world unless he had a clear intention of abandoning ownership, which could not be lightly inferred with respect to any objects of value.[80] On this score Bentham took up the same theme as Blackstone when he wrote about the origins of property.[81] The underlying point may be put the following way. If the initial position was as weak as Harris notes it is, then we have an unambiguous social improvement by attaching more heft to possession by projecting it forward in time. Why then stick with the miminalist account when it is in the interest of no one?

This critical move, moreover, does not deny the existence of the limited types of property interests that Cicero and Blackstone described. As noted earlier, the division between common and private property arises from the earliest times, and to this day the system of rights in a commons works exactly as Cicero described it. I can sit on the beach during the day, but cannot stake a permanent claim to it that carries over even one day. I may drive my car on the highway, but cannot occupy a section of the road that blocks the highway for transportation. However,

[78] W Blackstone, *Commentaries on the Laws of England* (1766) (U of Chicago Press, 1979), p. ii, 3–4.

[79] Ibid., 4 (quoting Cicero De Fin. L. 3. c. 20) (cited in Harris, *P&J*, n.1 above, 214).

[80] For the Roman treatment on this subject, see J Getzler, 'Roman Ideas of Landownership', in S Bright and J Dewar (eds.), *Land Law: Themes and Perspectives* (OUP, 1998); B Nicholas, *An Introduction to Roman Law* (Clarendon Press, 1962). For the common law approach, see F Pollock and RS Wright, *An Essay on Possession in the Common Law* (Clarendon Press, 1888).

[81] J Bentham, *The Theory of Legislation* (ed. CK Ogden, FB Rothman and Co., 1987), 112–13:

> The savage who has killed a deer may hope to keep it for himself, so long as his cave is undiscovered; so long as he watches to defend it, and is stronger than his rivals; but that is all. How miserable and precarious is such a possession! If we suppose the least agreement among savages to respect the acquisitions of each other, we see the introduction of a principle to which no name can be given but that of law.

the theatre example does not offer the right analogy. In that case, the limited use by licensees is in accord with the plan of the owner (public or private), who does far better with his theatre by selling tickets on a per show (or per series) basis than by being forced to suffer the ticket holder whom he allows in for a single show to remain in perpetuity. A theatre (like a government building) may be publicly owned, but it does not operate as a commons. Rather, the single owner of the theatre has the ability to admit patrons on whatever terms and conditions it sees fit, and to exclude others. Presumably, the owner of the public theatre has an obligation to raise as much revenue as it can, which can then be used to offset the public debts of all citizens. (I put aside here all complications that arise from any need to regulate common carriers that enjoy a monopoly position[82]). When multiple theatres operate in competition, it leads to an overall maximization of social welfare. Yet that system only works when the owner of the property has the strong set of ownership rights associated with possession, use, and disposition in all its forms.

More generally, we can see the weakness of weak systems of ownership by asking what happens to that fraction of rights that belongs in the strong bundle, but nonetheless is excluded from the weak bundle? These rights do not disappear into thin air, because in the end *someone* has to decide who gets to make what use of the asset in question. The great advantage of giving the whole gamut of control powers (subject to the constraint of respecting the like rights of others) is that it avoids divisions of authority that retard or block any efficient deployment of resources. The differences between the strong and weak systems is well revealed by looking at cases where individuals receive, usually from the government, only licences to use resources that might otherwise be fully owned. Harris is receptive to these possibilities when he discusses how various imaginary societies experiment with different constellations of property rights. Thus, in Redland, a modern society, he sets out the basic situation elegantly as follows.

> So far as unique items are concerned—like specific dwellings or library books—there is a system of licensing and rationed use. An applicant is granted privileges of use over these things by an appropriate bureaucrat or committee on suitable terms stipulating the mode of enjoyment. These licensed privileges of use are protected by trespasser rules. During the subsistence of the licence, everyone but the licencee is prohibited from meddling with the dwelling or the library book in any way which might frustrate the licence use. However, questions whether the terms of any licence have been infringed, or disputes about whether a trespassory rule has been broken, are not resolved by any reference to any notion that, during the persistence of the licence, the item is, in any open-ended sense, 'her house' or 'his book'. Such questions and disputes are settled according to the spirit of the licence having regard to the general goals of fraternal living.[83]

In just a few lines, Harris gets to the cardinal distinction between the governance of resources in the modern administrative state and the comparable institutions in

[82] On which see RA Epstein, *Principles for a Free Society: Reconciling Individual Liberty with the Common Good* (Perseus Books, 1998), ch. 10.

[83] Harris, *P&J*, n.1 above, 17–18.

a full-blooded regime of private property. He is without doubt correct to insist that modern societies can organize complex problems through the administrative state, and some would say that it is not possible to do otherwise. But it is on this point that I strongly disagree with the implicit ecumenicalism of being aware of the multiple approaches to single problems in particular contexts. Just because one believes that common and private property must coexist does not mean that he or she should be indifferent to whether water is owned privately and all land is held in common. There are good functional reasons that mean for each particular setting one approach is likely to work better than another. While the administrative state proves indispensable for dealing with complex issues that arise when multiple sources of pollution cause harm to multiple targets, in general, the kinds of discrete property matters that Harris addresses are badly handled through the administrative state that he sometimes champions. What follows is a snapshot explanation of why.

The key difficulty in organizing a system of private property with discrete resources is of course the boundary question given that ownership, as Harris constantly stresses, does not entail the right to make unlimited use of any object. Crossing or invading someone else's property or striking that person is the paradigmatic case of a wrong; and it is easily extended to cover threats of force that cause serious emotional distress to the person.[84] The physical and psychological boundaries in cases of harms to persons or property have to be policed one way or the other, and I am not unduly troubled if they are policed in some instances by a state board and in others by common law actions for trespass or nuisance. The mere thought of anti-pollution statutes is not an affront to limited government. But the key question for dispute concerns the full range of uses that do *not* involve boundary-crossing activities. Whenever 'an appropriate bureaucrat or committee' has to determine which uses are allowed and why, someone has to determine which individual or what committee will make that decision. They will also have to determine which individuals are in a position to apply for the resource in question, which individuals have standing to oppose the application, and which of the hundreds of potential licence permutations will be adopted in any given case. The upshot is a pattern of use restrictions that may give short-term competitive relief to certain objectors, but which hold back the rate of adaptive responses to social and market forces. Too many valuable rights are left on the table.

Here are two examples of how this all works. The decisions for land use today often require permits and licences from bureaucrats and committees who need not stop with the question whether a new factory or home poses a threat of nuisance against its neighbours. Rather, that group can decide to zone some land for commercial development, some for residential, some for open space, and the like. Ironically, oftentime the strict segmentation that is contemplated by the term zoning itself leads to the serious partition of neighbourhoods that

[84] See, e.g., *Wilkinson v Downton* [1897] 2 KB 57, for one conspicuous example.

ignores the positive interactive effects that everyone wants to see emerge in vibrant communities.[85]

The situation gets no better when we look at narrower economic values. The leading zoning case in the United States is *Euclid v Ambler Realty Co.*,[86] which involved a 68-acre manufacturing site that was zoned residential. However, it was located between two railroad tracks, such that it was ideal for the industrial use for which its owners planned.[87] Zoning is often justified as an administrative means to control externalities, but here the unified development of the plot under a single owner already did that job far better than any administrative system. The upshot was that the value of the property declined after zoning from $700,000 to $200,000. And the simple question to ask becomes: can anyone find $500,000 in public benefits that offset the losses that this system of regulation imposes on the owner—losses that no responsible social calculus could ignore? That question is particularly poignant because some ten years later, after endless wrangling with local officials, the land was put to its original use anyhow.[88] Thus, the government change was definitely not Pareto efficient and probably not Kaldor-Hicks efficient since, if compensation had to be paid to Ambler Realty, the zoning would most likely have instantaneously been changed to industrial. The competition over use that necessarily takes place within the political process under Harris's weak view of property would swell the political sphere to a vast bulk if not checked. But that political wrangling is largely dampened by the stronger view of property rights, which prevents public officials from blocking a project unless they can show, which they virtually never can, some violation of the trespassory rules.

These concerns are not specific in any way to the United States. Create by administrative fiat a green belt around London, and the one landowner who is lucky enough to negotiate an exemption from the general prohibition will make a killing while everyone else is saddled with land that could well turn out to have more liabilities than benefits. The basic point is this: the system of full-blooded use rights avoids the endless and destructive wrangling that takes place when everything inside the trespassory envelope is left up for grabs between the state and the weak property owner. This preference for the strong view does not slight public regulation. It may well be needed to police various kinds of violations that private actions will not disentangle because of the enormous co-ordination and free rider problems that are raised when many neighbours are hurt by nuisance-like activities of a single owner. But, even so, the following iron rule should apply: the *grounds* for public intervention do *not* expand simply because the system of enforcement moves from private action to public administrative law. The weak conception of private property always violates that constraint. The strong approach, on the other hand, only allows for public intervention when the

[85] See J Jacobs, *The Death and Life of Great American Cities* (Random House, 1961).

[86] 272 US 365 (1926).

[87] For a short discussion of the point, see RA Epstein, 'A Conceptual Approach to Zoning: What's Wrong with *Euclid*' (1996) 5 *NYU Envtl LJ* 277.

[88] Ibid., 287, n. 10.

individual owners could have filed suit on their own, but did not because of the problems of collective action.

The conclusion here is not restricted, moreover, to cases of land. It can apply with equal force to new resources made possible through advances in technology. Take the broadcast spectrum, which only has value after the ability to master radio waves.[89] One possible way to allocate the spectrum is to create full-blooded ownership rights that are modelled on the analogous institutions for land. Here the uses made of the spectrum are left to the owner so long as he does not interfere with (the perfect trespass analogy) broadcasts on neighbouring frequencies. Otherwise, the spectrum is an asset for him to do with as he pleases. That system could have developed in the United States by application of the first possession rule, but that progression was stopped short by administrative co-option of the spectrum. This co-option occurred in part for use by the United States Navy, and in part because of the efforts of the Department of Commerce in the 1920s under Herbert Hoover to bring national control and order to the system through the Federal Radio Act of 1927.

The consequences of this system are not benign, but result in systematic underutilization that manifests itself in all sorts of dimensions,[90] given the intricate restrictions that were placed on the system. The initial impulse beyond the system stemmed from the belief that the government could allocate frequencies, in the public interest, of course, in ways that avoided the 'chaos' of the market place, as Justice Felix Frankfurter wrote.[91] Frankfurter noted that the objectives of the Federal Communications Act were not modest, and amounted to an extension of the administrative state:

> The Act itself establishes that the Commission's powers are not limited to the engineering and technical aspects of regulation of radio communication. Yet we are asked to regard the Commission as a kind of traffic officer, policing the wave lengths to prevent stations from interfering with each other. But the Act does not restrict the Commission merely to supervision of the traffic. It puts upon the Commission the burden of determining the composition of that traffic. The facilities of radio are not large enough to accommodate all who wish to use them. Methods must be devised for choosing from among the many who apply. And since Congress itself could not do this, it committed the task to the Commission.[92]

[89] For the seminal paper on the issue, see RH Coase, 'The Federal Communications Commission' (1959) 2 *JL & Econ* 1. In responding to Mr Frank Stanton's, the head of the Columbia Broadcasting System, objection of the 'novel theory' of auctioning off the frequencies, Coase wrote: 'This "novel theory" (novel with Adam Smith) is, of course, that the allocation of resources should be determined by the forces of the market rather than as a result of government decisions': ibid., 17–18. Coase, of course, was no stranger to this question, having written just before he left England a strong criticism of the BBC. See RH Coase, *British Broadcasting: A Study in Monopoly* (Longmans, Green, & Co., 1950). For more recent confirmation of the political intrigue of the system, see TW Hazlett, 'The Rationality of U.S. Regulation of the Broadcast Spectrum' (1990) 33 *JL & Econ* 133.

[90] See, e.g., ER Kwerel and JR Williams, 'Moving Toward a Market for Spectrum' (1993) 16 *Regulation* 53; TW Hazlett 'Spectrum Tragedies' (2005) 22 *Yale J on Reg* 315.

[91] *National Broadcasting Co., Inc. v United States*, 319 US 190, 212 (1943).

[92] Ibid., 215–16.

But it has never worked out that way, for the restrictions on use have been massively destructive in all sorts of ways. Here are some examples. Broadcast licences require that licensees make individual determinations of the shows that they put on the air. Hence, a station lost its licence when it had the sensible idea to turn itself into a common carrier of sorts, by selling out blocks of time to individual users to do with as they pleased. The consequence was that all sorts of marginal ethnic voices that could not afford to obtain a licence were shut out from the market place under a state system that reduced the diversity of voices heard over the airwaves.[93] Other difficulties are technical. New advances in technology allow for the transmission of more content over a bandwidth originally assigned to a single station: sorry, the division of stations cannot take place without FCC approval, which never comes. A particular frequency is restricted to a particular use for which there is no demand: sorry, a shift in use is not possible. Thus, the nearby bandwidths allocated to areas of intense demand (e.g., mobile phones) are crowded, while other frequencies lie vacant. A new technology (e.g., digital) comes available but the licence requires the use of analogue technology. Again stasis. This list could be multiplied almost without end, but for little purpose. The fatal mistake of the rigid licence system is that pointless administrative restrictions undermine robust use rights and thereby destroy resource value. That can never happen in a system of full-blooded property rights. Individual owners could sell, swap, divide, or switch uses in endless variations, all without having to do battle with the FCC or some other commission. The social losses are easily estimated in the high billions of dollars.[94]

(iii) Constitutional Issues

In closing, I hope to explain how this principled distaste for the administrative allocation of use rights ties in with my own constitutional views on the takings clause, which Harris criticizes in his Maccabaean Lecture. To set the stage, it is imperative to note that throughout legal history there has long been a duality about the scope of liberty and property rights within the legal system. Thus, Blackstone, who is often taken as a strong defender of private property rights, often adopts, as Harris shrewdly notes, a more cautious view on the scope of these rights—one which places the emphasis on exclusion, not use and disposition. Therefore, in dealing with personal liberty, Blackstone took the position that liberty encompasses the right to go along one's way and to avoid false imprisonment.[95]

[93] See, e.g., *Cosmopolitan Broadcast Corp. v F.C.C.*, 581 F2d 917 (DC Cir. 1978).

[94] See TW Hazlett 'Spectrum Tragedies' (2005) 22 *Yale J on Reg*, (forthcoming) manuscript at 8.

[95] W Blackstone, *Commentaries on the Laws of England* (1766) (U of Chicago Press, 1979), i, 130:

> This personal liberty consists in the power of loco-motion, of changing situation, or removing one's person to whatsoever place one's own inclination may direct; without imprisonment or restraint, unless by due course of law.

All matters of occupational choice (within the bounds of trespass and nuisance law) are not captured by that definition. On the question of property, Blackstone did treat it as including the rights of possession, use, and disposition,[96] tolerant of various forms of economic protectionism, such as restrictions on imports that would work to the benefit of the wool trade. All of these restrictions fit in well with Harris's account of the ownership situation. That is, each allows some use of property, and all give full respect to the trespassory protections that property needs, even though they do not protect the full package, which includes rights of use and disposition along with exclusion.

What is critical to note is that the same cleavage that one can find on the private law side plays out as well on the constitutional law side. In dealing with liberty, we can find many cases that give its inclusion in the Fourteenth Amendment a broad reading, including the rights to marry and to pursue an occupation.[97] Within the American tradition, there are passages in cases that say that the bundle of rights in property includes the right to possession, use, and disposition.[98] But the dominant thread is surely in the opposite direction, such that the right to exclude is given paramount place, subject to virtually automatic protection. That cashes out to protection against arbitrary imprisonment of the person,[99] as the only protection for liberty, and protection of the exclusive right of possession for real and personal property.[100] The protection of the other rights, including the rights

[96] W Blackstone, *Commentaries on the Laws of England*, i, 134: 'The third absolute right, inherent in every Englishman, is that of property: which consists in the free use, enjoyment and disposal of all his acquisitions, without any control or diminution, save only by the laws of the land.' That last note of caution is later repeated, for 'all these rights and liberties it is our birthright to enjoy entire; unless where the laws of our country have laid them under necessary restraints': Ibid., 140.

[97] See, e.g., *Allgeyer v Louisiana*, 165 US 578, 589 (1897):

> The liberty mentioned in that amendment means not only the right of the citizen to be free from the mere physical restraint of his person, as by incarceration, but the term is deemed to embrace the right of the citizen to be free in the enjoyment of all his faculties; to be free to use them in all lawful ways; to live and work where he will; to earn his livelihood by any lawful calling; to pursue any livelihood or avocation, and for that purpose to enter into all contracts which may be proper, necessary and essential to his carrying out to a successful conclusion the purposes above mentioned.

See also *Pierce v Society of Sisters*, 268 US 510, 534 (1925) (nothing that liberty covers the right to educate one's own children).

[98] See, e.g., *United States v General Motors Corp.*, 323 US 373, 377–8 (1945).

[99] See, e.g., *Lochner v New York*, 198 US 45, 76 (1905) (Holmes J dissenting):

> I think that the word liberty in the Fourteenth Amendment is perverted when it is held to prevent the natural outcome of a dominant opinion, unless it can be said that a rational and fair man necessarily would admit that the statute proposed would infringe fundamental principles as they have been understood by the traditions of our people and our law.

See also C Warren, 'The New "Liberty" under the Fourteenth Amendment' (1926) 39 *Harvard* LR 431, 440 (disputing *Allgeyer*, and treating liberty as 'the right to have one's person free from physical restraint').

[100] See *Kaiser Aetna v United States*, 444 US 164, 179–80 (1979) ('[W]e hold that the 'right to exclude', so universally held to be a fundamental element of the property right, falls within this category of interests that the Government cannot take without compensation'.); *Loretto v TelePrompter Manhattan CATV Corp*, 458 US 419, 434 (1982) (noting that forced physical occupation of another's property destroys the right to exclude). See also TW Merrill, 'Property and the Right to Exclude'

of use and disposition of these resources, whether labour or capital, is much more restricted. In dealing with the labour questions, issues as to whether the state may impose minimum wage or maximum hour laws are subject only to a minimal level of scrutiny, while the same is true of most restrictions on land use.[101] This position is in marked contrast with some earlier efforts to provide a deeper set of protections to rights of use and disposition during what is sometimes called the heyday of substantive due process.[102]

The position that I first advanced in *Takings* is that the strong account of private property offers a better fit to the constitutional text, which, after all, does make explicit references to liberty and private property. Further, a full understanding of how that system of property rights is put together allows it to escape charges that this full-blooded reading is unresponsive to conditions of modern times. The key objective of that system is to avoid the gaps in rights of use and disposition that give full sway to the destructive social tendencies that can be observed in the labour, land use, and spectrum cases, as well as other areas of the law. The first move in that system is one that Harris would reject, which is that partial takings, including the elimination of, or limitations on, the rights to use property, count as a taking of private property. But recall that the constitutional provision does not say that private property shall not be taken without consent. Quite the opposite, it may be taken for public use on payment of just compensation. The ability of the state to initiate forced exchanges for limited purposes is meant to turn the system into one in which the government may initiate forced exchanges in cases where voluntary markets will not work, i.e., situations in which hold-out and co-ordination problems prevent the realization of socially desirable solutions that markets cannot reach.[103] The public use limitation, which has been arguably gutted

(1998) 77 *Neb LR* 730, 730 ('The Supreme Court is fond of saying that "the right to exclude others" is "one of the most essential sticks in the bundle of rights that are commonly characterized as property" ').

[101] See *Euclid v Ambler Realty Co.*, 272 US 365 (1926) (noting that land use could be restricted to residential only); *Penn Central Transportation Co. v City of New York*, 438 US 105, 123–8 (1978) (setting forth limitations on when use restrictions will be considered takings); *Lucas v South Carolina Coastal Council*, 505 US 1003, 1017 (1992) (noting that if all economically beneficial uses of property are restricted, it will finally become a taking).

[102] See, e.g., *Adair v United States*, 208 US 161, 176 (1908) (holding unconstitutional a criminal law that restricted an employer's ability to terminate an employee based on his membership in a labour union); *Coppage v Kansas*, 236 US 1, 10–11 (1915) (holding unconstitutional a state law doing the same); *Hitchman Coal & Coke Co. v Mitchell*, 245 US 229 (1917). These are both ostensibly labour cases involved with personal liberty, but the connection to property is inexorable. So long as one need not bargain with a union against one's own will, it is easy to respect the right to exclude. But once the duty to bargain collectively is accepted, see e.g., *National Labor Relations Board v Jones & Laughlin Steel Corp*, 301 US 1, 45–6 (1937), the property rights necessarily fall away as well, so that union representatives are allowed limited access to plants over the objection of the employer. See, e.g., *Republic Aviation Corp. v National Labor Relations Board*, 324 US 793, 804–5 (1945). For my defence of the old order, see RA Epstein, 'A Common Law for Labor Relations: A Critique of the New Deal Legislation' (1983) 92 *Yale LJ* 1357.

[103] For a discussion of how these forced exchanges separate my position from that of Robert Nozick, see RA Epstein, *Takings: Private Property and the Power of Eminent Domain* (Harvard UP, 1985), 334–8. Harris notes the evident parallels between myself and Nozick, see 'Mumbo Jumbo', n. 2 above, 456–7, but does not reflect on the differences between Nozick's views and my own.

in American law,[104] is an effort to make sure that the power of the state to take and pay does not allow one person to buy out his neighbour in ways that magnify the dangers of political abuse. But all of this is hemmed in, of course, by a sensible account of the police power, which on any reading allows the state to protect against unlimited use of private property in ways that cause trespassory (or fraudulent) conduct against neighbours. I have never been able to identify a sensible form of government regulation that could not be discharged within this framework in terms of the management of human or natural resources. In particular, the state enjoys considerable leeway in figuring out the best way to deal with environmental risks and common pool problems. And it certainly can purchase land for green belts, if it thinks such is desirable, and put them to common use.

Nor is anything here at odds with key values of community and transparency. The current rules on just compensation, which inexcusably ignore the subjective value of all owners, make it easy for government bulldozers to break up neighbourhoods without taking into account the enormous burdens often placed on the most vulnerable members of a community. The constant ability to hide behind regulations in order to achieve social ends means that legislative bodies never have to consider the full costs of their action, resulting in a loss of transparency in deliberative processes.[105] There are, in sum, huge reasons to favour a system that starts with robust property rights and works through corrections in ways that seek to prevent the under-utilization of resources on the one hand, and their dissipation through political intrigue on the other. The version of the takings clause that I have defended is *not* a covert effort to cement in privilege or undercut democratic processes. It is an effort to achieve the end that both J.W. Harris and I share, the improvement of the lot of all citizens within the framework of the modern state. Harris has done a great service in that connection by resisting all the efforts to marginalize and deconstruct questions of property rights. But his eloquent and learned defence of the weak position comes out, in my mind, second best to the more full-blooded conceptions of individual liberty and private property.

[104] See *Hawaiian Housing Authority v Midkiff*, 467 US 229, 241 (1984) ('But where the exercise of the eminent domain power is rationally related to a conceivable public purpose, the Court has never held a compensated taking to be proscribed by the Public Use Clause'). *Midkiff* survived its reexamination in *Kelo v City of New London*, 545 US__, 125 S. Ct. 2655 (2005).

[105] As noted in *City of San Jose v Pennell*, 485 US 1, 21–2 (1985).

7

Property and Ownership: Marginal Comments

*Tony Honoré**

(i) Introduction

Jim Harris's *Property and Justice*[1] is a major work. Its range, coherence, and depth put it in a different class from most modern writing on these intractable topics. The comments that follow concern his treatment of property, in particular the relation of his view of property and ownership to mine. The *ad hominem* strategy is suggested by the way in which Harris summarizes his conclusions in the introduction to *Property and Justice*:

> [I]t will emerge that the essentials of a property institution are the twin notions of trespassory rules and the ownership spectrum. By 'trespassory rules' is meant any social rules, whether or not embodied in law, which purport to impose obligations on all members of a society, other than an individual or group who is taken to have some form of open-ended relationship to a thing, not to make use of that thing without the consent of that individual or group... By the 'ownership spectrum' is meant the open-ended relationships presupposed and protected by trespassory rules.[2]

He then goes on:

> All attempts in the history of theorizing about property to provide a univocal explication of the concept of ownership, applicable within all societies and to all resources, have failed.[3]

The footnote to this sentence cites two articles of mine, one of 1961 describing the liberal concept of individual ownership[4] and another of 1977 concerned with the justification of property rights.[5] Did Harris think of them as failed attempts to provide a general explanation of ownership, or did they seem to him to favour the

* Regius Professor of Civil Law, Emeritus, at All Souls College, Oxford.

[1] JW Harris, *Property and Justice* (OUP, 1996). [2] Ibid., 5. [3] Ibid.

[4] Honoré, 'Ownership', in AG Guest (ed.), *Oxford Essays in Jurisprudence* (1961) (also published as T Honoré, *Making Law Bind: Essays Legal and Philosophical* (Clarendon Press, 1987), 161–92).

[5] T Honoré, 'Property, Title and Redistribution' (1977) 10 *Archiv für Rechts–und Sozialphilosophie*, New Series, 107 (also published as T Honoré, *Making Law Bind: Essays Legal and Philosophical* (Clarendon Press, 1987), 215–26).

idea that all such attempts are doomed to failure? I am not sure. But the reference invites comment. How far do our views coincide or diverge?

Harris's explanation of property has five leading features, to which he consistently adheres. They are: (a) the need for trespassory rules; (b) that property interests are relations between the holder of the interest and the resource (thing) subject to it; (c) that property interests lie along an 'ownership spectrum'; (d) that the privileges and powers that the holders of these interests possess are 'open-ended'; and (e) that items on the ownership spectrum authorize 'self-seekingness' on the part of the individual or group to whom they belong. Comments on these five features follow.

(a) Trespassory Rules

Trespassory rules are 'a necessary but not sufficient condition for property'.[6] This is surely true. If someone holds property, there must be reserved to the property holder an element of use, control, or benefit that is forbidden to others. There can be no property unless to intrude on that reserved sphere is a wrong for anyone who lacks the property holder's consent or some special authority conferred by law.

That trespassory rules need not be embodied in law carries with it the implication that there can be entitlements to property outside the law.[7] Indeed, it is a feature of legal concepts such as rights, obligations, and property that they have moral analogues outside the law. They apply in situations not governed by law that resemble those in which the corresponding legal concept applies. It is as if someone had, morally speaking, a right, obligation, or property interest with a certain content. In such cases morality derives its impetus from the law, just as in others the law derives its impetus from morality, or there is a reciprocal impact.

An example of moral property and its connection with trespass is brought to mind by a recent biography. Robert Scott first explored the Antarctic in 1902–4 and, in the course of his expedition, established a base at McMurdo Sound in the Ross Dependency. Ernest Shackleton, leading a later expedition in 1907–9, promised Scott that he, Shackleton, would approach Antarctica not from there but from some other base. McMurdo Sound was, as it were, Scott's property, though not in a legal sense. As a fellow explorer wrote to Shackleton: 'I do wholly agree with the right lying with Scott to use that base before anyone else'.[8] Shackleton broke his promise and landed at McMurdo Sound. His conduct was criticized as a trespass on Scott's preserves. Like the criticism the defence was quasi-legal. Was Shackleton, if he could find no suitable alternative, justified by necessity in landing at McMurdo? The trespass idea, along with justifications for trespassing, applies to property claims outside the law, as within it.

[6] Harris, n.1 above, 24–5, 33.
[7] Harris does not, so far as I can tell, mention this.
[8] Quoted in R Fiennes, *Captain Scott* (Coronet, 2003), 141.

(b) Interests in Things

Property relations all involve a juridical relation between a person or group and a resource,[9] in law a 'thing'. 'Resources' here includes things that do not exist apart from the law, such as patents and rights to software. This proposition, also, is surely correct. The relation between the holder of the interest and others arises from the fact that trespassory rules require others to respect the relation between the holder and the thing. So, property interests are not to be analysed merely as consisting in relations between people, but as relations between people and things, protected by rules that impose restraints on others. Indeed, Harris could argue that the relation of the holder of the interest to the thing is primary, since the main task of the law of property is to regulate the use of resources. The relation of the holder of the interest to other people, though a necessary element in a property relationship, is secondary in the sense that it presupposes and serves to uphold the relation of the holder to the thing.

The contrary view, that property is always concerned with relationships between people as to the use or exploitation of things is attributed, I am glad to say, to *illegitimate* inferences drawn from treatments of the topic by Hohfeld and myself.[10]

(c) The Ownership Spectrum

A central, but more controversial, element in Harris's analysis of property is that of the 'ownership spectrum'. In his view, property interests lie somewhere along this spectrum which runs from 'mere property' to 'full-blooded ownership'. 'Modern property institutions', he says, 'protect ownership interests well down the spectrum over some resources'.[11]

It is not clear why the range of property interests should be said to lie along an ownership spectrum. Those who hold long leases are not regarded as owning anything except possibly their lease. Indeed, 'owning' in this context is awkward. It is more natural to think of the holders as 'having' or 'possessing' the lease. It is true that they have many of the interests in the thing leased that a full, unencumbered, owner would have. But that does not make these interests 'ownership interests'. On the contrary, their interests are protected by law, but are distinct from ownership. It would have been better to talk not of an 'ownership spectrum' but of a 'property spectrum', since a spectrum of *property interests*, of which ownership is the summit, clearly does exist. We can take 'property', with Harris, to comprise items that are either the subject of direct trespassory protection or are separately assignable as parts of private wealth.[12] The property spectrum admits of

[9] Harris, n.1 above, 5.
[10] Ibid.,119–20, 125. Neither of us expressed this view. What is true is that property interests require that there should be legal relations of various sorts between the holder of the interest and others.
[11] Ibid., 125. [12] Ibid., 13, 47–54.

lesser and greater property interests, but does not merely reflect a historical evolution from simple to complex interests, including full ownership. Simpler and more complex, greater and lesser, property interests co-exist at the same time and in the same society. So, does appeal to an 'ownership spectrum' help us to understand the relationship between property interests and ownership?[13]

I do not think so. An alternative is to offer an analysis of 'full-blooded ownership' (for convenience, 'full ownership') and then compare full ownership of tangible things with lesser property interests or property interests in things created by the law ('ideational things').[14] To follow this route would have led Harris to an analysis of full ownership, which he does not provide. It would then have been easier to focus attention on the reasons for recognizing or denying recognition to interests less than full ownership, or interests in non-tangible things. I offered an analysis of this sort in the 1961 article on the 'standard incidents' of 'the liberal[15] concept of full individual ownership'.[16] And, while the discussion of method in legal philosophy is sometimes unprofitable, there is perhaps, in this context, a point in comparing different strategies.

The method adopted by Hart and myself in *Causation in the Law*, by Hart in *The Concept of Law*, and by me in the article cited above was to describe the incidents of the model case that the concept fits and from which defined normative consequences follow. One can then go on to examine cases in which one or more of the standard incidents are missing. What, in the light of the differences between the non-standard and the standard case, is the strength of the case for applying the same, or similar, normative consequences to them?

To take causation as an example, we delineated a 'central notion' of cause, where an agent's causing something to come about consists, roughly, in their manipulating the natural or human environment. Starting from this model, we sought to explain how causal notions could be applied for different purposes, in particular to explain puzzling occurrences and to attribute responsibility. As regards responsibility, we pointed out that, alongside cases where the core notion clearly applied, there were others, in some ways analogous, where one or more features of the core case was missing. Examples were where the agent provides an opportunity or inducement for another to do something that has a harmful outcome. In the core cases, responsibility, moral or legal, goes without saying. But in the analogous cases, where someone is said to be responsible for the outcome of a later voluntary act by another, it is debatable whether the normal consequences of being morally or legally responsible for harm caused should apply. The extension of responsibility to such cases is not automatic.

The advantage of adopting this technique is that cases that are described in law by the same portmanteau term, say 'proximate cause', or 'participating in crime',

[13] Harris, 125. [14] Ibid., 42–7, 139.

[15] I was using this term in a descriptive sense, to refer to both positive and negative freedoms: freedom to exercise a wide range of powers, and freedom from interference by others and by the state. I was not concerned with the justification of the institution, of which Harris has a good account in chs. 13 and 14. [16] N.2 above.

may be shown on a more careful analysis to be conceptually and morally different. When that is so, the original agent's responsibility should be discussed on its merits, not as a straightforward application of the core case which would automatically carry with it the defined normative consequences.

A similar technique may provide a good way of analysing those 'mere property' relationships that possess some, but not all, of the features of full ownership. What sort of rights and obligations should accrue to lessees, or to the owners of intellectual property such as copyrights or software can, arguably, best be judged against the background of the model of a person having full, unencumbered ownership of a physical thing. If the right to physical possession of a thing forms part of the 'full ownership' model, should the normative position of someone whose property interest is divorced from physical possession, such as a patent, or copyright holder, be the same as that of the full owner of a physical thing? To what extent should having a share in a company, or inventing a technique, or acquiring special knowledge be treated in the same way as owning a physical asset? It is here that a link between analysis and policy emerges. The case for vesting exclusive control over a tangible thing in some person or organization is stronger than that for vesting similar control over (in Harris's term) an ideational thing. Tangible things, if relatively scarce, and hence of some social value, require someone to manage them, and there is a limit to the extent to which control over them can be shared. So, there must be rules allocating them to a full owner, or dividing the control over them between a limited number of holders of lesser property interests. Ideational things, on the other hand, such as intellectual property, need not be recognized as capable of being owned or held as property at all. If they are so recognized, the extent to which the same incidents should apply, as in the case of tangible things, falls to be decided as a matter of social and legal policy.

The institution of property in tangible things is necessary and, in that sense, natural. It does not follow that any particular scheme about how title to them should be acquired, or how property interests in tangibles should be distributed, is to be preferred. Property in ideational things, on the other hand, is not necessary. Societies can choose whether to recognize particular ideational items, and on what terms.

Because Harris focuses on 'ownership interests', rather than ownership, he does not need to explain what he takes to be the incidents of full ownership, except, he says, that it starts from the assumption that the owner 'is entirely free to do what he will with his own, whether by way of use, abuse or transfer'.[17] 'Ownership interests' are, in his view, privileges and powers over things. 'All ownership interests comprise some use-privileges and some control-powers. Ownership interests in the upper half of the spectrum also comprise powers of transmission'.[18] In contrast, I listed eleven incidents of the 'liberal concept of full individual[19] ownership',

[17] Harris, n.1 above, 29. [18] Ibid., 5.

[19] This refers to private ownership by individuals. Harris (100–18) takes the view that 'conceptions of private property are logically prior to conceptions of non-private property and justifications for the latter are parasitic on justifications or disjustifications for the former'.

several of which are not privileges or powers: (i) the right to possess; (ii) the right to use; (iii) the right to manage; (iv) the right to the income; (v) the right to the capital; (vi) the right to security; (vii) the incident of transmissibility; (viii) the incident of absence of term; (ix) the duty to prevent harm; (x) liability to execution; (xi) the residuary character of ownership. This list describes not 'ownership interests', but ownership as a working institution. As a working institution, it is clearly not 'absolute' in the sense that 'the owner is entirely free to do what he will with his own'. It includes limitations on owners' interests such as those listed under (ix) and (x), while under (vi) the explanatory text refers to the possibility of expropriation. Liability to tax might well also have been mentioned. Nor does the list seek to provide a 'unitary conception of ownership' of the sort that is said to generate 'juristic puzzles'.[20] It is rather a model against the background of which lesser property interests, for instance tenure for a limited period under the doctrine of estates in land, can be assessed and evaluated.[21] The model is not invalidated by the fact that someone with an interest less than full ownership is sometimes regarded, socially, as an owner, or that the law may require this to be done on the ground that, in a certain legal context, the thing in question must have an owner. It may be that, in some legal contexts, 'possession' or 'occupation' is 'just another term for some kinds of ownership interests'.[22] But that does not convert possession or occupation into ownership.

According to Harris, some of the incidents listed above, along with their explanation, exemplify the inter-relationship between ownership interests and various kinds of property-limitation rules[23] or expropriation rules.[24] But these rules 'are none of them analytic features of ownership interests as such'.[25] This conclusion, however, depends on defining 'ownership interests' narrowly; indeed, confining them to privileges of use and powers of control or transmission. Yet the duties that go with ownership ('limitation-rules'), for example the landowner's duties towards those who come onto his land, are a feature of the institution of ownership in all modern (and one may suspect nearly all ancient) societies. The law of nuisance is treated as a species of 'property-limitation', because premised on the assumption that, but for the restriction, the owner would be free to act in a certain way, for instance to emit smoke from his own land so as to lessen his neighbour's enjoyment.[26] This branch of the law imposes restrictive duties on landowners. So to say that 'duties [are not] intrinsic to ownership interests'[27] is to focus on the privileges rather than the responsibilities of an owner to an extent that makes the analysis one-sided. The same is true of expropriation rules such as liability to execution and forfeiture. Harris recognizes that 'any property institution must, in practice, comprise property-limitation rules and expropriation rules as well as trespassory rules'.[28] Why are these rules not 'intrinsic' to ownership? That word plays a leading, but obscure, role in the analysis. In any society in

[20] Harris, n.1 above, 79. [21] Ibid., 133. [22] Ibid., 84. [23] Ibid., 33–6.
[24] Ibid., 29, 37–9, 93–9. [25] Ibid., 127. [26] Ibid., 34. [27] Ibid., 129.
[28] Ibid., 33–4.

which co-operation is a value—which is to say in all societies—there will have to be rules of this sort. That 'analytically... no liability or immunity is intrinsic to ownership interests'[29] is predicated, perhaps, on the idea that there might be a society, like the imaginary societies so entertainingly described in Chapter 2 of the book, in which there were owners, but no incidents of this type. But the real world is different.

Even if attention is focussed on incidents that benefit the owner, Harris takes a restrictive view. He does not accept that the claim to possession is a feature (intrinsic feature?) of ownership interests.[30] Yet it is clearly a necessary element in ownership:

> The crime of theft and tort of conversion would be meaningless unless it were presupposed that there was someone, the owner, who has specially privileged relations to chattels. The definition of wrongs and sanctions do not, however, vest in the owner an unqualified set of claims correlating to duties on others not to interfere with, or to restore, his physical control... It follows that claim-rights are not intrinsic to ownership interests.[31]

This view can have extraordinary consequences. 'In the case of cashable rights [e.g. shares] power of transmission is the only element of the ownership bundle which applies.'[32] But the shareholder needs to be able to claim dividends and, if he or she decides to sell the shares, the proceeds of sale. What value would shares possess otherwise? Why are these claims not a necessary, hence 'intrinsic', part of the shareholder's 'ownership bundle'? Is it because the claim to dividends or the proceeds of sale is normally founded on a contract? Perhaps that is the line of thought. But if such claims did not exist the shareholder would not be regarded as owning the shares.

The owner's right to possess must include a claim to possess that normally makes dispossession wrongful. Nothing, surely, can turn on the 'definition of wrongs and sanctions', especially if the definitions are derived from a particular legal system, such as English law. Whether the legal remedy for the violation of the right to possess in relation to a particular class of things is framed as a claim to possess, or as a remedy for dispossession, is not material. What is protected is the right to possess, which is not a mere privilege. This right would be meaningless in the absence of claims against thieves, trespassers, and, indeed, often possessors in good faith, even if these claims need not result in court orders for specific restitution of the thing taken or detained.

Certainly my list of the incidents of ownership is imperfect. Additions and deletions can plausibly be suggested. Moreover, it needs to be supplemented by a discussion of the leading incidents—benefit, management, and title—that justify treating someone as the owner of a thing in a particular case.[33] But to point to a set of privileges and powers 'intrinsic' to interests on the 'ownership spectrum' is no substitute for an analysis of ownership.

[29] Ibid., 130. [30] Ibid., 30. [31] Ibid., 127. [32] Ibid., 31.
[33] See text accompanying nn.37–38 below.

(d) Open-ended Privileges and Powers

The fourth element in Harris's analysis of property consists in the allegedly open-ended use-privileges and powers that those on the ownership spectrum possess. These privileges and powers 'cannot be concretely listed'.[34] For example, the holder of an estate in land has an open-ended set of use-privileges and control-powers, but the holder of an easement or licence does not.[35] But this appeal to open-ended privileges and powers is a mistake, whether 'open-ended' is interpreted as referring to specific actions or to types of action. The privileges exercisable over a thing do not together constitute a finite number of permissible actions.[36] This is as true of the privileges of the holder of an easement or licence as of a lessee or holder of an estate in land. The view that permissible actions can be listed rests on a fallacy about enumeration. The privilege of using the telephone in someone else's house is a privilege to telephone A, B, C, D, E, and anyone else not specifically excluded. Privileges and powers are privileges and powers to do an indefinite number of actions within a certain range. If, on the other hand, 'open-ended' is interpreted as referring to types of action, no one, whether the owner, the holder of a lesser property interest, or of a licence, or mere contractual interest, has an open-ended set of privileges or powers. All are limited by the general law and the terms of the transaction that entitle the holder to the privilege or power.

A more promising approach is to treat the distinctive features of limited interests in property as a combination of the negative and the positive. Negatively, their privileges and powers are more limited that those of an unencumbered full owner. Positively, the holder of a lesser property interest is privileged in the sense that his or her interest has, in law, to be given immunity or priority by the owner, the owner's unsecured creditors, and indeed by all who do not possess a property interest that ranks above the holder's. It is not just that the holder of a property interest is protected against trespassers. That is true of the holder of any interest. But the holder of a property interest is accorded immunities and priorities that are not accorded to the holder of a non-property interest. Property interests form a special legal category, which can only be explained in terms of how their holder fares legally in competition with other claimants.

(e) Self-seekingness

The items on the ownership spectrum are said to have in common that 'they authorise self-seekingness on the part of the individual or group to which they belong'.[37] This may not be true of all property interests, but if it is meant to characterize full ownership, it seems correct. The institution of ownership carves

[34] Harris, n.1 above, 5. [35] Ibid., 55. [36] Honoré, n.4 above, 125.
[37] Harris, n.1 above, 5.

out an area in which the full, unencumbered owner can pursue his or her interests subject only to the restraints and liabilities imposed by the general law, or by agreement. On the other hand, that is not the case when ownership is split, as with a trust, so that benefit, management, and (sometimes) title inhere in different people. The trustee is not free to pursue his or her own interests at the expense of the beneficiary's or the trust's objects.

The point is important because if the leading incidents of ownership—benefit, management, and title—are united in the same person, that person is in reality the owner of the thing, even if technically 'ownership' is located in, say, a limited company controlled by that person. The veil of a company or trust can properly be lifted if all the shareholders or beneficiaries are the same as the directors or trustees. In that case nothing restrains the pursuit by them of their own self-interest. They are, in effect, unencumbered owners of the assets. Conversely, if the leading incidents are split, as in the case of an ordinary trust, in which the trustees and beneficiaries are not identical, technical 'ownership' in the assets can be located as the law of the system finds convenient—in the trustees, the beneficiaries, a juristic person, or nobody.[38] No one fully owns the assets, because full ownership requires that the incidents of benefit, management, and title be united.

It is a pleasure to mull over Harris's well-argued themes in *Property and Justice*, to agree with some and disagree with others. Do the points of disagreement merely reflect the differing viewpoints of a common lawyer and a civilian? Is it important that 'ownership in common law systems is not a term of art'?[39] I think not, but others must judge.

[38] T Honoré, 'Trusts: The Inessentials', in J Getzler (ed.), *Rationalising Property, Equity and Trusts: Essays in Honour of Edward Burn* (OUP, 2003), 7–20; reprinted in (2003) 4 *Trusts e attività fiduciarie* 497–506.

[39] Harris, n.1 above, 86.

8

The Morality of James Harris's Theory of Property

*David Lametti**

People everywhere invoke 'justice' in political and ethical controversies and in criticizing and applying the law. Against that, two and a half millennia of speculative thought have yielded no agreement about what justice is. Indeed, in addition to diametrically opposed conceptions of justice, there are those who say justice does not exist. . . .

Such disagreements and scepticism about justice are familiar enough. More surprisingly, there is no consensus, and there is also scepticism, about the concept of property. All societies have property institutions of one kind or another. We all make plans and enter into transactions which take for granted the blindingly obvious fact that property institutions exist. We also, from time to time, disagree on moral and political grounds about how property should be allocated among us. Yet when speculative thought is brought to bear on the subject, it appears that the very idea of property is so malleable that, again, there is no agreement about what it is and, believe it or not, there are sceptics who deny that there is any such thing as property.

James Harris, Preface to *Property and Justice*[1]

(i) Introduction: In What Sense Moral?

So begins *Property and Justice*, James Harris's foundational work on the concept of property. *Property and Justice* answers the scepticism identified both in attempting to elaborate the question of what property is, and identifying and assessing the strength of various justifications for private property. In its two parts, Harris first provided a rich conceptual description of a 'malleable' institution, and then went on to assess the normative weight that ought to be given to various kinds of

* Associate Professor of Law and Member, Institute of Comparative Law, McGill University. My personal, professional, and intellectual debt to J.W. Harris cannot be measured. In addition to his intellect and scholarship, I am grateful for his kindness, guidance, and encouragement—especially when we disagreed. He was a paragon of human decency, and a truly remarkable man. I would like to thank the Facoltà di giurisprudenza, Università degli studi di Perugia for offering workspaces conducive to thought about property, and D. Gordon Cruess for his careful reading of the text and valuable comments.

1 JW Harris, *Property and Justice* (OUP, 1996), p. vii.

justificatory argument about the justice of the property institution ('property-specific justice reasons'). Filtering out the 'dross from the gold' with understandable temerity, Harris arrived at the following conclusion on justifying property:

> The upshot consists of a mix of morally viable property-specific justice reasons. I offer them to all those concerned with political and legal questions about distribution and property-institutional design. They are relevant to such questions because it is these same property-specific justice reasons which, I shall argue, support a moral right of every citizen of a modern State that his society should provide a property institution, but only one which is structured so as to take account of what justice does indeed require.

Herein lies an intriguing aspect of Harris's *opus*. He was—not surprisingly given his professional academic context—a legal positivist, maintaining to some degree the separation of law and morals,[2] though, as will become evident, an 'inclusive' or 'soft' positivist.[3] The first part of his book describes the hallmarks of an institution that has no necessary link to any specific set of moral underpinnings. That is, he wished to say something about the justness of property, without necessarily saying anything conclusive about the just society. Yet Harris was a profoundly moral person, and the conclusions he drew on property and justice, positing, in effect, property as a human right, seem to point to not only a contingently moral institution as a soft positivist might argue, but also a morally *necessary* institution, one that can form the basis of not only a claim-right but, indeed, also of a just society. In short, it is a requirement of justice that every society have a property institution of some sort.

Is there a contradiction here? Harris sidestepped the issue of the formal relationship between property and morality neatly:

> There is no 'true' property in the sense of a uniquely correct use of terminology. We shall also eschew any search for 'true property' in another sense. We assume that 'property' does not refer to a morally contested concept in the way that justice does. It would be a contradiction to affirm of a social institution both that it was perfectly just and also that it was devoid of moral status. We wish to preserve the sense of 'property' such that it is no contradiction to predicate of any particular property institution, or of all property institutions, that it or they flout the requirements of justice. We shall leave to one side that familiar jurisprudential controversy between those legal positivists who claim that the existence of a legal system is one thing, its moral merits another, and anti-positivists who deny this on the

[2] While not clearly stated by Harris, this is fairly inferred. In discussing Hart, Harris points out that even if morality hovers over the law, it is not intrinsic to it. Moreover, Harris notes that one can make sense of the legal duty without questioning whether it ought to be done. Later, discussing Fuller, Harris maintained that positivists were concerned with law as a matter of descriptive legal science, while others such as Fuller were speaking about the functioning of legal institutions. See the discussions in JW Harris, *Legal Philosophies* (2nd edn., Butterworths, 1997), chs. 9 and 11 *passim*, and at 127 and 154. Part I of *Property and Justice*, n. 1 above, attempts the neutral description of private property, while Part II addresses the institutional justification and design, and, by necessity, its morality.

[3] There is no need to cite the abundance of literature defining and distinguishing these terms as well as the debates over them. For my purposes, it is safe to say that a soft positivism allows for some legal rules to include or incorporate moral norms.

ground that the moral goodness enter into the very concept of law. Someone committed to the latter view either denies the propriety of speaking about 'unjust laws', or at least affirms that the word 'law' in 'unjust law' points to a derivative or non-central instance of the true concept of law. It might be possible to take a similar tack with property, and to insist that a complex of rules which imposed unjust obligations or which distributed wealth unfairly was not a true system of 'property'. To adopt such a position one would have to have already established the basis in justice of true property. We leave it aside because it would befuddle our entire enterprise.[4]

By avoiding an inquiry into the nature of 'true property', Harris wished to free himself of the trappings of all too familiar jurisprudential debates, focusing rather on what one might call the substance of property: its contours and its justifications. Indeed, in terms of the structure of the book, Harris appears to give both the legal and the moral their respective due: the formal division of his book is in two parts, one describing property in its social and legal practice, and the other setting out its justifications. In terms of what has famously been called descriptive sociology, any property institution was comprised of trespassory rules protecting rights along a spectrum of ownership, and none of the various 'property' outcomes were necessarily determined by some concept of 'true property'.[5] With respect to moral discourse, any specific property institution in any society had in some way to pass muster in a justificatory discourse focused on property itself: property-specific justice reasons (thus avoiding the larger philosophic debates about justice which are as old as Socrates). This formal separation of Parts (i) and (ii) is an aptly symbolic embodiment of the positivist reconciliation: contingent connections but no necessary one; a rich property institution, but no true one. And yet, by the end of the argument, property, and indeed private property, is infused with a great deal of moral weight: while not 'true', it is laced with a great deal of justice.

So in formal terms, the argument is rather open-ended with respect to the morality or moralities of the institution of property. How persuasive is this reconciliation, or indeed non-reconciliation, between property law and morality? My purpose here is to assess Harris's contribution by bringing to light some of his own moral assumptions, and by viewing his theory in light of some more explicitly moral theories of property. These latter theories tend to be North American in origin (perhaps a reaction to the excesses of rights talk in these parts), and not always framed in the analytic terms of Oxford legal discourse. The purpose of this chapter is to survey this terrain and look for commonalities and differences, and to identify and elaborate some of the implications of the divergent positions.

The conclusion that I shall reach is that Harris's overall theory of property does indeed exhibit an internal morality, one which is grounded in the fostering of individual autonomy and development and that can form the legitimate basis of

[4] See n. 1 above, 139–40.

[5] Harris would often put this question of 'true property' to me directly in conversation. He remained unconvinced that any formal inclusion of morality in the institution of private property did not import this particular implication.

a human right to property. The more weight one gives property in its role in human development, the closer one gets to positing it as a human right and calling it a component of justice. Thus Harris's view of property does contain what are, in effect, moral rules or assumptions, and the line between necessary and contingent becomes obscured by talk of property as a human right. This 'thin view' of justice differs from other defensible moral theories of property that have a wider grounding, particularly in non-individualistic goals. The differences between the two approaches will be most manifest in what one might call the clash between 'concept' and 'context', in both the understanding and justification for private property, a fundamental tension that runs throughout property scholarship. None of this means that there necessarily exists a form of 'true property' that can be deduced through reason, and that becomes the standard to adjudicate other manifestations of the property phenomenon.

(ii) Harris's *Property and Justice* in a Nutshell[6]

The outline of James Harris's theory of property will be familiar to the reader. In Part I of *Property and Justice*, Harris sets out to describe the elements of a private property which any private property system will exhibit. In the end, Harris identifies two necessary elements: trespassory rules and an ownership spectrum. The latter is the various *congeries* of entitlement that the holder of a property right might have with respect to some object of social wealth, varying in power from the most minimal or limited form of control right ('mere property') to the most powerful and exclusionary right of 'full-blooded ownership'. These entitlements, all of which are called 'ownership interests', are posited in the optic of a property relationship between the individual interest-holder and all other claimants. While not completely linear—there is a point of disjuncture on the spectrum at which point the power of transmission is included in the interest, increasing immensely the powers of ownership—the spectral metaphor ensures that the range of entitlements is generally ascending: one moves up the spectrum to more powerful rights. The spectrum is categorized by open-endedness, and permitted self-seeking for the interest-holder, except where expressly limited. Thus full-blooded ownership is almost completely unlimited, mere property much more limited.

The other necessary element of private property, trespassory rules, are those rules that protect the holder's right by excluding or limiting others from exercising

[6] I have dealt with some of the justificatory issues more fully in D Lametti, 'Property and (Perhaps) Justice' (1997) 43 *McGill LJ* 663. The gist of the argument therein is that while arguments grounded in autonomy are critical to understanding and justifying private property, they do not capture the fullness of the institution; indeed, without other non-rights-based arguments, autonomy-based arguments can distort our understanding of private property. While Harris had also built his justificatory argument in part on social convention, the structure of the argument, in my view, relegated it to a secondary role, allowing Harris's argument fairly to be characterized as rights-based.

similar rights on the same object of social wealth, or indeed, at the upper ends of the spectrum, from interfering at all with that object of social wealth. These are obligations imposed on an open-ended category of persons to respect the ownership interest of others.[7] While described first by Harris in the chronology of the argument in *Property and Justice*, in my view the ownership interests that these trespassory rules protect are conceptually prior; first the interest then the means by which it is secured.

Interesting are the occasional or contingent elements of property identified by Harris, which, for him, are by no means necessary features of the institution: property limitation rules, property duty and privilege rules, appropriation and property expropriation rules. These elements build upon the 'minimal structure' of the ownership spectrum and trespassory rules by limiting or enhancing the ownership spectrum in some way. What is of particular interest, in my view, is those specific kinds of rules which limit the exercise of ownership interests or constrain the allocation of ownership interests, and what their presence implies for property theory: limitation, duty, and expropriation rules. Harris notes that property limitation rules and property expropriation rules are omnipresent in most societies, though property duty rules are not. Yet even for property limitation and expropriation rules, given that they are not categorized as 'necessary', the conceptual picture given by Harris is one that could conceive a property system without them, notwithstanding their ubiquity in practice.

In the end, one is left with a set of descriptive categories that is quite flexible and able to accommodate any number of variations. There is no formal essence of property beyond these possibilities: Harris chose to describe these categories as flexible and changeable. Yet in the face of this flexibility he was not sceptical about the existence of this institution: private property is indeed a distinct, identifiable, and important legal and social institution, notwithstanding the absence of more formal rigid boundaries between property and other forms of socio-legal ordering.[8] And despite its elusiveness, people share an intuitive sense of what property is.[9]

The second part of *Property and Justice* deals with the justification of the institution of private property. As seen in the passage cited above, Harris circumscribed his analysis to only those justifications for private property which were limited to private property: *property-specific* justice reasons. These reasons were mid-level arguments about justice that were posited as independent of some larger master vision of private property, exhibited in wider theories of justice. That is, these larger, general-level arguments involved, in Harris's view, moral claims about property, and pointed towards an ultimate basis for property rights. These macro-level

[7] And what James Penner rather insightfully and incisively has called an *in rem* duty of non-interference: see J Penner, *The Idea of Property in Law* (OUP, 1998), 25–9.

[8] Such views of property's malleability have been attacked from all sides: see J Penner, 'The "Bundle of Rights" Picture of Property' (1996) 43 *UCLA LR* 711; and TC Grey, 'The Disintegration of Property', in J R Pennock and J W Chapman (eds.), *Property* (Nomos XXII, NYUP, 1980), 69.

[9] See n. 1 above, 6–8.

arguments were, first, natural rights to private property, secondly, social convention as, if not the sole basis, at least one of the ultimate bases of property rights, and, thirdly, that equality of resources should bear on the distribution and use of private property.

Each of these three categories of justification comprises a meta-group of argument, embedded in some wider grand theory. Applied at the highest level of abstraction, a necessarily moral master vision would mediate between these larger arguments to yield a justification for private property. On the other hand, mid-level justificatory arguments particular to private property, according to Harris, could be advanced without subscribing to such a (moral) master vision. Thus, one could fruitfully discuss property justification without making larger conclusions about justice.

Harris had grouped these property-specific justifications into four categories of argument. The first type of justificatory argument comes about as the result of an individual's specific interaction with the world. Arguments justifying private property based on claims emanating from protecting self-ownership, from rewarding deserving behaviour, from protecting 'creation-without-wrong', from protecting first acquisition, and from fostering personality or privacy, all fall into this category. Harris allowed no weight to be given to some of these arguments—protecting self-ownership, creation-without-wrong, and first acquisition—and only limited weight to others—protecting personality and privacy. Of particular note is that, where desert rewarding good property 'behaviour' can be linked to a property right, some justificatory weight should be given to a theory promoting those actions. Desert theories which attach to one's labour thus outline the 'shell of a natural right', and give support to the notion that one should be rewarded for labouring without necessarily specifying the desert. The exact nature of the reward or, more precisely, the content of the right must be supplied by the societal context, and, given our tradition, does often end up being the rewarding of the property right in the resource.

The second category contained the arguments for and against private property, based on promoting and protecting individual freedom and autonomy. All arguments fostering individual freedom are accorded some *prima facie* weight, according to Harris, because they have enough persuasive weight, given the value of individual freedom and autonomy in our society. At the end of the day, these arguments are accorded great justificatory weight by Harris, giving the individual pride of place in Harris's schema. They thus form the basis for the claim of a property institution as a basic human right.

The third type of argument gathers instrumental justifications. These utilitarian concerns assess the type of property institution one should have, given one's specific goals and objectives in utilizing the property institution. According to Harris, these play a primary role in the institutional design of private property, which is itself a second-order consideration to be broached when one has already opted for private property, as a justified means of social ordering. Incentives to create wealth and market-instrumental value can be important types of instrumental justification, say in the case of intellectual property.

Finally, in the fourth category, Harris places social convention and equality arguments. However, as mentioned above, he had already identified these as two larger, general, and meta-level arguments for private property. Social convention arguments hold that private property is a product of socio-political agreement. Equality arguments specifically serve as a benchmark for analysing the distribution of private property. Thus, these arguments seem to operate at both the middle and higher levels of justification, making it sometimes unclear how they remain property-specific justice reasons and how much weight is to be given to them at the middle level.

Harris examined each of the various strands of these four categories of justification under the light of his initial assumptions about justice, and the specific imperatives of institutional requirements. The requirements of minimal justice were three: (1) the protection of natural equality; (2) the value of autonomous choice; and (3) the protection of bodily integrity. In his casting, these assumptions served only to justify private property, and are not necessarily the foundation for larger claims for social ordering. Here Harris notes the normative significance of a variety of other considerations, most importantly that wealth disparity does not undermine the property institution, though some attention must be paid to the potentially nefarious impact that property might have in larger social relations: property's alleged domination potential.

Harris's conclusions are important. The boldest is that there are no natural rights to full-blooded ownership. According to Harris, full-blooded ownership, to the extent that it exists and is protected by legal trespassory rules, is a creation of human convention and must find its ultimate justification in one or more of the other identified rationales. With the stress on autonomy, all property freedoms are *prima facie* valuable, but none sacrosanct. Harris concludes that property can be a just and justified institution, offering his own summary conclusion as follows:

> [W]e have cleared the normative undergrowth by eliminating some hoary philosophical dead wood. Property institutions cannot be erected on natural rights to full-blooded ownership, because there are none. 'Self-ownership' may have a (rhetorical) role to play in the context of the bodily-use freedom principle, but its invocation in the context of external resources is illegitimate. The notion that persons constitute themselves by absorbing everything they own is bizarre fancy. Speculative assertions about the real pre-history of property have little to contribute....
>
> We have sorted other normative considerations into an ordering of approximate significance. Thing-fetishism is relevant to moral aspiration not to the legislator. Equality of resources has a role to play only in the context of that which is genuinely 'windfall' wealth. Domination-potential is of pervasive significance, wealth-disparity is not. Social convention, including juristic doctrine, has inescapable importance, but is never conclusive.
>
> In the end, we are left with a mix of property-specific justice reasons—property freedoms, labour-desert, privacy, incentives and markets, independence, and basic needs. None of these imports precise, context-free considerations, and their mix can do no more than

structure our answers to general or specific problems. On the contested planes of politics or adjudication, there can be no such thing as judgment-free determinacy. In any case, property questions are inseparably affected by the social setting in which a property institution exists.[10]

Thus we have the potential bases for a right to a property institution. In a sense, Harris has outlined a series of touchstones by which to assess the justification and design of the institution of private property. These conclusions point to a pluralistic justification of property rights. Such a justification admits the role of context: the various justifications might apply in different circumstances and no one justification is sufficient. A number of property-specific justice reasons may work together to justify the shell or the substance of a specific property right, with convention filling out the latter details of substance. Thus the role of convention is quite strong, even if understated.

This conclusion is also quite consistent with the idea put forward by Harris that there is no 'true property' by which to measure other less perfect forms of the institution. A malleable institution—there is plenty of scope for diversity on the property spectrum, not just for rights but limits and duties as well—justified in a pluralistic manner, certainly supports the initial hypothesis that no one true form exists. However, this insight does not mean that the institution is any less moral. In the case of a liberal Western society, the arguments which Harris finds most favourable are those linked to autonomy. And with respect to autonomy, Harris states that institutional options that allow for more choice are generally to be favoured over those that do the contrary.[11] Harris has not escaped the larger argument about justice at the meta-level; rather, he has expounded a theory based on a particular conception of justice and morality.

This is evident in the conclusions about the kind of property system which will meet the particular demands of justice. Despite the malleability of property, and despite there being no true property, not all systems will pass justificatory muster in a society that shares our values:

Beginning with our minimalist conception of justice which did not include property, we have reached the conclusion that total abolition of property would treat everyone unjustly. There is a moral background right vested in each citizen of a modern society that a property institution of some kind must be maintained.

It has emerged, however, that it is not every variety of property institution which will satisfy this background right. It must incorporate certain features, and justice requires

[10] See n. 1 above, 365.

[11] Ibid. 173. Harris writes:

Given that respecting personhood is intrinsic to just treatment, it follows that, other things being equal, it counts in favour of the justice of an institution if it accords a wider rather than a narrower scope for autonomous choice. In that sense, 'freedom' is a consideration of justice. Furthermore, other things being equal, the wider the range of autonomous choice the better. ... '[F]reedom' of any kind presupposes choice and, at the abstract level, more choices must entail more freedom. All liberals and most non-liberals would, it is thought, assent to the bald assertion that autonomous choice is to be valued, differ though they do as to the kinds of social arrangement which make genuine choices possible.

that any actual institution which does not incorporate them should be altered so that it does.

Most importantly . . . the social setting of the property institution must be such that the community shoulders the obligation to meet the basic needs of all citizens. The discharge of that obligation may have implications which have nothing to do with property, but it may also entail some particular requirements of property-institutional design—including expropriatory taxing rules, appropriation rules where discharge of basic needs itself requires conferring property, and quasi-ownership holdings by public agencies.

The property-freedom argument and the various instrumental arguments combine to make money and cashable rights indispensable features of a property institution. The same is true of full-blooded ownership of chattels. All dwellings must be the subject of ownership interests, the point on the ownership spectrum to be determined according to a mix of property-specific justice reasons—which includes the shell of a natural right to privacy, domination-potential in the case of family units, and incentive and market-instrumental considerations. The use-channelling and use-policing merits of property institutions, dangers of domination-potential, and market-instrumental and incentive considerations must all be taken into account on any question whether a major enterprise should be the subject of a (packaged) ownership or (packaged) quasi-ownership interest. Ownership interests over intellectual property should be recognized because, and only to the extent that, they have incentive and market-instrumental value, save where conventional assumptions about labour-desert have crystallized around them.[12]

In the end, we have a private property system predicated on ownership, subject to limits that ensure that a minimum 'justice threshold' is met, thus fostering a general basic level of equality. However, notwithstanding the claims of context on the final product, the archetypal minimal features of Harris's justified property system, some examples of which are seen in the preceding excerpt, are those that fall squarely within the purview of individual freedom and autonomy arguments, and in effect justify a *private* property system. Social arguments other than those ensuring a basic level of individual equality, whether instrumental or conventional, appear to be relegated to a secondary status.

I have argued elsewhere that the stress on autonomy and freedom arguments makes Harris, in the end, a rights-based thinker. That is, ultimately there is a master vision that is omnipresent in Harris's theory of justification; one based on individual autonomy, and one that is rights-based.[13] But our disagreement on this characterization—more than a quibble, but less than an intellectual schism—is more a question of including certain excluded arguments and emphasizing others, rather than disagreeing on the process of justification. What is more important for the purposes of this essay is that the justifications reflect a particular focus—the individual—and a particular goal—her ability to develop her potential freely and autonomously, and to flourish. This stress and these aspirations reflect a

[12] See n. 1 above, 305–6.

[13] See Lametti, n. 6 above, 720–5. Harris admitted this when commenting personally on a version of that cited text: he stated that, when push came to shove, he did indeed come down on the side of the individual.

functional morality, specific to our society, that is internalized in the property discourse that animates it. This is what I believe can accurately be called the internal morality of Harris's property theory. It may not necessarily be linked to all potential forms of private property, but it is strongly linked to our particular society and its chosen form of private property.

This morality is evident with respect to the underlying assumptions posited by Harris. The tenets held out as bases for assessing individual arguments are closely linked to a particular culture: one based on liberal Western values of freedom, equality and bodily integrity, where basic needs must be met. Thus, the core assumptions do a great deal more work than Harris admits: they are not simply property-specific, but tie the analysis to the very discourse on justice that Harris was trying to eschew.[14] Not that there is anything wrong with that! Indeed, a society's justification for private property must necessarily reflect its values.

The underlying assumptions also have an impact at the level of description of the institution of private property. Harris's initial assumptions not only imply that property rules are grounded in a sort of minimal morality, but they also explain the categories that organize Harris's description of private property. The first two assumptions, I believe, are particularly instructive. First, the natural equality of human beings gives a *prima facie* entitlement to natural resources. Equally important, the assumption of equality forces distribution and use of resources through a private property mechanism—by necessity creating inequalities—to be justifiable on some grounds. This effectively necessitates a moral discourse of some sort. Secondly, the assumption of individual autonomy shows that at a base level property is in service of a teleology, in this case framed in terms of an individual good. The goal of the property institution is based primarily on the goal of promoting individual well-being.

This internal morality evident in the underlying assumptions has an impact on other aspects of both the description of the institution and the justificatory discourse underlying property. Regarding the articulation of the parameters of property, the attempt at neutral description in Part I of *Property and Justice* is conditioned by a view of what is most significant in the property institution: the individual. If property-limitation rules are present in every society, and if ownership without any limits at all—totality ownership—is an empty concept, as Harris admits, then why are property-limitation rules not considered a necessary feature of the property institution? Clearly, the answer lies in the way in which the

[14] Moreover, these tenets were meant to transcend, according to Harris, both moral realism and conventionalism to overcome linguistic and conceptual scepticism. Harris tried to navigate a middle ground between the argument that there is an objective or transcendent moral standpoint, accessible to all human beings, and the position that all morals are relative, thereby forcing a society to agree on what its moral standards will be. While I am sympathetic to the attempt to pursue a balanced theoretical approach to questions concerning the ontology and the epistemology of justice, I remain unconvinced that Harris had succeeded in doing so. In the end, a morality at times realist, at times conventionalist, shines through the protection of the individual and her autonomy.

institution has been cast, mainly, if not only, in terms justifiable by individual rights-based arguments. This matter is raised in the third part of this chapter.

On the level of justification, this morality informs the relation between individuals and society, and in the role social context plays in justifying the right. While Harris is careful in formal terms to posit a role for social convention and instrumental considerations, with the exception of the collective responsibility for meeting and maintaining basic individual needs, the role is usually one of filling in the content of basic rights already defined and justified by a more individualistic argument, usually freedom and autonomy. Thus the 'concept' of private property as an individually-grounded, ownership-based notion, takes precedence over the 'context' where that context does not share the same autonomy-based assumptions: a minimally just private property regime, as outlined by Harris, can only be seen as a basic human right in these terms.

We can go further by stating the corollary: that some measure of this institution of private property, for these property-specific justice reasons, becomes a prerequisite for a just society, and suggests a privileged role for private property in social ordering. While Harris tries to limit his analysis to the 'property-specific', the discourse justifying property itself has wider implications about justice in the general sense. Given the link between the underlying morality of property-specific justice reasons to higher-order arguments about justice generally, the conclusion that some form of property constitutes a basic human right, grounded in justice, should not surprise. But we should be careful to note that we may now have moved from the contingent to the necessary, from a form of soft positivism to something more.

The important point for this chapter is that there is an internal morality present in Harris's theory; one that focuses on individual autonomy and that is rights-based. While I have disagreed on the weighting one gives to autonomy and rights, they remain one of the most important factors to be weighed. Thus, it must be conceded that Harris's specific conclusions on the structure and justification of the property institution are quite justifiable. But the larger points, implicitly supported by Harris's method, remain: justificatory discourse is necessary; it reflects societal values, and this underlying morality is reflected by the parameters of the institution itself. The room for disagreement on conclusions is achieved by altering the weight or priority given to any of the assumptions and associated reasons, even within a discourse where much of this remains shared by interlocutors.

So while Harris often questioned explicitly moral theories of property by asking, 'is there a true property?', it appears to me that the question is a red herring. Harris's own theory reflects a strong moral view of human beings, their autonomy, and their development. His conclusions reflect a widely shared and highly defensible view. Thus there is no need for a moral theory to posit a 'true' property: the morality is contextual. It is found in the assumptions behind, as well as the justifications for (and thus, the purpose of), the choice of private property over some other form of resource allocation and management, and in its actual design. This, I argue, is the inherent, or internal, morality of Harris's theory of property. The protection and promotion of individual autonomy forms an important—perhaps *the* most important—component of the dominant modern Western idea of property.

(iii) Thicker Moral Approaches to Property

Other moral approaches to property are possible. In recent years, a number of more explicitly moral approaches to property have surfaced, which move beyond the individual, rights-based moralities of a work such as Harris's.[15] These works attempt, *inter alia*, to portray private property as an institution understandable not simply in terms of rights, and most definitely not comprehensible in formal terms, such as an exclusive right of non-interference by others. Rather, private property is posited as being more inherently and fundamentally complex. Here private property is seen as having a social aspect, or, indeed, as being a social, contextual institution, and justified by a very moral or ethical discourse.

These moral approaches, in contrast to Harris's moral approach identified above, might be described as being more 'thick', either because of a heightened sensibility towards collective concerns, or going so far as to include obligations regarding property. Some are a reaction to environmental imperatives,[16] others to protecting the ongoing value of land,[17] others are motivated by distribution and poverty issues, and others by a more abstract sense that rights-based theories are inadequate on their own to explain or justify property.[18] Such attempts are not new. In the Oxford context, A.M. Honoré had begun to articulate a number of arguments in his various articles on private property.[19] While I shall not pretend

[15] See, e.g., J Penner, *The Idea of Property in Law* (OUP, 1997), and J Waldron, *The Right to Private Property* (OUP, 1987). Stephen Munzer's book is also mainly rights-based, though it does posit a more important role for the social through utilitarian justifications in ch. 8, and some accounting for the 'social aspects' of private property in Part II: see SR Munzer, *A Theory of Property* (CUP, 1988). However, he remains sceptical of defining private property in a manner that too greatly downplays autonomy: see SR Munzer, 'Property as Social Relations', in SR Munzer (ed.), *New Essays in the Legal and Political Theory of Property* (CUP, 2001).

[16] See the work of Eric Freyfogle, for example, 'Ownership and Ecology' (1993) 43 *Case W Res LR* 1269 and 'The Construction of Ownership' [1996] *U Ill LR* 173.

[17] See, e.g., WNR Lucy and C Mitchell, 'Replacing Private Property: The Case for Stewardship' (1996) 55 *CLJ* 566; K Gray, 'Equitable Property' (1996) 49 *CLP* 157, 161; and EJ McCaffery, 'Must We Have the Right to Waste?' in SR Munzer (ed.), *New Essays in the Legal and Political Theory of Property* (CUP, 2001) 76.

[18] See G Alexander, *Commodity and Propriety: Competing Visions of Property in American Legal Thought 1776–1970* (U Chicago Press, 1997).

[19] AM Honoré, 'Ownership', in AG Guest (ed.), *Oxford Essays in Jurisprudence* (OUP, 1961), and reprinted in AM Honoré, *Making Law Bind: Essays Legal and Philosophical* (OUP, 1987), 161; AM Honoré 'Property, Title and Redistribution' (1977) 10 *Archiv für Rechts-Fund Sozial Philosophiens* 107, and reprinted in AM Honoré, *Making Law Bind*, at 215; and AM Honoré 'Social Justice' (1962) 8 *McGill LJ* 77, and reprinted in AM Honoré, *Making Law Bind*, at 193. Honoré had included a minimal duty not to harm others in his elaboration of incidents in 'Ownership', and also specified that property was liable to seizure, a clear limit on absolute ownership. Moreover, as noted below, he appeared to have understood that the nature of a property right changed with the nature of the resource.

to cover the field, I will attempt to outline briefly three such recent arguments. Each of these offers, in my view, some augmentation or corrective to Harris's more minimal, individualistic view of property, and assists in enhancing the property picture. Two of these contain more explicitly moral views of property, affecting both the understanding of private property itself and its justification, while the third potentially posits a more open-ended sort of property discourse. All of these arguments draw from a less individualistic view of society, a view that has implications for property discourse.

(a) Joseph W. Singer: Property and Obligation

The first, and perhaps most explicitly moral, understanding of property is advanced by Joseph William Singer in his book, *Entitlement: The Paradoxes of Property*.[20] The text presents a powerful argument for a more limited notion of property. The style of Singer's book is narrative, orienting itself around a number of specific and paradoxical stories and cases involving private property. It thus stands in marked contrast to *Property and Justice*, whose style, we have seen, aims at neutral description and analysis. The examples serve to frame the central theses of the book: that property cannot be understood simply on the ownership model, that property is a limited concept, that property is a contextual relationship, and that obligations are an important part of the property relationship. Indeed, one might observe that the very form of Singer's work serves to illustrate that the content of a whole category of property norms should be made more explicit.

Harris had written of the *ownership* spectrum. According to Singer, the ownership model—that which posits private property as a relatively absolute[21] set of powers or rights in a bundle, which presents the institution as self-regarding from the perspective of the owner, and which orients ownership as the organizing idea of private property—while pervasive, is defective. Despite some progress, we remain mired in the absolutist paradigm.

In terms of the institution of private property, Singer argues that the ownership model presents a flawed description of the practice and structure of property, a practice and structure that in reality posits an understanding of property rights that is more limited and regulated. That is, Singer also points out that there are inherent tensions in the ownership model, which cannot be settled without some

[20] JW Singer, *Entitlement: The Paradoxes of Property* (Yale UP, 2000).

[21] I use the term 'relatively absolute' here and elsewhere in this text because, as Harris was fond of pointing out to me, very few writers would ever claim that property rights are totally absolute. Indeed, Harris identified such a completely absolute view, labelled it 'totality ownership', and called it an 'Aunt Sally' argument, erected to be knocked over with the first good throw: n. 1 above, 132–8. While I agree with this view, I posit that it is equally important to note that the positions on ownership which are *relatively* absolute, in that they contain only very few limits, such as Harris's full-blooded ownership on his ownership spectrum, are also defective. Like totality ownership, they remain part of the absolutist paradigm, and as such are simply too unlimited.

sort of government regulation, and that such regulation can never be neutral, but must choose which claim will prevail. The system also fails to describe how to resolve situations where property claims conflict with other sorts of claims based on personal rights. Which rights are to be given more weight?

In terms of the concept of property, Singer points out that the ownership model mis-describes the ideals underlying the institution, as well as the actual rules of the institution. Of particular import are Singer's conclusions that the model allocates 'burdens of persuasion' in a morally unacceptable manner, and, indeed, that the model is wholly premised on the position that the meaning of property is clear, and is not a matter of controversial political or moral judgement.[22] Rather, '[p]roperty does not come in a preset package. There is no simple definition of property that can be posited without making controversial value judgments about how to choose between conflicting interests'.[23] Finally, Singer argues that owners have obligations as well as rights; these obligations are moral, and some should be made legally binding:

> Owners have obligations both to share their wealth with the dispossessed and to use their property in a way that is compatible with the interests of non-owners in being able to enter the system to become owners. . . . All this means is that there is no core of property we can define that leaves owners free to ignore entirely the interests of others. Owners have obligations; they have always had obligations. We can argue about what those obligations should be, but no one can seriously argue that they should not exist.[24]

These conclusions, supported in the various narratives presented by Singer, challenge a number of Harris's presuppositions. The first is regarding the possibility of describing private property in some neutral manner. Harris concluded that only the ownership spectrum and trespassory rules were necessary parts of the property institution. If Singer's analysis is correct, then the other sorts of property rules identified by Harris that limit the individual owner—property-limitation, expropriation and even property-duty rules—would all necessarily be a part of the property institution. Thus Harris may have been guilty of underestimating the concept of limits in his description of private property as only necessarily including trespassory rules, and thus under-weighing these other non-right-based elements. In fairness to Harris, it is simply a question of weight, as he had, to his credit, identified these other kinds of rules as contingent, yet ubiquitous parts of a private property system.

This can further be illustrated in terms of Harris's ownership spectrum. If Singer is correct, the bias of the ownership model perhaps predisposed Harris to exclude *ab initio* these non-rights based norms in his description of property.

[22] While James Penner has done excellent work in helping to define private property in conceptual terms, he is guilty of playing down property's controversial nature, and its need of justification. I am reminded of Penner's view that private property need not be justified, as it is 'well-nigh justifiable': n. 15 above, 206–7.

[23] See n. 20 above, 7.

[24] Ibid., 18.

Singer explicitly tries to shift the normative weight from the concept of *title* to the concept of *entitlement*:

> Property law fulfills two major functions. It creates presumptions about who gets to control particular resources, placing the burden of persuasion on the non-owner to justify an alternative result, and it defines the property interest that it will protect.... Both of these functions of property law are achieved by adopting rules that shape the contours of social relations. Whether the rules distribute powers over property, allocate burdens of persuasion, or define the allowable bundles of rights, the law enacts some form of social life....
>
> Rather than asking whether owners are legitimately subject to regulation in the public interest, it is often more appropriate to ask which set of rules will produce results that best satisfy human needs and desires and that best promote a free society that treats its members with fairness, respect, justice, and common decency.
>
> The new model of ownership does not make ownership irrelevant, but it puts the concept in its proper place. Property law is about *entitlements and obligations, which shape the contours of social relations.*[25]

Thus the self-regarding nature of title or ownership does not give its due to the larger context in which ownership rights are determined and exercised. Simple title or ownership is too narrow a concept to capture the multiplicity of contexts; rather the question becomes what one is entitled to in a particular context. Given these limits, according to Singer, we need to recognize private property as consisting of varied and multiple 'bundles of entitlements' (or, if called ownership, then defining ownership as control of more limited estates),[26] with both the allocation and the contents of the entitlement to be determined in a given social setting.

While Harris had posited a flexible spectrum of ownership interests, the self-regarding nature of the spectrum is perhaps over-stated. Harris had recognized the powers associated with ownership, both as an organizing idea and as a principle, and tried to describe the institution in those terms. He had also acknowledged the domination-potential of property and power relations associated with the resource. However, while this exercise of neutral description is analytically possible, it is extremely difficult to achieve, and even so careful a scholar as Harris did not completely achieve such a description. The weight of a rights-based concept such as ownership, the essentially controversial nature of private property itself, and the general societal context of liberal individualism make an attempt at neutral description virtually impossible.

Does this completely undermine the usefulness of Harris's ownership spectrum in understanding property relations? That is, the strong inclusion of duties and limits may also point to a larger flaw in the use of an ownership spectrum, which is too focused on rights. While I have made an independent series of substantive arguments, many of which are similar to those posited by Singer, it remains my view that, while the spectrum is too focused on rights, it remains a useful analytic and descriptive tool. Whatever one may say about duties and limits—and there is

[25] See n. 20 above, 61 (emphasis original). [26] Ibid., 209.

a lot that these concepts add to the necessary understanding of private property—private property, in balance, remains a great deal, if not mainly, about individual rights. Even those arguing for more contextual understandings of private property must admit to this obvious point: rights are still the key element in property relations. Thus a spectral metaphor taken from the perspective of the owner is still a helpful grouping for heuristic purposes, especially as it conforms to a great deal of the lay understanding of the institution.[27]

The inclusion of duties and obligations nonetheless complicates the spectrum, since the duties may be owed to individuals (for example, specific duties *vis-à-vis* specific resources), or to the collective generally (for example, a duty of stewardship with respect to a specific resource). The end result is that the spectrum cannot be understood uniquely from the perspective of the owner, and cannot be framed conceptually along the lines of self-regarding powers of ownership. The institution is much richer and more complex than the original spectrum—notwithstanding its explicit open-ended nature—as conceived by Harris.

The point on the inclusion of duty in the private property institution is particularly rich in potential. It is already a well-established point in property theory that a private property system cannot exist without trust: each owner must be able confidently to assume that others will respect ownership rights.[28] But Singer goes further on duties and obligations. Duties and obligations are a necessary part of the property 'picture':'[o]wnership without obligation is a form of dictatorship'.[29] Singer states that the source of obligation is moral, and that sometimes such obligations ought to be reflected in legal norms. Obligations are needed to ensure that owners share their wealth and use their resources in such a way as to allow others to become owners. He also re-states the idea that the basis for obligation is contextual, and that justified expectations form the basis for both entitlements and obligations. Yet on this point, contrary to Singer, regarding both the allocative and use functions of a private property system, we need more than an extended narrative on a case where a 'good owner' was loyal to his employees, since it might be argued that this instance is not really about property at all, but rather about some other type of obligation. While Singer has expressly attempted to place the underpinnings of this discussion on duties in the social context of property, more needs to be said about how the analysis will remain property-focussed. The 'reliance interest' posited by Singer is potentially quite wide.[30] Even if context dictates that we cannot know the answers to specific legal problems in advance, we need at least to articulate more clearly how this contextual discourse will proceed,

[27] We are a long way from Ackerman's rather simplistic portrayal of the 'lay' view of property as things; most people do appreciate that property entails some sort of relationship to other people. See BA Ackerman, *Private Property and the Constitution* (Yale UP, 1977)

[28] Most famously pointed out by C M Rose: see her 'Trust in the Mirror of Betrayal' (1995) 75 *Boston U LR* 531; and 'Property as the Keystone Right?' (1996) *71 Notre Dame LR* 363.

[29] See n. 20 above, 209.

[30] See the discussion of Singer in Harris, n. 1 above, 137–8. As I argue below, putting objects back into focus allows us to discuss issues of duty without being sceptical of ownership itself.

and how it manifests itself in legal *property* norms. I shall have more to say on this point below.

If Singer is correct, then on justification and specifically with respect to the role of context in determining the parameters of the property relationship there must also be a change in emphasis. As I pointed out above, the inclusion of justificatory or explanatory considerations other than those favouring or fostering individual autonomy ought to be given some measure of greater weight. In particular, Singer advocates a concentration on the relationships created by property. Focusing on rights as they shape the contours of larger social relations will necessarily lead to a wider and deeper inquiry of private property as determining allocations and uses of valuable objects of social wealth. Moreover, if true, then it may also be the case that Harris's basic conditions do not satisfy the equality condition of his own work, cast as it is in individualistic terms. In particular, as mentioned above, owners need to act in such a way as to allow others to enter the system: only property rights that are inherently limited will allow for this fact, and will thus satisfy the egalitarian principle. Reconciling Singer and Harris on this point would force Harris to admit that at least some property-limitation rules are in fact necessary, in order to fulfill the basic condition of minimal equality.

The essential analytic point is this: resources are scarce, and valued for precisely the reason that they have an understood economic or social value. Since private property by definition entails scarcity, and since by allocating the resource through a private property regime to individuals we create inequality, it is thus entirely justifiable and understandable that the institution comes with strings attached. Private property must in some way serve some greater good in order to be justified. While definitely important, the promotion of individual autonomy cannot persuasively stand as the sole reason justifying property rights. Some other goals, including collective ones, must be served. The analysis is goal-driven and therefore utilitarian, but is expressly moral as well, in that the goals served are more clearly moral and certainly more plural and complex than those in the more 'single-minded' and traditionally well-known forms of utilitarian analysis. The essential justificatory point is similar: what is sauce for the goose is sauce for the gander. The same kinds of arguments that justify conferring rights in objects of social wealth necessitate limits and obligations.

(b) Laura Underkuffler: The Presumptive Powers of Property

A second contribution to a thicker approach to understanding the morality of private property emerges from the work of Laura Underkuffler, and is best exemplified in her most recent book.[31] While the argument is sophisticated and complex, one might summarize her central thesis as revolving around 'the

[31] L S Underkuffler, *The Idea of Property: Its Meaning and Power* (OUP, 2003). The title is not to be confused with James Penner's book, *The Idea of Property in Law*, n. 15 above, also published by OUP!

presumptive powers of property'. Here the description of the property institution is not posited with explicitly moral elements, but illustrates a process which helps to frame the moral discourse used to justify and identify the limits of property rights.

Writing in more traditional analytic terms, Underkuffler, like Singer, begins generally with a socially-oriented understanding of private property.[32] This understanding sees property as an idea *and* an institution, with both social aspirations and social goals accepted as an inherent part of the right to private property. Her definition of private property is more particularized: property has a variety of contours or 'dimensions'. The purpose of identifying these dimensions is to give the fullest understanding of the property institution. Underkuffler, like all property theorists, identifies rights as one of these dimensions. However, in addition to a theory of rights, of which there are a number that could help understand property, and for each of which there are implications for the conception of property, Underkuffler identifies the space of field, the stringency of protection, and time as the three other necessary dimensions of property.

The second dimension of property, spatiality, puts the focus on what I have called the 'property-as-object'. In this analysis, Underkuffler focuses her inquiry on the nature of the resource to determine what impact it has on property relations. The third dimension, stringency, takes the element of property which delimits the scope of the right—what Harris had called a trespassory rule—and determines how the property right is to function in context. Here the degree of protection will depend on the presumptive power to be given to the right in a given spatial dimension: the stringency or robustness of the property rules will be framed accordingly. The fourth dimension, time, is quite simply the length of time for which the interest endures. In my understanding of Underkuffler's argument, time can also be framed as an element of the third dimension. That is, the length of time protected might just as easily be cast as part of the robustness of the right. One might think of an estate which is full in terms of powers, but short in terms of time. Nevertheless, this is quibbling and both aspects go to the nature of the right and its limits.

These categories are a useful addition to property theory, organizing to some extent in principled terms a classification of the kinds of powers and duties listed by Honoré in his famous article on ownership: these are: (i) the right to possess; (ii) the right to use; (iii) the right to manage; (iv) the right to the income; (v) the right to the capital; (vi) the right to security; (vii) transmissibility; (viii) absence of term; (ix) the duty to prevent harm; (x) the liability to execution; and (xi) a residuary interest.[33] Honoré's listing of incidents is meant to be flexible, with not all incidents needing to be present to have an ownership right. Underkuffler eschews a list, but rather provides an overarching structure in which the incidents

[32] Originally set out in L S Underkuffler-Freund, 'Property: A Special Right' (1996)71 *Notre Dame LR* 1033, and now revised as ch. 12 of Underkuffler, n. 31 above, at 141–9.

[33] Honoré, 'Ownership', n.19 above, 165–79 (cited to *Making Law Bind*).

might be fitted. The mapping is not perfect though; while the absence of a term goes to 'time', and the duty to prevent harm to 'stringency',[34] most of the other incidents can fall within the dimensions of either 'rights' or 'stringency', depending on how one frames the power in question and the rule delimiting it. Put differently, perspective makes the determination and delimitation of categories somewhat flexible. What is interesting about Underkuffler's categories is not only the attempt to classify the various elements of the property right, but also the inclusion of space as an element, and the open-endedness of the other categories: they are wide, flexible, and potentially quite inclusive, going further than the rights, liability, and duty listed by Honoré. As I have intimated, it is the dimension of space that I believe to be the key innovation in Underkuffler's listing, as it implies that the nature of the resource—physical or non-physical—can have an impact on the contours of the property right. While developed implicitly throughout the rest of the book, her argument could be strengthened by bringing this dimension more clearly to the fore.

Notwithstanding the identification of the dimensions of private property, the definition remains malleable. Underkuffler then focuses this contextual approach on the question of limits to private property, and, in particular, to the relationship between the property owner and the community. The 'common conception' of property resembles the absolutist idea of property: property serves to protect individual interests against the collective. The 'operative' conception is much weaker from the standpoint of the individual; it certainly does not have the protective function. From protective versus non-protective conceptions of property, she goes on to identify instances where the very presumptive power of property rights changes in the face of conflict with other, non-property rights, precisely according to which of these conceptions is employed and justified. That is, the presumptive power of a property claim will depend upon the values asserted by both the property claim and the counter-claims raised against them. These claims are socially constructed, malleable, and contentious in nature.

Generally, the presumptive powers of property are stronger where the claimed property right is different in kind from the competing public interest, but these property powers should have no presumptive priority when the competing public interest is of the same nature. The first kind of cases, in which property rights *prima facie* trump collective claims, involves land titles, exclusion, patents, and similar individual interests. Here the individual interest grounding the right is different from the interests underlying the rights asserted by the collective, and the protection of the individual requires a weighting in favour of the property right. The second, or 'tier-two' case, where property claims do not have some presumptively superior claim, involves, by way of example, environmental laws, zoning controls, and similar public

[34] Or even a category not identified by Underkuffler—duty.

interests. In these cases, the normative weight of the public claim is equal to the property rights claimed:

> There is no reason why the property interests of one person should be presumptively superior to the property interests of many persons, simply because the interests of the many are asserted 'publicly' or 'collectively'. *It is the nature of the interests and the values that they assert—not the identities or numbers of the holders—that should determine normative (and presumptive) power.* If the claimed property right and the competing public interest involve interests and values of the same kind—if, for instance, the land-use or preservation claims of one landowner are opposed by the collectively asserted land-use or preservation claims of others—there is no reason to give the individual claim presumptive power.[35]

This characterization is novel and interesting, and I cannot assess it completely here. In addition to analysing the overall assumptions behind, and contours of, the proposed structure, the particular nature of property claims, as identified, needs to be examined against more general assertions of all kinds of rights, to see if Underkuffler has indeed made a plausible case for distinguishing rights from property rights. Here it would appear that the real distinguishing comes down to identifying where societal interests can validly trump property rights, and vice versa. In such an analysis, the actual applied examples need to be analysed in light of the chosen structure and other understandings of property, to see if they are helpful in both resolving claims, and in better understanding the nature of property. My intuitive sense is that the structure, at first blush, is still greatly weighted in favour of the individual. For the purposes of this chapter, however, I can safely conclude that there is an explicit role for social context in the property relationship, and that property rights are not unlimited.

Harris too had described a malleable institution, one whose content was articulated to a large extent by social conventions. There is also some similarity to Harris, in that the role of rights (as both a dimension of property and in its framing as a presumptive power), as posited throughout Underkuffler's argument, is still extremely strong; as such, she at times does appear to be, if not wholly rights-based, then at least mainly so. Thus Underkuffler's top-tier category is quite powerfully protected by presumptively strong property claim rights that are not unlike the *prima facie* autonomy-based rights identified by Harris. However, on balance the similarities, to my mind, appear more formal than substantive. Underkuffler's context is more formally attuned to the social elements of property than is Harris's, and her role for context more robust, notwithstanding the continued (and indeed necessary) importance of rights in the understanding of property. The difference is one of degree, but it is nevertheless important.

The essential point is that the contextual powers and role of property in society are, in some way, captured in this understanding of the varying dynamics of property relations. When one delves behind the structure, one finds a sensitivity

[35] See Underkuffler, n. 31 above, 97 (emphasis original).

to moral argument in resolving any particular claim. That is, moral argument is used to identify the competing claims and then balance them off. The practical process of resolving property claims, and elaborating the property system goes to the very relation between the individual and the collective. Underkuffler has attempted to articulate why property rights act as trumps in some situations but not in others. This approach goes some way towards supplementing, and perhaps re-calibrating, the approach described by Harris. While Harris did invoke explicitly the idea of social convention as a determiner of property rights—usually to fill out the content of a right *prima facie* justified by some other argument—Underkuffler's view of the role played by the social setting of property appears to be more robust. It is wider, in the sense that it encapsulates more issues, and is deeper, in that its role as posited is more pronounced from the outset (and not in some secondary justificatory analysis). As far as the elaboration of the presumptive powers of property goes, it clearly adds a level of nuance to the understanding of the institution of private property, with different presumptive weights given to property rights in different circumstances, with different legal results.

Most explicit is the weighing of purposes, again, for example, in environmental or zoning claims. In such an instance, the use to which a certain resource is put is expressly at issue, and is tested against the standard by which society deems that the resource *ought* to be used. Here the explicit weighing of justifications occurs, taking into account rights and duties, social goals and purposes, expectations (following Singer), and the relation of the individual to the collective. This weighing is a thoroughly moral process.

It is worth repeating that Harris had identified a number of analogous considerations. He had implicitly accounted for the purpose of property in his moral arguments based on autonomy. He also understood the metaphorical weight of property as both a concept and principle in chapters 5 and 6 of *Property and Justice*, and recognized that too much weight accorded to the individual could result in the domination of others in other spheres. However, both in terms of substance and process, I would argue that these considerations were not adequately weighed, and their impact not otherwise accounted for. Here Underkuffler's more explicit process, and more inclusive substantive bases, represents an improvement, even if more work still needs to be done to examine fully all the implications of her argument. It is also clear that for Underkuffler, as indeed was the case for Harris, that ownership is less than absolute; it is still quite powerful for both writers, either at the level of 'full-blooded ownership' (Harris) or on the 'top-tier' analyses (Underkuffler).

One also finds in the 'dimensions' of property set out by Underkuffler some sensitivity to the object of property. This is especially true with respect to space. While the application of this dimension is explicitly to be relegated to the balancing process articulated and defended later in the book, the implication remains that certain kinds of objects—land and patents, say—seem to embody stronger rights claims than other objects; however, where the context points to something unique about the resource—for instance, the environmental sensitivity of a parcel of land—the converse might be true. 'The nature of the interest', as identified by Underkuffler in the weighing process, accounts in part for some examination of the actual object of social wealth in question. In my view, her method could be strengthened by more explicitly taking the resource into account in both her 'dimensions' and in her balancing method.

(c) An Analytic Role for Objects

The third, more explicitly moral argument regarding private property is my own.[36] I have left this modest but ongoing contribution for last, as a means of filling in gaps which I perceive in the other two thicker moral theories, as well as Harris's, whose theory I have used as a starting point, and as a means of expressing some of these concerns in terms similar to those used by Harris and others. In addition to echoing a number of the concerns raised by Singer and Underkuffler, in terms more familiar to analytic legal discourse, I have also tried to make the argument explicitly that objects, definitionally, are a necessary part of the concept of private property, thus rectifying Hohfeld's glaring omission. In so including objects, one gives analytic backing to the idea that property is contextual, that it has a teleology, and that duties are part of the property picture. That is, the nature of the resource, either in general or specific terms, helps to condition the property relationship. The argument thus supplies the obligations aspect of Singer's narrative with more traditional argumentative support (though the argument does narrow Singer's field of application somewhat).

I have argued that the private property metaphor should be thought of as a relationship between or among individuals, filtered or mediated through objects of social wealth. Using this metaphor, I redefine private property as follows:

> Private property is a social institution that comprises a variety of contextual relationships among individuals through objects of social wealth and is meant to serve a variety of individual and collective purposes. It is characterized by allocating to individuals a measure of control over the use and alienation of, some degree of exclusivity in the enjoyment of, and some measure of obligation to and responsibilities for scarce and separable objects of social wealth.[37]

This revised understanding has a large impact on property theory. The new metaphor and re-definition, as seen in part in both Singer and Underkuffler, as well as in Harris to a lesser extent, encapsulates the contextual nature of property. I have argued that the change implies that the object of a property relation has an important impact on the property relationship itself. That is, the inclusion of objects into the formal understanding of private property allows for certain objects of property to determine the contours of the property relationship (as

[36] The argument is advanced most fully in D. Lametti, 'The Concept of Property: Relations *through* Objects of Social Wealth' (2003) 53 *U Toronto LJ* 325.

[37] Ibid. 326.

distinct from the other areas of private law), conditioning its rights, limits, and duties as manifested in both allocation and use rules.[38] This understanding is common in the practice of property law, where property systems classify objects of property and attach normative implications. However, it is mainly absent in property theory, where it is at best implicit, as I would argue we have seen with both Singer and Underkuffler, and indeed with Harris.

Contrary to the absolutist ownership paradigm, this re-casting allows specific objects of property to carry with them duties of stewardship, or obligations to use in a specific manner. Put differently, the understanding of what an object of social wealth brings to the property relationship is nothing less that the identification of the teleology of the property institution. However, the formal inclusion of objects in property's definition also provides a defence against a view of property that is *only* about social relations or context.[39] The focus on objects makes the 'context' more property-specific. For the inclusion of objects in the property equation necessarily imports all sorts of explicit and implicit analyses of the separable value of a given object of social wealth—the reasons for which that object has a relatively objective value to a large number of persons. Many of these relatively objective sources of value are often attached to the object's use in the fostering of individual autonomy, for reasons ranging from history to morality. Some attention to the object or resource also excludes from the purview of property relations other kinds of social and legal relationships, where the property resource is out of focus.[40]

Singer, in his postulating a limited property right, and in his inclusion of obligations as well as rights in the property picture, is closest to this view. The expectations of private property capture in part what I have called the ethics or teleology of property. The allocation and use of certain specific resources can only be justified where they conform to a larger set of social goals or societal expectations. Like Singer, there is a moral utilitarian aspect to this understanding of private property, but unlike Singer, the context is circumscribed in a very 'real' way. And as with both Singer and Underkuffler, there is an explicit recognition that property claims are not absolute, but that they need to be determined in a moral discourse which delimits and justifies property rights. Here I would go further than Harris in that the justificatory reasons need not be property-specific, but can be subsets of larger moral arguments. They need only be persuasive in the property setting.

[38] I have argued elsewhere that Honoré has also made this point in 'Ownership', but left it undeveloped: see Lametti, n. 36 above, 339 ff; and D Lametti, 'The (Virtue) Ethics of Private Property: A Framework and Implications', in A Hudson (ed.), *New Perspectives on Property Law, Obligations and Restitution* (Cavendish, 2003), 39, 61–2.

[39] See, e.g., Stephen Munzer's critique in 'Property as Social Relations' in SR Munzer (ed.), *New Essays in the Legal and Political Theory of Property* (CUP, 2001), 36.

[40] Thus I would not include the moral duties of Singer's good mill owner in an elaboration of *property* duties, as the relationship was contract: see n. 20 above, ch. 6. If I am correct, property duties will be fairly circumscribed, and linked to the particular nature of an object of social wealth: its scarcity, its unique environmental value, its unique social value, as determined by a myriad of valuation processes, etc.

Regarding obligations, I have argued that the inclusion of objects in the definition of property allows for a more robust inclusion of property-duties in the institution of property. That is to say, they can be attached in property norms specifically to a resource. As such, they go beyond merely trying to uphold a claim for equality of opportunity, or a minimal redistribution of wealth, as was the case for Singer. Indeed, the inclusion of strong duties might even justify unequal distributions of wealth, where some greater social good is being advanced. So, for example, patent rights, and the profits therefrom, are justified provided that the invention is put to use by the owner in such a way as to make its benefits available to society. When not so used, society is justified in otherwise licensing out the right, and sometimes even expropriating the right.

It may even be that virtue and virtuous behaviour provide a source of property justification. While not fully elaborated, an ethics of virtue with respect to resources might help justify the allocation of resources to particular individuals. While such Aristotelian arguments are not new, they have fallen out of favour in our day and age, though they remain for elaboration and rehabilitation.[41]

The two major differences between all of these works and Harris's are the sources of justification for private property, and the contours of the institution itself. Especially with regard to Singer and myself, there is a wider social context—wider than individual autonomy—that must be understood in the justification discourse of private property and in the articulation of its basic structures. While Harris has identified all the justificatory arguments, he did not weigh them as he might have, given a fuller (or at least alternative) view of property. The same is true for the property structures: while property-duty and property-limitation rules are identified, a more robust view portrays them as a necessary part of the property institution. All of this is bound together in a discourse which is moral.

The challenge for all of these morally thick theories is that the basis for morality cannot be articulated fully. There is indeed no one moral theory that yields a true form of property. This puts us back into the seemingly eternal discussions about morality—moral realism versus moral conventionalism, and justice—that Harris wished to avoid. This recourse is not a sign of underlying weakness in the theory. Given that private property is contextual, it is only in this moral discourse that it can be continually justified and re-justified. These larger debates about morality and justice simply cannot be avoided, but must be met head-on. Only in this way can an institution that creates inequality by definition be allowed to exist. In my understanding, Harris's analysis in *Property and Justice* struggles on this point of moral discourse, exhibiting an unresolved tension between levels of moral argument and their specificity to property analysis. A number of issues—even practical property issues, such as windfall gains—need to be resolved at the higher level of moral argument. While eschewing this discussion, the substance of

[41] See Lametti, n. 38 above, 41–2, and especially at n. 13 of the article. Similar themes are treated more fully in the American context by G Alexander in *Commodity and Propriety*, n. 18 above.

Harris's position—indeed its most convincing parts—relies on the persuasiveness of such higher moral arguments, and fluctuates from 'middle' to 'higher' levels of justificatory discussion.

Secondly, the institution of private property has a social dimension which influences both uses and allocation, and which helps us understand the definition and contours of the institution. Harris had identified this point implicitly, but not given it its full weight. The concept of property needs to be better calibrated by its context.

These differences between Harris and the alternative moral approaches mentioned here are a matter of emphasis. The perceptiveness and usefulness of both Harris's descriptive categories and justificatory analysis is most clearly evidenced in the fact that one can frame all of these alternative moral discussions around his seminal work. Harris remains the point of departure and critical point of comparison.

(iv) The Anti-commons: Property Limits by Another Name

Another current trend in North American property theory goes by the name of the anti-commons theory. Most explicitly identified with the writing of Michael Heller, the work seeks to provide remedies to situations where absolute property rights lead to nefarious results.[42] In the classical scenario posed by some efficiency-based property thinkers, common property inevitably leads to the over-exploitation of a given resource, the so-called tragedy of the commons. Heller by contrast has identified the 'tragedy of the anti-commons', in which too much private property, especially where ownership is fragmentary and absolute, can result in the under-use of resources. In this scenario, too many right-holders failing to put their resources to use, or even one right-holder neglecting to employ the resource, can result in the resource not being used at all. The best example is the single patent holder who refuses to use, or to allow the use of, a patent linked to other patents and applications, effectively putting a stop to a variety of other kinds of technology and thus hindering the development of various property rights and resources.

A great deal of literature has been spawned by anti-commons analysis, both in identifying anti-commons 'situations', and in proposing remedies for such situations. This research often uses the tools of economic analysis, whether these be in traditional areas of property law or in intellectual property law. As Stephen Munzer has observed, it is too early to tell how enduring this phenomenon will be.[43] This anti-commons literature 'took off' after the publication of *Property*

[42] See, e.g., MA Heller, 'The Tragedy of the Anti-commons: Property in Transition from Marx to Markets' (1998) 11 *Harvard LR* 621.

[43] SR Munzer, 'The Commons and Anticommons in the Law and Theory of Property', in MP Golding and WA Edmundson (eds.), *The Blackwell Guide to the Philosophy of Law and Legal Theory* (Blackwell, 2005), 148.

and Justice, so one can only speculate as to what Harris might have thought about its ongoing evolution. His description of property in chapters 4 to 7 did point to a number of different kinds of holding, and his argument in chapter 7, that private property was logically prior to common property, does lend support to an anti-commons analysis, which in effect takes ownership as its starting point and then allows for more limited formal or informal incursions by the collective.

In the context of the arguments contained in this brief chapter, I would point out the following. The thrust of anti-commons scholarship is a reaction to the problems created when ownership is taken to be absolute. Thus an owner can choose not to use his resource in a self-regarding fashion. In effect, the argument of Heller and others is a plea for limiting some of the impact of what is seen as the traditional purview of *dominium*, for purposes which do not always conform to those that the individual owner shares. Some of these purposes are social; for example, the wider diffusion of a base technology protected by a patent. Other purposes, however, are more individualistic, as where one individual patent-holder can only realize the value of that patent with the use of another patented technology that is not being deployed or blocked by the patent holder of base technology. In either case, one owner scuttles the commonly or individually held goals of other owners. Given what has been argued above, this initial assumption may not be plausible.

Thus it is a further question for anti-commons scholars whether a more realistic and less absolutist starting point for property would affect their analysis. That is, if property (or intellectual property) rights were not taken to be absolute, it is conceivable that a number of anti-commons situations might never occur. Put another way, if an obligation to put to productive use is understood to accompany the granting of a patent, a compulsory licence or outright expropriation of the patent takes care of the failure to put the patent to use, employing more traditional property understandings and tools without recourse to anti-commons analysis. Certainly where objects of social wealth as understood by society contain a strong sense of expected uses or destination, it is part of the contours of property analysis that, in granting a property right in the resource to the exclusion of others, society expects the resource to be used. This kind of argument coheres better with the conceptions of thicker moral approaches to property, as seen in the previous part.

(v) Moral Imperatives and Property

Harris was correct to say that the search for a true form of property would be befuddling. Indeed, it would have been a misguided enterprise, focusing on the validity of a particular property law or property scheme. There is no one true, valid, moral form of private property with which to compare all other schemes. The discussion of the morality of private property focuses not on its validity, but rather on its value as a system: its goals and functions in society, and how well the particular property institution attains these larger goals. Harris, happily, is just as guilty of this moralistic standpoint as other writers. As I have argued, Harris participated full-knowingly in this latter exercise. In his setting out of private property, he was sensitive to the contextual nature of private property. He was an anti-essentialist: property was a number of conceptual buckets to be used and applied in context.

However, Harris also understood that justificatory argument was necessary, and had an impact on the institution. Indeed, the structure of Harris's book appears to point to a necessary relationship between justifications for private property and its structure. So while trying to avoid pronouncing on the stultifying debate on the formal relationship between law and morality, he does in effect do so. By sidestepping the question, he points to the goals and functions which property might serve, and indeed must serve—at least in our society—in order to be justified. In his view, this was fostering autonomous choice. Harris was attentive to the role that private property has on personal development. Rather ironically, and indeed most powerfully, Harris has touched upon not only the nature of property, but also at least part of the source of its underlying morality. This I have called the implicit or internal morality of Harris's theory of property. It allowed him to posit private property as a fundamental human right, a right which any just society—founded on egalitarian principles, sensitive to individual freedom and autonomy, and respecting the inviolability of the person—would have to have. This last postulation of private property as a human right makes it unclear whether Harris has remained a soft positivist or become something more.

Some of us would go further. With Harris we would agree that the fundamental point is that the normative system we know as private property rules does attempt to deal with the questions of allocation and use of property. Given that these rules revolve around scarce objects of property, and that people ought to be treated presumptively equally—both points that Harris recognizes—then it becomes clear that the private property system is moral in its very enterprise: regulating the allocation and uses of scarce resources as amongst equals, according to justifiable arguments. Beyond Harris, we would argue that the property system is fundamentally moral in its purpose or aspiration,[44] and that this morality would manifest itself not in some sort of natural law calculus for determining the validity of property laws, but in the continuing moral discourse that is used to justify the continuing allocation and use of scarce resources by individuals.

[44] Harris once told me jokingly that he thought this argument could be labelled the 'Lon Fuller theory of property'. As one says in Italian: *magari* ('if only')!

In the end, we need to balance individual against collective concerns, understanding and articulating property norms according to larger goals of social ordering. Harris knew this, and most property scholars, property lawyers, and citizens would agree. The differences lie in effecting the balance. In the end, as stated in the preface to *Property and Justice*, we will continue to disagree on moral and political grounds about how property should be allocated, and indeed how we ought to describe and justify the institution. However, we need not be sceptical about it. J.W. Harris's work in property, in both its descriptive and justificatory aspects, has provided a formidable point of departure and standard of comparison for all those engaged in this crucial exercise.

9

Ownership, Co-Ownership, and the Justification of Property Rights

*James Penner**

One of the marks of Jim Harris's property scholarship was his clear elaboration of and sustained emphasis on the concept of 'ownership' and the way it figures in a proper understanding of property.[1] In this chapter I hope to elaborate a 'property-specific justice reason', Harris's term for those reasons which specifically worked to justify rights to property, which has not hitherto been given sufficient attention. To do so I will elaborate a distinction between two different kinds of property interest, the 'ownership' interest and lesser 'proprietary right'. With this distinction in hand, I hope to show that it is actually very difficult to use a Lockean 'state of nature' model of natural rights to justify the institution of ownership rights which is not merely instrumental, or incidental, to protecting these lesser, proprietary rights. However, I shall then propose a justification which is not instrumental in this way, one that trades heavily on a particular conception of co-ownership, and this, I hope, will reveal that the justification of ownership *per se* depends upon the premise that property will generally be shared or co-owned.

In doing so I will challenge the all too common idea that ownership is one of the most, if not the most, individualistic of rights. Our paradigm or standard 'picture' of property comprises the single owner, alone with their[2] goods, occupying their land, to the exclusion of others. While all basic human rights, for example the right to freedom of expression, the right to freedom of religion, the right to freedom of contract, and so on may be regarded as serving to enhance the autonomy of the individual, our understanding of these other rights seems necessarily

* School of Law, King's College London. I am grateful to Pavlos Eleftheriadis, Cecile Fabre, Joshua Getzler, William Lucy, Stephen Munzer, Seana Shiffrin, and Leif Wenar for comments on earlier drafts of this chapter. JW Harris read a version of this chapter and we discussed the ideas in it on several occasions. As ever, I learnt much. I am sad he did not have the chance to read the final version.

[1] JW Harris, *Property and Justice* (Clarendon Press, 1996), in particular chs. 2, 3, 5, and 6; JW Harris, 'Ownership of Land in English Law', in N MacCormick and P Birks (eds.), *The Legal Mind: Essays for Tony Honore* (Clarendon Press, 1986), 143.

[2] My use of their/they as singular personal pronouns is my attempt at non-sexist language. This is the common non-sexist rule-governed usage that has naturally arisen in spoken English.

to involve the interaction of the right holder with others: one expresses oneself to others, one (typically, at least) follows religious practices with other adherents, and contracts require at least two persons to agree about something. But ownership seems to work as much for the hermit as for anyone else, for, by operating as a norm that excludes others, it appears to contain no significant social dimension at all.[3] My aim here is to dislodge this picture with one in which ownership is seen primarily to provide a means, or resources, for significantly social activity, i.e. that our understanding of the institution of ownership only correctly reflects reality on the premise that property will generally be co-owned and shared.

(i) Ownership and Proprietary Rights

The basic difference between an ownership right and 'proprietary right', as I shall term it, is this: an ownership right is truly a right to a thing,[4] an exclusive right to engage with a thing to realize its value in any way that suits the right holder, a right which roughly corresponds with a duty on all others not to engage with that thing, to 'keep off', as it were. A proprietary right, on the other hand, is the right to realize a particular value by engaging with a thing in a particular way, for example, a right to graze one's cows in a particular pasture. Thus *ownership* provides owners with a realm of non-interference, in which they may realize the value of particular things which, in virtue of this protection, they are said to own. An ownership right, then, is a right of exclusive engagement or use, allowing the owner or co-owners to determine the disposition of a thing because all others are under a duty not to interfere with it. Importantly, no particular realization of the value of the thing is indicated. (Note ownership does not *empower* an owner in any

[3] Two points: (1) I am pointing out a matter of emphasis here, not elaborating a water-tight distinction between property and all other rights. The right to life, for example, can be framed as very much the right not to engage in any worthwhile life, but, rather, as simply the right not to be killed, which invokes no social aspect of living a life. But the general point, barring the right to life, holds, I think. To add to the list of examples which appear to invoke a necessary social context, we may cite the right of assembly, the right of political participation, the right to a fair trial, and the right to marry and reproduce. (2) Pointing out this individualistic aspect of our understanding of property rights is not intended to deny, of course, that the institution, communication, and following of any norm are dependent on social practices and conventions; in that respect all norms, the right to property included, are social. The point is that the substantial direction or guidance that the property right conveys does not refer to or depend upon any social interactions by the right holder for its sense, or at least, that appears to be our common understanding of it.

[4] By 'things' I mean first, tangible, moveable, physical objects, like cars, books, and apples, and, secondly, defined areas of land. While it is patently true that property rights in law extend beyond rights to tangible things of these kinds, and that any successful theory of property will show how one can have property rights in debts, bank balances, money, monopolies, and so on (see, e.g., JE Penner, *The Idea of Property in Law* (Clarendon Press, 1997), chs. 5 and 6), I will restrict my focus here to the tangible; first, because an exclusive right to a tangible thing is a paradigm case of ownership, from which other cases of property can be regarded as justifiable extensions, and, secondly, this will simplify the issues somewhat without detracting from the cogency of the analysis.

way—they can only do with their property what they are independently capable of doing, for their right correlates only with the duty of non-interference on all others; no others are under a duty to assist the owner to realize any particular value of the things they own.[5])

Proprietary rights, by contrast, are narrower. A proprietary right is the right of an individual to realize a *particular* value of a thing by engaging with it in a *particular* way. Examples of such rights are the rights of borrowers from libraries, or the holders of certain *proprietary* rather than *property* rights in land—for example, one kind of 'easement' in law gives the holder a right of way over another's land; to take another example, the holder of what in law is called a '*profit à prendre*' has the right to enter another's land to take something from it, e.g., to fish or cut timber.[6] Proprietary rights are 'defined', in the sense that the realization of a particular value provides the contour of the right itself. By contrast, the use-rights or use-values of an owner are not 'defined' in this way. An owner is able to take advantage of what Harris[7] has described as an open-ended set of use-privileges and control powers. I may do any number of things with what I own. This realm of freedom follows from, strictly speaking is entailed by, the kind of protection which ownership provides—it only imposes duties on others not to interfere with one's property; such duties work to protect indefinitely many kinds of use, but do not specially protect any particular ones.

Ownership rights and proprietary rights differ in their conception, in particular in terms of their genesis. The subject matter of ownership, what can be owned (parcels of land, objects like coats and cars, and so on), is determined by the general rules or conventions of society (typically rules of law), and the question about who owns what is determined by rules governing how title to these things is acquired, lost, or transferred. With respect to things which can be objects of property rights, they are conceived as putative items of property prior to any actual ownership, which explains why an individual can acquire the first title in something merely by, say, taking possession of it. The first acquirer does not have to create the subject matter of the property right by entering into any sort of legal transaction with others. Thus when Andrea takes possession of a tangible object, or of a piece of land, she possesses what was already there and may, by virtue of her possession, acquire a right to it. And when Betty sells Carl a house, this transaction does not create a property right in the house *de novo* for Carl. The

[5] See further, Penner, n. 4 above, 72–3.

[6] There is a difference between 'proprietary right' as used here and 'proprietary right' as used in the law: in the law a proprietary right is a right in property which 'runs' with the property, so as to bind subsequent holders of the property; an easement (e.g. a right of way) is such a proprietary right, as the easement can be enforced against a purchaser of the land over which it is held, not only against the owner who granted it; conversely, in general a contractual licence, a contractual right to occupy a piece of land, is not, for the licence only binds the owner with which it is made; a buyer of the property from the owner is not bound to give effect to the licence. For my purposes here, any *defined* interest in property, that is, defined in terms of a particular benefit to be taken from it counts as a proprietary right.

[7] Harris, n. 1 above, 5, 75–7.

right, or title, to the house is *passed* from Betty to Carl. By contrast, the subject matter of proprietary rights, i.e. particular uses or engagement to realize the values of things, do not have this kind of independent existence. They depend upon actual action by individuals so as to realize this or that particular value. In one sense, to point this out is merely to reiterate or elaborate upon the basic distinction by which ownership rights are not linked to any particular realization of value, while proprietary rights are. Determining the subject matter of proprietary rights is a matter of defining a particular realization of value. Typically, in law, proprietary rights are second-order in relation to property rights, for it is generally the owner who may create or 'grant'[8] proprietary rights to others over their property. Before such a grant is made, the subject matter of the right does not exist. The passing of someone over David's land, which could be the subject matter of a right of way, does not exist 'in the air' before and until David actually grants such a right to someone. Indeed, in law a person cannot acquire a *proprietary* right in unowned property—any engagement he makes with it will be regarded as evidence of his possession of the whole so as to justify ownership of it.[9]

Although the right to property protects any use I might make of the things I own, it is also clear that for a great deal of property, no one expects any one to explore the open-ended use possibilities.[10] I can use my bottle of champagne as a doorstop, but realistically champagne is there to be drunk and has little value otherwise. This is true of a great many, perhaps most, of the objects which the average person owns. Most of these have been manufactured or shaped specifically

[8] Although the distinction in law is not exactly the same as the one I have outlined here, English common law marked a distinction between rights in land which lay 'in livery', i.e. delivery, and those which lay 'in grant'. The former were true 'property' rights, the subject matter of which was tangible and existed independently of any act of an owner, and which could merely be transferred. The latter were those rights in the land of another which depended upon an act of creation by an owner. Title to the former could be acquired by mere possession, the best evidence of which was evidence showing the intention to exclude all others, e.g., by fencing off land; if possession was significantly long, the right of any previous possessor could be defeated. A right to the latter could be acquired by way of 'prescription', by which a right which might have been created by grant could be secured by long and continuous usage.

[9] Of course, the rules of society could be geared only to the first acquisition of proprietary rights, not property rights, as we shall consider below (text to n. 13 ff). It could be the case that you could only acquire a right to some unowned thing by using it in some way, and your right would only be to that use, and would last only so long as you kept using it; in short, you might only be able to acquire a proprietary right. The point of making reference to the law here is to provide an example of how the distinction, nebulous in some respects as it is, underlies an extant, functioning body of rules and, more importantly, shows that something different is required to establish a proprietary right from a property right, even if a system were to favour the recognition of one rather than the other.

[10] It should not need saying, but I shall say it anyway: the owner's open-ended use possibilities does not mean that owners can do anything they like, in the sense that owning a gun analytically comprises the right to murder someone with it, so that the prohibition of murder must count as a limitation on ownership in guns, knives, staves, and whatever else it occurs to one to use in a killing. The prohibition on murder is general, in that in this context it cuts across the issue of ownership. No one is allowed to use a gun to murder another, whether they own the gun or not. General restrictions on the behaviour of individuals which might involve things are not norms which limit or conflict with property rights. Cf. Harris, n. 1 above, 32–3.

for the purpose of a particular kind of use, and have essentially little value otherwise.[11] In contrast, proprietary rights may be more or less broadly defined, such that the proprietary right holder may have some substantial freedom of action in realizing the value of a thing. To maintain the distinction between property and proprietary rights is not to claim that there is an absolute scale of 'freedom' of action which distinguishes the rights of an owner from that of a proprietary right holder. What must be remembered is that in conception the two are distinct, as the general or indefinite is distinct from the specific or defined. As we shall see when we turn to Locke's state of nature, it is a mistake to elide the two and treat the grounds justifying a proprietary right, to use a thing in a particular way, with those for full ownership. Ownership is a right to realize, or not realize, any value or no particular value, as one wishes and is able, and is a *right to the realization of value* only in so far as the right to exclude others contributes to that realization. Justifying this 'global' right to a thing cannot be simply a matter of justifying a person's right to extract a particular value from it.

Before going on I must mention an alternative analysis of ownership that has become popular, which treats the ownership as a 'bundle' of particular rights to use property in particular ways. This analysis gives logical priority to the right to realize values over the right to exclude. Its effect is obviously to abolish the distinction between ownership and property, as ownership is defined merely as an agglomeration or a series of proprietary rights in respect of a particular thing; a 'big enough' agglomeration, or an agglomeration with enough significant proprietary rights to pass some threshold, delivers ownership. The basic defect with this analysis, which cannot be fully explained here,[12] is that it confuses potentiality with actuality. Intuitively this seems fairly clear. Grasping the concept of ownership is grasping that an owner has a realm of freedom secured by the non-interference of others with respect to some thing; it does not require being able to enumerate, even inadequately, a battery of value-realization rights over any particular thing; much less does it require us to regard all these potential value-realizations as the current subject matters of existing rights. But if we do so, and this seems part of the rationale of the analysis, we can simplify property rights: by denying the distinction, we can treat any *creation* of a proprietary right, e.g., when an landowner grants an easement, as a transfer from the owner to the easement holder of a pre-existing right, just one of the bundle which the owner already has. The problem is that the facts are not so simple, and if we think, as we should, that the genesis of proprietary rights in this way gives rise to different considerations about their nature and justification, as I hope will become apparent, then the simplification is illegitimate.

[11] This reduction of use-possibilities reaches its extreme form in the case of rights such as debts, bank balances, money (roughly), where to realize their value is to exchange them, perhaps for other such rights, but finally for something tangible, whose value can directly be realized to serve one's interests.

[12] See JE Penner, 'The 'Bundle of Rights' Picture of Property' (1996) 43 *UCLA Law Review* 711; Penner, n. 4 above, 23–31; JL Schroeder, 'Chix Nix Bundle-O-Stix: A Feminist Critique of the Disaggregation of Property' (1994) 93 *Michigan LR* 239.

(ii) The Justification of Rights to Things in a Plentiful Lockean State of Nature

Let us now consider a mythical state of nature, such as that described by Locke[13] in the passages in which he seeks to justify property rights. The first thing to notice, something I want to emphasize, is the *asocial* character of the state of nature. I take it that the whole idea of a state of nature is to depict a situation arising before the advent of a civil society, in which the state of individuals is characterized by significant social relations, that is, relations of co-ordination and co-operation either between particular individuals or between groups, relations which can give rise to particular rights and duties against each other. The general point of state of nature models is to determine those rights which individuals bring with them when they enter civil society, rights which therefore cannot be stripped of individuals by the social contract, or, at least, may be used as bargaining chips, so that if individuals are to be stripped of them this can only be by their own fully-informed consent. Thus, whatever rights and duties there are in a state of nature exist purely in virtue of the human status of so-called 'atomized' individuals, not in virtue of their co-operative social relations. I am well aware that Locke introduces relations of contract (in the form of barter) into his passages on the justification of property, but I shall avoid doing so, for it is not clear at all that one can simply introduce contracts of barter into the state of nature as casually as Locke does, without unsettling important aspects of the justification. To take but one example, it is not clear how the justice of barter could somehow contribute to the justification of property rights, since the justice of bartering presumes that the barterers are the just owners of what they barter with.[14] If we can elaborate rights to things without introducing a contractual mode of social co-operation, then we will have a surer grip on what the state of nature can tell us about such rights.

Addressing Nozick's[15] interpretation of Locke, Cohen points out that there are two fundamentally different ways in which one may conceive of the individual's right to things in the state of nature,[16] 'common ownership' and 'joint ownership'. Under the former, any individual may access any external resource in the world (so long as someone else is not using it) without consulting, much less getting the consent of, anyone else. It is *common* in that all individuals have identical rights to

[13] J Locke, *Second Treatise of Government* (1690) in *Two Treatises of Government* (ed. P. Laslett, CUP, 1952), paras. 25–51.

[14] The actual nature and extent of the social relations and social interactions that Locke intended to form part of the state of nature he described are pretty much impossible to determine from the text; the obvious conclusion to draw is that Locke did not attend to it sufficiently. Locke tends to refer to the interactions of individuals whenever it serves his purpose, e.g., when he makes reference to barter. For a detailed discussion of how Locke's inattention to characterize the social relations in his state of nature undercuts his thesis about property, see Penner, n. 4 above, ch. 9.

[15] R Nozick, *Anarchy, State, and Utopia* (Basil Blackwell, 1974), 174–82.

[16] GA Cohen, 'Nozick on Appropriation' (1985) 150 *New Left Review* 89, 98–9.

all resources, so all resources are held 'in common', and *ownership* because this right of access is protected or instantiated by the right to exclude others from a resource, so long as one is actively using it oneself. Under *joint ownership*, any decision to use any thing must be unanimous. Everyone is a co-owner of all resources. Ownership is *joint*, in that each individual must agree to every disposition of every resource, and so only those dispositions of resources upon which all unanimously agree are permitted. It is *ownership*, and more extensively so, because ownership here amounts to a full right of exclusive use, i.e. the right permanently to exclude anyone without the status of owner from access to the property in question, irrespective of whether any use is being made of it. Now the notion of 'exclusion' may seem odd in the case of global joint ownership, i.e. where all are equally owners; if all are owners, how can anyone be excluded? One needs to realize, however, that no *individual* counts as an owner, but rather only the body of all individuals does; *qua* individual each person has the general duty of keeping off or away from the property—their access is permitted only as a consequence of the decision of the owner, the body of all, to allow a use in which they take part. *Qua* individual, each person is a non-owner, and if he engages the property without the consent of all, he is a trespasser.

Now on the asocial characterization of the state of nature that I have opted for above, common ownership seems clearly to be the appropriate model for realizing its potential as a thought experiment for just appropriation. Whatever rights there are in the state of nature, these must be the rights of more or less lone individuals against other lone individuals, who come across each other more or less at random. The rights cannot depend upon the sort of social organization and co-operation which joint ownership demands, for that would, in essence, import civil society into the state of nature, indeed a rather well-organized democratic civil society. It is worth remarking that because joint ownership requires joint decision-making, in which to act at all, people must act together, i.e. socially,[17] it describes the antithesis of ownership as normally conceived; in contrast to the individual owner being able to do what he likes with his own subject to the veto of no one, under this global joint ownership one's relation to things in the world is subject to the veto of every other individual. Neither an individual, nor a group of like-minded individuals, indeed no group smaller than everyone, has the right to determine the disposition of any property whatsoever.

Moreover, if the asocial character of the state of nature is taken seriously, any claim for joint ownership there is vexed for another reason. Consider Locke's idea that the world is given by God to man in common. Sitting here in England, is it

[17] While related, this is not the point that Cohen forcefully makes about the demise of *self-ownership* under a joint ownership regime, i.e. that to act at all involves using some resources of the external world, if only to occupy the space where one stands, and so to the extent that even the most minimal activity would require the consent of everyone else, one has no freedom to act, no 'self-ownership', at all: GA Cohen, 'Self-Ownership, World Ownership, and Equality: Part II' (1986) 3 *Social Philosophy and Policy* 77, 82–3.

churlish to think that God made a poor job of giving me a right (in common with all others, of course) to Australia? The bottom of the Pacific Ocean? Mars? People, whether acting as individuals or in groups, give the world to themselves. No one has any normatively significant relationship with respect to realizing the value of any thing until it is brought into some relation, either with themselves, or with other individuals with whom they have relations, such that they might possibly realize some value from it. The unspoken premise behind the concept of joint ownership is that I as an individual, simply by existing, have some normatively significant relation to every piece of matter in the universe concerning the realization of its value, a relation that all others must acknowledge and respect. The implausibility of this is obvious as soon as it is stated. Any sensible characterization of what is owned by joint owners involves the summation of what each has access to, in a way that value might be realized. And what underpins any possible normativity in respect of my relationship to things with which I have never been in any relation, such that I might realize their value, is the fact that *other people* have put themselves in such a relation with those things and that I, by virtue of my relation to those other people, may *through them* have some normative relation to those things. Thus the idea of joint ownership implicates some sort of real society once again, and so, once again, is inappropriate to the state of nature.

If this is right, and we must embrace common ownership as our model for examining the justice of rights to things acquired in the state of nature, it can be shown that in the condition of plenty, the most we can justify are rights to realize the particular value of things, i.e. proprietary rights, and not ownership.

The result we want in the state of nature is to secure to individuals the realization of values, in so far as each of them can individually accomplish this by engaging with things; this involves two aspects; the first is securing their access to things so as to provide an opportunity to realize value, and the second is to secure to them the values that they realize by engaging particular things. The first is secured by a personal right not to be assaulted, i.e. a right not to be interfered with when one acts, here acting to take advantage of the plentiful resources. There is no need to institutionalize any form of ownership right, i.e. an exclusive realm of non-interference over particular things, to secure the opportunity to access things and realize their value, because perfectly adequate access is secured by plenty itself. The second aspect is secured by instituting proprietary rights. If the only way to realize the value of a thing required one to be actually, actively engaged with it, then we would not even require the institution of proprietary rights, but simply a right against assault. But because certain realizations of value are more than a matter of immediate engagement in this way, such as the alteration of things so as to create improvements (ploughing land, turning wood into a table), then interfering with the improved thing itself (by destroying it, for instance), rather than with the improver themselves, would still be to interfere with the improver's realization of value. In consequence, there is a requirement for the institution of proprietary rights, rights to allow a person to realize the value of particular things, to prevent this sort of interference. The right, in other words, must apply also to interfering with the improved thing itself.

Notice how this institution of proprietary, rather than ownership, rights lends itself to the multiple uses of property by different individuals. Recall, a property right is the right to exclude all others from engaging a thing, *irrespective* of how that engagement might affect the owner's own realization of value. This is a familiar feature of property rights. Someone who interferes with another's property can enrich himself by engaging with the owner's property without causing the owner any loss. My quiet use of your library while you sleep upstairs may upset nothing at all in the way of your realizing the value of your property. My taking your horse for a gallop may interfere not at all with your plans—your horse may be better for the exercise. There would seem to be no reason in principle why such multiple non-interfering uses should not be permitted in our state of nature, which undermines any case for instituting ownership. What justification could there be, deriving from the protection of individuals' rights to realize the value of things, to stop A from picking the daffodils in the field B uses to graze cattle, so long as A did not harass the cattle?

To summarize, ownership secures the owner the *opportunity* to realize value, not any particular realization. In the state of nature, though, plenty itself secures this, and there seems to be no other obvious principled basis for instituting individual ownership, and, indeed, some reason not to, for it would diminish the full scope of common ownership, whereby individuals have common access to all things—even those which are used by others to realize value—so long as they do not interfere with anyone else's realization of value. By contrast, proprietary rights do seem necessary in principle, in order to protect the rights of improvers to values which can only be realized by modifying things. Even so, on further examination of the features of the state of nature, there may be a valid *instrumental* reason for instituting ownership.

Consider the duties which correlate with ownership rights. The standard way of putting the right–duty correlation that attends ownership is something like this: when I own some thing, all others have a duty not to interfere with it. While correct as far as it goes, to understand the correlation fully we must understand that the normative relationship between persons conceived as owners and persons conceived as non-owners (though almost everyone will be both) is mediated through a practice, a way in which we deal with things, the essence of which is very simple: we are under a duty not to interfere with, or use, or occupy things which are typically things which are owned (houses, for example, as opposed to pigeons), and which are not ours. Basically, unless we own it or have been given permission by the owner, we must not interfere with such things. To own property is to take part in this practice by benefiting from the general duty which everyone has in respect of what they do not own. It is thus an existence condition of ownership that such a practice exists, and it is an essential aspect of this practice that the relation between individuals *qua* owners and individuals *qua* respecters of property, i.e. duty-owers, is mediated by their relations to things.[18] In short, things stand between the owner and the duty-ower, for the duties are understood and followed by duty-owers, via their behaviour in respect of things which are not their own—they are not duties which implicate any direct contact or engagement between right holders and duty-owers themselves. As already mentioned, there must also be fairly well-defined and *generally appreciated* conventions about what is owned and what is not; houses, but not pigeons. So, for example, in most western countries, all land other than public highways, parks, and other well-known exceptions is owned, and therefore one must not trespass upon it. In respect of chattels, the general exclusionary picture is even clearer—with the exception of wild animals, basically all tangible objects are owned.

Now, if we are trying to frame the relations between individuals in the state of nature as those between 'atomized' individuals with the minimum of social relations, then a property practice giving effect to individual ownership seems more *practically* suitable for governing rights to things than does the institution of proprietary rights. In the case of the latter, we need some kind of boundary which allows any individual to know when he is interfering with another's right to value of a thing, i.e. with his proprietary right to take a specific value from it. Such a boundary definition might be simplified if any individual could only have one particular proprietary right in any particular thing. Thus if Monica has enclosed a field for grazing cattle, I would be forbidden from harvesting the grass but could still play cricket there, so long as I did not interfere with the cattle unduly. Boundaries would also be clear in the case of things where for all intents and purposes only one particular value can be realized, such as food. In such a case, one would pretty much only respect the proprietary right of Ben to his chocolate bar by not interfering with the chocolate bar *tout court.* Despite one-use items, there will remain any number of proprietary rights whose character and extent will not be apparent just by coming into contact with things *per se.* Determining the extent of someone's proprietary rights will involve dealing with the appropriator, to see the extent of their realization plans; this is simply a facet of the fact that the realization of any particular value is a matter of deciding to do something particular with a thing, as opposed to merely treating it as out of bounds to others. But dealing with an appropriator to determine the precise scope of their realization plans, thus to determine the scope of their proprietary right, looks a great deal like co-operative activity, not in the sense of individuals directly assisting each other in the realization of value from a thing, but in terms of co-ordinating their activities in the sense that Paul lets Mary know the extent to which he is using a thing, so that she may realize a non-interfering value from the same thing herself. In order to avoid requiring this kind of social interaction so as to keep our state of nature innocent of civil society, it would seem necessary to institute ownership rights, for no question of this kind of co-ordination arises if any particular thing may only be used by

[18] See further Penner, n. 4 above, 23–31.

one individual. Thus one of the features of proprietary rights is typically that assessing their contours, in order to respect them, will typically require social interaction; since we are trying to frame the character of rights in things in a context which is as close to a social vacuum as we can manage (in order to glean whatever value we can from this state of nature parable), having resort to proprietary rights to explain the normative boundaries in respect of things, while perfectly justifiable in principle, seems less satisfactory than the institution of ownership rights for these practical reasons. Another way of putting this is to say that, in a state of plenty, the values proprietary rights serve are most easily protected by ownership rights, where the duty not to interfere is framed in terms of any thing which has somehow been set off from the common in an appreciable way, land by fencing, apples by being gathered in baskets, and so on. Since there is an abundance of all things, no one suffers by having to refrain from engaging with any particular item, and so, out of an abundance of caution to ensure that no proprietary right is violated, full ownership would provide the best means available. So, though the justice of rights to things in the state of nature indicates only proprietary rights, instrumental considerations of this kind suggest that ownership is justified.

However, these considerations weighing in favour of ownership are upset with the coming of scarcity. Now the importance of scarcity in the state of nature, as regards the justification of rights to things, seems to me to have been generally misunderstood; misunderstood as the situation where so many things are owned that there is not enough and as good for those who have not yet appropriated. But if I am right about the character of rights in the plentiful state of nature, in particular that ownership rights arise there because of instrumental considerations, this is misconceived.

(iii) Scarcity in the State of Nature

When scarcity looms in the state of nature, in the sense that if all ownership rights were respected, then some individuals at least would be thwarted in their attempts to access things and realize values as they chose, then ownership rights, being instituted for instrumental reasons to protect proprietary rights, must give way. A more social environment, in the sense of increased social co-ordination, must arise. At a minimum, individuals must co-operate to the extent of giving genuine effect to proprietary rights, i.e. by communicating to the extent of permitting, where possible, the multiple use of the same resources by different individuals, shaped in terms of rights by each individual's proprietary, not ownership, rights. Prior realizors of value, those with 'vested' proprietary rights, must co-operate with others by informing them of the extent of their particular realizations of value, so that others may realize the value of those things to the extent compatible, in order to squeeze their own realizations of value into the available gaps, so to speak. Not only does this seem to follow from a robust reading of Locke's proviso that an appropriator may not allow what he appropriates to spoil[19] (read 'go to waste'), it would also seem to fit nicely with his approval of labour as a means of forestalling scarcity;[20] if it is true that an individual needs less land to the extent that he tills it, i.e. uses it more intensively, then it is also true that when two or more individuals are able each to realize the value of a thing by co-ordinating their different realizations of value from it, scarcity is forestalled even further. Two can live as cheaply as one, as they say.

True scarcity only looms when things are being used as intensively as practically possible by the activity of individuals, but individuals are yet thwarted because they cannot realize all the values of using things which they wish to, because now no gaps remain. What happens now?

At the outset, we must assume that all individuals will be concerned both to introduce new value-realizing uses of things, and be concerned to hold onto those they currently enjoy, i.e. to hold onto the proprietary rights they have managed to acquire. To the extent that we are concerned with the living, all are realizing the value of some things. And as scarcity arises, all are deprived, at least theoretically, of the liberty to realize whatever values of whatever things they wish, which was formerly secured by plenty. In short, once scarcity arises it affects everyone equally, in the sense that there is now not 'enough and as good' remaining for anyone. This is not to deny that there might be significant relative disparity in property rights. Scarcity, when it comes, might well hit some harder than others, and I am not denying that issues of justice arise because of this. The question that must be addressed is: given the structure of rights that operates in the plentiful world, is there any operation of those rights which allows individuals to deal in some practically justifiable way with the problems that arise when scarcity does? My argument will conclude that in this 'thinly' social world, there is no possible way of framing the claims of the thwarted, either in terms of proprietary rights or ownership rights, that works to generate a reasonably justified institution of property rights of either kind. I must tread carefully to show why this is so, but if it is correct, it suggests that when true scarcity arises in the state of nature as I have depicted it, claims to ownership rights can be made on a principled, as opposed to instrumental, basis, in just the circumstances where, paradoxically, they are not justifiable.

Consider the sort of claim a would-be introducer of a new realization of value, call her Tess, could make against a particular proprietary right holder, call him Alec. Now if we frame Tess's claim merely as a claim that Alec withdraw from a thing so as to allow her to make some use of it, i.e. just to exclude himself to some extent, on the premise that while her use might displace one currently enjoyed by Alec, such a use would not itself unjustly take advantage of him, on the assumption, say, that she is currently worse off than he. That claim could be complied with fully. Alex is, of course, entitled to withdraw from any thing he

[19] Locke, n. 13 above, paras. 31, 37, 38. [20] Ibid., para. 37.

uses, to abandon it, as it were. Of course, abandonment is not directional, in the sense of leaving something *to* any particular person.[21] As a matter of right, Alec's abandonment does not accord Tess any right to make use of what Alec abandons; a third party standing by, Boris, has just as much right to take advantage of Alec's withdrawal as Tess does. Now, if we suppose a requirement that any person with greater proprietary rights than another is subject to a duty to withdraw from some of his rights when demanded to do so by that other, up to the point where their total rights are equal, then we can also suppose that iterative claims of this kind might operate eventually to distribute all holdings equally. Thus if Boris jumps in where Alec withdraws, and Boris is 'poorer' (has fewer rights) than Tess, Boris cannot be challenged by Tess, whereas if she is the poorer, she can make the same claim against him as she did against Alec. And such claims and abandonments might proceed repeatedly so as to deliver a parity of rights holdings. We might call this the 'crowded dance floor' model of property equalization; by the closing of distances between dancers as new dancers squeeze in, in some space of time the floor will become more or less equally densely occupied.

While this 'crowded dance floor' model accords with the thinness of the social relations in the state of nature, I think it represents a very poor model for understanding the issues involved in the sort of claim the Tesses of the world really make. In particular, I doubt that the claim Tess makes can be fully comprehended without in some way regarding Alec as the owner of his proprietary rights, i.e. treating Alec as not being limited merely to withdrawing from his uses in order to make space for others, but as having the power actually to confer or transfer his proprietary rights *to* specific others. If we can only make sense of Tess's claim if we assume that Alec can transfer his rights to specific others, then of course we tacitly treat Alec not merely as having proprietary rights acquired by his use of things, but as an owner of those rights. Alec is treated as having the typical 'incident' of ownership, i.e. that one may transfer the property rights one has. The transfer of pre-existing proprietary rights is, of course, perfectly coherent in an established system of ownership and proprietary rights, and the transferability of mere proprietary rights partakes, in a derivative way, of our tacitly assuming the existence of the typical incidents of ownership. Since things, like defined patches of the earth, or goods like apples, and so on, are regarded as individuated subject matters of ownership rights, i.e. rights of exclusion, we can easily conceive of them, and the rights to them, being transferred from one person to another. The idea is, as we have seen, implicit in the notion of title.[22] We can then apply this facility of transferability to any other defined right we wish, such as a proprietary right, the right to realize a particular value of a thing.

The basic problem is that it is difficult to understand the force of any claim the 'poor' can make against the 'rich', which does not also entail, given the legitimacy,

[21] Although by abandoning property in a certain context, a directional transfer can effectively be achieved. See Penner, n. 4 above, 80–7.

[22] Text following n. 7, above.

ex hypothesi, of the proprietary rights which the rich have acquired, that the rich might transfer, not merely abandon, their rights. It is a simplistic reading of the situation, prompted by the 'crowded dance floor' model of redistribution of rights, to frame the claims of the crowded against the uncrowded as the latter's simply 'taking up too much space'. That is a comprehensible claim from the perspective of waste or spoilage, i.e. that a person misuses resources in some vice-like way, as a glutton, for instance. This of course has nothing to do with the position of others; such a claim can be made where there is abundance. Clearly the claim must be understood in the sense of 'too much space' *relative* to what others have. Now, given the social relations which characterize the state of nature, where the model of right concerns not interfering with others, rather than having in any way positively to care for others, it is arguably impossible to provide any basis for the kind of claim the poor might make, but that is not the salient point here. The point is rather that once such a claim is accepted as legitimate, it seems impossible to deny the rich the power of ownership, and the right of the poor to take advantage of it.

Why is that? Consider again the legitimacy of Alec's proprietary rights. They are *ex hypothesi* his because he has acted on resources to make valuable use of them. In doing so he has, *ex hypothesi*, violated no one else's proprietary rights. At first glance, he is entirely immune from the claims of anyone else *vis-à-vis* these rights. But we accept that he must answer to the poverty of others. Why must his answer lie in abandonment of his rights? As we have seen from the 'crowded dance floor' model, his doing so in response to the claims of the poor will, over time, result in a more or less equal distribution, but remember, the claim cannot be framed in terms of 'there are poor out there—abandon some of your rights', for there is no collective voice of this kind in the state of nature. The procedure of equalization must operate through the iterated claims of individuals one against the other, brushing shoulders on the dance floor. But if the claims are framed in terms of pair-wise comparisons of rich person with poor, does this not suggest a level of social interaction and 'sharing' of concern which would entitle Alec simply to co-operate with Tess, so as to share the use and value of his holdings? What reason, other than a seemingly peremptory denial of individual co-operation of this kind in the state of nature, would make it a matter of right that the only way in which Alec and Tess could deal with each other to allay Tess's material disadvantages is for Alec to abandon his rights and let Tess, and any other who came along, have a go at realizing values for themselves? The point is that, having crossed the Rubicon and made it a condition for the justice of holdings that, relative to others, one may not take for oneself too much, it is an entirely arbitrary stopping point to say that this condition of justice can only be made operational by the abandonment by the rich of (some of) what they have. Taking into account the interests of others in this way is oddly, perhaps pathologically, bloodless. Indeed, it smacks of not really taking others' interests into account at all, but merely dealing with them so as to protect one's own self-interests, providing a dole so that the rabble do not rise and threaten the wealthy.

Let us retrace our steps for a moment. We saw how ownership rights, instituted for instrumental reasons, give way when scarcity looms. Notice again that when this occurs, intensive use of things requires a minimal level of social interaction, so as to allow individuals to co-ordinate their behaviour. It would seem that when genuine scarcity arises, the natural development from this is not iterative abandonments of rights, but enhanced *co-operation* between individuals and groups, so as to provide for the less well off, according individuals the right to dispose of their proprietary rights in favour of specific individuals. There is, it seems, a genuine tension between treating proprietary rights as justified because acquired by not interfering with others, and yet taking the interests of others into account, so as to redistribute them, in the sense that the character of the former minimizes any actual social relations between individuals, operating on the model of acquisition by individual use and loss only through abandonment, while the latter is an expression of their existence. In giving effect to the latter, i.e., in accepting social relations which manifest an interest in the welfare of others, the natural model of property rights would be one where people are entitled to share with and give to individual others, i.e., a model encompassing true property rights, not a model by which my concern for others is effected not by in any way embracing them and their lives, but withdrawing from my engagement with the world of things into a smaller space, by becoming a more frugal hermit, as it were. Nevertheless, given the resources of the state of nature model, I think this tension is unavoidable, and results in an air of paradox.

To put this precisely in terms of the distinction between ownership and proprietary rights, we have reached the paradoxical position that, on the state of nature model, ownership rights are justified only instrumentally—provisional on a condition of plenty—and that only when scarcity arises, and Tess's sort of claim becomes pressing, does a real need for ownership arise; for only by allowing genuine giving and sharing do we really give effect to an interest in the welfare of others. Furthermore, the person whose claim is realized best by the institution of ownership is not the one who has appropriated and diligently laboured to realize the value of things—mere proprietary rights do for them—but the one who has not been able to appropriate enough. This rather stands Locke on his head, to put it mildly.

It seems to me that there is no way out of this paradox, given the structural features of the state of nature. One way to proceed is to bite this bullet in the following sense: it is true that scarcity undermines the instrumental foundation for property rights which operates in the world of plenty, but it also may force a kind of social interaction in which everyone has to take some notice of the interests of others, since, unless some plausibly fair mechanism for the distribution (or re-distribution) of rights to things can be worked out, no claims to things of any kind, neither ownership rights nor proprietary rights, can be sustained. Thus we may be led to what might be called the 'liberal settlement': we justify both ownership rights and proprietary rights of various kinds on consequentialist considerations, following a political settlement of some kind, under which no individual is so badly off, by virtue of the ownership and proprietary rights of others, as to be able to claim that the institution of these rights is unjust.[23] So, for example, in a welfare state where education and health care are universally available, and the worst off are provided with a source of income, familiar consequentialist considerations may properly be taken as sufficiently weighty to justify such an institution: the award of proprietary rights provides an incentive to those who would improve things; instituting ownership rights makes the determination of the boundaries of individuals' rights easier to determine; where contractual transactions are recognized, ownership rights allow goods to move to their highest value users, and so work to maximize utility, and so on.

However I would like to suggest a different, non-provisional justification for ownership rights, which turns on a social interaction of individuals which goes beyond the mere co-ordination of their behaviour, so as to prevent their violating each other's rights.

(iv) Justifying Property Rights by Essential Reference to Co-ownership

Elsewhere I have approached this issue by considering the different character of the social relations underlying gifts, versus those underlying contracts. There, I argued that, whereas the right to property encompasses the right of an owner to share their property and to give it away, it does not comprise, nor does it entail, any right to sell their property,[24] as follows:

(1) The right to property protects the owner's interest in making use of the thing they own to realize some value from it in such a way as they determine, by imposing a general duty on others not to interfere with it.

(2) Owners, however, just like the rest of us, are social beings, and therefore many realizations of the value of things will be social realizations; since taking up the right to property is not to commit oneself to the social isolation of a hermit, the owner is permitted, as they determine, to realize the value of their property with others, i.e. share it, by releasing particular others from the duty not to engage with the property.

(3) The essence of the justification of sharing is that people can share in the realization of values in two importantly distinct ways: first, more than one person may realize the value of the same thing; thus, A and B may both realize the aesthetic value of the same painting by looking at it; furthermore, realizing the

[23] Quite what the appropriate way of determining when someone 'at the bottom' is so badly off as to indicate that the institution is unjust is, clearly, a difficult problem, and I will not venture a solution here.

[24] Penner, n. 4 above, 87–93.

value of some things, e.g., tennis rackets, requires co-operative activity—unless two or more realize a value no one will. In these cases, then, we are concerned with different individuals realizing their own self-interests, narrowly conceived. However, the idea of sharing encompasses a distinct second idea, that of truly shared interests, i.e. the sharing of one person in the interests of another. One person can share in another's realization of value: A may realize a value in B's realizing the value of the painting (and vice versa, of course); that is, A's interests may be served when B's interests are served, because A's interests encompass, or include, or turn on B's interests. This second aspect of sharing is somewhat difficult to articulate but trivially easy to appreciate. Parents and children, friends, lovers, colleagues, and so on, typically understand their own interests to be bound up with the interests of those others; it is part of the value of seeing a marvellous painting, or eating a good meal, or achieving a project that (certain) others appreciate the painting, the meal, or the achievement, as well. We identify our interests 'broadly', in the sense that they extend beyond our so-called self-interest, narrowly conceived. (Indeed, why else should we have the concept 'self-interest', as opposed to just 'interest' *tout court*?) It is the latter aspect of the sharing of the realization of value that is the essence of sharing, for it is this aspect which brings sharing within the justification of ownership. Rights are only justified in so far as they serve the right holder's interests, and so, by showing how sharing serves the owner's own interests, we show how the right to share is justifiably encompassed by ownership.

(4) The analysis, however, cannot end with sharing, but must extend to outright giving as well, i.e. the transfer of property to a donee who thenceforth has the right to realize the value of the property as they shall determine (once again, of course, including social uses of sharing and giving). Why? Because I can be interested in another's interests, I can be interested in another's realization of the value of a thing, though I no longer realize the value of the thing directly myself. Giving property to someone so that they may serve their interests with it in various ways can serve my interests. Thus I can serve my interests by giving things of various kinds to others in whom I am interested, giving them things 'without strings attached'. This sort of giving is probably most typically realized in cases of loving family relationships and friendships. If I am truly interested in someone, I am interested in their interests being served, am interested in their realizing the values of life which make living worthwhile. I cannot, however, realize such values for them; they must do it themselves. Thus if I am truly interested in someone I am interested in their autonomously choosing to realize these life-enhancing values. But I can encourage and assist them indirectly. I can give my daughter a cello if it looks as if she will learn to play and appreciate the value of playing music well. I can give a friend money in the hope that it will assist him to finish his doctorate. Once given, such gifts, like one's children and friends themselves, are not to be under my control. My hopes may be thwarted by their failure to make value-realizing uses of what I provide them. But that is the price of treating them as autonomous individuals, and there is no other way to treat persons whose

interests I genuinely share, or 'take on board' as interests of my own. This explains how the making of outright gifts counts as a case of an owner disposing of property in a way which serves their own interests. When I make a gift, it is not my use of the property, in the sense that I used up or directly engaged the property myself, nor directed its precise use, but my use in the equally robust sense that I provided my property for use in a way which directly implicates my interests, and it was given with just that understanding in mind.

(5) This analysis comes to an abrupt end, however, when we come to contractual exchanges (or lending, leasing, or licensing the use of my property under a contract). The essence of a contractual exchange is not that my interests will be served by my determination of the use of the property in question; rather the opposite. I receive the contractual *quid pro quo*, the consideration as lawyers say, precisely on the footing that I will no longer regard the thing that I transfer under the contract as continuing to serve my interests in any way whatsoever. It is the buyer who now realizes the value of the property, in a way that they determine will serve their interests. My interest is to be served through my realizing the value of whatever I receive in exchange, whether other property, say a bottle of wine, or a service, say a haircut. To make this point as clear as possible: the property in question, which I exchange, is, following the exchange, no longer in any position to serve my interests.[25] My relationship to it is now such that I cannot serve my interests through any realization of its value. In this respect, my relationship to what I have sold is no different from my relationship to a thing which I have never owned, or which I have abandoned, or which has been expropriated from me.

(6) The right to exchange the very things one owns, then, is not a right which flows from the right to determine the use of those very things. It is important to realize how radical the step is from the right to determine the valuable use of one's property, even broadly framed above to include the right to share and give away, to the right to exchange one's property. The latter right depends not only on the right to make binding agreements *per se*, roughly the right to contract, but also to allow the owner of property to treat his right of exclusive use over his property as an entitlement, in respect of which he is *entitled* to contract. This allows the owner not only to capture any value they themselves might realize from what they own, but to capture (some contractually negotiated share of) the value which *others* might realize from the use of it. Thus, even if I find no value in this lump of gold as it is, or in any jewellery into which it might be made, nor have any skill to render it into jewellery, so long as I am the owner of it, and have the right to exchange what I own by contract, I can enter into an agreement to exchange it so as to capture some of the value that the gold has for one who appreciates gold jewellery.[26]

[25] Except adventitiously, of course, in the same way that I may realize certain values of the property of others, for example when I admire the beauty of my neighbour's garden.

[26] Christman discusses an essentially identical point in economic terms when he distinguishes control rights and income rights. See JL Christman, *The Myth of Property* (OUP, 1994), 132–9.

Though this gift/contract distinction presents an overly pure or ideal characterization, which represent ends of a spectrum,[27] it does, I submit, capture two essentially different ways in which our interests may be served by co-operative activity. I can serve my own self-interests, narrowly conceived, by engaging in co-operative activity with another or others, who equally serve their own self-interests by the arrangement. Or I can serve my interests, my broader shared interests with others, by participating in an activity wherein all of our interests are linked in the sense described above, where the serving of your interests is constitutive of the serving of my interests. As mentioned above, this is most easily seen in the case of relationships of family and friends, but it extends beyond this to what might broadly be called 'cultural' activities, where people create a sense of belonging to each other, through carrying out projects of various kinds whose achievement provides the basis for the realization of values which express their common humanity.

In the world of 'atomized' individuals in the state of nature, it seems to me that there can be no sharing of interests akin to that which operates where property is shared or given. The co-operative activity, which is forced when scarcity looms and property rights break down, is the co-operative activity of those who are trying to stay out of each other's way when they are pressed to realize their own individual values, yet by using the same things. This meagre interaction can be illustrated by two persons approaching each other on a narrow path. They respect each other's rights by each moving left or right, so that they may pass by each other, but the interaction has no more substance than that. In such a world, we might say that individuals must respect each other's rights, but do not (or certainly need not) care a fig for each other's interests. Accordingly, the sort of co-operative social relations envisaged by a more or less 'Lockean', 'everyone for himself' state of nature will be regarded as relations on the contractual model of serving one's own interests, not the sharing-gift model, as indeed Locke does regard them when he introduces barter as the only significant person to person interaction.[28] But this sort of resort to social interaction cannot overcome the 'paradox' or impasse described above in justifying ownership, for the resort to exchange or barter or contract depends upon the pre-existing legitimacy of ownership. It cannot dig any justification of ownership *per se* out of the state of nature, but rather leads to the result that the model cannot justify ownership at all. Or rather, it pushes one to search for something like the 'liberal settlement', described above.

Armed, however, with a different version of co-operative behaviour, in which the sharing of interests can be frankly acknowledged, and modelling a state of nature in which that sort of co-operative behaviour takes place, I shall argue that we can begin to perceive a justification of ownership which does flow from a state of nature model.

Let us then assume a state of nature, but this time allow that individuals can work together to realize the values of things, both to serve their self-interests but,

[27] See JE Penner, 'Voluntary Obligations and the Scope of the Law of Contract' (1996) 2 *Legal Theory* 325.

[28] Locke, n. 13 above, para 46.

importantly, also to serve their shared interests. Allow them, in other words, to care for others, but do not immediately falsify this positive step by assuming that every (or any) individual cares for *all* others. All we are admitting is the fact that almost all will share interests with some others.

This is a good move, for otherwise everyone would be long dead. Humans are not cut out to survive alone. It puzzles me, in fact, why this is not pointed out more often in discussions of the state of nature, given that it is supposed in some way to model some conclusions for humans. Even G.A. Cohen, of all people, entertains the differing life chances of Able and Infirm, two inhabitants in the state of nature, without wondering whether even Able himself would survive on his own.[29] I think this point must be taken extremely seriously. Humans, *qua* humans, depend upon co-operative activity to survive as a matter of their very nature, for without the transmission of cultural knowledge humans die. We have insufficient instincts to survive without it. The picture of the lone camper in their all-weather clothing and books on edible plants is not the right one. Rather, drop a naked, native, New Yorker in the middle of the Serengeti. The point here is not to argue that by virtue of the contribution that cultural input makes to the realization of value from things, all proprietary rights in the state of nature are communally co-owned.[30] The point is rather that social activity is essential to human life, and so, even in the state of nature, some characterization of the terms of that social engagement is necessary. Otherwise, the state of nature simply does not serve as an enlightening thought experiment by which we can begin to understand the character of property rights.

We shall also not falsify the positive step of recognizing sharing and giving by abolishing the contractual model of co-operative behaviour, claiming that all social interactions involve interactions between those who share interests. Contractual co-operative behaviour has a nobility all its own, where, by forming agreements, even those who do not share interests can together advance their interests better than they could have done without this facility. Recognizing both kinds of co-operative behaviour is essential. The argument that I shall make is that property rights arise in consequence of characterizing a social context, in which these two basic kinds of co-operative activity exist.

Recall how property rights were provisionally introduced in the individualistic state of nature, on the provisional ground that it made it easier to avoid interferences with proprietary rights, and furthermore, that protecting proprietary rights *per se* would tend to introduce co-ordinating activity which, before the pressure of any scarcity, would seem somewhat inappropriate to that state of nature as envisaged. But, if we start first with the assumption that quite a lot of property, in particular land, is, as a rule, shared, i.e. co-operatively, communally exploited, *whether there is plenty or not*, it is likely to be the case that for all intents and purposes any non-trivial engagement to realize value by someone outside the

[29] Cohen, n. 17 above, 80–7. [30] Cf. Nozick, n. 15 above, at 93–5.

co-operative group with something which the co-operative group is presently using will interfere with the proprietary rights of those in the co-operative group, for 'working' the property communally is likely to be intensive, i.e. fully to exploit the property. So we move towards the *de facto* ownership of land, by the complete exploitation of value-realizing uses by members of the co-operative group acting together. *Vis-à-vis* others, their full exploitation essentially presents others with a duty to exclude themselves entirely, so, to that extent, ownership appears to have arisen. But it only works this way because the group acts co-operatively to exploit fully the value of the thing, so in so far as it is ownership, it is co-ownership, a co-ownership where the terms of the co-owners' relations *inter se* are governed by their mutual sharing of each other's interests. Consider this, if you want, a kind of family or tribal ownership.

The gift/contract distinction tracks, in a significant way, the proprietary rights/ownership distinction. Proprietary rights naturally align with *contractual* co-operative activity, while ownership rights *per se* align with *shared* or *cultural* co-operative activity. Proprietary rights are rights to defined realizations of the value of things. They are the sort of values that represent what might be called the production and consumption values of economic life, the goods of food, shelter, housing, and so on. It is easy to conceive the kinds of 'contractual' negotiations which may go on to determine which proprietary rights, which 'shares' as it were, will go to whom, based upon different individuals' actions or contributions to the productive enterprise. The array of values can thus be distributed in a way which allows individuals better to serve their own interests by negotiating with others seeking to serve their own interests. This view of property, in which ownership is regarded in its very essence as a 'bundle' of individuated rights to value, is much favoured as a modern analysis because it fits so well with the creative power of contracting 'efficiently' to allocate rights to the realization of value, and also with the economic analysis of law that treats every valuable entitlement as an ownership right.[31] Ownership, on this view, is not an open-ended right to a thing, but consists of any amalgam of rights to the disparate, actual, and potential values of a thing, i.e. any amalgam of proprietary rights.

On the other hand, the co-operative activity of the second kind cannot be reduced to individual rights to value in this way, since interests are shared. On this model, the benefits of giving and sharing cannot be fractioned into particular benefits to particular individuals, so cannot be the subject matter of individual rights; my interest in my friend's becoming educated, or my child's experiencing the values of music and musicianship, cannot be framed as a proprietary right to value in a sum of money, or a cello, which I gave them. My 'right' to realize this value in making a gift exists with, not apart from, their own rights freely to use the sum of money or cello as they wish, and their own rights to realize the value of these properties. Similarly with sharing: if I invite you to my flat to share a bottle

[31] See Penner, n. 4 above, at 63–4.

of whisky, my continuing ownership of the flat and the whisky, which entitles me to let you have a drink with me, are not proprietary rights in the right of access I endow you with, which entitles you to be there and have a drink. My right to use goes hand in hand with your right to take, and the value realized is one we share by exercising those rights. It would amount to a complete mischaracterization (albeit one which is often mistakenly and unfortunately made) to treat this sort of activity as one which represents the results of an unspoken contractual negotiation by which you and I have acquired particular self-interest-serving rights.

Taking full account of this activity explains why the use of property in these circumstances, whether real property rights to actual places or spaces, or personal property interests in things like bottles of wine, provide a *location* or a *site* or the *means* for the unfolding of this sort of activity; rights to the realization of shared values of this kind must be actual *ownership rights*, for these kinds of uses are, by their very nature, creatively open-ended, in that they depend upon a continuing interaction of interests the particular course, success, or failure of which cannot be spelled out in advance. There is no value of a proprietary character, no defined value, whose result can be assured in advance, and so no right to such a value can be claimed, any more than you can seriously promise to love someone forever. The point is not that social uses serving shared interests in this way are too vague to be defined—contractually negotiated rights and duties too can be more or less vague. The point is rather that the values that are created cannot properly be allocated through a system of individual rights protected by correlative duties.

The result is that property devoted to this kind of co-operative activity must inherently be 'co-owned', and the uses by individuals only loosely defined. The difference is, perhaps, along the lines of the difference between the sort of relations individuals have as guests in a hotel and the relations they have as members of a college. The necessary rights and duties of college members are the rights to: (1) a kind of common ownership—the right of each to access all, with general understandings as to the sort of conduct that is permitted and expected, and the right and duty to participate in the joint exploitation of the property for the benefit of all; and (2) co-ownership of the property in question *vis-à-vis* all others. Those who are not co-owners are subject to the duty not to interfere with the thing in question *per se*, for only by 'keeping off' is space provided for a realization of value, which cannot be framed in terms of proprietary rights. Incidentally, this is, roughly, the normative situation which we find in common law legal systems regarding the co-ownership of land.[32] And as co-owners, individuals may together act as a party to engage in the second, contractual form of social co-operation, where parties do not base their co-operation on their sharing of interests, but on serving their own.

[32] Cf. H Dagan and MA Heller, 'The Liberal Commons' (2001) 110 *Yale LJ* 549, in which it is speculatively argued that, in comparison with certain civil law systems, in American law the current rules of co-ownership insufficiently support communal co-ownership activity.

If this is right, then in a justifiable property system, ownership *per se*, that is, actual open-ended rights to things like land, can be justified on a non-provisional non-instrumental basis only when they draw their justification from the values arising from co-ownership as described. Thus Eric's individual ownership of his house is, on this view, justified because he will share it; not with everyone, but with some people, presumably those he likes. If Eric is a sociopath so that he truly has only self-interests, then, in justice, he should not be entitled to ownership, but merely proprietary rights to things. However, cases like Eric's are rare enough that we give everyone the benefit of the doubt.

This justification of ownership is neither romantic nor cynical. It is not romantic because we know that many people will join with others to form bonds of shared interests which are not particularly praiseworthy. However, if we have any commitment to autonomy, encourage though we may, we will have to live with the fact that many will not make the most of their capabilities. Neither, however, is it cynical, for it takes for granted that people will, in serving their own interests, serve interests they truly have in others.

In view of the foregoing, then, it appears that there may indeed be a non-provisional justification for ownership *per se*, a justification which points out how the open-ended right to the use of property may serve values (the sharing of interests) which simply cannot be accommodated if only proprietary rights, rights to specified values in things, are permitted. And it quite nicely dissolves the individualistic taint which has attached itself to ownership, at least amongst legal and political philosophers. It also, I think, reflects a great deal of common sense, for it must be the case that there are very few hermits, and furthermore that most others would regard it as a gross mischaracterization to say to them of their property that they hold it only for what they individually can get out of it.

10

Plants, Torts, and Intellectual Property

*Stephen R. Munzer**

Time was when anyone interested in intellectual property and genetics would concentrate on humans or other animals and on utility patents. But, as my thinking slows, I find that I identify more readily with plants. This shift in focus does not make the inquiry into intellectual property easier. On the contrary, the intellectual property rights available in plants are more diverse than those in humans or other animals. This diversity is itself part of the problem, for it creates unwieldy overlapping regimes of legal protection.

My aim is to show that systems of protection need improving. I propose and defend three specific improvements. First, the US system of separate and divergent protection of new plants depending on the mode of propagation should go. There should instead be a unified system for protecting intellectual property in asexually reproduced and sexually reproduced plants.

Secondly, on the issue of liability for genetic drift, there should be an alternative legal scheme, if pervasive and enduring prejudice disrupts the application of otherwise fair rules of tort law. If judges and juries harbour no prejudice, *pro* or *con*, toward genetically engineered crop plants, the usual rules governing negligence, nuisance, trespass, and strict liability under *Rylands v Fletcher*[1] would not usually lead to verdicts of liability for genetic drift. But if they are prejudiced for or against these crop plants, and if the prejudice is widespread and long-lasting, then prophylactic adjustment of the usual tort rules is justifiable. For instance, were there prejudice *against* transgenic crop plants, no one should be able to get legal relief from an owner of farmland for genetic drift—be the crops genetically engineered, conventional, or organic—unless the owner intended to harm neighbouring landowners, was reckless, or grew genetically engineered crops with a foreign gene

* My thanks go to Alison Grey Anderson, Carl Cranor, Richard A Epstein, Mark F Grady, Gregory C Keating, Neil Netanel, A Gregory Pinto, Kal Raustiala, Christen Raymond, and Daniel Tix. Presentations in 2004 to meetings of the American Philosophical Association in Pasadena, California, and the Law and Philosophy Discussion Group in Los Angeles led to improvements in this chapter. For material support I am grateful to the Academic Senate and the Dean's Fund at the University of California, Los Angeles.

1 (1865) 3 H & C 774, 159 ER 737 (Exch), rev'd, (1866) LR 1 Exch (Exch Chamber), aff'd, (1868) LR 3 HL 330.

that the owner knew to be dangerous. Legal relief should also be unavailable from a seed company for genetic drift unless the company knew that neighbours would suffer harm, was negligent, or sold seeds it knew, or should have known, to be dangerous. Differently, if there were a widespread and long-standing prejudice *in favour of* transgenic crop plants, it would be justifiable to hold seed companies to a standard of strict liability, as used in the case of defective products, for harm to farms.

Thirdly, a landowner should not be liable for patent infringement for using genetically modified seeds that blow onto his or her land from neighbouring property. *Monsanto Canada Inc. v Schmeiser*[2] was in significant part wrongly decided.

How can an essay of modest length address such different legal areas as tort and intellectual property? J.W. Harris, whom this volume honours, suggests an answer. The essentials of an institution of property, he writes, 'are the twin notions of trespassory rules and the ownership spectrum'.[3] The former notion is pertinent here. For Harris trespassory rules are 'any social rules, whether or not embodied in law, which purport to impose obligations on all members of a society, other than an individual or group who is taken to have some form of open-ended relationship to a thing, not to make use of that thing without the consent of the individual or group'.[4] In Bentham's memorable phrasing, ' "Let no one, Rusticus excepted," (so we will call the proprietor) "and those whom he allows meddle with such or such a field." '[5] My first and third proposals revise the trespassory rules applicable to intellectual property rights in plants. My second proposal conditionally adjusts the trespassory rules embodied in the law of tort, especially negligence, trespass, nuisance, and strict liability, that govern neighbouring plant growers. The second and third proposals alter trespassory rules in justifiable balance. In effect, the second favours, and the third disfavours, the interests of farmers or seed companies specializing in genetically engineered crop plants.

The structure and content of this chapter exemplify an intellectual experiment. The experiment tests a hypothesis about legal and philosophical casts of mind: that lawyers, including academic lawyers, typically seek judicious solutions to problems, whereas philosophers more often venture daring or counterintuitive solutions, or pronounce that no solution exists, or even that earlier thinkers misconceived the problems. In this article, I explore my own experience in trying to integrate legal and philosophical approaches. Harris would have understood the experiment. He was, temperamentally, part philosopher and part academic lawyer. Whether he would have thought the hypothesis true or false, alas, we shall never know.

[2] (2004) 239 DLR (4th) 271.

[3] *Property and Justice* (Clarendon Press, 1996), 5.

[4] Ibid. For Harris's account and use of trespassory rules, see ibid., 18–22, 24–6, 30–2, 43–6, 52–3, 55–6, 59–60, 86–90, 128–30, 334–5, 342–3, 345–6, 348, and 367–8.

[5] J Bentham, *Of Laws in General*, ed., HLA Hart (Athlone Press, 1970), 177.

(i) Making the US System More Uniform

At present in the United States, new plants can receive legal protection as trade secrets, by utility patents, by plant patents, and by plant variety certificates. I have no quarrel with the first two modes of protection. Trade secrets in information pertaining to plants are of middling practical importance, because they are vulnerable to independent discovery and reverse bioengineering. Utility patents under the Patent Act of 1952[6] can have great commercial significance. Such patents have been issued since *Ex parte Hibberd*.[7] The Supreme Court endorsed the practice by holding that if a plant satisfies the criteria of the Patent Act, it is a 'composition of matter' protectable by a utility patent.[8] The commercial significance of these cases is that a utility patent offers a more robust package of protection than either a plant patent or a plant variety certificate. Because a utility patent must satisfy more demanding criteria than a plant patent or a plant variety certificate, I have no problem with the stronger protection afforded by a utility patent on plants.

My quarrel is with the different legal protection that US law gives to asexually reproduced plants on the one hand, and sexually reproduced and tuber propagated plants on the other.

The Plant Patent Act of 1930, or PPA, affords patent protection to anyone who 'invents or discovers and asexually reproduces any distinct and new variety of plant.... other than a tuber propagated plant or a plant found in an uncultivated state'.[9] A plant patent is limited to a single claim on the plant itself as 'shown and described'.[10] Unauthorized reproduction of the plant or using or selling plants or parts of plants derived from unauthorized reproduction, infringes the patent. The statute incorporates by reference the usual requirements of originality, novelty, inventiveness, and utility.[11] But it waters down the written-description requirement for utility patents[12] to make it easier to get a plant patent than a utility patent. The description suffices if it is 'as complete as is reasonably possible'.[13] *Imazio Nursery, Inc. v Dania Greenhouses*[14] maintains that it is not enough that the patentee show that the alleged infringing plant has the same essential characteristics as the patented plant. To constitute infringement the defendant must have asexually reproduced the questioned plant from the patented plant.

[6] 35 USCA ss. 101–376 (2002).

[7] 227 USPQ 443 (PTO Bd App & Int 1985).

[8] *J.E.M. Ag Supply, Inc. v Pioneer Hi-Bred International, Inc.*, 534 US 124 (2001) (interpreting 35 USC s. 101). Cf. Transgenic plant/NOVARTIS II, OJ EPO (Mar. 2000) 111.

[9] 35 USC s. 161 (2000). The Plant Patent Act of 1930, Pub L No. 71–245, 46 Stat 376 (1930), is codified as amended in 35 USC ss. 161–164 (2000).

[10] 35 USC s. 162, para. 2.

[11] 'The provisions of this title relating to patents for inventions shall apply to patents for plants, except as otherwise provided': ibid., s. 161, para. 2.

[12] Ibid., s. 112, para. 1.

[13] Ibid., s. 162, para. 1.

[14] 69 F3d 1560, 1569–70 (Fed Cir 1995). The court held that under 35 USC s. 163 no infringement existed where the patent holder failed to show that a rival nursery's early-bloom heather derived asexually from the patentee's early-bloom heather.

Imazio Nursery rejects the view that the patented plant is a 'variety' as that word is used in the Plant Variety Protection Act of 1970, which I shall come to momentarily.[15] Thus, a plant patent gives the holder a modest package of intellectual property rights. The narrow conception of infringement effectively requires a physical taking of, or interference with, the plant or its parts.[16] Accordingly, the duties and restrictions placed on other persons are limited.

Two factors justify relaxing the written-description requirement for a plant patent, compared to a utility patent, on an asexually reproduced plant. First, it is fiendishly difficult to describe any such plant completely. Virtually all descriptions prove to be either over-inclusive or under-inclusive. Consider a rosebush whose yellow blossoms have black stipples. A description of it as black-stippled may include too much (other brighter-yellow roses may have black stipples also) or too little (the same variety may have grey rather than black stipples if the soil is different). Even if one had the entire genome of the rosebush in question, one might not know what causes various genes to switch on or off. Hence rosebushes with the same lineage and genetic make-up could have morphologically different blossoms due to epigenetic factors.

Secondly, because utility patents require a full written description, largely to enable a person skilled in the pertinent art to practise the invention, the self-propagating nature of an asexually reproduced plant makes this requirement far less important for plant patents. Besides, though hybridizing techniques are well known, obtaining a new rosebush may be as much a matter of luck as skill. Even with ample disclosure, a skilled rosebush breeder might not get the black-stippled yellow roses from the original crosses.[17]

The Plant Variety Protection Act of 1970, or PVPA, protects varieties of plants that are tuber propagated or sexually reproduced, including commercially important vegetables, beans, rice, and cereals.[18] A *plant variety* is a class of plants below the species level that display a particular defined characteristic. If a plant variety results from cultivation rather than occurs naturally, it is known technically as a cultivar (a contraction of *culti*vated *var*iety).[19] Protectable varieties are registered

[15] 69 F3d, at 1567–8 (interpreting 35 USC s. 161 versus 7 USC s. 2401(a)(9)).

[16] Ibid., at 1570.

[17] Benjamin Pi-Wei Liu clarified these matters for me.

[18] Pub L No. 91–577, 84 Stat 1542 (1970), codified as amended in 7 USC ss. 2321–2582 (2000).

[19] HT Hartmann and DE Kester, *Plant Propagation: Principles and Practices* (4th edn., Prentice-Hall, 1983), 12. The complete scientific name of a cultivated plant variety is given by its genus and species (in Latin) and its cultivar name (in a modern language)—for instance, *Syringa vulgaris* 'Mont Blanc', which is the Mont Blanc variety of lilac. To prevent confusion, the International Code of Nomenclature for Cultivated Plants governs the assigning of names to cultivars. It defines a cultivar as 'an assemblage of cultivated plants which is clearly distinguished by any characters (morphological, physiological, cytological, chemical, or others) and which when reproduced, sexually or asexually, retains its distinguishing characters': ibid. This definition explicitly allows for *asexually* reproduced cultivars, whereas the Plant Variety Protection Act of 1970 applies only to varieties that reproduce *sexually* or are *tuber propagated*: 7 USC s. 2401(a)(9) (2000). The language of the PVPA might make it seem that tuber propagation is some form of reproduction that is neither sexual nor asexual. In fact, propagation by tubers is asexual. Some botanists view varieties as subcategories of subspecies, whereas others see them as equivalent to subspecies. See PH Raven, RF Evert, and SE Eichhorn, *Biology of Plants* (6th edn., WH Freeman and Company/Worth Publishers, 1999), 264, 913.

with the US Department of Agriculture. There is no innovation or utility requirement for registration. The plant variety must, however, be new, distinct, uniform, and stable over generations. The registrant must establish these features and explain the genealogy and breeding procedure.[20] Infringement lies in others' planting, selling, distributing, importing, exporting, or reproducing the registered variety or its offspring. There are exceptions for research and non-commercial use.[21] Legal protection for most varieties lasts for twenty years from the date a certificate is issued. Protection for trees and vines lasts for twenty-five years.[22]

There is a quirk in the coverage of the PVPA. In the main, it applies to plants that reproduce *sexually*. But at the request of the potato industry, Congress amended the PVPA in 1994 to include tuber propagated plants.[23] Tuber propagation is a form of *asexual* reproduction. Potatoes and other tubers do not receive double protection, for the PPA does not apply to tuber propagated plants.[24] If, however, we leave tubers to one side, it is correct to say that the PVPA applies to sexually reproduced plants and the PPA to asexually reproduced plants.

The PVPA limits the legal protection it confers on plant varieties. One limit is a compulsory licensing requirement. It provides for a licence of up to two years at a reasonable royalty, if the Secretary of the USDA declares that licensing is necessary to ensure an adequate food supply.[25] Another limit is a 'saved seed' exemption. It permits farmers who grow protected varieties of, say, wheat or corn, to save harvested seeds for later 'use on the farm' to produce a subsequent crop.[26] Still another, and for now final, limit allows the Secretary to shorten the period of protection if the applicant delays in prosecuting its application for a certificate.[27]

I object to the differential protection of the PPA and the PVPA. First, the line between the PPA and the PVPA is arbitrary from the standpoint of plant propagation. Cultivated varieties can be reproduced asexually (by cuttings, graftings, divisions, and stored tubers) as well as sexually (by seeds). These differences, though relevant to botanists' classifications, do not justify divergent forms of intellectual property rights granted by different governmental agencies under different statutes. Secondly, obtaining a certificate under the PVPA is an onerous process, and yet the financial rewards are quite small. A recent empirical study indicates that licensing and enforcement activities under the PVPA are rare. Such activities are, however, common in the case of utility patents on plants.[28] Thirdly, the PVPA's meagre pay-off gives little incentive for research in plant breeding.[29] The statute

20 7 USC ss. 2402, 2422. 21 Ibid., ss. 2541, 2543, 2544. 22 Ibid., s. 2483(b)(1).

23 HR Rep No. 103–699, 103d Cong., 2d Sess, at 9. 24 35 USC s. 161 (2000).

25 7 USC s. 2404.

26 Ibid., s. 2543. *Asgrow Seed Co. v Winterboer* 513 US 179, 183–6 (1995), refused to extend the saved-seed exemption under ss. 2401(b)(1) and 2543 to certain sales of 'brown-bagged' seed.

27 7 USC s. 2483(b)(2).

28 MD Janis and JP Kesan, 'U.S. Plant Variety Protection: Sound and Fury . . . ?', (2002) 39 *Houston LR* 727, 753–77 (hereafter Janis and Kesan).

29 JR Kloppenburg, Jr., *First the Seed: The Political Economy of Plant Biotechnology, 1492–2000* (CUP, 1988), 141. He gives a concise, shrewd history of plant breeders' rights in the US: ibid. 130–51.

may, of course, provide something stronger than a trade secret and help in marketing a new plant. And the United States may need to keep the PVPA, or something like it, to honour its international obligations.[30] But for serious incentives to innovate and invest in developing new plant varieties, as the PVPA defines them, it is necessary to look to utility patents.

The legislative history of the PPA reveals why it was limited to asexually reproduced plants. After failed efforts in the early 1900s to bring plants within the scope of utility patents, nursery operators lobbied for statutory protection of asexually reproduced varieties. Such varieties were dear to their hearts, because nurseries developed and sold mainly ornamental plants and trees that reproduce asexually. Seed companies, in contrast, dealt mainly in food crop plants, and might have sensed that there would be political opposition to protecting seed plants during the Great Depression.[31] Later efforts to bring sexually reproduced plants under the PPA failed for various reasons.[32] As Mark D. Janis and Jay P. Kesan caution, one should not attribute 'to Congress a more coherent vision than the historical facts support. Plant variety protection in the United States owes its existence as much (or more) to expediency in the politics of plant patenting as to a clear-eyed normative vision of the appropriate range of protection for types of plant innovation.'[33]

It would be far better to have a single statute for all plant varieties, as botanically defined, to complement utility patents. A single statute would simplify US law and give uniformity to plant variety rights. The level of protection could be set so as to supply at least a modest incentive for plant breeding. Carefully drafted, a statute would satisfy US obligations under UPOV. It would reduce information costs to third parties, in the US and elsewhere, of ascertaining the sweep of plant variety rights, of making sure those rights were not violated, and of deciding whether to purchase them outright or obtain licences to produce or market the plants, and so on. Obviously, a sensible statute would allow the mode of propagation to make some difference. It would, for example, be a spark of sound sense to limit a farmer's entitlement to a saved-seed exemption to plants that reproduce sexually by seed. The heart of the proposal, then, is a plant variety statute that applies to all plants, no matter what the mode of propagation, gives weaker legal protection than a utility patent in return for having to satisfy less demanding criteria, and yet provides enough protection to yield an incentive for plant innovation.

[30] Janis and Kesan, n.28 above, 776–8. The international obligations come from the Union Internationale pour la Protection des Obtentions Végétales (UPOV) (1961). UPOV was revised in 1972, 1978, and 1991. The United States deposited its instrument of ratification on 22 Jan. 1999: ibid., 740–5, 778.

[31] C Fowler, 'The Plant Patent Act of 1930: A Sociological History of its Creation' (2000) 82 *Journal of the Patent and Trademark Society* 621, 634–5; Janis and Kesan, n. 28 above, 730–7; EM Thomas, 'Outline of the History of the United States Patent Office' (1936) 18, no. 7 *Journal of the Patent Office Society* 11, 122.

[32] Janis and Kesan, n. 28 above, 737–9; Kloppenburg, n. 29 above, 139.

[33] Janis and Kesan, n. 28 above, 737.

As a practical matter, the proposed statute would have to give legal protection closer to that of the PPA than that of the PVPA, except that the proposed statute, unlike the PPA, would have to create rights in plant varieties (rather than in an individual plant) and to prohibit much more than the physical taking of, or interference with, protected plants.

Space hardly exists to draft and defend such a statute here, and, in a predominantly jurisprudential collection, it is more fitting to consider objections in principle to the proposal. One potential criticism is that, even if the proposal is sound for one writing on a clean slate, it would be unwise, given that the United States has existing plant protection statutes. Legislative revision involves substantial costs. These include the time, energy, and money spent on drafting and passing a new statute and expended by farmers, lawyers, and others in rearranging their affairs accordingly. In short, the costs of substituting a new statute for the PPA and the PVPA should rule out substitutions that, if costless, it would otherwise make sense to make.

This objection proceeds too swiftly. True, no legislative reform is costless. But even judged from an economic perspective, the question is whether the costs of reform exceed the gains from reform. Often the answer is no. For example, if the PPA and the PVPA were repealed, and if all plants were covered by a new statute that elicited more plant innovation, then the gains could well exceed the costs of statutory reform.

A new objection rises from the ashes of the old: even if one grants that the foregoing reply is sound, the new statute would alter retroactively the legal position of existing holders of plant patents and plant variety certificates. Retroactive legislation is highly disfavoured and may take private property without compensation in violation of the takings clause of the Fifth Amendment. Also, the upset expectations of existing holders are costs, and these costs may be large enough to make legislative reform unwise from an economic point of view.

In response, I grant that retroactive legislation imposes costs and is disfavoured. Yet even granting these points, I can still disable the objection. First, in cases where existing holders of plant patents or plant variety certificates would be unjustifiably harmed by retroactive imposition of the new statute, the legislature should draft the statute so as to 'grandfather in' these existing holders. So, in these cases usually the new statute would apply only to plant innovations made or filed after the statute was passed. I am receptive to flexible transition strategies from the old PPA–PVPA regime to the new legislative regime.[34] Secondly, one must state the costs accurately. Plant certificate holders would probably prefer the new statute to the PVPA because the PVPA provides little incentive to innovate. Plant patent holders might not much mourn repeal of the PPA if the new statute applied to plant varieties and protected against more than physical takings and interferences. In short, the costs stemming directly from retroactivity are unlikely to be as high

[34] L Kaplow, 'An Economic Analysis of Legal Transitions' (1986) 99 *Harvard LR* 509, offers sophisticated transition strategies.

as the objection supposes. Thirdly, some retroactive statutes are far more disfavoured than others. The *ex post facto* clause prohibits retroactive penal legislation.[35] It does not apply to retroactive legislation affecting property, contracts, and taxation. I argue elsewhere that statutes retroactively modifying property rights are, more often than is generally supposed, both constitutional and justifiable on policy grounds.[36]

A different, and for present purposes final, objection is political. Assume, the objector says, that the proposed statute would retroactively affect some existing plant patent and plant variety certificate holders adversely, that the statute would be constitutional and justifiable on policy grounds, and that grandfathering would be unwarranted. Then, those who stand to be harmed by the proposed statute would lobby vigorously against it. The ivory tower is no match for the sturdier halls of Congress. The statute would never be enacted.

I answer: don't bet on it. In its history, Congress has passed statutes over the objections of powerful interest groups many times. Statutes cleaning up slaughter-houses, laying the foundations of the New Deal, and granting civil rights without regard to race or creed are premier examples. Anyway, the statute I envision will tend to improve the position of large seed companies, which currently have to settle for PVPA protection or satisfy the more demanding conditions for a utility patent. Further, nursery operators, who are the main holders of plant patents, and trade associations representing their interests, have much less political power than large seed growers. Doubtless some opposition will arise to any new proposal. But the opposition I anticipate lacks overwhelming force.

Whilst reforming protection of plants lacks the urgency of securing civil rights, most legislators and legal scholars in the US seem scarcely aware that the double regime of the PPA and the PVPA is an utter outlier on the global scene. The International Convention for the Protection of the New Varieties of Plants (UPOV, Act of 1991) provides a short model statute. The Australian Plant Breeders' Rights Act of 1994, as amended by Act No. 148 of 2002, is a fine example of a more detailed statute. Members of the EC have a supranational Community statute based on UPOV (1991), which they can supplement with their own national legislation. The UK, for example, does so with the Plant Varieties Act 1997 and later 'statutory instruments' and regulations. Worldwide, some ninety-one countries now offer intellectual property protection to plant varieties; another twenty-nine countries are considering legislation; the systems in India and the Andean Community diverge markedly from most western models.[37] Among the fifty-five members of UPOV, only the US has a statutory regime with different rules, depending mainly on the mode of propagation. Proving a negative is treacherous, but, as yet, I have found no other country that has twin statutes

[35] US Const art. I, s. 9, cl. 3; ibid., art. I, s. 10, cl. 1; *Calder v Bull*, 3 US (3 Dall) 386 (1798).

[36] SR Munzer, 'A Theory of Retroactive Legislation' (1982) 61 *Texas LR* 425.

[37] Bonwoo Koo, C Nottenburg, and PG Pardey, 'Plants and Intellectual Property: An International Appraisal' (2004) 306 *Science* 1295.

akin to the PPA and the PVPA. Just as the US made certain concessions for the uniformity of TRIPs, it should now enact a uniform statute for all plant varieties without regard to the mode of propagation.

To be sure, many features of US law pertaining to intellectual property differ from those of other legal systems. Sometimes the differences, such as first-to-invent versus first-to-file regimes of patent law, are fundamental. I do not claim that the bifurcated arrangements for plants under the PPA and PVPA are legally the most fundamental or economically the most significant differences. Nevertheless, the split protections of the PPA and the PVPA are far from optimal. A uniform US statute for all plant varieties is eminently justifiable.

(ii) GMOs and Liability for Harm

So far I have dealt almost entirely with traditional methods of creating new plants. I now shift to the genetic engineering of new plants—genetically modified organisms, or GMOs for short. Methods of inserting foreign genes into an existing plant include using DNA-coated metal microprojectiles, benign plasmids as vectors, and direct uptake by protoplasts of plant cells. A foreign gene can impart resistance to herbicides or pesticides in the resulting new plant, or endow the edible portion of the new plant with better appearance, a longer shelf life, or increased nutritional value. One can confer resistance to the herbicides glyphosate, glufosinate, and bromoxynil by genetic engineering. Resistance to the herbicide imidazolinone results from mutagenesis and, thus produced, does not qualify as transgenic.[38]

Cool though this description may be, hot is the word for the fierce debates generated by GM crop plants. The real heat comes from debates over GM *food* crop plants and GM *foods*. The most common non-food GM crop is cotton. People the world over wear clothes made of GM cotton without much complaint. In due time, GM maize or sugar may be used instead of petroleum to make bio-fuel or bio-plastics.[39]

In this section I pursue a complicated strategy. I first investigate liability for harm caused by growing GMOs. The investigation assumes that judges and juries are free from prejudice—*pro* or *con*—regarding the risks of GMOs and use standard doctrines pertaining to tort liability. I then consider the possibility of prejudice and how one might adjust legal doctrines to correct for it. People could be prejudiced *against* GMOs—'they'll damage the environment and make you sick, no matter what the corporate lackeys say'. For purposes of argument, I assume here that genetically engineered crops merely extend other forms of agricultural innovation and consider how to adjust legal doctrines in order to offset a prejudice against GMOs. Alternatively, people could be prejudiced

[38] HJ Beckie, G Séguin-Swartz, H Nair, SI Warwick, and E Johnson, 'Multiple Herbicide-Resistant Canola Can Be Controlled by Alternative Herbicides' (2004) 52 *Weed Science* 152.

[39] 'The Men in White Coats are Winning, Slowly', *The Economist*, 9 Oct. 2004, at 63.

in favour of GMOs—'they won't hurt you a bit despite hysterical cries to the contrary'. In discussing this possibility, I assume that GM crop plants do more than merely extend other forms of agricultural innovation and consider how to mould legal doctrines to offset a prejudice in favour of GMOs. I take no position on what risks GMOs actually carry.

To make my strategy clear I distinguish among bias, prejudice, risk, risk assessment, and risk distribution. As understood here, bias is a mental leaning in favour of, or against, someone or something. Ordinarily, one should strive to be unbiased, which requires figuring out one's mental inclinations and the reasons underlying them. Prejudice is a preconceived and unreasonable opinion or judgement. 'Prejudice' is a stronger word than 'bias', for prejudice implies that the unreasonable opinion or judgement is tinged by suspicion or fear, or, differently, by enthusiasm and strong attraction. Subsections (b) and (c) below deal with widespread and long-lasting prejudice. I want to investigate how the legal system might correct for this form of irrationality and decisions influenced by it.

Risk, as understood here, is the product obtained by discounting (multiplying) the gravity of an adverse outcome by the probability of that outcome. This 'product' is often only quasi-mathematical. Sometimes we can both put a value on the gravity of an outcome and specify its probability. Sometimes we can do one, or the other, but not both, and sometimes we can do neither. Hence, sometimes we can express the product (expected value) mathematically and sometimes we can only specify a range of expected values or make a rough estimate. Risk assessment compares the risk of one adverse outcome with other risks and with possible benefits. Risk distribution is a specification of the individuals or groups that bear a given risk.[40]

The relevance of these distinctions to this treatment of GMOs and liability for harm is as follows. With effort, people can avoid *prejudice* and *bias* on this topic but not *risk*. In making decisions about GMOs and liability, we must not only identify risks but also engage in *risk assessment*. Assessing risk is especially difficult when probabilities, the nature and gravity of adverse outcomes, precaution costs, and pertinent benefits, are unknown. The difficulties mount when we bring *risk distribution* into the matter. Although I cannot argue the matter here, I doubt that decisions involving such uncertainties surrender justifiably to consequentialist considerations of maximizing, say, average or aggregate preference-satisfaction. Instead, such decisions, and especially decisions made under uncertainty about harm from GMOs, have to attend to the effects on particular individuals or groups. Above all, they have to take into account the effects on the life prospects of the least well off in societies or those most burdened by decisions about GMOs. In effect, I am sympathetic to Rawlsian and Scanlonian approaches to these decisions.[41]

[40] These distinctions partly follow JE Krier, 'Risk Assessment', in P Newman (ed.), *The New Palgrave Dictionary of Economics and the Law* (Macmillan Reference Limited, 1998), iii, 347–50.

[41] J Rawls, *A Theory of Justice* (Harvard University Press, 1971); TM Scanlon, *What We Owe to Each Other* (Harvard University Press, 1998).

After this uncomfortably Olympian preamble, it is time to get down to brass tacks. Consider three farms situated as follows:

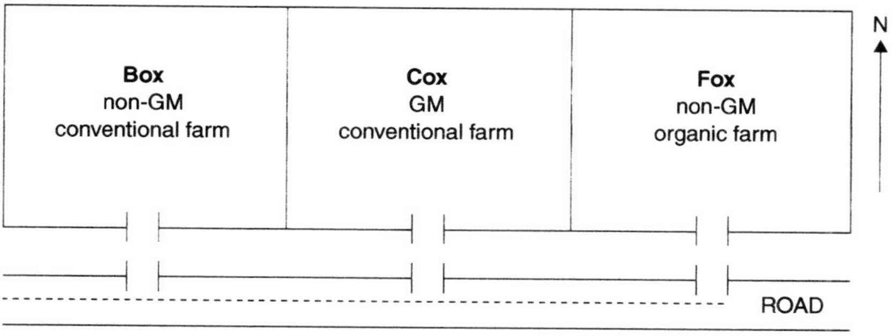

Box grows non-GM soya beans using conventional methods. Cox grows GM soya beans by conventional means. Cox's soya beans contain a foreign gene making them resistant to the herbicide glyphosate ('Roundup') and a foreign gene from the Brazil nut that increases the soya beans' protein content. Fox grows non-GM soya beans in accordance with organic standards.[42] All three begin farming at the same time. When the wind blows from east to west, genetic material from Cox's soya beans spreads to Box's farm. When it blows from west to east, genetic material from Cox's soya beans spreads to Fox's farm. Insects common to agricultural areas also spread pollen and seeds from farm to farm.

What harm results? Box alleges that Cox's 'Roundup Ready' soya beans have conferred glyphosate-resistance on weeds on Box's farm. Consequently, Box has had to use a different herbicide to kill weeds. By contrast with *Plant Genetic Systems*,[43] where the spread of herbicide-resistance to weeds was considered speculative, Box asserts that he has solid evidence of its spread to weeds on his farm. Furthermore, Box says, he sold his soya beans to a manufacturer who was held liable when its product caused an allergic response in a sensitive consumer. Box seeks an injunction against Cox's growing GM soya beans. Box also seeks damages for the costs of more herbicide and ridding his farm of genetically altered weeds, indemnification for damages that he paid to the manufacturer, and injury to Box's reputation as a non-GMO farmer.

Fox alleges that genetic material from Cox's soya beans has infiltrated Fox's own soya bean crop. No longer can Fox market his soya beans as 'organic'. Organic foods fetch a premium compared to both GM foods and non-GM conventionally grown foods. Fox prays for an injunction against Cox's growing GM soya beans. Fox also seeks damages for the loss of his organic certification and subsequent loss

[42] See the Organic Food Production Act of 1990, 7 USC ss. 6501–6523 (2000). Under USDA standards proposed on 7 Mar. 2000, food from GM crop plants does not qualify as 'organic' even if the plants are grown in conformity with organic standards. Under EC law, 'Genetically modified organisms (GMOs) and products derived therefrom are not compatible with the organic production method': Council Regulation (EC) No. 1804/1999 of 19 July 1999 [1999] OJ L222/1, Recital 10.

[43] O J EPO (Aug. 1995) 545, 566–7.

of profits, the cost of ridding his farm of genetic material from Cox's soya beans, and injury to his reputation as an organic farmer.

(a) Decisions without Prejudice: Four Torts

Assume that Box and Fox can prove their allegations and damages. Under what legal theories may they seek relief? The obvious candidates are negligence, trespass, strict liability, and nuisance. I investigate these theories under the assumption that judges and juries have no prejudice in favour of, or against, GMOs.

Negligence, as an independent tort, is a breach of a legal obligation of care that causes loss or damage to another's interests. The duty of care is circumscribed by a foreseeable likelihood of loss in the event someone fails to conform to a pertinent standard of conduct. A theory of negligence can succeed in cases involving a landowner's using his or her property so as to cause harm to another's property. For instance, a pharmaceutical factory's low-level radiation emissions can make the factory owner liable for damage to adjacent business property.[44]

Trespass is a physical invasion of another's interest in the exclusive possession of his or her land. Liability is strict; the invasion need not be negligent. The wrongdoer need not have to intend to invade, but must engage voluntarily in the activity—here, the farming of GM soya beans—that causes the invasion. The invasion must be physical; excessive light or sound is not enough; microscopic particles suffice.[45] Extent, duration, and even harm are not pertinent to liability, yet do affect the amount of damages.[46]

Somewhat akin to trespass is the doctrine of strict liability under *Rylands v Fletcher*.[47] Water in the defendants' reservoir broke through into an abandoned coal mine shaft on their property and eventually flooded the plaintiff's adjacent coal mine. Under the English law of the day, trespass did not lie because the flooding was neither immediate nor direct, and no nuisance existed because the damage was neither recurring nor continuous and the water did not offend the senses. American courts interpreted the rule of *Rylands v Fletcher* as applicable mainly to abnormally hazardous things or activities. In due time most American courts accepted the rule so understood.[48]

Nuisance is an unreasonable and substantial interference with the use and enjoyment of land that harms the owner or possessor. To be substantial, the interference must exceed some threshold. A momentary bad smell is not enough, but in most locations a continuing stench is. Non-physical interferences, such as prolonged noise or excessive light, can be nuisances. Yet so can interferences that involve small particulates such as smoke; in this respect, nuisance and trespass

[44] *Maryland Heights Leasing, Inc. v Mallinkrodt Inc.* 706 SW2d 218 (Mo Ct App 1985).

[45] *Martin v Reynolds Metals Co.* 221 Ore 86, 342 P2d 790 (1959), involved microscopic fluoride particles.

[46] WP Keeton (gen. ed.), *Prosser and Keeton on the Law of Torts* (5th edn., West, 1984), 67–85 (hereafter *Prosser and Keeton on the Law of Torts*).

[47] (1866) LR 1 Exch 265, aff'd., (1868) LR 3 HL 330.

[48] *Prosser and Keeton on the Law of Torts*, n. 46 above, 548–68.

overlap. Harm is an element of nuisance, but not of trespass. To qualify as a nuisance, the wrongdoer's interference must be unreasonable. Many cases turn on whether the defendant's conduct, in light of the locality and the harm inflicted on the plaintiff, is nevertheless a reasonable use of the defendant's own land. Case law constantly adjudicates and adjusts the rights and duties of both parties. Courts often look at the social and economic value of the parties' respective uses of their land. Economists often insist that an injunction should issue only if the defendant can prevent the harm at a lower cost than the plaintiff.

With this dismally blackletter summary in hand, we can assess Box and Fox's prospects. Cox is not liable to either Box or Fox in negligence. The existence of a duty of care on Cox is disputable. If such a duty exists, its scope is disputable, for a foreseeable likelihood of injury to conventional and organic farmers is in doubt. Box and Fox may well find that their scientific evidence and expert testimony are more than offset by Cox's scientific evidence and expert testimony. Besides, they would still have to show that Cox's farming practices fell short of a pertinent standard of conduct.[49]

Nevertheless, Cox is liable in trespass to Box. Genetic material from Cox's soya beans has physically invaded Box's farm and infringed Box's right to exclusive possession. Box can recover money damages for the resulting harm. However, Box gets nothing for injury to his reputation as a non-GMO farmer, because there is no evidence that Cox intended to harm Box's reputation. The same applies to Fox's lawsuit. Fox can recover in trespass for all items of damage except injury to his reputation as an organic farmer. Neither Box nor Fox is likely to obtain an injunction unless balancing the equities so requires.

The rule of *Rylands v Fletcher*, as understood by American courts, is unlikely to get the plaintiffs any equitable or legal remedy. It is highly doubtful that a judge or jury would regard Cox's growing GM soya beans as an abnormally dangerous or ultra-hazardous activity. True, a few cases have awarded damages for the misalliance of an escaped scrub bull with a pedigreed heifer.[50] But depredations of escaped animals, including the impregnation of prized females of the same species, form a distinct topic in the jurisprudence of strict liability. These cases afford scant prospect of liability for escaped seeds or pollen, for they deal with mammals and a few other vertebrates. As for insect-aided gene flow, Cox should not be liable if he fails to interfere with the normal movement of non-disease-carrying insects. It would be different if, as in *Greyvensteyn v Hattingh*,[51] Cox shooed insects from his land onto the farms of his neighbours. Conceivably, liability could exist for insects that transmit disease, such as mosquitoes that carry the parasite that causes malaria. Still, insects common to agricultural areas that spread seeds or pollen from one farm to another are not a plausible basis for liability.

Recovery for nuisance is even less likely. The key issue is whether Cox's growing GM soya beans is unreasonable. Judges instruct juries on the law, and almost

[49] RA Repp, 'Biotech Pollution: Assessing Liability for Genetically Modified Crop Production and Genetic Drift' (2000) 36 *Idaho LR* 585, 614–6.

[50] e.g., *Kopplin v Quade* 145 Wis 454, 130 NW 511 (1911).

[51] [1911] AC 355 (PC).

always juries must decide whether the defendant's land use is unreasonable. In the United States, where many people regard growing GM crops as reasonable, juries are likely to decide in favour of Cox. Nuisance allows no damages for injury to reputation. Precisely the same applies to Fox. In sum, nuisance and strict liability under the rule of *Rylands v Fletcher* are less promising causes of action for the plaintiffs than is trespass.

The best precedent for Box and Cox is probably *Langan v Valicopters Inc.*[52] Patrick and Dorothy Langan were organic farmers whose crops were damaged by aerial spraying. They sued the spraying company, the firm that sold the pesticide, and the neighbouring conventional farmers whose land was the intended target of the spraying. Pesticide dispersed by the company's helicopter contaminated the Langans' organic crops. Their entire property was decertified as an organic farm. Their crops were pulled out to prevent further contamination of the soil. The jury found in the Langans' favour. The Washington Supreme Court affirmed on grounds of strict liability and negligence.

Valicopters is, however, distinguishable from the cases of Box and Fox. To begin, *Valicopters* helps Box little, for only Fox is an organic farmer. Next, the main defendant in *Valicopters* engaged in aerial crop spraying, whereas Cox grows GM crops. Thus, the strict liability theory used in *Valicopters* is the robust tort version, not the watered down version of *Rylands v Fletcher*. Lastly, Patrick Langan testified that the company's helicopter, during one pass, had the spray on while it flew directly over his property. At no point did Cox enter or fly over Fox's farm whilst disseminating genetic material. The genetic drift came from insects and the wind.

We see broadly similar results in the UK. The English law of negligence, in action, differs somewhat from its American counterpart.[53] It is more unified, uses bench trials rather than juries, and compensates plaintiffs' lawyers on a non-contingent basis.[54] And yet, the central components of negligence are highly similar: duty, scope, standard of conduct, foreseeability, breach, causation, and loss. So negligence is not a promising theory for plaintiffs.

Contemporary British treatises on tort usually contain a brief treatment of trespass to land.[55] The tort is unjustifiable interference with its possession. But the interferences discussed are chiefly those of persons or animals over which owners fail to exercise enough control, or landowners who place rubbish or stones near the boundary line which then topple onto another's land.

For interferences potentially relevant here, the strict liability rule of *Rylands v Fletcher* does the heavy lifting. Over nearly a century and a half, British courts and scholars have interpreted and adjusted this rule differently from their American counterparts. The rule, as stated by Blackburn J in the Court of

52 88 Wash 2d 855, 567 P2d 218 (1977).

53 BS Markesinis and SF Deakin, *Tort Law* (4th edn., Clarendon Press, 1999), 69–237 (hereafter Markesinis and Deakin).

54 Ibid., 203–5.

55 Ibid., 413–21; WVH Rogers, *Winfield and Jolowicz on Tort* (17th edn., Sweet & Maxwell, 2002), 487–502.

Exchequer Chamber, is:

> [T]he person who for his own purposes brings on his lands and collects and keeps there anything likely to do mischief if it escapes, must keep it in at his peril, and, if he does not do so, is prima facie answerable for all the damage which is the natural consequence of its escape.[56]

The House of Lords affirmed. There, Lord Cairns opined that, to be liable, the defendant must make a 'non-natural use'[57] of his or her land. Forty-five years later, Lord Moulton parsed this requirement as:

> some special use bringing with it increased danger to others, and must not merely be the ordinary use of the land or such a use as is proper for the general benefit of the community.[58]

The strict liability rule required accumulation (being brought to the defendant's land), non-natural use (as explained by Lord Moulton), escape, and foreseeability.

One might suppose that a British judge could be quite sympathetic to Box and Fox. Yet two factors complicate the matter. One is that *Cambridge Water v Eastern Counties Leather plc*[59] saw *Rylands v Fletcher* as a specimen of private nuisance, which blurs the distinction between strict liability and nuisance.[60] Another complicating factor is that UK administrative regulations, including site-specific regulations, may restrain judges from allowing a jury to conclude that Cox's growing GM soya beans is either non-natural or unreasonable.[61] These factors may make strict liability in the UK less promising for plaintiffs than trespass in the US.

The English law of nuisance is no more reassuring for Box and Fox than its American cousin. Cox is liable only if he unlawfully interfered with the plaintiffs' use of their land. To be unlawful, Cox's use must be unreasonable. Much as in the US, judgments of unreasonableness have to consider the nature of the locality, the intensity of the interference, and the sensitivity of a plaintiff's use (which is pertinent to Fox, the organic farmer)—all assessed with respect to the 'give and take as between neighbouring occupiers of land'.[62]

Every silver lining has its cloud, and the cloud of proof further darkens the prospects of both Box and Fox. Earlier I assumed that they could prove their allegations and damages. This assumption may well be false. Genes coding for resistance to herbicides (or pesticides) do not often jump from crop plants to weeds. Ordinarily, genes jump more readily between plants of the same or a related species, such as between grasses.[63]

56 *Fletcher v Rylands* (1866) LR 1 Exch 265, 279.

57 *Rylands v Fletcher* (1868) LR 3 HL 330, 339.

58 *Rickards v Lothian* [1913] AC 263, 280.

59 [1994] 2 AC 264 (HL).

60 It does not erase the distinction: Markesinis and Deakin, n. 53 above, 504. *Crowhurst v Amersham Burial Board* (1878) 4 Exch D 5, imposed strict liability for poisonous vegetation. Only staunch opponents of GM crop plants regard all of them as poisonous.

61 M Lee and R Burrell, 'Liability for the Escape of GM Seeds: Pursuing the "Victim"?' (2002) 65 *MLR* 517, 529–35.

62 Ibid., 530–2; *Cambridge Water v Eastern Counties Leather plc* [1994] 2 AC 264, 299.

63 LS Watrud, EH Lee, A Fairbrother, C Burdick, JR Reichman, M Bollman, M Storm, G King, and PK van de Water, 'Evidence for Landscape-Level, Pollen-Mediated Gene Flow from Genetically Modified Creeping Bentgrass with *CP4 EPSPS* as a Marker' (2004) 101 *Proceedings of the National Academy of Sciences USA* 14,533.

When genes jump from cultivar crop plants to weeds, often the cultivars belong to the same 'weedy' species. For example, 'canola' applies to a number of cultivars of *Brassica napus* (oilseed rape). Canola is desirable because its seeds are lower in saturated fats and fatty acids than those of wild *B. napus*, whose progenitors are *B. campestris* (birdsrape mustard) and *B. oleracea* (a species that includes cruciferous plants such as kale, cauliflower, broccoli, and cabbage).[64] Cross-pollination occurs at low frequencies from commercial herbicide-resistant canola cultivars to wild *B. napus* and related weedy species.[65] If some canola or oilseed plants become resistant to one or more herbicides, farmers can control the plants by using other herbicides.[66] Even so, scientists genetically engineer many species and varieties of plant for many traits besides resistance to herbicides and pesticides. Evidence exists for both crop-to-crop and crop-to-wild transgene flow.[67] Debate persists on how risky genetic drift is.[68] At present, however, Box and Fox seem unlikely to prove their allegations and damages.

Furthermore, Box's allergic response claim is implausible. GM foods receive pre-market testing. If the foreign gene comes from a Brazil nut, it is almost certain to be tested because many people have nut allergies.[69] Post-market testing, though, is perhaps spottier; the most notable example so far is the StarLink incident, in which potentially allergenic genetically modified corn, limited to use for animal feed and industrial purposes, found its way into corn products for human consumption.[70] Still, no such lapse is present in the facts before us. Box's case is on the verge of collapse.

Fox may fare somewhat better, at least on a theory of trespass in the US. The facts are likely to be more complicated than his original allegation. His farm probably has three varieties of soya bean plants: his original organic variety, Cox's GM variety, and a cross of the two. To the naked eye the three will be indistinguishable. To discover which plants have a gene for herbicide resistance, it will be necessary either to do some sophisticated testing (generally for a 'marker' rather than the gene

[64] L Hall, 'Pollen Flow between Herbicide-Resistant *Brassica napus* is the Cause of Multiple-Resistant *B. napus* Volunteers' (2000) 48 *Weed Science* 688, 689.

[65] Ibid.; MA Rieger, M Lamond, C Preston, SB Powles, and RT Roush, 'Pollen-Mediated Movement of Herbicide Resistance between Commercial Canola Fields' (2002) 296 *Science* 2386, 2388; MA Rieger, TD Potter, C Preston, and SB Powles, 'Hybridisation between *Brassica napus* L. and *Raphanus raphanistum* L. under Agronomic Field Conditions' (2001) 103 *Theoretical Applications of Genetics* 555.

[66] Beckie *et al.*, n. 38 above; IJ Senior, C Moyes, and PJ Dale, 'Herbicide Sensitivity of Transgenic Multiple Herbicide-Tolerant Oilseed Rape' (2002) 58 *Pest Management Science* 405.

[67] NC Ellstrand, 'When Transgenes Wander, Should We Worry?' (2001) 125 *Plant Physiology* 1543.

[68] e.g., National Research Council, *Environmental Effects of Transgenic Plants: The Scope and Adequacy of Regulation* (National Academy Press (USA), 2002).

[69] Pioneer Hi-Bred International, Inc. tried to insert such a gene into soya beans in the mid-1990s. Independent testing revealed that the gene encoded an allergen and the plant never made it to market: JA Nordlee, SL Taylor, JA Townsend, LA Thomas, and RK Bush, 'Identification of a Brazil-Nut Allergen in Transgenic Soybeans' (1996) 334 *New England Journal of Medicine* 688. Genetic engineering can also be used to *remove* allergens from GM crop plants: A Pollack, 'Gene Jugglers Take to Fields for Food Allergy Vanishing Act', *New York Times*, 15 Oct. 2002, D2.

[70] MR Taylor and JS Tick, *Post-Market Oversight of Biotech Foods: Is the System Prepared?* (Pew Initiative on Food and Biotechnology/Resources for the Future, Apr. 2003), 1–3, 73–5, 78–93.

itself) or, more crudely, to treat the plants with Roundup. If Fox can prove contamination of his farm by Cox's GM soya beans, Fox has a respectable chance of getting money damages for his economic loss, but not for injury to his reputation.

(b) Decisions resulting from Prejudice against GMOs: Two New Rules

To this point I have shown that Box and Fox are unlikely to prevail under current law so long as neither judges nor juries are prejudiced. If, however, judges and juries were prejudiced *against* GMOs, then triers of fact could engage in a sort of civil 'jury nullification'. They could misinterpret, misapply, or simply disregard the four tort doctrines just discussed. The question then arises as to how one might correct for the effects of prejudice, given the working assumption that GM agriculture is an extension of other forms of agricultural innovation. More fully, the assumption and the intended corrective or prophylactic go like this. Non-GM innovations, as by cross-breeding, often depend on the shuffling of genes. The aims are to produce crops that are hardier or whose edible products are tastier, or more nutritious, or stay fresh longer. GM innovations add or delete genes and have the same aims. No reason exists to treat GM crops differently from non-GM crops, except for the prophylactic reason of preventing the consequences of prejudice. To my knowledge no tort liability exists for genetic drift in the case of adjacent non-GM farmers. Accordingly, no tort liability should exist for genetic drift in the case of adjacent farmers, only one of whom grows GM crops, or, for that matter, of adjacent GM farmers, save in exceptional circumstances.

Designing prophylactic rules against hypothetical prejudice might seem to be a curious intellectual enterprise. Often, we let the tort system career on its way, despite inadequate scientific evidence. Consider silicone breast implant litigation in the US from 1984 to 1994. American juries awarded individual plaintiffs damages of up to $25 million for connective tissue diseases and other disorders, despite the fact that evidence was, at best, preliminary that the implants caused the diseases. Dow Corning, the implant manufacturer which faced astonishing potential liability, entered into a multi-billion dollar settlement in 1994. After the settlement agreement fell apart, the company filed for bankruptcy in 1995. Large epidemiological studies published in 1994 and 1996 showed that women with silicone implants had no larger risk or incidence of connective tissue diseases or other disorders than did otherwise similar women who had no breast implants. Juries awarded staggering damages and helped to plunge a large company into bankruptcy on the basis of faulty evidence.[71]

[71] SE Gabriel, WM O'Fallon, LT Kurland, CM Beard, JE Woods, and LJ Melton III, 'Risk of Connective Tissue Diseases and Other Disorders after Breast Implantation' (1994) 330 *New England Journal of Medicine* 1697; BG Silverman, SL Brown, RA Bright, RG Kaczmarek, JB Arrowsmith-Lowe, and DA Kessler, 'Reported Complications of Silicone Gel Breast Implants: An Epidemiologic Review' (1996) 124 *Annals of Internal Medicine* 744. Cf. M Angell, *Science on Trial: The Clash of Medical Evidence and the Law in the Breast Implant Case* (W.W. Norton, 1996).

Yet, sometimes, we interfere with the tort system. Medical malpractice is a good illustration. At least through the first half of the twentieth century, US juries were chary of finding liability and imposing appropriate damages in a significant number of malpractice cases. A key reason was that Americans held physicians and surgeons in high esteem and were reluctant to second-guess defendant doctors. When the pendulum swung in the other direction, the frequency and amount of jury awards rose, as did medical malpractice insurance premiums. Medical associations and other groups lobbied state legislatures to adjust tort rules pertaining to liability and damages. Caps on non-economic damages, limitations on lawyers' contingent fees, and insistence on high qualifications for expert witnesses were especially common.

Neither breast implant litigation nor changes in medical malpractice rules are wholly parallel to tort liability for genetic drift. The implant litigation ran its course in about ten years and did not involve prejudice. Tort law made no changes specific to this litigation. Medical malpractice may have involved some prejudice, or at least bias, in favour of doctors in the first half of the twentieth century. Even though some tort rules were changed, the changes did not spring from a new-found prejudice against doctors.

All the same, there are some analogies. Scientific evidence regarding genetic drift is preliminary and unlikely to become conclusive in the next ten years. Prejudice, or at least bias, is common in regard to GM crops and GM foods. This phenomenon is not uniform, but divides along geographical and cultural lines. In the main, Americans are receptive to these crops and foods, whereas Europeans are not. Given these, at least limited, analogies, considering prophylactic adjustments to tort liability doctrines concerning liability for genetic drift is not such a curious enterprise after all.

I now propose two new rules. One is directed to farmers and the other to seed companies. Their net effect is to reduce the chance that farmers, including GM farmers, will be liable to their neighbours but to leave room for a justifiable level of tort liability on seed companies. Space does not permit examination of alternative correctives such as science courts, specialized administrative agencies, judicial power to stay proceedings until better scientific evidence is available, or expansion of post-judgment relief.[72]

The first proposed new rule is: no one may obtain an injunction against or damages from an owner of farmland for genetic drift—be the crops GM, non-GM, or organic—unless the owner (1) intended to harm neighbouring landowners, (2) acted with reckless disregard of neighbours' interests, or (3) grew GM crops with a foreign gene which the owner knew to be dangerous. Probably few will quarrel with this rule as applied to non-GM or organic crops. So I shall concentrate on its application to GM crops.

The proposed rule creates three exceptions. The first involves intended harm to neighbouring landowners. Quite justifiably, tort law separates unintentional harm, whether caused knowingly, unknowingly, or negligently, from intentional

[72] EK Cheng, 'Changing Scientific Evidence' (2003) 88 *Minnesota LR* 315.

harm. There is no reason to shield GM farmers or non-GM farmers from liability for harm that they cause intentionally. To be explicit, this exception requires more than an intention to grow GM crops. It requires either an intention to cause harm by growing GM crops or at least an intention to grow GM crops with the knowledge that harm will result and an indifference to that harm.

The next exception creates liability for recklessness. The exception involves more than, say, a GM farmer's negligently failing to observe a seed company's instructions in regard to planting. Negligent departures from instructions may be difficult to establish. If American juries or English judges harboured a prejudice against GM crops, it makes no sense to give them the chance of transmuting negligence into recklessness. Still, recklessness can occur. Although reckless behaviour by farmers with respect to GM crops is almost surely rare, such behaviour suffices to ground tort liability.

The last exception creates liability for a farmer's use of GM crops containing a dangerous foreign gene. Liability results only if the farmer knew that the gene was dangerous. What makes a gene dangerous? It is a start that an entity, generally an agribusiness firm, inserted a foreign gene into a crop plant knowing that it would harm, or create a significant risk of harm to, the person or property of others. To illustrate, had Pioneer Hi-Bred International known that the Brazil nutgene inserted into its soya bean plant coded for an allergen, and then marketed the plant anyway, the gene would qualify as dangerous.[73] Merely knowing that the foreign gene came from a Brazil nut would not suffice to make the gene dangerous. As a practical matter, few *farmers* would know whether the foreign gene in a GM plant is dangerous.

One significant effect of the proposed rule is procedural. It allocates significant power to the judge as the enunciator of the pertinent law. It reduces the latitude of the finder of fact, be that judge or jury, to make case-by-case determinations of liability. Of course, the judge will have to announce and, if need be, clarify the rule. The trier of the fact will have to decide, on the evidence, what the GM farmer intended, whether the farmer acted recklessly, and whether the farmer knew that the foreign gene was dangerous. On the whole, however, the proposed rule gives the trier of the fact less influence on deciding liability than do traditional rules of negligence, nuisance, trespass, and strict liability under *Rylands v Fletcher*.

The rule does not cover all possible situations. For illustration, in the third exception, the rule does not specify the duty of plant innovators to test foreign genes and make the results of the tests known to farmers. Relevant genes are likely to have extensive database annotations to guide researchers, and, in some measure, it is a judgement call whether any given gene merits careful pre-market testing. On these matters, then, the rule leaves room for case-by-case development of the law by judges and juries.

Another effect of the proposed rule is doctrinal. It offers no exceptions for firstness or sensitive uses. The doctrine of 'coming to the nuisance' sometimes gives mild priority to existing uses over new ones.[74] Ordinarily, I cannot make your

[73] See n. 69 above.

[74] Markesinis and Deakin, n. 53 above, 443–6; *Prosser and Keeton on the Law of Torts*, n. 46 above, 634–6.

existing feedlot a nuisance by building my new house twenty yards from your property.[75] My earlier example elides this issue by stipulating that Box, Cox, and Fox all began farming at the same time. The proposed rule would not grant priority to existing farmers; liability determinations would be independent of 'who started when'. Nuisance law says that putting your land to a sensitive use does not increase your neighbour's liability.[76] If you build a drive-in theatre next to a track that uses bright lights for night dog racing, your light-sensitive use does not enlarge the track owner's duty.[77] Because the proposed rule follows this component of the law of nuisance, Cox is no more likely to be liable to Fox, the sensitive organic farmer, than he is to Box, the conventional non-GM farmer.

So much for the first rule. The second proposed rule is that no one may obtain an injunction against or damages from a seed company for genetic drift unless the seed company (1) knew that neighbouring landowners would suffer harm, (2) acted negligently with respect to neighbours' interests, or (3) sold GM seeds which it knew or should have known were dangerous. For purposes of this rule a 'seed company' is a firm that creates or produces seeds for eventual commercial sale to farmers. Brokers, retailers, and other middlemen do not count as 'seed companies'. Firms such as Monsanto and Pioneer Hi-Bred International do. As before, I concentrate on GM crops and GM seeds.

The strategy behind the second rule is obvious: to make seed companies more likely to be liable for genetic drift than farmers. The justifications for this strategy are that seed companies, compared to farmers, know much more about the risks of genetic drift, can take precautions to prevent these risks from materializing, and can issue warnings as needed. Thus, exception (1) lowers the standard from intended harm to known harm. Exception (2) reduces the threshold from recklessness to negligence. And exception (3) counts on the fact that seed companies are vastly more likely than farmers to know that certain genes are dangerous.

The second proposed rule allocates more power to the trier of fact than does the first rule. But, like the first rule, it creates no exceptions for firstness or sensitive uses. For reasons of space, I shall not try to craft a rule for middlemen, though on the whole they occupy a position more similar, in pertinent respects, to farmers than to seed companies. The second rule exposes seed companies to a justifiable level of tort liability. Still, that level is probably lower than that of the four common-law torts discussed.

Undoubtedly, the most significant practical effect of the two suggested rules is to favour GM farming and GM foods. The rules slightly favour GM farmers and, to a lesser extent, GM seed companies more than does current law. My justification for these rules rests on two assumptions: that GM agriculture merely extends other forms of agricultural innovation, and that a pervasive and enduring prejudice

[75] But see *Spur Industries, Inc. v Del E. Webb Development Co.* 108 Ariz 178, 494 P2d 700 (1972). Although an existing feedlot was considered a nuisance after a large residential development was built nearby, the court required the developer to indemnify the feedlot owner for the cost of shutting down or relocating.

[76] Markesinis and Deakin, n. 53 above, 431; *Prosser and Keeton on the Law of Torts*, n. 46 above, 628.

[77] *Amphitheatres, Inc. v Portland Meadows* 184 Ore 336, 198 P2d 847 (1948).

harboured by judges and juries would disrupt the application of otherwise fair rules of tort law. So, my argument amounts to an intellectual enterprise of designing prophylactic rules in the face of hypothetical prejudice. We shall see that my third proposal counterbalances any benefit to seed firms that specialize in GM crops.

(c) Decisions resulting from Prejudice in Favour of GMOs: Strict Liability

Previously, I assumed that judges and juries either are unprejudiced, or are prejudiced against transgenic plants. In the former case the usual tort rules need no adjusting, and, in the latter case, I suggested two rules that would correct for the prejudice. Assume now that judges and juries are prejudiced *in favour of* GMOs. They have a preconceived and unreasonable opinion or judgment that is marked by enthusiasm for or strong attraction to GMOs. They dismiss warnings from scientists and environmental groups as so much claptrap. Accordingly, their decisions about liability for harm do not take adequately into account the risks of GMOs or the uncertainty that surrounds the effects of GMOs.

Mercifully, I can tell a much shorter story about how to correct for this prejudice than its opposite number. I start simply: there are two different doctrines of strict liability. Strict liability under *Rylands v Fletcher* was always somewhat hedged and is now, in both the US and the UK, even more watered down. Then there is the doctrine of strict liability that applies to defective products as well as abnormally dangerous activities. It is serious business.

In the interest of dispatch, I confine myself to American law, as summarized in the pertinent *Restatement*. Commercial sellers and distributors are liable for harm caused by products that are defective in manufacture or design, or come without adequate instructions or warnings.[78] Liability exists both at the time of sale and for post-sale failure to recall the product or to warn.[79] It extends specifically to defective food products.[80] Of course, the plaintiff must establish a causal connection between the defect and the harm, and the defendant can set up some affirmative defences.[81] Most important, liability exists without regard to fault in the case of manufacturing defects and approaches that position in the case of design defects and defects in instructions and warnings.[82]

As a general matter, product liability rules do not govern liability between neighbouring farmers. True, the rules make some provision for harm to the plaintiff's property other than the defective product itself.[83] But, in our example, Box, Cox, and Fox are neither commercial sellers nor consumers with respect to each other. And crops growing in a field are not considered food products. Product liability rules do not apply to genetic drift between or among their farms.

[78] *Restatement Third, Torts: Product Liability* (American Law Institute, 1998) ss. 1 and 2.
[79] Ibid., ss. 10–11. [80] Ibid., s. 7. [81] Ibid., ss. 15, 17–18.
[82] Ibid., s. 1, Comment *a*; s. 2, Comments *a* and *n*, and Reporters' Note, Comment *a*.
[83] Ibid., s. 21(c) and Comment *e*.

All the same, under the prejudice just described, it makes sense, as a matter of prophylaxis, to hold seed companies strictly liable for harm caused by transgenic seeds that they sell to farmers. If the seeds, blown by the wind or carried by insects, alight on a neighbouring farmer's property and cause harm, the seed company should be liable without regard to fault. This corrective measure will give an incentive to seed companies to test their transgenic seeds carefully and to issue appropriate instructions and warnings to farmers who purchase their seeds. It is economically efficient to impose this liability on seed companies rather than neighbouring farmers because seed companies are in the best position to understand the genetic engineering of crop plants and to assess the risks and uncertainties of GMOs. They are also in the premier position to issue needed instructions and warnings.

The situation of middlemen, such as seed retailers, is closer to that of farmers than that of seed companies. Middlemen are not in nearly as good a position as seed companies to understand transgenic plants and their risks, to undertake risk assessment, or to issue instructions and warnings. Accordingly, strict liability applies only to seed companies. Negligence is the proper standard for farmers and middlemen.

(iii) GMOs and Patent Infringement

Percy Schmeiser and Schmeiser Enterprises Ltd owned twenty fields totalling some 1,000 acres in Saskatchewan. He grew peas, wheat, and canola in a large-scale farming operation. In the 1990s, five farmers in Schmeiser's area started to grow Roundup Ready Canola. Monsanto Canada Inc owned a patent on genes and cells from the herbicide-resistant canola variety. Monsanto investigators discovered that, by 1998, 95 to 98 per cent of Schmeiser's canola crop, spread over 1,000 acres, consisted of Roundup Ready Canola. How the herbicide-resistant plants came to be on Schmeiser's property was never ascertained. Eventually Monsanto sued Schmeiser and his company. In 2004 the Canadian Supreme Court held, in a 5–4 decision, that Schmeiser had infringed Monsanto's patent.[84]

As my aim is to defend a general position on such cases, rather than to write a case note, I mark only briefly two distinctive features of *Schmeiser*. First, under Canadian law, Monsanto's patent covered only glyphosate-resistant cells and the genes for encoding this resistance. It did not cover the transgenic canola plants themselves. Arbour J, dissenting, made much of this point. She argued that the majority had ignored *Harvard College v Canada* (*Commissioner of Patents*),[85] which held that a transgenic mouse, and by implication other life forms such as plants, is not, except for genetically engineered bacteria, patentable. Justice Arbour reasoned that, in light of *Harvard College*, a narrow construction of Monsanto's claims would render them valid but not infringed, while a broad construction would render them invalid.[86] Secondly, there is the puzzling matter of how the herbicide-resistant

[84] *Monsanto Canada Inc. v Schmeiser* (2004) 239 DLR (4th) 271.

[85] [2002] 4 SCR 45.

[86] *Schmesier*, n. 84 above, 302, citing *Gillette Safety Razor Co. v Anglo-American Trading Co.* (1913) 30 RPC 465, 481 (HL).

plants came to be on Schmeiser's land, and indeed what to make of Percy Schmeiser himself. Possible explanations include the transfer of seeds and pollen by insects and the blowing of canola seeds onto his property or onto public land near roads. But these explanations seem inadequate to show why 95 per cent or more of Schmeiser's canola crop was Roundup Ready. Or did Schmeiser go onto neighbouring farmers' land to get the hardy plants? As for Schmeiser himself, it is an unusual patent-infringement defendant who sets up his own web site and attracts a bevy of supporters ranging from the Action Group on Erosion to the Sierra Club of Canada. The lengthy law review comments one can expect on *Schmeiser* will no doubt pursue these two features of the case.

I wish to confront a harder case. Suppose that Monsanto has patented not only a foreign gene and cells containing that gene but also plants that contain the gene and cells. Some legal systems do not issue patents on plants (GM or non-GM) themselves, but since *Ex p Hibbard*[87] and *J.E.M. Ag Supply Inc.* v *Pioneer Hi-Bred International Inc.*,[88] the US system does. A foreign gene can confer glyphosate-resistance, as with Roundup Ready soya beans or canola, or repel insects, as with Monsanto's Bollgard Cotton. In fact, Monsanto sells cottonseed with both genes marketed as Bollgard with Roundup Ready Cotton. Suppose also that Monsanto sells GM seeds to retailers, who, in turn, sell them to farmers under licence. The licence allows farmers to use the seeds for a single growing season. It bars them from saving any seeds from the resulting crops and from selling or otherwise transferring the seeds to anyone else for planting. Retailers collect a licensing fee from the farmers and pass the fee along to Monsanto.

In what circumstances should an unlicensed farmer be liable to Monsanto for patent infringement for using seeds, pollen, or other genetic material from Monsanto's patented genes, cells, or plants? Consider two farms situated as follows:

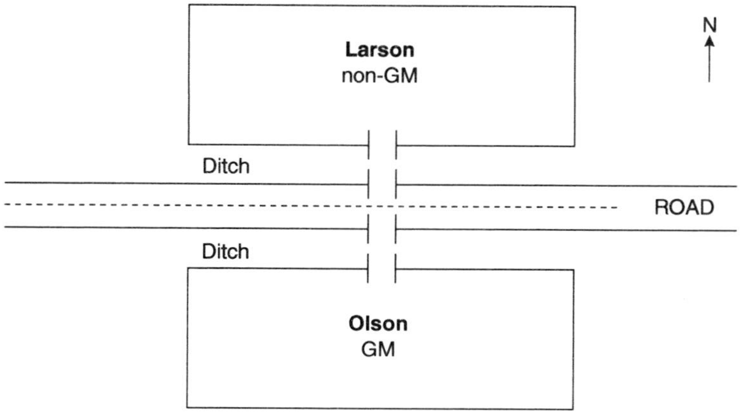

[87] 227 USPQ 443 (PTO Bd App & Int 1985).

[88] 534 US 124 (2001).

Larson grows non-GM canola. Olson grows Roundup Ready canola under licence from Monsanto. Prevailing winds are from south to north. Both farms have insects common to agricultural areas. Now attend to the following scenarios.

(a) Three Scenarios: Provisional Reactions

1. Genetic Material Blown onto Private Land

Assume that seeds from Olson's GM canola blow onto Larson's land and grow into adult plants. Larson harvests them and saves the seeds. Next year Larson plants the saved seeds. Monsanto sues Larson. What result?

Larson should win. Larson is violating no contractual duty to Monsanto. There is privity of contract between Monsanto and the seed retailer and between the seed retailer and Olson. Perhaps there is even privity of contract between Monsanto and Olson. But Larson has no contract with any of them, and certainly not with Monsanto.

Nor is it plausible to say that Larson is infringing Monsanto's patent. Granted, the point of a patent is to protect the holder from unlicensed use of the invention by others. To identify the perimeter of legal protection, however, it is necessary to specify the duties of unlicensed individuals to the patentee. If someone found a patented machine on his or her land, he or she would not be able legally to use it without the patentee's permission. Now it would be a great surprise to stumble over a stray patented machine in a canola field but no surprise at all to see lots of canola plants. To the naked eye, GM canola plants look the same as non-GM canola plants. The physical arrangement of the farms does not ground any duty on Larson to return the genetic material to Olson, the retailer, or Monsanto or to refrain from using it. 'The wind bloweth where it listeth' (John 3:8). The gospel author, though no meteorologist, is correct about the weather. Monsanto cannot create a duty on Larson out of moving air or insects and the existence of Olson's farm across the road.

Schmeiser does not compel a different result. McLachlin CJC and Fish J 'are not concerned here with the innocent discovery by farmers of "blow-by" patented plants on their land or in their cultivated fields'.[89] Monsanto could protect its economic interest by requiring Olson to erect high fences around his farm, or by using a genetic use restriction technology (GURT) to shield its patented plant. GURTs, which are highly controversial, fall roughly into two groups. V-GURTs deny use of the plant variety. Examples include seeds with a promoter sequence that activates a toxin that prevents germination (so-called 'terminator technology') and seeds that do not grow unless a separate chemical activates them. T-GURTs protect from illicit use the specific trait that adds value to the transgenic plant. Over thirty GURT patents were issued in the US and the EU between 1997 and 2002, but these plant technology protection techniques were, as of 2003, not yet

[89] *Schmeiser*, n. 84 above, 279.

commercially available.[90] Either method could protect Monsanto but would likely lower its profits. Monsanto cannot have it both ways by keeping its profit margin on GM crops steady, while collecting damages from Larson for patent infringement.

Monsanto might counter that, in a key respect, canola plants are more like computer software than machines. Software, like plants but unlike machines, is easily replicated. If a firm has a patent on or other intellectual property rights in software, the firm need not use the best available encryption or other method of copy protection, or any method at all, to keep a finder of the software from using it. By parity of reasoning, Monsanto might conclude that it should not have to use a GURT to protect its transgenic canola plants.

I reply that canola plants differ in at least two particulars from software. First, the wind rarely blows and insects never carry software from one farm to another, but they often blow or transfer genetic material from one canola field to another. Secondly, a farmer can readily identify stray software, but not blow-by canola pollen, seeds, or plants, as 'foreign' material in a canola field. Given these differences, Monsanto needs to do something—for instance, use a GURT, contract with Olson to erect a high fence, or contract with Larson to remove GM canola pollen, seeds, and plants from Larson's farm—to make Larson liable for patent infringement.

2. *Trespass on Neighbouring Private Land*

Assume instead that Larson's lust for Roundup Ready canola is so great that he cannot wait for insects and the southerly zephyrs to do their work. In the dead of night Larson sneaks onto Olson's farm through a hole in Olson's fence and snatches up as many canola seeds as he can without leaving obvious evidence of his pilfering. Next year, Larson plants the glyphosate-resistant seeds and raises a fine crop of transgenic canola.

Alas for Larson, his midnight roving under a full moon was descried by Olson's daughter, Helga, who was coming home from a date. She also saw the burlap sack in which Larson carried off the seeds. Helga reported as much to her father, who told the retailer, who reported the matter to Monsanto. Olson sued Larson for trespass and conversion. Monsanto sued Larson for patent infringement. The county prosecuted him for theft. What results?

Larson should lose all the way round. Clearly he trespassed on Olson's land. Conversion, an elusive tort, lies in cases of trespass, theft, and removing severed

[90] AE Segarra and JM Rawson, 'The "Terminator Gene" and other Genetic Use Restriction Technologies (GURTs) in Crops', in S Eldridge (ed.), *Food Biotechnology: Current Issues and Perspectives* (Nova Science Publishers, 2003), 65–75. Common criticisms of GURTs are that they unwisely promote concentration and vertical integration in the seed industry, unduly limit seed choices for farmers in developing countries, and reduce crop biodiversity: ibid., 69–75. When Monsanto was on the verge of acquiring 'terminator technology' from the Delta and Pine Land Co, the widespread furore led Monsanto's CEO to promise not to commercialize the genetic engineering of seed sterility: 'Terminator Genes: Fertility Rights', *The Economist*, 9 Oct. 1999, 104. I do not know whether Monsanto considers itself still bound by this promise, whether it has acquired other sterile-seed technology, or whether it owns either V-GURTs or T-GURTs that do not involve sterile-seed technology. For a perceptive legal discussion of GURTs, see Dan L Burk, 'DNA Rules: Legal and Conceptual Implications of Biological "Lock-Out" Systems' (2004) 92 *California LR* 1553.

crops from the land.[91] The illegality of Larson's actions plainly infringes Monsanto's patent on Roundup Ready canola. A good prosecutor should have little trouble persuading a jury that Larson is guilty of theft. It seems unlikely that these results would be much different if Larson stood just outside Olson's fence and reached over it to pluck the seeds, or even if Larson stood on his own land and used the world's longest golf ball retriever to snatch up seeds from Olson's property.

3. Getting Seeds from Public Lands

The diagram shows that the Larson and Olson farms are separated by a road that has ditches on both sides. Assume now that the road and ditches are public property. Anyone may walk or travel on them for any legal purpose in conformity with the traffic laws. The road is paved with asphalt. The ditches on either side are covered with soil. As the south wind blows and insects move around, seeds from Olson's canola crop are carried into the ditches, where they germinate and grow into mature plants with seeds of their own. Larson walks along the ditches and bags as many Roundup Ready canola seeds as he can. Next season, he plants the seeds, harvests the plants, and saves enough seeds from the crop to plant his entire farm with Roundup Ready canola the following season. Monsanto learns of Larson's activities and sues him for patent infringement. What result?

This hypothetical case does not fall within Chief Justice McLachlin's exception in *Schmeiser*. We do not have 'innocent discovery' by Larson of ' "blow-by" patented plants' on Larson's 'land' or in his 'cultivated fields'.[92] Larson discovered something in the ditches. But the ditches are public land. And Monsanto would dispute the innocence of the discovery.

A plausible result is that Monsanto should prevail. Were the courts to rule in Larson's favour, the decision would create an incentive for gleaners to explore publicly owned ditches near fields of GM crops. By no means would the only gleaners be neighbouring farmers. It would be easy for enterprising individuals or firms to find out who is growing GM crops and hire people to patrol nearby ditches in search of GM seeds. The consequences of this incentive would be a use of ditches different from that intended and the interception of the financial benefits of Monsanto's patented plants. In contrast, to rule in Monsanto's favour would create no such incentive or consequences.

To call the foregoing result plausible is not to say that it is obviously sound. In part, the issue is who best bears the costs of wind-driven or insect-aided seed transfer. A rule that puts liability on alleged gleaners from public land pushes up administrative costs—viz. the costs of finding out where, exactly, the gleaners obtained the transgenic seed. Some of them might claim that powerful winds or moving insects carried it onto their distant fields. In contrast, a rule that makes all free-moving seed

91 *Prosser and Keaton on the Law of Torts*, n. 46 above, 91, 93.
92 *Schmeiser*, n. 84 above, 279.

alighting on public land fair game for gleaners would hold down administrative costs. It would also give Monsanto an incentive to eliminate or drastically reduce the wind-blown and insect-abetted movement of fertile transgenic seeds.

(b) Differential Analysis

Now we have in hand provisional results from three scenarios. The next question is whether the tentative results in the last two scenarios subvert the provisional result in the first. Scenario 2 does not. It involves trespass and theft plain as the moonlit night on which they occurred. Scenario 1 involves neither.

Scenario 3 creates more of a problem if the optimal rule bars Larson and gleaners from picking up transgenic seeds from publicly owned ditches. Scenario 1 involves a neighbouring farmer's own private land, whereas Scenario 3 involves public land. The provisional result in Scenario 1 could offer an incentive for others besides Larson to get the benefit of GM seeds carried by insects or blown by the wind from Olson's land onto Larson's farm. Imagine that Larson has no interest in growing GM crops himself. Yet he likes money. Enterprising individuals and firms approach Larson and other non-GM farmers whose fields are close to those of GM farmers. They offer Larson and other non-GM farmers either a flat fee or a scaled fee, based on the amount of GM seed recovered, for the privilege of coming onto their land to bio-prospect for GM seed. The entrepreneurs then sell the GM seed to seed retailers who in turn sell it to farmers at a lower price than Monsanto-licensed seed. This practice is starting to smell like patent infringement somewhere down the line of non-GM farmers, gleaners, seed retailers, and customers who buy from them.

This problem created by Scenario 3 favours adjusting the provisional result in Scenario 1. Larson should be limited to the amount of blow-by seed coming from Olson's farm that Larson can and does plant on his own fields. In effect, Larson gets a saved-seed exemption from infringing Monsanto's patent but nothing more. It is unconvincing for Monsanto to say that patent protection is good against all the world—*in rem* rather than *in personam*, for the issue is how strong its *in rem* protection should be when insect-aided or wind-borne genetic material alights on the property of an unlicensed farmer. Neither any contract, nor the scope of Monsanto's patent, nor the prevailing winds, nor the movement of insects, nor even all of these together, impose any duty on Larson not to use the saved seed on his own property. If Monsanto wants to protect its financial interest, it can employ a genetic use restriction technology, contract specifically with Larson and others like him, or require Olson and other licensed seed purchasers to build high fences. This solution makes more sense than, say, an innocent-conversion theory under which Monsanto can repossess the plants subject to Larson's lien for the labour and other resources expended in growing them.

(iv) The Intellectual Experiment

I hypothesized in the Introduction that lawyers, including academic lawyers, generally offer judicious, balanced solutions to problems, whereas philosophers more frequently propose daring or counter-intuitive solutions, or say that no solution exists or even that earlier philosophers misunderstood the problems. Lawyers have practical problems to solve. Even academic lawyers, in so far as they aim to reform the law, must craft solutions that judges or law-makers might accept. To achieve the desired effect, the solutions on offer must seem balanced, not hare-brained. I hardly suggest that lawyers are unimaginative. Without the celebrated conveyancer Sir Orlando Bridgman (1606–74) to create trust indentures to shield the Earl of Arundel's family from the consequences of the lunacy of the Earl's eldest son,[93] we might never have had the rule against perpetuities, a rule beloved by law students in all common law countries. But celebrated philosophers are a breed apart. Leibniz argues that the world is composed of monads.[94] Hume confesses that whenever he enters most deeply into himself he finds only perceptions.[95] Russell deploys his theory of descriptions to solve a problem about 'denoting phrases' whose nature and importance escaped the attention of earlier philosophers.[96] Strawson contends that Russell's theory embodies some fundamental errors and that his solution is mistaken.[97]

There are exceptions. Hohfeld claimed, boldly, that his octet of fundamental legal conceptions gives the 'lowest common denominators of the law'.[98] In our own day Richard A. Epstein gives simple rules as solutions to intricate, highly difficult problems.[99] Among contemporary Anglo-American analytic philosophers, even highly regarded ones, daredevils are hard to find. Jones replies to Smith, who attacked Jones's earlier article incrementally adjusting someone else's interpretation of Kant's categorical imperative. Colleagues and peer reviewers rigorously vetted all of these contributions except Kant's.

In this chapter I have tried to write more boldly than I ordinarily would about trespassory rules pertaining to plants. The bifurcated system in the US for protecting intellectual property rights in plants, based chiefly on the mode of propagation, seemed unjustifiable. So I argued for a unified system similar in principle to plant variety legislation in Australia and the UK. Next, the usual rules of tort law may work well enough, in the absence of prejudice, in cases of genetic drift. Yet, if

93 *Duke of Norfolk's Case*, (1681) 3 Ch Cas 1, 27, 36; 22 ER 931, 947, 952–3.

94 GW von Leibniz, *The Monadology*, in *Basic Writings* (trans. GR Montgomery, Open Court Publishing, 1968), 251–72.

95 D Hume, *A Treatise of Human Nature* (ed. LA Selby-Bigge, Clarendon Press, 1960), 252.

96 B Russell, 'On Denoting' (1905) 14 *Mind* 479.

97 PF Strawson, 'On Referring' (1950) 59 *Mind* 320.

98 WN Hohfeld, *Fundamental Legal Conceptions as Applied in Judicial Reasoning* (ed. WW Cook, Greenwood Press, 1978 [1919]), 64.

99 RA Epstein, *Simple Rules for a Complex World* (Harvard University Press, 1995).

judges and juries harboured a pervasive and enduring prejudice *against* genetically modified crops, I brashly argued, on prophylactic grounds, for new rules that would limit the chances of getting damages or an injunction when GM crop plants harm neighbouring landowners. If, instead, judges and juries had a pervasive and enduring prejudice *in favour of* transgenic crops, I argued with equal brashness for imposing liability without regard to fault on seed companies whose genetically modified seeds cause harm to neighbouring farms. Lastly, I contended that farmers should not be liable for patent infringement if they use genetically modified seeds that winds blow or insects carry onto their fields. With respect to none of these proposals did I follow out all the consequences or rebut all the objections. In US law reviews, each proposal would have required at least a sixty-page article with footnotes easily passing the double-century mark. Thus, I have the acute sense of having crept out onto a branch only to hear the sound of a saw cutting behind me.

Like Harris, I am by temperament part philosopher and part academic lawyer. The philosophical half of me would like to get to the heart of the matter and omit the tedious documentation that law reviews typically require. The legal half is nagged by the worry that I have omitted too many issues,[100] dived in too quickly, not made myself sufficiently familiar with either the biotechnology or the cases and statutes, given short shrift to political difficulties with each proposal, and not canvassed and responded in a balanced way even to the obvious objections. If my split-minded reactions are typical, that would tend to confirm my hypothesis.

I can, even now, anticipate the following question about these reflections: do you really believe that an essay with 100 footnotes is *bold*? Though perhaps not a high-wire act, this article is bolder than much legal academic writing. I have, admittedly, struck a compromise between confining myself to legal analysis and allowing myself the traditional freedom of philosophy. I shall never be in the club that includes Leibniz, Hume, Kant, Russell, and Strawson, nor in that of Bridgman, Hohfeld, and Epstein. As Harris has shown, however, there is fertile academic ground between the two.

[100] Among these issues are whether the economic loss doctrine bars farmers' public nuisance and negligence claims against producers of GM seeds: *Sample v Monsanto Co.* 283 F Supp 2d 1088, 1092–4 (ED Mo 2003); whether indirect as well as direct purchasers of GM seeds have standing to sue producers for antitrust violations: ibid., 1094; whether either 'willful' or 'malicious' injury inflicted by a violator of a GM seed patent makes the producer's pre-petition award of damages for patent infringement non-dischargeable in bankruptcy: *In re Trantham* 304 Bankr Rptr 298 (6th Cir BAP 2004); whether a replanting prohibition in a GM seed producer's licensing agreement constitutes patent misuse: *Monsanto Co. v McFarling* 363 F3d 1336 (Fed Cir 2004); whether a reasonable royalty awarded for an infringer's planting or transferring patented seed that he saved at the end of a season after agreeing to use the seed only in a single season could exceed the infringer's anticipated profits from use of the seed: *Monsanto Co. v Ralph*, 382 F3d 1374 (Fed Cir 2004).

11

The Legacy of *Penn v Lord Baltimore*

*Edwin Peel**

The reason for my involvement in this collection of essays is a little different from those of the other contributors. Rather than a shared interest in one of the branches of the law in which he worked, it was instead my privilege to have worked closely with Jim Harris for ten years as one of the two Law Fellows at Keble College. I have had the opportunity already to say how rewarding and valuable that experience has been.[1] On this occasion I shall confine myself to this one thought, that I should be fortunate to leave but half the mark on those whom I have taught which I have seen for myself that Jim left on his former students, through his kindness, his self-effacing good humour, and his moral courage.

(i) Introduction

This chapter is prompted, in part, by the case of *Griggs Group Ltd v Evans*[2] and the issues raised therein by the judgment of Mr Peter Prescott QC, sitting as a Deputy High Court Judge. The facts are simple enough. Under a contract found to be governed by English law, a commercial artist (Evans) had designed a logo for the claimant, Griggs, for use in the marketing of its footwear, both in England and in numerous other countries. By the time of the events which were the subject of the litigation the logo had acquired considerable business value.[3] It was an implied term of the contract that any copyright in the logo, both British and foreign, would belong to Griggs, so that Griggs was the owner in equity.[4] Before Griggs had acquired legal title in the copyright,[5] Evans purported to assign it to the defendant (Raben), an Australian company in competition with the claimant.

* Keble College, Oxford. I am very grateful to my colleagues Adrian Briggs, Joshua Getzler, and James Edelman for their helpful comments on an earlier draft of this chapter. I am responsible for the errors which remain.

[1] *Oxford Law News*, 2004. [2] [2005] 2 WLR 513.

[3] The logo is applied to the iconic range of Dr Martens boots and shoes.

[4] This was the finding of the same judge in earlier proceedings: [2003] EWHC 2914 (Ch).

[5] Which it sought to do by way of negotiation and payment, rather than litigation.

Since Raben had notice of the facts giving rise to Griggs's prior equitable interest, the judge held that it should be ordered to assign the copyright to Griggs. Almost as an afterthought,[6] Raben objected that the judge had no jurisdiction so to order in relation to the foreign copyright on the basis of the *Moçambique* rule. As the judge pointed out, this afterthought raised issues of equity, private international law, land law, intellectual property, and English civil procedure. It is with the issues of private international law that this chapter is primarily engaged. It assesses, and re-assesses, the extent to which the English courts may, and should, adjudicate claims which concern foreign land and foreign intellectual property.

(ii) The *Moçambique* Rule and Its Exceptions

It is only relatively recently that the *Moçambique* rule has been applied to claims based on foreign intellectual property rights.[7] In origin, it is a rule concerned with foreign land and it is with such property that this assessment of it begins.

(a) Foreign Land

At the time when southern Africa was being carved up by the European imperial powers, Britain found itself in dispute with Portugal over lands that were later to form parts of Rhodesia and Mozambique. Part of this dispute ended up in the House of Lords when Companhia de Moçambique, a Portuguese company, sued for trespass British South Africa Co, a British company controlled by Cecil Rhodes.[8] The essence of the claim was that Rhodes's company had invaded the territory known as Manicaland with a military force and seized the lands and minerals, doing injury to the Portuguese company's business. In order to succeed in its claim, it was necessary for the Portuguese company to assert its title to the land in question[9] and it was principally over this issue that the House of Lords held that it had no jurisdiction.

The origin of the rule that an English court will not adjudicate over title to foreign land lies in the distinction drawn between local and transitory actions. With the former, the ancient practice prevailed whereby juries could only be

[6] Indeed, the challenge to the jurisdiction of the court was only made after the final version of the judgment had been delivered and the judge had heard the parties concerning costs, but before the order had formally been drawn up and entered. There was little prospect of the defendant meeting the requirement of 'exceptional circumstance' necessary to allow a submission after judgment has been delivered (*Stewart v Engel* [2000] 1 WLR 2268), but since the point taken was to assert that the court had *no jurisdiction* to order as it proposed the late submission was allowed to proceed.

[7] At least in England; for Australia, see text to n.61 below.

[8] *British South Africa Co v Companhia de Moçambique* [1893] AC 602.

[9] Even if, in the Court of Appeal, the claimant formally abandoned its other claims for a declaration that it was lawfully in possession and occupation of the lands, mines, and mining rights and an injunction restraining the defendant from continuing to occupy or from asserting any title to the said lands, mines, and mining rights.

assembled from persons acquainted with the facts of the case. With the latter, this requirement could be evaded by the fiction of *videlicet*, i.e. by adding after the statement of the foreign place the words 'To wit at Westminster, in the county of Middlesex' or whatever else might happen to be the venue in the action.[10] An action was transitory where the facts might have occurred anywhere. An action was local where the facts could only have occurred in a particular place. Actions relating to foreign land were clearly local, and this led to the impossibility of summoning a jury. With the abolition of local venues in the Judicature Act 1873 and the Rules of Court created thereunder,[11] the opportunity was created, at least as a matter of procedure, for English courts to decide questions of title to foreign land. It was this opportunity which was rejected by the House of Lords in the *Moçambique* case. According to Lord Herschell the grounds upon which the courts refuse to decide questions of title to foreign land are 'substantial and not technical', so that the changes introduced by the Judicature Act did not affect the rule at hand. The requirement of a local venue may have proved to be an additional difficulty, but the real basis of the rule was that the English courts simply do not exercise their jurisdiction in matters arising abroad which 'are *in their nature* local'.[12] This much may be stated with some clarity, but when it comes to articulating what are, or were, the substantial grounds for the *Moçambique* rule, matters are 'less clear'.[13] To a large extent, it seems to have been enough for the House of Lords simply to rely on its universality and venerability. Lord Herschell noted that Story, after stating that in Roman law a suit might in many cases be brought either where property was situated or where the party sued had his domicile, proceeds to say that:

> even in countries acknowledging the Roman law, it has become a very general principle that suits *in rem* should be brought where the property is situate; and this principle is applied with almost universal approbation in regard to immovable property. The same rule is applied to mixed actions, and to all suits which touch the realty.[14]

He also referred to passages[15] in which Story quotes the following language of Vattel:[16]

> as property of this kind (i.e. land) is to be held according to the laws of the country where it is situated, and as the right of granting it is vested in the ruler of the country, controversies relating to such property can only be decided in the state in which it depends.

[10] *British South Africa Co v Companhia de Moçambique* [1893] AC 602 at 618, *per* Lord Herschell LC; see WS Holdsworth, *History of English Law*, vol.5, 140–2; *Dicey & Morris: The Conflict of Laws* (13th edn. ed., L Collins, Sweet & Maxwell, 2000), para. 23–034 (hereafter 'Dicey & Morris').

[11] In particular, the then RSC Ord. 36, r. 1.

[12] *Doulson v Matthews* (1792) 4 Term Rep 503, 504, *per* Buller J (emphasis added).

[13] *Pearce v Ove Arup Ltd* [2000] Ch 403, 427, *per* Roch LJ.

[14] J Story, *Conflict of Laws* (8th edn., Hilliard, Gray & Co, 1883), s.551.

[15] Ibid., ss.553–4.

[16] *Vattel's Law of Nations* (GG and J Robinson, 1797). See A Watson, *Joseph Story and the Comity of Errors: A Case Study in Conflict of Laws* (University of Georgia Press, 1992) in which it is argued that Story got many of the civilian sources wrong.

Lord Herschell may have taken the view that there are 'solid reasons why the courts of this country should in common with those of most other nations have refused to adjudicate upon claims of title to foreign land', but he then only went on to speculate on one possible inconvenience:[17]

> Supposing a foreigner to sue in this country for trespass to his lands situate abroad, and for taking possession of, and expelling him from them, what is to be the measure of damages? There being no legal process here by which he could obtain possession of the lands, the plaintiff might, I suppose, in certain circumstances, obtain damages equal in amount to their value. But what would there be to prevent his leaving this country after obtaining these, and repossessing himself of the lands?

The problem of 'double jeopardy' which seems to have exercised Lord Herschell is not one which is confined to claims involving land. A claimant might obtain an order for damages in conversion from an English court and then seek to recover the converted chattels themselves from the courts in another jurisdiction. The problem may be more acute with land because of the likelihood that the English court's order would not be recognized by the foreign court. But the reason why the foreign court would not recognize the order would be because of the universal recognition of the *Moçambique* rule. In that sense, it has become something of an axiom: the English courts will not decide questions of title to foreign land because their decisions will not be recognized by other courts who also adhere to the same rule.[18] Consequently, of course, the English courts will not recognize a foreign court order which purports to resolve a question of title to English land.[19]

In his search for the underlying rationale of the *Moçambique* rule, the judge in the *Griggs* case was also guilty, despite his better efforts,[20] of resorting to bald assertion and tautology:

> The answer must be that it is understood that in the case of land the sovereign is or may be asserting a double prerogative. It is not only a prerogative to make laws for his own country, but a prerogative to have those laws adjudicated in his own courts exclusively. That was the traditional understanding when it came to land.[21]

There is no doubt that this was, and is, the traditional understanding, but one is still left to ask: why? In the final analysis one is perhaps left simply to acknowledge that land has a 'rather special position in most legal systems'.[22]

[17] At 625.

[18] It is for this reason that the rule might best be described as 'pragmatic': A Briggs and P Rees, *Civil Jurisdiction and Judgments* (4th edn., Lloyds of London Press, 2005), 292.

[19] And without exception, it seems: Rule 40(2) in Dicey & Morris, n. 10 above, and commentary thereon in para. 14–105.

[20] [2005] 2 WLR 513, paras. [72]–[79] and [118].

[21] Ibid., para. [78].

[22] Dicey & Morris, n. 10 above, para. 23–003 where the editors go on to suggest that 'a modern justification for this is that important social questions may be involved, such as housing policy and tenants' rights, and the relevant legislation may be regarded as embodying public policy'. That may well be true, but there is a good deal of social and public policy embodied in the law of obligations in each legal system, and if it is felt that there may be cases where it is better for the local courts to apply local law that would seem to militate in favour of a discretion to stay rather than an exclusionary rule.

As the judge went on to observe:

In former times the ownership of land might confer obligations of a military character. In unruly times the very puissance of the sovereign might depend on his ability tightly to control land ownership. Later on, ownership of land might confer a right to vote or to seek election to the legislature. For a foreign court to determine titles to land might amount to undermining the constitution of the country. Those considerations are obsolete now in civilised states, but may have shaped the law.[23]

An acknowledgement that whatever historical reasons there may have been for the *Moçambique* rule might now be obsolete invites speculation as to whether it is really any longer justified, or necessary. This is examined below,[24] but, for now, it is necessary to establish the precise scope of the rule.

The only action left before the House of Lords in the *Moçambique* case may have been in trespass, but there is no doubt that the dispositive issue was the ownership of the lands in question. The British South Africa Company was claiming a title to the mineral rights granted by Umtassa, the paramount chief of Manicaland, while the Portuguese claimed that the territory had been ceded to them by the same chief some twenty years previously and sent in an invading force on news of the concession to the British Company.[25] As the judge was to note in the *Griggs* case, not only was this indisputably a claim which turned on the question of title, but also 'a more political dispute can scarcely have been imagined'.[26]

The facts in *Hesperides Hotels Ltd v Aegean Holidays*[27] were scarcely less political but the principal significance of this further decision of the House of Lords lies in the rejection of the argument that the *Moçambique* rule was confined to claims in which it was necessary to decide a question of title to foreign land. That may have been the context of the *Moçambique* case, but the speeches of their Lordships therein were said to make it clear that the court had no jurisdiction to entertain claims of trespass on foreign land, whether or not title was in issue.[28] Had the rule

[23] [2005] 2 WLR 513, para. [118].

[24] See Part (iv), below.

[25] For a somewhat partisan account of these events, see H Hensman, *A History of Rhodesia* (Wm Blackwood & Sons, 1900), ch. 4, which is believed to be out of print but is available at: http://home.wanadoo.nl/rhodesia/henspref.htm. See also: B Williams, *Cecil Rhodes* (Constable and Company Ltd, 1938), 169–70.

[26] [2005] 2 WLR 513, para. [64]. The judge's observation cannot be faulted, but he may have erred a little in his history and his geography. He notes that the 'incident led to a serious diplomatic confrontation and eventually the British Government told Cecil Rhodes to back off. Thus Manica became a province of Mozambique, not Rhodesia (Zimbabwe), and is so to this day.' Rhodes was told to back off, but the treaty which would have given the whole of Manicaland to Portugal was not ratified and, in the following year, the British and the Portuguese came to terms under which the British South Africa Company acquired the greater part of Manicaland: see Williams, n. 25 above, 170. Manica is indeed a province of Mozambique, but the relevant events appear to have taken place in what is still known as Manicaland, which remains a province of Zimbabwe.

[27] [1979] AC 508.

[28] Lord Mansfield had rejected the rule in two cases of trespass to land in Nova Scotia and Labrador, referred to in *Mostyn v Fabrigas* (1774) 1 Cowp 161, where there was no dispute as to title, but his view was overruled in *Doulson v Matthews* (1792) 4 Term Rep 503, 504. In the later case of *The Tolten* [1946] P 135 the supposed limitation of the *Moçambique* rule was rejected by the Court of Appeal.

been so confined in *Hesperides Hotels* then the political dimension would have been very much to the fore. Following the Turkish invasion of Northern Cyprus, the defendants had taken possession of hotels in Kyrenia, on the north coast, which had been in the ownership of the claimants. If it had been necessary to raise a dispute as to title to invoke the *Moçambique* rule, it seems clear that the defendants would have sought to rely on 'laws' passed by the Turkish Federated State of Cyprus. The courts would have had the obvious difficulty of determining what effect, if any, to give to such laws given that the British Government had certified that it did not recognize the Turkish Federated State of Cyprus.[29]

If the *Moçambique* rule was not already confined to claims in which it was necessary to decide a genuine question of title to foreign land, the House of Lords in *Hesperides Hotels* resisted the formidable body of academic opinion calling for it to be so limited.[30] This issue is no longer open for debate,[31] since Parliament intervened in the form of section 30 of the Civil Jurisdiction and Judgments Act 1982, which states:

> The jurisdiction of any court in England and Wales or Northern Ireland to entertain proceedings for trespass to, or any other tort[32] affecting, immovable property shall extend to cases in which the property in question is situated outside that part of the United Kingdom unless the proceedings are principally concerned[33] with a question of the title to, or the right to possession of, that property.

So, to take stock. So far as foreign land is concerned, the *Moçambique* rule is now confined to claims which turn on a disputed question of title to the land. The two leading cases not only either raised such questions (*Moçambique*), or would have done if the case had got that far (*Hesperides Hotels*), but the resolution of them

[29] Resolution of this sort of issue is no easier now that the Foreign Office has ended its practice of according recognition to governments: see Dicey & Morris, n. 10 above, para. 25–004. In the Court of Appeal in the *Hesperides* case ([1998] QB 205, 218), Lord Denning, based on dicta of Lord Wilberforce in *Carl Zeiss Stiftung v Rayner & Keeler Ltd (No 2)* [1967] 1 AC 853, 894, would 'unhesitatingly' have held that the courts of this country can recognize the laws or acts of a body which is in effective control of a territory even though it has not been recognized by Her Majesty's Government *de jure* or *de facto*. The point was not considered in the House of Lords.

[30] See, at the time: *Dicey & Morris: The Conflict of Laws* (9th edn ed., JHC Morris, 1973), 516–18, 525; *Cheshire's Private International Law* (9th edn ed., PM North, 1974), 495; *American Law Institute, Restatement of the Law, Second, Conflict of Laws* (West, 1957), ss.10, 87; JH Beale, *A Treatise on the Conflict of Laws* (Baker, Voorhis & Co., 1935), s.614(1); HF Goodrich, *Handbook of the Conflict of Laws* (4th edn., West Publishing Co, 1964), s.96; Ehrenzweig, *A Treatise on the Conflict of Laws* (West Publishing, AA 1962), s.39.

[31] Unless it is to be argued that the *Moçambique* rule should be given a broad scope again. It is one of the theses of this chapter that, if anything, it should be narrowed further still.

[32] It was at least implied by the decision of the Court of Appeal in *The Tolten* [1946] P 135 that the *Moçambique* rule applied to other torts since that case involved a claim for negligence where, instead of holding that the rule was confined to trespass, the court created a further exception to allow for an action *in rem* against a ship to enforce a maritime lien for damage done to foreign land (a bulk oil wharf in Lagos). The action could now be heard by virtue of s. 30 since there was no question that the claimants were owners of the land in question.

[33] For a narrow interpretation of this proviso, see *Re Polly Peck International Plc (No.2)* [1998] 3 All ER 812, CA which is discussed in Part (iv)(a), below.

would also have touched upon issues of considerable political sensitivity. Where the land in question is situated in a Member State of the European Union, the *Moçambique* rule is replaced with an equivalent, but not identical,[34] rule in the form of what is now Article 22(1) of Council Regulation (EC) 44/2001. The possible impact of the interpretation put upon this provision by the European Court of Justice is considered below.[35]

There are two exceptions to the *Moçambique* rule.[36] The first need not be dwelled on for too long, other than to note one consequence of its existence. The English courts will entertain proceedings for the determination of title to foreign land where 'the question has to be decided for the purpose of the administration of an estate or trust and the property consists of movables or immovables in England as well as immovables outside England'.[37] As the editors of Dicey and Morris note: '[t]his exception has not been precisely formulated by English judges, but its existence can scarcely be doubted'.[38] It is probably based simply on convenience since, without it, it could be difficult to find any court with jurisdiction to deal with the administration of the whole estate. Whatever its justification, it does mean that the English courts have sometimes been required to resolve questions of title to foreign land, to which, of course, they have applied the *lex situs*.[39]

The second exception to the *Moçambique* rule had already existed for some 200 years by the time of the case from which the rule now derives its name. Lord Herschell acknowledged that: '[w]hile courts of equity have never claimed to act directly upon land situate abroad, they have purported to act upon the conscience of persons living here'.[40] This exception may be traced back to the case of *Arglasse v Muschamp*,[41] decided in 1682, but *Penn v Baltimore*[42] is usually regarded as the leading case. Mindful that the scope[43] of this exception is uncertain, and is the subject of later consideration in this chapter, we may begin by saying: where the English courts have jurisdiction over a person they may order him to deal with foreign land so as to give effect to an obligation incurred with respect to the land in question. If complied with, such orders can, of course, affect title to foreign land, but this has not prevented the English courts from exercising their *in personam* jurisdiction; so much so that the Court of Chancery in *Penn v Baltimore*

[34] Not least because Art. 22(1) also extends to tenancies of immovable property.

[35] See Part (iv)(a).

[36] A third, in the form of the decision in *The Tolten*, has been superseded by s. 30 of the 1982 Act: see n.32 above. It may be more accurate to see s. 30 itself as an exception to the rule as promulgated in the *Moçambique* and *Hesperides Hotels* cases (see Briggs and Rees, n. 18 above, 292), meaning that there are still three in total.

[37] Dicey & Morris, n. 10 above, rule 114(3)(b).

[38] Ibid., para. 23–049. See: *Nelson v Bridport* (1846) 8 Beav 547; *Bunbury v Bunbury* (1839) 1 Beav 318; *Hope v Carnegie* (1866) LR 1 Ch App 320; *Ewing v Orr-Ewing* (1883) 9 App Cas 34; *Re Piercy* [1895] 1 Ch 83; *Re Moses* [1908] 2 Ch 235; *Re Stirling* [1908] 2 Ch 344; *Re Pearse's Settlement* [1909] 1 Ch 304; *Re Hoyles* [1911] 1 Ch 179; *Re Ross* [1930] 1 Ch 377; *Re Duke of Wellington* [1948] Ch 118.

[39] In accordance with the choice of law rule for all rights over or in relation to immovable property: Dicey & Morris, n. 10 above, rule 115.

[40] [1893] AC 602, 626.

[41] 1 Vern 75.

[42] (1750) 1 Ves Sen 444.

[43] Not to say its existence: see text to n.114 below.

felt able to decree an order for specific performance of a contract to fix the original Mason–Dixon line which divided the then privately owned territories of Maryland, Pennsylvania, and Delaware.

The key to this exception is said to lie in the existence of some personal equity between the claimant and defendant. In addition to the decision in *Penn v Baltimore*, for example,[44] this has been found to be present in actions to recover the rent due under a lease of premises in Chile,[45] to foreclose a mortgage of land in Sark,[46] to take accounts between tenants in common of land in Jamaica,[47] and to redeem the gift by a wife of a flat in Athens and other land in Greece made under the undue influence of her husband.[48] The courts will not exercise their jurisdiction if the *lex situs* would prohibit the enforcement of their order,[49] nor if the court cannot effectively supervise its execution.[50]

The principal issue with which this chapter is concerned, so far as the scope of the *Penn v Baltimore* exception is concerned, is the extent to which it can be invoked where the defendant is a 'stranger to the equity' upon which the claimant relies. This is dealt with later when analysing three difficult cases, one of which is the *Griggs* case with which this chapter began. Before that can be done, one must first consider the scope and effect of the *Moçambique* rule in the context of foreign intellectual property.

(b) Foreign Intellectual Property

The extent to which the *Moçambique* rule applies to claims concerning foreign intellectual property was analysed by Roch LJ in *Pearce v Ove Arup Ltd.*[51] The claimant alleged that drawings produced for the construction of a public building in Rotterdam amounted to a breach of his English and Dutch copyright. One of the defendants was domiciled in England, so that the courts had jurisdiction over the claim against him under Article 2 of the Brussels Convention. The other defendants were domiciled in the Netherlands,[52] but the English courts had jurisdiction over the claims made against them as co-defendants pursuant to Article 6(1). There was no question of the claims falling within Article 16(4) of the Convention,[53] which states:

> (the following courts shall have exclusive jurisdiction, regardless of domicile)... 4. in proceedings concerned with the registration or validity of patents, trade marks, designs, or

[44] For other instances of an action for specific performance of a contract for the sale of foreign land, see *Richard West and Partners (Inverness) Ltd v Dick* [1969] 2 Ch 424 (a house in Scotland). For further illustrations in addition to those mentioned in the text, see Dicey & Morris, n. 10 above, paras. 23–043, and 23–054–23–055.

[45] *St. Pierre v South American Stores Ltd* [1936] 1 KB 382.

[46] *Toller v Carteret* (1705) 2 Vern 494.

[47] *Scott* v *Nesbitt* (1808) 14 Ves 438.

[48] *Razelos v Razelos (No.2)* [1970] 1 WLR 392.

[49] *Re Courtney, ex p Pollard* (1840) Mont & Ch 239, 250, *per* Lord Cottenham.

[50] *Grey v Manitoba Co* [1897] AC 254.

[51] [2000] Ch 403.

[52] It seems that one of them may also have been domiciled in England.

[53] Now Art. 22(4) of Council Regulation (EC) 44/2001 [2001] OJ L12/1.

other similar rights required to be deposited or registered, the courts of the contracting state in which the deposit or registration has been applied for, has taken place or is under the terms of an international convention deemed to have taken place.

Article 16(4) did not apply because copyright requires no deposit or registration. The English courts therefore appeared to have a jurisdiction which, since it arose under the Convention, they were obliged to exercise.[54] The defendants argued that, so far as the claims in relation to Dutch copyright were concerned, the *Moçambique* rule applied so as to override even the jurisdiction conferred by the Convention, i.e. any personal jurisdiction was defeated by the subject matter limitation in the form of the *Moçambique* rule.[55]

From his analysis of the speeches in the *Moçambique* case, Roch LJ concluded that the rule was one of non-justiciability based on international comity or 'generally accepted principles of private international law'.[56] If it applied to intellectual property, it was limited to claims which required the court to determine the existence or validity of the foreign intellectual property in question. Only two previous cases bore directly on the issue.[57] In *Potter v Broken Hill Pty Co Ltd*[58] an action was brought in Victoria for an injunction and damages in relation to the alleged infringement in New South Wales of the claimant's New South Wales patent. The defence was that the patent was invalid. It is clear that validity was the dispositive issue in the case, and it was this which was central to the decision and the reasoning of Chief Justice Griffith in the High Court of Australia:

I am of the opinion that the substantial question sought to be raised by the defendant is the *validity of the act of the governing power of New South Wales* in granting the patent sued on, and that such a question can only be dealt with by the proper courts of that state.[59]

[54] The proposition that they would have enjoyed a discretion not to hear the claims and stay their proceedings if the alternative forum had been a non-Contracting State then held good in the English courts, but it has since been rejected by the European Court of Justice: Case C–281/02 *Owusu v Jackson (t/a Villa Holidays Bal-Inn Villas) and others* [2005] 2 WLR 942. There may still be room for the courts to decline to hear a claim in relation to which the analogous (or 'reflexive') application of Art. 16(4) (now 22(4)) would point to the exclusive jurisdiction of a non-Contracting State. This possibility (and other examples of 'reflexive' effect) were left open by the European Court: see E Peel, '*Forum Non Conveniens* and European Ideals' [2005] *LMCLQ* 363; A Briggs, '*Forum Non Conveniens* and Ideal Europeans' [2005] *LMCLQ* 378.

[55] An additional argument at the time was that a claim before the English courts for infringement of a foreign intellectual property right could never satisfy the common law choice of law rule in torts which requires double actionability. For claims other than defamation, the common law choice of law rule has been replaced by a statutory rule which abolishes double actionability (see Private International Law (Miscellaneous Provisions) Act 1995, Part III). See Dicey & Morris, n. 10 above, para. 35–029.

[56] [2000] Ch 403, 431F.

[57] Of the others which were put to the court, some raised the very different issue of whether an action can be brought in England for the infringement of UK copyright by acts done outside the UK, to which the answer is no: *Def Lepp Music v Stuart-Brown* [1986] RPC 273, cf. J Fawcett and P Torremans, *Intellectual Property and Private International Law* (OUP, 1998), 600–4. See also: *James Burrough Distillers plc v Speymalt Whisky Distributors Ltd* [1989] SLT 561; *Norbert, Steinhardt and Sons Ltd v Meth* (1960) 105 CLR 440.

[58] (1906) 3 CLR 479.

[59] Ibid., 500 (emphasis added).

He went on to say:

I apprehend that any exercise by a de facto repository of any power of sovereignty, which results in the creation of a right of property that can only be created by such an exercise, must be regarded as an act of the state itself. This appears to be the foundation of the doctrine referred to in the passage cited by Story from Vattel[60] . . . the right of creating a title to such property as land, being vested in the ruler, that is in the sovereign power, of the country, controversies relating to such property can only be decided in the state in which property is situated. The reason appears equally applicable to patent rights, which, as already pointed out, are created by a similar exercise of the sovereign power.[61]

The last sentence of this passage suggests a precise equation between land and intellectual property, but there is a significant difference. Chief Justice Griffith refers to the 'granting' of a patent and the 'creation of a right of property', both of which are apt to describe the issue which must be resolved when the validity of an intellectual property is challenged; this always involves a reference back to, and consideration of, the original grant or creation of the right. It is far from obvious that this is an apt description in all cases where the question of title to land is in issue; say, for example, where two parties dispute which of them is the rightful owner in cases where they each claim to have purchased the land from the previous owner.[62] If confined to issues of validity, the *Moçambique* rule (if it is right to call it that) appears to be narrower in its application to intellectual property.

As far as English cases were concerned, only *Tyburn Productions Ltd v Conan Doyle*[63] provided direct support for the application of the *Moçambique* rule to claims for breach of a foreign intellectual property right. Although there are passages in the judgment of Vinelott J which appear not to distinguish between claims where the validity of the right in question is in issue and those where it is not, that was the dispositive issue in *Tyburn* itself. The daughter of the late Sir Arthur Conan Doyle claimed that she enjoyed rights under the copyright or trade mark laws of the United States[64] which entitled her to prevent the claimants from distributing in the US a film which featured the characters Sherlock Holmes and Dr Watson. The claimants applied for a declaration that no such rights were enjoyed by the daughter, so that all that Vinelott J was actually required to decide was whether he had jurisdiction to investigate the existence and validity of the rights claimed. His decision that he did not is entirely consistent with a narrow application of the *Moçambique* rule which confines it to questions of validity.

There is an element of ambiguity in the final conclusion reached by Roch LJ in *Pearce*, which was simply that 'the *Moçambique* rule does not require the English court to refuse to entertain a claim in respect of the alleged infringement of Dutch copyright'.[65] That conclusion can be reached on the basis that the rule has no

60 See text to n.16 above.

61 (1906) 3 CLR 479, 496–7.

62 See further Part (iii), below.

63 [1991] Ch 75.

64 As well as under US laws of unfair competition.

65 [2000] Ch 403, 445A–B.

application in the context of the Brussels Convention,[66] or by rejecting the application of the *Moçambique* rule to intellectual property. It seems clear, however, from the whole tenor and approach of Roch LJ that he was advocating the retention of the rule, but limited to its proper scope, i.e. the English courts have no jurisdiction to determine the validity of any foreign intellectual property right. Within what is now Council Regulation (EC) 44/2001 (i.e. intellectual property rights in the Member States) this result is achieved through the application of Article 22(4).[67] Outside the Regulation (i.e. intellectual property rights in non-Member States) this result is achieved through the application of the *Moçambique* rule as interpreted by Roch LJ. [68] In *Pearce*, where the claim was for infringement of foreign copyright, but there was no issue as to the validity of the copyright in question,[69] there was nothing to prevent the English courts exercising their jurisdiction.

(iii) Three Difficult Cases

The *Moçambique* rule deprives the English courts of jurisdiction to determine any genuine question of title to foreign land, or the validity of foreign intellectual property. The *Penn v Baltimore* exception allows them to exercise their *in personam* jurisdiction so as to give effect to an obligation incurred with respect to foreign land and foreign intellectual property.[70] Since this exception depends upon the proof of a personal equity between claimant and defendant, there is one situation which raises the question of the borderline between rule and exception more clearly than any other: A, the owner of foreign land or the holder of a foreign intellectual property right, agrees to sell the land or the right in question to B but, before title has been conveyed, he agrees to sell the same land or right to C

[66] And now the Regulation.

[67] Case 288/82 *Duijnstee v Goderbauer* [1983] ECR 2383; *Coin Controls Ltd v Suzo International (UK) Ltd* [1999] Ch 33; *Fort Dodge Animal Health Ltd v Akzo Nobel NV* [1998] FSR 222; *Napp Laboratories v Pfizer Inc* [1993] FSR 150; *Chiron Corporation v Evans Medical Ltd* [1996] FSR 863; Case C–4/03 *Gesellschaft für Antriebstechnik mbH & Co. KG (GAT) v Lamellen und Kupplungsbau Beteiligungs KG (LuK)*, Opinion of 16 Sept. 2004. As noted in *Griggs*, Art. 22(4) does not apply to copyright, which is not 'required to be deposited or registered'. It remains to be seen what the English courts will do if they have jurisdiction under the Regulation, but the claim turns on the validity of a claim to copyright in another Member State.

[68] If seen as an aspect of *forum non conveniens* this approach is vulnerable to the argument that it has been excluded by the decision of the European Court of Justice in Case C–281/02 *Owusu v Jackson (t/a Villa Holidays Bal-Inn Villas) and others*, n. 54 above. The better view, to which this chapter subscribes, is that it is a separate issue of non-justiciability, unaffected by any exclusion of resort to *forum non conveniens*: A Briggs, 'Two Undesirable Side-effects of the Brussels Convention' (1997) 113 *LQR* 364.

[69] It follows that the defendant may raise a defence of validity solely to remove the claim from the English courts; it is far from clear what test should be employed to distinguish the genuine defence from the bogus one which amounts to forum shopping by the defendant: for a suggestion, see Briggs and Rees, n. 18 above, 295.

[70] The *Griggs* case itself appears to be the first instance of this.

and conveys it to C. In proceedings before the English courts, B claims that C is obliged to convey title to B. This part considers three cases in which this situation has presented itself to the English courts in slightly different guises. I have referred to them as three 'difficult' cases. At the time they were decided, one suspects that the first two were thought of as anything but difficult,[71] and it may still be that that is the way they should be viewed. It is the judgment in the third of the cases, *Griggs*, which purports to cast on them a new light which invites their reconsideration.

(a) *Norris v Chambres*

John Sadleir, a founder of the Anglo-Prussian Mining Company, personally paid £40,000 towards the purchase price for two mines in Prussia to be bought by the company. Some time afterwards he committed suicide. One of the mines was then sold to a new company, The Maria Anna Steinbank Coal and Coke Company, under a contract which gave the new company credit against the price for the sum already paid by the deceased Sadleir. In *Norris v Chambres*[72] proceedings were commenced in England by Sadleir's personal representative against the new company[73] claiming, *inter alia*, a declaration that the defendants had purchased the mine subject to Sadleir's lien and that they might pay the amount due, or in default that the colliery might be sold and the produce applied in payment.

According to Sir John Romilly MR, there was no prospect that such a claim might be brought within the *Penn v Baltimore* exception:

> I am told that according to late decisions, and according to the law of England, if a man sell an estate to B. and receive part of the purchase-money and then repudiate the contract, and sell the estate to C., who has notice of the first contract and of the payment of part of the purchase-money by B., B. shall, in that case, have a lien on the estate in the hands of C., for the money paid to the original owner. But assume this to be so, this is purely a *lex loci* which attaches to persons resident here and dealing with land in England. If this be not the law of Prussia, I cannot make it so, because two out of the three parties dealing with the estate are Englishmen[74] and I have no evidence before me that this is the Prussian law on this subject, and if it be so, the Prussian Courts of Justice are the proper tribunals to enforce these rights.[75]

[71] In *Norris v Chambres*, n.72 below, it was put to Sir John Romilly MR that an opinion had been given 'by three of the most eminent leaders of the English Bar, to a contrary effect' to his ruling that *Norris* was an example of the rule and not the exception (at 258). His terse response was that 'such an opinion must have been given upon a different state of facts than that before me, or upon some imperfect representation of them' (ibid.)

[72] (1861) 29 Beav 246; affd., 3 De GF & J 583.

[73] The named defendant, Chambres and Slatter, acted for the new company; one presumes as their lawyers, but this is not made clear in the judgment of the Master of the Rolls.

[74] The second 'Englishman' was, presumably, the new company (or perhaps those acting on its behalf); the original owner of the mine, Michael Simons (i.e. party A), was described as a 'foreigner resident out of the jurisdiction'; proceedings against him for repayment of the sum obtained from Sadleir were on foot in Prussia.

[75] 29 Beav 246, 254.

It is clear from this passage that the question whether a third party is bound to recognize the interest of another in land, where the two parties have no prior relationship, is a question for the *lex loci*, i.e. the *lex situs*. But once the point is reached at which the issue is for the *lex situs* to resolve, the English courts have no jurisdiction to adjudicate. Under the *Penn v Baltimore* exception, their jurisdiction is confined to the enforcement of a personal equity which exists independently of any question of title to the land in question and not as a consequence of resolving a dispute as to title:

> in this case, the very foundation is wanting, for independently of the lien which this Court is asked to declare . . . there is no equity between the parties; here the Plaintiff is entitled to no decree against the Defendants for payment of any sum of money, nor is any such claimed, but the equity and relief sought begin and end with a prayer to make a certain transaction between other persons, one of whom is a stranger to this Plaintiff, an interest in an estate in Prussia, belonging to that stranger, and this independently of all personal equities attaching upon him. I never heard of any such case and I will not be the first Judge to create such a precedent . . .[76]

In sum, in the basic situation with which this section began, the competing interests of B and C raise a question of title which may be determined by the *lex situs*, but since it is a question of title which is the dispositive issue in the case, the *Moçambique* rule denies the English courts any jurisdiction to entertain the claim at all.

(b) *Deschamps v Miller*

On 6 October 1831, Jean Deschamps, a Frenchman, married Marie Taris, a Frenchwoman, under a French contract of marriage which provided that the marriage should be governed by the *régime dotal*. As a consequence, all after-acquired property was to be shared equally between M and Mme Deschamps. In 1836 Jean left France, and his wife, for India, where he bigamously married Cecilia Taylor. In a settlement of 1865 he placed his business premises in Madras on trust for Ms Taylor.[77] In *Deschamps v Miller*,[78] after the death of M and Mme Deschamps and Ms Taylor, Thomas Deschamps, the son of the first marriage, commenced proceedings against the trustees of the 1865 settlement for a declaration that the properties comprised in that deed were after-acquired property, such that Thomas was entitled to one-half as the administrator of Marie Deschamps.[79]

As with Sir John Romilly MR in *Norris v Chambres*, Parker J entertained no doubt that the claim made by Thomas Deschamps fell within the *Moçambique*

[76] 29 Beav 246, 254

[77] Other real estate was conveyed to the trust in 1866 and 1869.

[78] [1908] 1 Ch 856.

[79] For those wondering how the English courts had jurisdiction over these proceedings in the first place, the report reads that the plaintiff and the defendants were all within the jurisdiction of the English courts and Thomas Deschamps had taken out English letters of administration of the personal estate of his deceased mother.

rule and not within the *Penn v Baltimore* exception:

It is obvious . . . that whether the wife (Marie Deschamps) could assert any interest against the land outside France would be governed entirely by the law of the place where the land is situate . . . In order, therefore, to decide whether the plaintiff can succeed in following the property into the hands of the defendants I should have to consider the law relating to immovable property in India . . . The question is whether under these circumstances the Court ought to entertain jurisdiction. In my opinion the general rule is that the Court will not adjudicate on questions relating to the title or to the right to possession of immovable property out of the jurisdiction. There are, no doubt, exceptions to the rule, but without attempting to give an exhaustive statement of those exceptions, I think it will be found that they all depend on the existence between the parties to the suit of some personal obligation arising out of contract or implied contract, fiduciary relationship or fraud, or other conduct which, in the view of a Court of Equity in this country, would be unconscionable, and do not depend for their existence on the law of the locus of the immovable property.[80]

Once again, the claims of B (Thomas Deschamps, as administrator for Marie Deschamps) against C (the trustees of the 1865 settlement) turned on the question of the nature and priority of the interests he enjoyed in the land in question: 'such obligation . . . as exists (between the plaintiff and the defendants) depends on the Indian law relating to immovable property, and on that alone'.[81] But once that point was reached the English courts had no jurisdiction to adjudicate.

(c) *Griggs Group Ltd v Evans*

If, as is advocated herein, the *Moçambique* rule is confined to questions of *validity* when applied to intellectual property rights, this would provide a short answer to the issue raised in *Griggs*.[82] In line with *Norris* and *Deschamps*, the question whether Raben (C) should be ordered to assign to Griggs (B) the copyright sold to it by Evans (A) would appear to turn on the question whether Raben obtained the rights free of Griggs' interest in them. That is, or may be, a question of *title*, but it is not a question of *validity*. The parties were disputing which of them was to be regarded as the owner of an entirely valid bundle of rights. Although the judge did go on to decide that there was nothing in the previous cases dealing with intellectual property rights which prevented him from adjudicating,[83] the principal ground for allowing Griggs' claim to proceed was his finding that the *Moçambique* rule would not have prevented this even if the foreign property in question had been land.

It is difficult, at first sight, to see how such a conclusion could have been reached, in light of the decisions in *Norris* and *Deschamps*. The judge's answer is to suggest that both cases might be viewed differently today. The problem they dealt with should be treated as a question of choice of law, or the English courts should

[80] *Deschamps v Miller* [1908] 1 Ch 856, 863.
[81] Ibid., 864.
[82] *Griggs Group Ltd v Evans* [2005] 2 WLR 513.
[83] Ibid., para [140].

decline to hear the case, not on the basis of a lack of subject-matter jurisdiction, but on the basis of their power to stay proceedings under the doctrine of *forum non conveniens*.[84] The latter certainly did not exist at the time of the earlier decisions and is still only a relatively recent development in English private international law. The same cannot be said about the former.[85] Indeed, there was explicit acknowledgement by Sir John Romilly and Parker J that, as a matter of choice of law, it was Prussian law and Indian law respectively which would apply. It has been said of cases like *Norris* and *Deschamps* that 'instead of applying choice of law rules to a dispute the Court insisted that there be a sufficient connection between the parties or the cause of action and England'.[86] It may be more accurate to say that, rather than not applying choice of law rules, the two judges in question declined to apply the foreign law which they could see should apply, and did so because it was clear that it was the law applicable to a question of title to foreign land. In this sense there is a link between the *Moçambique* rule and choice of law. Once it is realized that the claim before the courts turns on the application of the *lex situs*, the point is reached at which the real issue is the question of title to the foreign land.

The solution to this 'conundrum' as it was seen by the judge is to be found in the following passage from Millett J in *Macmillan v Bishopsgate Trust (No 3)*:[87]

> The case [*Norris v Chambres*] was treated as one of jurisdiction, but it would today more properly be regarded as one of choice of law; whether the claim be brought against the vendor himself or against his transferee, the plaintiff would be invoking the in personam jurisdiction of the court against a defendant who was amenable to that jurisdiction. The difference between the two cases is that in the second there is no equity or privity between the parties which the court can enforce except such equity, if any, as may arise from the transferee's notice; while the sufficiency of such notice to affect the transferee's title is a matter for the *lex situs*. If, by that law, the transfer to the defendant extinguished the plaintiff's interest notwithstanding the defendant's notice, the plaintiff no longer has any proprietary interest upon which he can base his suit in England...

It is on the basis of this passage that Judge Prescott concluded that 'private international law has moved on'.[88] In the exercise of their *in personam* jurisdiction the English courts will apply English equity to determine whether a third party transferee is under an obligation to transfer the foreign land in question to the claimant, but subject to the proviso that such equity may be extinguished by the *lex situs*. With foreign land, for example, the *lex situs* will be determinative if B's interest is unenforceable for want of registration, irrespective of any notice of it

[84] For example, he suggests that *Deschamps* might have been a case in which the English proceedings would have been stayed in favour of proceedings in India if the doctrine of *forum non conveniens* had been available to Parker J in 1908: para [112].

[85] That is not to say that, historically, jurisdiction may not have been used as a proxy for underdeveloped, or under-applied, choice of law rules: RW White, 'Equitable Obligations in Private International Law: The Choice of Law' (1986) 11 *Sydney L Rev* 92, 106; TM Yeo, *Choice of Law for Equitable Doctrines* (OUP, 2004), 22–3.

[86] White, n.85 above.

[87] [1995] 1 WLR 978, 989.

[88] [2005] 2 WLR 513, para [110].

by C as third party transferee. Since, in *Griggs*, there was no evidence to suggest that the laws of the foreign countries in which copyright was said to exist would extinguish the equity enjoyed as against Raben,[89] the judge held that Griggs was entitled to the order requiring Raben to assign the copyright, both English and foreign, to Griggs.

(iv) Logical Conclusions and Re-evaluation

In *Griggs*, it is easy to understand the judge's preference for deciding that he had jurisdiction to hear the claims by confining the relevance of the foreign copyright to choice of law. As he points out, if he were obliged to decline jurisdiction, a contracting party (in this case, Evans) who *would* fall within the *Penn v Baltimore* exception would always be able to defeat the claimant's right to specific performance[90] with respect to foreign property by assigning it to a third party (in this case, Raben), even though that party is well aware of the circumstances and might even be an associate company.[91]

Ultimately, however, the judge falls into the trap which has bedevilled the role of equity in the conflict of laws, of transposing its characterization in English domestic law onto the private international law plane. This has tended to manifest itself as a matter of choice of law in the 'forum-centric' approach under which the *lex fori* is always applied, on the basis that the application of English equity is dependent only upon the court's having personal jurisdiction over the defendant and his conscience.[92] The novel aspect of the judge's approach in *Griggs* is also to assert that, since equity only operates *in personam*, it is to be characterized as part of the law of obligations. It therefore falls within the *Penn v Baltimore* exception and not within the *Moçambique* rule, even in the absence of any personal equity between the parties:

> a claim to have foreign land conveyed to one, based on an English contract and made against a purchaser of the land with prior notice of that contract, could in principle succeed, provided the foreign law would not overreach our doctrine of notice. It would be a claim in personam, not in rem. The claimant would succeed, not by proving that he already had a title to the land arising out of the foreign land law, but upon a personal obligation owed to him by the defendant arising out of the contract and his unconscionable conduct. Internationally, it would be classified under the rubric

[89] And none likely since copyright is a 'non-registration system': ibid., [140].

[90] One imagines that damages in lieu would have been worth little against the impoverished Evans, or perhaps it is commercial artists who are the exception to the rule?

[91] [2005] 2 WLR 513, para. [14].

[92] *National Commercial Bank v Wimborne* (1978) 5 Butterworths Property Reports 11958 (NSW Sup Ct); *United States Surgical Corporation v Hospital Products International Pty Ltd* [1982] 2 NSWLR 766, 797–8, affd., [1983] 2 NSWLR 157 (NSW CA), revd. on different grounds, (1984) 156 CLR 41; *Paramasivam v Flynn* (1998–9) 160 ALR 203, 214–18 (HCA and Fed Ct of Australia).

'Obligations' ... He would be relying on a personal obligation: an equity arising from the English contract which had not been extinguished by the lex situs.[93]

The concession that foreign law might be 'taken into account' so as to defeat English equity has echoes of the approach taken in some recent cases to choice of law in claims of dishonest assistance.[94] In *Griggs* it seems that it is only 'taken into account' so as not to lose sight of the fact that it is an English equity which is to be enforced by the English courts in the exercise of their *in personam* jurisdiction. This is not just to elevate a domestic characterization of English law onto the private international law plane; it is to elevate a characterization based on an historical fiction. As is explained in *Snell's Equity*:

When it would have been unconscionable for the legal owner of property to keep the property for himself, the Court of Chancery acted on his conscience and compelled him to hold the property for the benefit of another person. In their origin, therefore, equitable rights were merely rights *in personam*. However, in the fifteenth and sixteenth centuries the chancellors began to enforce equitable interests not only against the person originally bound, but also against his heir, or a donee, or a purchaser who took with notice.[95] Finally, equitable rights became enforceable against all except a purchaser without notice, and so it became possible to treat them as rights *in rem*, or proprietary rights.[96]

It is true that Maitland, who is invoked in this passage from *Snell*, argued that a beneficiary's rights under a trust were only personal because the rights could be enforced against trustees and third parties who interfered with the rights, but not against a bona fide purchaser without notice.[97] And there are those who have argued that because of the immunity of the bona fide purchaser, equitable rights cannot be regarded as rights *in rem* in the same way as legal rights, so that they are best regarded as some form of hybrid.[98] Whichever way *this* debate should be resolved, the point to be emphasized is that it is the relevant debate only at the level of English domestic law. What really matters in cases like *Griggs*, and others said to fall within the *Penn v Baltimore* exception, is how the rights relied upon by the parties should be characterized as a matter of private international law.

Although one hesitates to say it, even Lord Millett may have lost sight of this in the passage from *Macmillan* upon which the judge in *Griggs* relies. Jeffrey Hackney has argued convincingly that the rule in *Pilcher v Rawlins*[99] is 'a matter of jurisdiction, not a matter of policy'.[100] It is the bona fide purchaser of a legal estate

93 At para [111].

94 *Grupo Torras SA v Al Sabah (No 5)* [2001] Lloyd's Rep Bank 36; *Kuwait Oil Tanker Co SAK v Al Bader (No 3)* [2000] 2 All ER (Comm) 271.

95 FW Maitland, *Equity: A Course of Lectures* (ed. AH Chaytor and WJ Whittaker) (ed. J Brunyate, 1936 revised edn., CUP), 112.

96 *Snell's Equity* (31st edn ed., J McGhee, Sweet & Maxwell, 2005), para. 2–02.

97 N. 95 above, 106–16.

98 See AW Scott (1917) 17 *Col LR* 269; HG Hanbury 'The Field of Modern Equity' (1929) 45 *LQR* 196.

99 (1872) LR 7 Ch App 259.

100 J Hackney, *Understanding Equity and Trusts* (Fontana Press, 1987), 24. See also J Hackney, 'Usucapio and the Law of Trusts', in J Getzler (ed.), *Rationalising Property, Equity and Trusts: Essays in Honour of Edward Burn* (OUP, 2003), 21, 31–2.

from a trustee for value and without notice who is able to discharge the heavy burden of proving that 'his assertion of his common law title is not unconscionable'.[101] He wins (in the common law courts) because the claimant is non-suited for lack of jurisdiction in the Court of Chancery. The purchaser with notice does fall within the jurisdiction of the Court of Chancery. In that sense,[102] the presence or absence of notice is jurisdictionally significant, but the relevant question for private international law purposes is whether the claim against the purchaser falls within the jurisdiction of the English courts at all. In that context, a purchaser with notice is just one variety of third party transferee; a purchaser without notice is another.

It is beyond the confines of this chapter to consider fully the characterization of equitable rights in the conflict of laws. For that the reader is referred to the masterly work of Yeo.[103] His principal concern is with choice of law. In that context, he proffers the same cautionary note which has been emphasized herein: 'in view of the fact that the category of property is intended to deal with different concepts of property in different countries, one should be careful not to let technicalities of domestic law have too great an influence over the characterisation of issues for choice of law.'[104] One such 'technicality' is the enforcement of court orders by compulsion of defendants personally. [105] As Yeo points out, that should have no bearing on the nature of the right being enforced:

> It is the substance of the claim, and not the form in which the claim is made, that is important. Where the claimant is asserting that the defendant owes an obligation to transfer property to the claimant, but that obligation arises only out of the claimant's property right, the claim should be characterised as a proprietary one. If an obligation is merely incidental to ownership, the predominant characteristic of the claim remains the reliance on the law of property. Thus, claims to recover property from third-party transferees are generally proprietary, even if the claim is couched in terms of an obligation of the third party to transfer the property to the claimant. The third party owes no independent obligation to the claimant apart from the duty arising from being a constructive trustee to convey the property, and the third party is a constructive trustee because he had not acquired the beneficial title. Such claims are functionally no different from revendication claims in civil law systems; the basis of the claim is an assertion of property rights.[106]

As an illustration of this approach to characterization where equitable claims are made in the English courts, based on dealings with foreign property, it is the decision of the Court of Appeal in *Macmillan v Bishopsgate*[107] which is more instructive than the passage from Millett J which was relied upon by the judge in the *Griggs* case.

[101] Ibid.

[102] And it is in this sense only that one should read the passage from Millett J in *Macmillan*, and in other cases: *El Ajou v Dollar Holdings plc* [1993] 3 All ER 717, 736 (revd. on other grounds: [1994] 2 All ER 685 (CA)). See Yeo, n. 85 above, 144.

[103] N. 85 above.

[104] Ibid., 144.

[105] 'One can protect rights *in rem* by judgments *in personam*': Hackney, n. 100 above, 27.

[106] N. 85 above, 151–2.

[107] [1996] 1 WLR 387.

When it transpired that the late Robert Maxwell had transferred shares in Berlitz International Inc from the name of the claimant to a nominee and then to a number of banks as security for loans to finance his group of companies, the claimant sought their recovery from the banks which had come into possession of them. The claim was for a declaration that the shares were held on a constructive trust, along with orders for them to be restored to the claimant, and damages for breach of trust. Although the *claim* might be characterized as restitutionary in nature (i.e. based on obligation, not property), it depended for its existence on the question whether the claimant could establish that it was the equitable owner of the shares in the face of the banks' defence that they had acquired them as bona fide purchasers without notice of the claimant's interest. That was the relevant *issue* and it raised a question of property, for which the normal choice of law rule is the *lex situs* of the property at the time of the transaction which is said to give rise to the competing interests of claimant and defendant. For shares that was the *lex incorporationis*,[108] the law of the place where the company (Berlitz) was incorporated;[109] in *Macmillan*, that was the law of New York.

Macmillan v Bishopsgate involved, therefore, a claim for the enforcement of an equitable obligation, but one where the 'obligation arises only out of the claimant's property right'. If the property in *Macmillan* had been immovable property, the *Moçambique* rule would have been engaged and the court would have been left with no jurisdiction to hear the claim at all.[110] The parallels with *Norris v Chambres* and *Deschamps v Miller* are obvious. There, the underlying equitable right upon which each claimant had to rely and upon which the courts were being asked to adjudicate was a right in immovable property. It is submitted that both cases were decided correctly, both at the time they were decided and now, on the basis of the *Moçambique* rule as it currently exists.

None of this should call into question the exception in *Penn v Baltimore* where the claimant is able to rely on an 'independent obligation', i.e. one not dependent on the prior determination of the claimant's property right. Where there is a contract between the parties or some unconscionable conduct *vis-à-vis* the claimant himself as opposed to his interest in the land, it is entirely appropriate, for the purposes of private international law, to characterize under the rubric

[108] Millett J adopted the same approach as the Court of Appeal, but held that the relevant law to determine the competing interests of the claimant and the banks was the *lex loci actus*, i.e. the law of the place where transactions took place on which the defendants relied as creating priority over the claimant's claim; that was also the law of New York.

[109] Unless (according to Staughton and Auld LJJ) the shares were negotiable instruments, in which case the *lex situs* is the place where the paper constituting the negotiable instruments is at the time of the transfer.

[110] Cf. a number of cases in which the courts have reached this point in their analysis, but proceeded to decide the case on the basis of the *lex situs* rather than declare that they had no jurisdiction: *Hicks v Powell* (1869) LR 4 Ch App 741; *Martin v Martin* (1831) 2 Russ & M 507. In *Norton v Florence Land & Public Works Co* (1877) LR 7 Ch D 332, Jessel MR found that the claim failed as a matter of the *lex situs* but also held that it should have been brought in the courts of Florence, where, in fact, litigation was already underway.

'Obligations' a claim to enforce the obligation created. In this sense it may be more helpful to refer to a 'privity of equity'[111] as opposed to a 'personal equity' and 'strangers' thereto.[112] In such cases, the English courts may still have been guilty of applying English law simply as the *lex fori* without any consideration of whether a different characterization might be appropriate for choice of law purposes, though, in some, English law would have applied in any event, e.g. as the law applicable to the contract which created the personal equity between the parties. This may help to explain why the judge in *Griggs* emphasizes on a number of occasions that his decision is reached in the context of a contract governed by English law.[113] But the contract in question was between Griggs (A) and Evans (B), and it is one which has no effect on Raben (C) unless the law applicable to Raben's acquisition of the property gives it any.

If one is left unpersuaded by the judge's final conclusion in *Griggs*, there is nonetheless much to commend in his attempt to discern the underlying rationale of the *Moçambique* rule and his willingness to question whether other solutions are now to be found in more fully developed choice of law rules and the doctrine of *forum non conveniens*. If one takes his approach to its logical conclusion, one finds that, rather than decline jurisdiction, the English courts should hear a claim even where a disputed question of title is central to its resolution, provided this question is resolved by applying the *lex situs*. In the case of immovable property that law would be literally the *lex situs*, the law of the place where the property was situated. In the case of intellectual property, by analogy with the approach to shares in *Macmillan v Bishopsgate*, that law would be the *lex protectionis*, or the *lex creationis*, the law of the territory from which the monopoly of rights which makes up the particular intellectual property is derived.

Of course, this represents a direct challenge to the *Moçambique* rule and this was not a luxury open to the judge. There are, perhaps, three reasons why the time may be ripe for its re-evaluation: the courts may be moving in this direction already in the decisions they have been prepared to reach; it may be possible to replace, or refine, the *Moçambique* rule so that it continues to apply in those cases which perhaps illustrate its true rationale; and a re-evaluation may be forced on the courts in any event through the involvement of that area of law

[111] It is this 'privity of equity' which lies at the heart of the courts' jurisdiction to grant an 'anti-suit injunction', but submissions to this effect seem to have carried little weight with the European Court in its ruling that such injunctions are not compatible with the Brussels Convention (and, now, the Regulation) (Case C–159/02 *Turner v Grovit*, [2005] 1 AC 1, a ruling which appears inconsistent with its approach in Case C–294/92 *Webb v Webb* [1994] ECR I–1717, which is discussed below: text to n.123. See: A Briggs, 'Anti-suit Injunctions and Utopian Ideals' (2004) 120 *LQR* 529.

[112] A purchaser with notice may not be a stranger to 'the equity' so that, as we have seen, the jurisdiction of the Court of Chancery could have been invoked, but it would still be inappropriate for private international law purposes to characterize the claim against him as anything other than proprietary. However, there seems to be no reason why the beneficiary may not assign the *benefit* of the trust and the assignee claim the privity of equity which would enable him to invoke the *Penn v Baltimore* exception.

[113] [2005] 2 WLR 513, paras. [115] and [140].

with which Jim Harris was so closely engaged just before his untimely death: human rights.

(a) The Practice of the Courts

There are some who would point to *Penn v Baltimore* itself as indicative of a less than full adherence to the *Moçambique* rule since it 'seems open to the strong objection that the court is doing indirectly what it dare not do directly'.[114] It may not have been the preferred solution of those who considered the exception as anomalous to reconsider the rule from which it departed, but this part looks to two much more recent decisions to illustrate, at the very least, a judicial willingness to narrow down the scope of the rule. One is decided in the context of the European instruments which now determine much of the jurisdiction of the English courts; the other in the context of the 'traditional rules' within which the *Moçambique* rule has largely been encountered.

Within the scheme of the 'Brussels Regulation'[115] there is no room for the *Moçambique* rule itself,[116] but a counterpart exists in the form of Article 22(1) which states:

> The following courts shall have exclusive jurisdiction, regardless of domicile: (1) in proceedings which have as their object rights *in rem* in immovable property or tenancies of immovable property[117] the courts of the Member State in which the property is situated.

The scope of this rule[118] was considered by the European Court in *Webb v Webb*. The constraints of exchange control led George Webb to 'purchase' a flat in the Antibes by having it conveyed into the name of his son, Lawrence. When the two fell out and Lawrence showed no inclination to give up the flat, his father commenced proceedings in England for a declaration that the flat was held for him on a resulting trust and for an order that Lawrence re-convey it.[119] A reference to the European Court[120] led to a ruling that the father's claim did not

[114] *Companhia de Moçambique v British South Africa Co* [1892] 2 QB 358, 404–5 (CA), *per* Lord Esher.

[115] Council Regulation (EC) 44/2001 on Jurisdiction and the Recognition and Enforcement of Judgments in Civil and Commercial Matters, [2001] OJ L12/1.

[116] This begs the question of what is meant by the 'scheme of the Regulation'. For example, may the English courts apply the *Moçambique* rule if they have jurisdiction under the Regulation but the claim revolves around a question of title to land in a non-Member State? This is an area of some uncertainty: see Briggs and Rees, n. 18 above, para. 2.225. The issue might have been resolved if the European Court of Justice had been willing to be a little more helpful in its recent ruling in Case C–281/02 *Owusu*, n. 54 above (see Peel, n. 54 above; Briggs, n. 54 above).

[117] A lease is, of course, a rather obvious example of 'privity of equity', at least as between the original parties; the likely reason for its inclusion in the exclusionary rule found in Art. 22(1) is assessed at n. 149.

[118] Or rather its predecessor, Art. 16(1) of the Brussels Convention. The Convention was superseded (save in Denmark) by the Regulation, which applies to proceedings commenced after 1 Mar. 2002.

[119] [1991] 1 WLR 1410.

[120] Case C–294/92 *Webb v Webb* [1994] ECR I–1717. See A Briggs, 'Trusts of Land and the Brussels Convention' (1994) 110 *LQR* 526.

fall within the terms of Article 22(1) so as to confer exclusive jurisdiction on the French courts. The reasoning of the Court, such as it is, is reminiscent of the Court of Chancery in *Penn v Baltimore*. George Webb did not seek to rely on any existing right *in rem*, and so far as he relied on his existing equitable right he was relying on a right *in personam* as against a person who was privy to it. The decision has been described as 'controversial' and 'the reasoning almost wholly spurious'.[121] Perhaps all that needs to be noted here is that, if the decision in *Webb* is just as anomalous as the decision in *Penn v Baltimore*,[122] it is an anomaly with which the European Court was happy to live so as to limit the scope of Article 22(1).[123]

If Article 22(1) of the Brussels Regulation represents a counterpart to the *Moçambique* rule in Europe, the rule itself is to some extent now enshrined in section 30 of the Civil Jurisdiction and Judgments Act 1982,[124] under which the English courts may entertain proceedings for trespass or any other tort affecting foreign land 'unless the proceedings are principally concerned with a question of the title to, or the right to possession of' that land. The question of when proceedings are 'principally concerned' with a question of title was considered by the Court of Appeal in *Re Polly Peck International plc (No 2)*.[125] The facts are very similar to those in the *Hesperides Hotel* case. The claimants' hotels in Northern Cyprus were expropriated by the unrecognized Turkish Republic of Northern Cyprus and leased to Polly Peck International (PPI), which was alleged to have derived substantial financial advantage as a result. After PPI had gone into administration, the claimants applied for leave, under section 11(3)(d) of the Insolvency Act 1986, to commence proceedings against PPI and its administrators. The claim was that sums received by the administrators represented the proceeds of PPI's wrongdoing and were subject to a remedial constructive trust for the benefit of the claimants.

Leave was refused on the basis that the court had no power under the 1986 Act to impose the trust being claimed, but Mummery LJ went on to reject the argument that the court had no jurisdiction to entertain the claim at all in so far as it related to title in foreign land.[126] He held that the proceedings were not 'principally concerned' with a question of title for the purposes of section 30 of the 1982 Act. It seems clear that it would have been necessary to resolve the question of

[121] Briggs and Rees, n. 18 above, para. 2.43.

[122] 'Given the doubts of our masters of equity, the airy certainty of the court comes as something of a surprise': Briggs, n.120 above, 529.

[123] It must be conceded that this was motivated in part by the approach which regards the general rule in Art. 2 (the defendant shall be sued in the courts for the Member State where he is domiciled) as the paramount rule from which all others are derogations which must be narrowly construed.

[124] S. 30 is, strictly speaking, an exception to the rule. For the full text of the section, see text to n.33 above.

[125] [1998] 3 All ER 812.

[126] He accepted that the *Moçambique* rule applied and did not think the claim fell within the *Penn v Baltimore* exception since 'the applicant's claim for relief by way of constructive trust is not founded on a contractual or equitable right. It is founded on the legal ownership of properties in Northern Cyprus': ibid., 828e.

title to the hotels in question,[127] but Mummery LJ relied on the use of 'principally' in its ordinary sense to mean 'for the most part' or 'chiefly' and that was 'a matter of judgment, one of fact and degree'.[128] While only *obiter dictum*, it has been observed that this interpretation would 'open the door to jurisdiction to such an extent that it calls into question the basic justification for the *Moçambique* rule'.[129]

(b) Alternative Rules

In this Chapter, as elsewhere, the tendency has been to assess whether a rule to deal with foreign intellectual property can be derived from, or by analogy with, the rule applied to foreign land, i.e. the *Moçambique* rule. But perhaps that is to work in the wrong direction. It has been suggested that the proper scope of the jurisdictional rule applicable to intellectual property is that the English courts should not seek to resolve any question as to the *validity* of foreign intellectual property. It is in the granting, and maintaining, of the monopoly of rights which makes up an intellectual property right that an exercise of prerogative power is involved; an exercise which is confined to the limits of territorial sovereignty enjoyed by the state in question, and which can only be reviewed by the courts of that state. Validity is not the same as title. Once acknowledged as valid, an intellectual property right is like any other commodity; it can be bought and sold and the rights which it represents can be infringed by the wrongdoing of others. There is no compelling reason why the effect of the transfer of such rights, or claims based upon their infringement, should not be heard by the courts in just the same way that they would entertain claims based on tangible movable property and other forms of intangible movable property, even if located abroad.

The same approach may be taken to foreign land. The question of which of two parties is the true owner of land only raises a question of 'validity' if one subscribes to the view that each and every disposition of land must be validated by the state, i.e. that each disposition is conditional on the approval of the state so that all land ultimately remains in the gift of the state. That may not have been an unrealistic description in times of Roman law, or even at the time that Vattel and Story were offering their justification for the *Moçambique* rule, but it cannot be sustained in the modern world where land is treated, for the most part, just like any other commodity.[130]

[127] See n.145 below.

[128] He derived support for this view from the approach taken to the meaning of that expression in Art. 19 of the Brussels Convention (now Art. 25 of the Regulation) in two cases concerned with the validity of foreign intellectual property rights: *Fort Dodge Animal Health Ltd v Akzo Nobel NV* [1998] FSR 222, and *Coin Controls Ltd v Suzo International (UK) Ltd* [1999] Ch 33, 47.

[129] Briggs and Rees, n. 18 above, para. 4.06, where the correctness of this interpretation is called into doubt as a result.

[130] It is submitted that this analysis is not affected by the widespread adoption of registration schemes for the disposition of land. They represent a formal record of ownership, necessary so as to avoid the need for cruder physical delineation of boundaries and to ease subsequent disposition.

It is at this point, if not at any others, that Jim Harris would have raised an eyebrow.[131] As late as 1973, Megarry J was to observe: 'it is a fundamental of English land law that nobody save the crown owns any land'.[132] But even if ultimate or 'radical' title may be located in the Crown and this may still have some practical importance,[133] 'the crown's radical title is, in truth, no proprietary title at all, but merely an expression of the *Realpolitik* which served historically to hold together the medieval theory of land tenure'.[134]

The only sense in which land can be said still to be in the gift of the state so that its ownership is subject to the validation of the state, or the only sense in which it matters, is that, as with other forms of property, the state can always take it away by expropriation. The effect of expropriation, as an exercise of the prerogative power of a state, can be dealt with largely as a matter of choice of law, with recourse, when necessary, to a much narrower rule of non-justiciability than the *Moçambique* rule. A brief consideration of the courts' approach to questions of title to movable property should indicate how this would work in practice.

Any question of title to movable property is determined by the *lex situs*, i.e. the law of the place where the property was located at the time of the transaction, or event, said to have affected title. If the transaction, or event, in question consists of an expropriation by the state at the time when the property was situated in that state, it will be recognized by the courts,[135] save only in those cases where the result is said to offend public policy.[136] The *lex situs* for land is, with one exception, immutable, so that the single prerogative of having its own law applied would be reserved to the state in question, if not the 'double prerogative' of having its own courts adjudicate.[137] There would be an understandable concern at the prospect of an English court having to assess whether the land law of another state was contrary to public policy, but it is clear from cases in which movable property has been involved that there could be no question of the courts of one property-owning regime sitting in judgment on the law of another very different property-owning regime. Consider, for example, the view of Bankes LJ in the leading case of *Luther v Sagor*[138] on the expropriation of private property in the aftermath of the Russian Revolution of 1917:

I do not see how the courts could treat this particular decree otherwise than as the expression by the de facto government of a civilised country of a policy which it considered to be in

[131] For many years, Jim gave a superb series of lectures on 'Interests and Estates in Land'; see also his essay 'Ownership of Land in English Law', in N MacCormick and P Birks (eds.), *The Legal Mind: Essays for Tony Honoré* (Clarendon Press, 1986), 143–61.

[132] *Lowe v J.W. Ashmore Ltd* [1971] Ch 545.

[133] e.g., in the law of escheat.

[134] K Gray, *Elements of Land Law* (4th edn., OUP, 2005), para 1.122; on the demise of the theory of tenure, see paras 1.142–1.153.

[135] Either as a consequence of the ordinary application of the choice of law rules for tangible movable property, or that version of the act of state doctrine under which the court will not enquire into a sovereign act done within the territory of the foreign state: *Underhill v Hernandez* 168 US 250, 252 (1897). See Dicey & Morris, n. 10 above, para. 5–040.

[136] *Kuwait Airways Corp v Iraqi Airways Co* [2002] 2 AC 883.

[137] *Griggs Group Ltd v Evans* [2005] 2 WLR 513, para. [78]; see text to n.21 above for the full quotation.

[138] *Aksionairnoye Obschestvo AM Luther Co v James Sagor & Co* [1921] 3 KB 532, 546.

the best interest of that country. It must be quite immaterial for present purposes that the same views are not entertained by the Government of this country, are repudiated by the vast majority of its citizens, and are not recognised by our laws.

If, however, the application of the *lex situs* were to constitute a flagrant breach of international law, in particular a breach of human rights, the courts should not shy from denying its recognition. In *Oppenheimer v Cattermole*[139] the House of Lords made it clear that, if necessary,[140] they would have refused to recognize a German decree of 1941 which deprived absent Jews of their German nationality and their property. If the property had consisted of land and a question of title based on the decree had arisen in the proceedings, would it have been a satisfactory response for the courts to say: 'of course, we would not have applied the *lex situs*, but, in fact, we decline to adjudicate this claim at all'?

The one exception to the immutability of the *lex situs* is that, while the *situs* cannot change, the *lex* might. How are the courts, in the absence of the *Moçambique* rule, to deal with claims where the question of title can only be resolved by first establishing who or what is the relevant authority? And what if it is two sovereign states themselves who are disputing title? Here, it is necessary to retain a rule of non-justiciability, but it need not be couched in quite such broad terms as the *Moçambique* rule. Indeed, it, or something very like it, may already exist. In *Buttes Gas and Oil Co. v Hammer (No.3)*[141] the resolution of claims and counterclaims for defamation and conspiracy depended, at least in part, on determining the competing claims of sovereign states to the ownership of, and right to exploit, the sea bed off the coast of Abu Musa, an island in the Arabian Gulf. The courts were therefore being asked to adjudicate, albeit indirectly, on an extant dispute in international law. The House of Lords declined to do so according to Lord Wilberforce because 'there are . . . no judicial or manageable standards by which to judge these issues'.[142] This principle, which was described as one of 'judicial restraint or abstension . . . inherent in the very nature of the judicial process',[143] may be more apt to deal with cases like the *Moçambique* and *Hesperides* cases.[144] Although the question of title raised therein might, strictly speaking, have amounted to a dispute between private parties, indirectly their resolution raised the same sort of political sensitivities: to whom had the tribal chief Umtassa really ceded the territory in Manicaland, the Portuguese or the British (*Moçambique*); what was the status of the Turkish Republic of Northern Cyprus and what effect should be given to the legislation it issued dispossessing the Greek Cypriot community of their property (*Hesperides, Polly Peck*[145])? As a rule of non-justiciability,

139 [1976] AC 249, 265, 276–8, 282–3.

140 The appeal was decided on different grounds.

141 [1982] AC 888.

142 Ibid., 938.

143 Ibid., 931–2.

144 It may be noted that Lord Wilberforce referred to the *Moçambique* rule as that 'much criticised rule': ibid., 926.

145 Mummery LJ had indicated, *obiter*, that he might have got as far as confronting these questions, but it is far from obvious how he would have resolved them, or whether he would have had the 'judicial or manageable standards' to do so.

this slightly extended application of the *Buttes Gas* principle would probably be less certain than the *Moçambique* rule, but it would be narrower in scope, possessed of a clear rationale, and kept within appropriate limits by the test of proportionality referred to in part (c) below.

If cases like the *Moçambique* and *Hesperides* cases might be decided the same way, others such as *Norris v Chambres* and *Deschamps v Miller* would be decided differently.[146] While these cases may not have involved issues of 'validity', or sovereignty, of the type which the courts are ill-suited to resolve, the judge is right to point out in *Griggs*[147] that they may nonetheless be cases which the English courts think are more appropriately resolved in another forum.[148] Outside the Brussels Regulation the option of staying proceedings would be available after any abolition or narrowing of the *Moçambique* rule by recourse to the doctrine of *forum non conveniens*. That would not be possible under the Regulation where all that is available is the rule in Article 22(1). But this is just the sort of problem one has when a discretion-based jurisdictional regime is replaced with a rule-based jurisdictional regime. One has to put something in the rule, but, as we have seen, the European Court has been keen to narrow its scope.[149]

(c) Human Rights

The more radical aspect of this Chapter lies in the suggestion that the courts should be invited to reconsider the *Moçambique* rule and slaughter a few sacred cows along the way. It may be surmised that they will not be queuing up to do so, so this Chapter finishes by speculating on how they might be forced into a reassessment in any event.

In 1946 the former Czechoslavakia confiscated the property of the monarch of Liechtenstein which was situated in Czechoslavakia, including the painting *Szene an einem römischen Kalkofen*.[150] It was taken under Beneš Decree No 12 which allowed, *inter alia*, for the confiscation of the property of those having 'acted as enemies of the Czech and Slovak people'.[151] In 1991 the painting arrived in Cologne under temporary loan and the claimant, the present monarch of Liechtenstein, saw his chance to recover it. His application to do so was met with the response

[146] Of course, *Penn v Baltimore* would be decided the same way, but now because it would no longer be caught by the *Moçambique* rule in the first place.

[147] [2005] 2 WLR 513, para. [112].

[148] That may be particularly true where the local land law is imbued with issues of social policy which it would be more appropriate for the local courts to assess.

[149] The issues of social policy referred to in the previous note are most likely to arise in landlord and tenant disputes so it is no real surprise to find them included in Art. 22(1) but, even here, there has been a narrow reading of what this covers: Case C–280/90 *Hacker v Euro-Relais GmbH* [1992] ECR I–1111.

[150] The oddly-named 'Scene at a Roman lime-kiln', though something may have got lost in the translation. The alternative title, *Der Großen Kalkofen*, is no less odd.

[151] It seems that it was 'generally known' that the monarch of Liechtenstein was a person of German nationality.

that the German courts had no jurisdiction to hear his claim. This was the consequence of the Convention on the Settlement of Matters Arising out of the War and the Occupation entered into between the occupying powers and Germany after the end of the second World War,[152] chapter 6 of which stated:

> 1. The Federal Republic of Germany shall in the future raise no objections against the measures which have been, or will be, carried out with regard to German external assets or other property, seized for the purpose of reparation or restitution, or as a result of the state of war.
>
> . . .
>
> 3. No claim or action shall be admissible against persons who shall have acquired or transferred title to property on the basis of the measures referred to in paragraph. 1....

The claimant argued that the refusal of the German courts to entertain his claim amounted to a breach of Article 6(1) of the European Convention for the Protection of Human Rights in depriving him of his right to a fair hearing.[153] This issue was considered by the European Court of Human Rights in the case of *Prince Hans-Adam II of Liechtenstein v Germany.*[154]

The Court observed that the right of access to the courts secured by Article 6(1) is not absolute. The Contracting States enjoy a margin of appreciation, but a limitation will not be compatible with Article 6(1) 'if it does not pursue a legitimate aim and if there is not a reasonable relationship of proportionality between the means employed and the aim sought to be achieved'.[155] The Court ruled that the test of proportionality had been satisfied. It is not the aim of this part to dwell on the merits of this decision, but it may be noted that the Court based its finding on the 'unique circumstance'[156] that the retention of Chapter 6, Article 3 of the Settlement Convention was one of the conditions under which the Occupation Regime was finally brought to an end and sovereignty was restored to a unified Germany in 1990.[157] If this is indicative of the sort of circumstances necessary to meet the test of proportionality, then the routine application of the *Moçambique* rule may soon be open to a challenge not easily met by some of the axiomatic

[152] Originally drawn up as one of the Bonn Conventions in 1952, but given legal force as one of the 'Paris Agreements' in 1954.

[153] For those wondering how he would have got round the application of Czech law, the claimant would have argued that the application of the *lex situs* on this occasion would have led to a result incompatible with German public policy (s. 6 of the Introductory Act to the Civil Code).

[154] [2001] ECHR 42527/98, 12 July 2001. There were also alleged violations of Art. 1 of Protocol No 1 and Art. 14, neither of which was upheld. I am grateful to my colleague, Professor Adrian Briggs, for suggesting the potential relevance of this decision.

[155] Ibid., para 44, citing *Waite and Kennedy v Germany* [1999] ECHR 26083/94, 6 BHRC 499, para. 59; *TP and KM v United Kingdom* [2001] ECHR 28945/95, para. 98; *Z v United Kingdom* [2001] ECHR 29392/95, 10 BHCR 384, para. 93.

[156] Ibid., para 59.

[157] Under the Treaty on the Final Settlement with respect to Germany, signed on 12 Sept. 1990 and which came into force on 15 Mar. 1991 (the so-called 'Two-Plus-Four Treaty').

arguments which now seem to sustain it. If not modified as advocated in this Chapter, it may be that, in practice, such challenges will depend on whether the courts of the *situs* were reasonably available,[158] but that would, at least, have converted what is currently a rule into something more like a discretion.

(v) Conclusion

This Chapter has ranged across a number of issues, but it had two principal aims. First, it has sought to clarify the *Moçambique* rule and the exception in *Penn v Baltimore*, both in relation to foreign land and foreign intellectual property. Secondly, and more radically, it has sought to challenge the need for the rule. In that regard, this Chapter has taken the underlying argument put forward by the judge in the *Griggs* case to its logical conclusion and suggests that solutions to the issues raised in such cases can be provided by recourse to other, now established, rules of private international law: choice of law, *forum non conveniens*, and the narrow principle of non-justiciability in the *Buttes Gas* case. It is a paper which has undoubtedly been improved by the comments of those who were kind enough to read an earlier draft, but I am certain that it would have been improved further if I had been able to show it to my much missed colleague in whose honour it has been a pleasure to write it.

[158] In the context of an application for an anti-suit injunction based on an exclusive jurisdiction agreement, it has been held that Art. 6 only enshrines a right to be heard; it does not guarantee an unfettered choice about which court should do the hearing: *The Kribi (No. 1)* [2001] 1 Lloyd's Rep 76.

12

Property, Personality and Violence

*Joshua Getzler**

Jim Harris taught criminal law and Roman law over the years, as well as property and jurisprudence, and his broad legal culture left its mark on the planes of his great work on property theory. I cannot help but wonder if the clear positions of classical Roman law did not somewhere inform Jim's strong rejection of self-ownership. 'Who Owns My Body?' is the rhetorical title of one of Jim's finest essays. 'Nobody owns my body, not even me' is the laconic conclusion.[1] The language is telling. According to the Roman jurist, Ulpian, a free man could not sue for property damage under the *lex Aquilia* for a culpable but non-intentional harm inflicted on his own person, 'because no one is deemed to be the owner of his own limbs'.[2] Only if the attacker intended to harm the person could one sue, and then, not for economic harm nor even for physical pain and suffering, but only for the *injuria*, the attack on the dignitary interest of the human personality. This important ruling suggests how persons and property formed a polarity in legal analysis from the early days of the Western legal tradition.

Building on the rejection of self-ownership, Jim insisted that property rights involved relations with external assets strictly and analytically separate from the right-holding subject. These positions led to his demolition of the Lockean theory that one mixed one's labour onto the world and, by this active possession, made parts of the world one's property. More generally, property metaphors could not rightly be used to articulate the justice claims of persons based on projections of

* St Hugh's College and Faculty of Law, Oxford. For their generous help I am grateful to Eyal Benvenisti, Timothy Endicott, Alon Harel, Jeremy Horder, Amnon Lehavi, Andrew Simester, James Whitman, and to Lucia Zedner. All remaining errors are my responsibility alone.

1 See JW Harris, 'Who Owns My Body?' (1996) 16 *OJLS* 55, 84; JW Harris, *Property and Justice* (Clarendon Press, 1996), 8–13, 182–212, 230–46.

2 Ulpian, *Edict, book 18*, in *The Digest of Justinian* (ed. A Watson, University of Pennsylvania Press, 1985, rev. 1988), D.9.2.13.pr. We can see such ideas operating in the recent House of Lords case of *R v Bentham* [2005] UKHL 18, para 8, where Lord Bingham refused to find that a hand concealed under a jacket could be 'possession [of an] imitation firearm' under s. 17(2) of the Firearms Act 1968: '[o]ne cannot possess something which is not separate and distinct from oneself. An unsevered hand or finger is part of oneself. Therefore, one cannot possess it. Resort to metaphor is impermissible because metaphor is a literary device which draftsmen of criminal statutes do not employ. What is possessed must under the definition be a thing. A person's hand or fingers are not a thing.'

their bodies, or their labour power, or their rational purposive will into the world. There was room in his analysis for intangibles, for 'ideational entities' such as intellectual rights; one could own assets created by the legal mind.[3] Again this was in a tradition; the Romans since the time of Gaius were well used to reification of legal concepts, of incorporeities, of mental objects.[4] But the analytical line between persons proper and the things external to the person, tangible and intangible, which could be owned, was, for Jim, essential to clear thinking about the nature of both property and justice in property institutions.

I would like to harness some doctrines of the criminal law to approach this central plank of Jim's property theory from a new, slightly tangential angle. We can possibly see the rootedness of the distinction between persons and property by measuring the permissible levels of reaction to violent attacks on persons and property. The particular doctrine I want to discuss—the right to use force, even deadly force, to repel those who attack one's property, in particular the invader of one's home—has now become a matter of public and party-political controversy. I hope that the distractions of today's politics will not blunt the readers' appreciation of the serious jurisprudential issues regarding property and persons lying within this pocket of law. It is the initial hypothesis of this Chapter that the legal permission of violence in defence of property does derive from the analytical and normative relationships between property and personhood in ostensibly liberal societies. The argument moves in two steps. The law licenses self-help to repress all forms of crime, with forceful defence of property or of persons being just two (partially entwined) categories of a larger class. But at steeper levels of violent self-help, defence of the person is the key justifying factor, and the pursuit of other goals—such as defence of property or resistance to generic criminal acts—will destroy the legal validity of the self-help.

In *Property and Justice* Jim Harris postulated 'imaginary' or ideal-typical societies in order to illustrate different property regimes, giving us Forest Land, Status Land, Red Land, Contract Land, Wood Land, and Pink Land.[5] We might conceivably borrow his expository technique in order to help us frame our inquiry and suggest what is at stake where persons use violence to defend their property. One can see the evolution of a natural property and crime regime in simplest form by observing children at play. So, let us pay a visit to a (not so) imaginary place that we shall call Toy Land. On occasion, children in this innocent land will argue

[3] Harris, *Property and Justice*, n. 1 above, 8–13, 42–7.

[4] P Birks, 'The Roman Law Concept of Dominium and the Idea of Absolute Ownership' (1986) *Acta Juridica* 1; G Diosdi, *Ownership in Ancient and Preclassical Roman Law* (Akadémiai Kiadó, 1970), 121–36; J Getzler, 'Roman Ideas of Landownership', in S Bright and J Dewar (eds.), *Land Law: Themes and Perspectives* (OUP, 1998), 81. Modern German legal science complicated the matter with the doctrine that the subjective right to property or *Eigentum* had to comprise a tangible thing or part of the material world and could not comprise immaterial obligations: see W Mincke, 'Property: Assets or Power? Objects or Relations as Substrata of Property Rights', in JW Harris (ed.), *Property Problems. From Genes to Pension Funds* (Kluwer Law International, 1998), 78.

[5] Harris, *Property and Justice*, n. 1 above, ch. 2, 15–22.

over who has the better right to possession of a toy, interrupting the happy flow of play. If one child asserts exclusive possession by snatching, the other may use force against the rival to attempt recovery, and the upset caused by the ensuing cycle of violent reprisals against persons will soon dwarf the disruption caused by the original property offence. To escape from this unhappy state of nature, parents in Toy Land try to teach children that any form of self-help and, in particular, personal violence, as a means to sanction and reverse recent dispossession of a doll or a ball, is not allowed, but rather that return of the valued object must be sought through the agency of a neutral third-party judicial authority, namely a parent or other responsible adult. However, the instinct to forceful self-help is difficult to eradicate; moreover parental coercion may only add to the violence by teaching that superior force prevails; children will constantly ask for parental force to be applied in their favour. Toy Land, like all societies, is not so easily pacified, for the participants can barely distinguish between self-help, assault, and punishment.

(i) The Problem of Excessive Defence of Property

If one ends up in court over such quarrels, the question is juridified and narrowed: can one lawfully use force to protect one's property, and if so how much? The common sense answer would be yes, to a reasonable degree, and the legal answer is similar. I can thrust away a purse-snatcher, I can shove a door shut in the face of a house-breaker, I can forcefully restrain a vandal from damaging my goods, and surely, in these cases, the police will not arrest me and the prosecutor will not arraign me for assault? I need not fling up my hands and submit to the criminal, and then go home to brief policeman and lawyers to find me redress.

It is a long-held common-law policy that anyone may lawfully use force to repel or arrest a criminal threatening property; *a fortiori* force may be used to defend one's own property. But there are limits to these powers. If I loose off a shotgun against a night-time burglar and kill him in the absence of a belief in personal danger, I may find myself guilty of murder or, at least, a lesser offence of culpable homicide. In cases where some amount of violence is justified but excessive force is used, some common law jurisdictions will deny any defence to murder. The killing through excessive force is neither justified nor excused. Other jurisdictions will allow a partial defence, excusing from the fullest penalty and reducing the offence to manslaughter or unlawful homicide, on the basis that the actor should be punished for a grievous miscalculation. But this divergence, important as it is, does not directly impact upon our primary question, which is: how does the law justify and calibrate the use of private force to defend one's property?

The common law, like the civilian systems, has fumbled for answers in defining excessive force in defence of property. Typically, it takes refuge in the unstructured fact discretion of the jury.[6] This may suggest that the doctrinal issue of excessive property defence contains within it contested ethical considerations that cannot be juridified. Perhaps three general ideas may be isolated from the legal sources. First, property cannot easily be conceived as a value worth protecting by force where there is no accompanying threat to the person. Secondly, the law may nonetheless see a presumptive identity between an owner's person and his property that is external to his person, so that violent defence of property becomes justified, even where there is no threat to bodily or personal safety. Finally, intentionality and purpose, i.e. *mens rea*, plays an important role in attributing legal blame for excessive force in protecting property; the test of allowable quantum of force is not objective. Lying beneath these relatively simple rules, however, we find many difficulties.

(ii) State and Non-state Coercion

Weber defined the state as an authority with the monopoly of legitimate violence.[7] As a pungent example of Weberian ideal typing this definition has been extraordinarily influential in modern social thought; yet it has only ever partially been true. James Whitman has argued that it is not the case that the modern state rises to replace more primitive self-help or vengeance with orderly, legalized, punishments and compensations. It is easier to say that both forms of social discipline have always coincided and cross-bred, with public agencies sometimes helping or encouraging individuals pursue their vengeance. Thus, in ancient societies mutilations inflicted by individuals upon each other in retaliation, or compositions in lieu, were tolerated or permitted as useful signals issued by individuals to the rest of society, signals that promoted deterrence and affirmed shared values, often of a ritual or religious quality. The state thus did not supersede self-help, but coincided with it and buttressed it.[8]

In the blood feud societies of the early to high middle ages, there was no omnicompetent state but, rather, interlocking jurisdictions generating fierce loyalties and rivalries; organized private violence was the norm with the state only slowly emerging to dominance.[9] The omnicompetent state which many assumed to be the endpoint of political modernization in the twentieth century has itself turned

[6] The policies of the common law in using jury discretion are examined in J Getzler, 'The Fate of the Civil Jury in Late Victorian England', in JW Cairns and G McLeod (eds.), *'The Dearest Birth Right of the People of England': The Jury in the History of the Common Law* (Hart Publishing, 2002), 217.

[7] Max Weber's famous definition is from *Politics as a Vocation* (Berlin, 1919), in HH Gerth and C Wright Mills (trans. and eds.), *From Max Weber: Essays in Sociology* (OUP, 1948, repr. Routledge, 1991), 77, 78: '[A] state is a human community ['authority association', *Herrschaftsverband*] that (successfully) claims the *monopoly of the legitimate use of physical force* within a given territory... the right to use physical force is ascribed to other institutions or to individuals only to the extent to which the state permits it. The state is considered the sole source of the "right" to use violence.'

[8] JQ Whitman, 'At the Origins of Law and the State: Supervision of Violence, Mutilation of Bodies, or Setting of Prices?' (1995) 71 *Chicago-Kent LR* 41; JQ Whitman, 'Between Self-Defense and Vengeance/Between Social Contract and Monopoly of Violence' (2004) 39 *Tulsa LR* 901.

[9] WI Miller's work on medieval Iceland, *Bloodtaking and Peacemaking: Feud, Law, and Society in Saga Iceland* (University of Chicago Press, 1990), and PR Hyams' monograph on blood feud in

out to have been only a temporary stage. Contemporary societies in the capitalist Western states are increasingly delegating or franchising coercive, as well as economic, powers to non-state actors. Examples are corporate providers of security services in America and Europe who substitute for national police, or even for military forces overseas.[10] Indeed, private security providers now exceed police in number many times over in Western countries.[11] An alternative model found in less-well-developed capitalist or transitional regimes involves the state tolerating the informal wielding of coercive powers, not just to repress extraordinary assaults but for the regular maintenance of contract rights and property claims. Modern Russia is a notable case in point; at a further extreme there are weakened or collapsed states where there is *only* private enforcement without state oversight or restraint. For one example, the skyrocketing crime rates in South Africa have led to a large amount of violent self-defence, and this has become a matter of sharp controversy, especially where whites readily kill violent blacks—or mistakenly kill their own family in response to a perceived attack.[12] Is a mistaken killing more easily excused in a social context where defensive violence is widely perceived as justified? Or is this a recipe for the warfare of every man against every man? Since Hobbes, theorists have acknowledged that even in the *Rechtsstaat* or legally-ordered society, persons retain a natural power of self-defence; and Hobbes himself struggled to explain why this natural right did not call into question the authority of the state to claim total allegiance and surrender of force.[13]

Examples of troubled, violent, splintering societies and weakened states in today's 'global' world could be multiplied. They present a spectrum extending from state-of-nature anarchy at one extreme through to more organized private enforcement regimes—mafia capitalism or armed crony capitalism—and on to regularized state-controlled and rule-bound coercion at the other end, with many cross-bred examples of regulated and corporatist security along the way.[14] The spectrum drawn here proceeds along a conventional private-public dimension,

Angevin times, *Rancor and Reconciliation in Medieval England* (Cornell University Press, 2003), are here highly suggestive.

[10] Non-state security agents have outnumbered state police in Great Britain since 1961: see T Jones and T Newburn, 'The Transformation of Policing? Understanding Current Trends in Policing Systems' (2002) 42 *Br J of Criminol* 129, and *Private Security and Public Policing* (Clarendon Press, 1998). The Iraq crisis and the deaths of civilian security contractors in Fallujah have highlighted this trend affecting military personnel. See the letter from 13 liberal Democrat senators to Secretary Rumsfeld of 8 Apr. 2004, protesting at the use of private security forces in Iraq outside military control: http://reed.senate.gov/iraq.htm. The world press is full of stories of the numbers (over 15,000 and growing), the dangers, the high pay, and the control problems surrounding the private security forces in Iraq; see e.g. 'Private contractors in Iraq', *The Economist*, 7 Apr. 2004.

[11] L Zedner, 'Too Much Security?' (2003) 31 *Int'l J Soc'y of L* 155.

[12] See R Carroll, 'Self-defence killings divide S Africa', *The Guardian*, 7 Jan. 2003, 'Former Springbok kills daughter in mistake for thief', *The Guardian*, 25 May 2004.

[13] See T Hobbes, *Leviathan* (ed. C B Macpherson, Penguin, 1968, 1981), 189 ff, 268 ff, on the residual natural right of violence within a state-governed society.

[14] F Varese, *The Russian Mafia: Private Protection in a New Market Economy* (OUP, 2001; Meulenhoff, 2004); F Varese, 'Mafia Transplantation', in J Kornai, B Rothstein, and

but we have noted how the structure of ancient and feudal societies challenges any axiomatic split between public and private coercion. We might approach the same problem abstracting from history and instead finding tools in political and social theory. To take a Marxisante view, if interests or hegemonic groups govern state power, then legal protection of property through legalistic coercion is really organized class violence. The legalism by which such power is mediated and governed may be significant, but no sharp line can be drawn between the powers wielded by state agents and the legal or extra-legal powers accorded by the state to certain privileged individuals.[15] From yet another vantage, thinkers of a more individualistic strain, from Thomas Hobbes and John Locke through to Albert Venn Dicey and Friedrich von Hayek, might characterize state law and coercion as merely the delegated power of sovereign individuals; the private defence of rights is not analytically separate from the police action of the state. All that a police force offers is a professionalized wielding of private policing powers, and conversely police officers or any public functionary ought not to be regarded as enjoying any special state privileges or immunities. Both state and non-state security forces work within the same framework, wielding the normal or inherent policing powers of the citizen, but with a professionalism and regularity that enhances security to the consumer of such services and that maximizes deterrence against delinquents. On this view, state officials just belong to a larger protection firm.

There is of course a median position. Public and private powers and rights may blur into each other in practice, but this does not mean that they cannot be conceived as distinct, if mutually supporting spheres. The postulates of an independent private sphere, albeit one supported and protected by communal action, and of a public sphere rising above private interests and passions, are touchstones of modern liberalism.[16] In particular, there are good reasons why, in a liberal society, we should want to reserve powers of punishment, coercion, and indeed policing to the authority and machinery of the state, such as preserving impartiality in the distribution of security and risk, and preventing abuse of state power by private and corporate persons seeking a noxious advantage or domination over others.[17]

S Rose-Ackerman (eds.), *Creating Social Trust: Problems of Post-Socialist Transition* (Palgrave Macmillan, 2004); D Gambetta, *The Sicilian Mafia: The Business of Private Protection* (Harvard University Press, 1993); B Dupont, P Grabosky, and C Shearing, 'The Governance of Security in Weak and Failing States' (2003) 3 *Criminal Justice* 331.

[15] Two key texts are D Hay *et al.* (eds.), *Albion's Fatal Tree: Crime and Society in Eighteenth-Century England* (Allen Lane, 1975) and EP Thompson, *Whigs and Hunters: The Origin of the Black Act* (Allen Lane, 1975). Thompson, in the famous epilogue to *Whigs and Hunters*, ibid., 258–69, made the claim that the cross-class protections afforded by the rule of law can transcend class hegemonic interests and become a universal benefit. Some say he ceased to be a Marxist at that point: see DH Cole, ' "An Unqualified Human Good": E.P. Thompson and the Rule of Law' (1 June 1999), http://ssrn.com/abstract=169264.

[16] The stream of social democratic or 'new' liberalism stretches back at least over the past century: to pluck out two texts from a rich tradition: see LT Hobhouse, *Liberalism* (OUP, 1911) and J Habermas, *The Structural Transformation of the Public Sphere* (Polity, 1989).

[17] Cf. N Lacey, *State Punishment: Political Principles and Community Values* (Routledge, 1994); I Loader and N Walker, 'Policing as a Public Good' (2001) 5 *Theoretical Criminology* 9.

If we accept the assumptions of state impartiality and competence, some licensing and resort to self-help may yet be an efficient way of setting incentives for good behaviour. If persons are expected to take some care for themselves, their dependants, and their possessions, as governments increasingly assert, and afforded limited coercive powers to do so, then arguably foreknowledge of these decentralized coercive powers might help potential criminals decide not to commit crimes. The revised assumptions are that state agencies and the law can be a blunt and inefficient instrument for maintaining order, and private ordering can usefully supplement state action. Other strategies for protecting persons' interests without hands-on state control include insurance pools and self-policing community institutions enforcing social norms. Such extra-legal devices can be praised as outgrowths of a rich civil society impregnated with co-operative norms and profuse market and social capital—and simultaneously criticized as inegalitarian, alienating, and demoralizing forms of power and governance.[18]

We will return to the question of the political justification for policing powers in a later section. Our next concern is to determine whether in legalistic countries, in particular the common law countries, individuals can be said to wield a right or privilege to use violence in defence of their property, either as a facet of self-defence of the person, or as a stand-alone right to police one's possessions outside state protections.

(iii) Tony Martin

At common law there are three main forms of attack on property which warrant forceful defence: theft, criminal damage, and criminal trespass such as burglary or housebreaking. I will concentrate on the latter and will have little to say about theft and criminal damage, which raise similar issues, but to a lesser degree.[19] One recent case dominates attention and, indeed, has become one of the most notorious criminal cases in England in the past decade, namely *Martin v R*.[19A] Tony Martin, a solitary Norfolk farmer, shot dead a burglar and was then prosecuted for murder. He was convicted and given the mandatory life sentence. Martin had suffered numerous burglaries at his secluded farm and believed that the police had decided not to make such break-ins a high priority either for prevention or investigation, since more serious crime demanded their attention. He argued that, in his unprotected circumstances, it was reasonable to use deadly force in self defence against

[18] Compare RC Ellickson, *Order Without Law: How Neighbors Settle Disputes* (Harvard University Press, 1991) with D Garland, *The Culture of Control: Crime and Social Order in Contemporary Society* (OUP, 2001), and RV Ericson, A Doyle, and D Barry, *Insurance as Governance* (University of Toronto Press, 2003).

[19] For general treatments see AP Simester and GR Sullivan, *Criminal Law: Theory and Doctrine* (2nd edn., Hart Publishing, 2003), 622–31; JC Smith, *Justification and Excuse in the Criminal Law* (Hamlyn Lectures, Stevens, 1989), ch. 4. As will be seen, the pure common law position is now overlaid by statute.

[19A] The trial was held on 19 April 2000 in the Crown Court at Norwich before Owen J; the 2001 appeal is reported at [2003] QB1 (CCA).

home-invaders. When Martin suffered yet another burglary, he claimed that he had acted in fear of three burglars who might have attacked him, and had therefore fired at two of the intruders from the top of his stairs. However, the prosecution argued that he had lain in wait at the ground floor and shot the burglars from behind as they exited the premises. One of the two, a 16-year-old traveller, bled to death; another was injured in the legs but escaped. The exact story was important because if Martin had shot egressing burglars then he could not have been acting in fear of his personal safety at that very moment and he could not have held any belief that he was acting in defence of his person, even an unreasonable belief. He would, rather, have been acting and, indeed, purposing to act as judge and executioner, levying a harsh personal punishment or revenge; or else trying to arrest burglars with unreasonable deadly force. Martin's story was disbelieved at trial; though on appeal further 'expert' evidence was readily admitted of his paranoid mental state, allowing the court to bring in a conviction of manslaughter on the grounds of diminished responsibility. Significantly, the appeal court agreed that an unreasonable but honest belief as to the facts of a dangerous situation could give rise to a claim of self-defence, but seemed to require an 'objective' assessment of the danger posed by such unreasonably believed facts. This contorted doctrine therefore put self-defence out of Martin's reach;[20] hence the turn to diminished responsibility. Martin was set free after serving the full five-year sentence for the unlawful killing; early release on parole was unavailable because he staunchly refused to concede that he had done anything wrong.

Martin v R. provoked a storm of debate with a wave of public sympathy going to the defendant. Martin's cause was taken up by conservative newspapers, Tory politicians, and the rural community who thought that justice had gone awry; the *Sun* newspaper polled one quarter of a million people and only 4 per cent agreed with Martin's conviction. It may be that the turn to repressive crime policies by the New Labour government can be pinned to the government's sensitivity to the depth of popular outrage caused by Martin's conviction for shooting a burglar.[21] The Tories raised home invasion as an electioneering banner in 2004–5, campaigning against the 'chaos and confusion' of the existing law permitting an unspecified 'reasonable force' and no more; instead the Criminal Law (Householder Protection) Bill, proposed in the form of a private Member's bill with massive support from the Tory benches, stipulated that the law should ensure that householders need not fear prosecution, let alone conviction, unless they used 'grossly disproportionate force' against burglars.[22] By the 2005 general election the Tory campaign to license householder use of disproportionate force with legal

[20] Simester and Sullivan, n. 19 above, 552 and update on *Self-defence, other defences, and subjectivity* at: http://www.hartpub.co.uk/Updates/upcrimlaw_selfdefence.htm, pointing out that the approach of the Court of Criminal Appeal is at odds with *Shaw v R.* [2001] 1 WLR 1519; [2002] 1 CAR 10; [2002] 1 CAR 77; [2002] Crim LR 140 (PC) and with *Beckford v R.* [1988] AC 130.

[21] Cautious use may be made of Tony Martin's own account recently ghosted by journalists: J McVicar and D Wallace (eds.), *Tony Martin, A Right to Kill?* (Elmstock, 2004).

[22] BBC News, 4 Feb. 2005.

immunity seemed to have stalled. Opposition forces, especially rural interests, by now were more exercised by the expressive right to use lethal violence against foxes.[23] The Crown Prosecution Service and the Association of Chief Police Officers have somewhat cooled the debate by issuing guidelines showing how householders can use extensive force against intruders within the bounds of a reasonableness standard.[24]

(iv) Housebreaking as Threat to Persons and Threat to Peace: Old and New Historical Perspectives

The Tony Martin case that kicked off this debate seemed to turn on whether an attack on a particular type of property—the dwelling or home—could reasonably be interpreted as a presumptive threat to personal safety. The perception of threat might be actuarial or predictive. A regular proportion of housebreaking and burglary in Britain is committed by non-professional criminals, often juvenile drug-addicts of small self-control, so fears for safety at their hands might contain a grain of good sense; normal levels of risk aversion might induce a victim of housebreaking to shoot and then ask questions.[25] We can see long historical antecedents to this surmise. Roman law allowed the slaying of a thief at night but not one by day,[26] and Jewish law took a

[23] The nature of hunting in English law and society is considered in J Getzler, 'Judges and Hunters: Law and Economic Conflict in the English Countryside, 1800–1860', in C Brooks and M Lobban (eds.), *Communities and Courts in Britain 1150–1900* (Hambledon Press, 1997), 199.

[24] See Crown Prosecution Service website, 1 Feb. 2005: http://www.cps.gov.uk/publications/prosecution/householders.html

[25] Home Office statistics suggest that England and Wales have one of the highest burglary rates in the world, hitting some 3.5 per cent of homes per year; and both fear of burglary and harm suffered from this crime are commonly reported in crime surveys: see J Herring, *Criminal Law: Text, Cases and Materials* (OUP, 2004), 579–81; N Lacey, C Wells, and O Quick, *Reconstructing Criminal Law: Text and Materials* (3rd edn., LexisNexis UK, 2003), 345–50. Interestingly the crime of burglary has fallen every year over the past decade and is continuing to drop, perhaps a reflection of full employment. UK figures provided by the Home Office record some 5.2 million offences in 2000–1, of which 82 per cent were property offences, with 16 per cent of all crime being burglaries (836,000), and 14 per cent violent crime (601,000). Only 12 per cent of burglaries were detected. In 1990 there were 250,000 violent offences, 1 million reported burglaries, 3.3 million other property offences, and 4.54 million offences overall. The classifications are of course contentious and the real crime rates may be very much larger. See http://www.archive.official-documents.co.uk/document/cm53/5312/crimestats.pdf for 2000–1; and http://www.homeoffice.gov.uk/rds/patterns1.html for historical trends. United States statistics tell a rather different story: in 2001 burglary amounted to 2.11 million incidents out of a total of property crimes of 10.41 million, down from 3.07 million and 12.65 million respectively in 1990; these figures are overshadowed by some 11.85 million violent crimes in 2001, down from 14.48 million in 1990. See Bureau of the Census, US Dept. of Commerce, *Statistical Abstract of the United States*, http://www.census.gov/prod/2004pubs/03statab/law.pdf.

[26] Starting with the Twelve Tables, VIII.3: 'If one is slain while committing theft by night, he is rightly slain'. Justinian's *Digest*, n. 2 above, D.9.2.4.1. (Gaius) gives the rule as follows: 'The law of the *Twelve Tables* permits one to kill a thief caught in the night, provided one gives evidence of the fact by shouting aloud, but someone may only kill a person caught in such circumstances at any other time if he defends himself with a weapon, though only if he provides evidence by shouting'. This ancient rule

similar position.[27] How can we account for this rule? On one view, it may be because detection and apprehension are more difficult at night; hence the power of forceful self-help against the night-time miscreant is ratcheted up to level the playing field.[28] But another interpretation, favoured in ancient legal sources, holds that the night-time intruder creates a higher risk to personal safety for members of the household, making robust or even lethal force reasonable. Daytime intruders usually calculate to break in when no-one is home. Night-time intruders can more likely expect to confront the inhabitants, and a prepared and watchful intruder might easily prevail against sleepy and surprised dwellers. Again, licensing high levels of defensive violence serves as deterrent and remedy.

English law has long taken a special concern with theft or other felony allied to trespass and housebreaking, especially housebreaking at night. In the old Anglo-Saxon law housebreaking was a well-established category of disturbance. Maitland suggests that any thief might be killed to prevent escape, whether or not the house was broken into, but that housebreaking made the crime more atrocious. In this context:

> An outlaw might . . . be slain with impunity; and it was not only lawful but meritorious to kill a thief flying from justice. A man who slew a thief . . . was expected to declare the fact without delay, otherwise the dead man's kindred might clear his fame by their oath and require the slayer to pay wergild as for a true man.[29]

Hyams has recently shown how in the vendetta culture that continued after the Conquest into Angevin England, attacks on the household were a particularly common form of feuding behaviour; to assault or kill a man in his house or *domus*

was mitigated in later law but left its traces: see further Gaius, *Institutes*, III.184–185, 189–190 (ed. F de Zulueta, Clarendon Press, 1946); Justinian, *Institutes*, 4.1.3, 4.1.5. (ed. P Birks and G McLeod, Duckworth, 1987); Justinian's *Digest* at D.3.2.13.7, 47.2.1.-3., 47.18.2, n. 2 above. Compare *Digest*, 9.2.5.pr (Ulpian): 'if for fear of death someone kill a thief, there is no doubt that he will not be liable under the *lex Aquilia*. But if, although he could have arrested him, he preferred to kill him, the better opinion is that he should be deemed to have acted unlawfully (*injuria*)'.

27 *Exodus* 22:1–2: 'If the thief is seized while tunnelling [i.e. housebreaking] and he is beaten to death, there is no blood guilt in his case. If the sun has risen on him, there is bloodguilt in that case'. One explanation for the rule is that the thief would be more ready to kill at night when unobserved by witnesses: see *Mishnah*, Sanhedrin, 8:6 (ed. H Danby, Clarendon Press, 1933), 395; *The Jewish Study Bible* (ed. A Berlin, MZ Brettler, and M Fishbane, Jewish Publication Society and OUP, 2004), 155. Another explanation, found in Rashi's *Commentary on the Chumash, Shemoth* (trans. AM Silbermann, Silbermann and Feldheim, 1934), 116–17, and the Talmud Bavli, *Sanhedrin*, 72a, b at xix (trans. and ed. A Steinsaltz, Random House, 1999), 47–57 is that people carefully guard their possessions in the security of the home and an intruder knowing this is likely to kill to steal them, if not on this occasion then maybe on another. Both explanations justify the rule for deadly force as preemptive and presumptive self-defence. See further JD Jacobs, 'Privileges for the Use of Deadly Force Against a Residence-Intruder: A Comparison of the Jewish Law and the United States Common Law' (1990) 63 *Temple LR* 31.

28 Cf. RA Posner, *Economic Analysis of Law* (6th edn., Aspen Publishers, 2003), 219–27, 234–5.

29 F Pollock and FW Maitland, *The History of English Law Before the Time of Edward I* (2nd edn., CUP, 1898, repr. 1968), i, 53.

and humiliate his household was the ultimate form of public retribution, of destruction of *dominium*. This power-mongering was the obverse of the familiar claim of Sir Edward Coke that 'a man's house is his castle, *et domus sua cuique est tutissimum refugium* [and each man's home his safest refuge]'.[30]

In an ambitious new work of historical political science, Markus Dubber argues that it is not the case that the state or Crown simply licensed violence by the householder in defence of his home. He suggests that private coercive power of the householder in Western law rather provided the urtext of state power, and that this form of power is inherently vague and limitless.[31] Dubber suggests that the state can be seen as wielding two ideal types of coercion: a defined power of law, which provides rules for autonomous individuals to coexist harmoniously; and a discretionary power of police, which derives from the functions of the patriarch in defending his family and advancing its sectional interests. Dubber cites the *patria potestas* of the classical world, which gave unconstrained powers of coercion of male heads of houses over women, children, and slaves, and he locates a like coercive power in the head of the medieval household, dwelling on the stringencies of petty treason. The law of petty treason in medieval England exacerbated the punishment where a servant killed a master, or a wife a husband, or a child a parent, on the basis that the insubordination rendered the homicide particularly atrocious and destabilizing to the natural order of the realm.[32] Church, Crown, and lords wielded

[30] Sir Edward Coke, *The Third Part of the Institutes of the Laws of England: concerning high treason, and other pleas of the crown, and criminall causes* (M Flesher, for W Lee, and D Pakeman, 1644; 4th edn., E and R Brooke, 1797, reprinted W Clarke and Sons, 1817), 162. The famous Cokean slogan is expanded in an important passage in *Semayne's Case* (1603) 5 Co Rep 91a; 77 ER 194 (KB):

> [T]he house of every one is to him as his castle and fortress, as well for his defence against injury and violence, as for his repose; and although the life of man is a thing precious and favoured in law; so that although a man kills another in his defence, or kills one *per infortuna*, without any intent, yet it is felony, and in such case he shall forfeit his goods and chattels, for the great regard which the law has to a man's life; but if thieves come to a man's house to rob him, or murder, and the owner of his servants kill any of the thieves in defence of himself and his house, it is not felony, and he shall lose nothing . . . [a]nd the reason of all this is, because *domus sua cuique est tutissimum refugium*.

We find modern echoes and inversions of the medieval sense of the house-as-castle in the perverse behaviour of some burglars who seem to delight in trashing homes and intruding into personal spaces—one burglar who came to visit on Christmas Eve is reported to have opened all the family's presents (but stole none): see D Aaronovitch, 'The Tony Martin in all of us', *The Guardian*, 29 July 2003. Wilful destruction by intruders is, however, quite rare: see M Maguire and T Bennett, *Burglary in a Dwelling: The Offence, the Offender, and the Victim* (Heinemann, 1982).

[31] MD Dubber, *The Police Power: Patriarchy and the Foundations of American Government* (Columbia University Press, 2005).

[32] Ibid., pp. xi–xvi, 3–62. It is tolerably clear that the common law quickly regulated and reduced the incidence of petty treason, mildly undermining one of the planks of Dubber's argument. Petty treason was certainly taken seriously, being the first offence to be excluded from benefit of clergy by declaration of Parliament in 1496; but by 1551 Robert Brooke had demonstrated that the distinction between murder and petty treason had shrunk in significance and turned on technicalities of marriage law. In 1554, a case decided that a parricide who did not earn his board in the household through service to his slain parent was not within the scope of petty treason, and by such devices the ambit of the crime was steadily narrowed. See JH Baker, *The Oxford History of The Laws of England, Vol. VI, 1483–1558* (OUP, 2003), 520–1, 556–8.

such punishments on a grander scale as 'macro-households', or heads of families writ large. Early modern political theorists emphasized the non-contractual, centralizing powers of the patriarchal sovereign, such as Jean Bodin and Robert Filmer, with Filmer in particular claiming biblical authority for his positions. John Locke in his two *Treatises of Government* attacked the illiberalism of the patriarchal theorists and argued for a bounded legislator governing by consent, but even he accepted the unlimited executive police power of the state in repressing disorder.[33] William Blackstone and Adam Smith also emphasized the police power, and they in turn had a powerful influence in colonial and revolutionary America.[34] The licence to use violence against burglars in Dubber's view traces its lineage to the very same conception of an intrinsic householder police power to defend the family interest, however that family is defined. Dubber's 'householder' theory of policing and the state is highly suggestive and is raising interest amongst theorists of crime and policing in Britain.[35]

James Whitman has argued in another major new historical study that the foundations of common law punitive attitudes to criminals, which include the licensing of personal violence against intruders, lie in an egalitarian and libertarian cultural legacy that values negative freedom as a sphere of sovereignty excluding state power. English, and especially American, law sees the integrity of the home, and the right to defend it, as a hallmark of individual freedom and independence. Whitman contrasts this libertarian independence with continental European (i.e. French and German) notions of individual dignity and autonomy, and the concomitant immunity of the human personality from degradation. He argues that the dignitary concept of individuality makes for a milder approach to punishment, as miscreants who trench on the freedoms of the community yet retain personal rights. These notions he links to an 'aristocratic' honour-based cultural praxis, which leads modern European social democracies to raise up the malfunctioning bottom end of society rather than simply repress it as a threat to the majority.[36] We shall see that European law has in fact tilted at times towards allowing disproportionate force against criminals, such as home intruders, who threaten their victims' autonomy and personality; but this may be an exception probing Whitman's overall thesis, rather than overthrowing it.

[33] See J Locke, *Two Treatises of Government* (ed. P Laslett, CUP, 1960); J Waldron, *God, Locke, and Equality: Christian Foundations of John Locke's Political Thought* (CUP, 2002); D Engster, 'Jean Bodin, Scepticism and Absolute Sovereignty' (1996) 17 *History of Political Thought* 469 and *Divine Sovereignty: The Origins of Modern State Power* (Northern Illinois University Press, 2001).

[34] Dubber, n. 31 above, 47–77.

[35] See, e.g., L Farmer, 'Tony Martin and the Nightbreakers: Criminal Law, Victims and the Power to Punish', in S Armstrong and L McAra (eds.), *Perspectives on Punishment: The Contours of Control* (forthcoming, OUP, 2005).

[36] JQ Whitman, *Harsh Justice: Criminal Punishment and the Widening Divide between America and Europe* (OUP, 2003); JQ Whitman, 'The Two Western Cultures of Privacy: Dignity Versus Liberty' (2004) 113 *Yale LJ* 1151.

(v) The Old Common Law Definition of Burglary and Blackstone's Restatement

Let us now return to the positive law. Burglary was defined by ancient common law and by statute as a felonious housebreaking in time of peace. It came to include intruding into a house without force but with intent to commit another different felony. Felonious intent as an element of the offence took time to crystallize; Mountford in 1527 tended to define the mental element negatively by listing the instances of housebreaking that were not felonious (putting out fires, legally taking one's own goods, arresting other felons, or separating fighters). Earlier cases seemed to require either intent to murder or a completed lesser felony as required in order to convert non-felonious housebreaking into the greater offence of burglary. Fitzherbert writing in 1538 held that burglarious intent had broadened to encompass other intended felonies such as rape and theft. Non-felonious but wrongful intentions were insufficient—a mere intentional trespasser or even one who intruded intending to harass or beat another did not necessarily become a burglar. Where the felony was incomplete, but intention proved, the *mens rea* could be added to the act of unlawful entry or invasion in order to construct the separate felony of burglary, and so was a useful surrogate for a law of attempts. Many sixteenth-century writers argued that the *actus reus* of burglary involved breaking into a dwelling or church (but not an ale house or inn) by night, the nocturnal requirement possibly being an echo of Roman doctrine. A 1503 writer states categorically that housebreaking by day was not a felony. But leading writers such as Fitzherbert and Mountford omitted the nocturnal requirement. The situation was further confused by a 1547 statute that removed benefit of clergy from housebreaking by day or night; a reform that tilted housebreaking towards becoming a twenty-four-hour offence of serious gravity, but still not necessarily a felony if committed by day.[37]

Sir William Blackstone's extensive reflections on burglary summarize much of the earlier legal history from the medievals to Coke, and further suggests a philosophy determining how much force could be used in defence of property:[38]

BURGLARY, or nocturnal housebreaking, burgi latrocinium, which by our antient law was called hamesecken, as it is in Scotland to this day, has always been looked upon as a very heinous offence: not only because of the abundant terror that it naturally carries with it, but also as it is a forcible invasion and disturbance of that right of habitation, which every individual might acquire even in a state of nature; an invasion, which in such a state,

[37] The above paragraph is derived from Baker, n. 32 above, 572–3.

[38] W Blackstone, *Commentaries on the Laws of England* (Clarendon Press, 1765–9), iv, ch. 16, 223–8. Important earlier treatments include Coke, n. 30 above, ch. 14, 63–5, and W Hawkins, *A Treatise of the Pleas of the Crown* (1st edn., J Walthoe, 1716–21; 8th edn., ed. J Curwood, S Sweet, 1824), i, ch. 17, 129–37. An especially detailed treatment of the historical law is given in E Hyde East, *Pleas of the Crown* (A Strahan and J Butterworth, 1803, Professional Books, 1972), ii, ch. 15, 481–523.

would be sure to be punished with death, unless the assailant were the stronger. But in civil society, the laws also come in to the assistance of the weaker party: and, besides that they leave him this natural right of killing the aggressor, if he can, . . . they also protect and avenge him, in case the might of the assailant is too powerful. And the law of England has so particular and tender a regard to the immunity of a man's house, that it stiles it his castle, and will never suffer it to be violated with impunity: agreeing herein with the sentiments of antient Rome. . . . For this reason no doors can in general be broken open to execute any civil process; though, in criminal causes, the public safety supersedes the private. Hence also in part arises the animadversion of the law upon eaves-droppers, nusancers, and incendiaries: and to this principle it must be assigned, that a man may assemble people together lawfully (at least if they do not exceed eleven) without danger of raising a riot, rout, or unlawful assembly, in order to protect and defend his house; which he is not permitted to do in any other case.

Blackstone repeated Coke's definition of a burglar as 'he that by night breaketh and entreth into a mansionhouse, with intent to commit a felony'. The legal definition broke into four components: time, place, manner, and intent. First, a burglary had to be nocturnal; this tracked the policy that saw any night-time attack as particularly atrocious, making homicide in self-defence more justifiable. The test was not whether there was any light to see the assailant, for:

then many midnight burglaries [by moonlight] would go unpunished: and besides, the malignity of the offence does not so properly arise from it's being done in the dark, as at the dead of night; when all the creation, except beasts of prey, are at rest; when sleep has disarmed the owner, and rendered his castle defenceless.

Secondly, the place had to be a 'mansion house', which could include a church being '*domus mansionalis Dei* . . . it may also be committed by breaking the gates or walls of a town in the night; though that perhaps Sir Edward Coke would have called the mansion-house of the garrison or corporation'. A deserted house or uninhabited structure such as a barn could not be burgled as no-one dwelt, or more particularly slept, there and there were not 'the same circumstances of midnight terror'. There was a complex body of law dealing with how permanent a structure a dwelling had to be to attract the law's protection from burglary, and also whether subdivided rooms, gardens, barns, and so on fell within the rule. Blackstone then described the third element of *actus reus* as involving a breaking and an entry; merely crossing a boundary might not be enough. But knocking on a door, lifting a latch, or entering on a pretext could all amount to housebreaking. Jurists of Blackstone's time and after differed over whether a peaceable entry with felonious intent could involve an implied or fictitious breaking. 'As to the intent', concluded Blackstone:

it is clear, that such breaking and entry must be with a felonious intent, otherwise it is only a trespass. And it is the same, whether such intention be actually carried into execution, or only demonstrated by some attempt or overt act, of which the jury is to judge. And therefore such a breach and entry of a house as has been before described, by night, with intent to commit a robbery, a murder, a rape, or any other felony, is burglary; whether the thing be actually perpetrated or not. Nor does it make any difference, whether the offence were felony at common law, or only created so by statute.

Blackstone also noted how Tudor statutes had removed benefit of clergy from burglary to underline its seriousness.[39] But outside the severity of state punishment, the main importance of the definition of the offence of burglary was that it licensed the householder to kill the criminal without more. Neither theft nor malicious property damage warranted such defence. If the eighteenth-century legal system upheld a 'Bloody Code' of capital offences to protect property, it did not commonly license private actors to execute such punishments but applied them by strict legal process.[40] Burglary was the striking exception.

(vi) Modern English Law

The modern definition of burglary is now found in section 9 of the Theft Act 1968, and involves two elements, namely entry into a building by a person as a trespasser, with the added component of intending to steal, inflict grievous bodily harm, or cause unlawful property damage, whether the offender commits any of these offences or merely intends to do so. Entry as a trespasser with intent to rape was historically part of the definition but was removed in 2003.[41] The current definition also embraces a case where there is not necessarily an intention to commit a serious crime at the very time of entry, but where such a criminal attempt is made after the trespassory entry into a building. Burglary is punished more severely where the building is also a dwelling; and the definition of the offence is extended to include trespassory entry into an inhabited vehicle or vessel, even where the inhabitant is not present at the time of trespass.[42]

The gist of the offence seems to be that invasion of a person's physical space by the burglar makes for a serious crime that is separate from the ulterior crime or attempt that accompanied the trespass. To steal from or attack a person, or intentionally destroy his property, is a crime; to invade his dwelling in order to do such is a further crime that causes a distinct, superadded type of harm, an *injuria* or attack on personality, security, and dignitary interests. The extension of the crime to protect people's space in any building, including non-dwellings, such as places of business, as well as their vehicles, can be seen as a fencing device protecting the core interest of protection of home or dwelling place.[43]

[39] Blackstone, n. 38 above, iv, 228, 366–7.

[40] Thompson, n. 15 above; P King, *Crime, Justice, and Discretion in England 1740–1820* (OUP, 2000).

[41] Sexual Offences Act 2003, Sch. 7, Para 1.

[42] See Herring, n. 25 above, 566–74; ATH Smith, *Property Offences* (Sweet and Maxwell, 1994), ch. 28, 889–922; P Pace, 'Burglarious Trespass' [1985] *Crim LR* 716.

[43] Compare Theft Act 1968, s. 9(4), with other statutory codifications, such as the Western Australian Criminal Code 1913 (as amended), s. 244, which protects an occupant in peaceable possession of a dwelling or 'associated building' against 'home invasion', but does not extend like

The modern definition of the offence throws no light on what type of force may be used to repel the intrusion. Modern authorities provide that, in general, reasonable force may be used to prevent a crime, including property crime such as burglary, and it may be that more force is allowed in crime prevention generally than in self-defence.[44] There is little authoritative guidance as to the permissible quantum of force in the case law. The question is a mixed one of fact and law and is ultimately decided through the black-box discretion of the jury. Lord Hewart, in the case of *Hussey*[45] in 1924, stated that a householder could kill a trespasser who was forcibly trying to dispossess or evict him, and, importantly, that the householder had no duty to retreat as with normal self-defence. In other words, a householder could not be expected to flee his home to avoid confrontation with a burglar. Lord Hewart was purportedly following the 1922 edition of *Archbold's Criminal Pleading, Evidence and Practice* which stated that: '[i]n defence of a man's house, the owner or his family may kill a trespasser who would forcibly dispossess him of it, in the same manner as he might, by law, kill in self-defence a man who attacks him personally', but, in the *Hussey* formulation, home defence was even less restricted than personal self-defence, which was based on the necessity of using lethal force. There are other indications that, at the turn of the last century, judges acted as if a burglar or other trespasser in the home had forfeited all protection of the law.[46] But even at the time, the judgment in *Hussey* appeared as something of an archaic throwback; Hewart was a notoriously tough judge and later editions of *Archbold* did not follow his lead. A similarly harsh result was reached in a German case in 1920, where a farmer shot some thieves stealing fruit from his farm after warning them that he would do so if they tried to flee. The German Supreme Court held that the use of force in this case, whilst harsh, was not excessive, as the farmer could not be expected to weigh his own interests in protecting his property against the right of the thieves to bodily safety.[47] Neither of these pro-owner authorities would be followed today, but they were read as legitimate, if controversial, decisions in the interwar period.

If some doubt has attached to the right to kill a burglar, it was early made clear in the common law that one could not kill or harm a mere trespasser in the

protection to other forms of property. The New Zealand Crimes Act 1961, ss. 52–56 differentiates between persons in possession of moveable property or land without claim right, who may use reasonable force to repel a trespasser or defend possession, but who may not strike or inflict harm upon the body of the attacker; and a person in a dwelling house who may use reasonable force to repel a forcible entry, with no added restrictions. For the varied US position, which on a state by state count tends to be harsher to assailants and more tolerant of violent reprisal: see SP Green, 'Castles and Carjackers: Proportionality and the Use of Deadly Force in Defense of Dwellings and Vehicles' [1999] *U Illinois LR* 1. The innovative Canadian legislation is analysed below.

44 Simester and Sullivan, n. 19 above, 626–8; cf. AJ Ashworth, 'Self-Defence and the Right to Life' (1975) 34 *CLJ* 282, 290–2.

45 (1924) 18 Cr App Rep160 (CCA).

46 See Smith, n. 19 above, 109–12, for some telling examples, such as an elderly Irishman who was knighted for slaying four burglars with his carving knife in 1911.

47 (1920) 55 Reichsgericht in Strafsachen 82, cited in TM Funk, 'Justifying Justifications' (1999) 19 *OJLS* 630.

absence of personal danger. This was stated in the case of *Scully* by Garrow B as early as 1824, holding that it was not justified to shoot an intruder merely to apprehend him. In the case before the court 'the life of the prisoner was threatened, and if he considered his life in actual danger, he was justified in shooting the deceased as he had done; but if, not considering his own life in danger, he rashly shot this man, who was only a trespasser, he would be guilty of manslaughter'.[48] In 1823, in *Mead and Belt*, Holroyd J instructed a jury that violence could not be used against a civil trespasser, adding: '[b]ut, the making an attack upon a dwelling, and especially at night, the law regards as equivalent to an assault on a man's person; for a man's house is his castle and therefore, in the eye of the law, it is equivalent to an assault'.[49] Later cases repeat that lethal force might not be used to arrest or apprehend a trespasser committing a felony (such as a chicken thief on a farm[50]), excepting cases of burglary where personal danger was commonly presumed.[51] The saga of spring guns and man-traps in the eighteenth and early nineteenth century is here instructive. The courts were clearly troubled by this problem. In *Ilott v Wilkes*,[52] Abbott CJ squeamishly legitimized these cruel devices in the following terms:

> We are not called upon in this case to decide the general question, whether a trespasser sustaining an injury form a latent engine of mischief, placed in a wood or in grounds where he had no reason to apprehend personal danger, may or may not maintain an action. That question has been the subject of much discussion in the Court of Common Pleas, and great difference of opinion has prevailed in the minds of the learned Judges, whose attention was there called to it. Nor are we called upon to pronounce any opinion as to the inhumanity of the practice, which in this case has been the cause of the injury sustained by the plaintiff. That practice has prevailed extensively and for a long period of time, and although undoubtedly I have formed an opinion as to its inhumanity, yet at the same time I cannot but admit that repeated and increasing acts of aggression to property may perhaps reasonably call for increased means of defence and protection. I believe that many persons who cause engines of this description to be placed in their grounds do not do so with the intention of injuring any one, but really believe that the notices they give of such engines being there will prevent any injury from occurring, and that no person who sees the notice will be weak and foolish enough to the perilous consequences likely to ensue from his trespass.

Automatic devices to shoot intruders were banned in an 1828 statute, but an exception was made, allowing lethal devices to be set to protect the dwelling against felons. In particular, devices could be placed in a house between sunset and sunrise as a protection against burglars.[53]

48 *R v Scully* (1824) 1 C and P 319; 171 ER 1213.

49 *Mead and Belt's Case* (1823) 1 Lew CC 184; 68 ER 1006.

50 *R v McKay* [1957] VLR 560, with similar facts to *Scully*.

51 *R v Price (R v Moir)* (1825) 7 C and P 179; 173 ER 78; *R v Symondson* (1896) 60 JP 645. See D Lanham, 'Defence of Property in the Criminal Law' [1966] *Crim LR* 368, 426.

52 (1820) 3 B and Ald 304, 308–9; 106 ER 674, 676 (CP).

53 Spring Guns and Man Traps Act 1828, s. 12.

Presumably, a legally set gun that shot a non-felonious entrant would bring criminal liability to the householder. Further issues of line-drawing arose from man-traps that did not threaten grievous bodily harm, and from fierce guard dogs that did. Notice of the danger set by the owner was often sufficient to dispel liability on the basis that the intruder was author of his own misfortune. In the famous case of *Bird v Holbrook* in 1828, the Court of Common Pleas led by Best CJ (who as a puisne justice had agreed with Abbott CJ's reluctant decision to allow spring guns in *Ilott v Wilkes*) held that a man who set a spring gun without notice or warning was liable for injuries caused to an under-age trespasser—even though the gun had been set at night in his dwelling, as envisaged by the 1828 statute. The plaintiff was a 19-year-old lad innocently retrieving a pea-fowl that had strayed; the defendant had put the gun in place after having suffered theft of some £20 worth of plants. Best CJ based his decision largely on the moral revulsion he felt at the practice of setting a spring gun, especially without notice:

> It has been argued that the law does not compel every line of conduct which humanity or religion may require; but there is no act which Christianity forbids, that the law will not reach: if it were otherwise, Christianity would not be, as it has always been held to be, part of the law of England. I am, therefore, clearly of opinion that he who sets spring guns, without giving notice, is guilty of an inhuman act, and that, if injurious consequences ensue, he is liable to yield redress to the sufferer. But this case stands on grounds distinct from any that have preceded it. In general, spring guns have been set for the purpose of deterring; the Defendant placed his for the express purpose of doing injury; for, when called on to give notice, he said, 'If I give notice, I shall not catch him.' He intended, therefore, that the gun should be discharged, and that the contents should be lodged in the body of his victim, for he could not be caught in any other way. On these principles the action is clearly maintainable, and particularly on the latter ground.[54]

Later cases blurred the rule that hazards could only be laid defensively with ample notice,[55] but still an important line had been drawn restricting use of violence against trespassers.

Today the matter is partially codified in England and Wales by section 3 of the Criminal Law Act 1967, which states that '[a] person may use such force as is reasonable in the circumstances in the prevention of crime' or in arresting offenders or suspects. The courts have glossed this defence as involving the objective standard of a reasonable man holding the subjective knowledge of the actual person involved, including his state of belief as to facts, even if mistaken. The jury must also take into account the fact that the person using force was likely acting in crisis and might not have had an opportunity to judge the level of force to a nicety. Even allowing for mistaken belief and judgement formed in crisis, the amount of force must be proportionate and reasonable in light of the interests being protected and the likely harm caused by use of force. Jurists have speculated whether grievous

[54] 4 Bing 628, 641–2; 130 ER 911, 916. See further Getzler, n. 23 above, 199; F H Bohlen and JJ Burns, 'The Privilege to Protect Property by Dangerous Barriers and Mechanical Devices' (1926) 35 *Yale LJ* 525.

[55] See, e.g., *Wootton v Dawkins* (1857) 2 CBNS 412, 140 ER 477.

bodily harm or death may reasonably be inflicted on a criminal in order to prevent theft of a large sum of money or destruction of a very valuable object. Some take the position that, without threat to a person, property by itself cannot reasonably provide a justification for inflicting serious physical harm; yet there are judgments approving considerable violence to arrest criminals offending against property, as where a butcher used his knife to stop a robber escaping with his loot, leading to the criminal's death. The coroner approved of the butcher's self-help.[56] More recently, a court approved of a builder who beat a drug-addicted burglar with a metal baseball bat, breaking his limbs and skull;[57] and a few months ago a court approved of the actions of a blind man in stabbing to death a drunken intruder who had forced in the door to his home.[58] Certainly, police regularly kill fleeing suspects and cases such as *Clegg*[59] (where the court convicted a young soldier of murder when he shot at a car which went through a checkpoint after the potential for danger had passed) are notable, precisely because they rupture an expectation that suspected criminals may be arrested with deadly force.

(vii) Justification, Excuse, and Partial Defences

In the old common law, a distinction was drawn between defences to homicide involving justification and excuse; both varieties were defences to the felony but in cases of excuse forfeiture of goods was levied by the Crown.[60] Today, theorists use the two categories to distinguish between actions that society approves of with respect to purpose or motivation[61] or consequences,[62] and those where the behaviour cannot be approved of, but some excuse may be found in the capacity or situation of the defendant, such as insanity or provocation.[63] In slogan form, justification describes the quality of the act; excuse pertains to the intentionality of the actor. It would seem most conformable to place use of force to prevent crime (including property crime) within the justificatory category, in that society positively approves of the act and result where a person uses reasonable force against a criminal or suspect. But the excuse/justification distinction cannot always cleanly discriminate between cases, especially where a person acts in a mistaken or

[56] *The Times*, 16 Sep. 1967.

[57] 'Judge reignites self defence row', *The Guardian*, 5 May 2000.

[58] 'Blind man killed intruder in self-defence', *The Guardian*, 19 Mar. 2004.

[59] *R v Clegg* [1995] 1 AC 482 (HL).

[60] See *Semayne's Case*, n. 30 above.

[61] GP Fletcher, *Rethinking Criminal Law* (Little, Brown, 1978; repr. OUP, 2000), 855–75, esp. 870–5.

[62] PH Robinson, 'Criminal Law Defenses: A Systematic Analysis' (1982) 82 *Col LR* 199, 203–36; PH Robinson, 'Competing Theories of Justification: Deeds v Reasons', in AP Simester and ATH Smith (eds.), *Harm and Culpability* (Clarendon Press, 1996), 45; cf. J Gardner, 'Justifications and Reasons', and GR Sullivan, 'Making Excuses', in Simester and Smith, ibid., 101 and 131; J Gardner, 'The Gist of Excuses' (1998) 1 *Buffalo Crim LR* 575.

[63] J Horder, *Provocation and Responsibility* (Clarendon Press, 1992); J Horder, *Excusing Crime* (OUP, 2004); Simester and Sullivan, n. 19 above, 342–60, 571–83.

objectively unreasonable state of belief. The celebrated case of *R v Dadson*[64] is key here. In that case, a policeman shot and wounded an escaping thief, not knowing that the man he shot was a felon. Had he known of the victim's status he would have had a complete defence, since force was at that time justified in order to arrest a fleeing felon.[65] Because the policeman did not know of this essential fact, he was convicted of intentionally causing grievous and unlawful bodily harm. Notwithstanding the beneficial consequences of his actions, his mental state in shooting the thief was not justified, and so conviction was required. Simester and Sullivan in their review of the justification–excuse debate have argued that many so-called defences entail failure of proof of a complete offence rather than the addition of some extra factor to relieve of liability. For example, an insane killer could be said to lack the requisite mens rea and, indeed, actus reus of purposeful action; hence, no crime is committed, rather than a crime plus a defence. Simester and Sullivan proffer a more intricate taxonomy of defences, in which prevention of crime amounts to permissible conduct. Objectively, reasonable response to a situation affords additional reasons to eliminate liability for what otherwise would be a completed crime.[66]

One important practical implication emerging from this involved defences debate is whether excessive use of force in defence of persons or property wholly eliminates any possible justificatory defence, or can yet serve as a partial defence by nature of excuse. In *McKay*, where a farmer shot and fatally wounded a chicken thief, it was decided that some force was justified, but that excessive or unreasonable force had been applied here. The defence could not therefore be total, but could operate partially so as to excuse and reduce the charge to manslaughter.[67] This may have been predicated on the existence of mandatory severe punishment for murder, a context that might lead juries into refusing to find excessive force in order to allow acquittal. The Australian courts later adopted a rule that, where a person subject to felonious attack uses more than reasonable lethal force, but honestly believes himself to be using necessary force only, then a manslaughter conviction is appropriate. This partial defence rule was rejected by English courts,[68] but long formed a pillar of Australian criminal law. It was ultimately thrown out by

[64] (1850) 2 Den 35; 169 ER 407; 3 Car and Kir 148, 175 ER 499.

[65] Compare *R v Scully* (1824) 1 C and P 319; 171 ER 1213, which held that a guard is not justified in shooting at trespassers in order to apprehend them or to stop the commission of a crime, even if they were seen going into the owner's chicken roost in order to steal. As it happened, the trespasser who was killed by the warning shot turned out to have stolen three fowls and carried tools showing he had broken and entered the premises. Yet it was not argued that the status of the deceased as a criminal or possibly a felon was material. Garrow B, indeed, suggested that the plaintiff had not shot in order to apprehend a felon, but, rather, had shot at another intruder in order to scare him off and so protect himself from harm. The final verdict appeared to be not guilty.

[66] Simester and Sullivan, n. 19 above, chs. 16, 20, 21; and see AP Simester, 'Mistakes in Defence' (1992) 12 *OJLS* 295. A piecemeal approach to excuses is also defended by V Tadros in 'The Characters Of Excuse' (2001) 21 *OJLS* 495. For a sustained effort to re-systematize see Horder, *Excusing Crime*, n. 63 above.

[67] N Morris, 'The Slain Chicken Thief' (1958) 2 *Sydney LR* 414; cf. *R v McKay* [1957] VLR 560.

[68] *Palmer v R* [1971] 2 WLR 831; *R v McInnes* [1971] 1 WLR 1600; *R v Clegg* [1995] 1 AC 482; see Law Com. no. 173: *Partial Defences to Murder* (TSO, 2003), paras 4.29—4.45.

the High Court of Australia in 1987, but was reinstated by legislation in two Australian states and has recently attracted support from the English Law Commission, driven in part by the sentencing rigidities set in place for punishing murder.[69] The partial defence debate is concerned with excessive force used to kill in general, and excessive defence of property is only a subset of that larger subject.

(viii) Deemed Assault and Proportionality

The Canadian Criminal Code makes a novel juristic analysis of the circumstances where force is justified in defending property, enlarging upon early nineteenth-century common law doctrine. Where a trespasser attempts to take personal property from a person in peaceable possession, the trespasser's continuing attempts to take the property are defined by the statute to be launching an assault. Hence, the self-help of the victim in repelling the property attack is converted in the eyes of the law into a form of personal self-defence against assault, provided that the possessor uses no more force against the trespasser than is 'necessary'.[70] Likewise, a person in peaceable possession of a dwelling house may use force to prevent another breaking in, and any person in possession of any land may use force to prevent or repel trespass, again subject to the requirement of necessity. If the trespasser resists that resistance he is deemed by the statute to be launching an assault on the possessor.[71] The provisions are complex and interlocking, and trouble has been caused by the focus on the possessor rather than the superior right-holder. The possessor is allowed to use reasonable force against a stranger to the goods but not against a person with a superior possessory right. But a squatter can repel the true owner or a person with a superior possessory claim who tries to enter real property in order to retake possession. Thus, in the case of land, the Code cleaves to a deep legal instinct prohibiting self-help in the recovery of property—but it reverses that policy with respect to personal property.[72] The courts have held that necessary force does not include killing to defend property in the absence of personal threat, but this does not sit easily with the legislative deeming of a trespasser's resistance as a species of assault. The Department of Justice has proposed legislative reform to introduce an overt requirement of

[69] *Zecevic v DPP (Vic.)* (1987) 162 CLR 645; cf. Criminal Law Consolidation (Self-Defence) Amendment Act 1991 (SA) and Crimes Amendment (Self-Defence) Act 2001 (NSW). See further Law Com. no. 173, n. 68 above, Part IX; S Yeo, *Unrestrained Killings And The Law: A Comparative Analysis of the Laws of Provocation and Excessive Self-Defence in India, England and Australia* (OUP, 2002), with a compressed treatment in S Yeo, 'Killing in Defence of Property' (2000) 150 *New LJ* 730.

[70] Canadian Criminal Code 1985 (as amended), s. 38(2).

[71] Criminal Code, ss. 40, 41(2).

[72] Criminal Code s. 39(1)(2), contrasting defence of personal property with and without claim of right; s. 42(2) allowing force to prevent a rightful owner entering land to take possession. Roman law and common law set their face against recovery of possession by self-help, instead according claimants possessory interdicts or assizes.

reasonable and proportionate force, but this has not been pursued to date.[73] It may be that the current legislative approach of deemed assault in practice is little more than a drafting technique; but it might also suggest that the law regards sustained property attack as a presumptive attack on the person, making available a wider array of self-defence powers.

The German position, which has evolved since the 1920 case of the shooting of a fruit thief described above, is that where there is a culpable aggressor who intentionally inflicts a wrong, the right-holder can respond with all necessary force to defend his or her autonomy and rights. In such a case, protection of autonomy and right has priority over utility and, hence, there is no requirement of safe retreat, nor must the defender avoid disproportionate force. The legal risk of infliction of harm disproportionate to the offence therefore lies on the initial attacker. Attempts to interpret section 32 of the Criminal Code to impose proportionality through 'appropriate' self-defence measures have attracted only minority juristic support, with the commitment to generous protection of autonomy prevailing.

Theorists such as George Fletcher[74] and Robert Schopp[75] have taken this Germanic concern with autonomy and placed it at the heart of their liberal theories of justification and self-defence. Because the criminal law's concern with justification is not welfarist, disproportionality of itself cannot eliminate justification for severe self-defence measures. One cannot trade off autonomy by measuring it on a balance of utilities. However, extreme disproportionality on this view can still take the wielder of force out of the terrain of self-defence entirely; the initial attack becomes a pretext for violence and the self-defence right is abused and so voided. Hence, 'abuse of rights' theory, a concept largely alien to Anglo-Commonwealth common law,[76] is propounded as the main control device or backstop, rather than any direct test of necessity or reasonableness, with their implications of proportionality.[77]

The American law on defence of property is typically fissured, with caselaw overlaid by state laws and the Model Penal Code. Joshua Dressler[78] has argued that American criminal law distinguishes (or ought to distinguish) between defence of property in the sense of self-help to guarantee rightful possession,

[73] See Department of Justice, Canada, *Reforming Criminal Code Defences—Provocation, Self-Defence and Defence of Property* (June 1998), in particular Part Three: Defence of Property: see http://canada.justice.gc.ca/en/cons/rccd/partie3p3.html.

[74] See, e.g., Fletcher, n. 60, above 855–75.

[75] R F Schopp, *Justification Defenses and Just Convictions* (CUP, 1998).

[76] M Taggart, *Private Property and Abuse of Rights in Victorian England* (OUP, 2002); cf. J Getzler, 'Review' (2003) 66 *MLR* 819. Note however that motive may have some place in the assessment of criminal mens rea: see *R v Thain* [1985] NI 457, and GR Sullivan, 'Bad Thoughts and Bad Acts' [1990] *Crim LR* 559. Blackmail is a possible example, where the selfish motive of the blackmailer issuing coercive threats converts an otherwise legal act into a crime: cf. G Lamond, 'Coercion, Threats, and the Puzzle of Blackmail', in Simester and Smith, n. 62 above, 215.

[77] Cf. J Horder, 'Self-Defence, Necessity and Duress: Understanding the Relationship' (1998) 11 *Can J of L and Jurisp* 143.

[78] J Dressler, *Understanding Criminal Law* (3rd edn., Matthew Bender, 2001), ch. 20.

where some reasonable and proportionate use of force is permitted but never deadly force, and defence of habitation, where deadly force may be used. Dressler finds different levels of licence for deadly force in the case law, and indicates dissatisfaction that the Model Penal Code tends to the severe position, allowing deadly force to be used against a home invader who threatens to dispossess, even where there is no threat, perceived or real, to the safety of the inhabitant.[79] However a non-disseising and non-threatening intruder may not lawfully be killed under this provision.

A sophisticated study of American defence of property law has been given recently by Stuart Green.[80] He notes that American law generally does not have a sturdy rule requiring proportionality of response to home invasion. Various defences of the non-proportionality rule are on offer: a rule-utilitarian calculus that favours the householder's interests in deterrence and repulsion of attack, as against the attacker's interest in life and limb; a theory that the attacker has forfeited his right to life through aggression; a theory that the defender has an inalienable right to repel aggression; a theory that the killing of an intruder is not directly purposed or intended but is only a by-product of the rightful defence of home; a theory that the householder's autonomy interests cannot be put into a balance with the aggressor's interests but may be defended absolutely. These justifications of non-proportionality are buttressed by the typical proneness and vulnerability of a householder under attack, who has nowhere to retreat and who may therefore panic and over-react, and also by the fact that attacks on dwellings can be seen as attacks on the security and identity, the dignity and autonomy of the house-dwellers, harms superadded to the physical and economic degradation caused by the trespass. Ultimately, Green finds all these theories lacking in explaining why proportionately can be discarded and a life taken to defend property, and he suggests that the law as it stands can only be justified by aggregating the entire set of disparate policies. His positive assessment of the non-proportionality rule is somewhat undercut by his demolition of the separate justifications commonly given for allowing householders to kill intruders absent self-defence.

Turning from American to European experience, it may be noted that all of the justifications for allowing unlimited force listed by Green cropped up recently in Italy. Laws were proposed in 2003 and 2004 allowing householders to kill intruders with a broad immunity from prosecution or punishment, propounded by Roberto Castelli, a right-wing populist leader of the Northern League without legal training, who serves as Justice Minister in Silvio Berlusconi's government in Italy. One clause of the bill adds in a radically subjective defence: '[one] is not to be held punishable who exceeds the limits of self-defence, because of panic,

[79] Model Penal Code, §3.06(3)(d)(i). The right to kill thus exceeds any justification of self-defence, as the American Law Institute apologetically notes in its Comment to §3.06, at 93.

[80] Green, n. 43 above. The American literature is otherwise remarkably sparse; cf. 'A Rationale of the Law of Burglary' [1951] *Colorado LR* 1009.

fear or distress'.[81] The bills for these changes are currently before the Camera and Senate of the Italian Parliament, but any such laws would likely collide with Article 2 of the European Convention of Human Rights.

In Britain, the echo of this approach in conservative politics has already been noted with the favouring of a rule permitting householders to use anything up to 'grossly disproportionate' violence, which, on its face, accepts the use of objectively disproportionate violence as being justified by the extreme circumstances of home invasion. But it is equally clear that the English courts have set their face against such a norm. The modern approach was stated in the 1995 appeal of *Revill v Newbery*,[82] involving a claim in tort for damages by a burglar who had been shot by a householder. The latter was an elderly man who, after repeated burglaries, had hidden in his garden shed with a gun in order to apprehend the culprits. He had bored a hole in the door and shot through the hole when he heard the burglar approaching, there being no suggestion that he felt personally threatened. He was held guilty of carelessly or recklessly causing harm, though the burglar's damages were steeply reduced for contributory fault. The Court of Appeal rejected the idea that the criminal nature of the plaintiff's trespass barred his claim regarding harm suffered in the course of his trespass. Millett LJ stated:

> For centuries the common law has permitted reasonable force to be used in defence of the person or property. Violence may be returned with necessary violence. But the force used must not exceed the limits of what is reasonable in the circumstances. Changes in society and in social perceptions have meant that what might have been considered reasonable at one time would no longer be so regarded; but the principle remains the same. The assailant or intruder may be met with reasonable force but no more; the use of excessive violence against him is an actionable wrong.[83]
>
> It follows . . . that there is no place for the doctrine ex turpi causa non oritur actio in this context. If the doctrine applied, any claim by the assailant or trespasser would be barred no matter how excessive or unreasonable the force used against him.

English law thus disallows a disproportionate response against miscreants, even in necessary defence of one's rights and autonomy. Yet this balance of law and policy may be fragile. *Revill v Newbery* caused public outcry, adumbrating the *Tony Martin* case four years later; and, ultimately, the defendant Newbery's costs and damages bill was paid by public subscription. In a sense, the court of public opinion reversed the Court of Appeal.

[81] See e.g. Proposta di legge N.4926 (22 Apr. 2004): www.camera.it/_dati/leg14/lavori/stampati/pdf/14PDL0059690.pdf. I am grateful to Alessandro Spina for information on this point. See also J Hooper, 'Italy plans law to allow property owners to shoot intruders', *The Guardian*, 19 Apr. 2004.

[82] [1996] QB 567 (CA, 1995) (Eng.), noted in T Weir, 'Swag for the Injured Burglar' (1996) 55 *CLJ* 182, 182–4 (1996); T Weir, 'ALL or Nothing?' (2004) 78 *Tulane LR* 511, 531–2.

[83] [1996] QB 567, 580.

(ix) The Role of Property Theory

Rights cannot easily be described without scrutiny of the underlying interests that those rights articulate.[84] The trespassory rules that protect crystallized interests may be highly varied, and thereby present an ungoverned set of pragmatic choices to the lawyers designing legal institutions. At the same time, the contours of those remedial rules can fold back onto the protected interests and help define their content. If we chose to uphold contractual performances with the death penalty, this would have some impact on our concepts of promissory obligation; the intensified remedy would mean more than just a machinery of enforcement. The right to use force to defend property therefore rests, to a degree, on our understanding of the interest in peaceable possession of property; and, likewise, the allowance of reasonable private force to defend property may teach us something about the law's regard for property interests.

The interest in peaceable possession is now enshrined in human rights legislation,[85] and we saw earlier how the concept of peaceable possession was employed to generate rights within the Canadian Criminal Code. Human rights discourse in both private law[86] and criminal law[87] is of course still emerging in the common law countries outside the USA. The nature of Article 1 of the First Protocol of the European Convention on Human Rights protecting property is not well-explored. The importance of human rights in this area may lie in requiring courts to balance the interest in self-defence, property defence and crime prevention against the right to life.[88] This is a generic problem in the area of justification, excuse, and defences, and says little distinctive about use of force in protecting property. We may, in fact, learn more about the precise interests at stake by drawing insights from property theory per se rather than looking at extant human rights institutions.

There are two major tasks pursued in property theory. The first is analysis of conceptual distinctions between persons as right- and duty-bearers, property as external things of value, and personal rights and duties that tie together both

[84] The literature on the interest theory of rights is burgeoning, most notably with J Raz, 'Legal Rights' (1984) 4 *OJLS* 1; J Raz, *The Morality of Freedom* (Clarendon Press, 1986), 166; J Raz, *Ethics in the Public Domain* (OUP, 1994), ch. 11. For recent work see A Harel, 'Theories of Rights', in MP Golding and WA Edmundson (eds.), *Blackwell Guide to the Philosophy of Law and Legal Theory* (Blackwell, 2004), ch. 13; A Harel, 'What Demands Are Rights? An Investigation into the Relation between Rights and Reasons' (1997) 17 *OJLS* 101; JW Harris, 'Human Rights and Mythical Beasts' (2004) 120 *LQR* 428.

[85] Art. 1 of the First Protocol of the European Convention on Human Rights; FG Jacobs, RCA White, and C Ovey, *The European Convention on Human Rights* (3rd edn., OUP, 1996), ch. 15.

[86] The most important case to date which is restrictive of human rights applications to contract and property is *Wilson* v *First County Trust Ltd (No. 2)* [2004] 1 AC 816 (HL); and see also *Parish of Aston Cantlow* v *Wallbank* [2004] 1 AC 546.

[87] See AJ Ashworth, *Human Rights, Serious Crime and Criminal Procedure* (Hamlyn Lectures, 53rd ser., Sweet and Maxwell, 2002); B Emmerson and A J Ashworth, *Human Rights and Criminal Justice* (Sweet and Maxwell, 2001).

[88] See Ashworth, n. 44 above, 282.

persons and things. Inquiry into these categories is one of the oldest themes in Western legal tradition: 'all the law we have is persons, things and actions', proclaims the classical Roman jurist, Gaius. The Hohfeldian denial of property as a meaningful juristic category is now on the defensive, as modern theorists have (re)discovered property to be an irreducible building block of the legal and social order. [89] The analytical exercise merges into a justificatory enquiry: does respect for the autonomy and interests of persons require a respect for property rights, and, if so, in what form? Locke's theory begins with self-ownership and hence justifies claims to fruit of labours, including appropriated resources. Hegel proclaims the need for individuals to master the world through property holdings expanding the sphere of rational choice. Bentham sees property as the key social device to enable individuals to enhance their utilities through stable investment and trade. The classical theories have had new bursts of life, with modern restatements of Lockean labour and appropriation theory by Nozick and Epstein, [90] of Hegelian personhood theory by Waldron, Radin, and Brudner;[91] of Benthamite utilitarian theory by Coase, Demsetz, Barzel, and others in the law and economics tradition.[92] Jim Harris's synthesis in *Property and Justice* took the debate in a new direction. He undermined natural right theories and argued instead that property was justified by a mix of instrumental and freedom-promoting benefits, all resting ultimately on social convention. It was a key part of Jim's critical work to attack not only the self-ownership fallacy,[93] but also the concomitant natural-right idea that trespass upon property could be analogized as an assault on the person of the owner. Perhaps an attack on intimate articles of property—destruction of a wedding ring, arson of a family home—could be seen as attacks on the person of the owner because such items of property are invested with emotion or personal sentiment. But attempts by theorists such as Radin to place such cases at the core of the property concept are unconvincing; they are rare anomalies, and the harm to the owner's interests caused by the trespass is better seen as a species of *injuria* or direct contempt for personality, rather than interference with property as some kind of surrogate extension of personality.[94] Property, as James Penner puts it, is

[89] See, in addition to Harris, n. 1 above, the following: T Honoré, *Making Law Bind: Essays Legal and Philosophical* (Clarendon Press, 1987), 161–92, 215–26; J Waldron, *The Right To Private Property* (Clarendon Press, 1988); SR Munzer, *A Theory of Property* (CUP, 1990); C M Rose, *Property and Persuasion* (Westview, 1994); J Penner, *The Idea of Property in Law* (Clarendon Press, 1997); D Lametti, 'The Concept of Property: Relations *Through* Objects of Social Wealth' (2003) 53 *U of Toronto LJ* 325.

[90] R Nozick, *Anarchy, State and Utopia* (Basic Books, 1974), 150–3, 167–82; R Epstein, *Takings: Private Property and the Power of Eminent Domain* (Harvard University Press, 1985), 10–11, 61, 217–19, 253, 304–5, 346–9.

[91] Waldron, n. 89 above, chs. 10 and 12; MJ Radin, *Reinterpreting Property* (Chicago, 1993), esp. ch. 1; A Brudner, *The Unity of the Common Law: Studies in Hegelian Jurisprudence* (University of California Press, 1995).

[92] RH Coase, 'The Problem of Social Cost' (1960) 3 *J of L and Econ* 1; H Demsetz, 'Toward a Theory of Property Rights' (1967) 57 *Am Econ R* 347; Y Barzel, *Economic Analysis of Property Rights* (2nd edn., CUP, 1997).

[93] See text to nn. 1–4 above.

[94] Harris, n. 1 above, 165 ff.

not 'personality rich'; the personal qualities of even intimate objects can be stripped away by gift, bequest, sale, or other modes of transfer.[95] It is true that land-based feudal societies sometimes saw an identity between an owner and his estates, but this was more a case of the land imprinting qualities on the person than the other way around, and the existence of free transmission of estates in all developed feudalisms snapped or weakened the link between personality and property.[96] Thus, where the older legal sources state that attacks on intimate property, such as the family home, are tantamount to personal assault, this is really identifying a presumptive danger to the body. The modern requirement of a direct threat to the person as a justification for violent attack on intruders therefore lies squarely within the dominant common law tradition, but modifies that tradition by reducing the presumption of personal danger. We are left with no special licence to use force to defend property as an extension of the person, but merely the normal principles that force may be used within bounds for self-defence, or to repress the commission of crimes where intervention by state officials might be ineffective.

The perceived legitimacy of violent self-help today may ultimately be tied to the rise or fall of the policing capacities of the state; violence becomes necessary and therefore reasonable where there is no other recourse. Be that as it may, the instinct of the law is that resort to violence cannot be justified by a blurring of the line between persons and property. The intuition with which we began—that persons cannot be identified with what they own, and that personality is not constituted by property—remains intact.

Jim Harris made one important exception in his own sharp critique of theories of property as constitutive of personality. A group, such as a nation, which depended for its collective existence on a certain territory, could be said to derive its identity from that property over which it claimed *dominium*—the latter being a convenient word to connote both ownership and sovereignty.[97] Trespass on group property could of itself be seen as assault, without presumptions or surrogates, metaphors or metaphysics. Such trespasses were an intrinsic attack on the group's basic interest in survival.[98] But this takes our enquiry out of the terrain of private property and criminal law, and into international law. It would be interesting to test how far international law uses concepts of necessity, subjective belief, proportionality, and autonomy in its measures of excessive self-defence of territory, and how much could be learnt from the filigree detail of domestic law.

95 Penner, n. 89 above, 105 ff.

96 See further A Pottage, 'Proprietary Strategies: The Legal Fabric of Aristocratic Settlements' (1998) 61 *MLR* 162.

97 On the relation of property to ownership see JW Harris, 'Ownership of Land in English Law', in N MacCormick and P Birks (eds.), *The Legal Mind: Essays for Tony Honoré* (Clarendon Press, 1986), 143–61; Harris, n. 1 above, 63–84; T Honoré, 'Property And Ownership', and J Penner, 'Ownership, Co-ownership, and the Justification of Property Rights', chs. 7 and 9 in this volume.

98 Harris, n. 1 above, 216–20. See further A Harel, 'Whose Home Is It? Reflections on the Palestinians' Interest in Return' (2004) 5 *Theoretical Inquiries in Law* 333.

Jim Harris's work, from his studies of positivism and precedent through to his property and human rights analyses, showed how much potential there was for jurisprudence to benefit from close engagement with the intricate details of positive law, even whilst maintaining its conceptual edge in analysing the possibilities of 'legal science'.[99] Jim's contribution has become so central to our thinking about property institutions that it is hard to remember how we managed before *Property and Justice* was published just a decade ago. Part of the potency of Jim's writing derived from his gifts as a teacher. Jim led students through his thinking on law, philosophy, history, and economics by the most artful discourse, often delivered with startling dramatic force, and always with good humour. Many students across the world will recognize that unique voice in Jim's sparkling introductory text, *Legal Philosophies*.[100] In graduate seminars, he especially enjoyed arguments with those who clung to the benighted idea that they owned themselves, and, even more, relished moments when his students contributed novel ideas from the legal and political systems of India or China, Ireland or Australia, New Zealand or Canada. In his last year of teaching, he raised his students to new heights, transcending any physical weakness. He offered unfailing warmth and loyalty to his many friends and colleagues. Even to the end his pleasure in learning, conversation and company never dimmed.

[99] JW Harris, *Law and Legal Science: An Inquiry into the Concepts 'Legal Rule' and 'Legal System'* (Clarendon Press, 1979).

[100] JW Harris, *Legal Philosophies* (Butterworths, 1980, 2nd edn., 1997).

PART III

PRECEDENT

13

Towards Principles of Overruling in a Civil Law Supreme Court

*Isabelle Rorive**

Professor Jim Harris dedicated a fair amount of his research to the issue of precedent in English law and in the common law system. He developed a very fine analysis of the attitude of the House of Lords towards its own precedents. His work is crucial for anybody interested in the way supreme courts are developing and changing the law on their own, with no legislative intervention whatsoever. Today, writing about judge-made law does still bring back to me the long hours spent in his room at Keble College, discussing the subtleties of overruling and distinguishing. During these valuable moments, I was following a fascinating guide in the rambling development of judicial reasoning. Jim Harris had amazing teaching skills and unfailing availability. I owe him a lot. Nowadays, I try to pass on what he taught me, not only from the scholarly point of view, but also from the human one.

(i) Introduction[1]

The contrast between the attitudes of civil and common law systems has often been portrayed 'as one between logical and empirical methods, between deductive and inductive thinking, between the rule of reason and the rule of

* Professor at the Law Faculty and Fellow at the Centre for Comparative Law and History of Law, University of Brussels (*Université Libre de Bruxelles*).

[1] This Chapter is based upon 'Diverging legal culture but similar jurisprudence of overruling: The case of the House of Lords and the Belgian *Cour de cassation*' (2004) 3 *ERPL* 321–346. Both contributions spring from a Master's degree in Legal Research supervised by Professor Jim Harris: *A Jurisprudence of Overruling? A Comparison between the Practices of the House of Lords and the Belgian Cour de cassation* (Oxford University Law Faculty, 1998). For further developments, consult I Rorive, *Le revirement de jurisprudence. Etude de droit anglais et de droit belge* (Bruylant, 2003), 565. I would like warmly to thank Silke Semeticolos, solicitor of the Supreme Court of England and Wales and legal practitioner of the Supreme Court of New South Wales (Australia), for having accepted the task of helping me with my English writing.

experience'.[2] This contrast has had a profound influence throughout comparative law, leading to an essential place being given to the nature and the scope of the judicial function. In civil law countries, the task of the judge would solely consist of an application of general statutory rules to the special facts of the case. Conversely, the common law judge would proceed from case to case, giving particular weight to the rulings of his predecessors.

According to the conventional view, the attitude towards precedent is one of the most important differences between common law and civil law systems.[3] And even if several academic writers have suggested that the gap between the two systems might be more apparent than real,[4] the rule of precedent is still one of the major criteria on which the division between common law and civil law families rests.[5]

The phenomenon of overruling, as practised both by the Belgian *Cour de cassation* and the Appellate Committee of the House of Lords, casts doubt on the cogency of such a perception. As a matter of fact, the Belgian and English systems exhibit a very similar jurisprudence with respect to departure from existing case law, as practised at the highest level in the judiciary. By jurisprudence of overruling, I mean *the revealed motivations behind the phenomenon of departure from existing case law*; in other words, the overtly discussed principles underlying the rules of change in case law. In order to bring the jurisprudence of overruling developed by the *Cour de cassation* into perspective, the status of judicial decisions in Belgium has to be reviewed.

[2] W Friedmann, '*Stare Decisis* at Common Law and Under the Civil Code of Quebec' (1953) 31 *CLR* 724. See also Lord MacMillan, 'Deux manières de penser', in *Recueil d'études en l'honneur d'Edouard Lambert. Introduction à l'étude du droit comparé* (LGDJ, 1938), 4; R Dekkers, *Le droit privé des peuples* (Editions de la librairie encyclopédique, 1953), n° 259, 230; CK Allen, *Law in the Making* (7th edn., Clarendon Press, 1964), 161–2; L-J Constantinesco, *Traité de droit comparé*, (Economica, 1983), iii, 383–4; C Jauffret-Spinosi, 'Comment juge le juge anglais?' [1989] *Droits (Revue Française de Théorie Juridique)*, 57–8; GA Zaphiriou, 'Introduction to Civil Law Systems', in RA Danner and M-LH Bernal (eds.), *Introduction to Foreign Legal Systems* (Oceana Publications Inc., 1994), 51–2; G Samuel, 'Entre les mots et les choses: les raisonnements et les méthodes en tant que sources du droit' [1995] *Revue internationale de droit comparé*, 512; D Poirier, *Sources de la Common Law* (Bruylant, 1996), ii, 103–07; P Legrand, 'Are Civilians Educable?' (1998) 18 *LS* 216, 219–221 and 7; HW Baade, 'Stare Decisis in Civil Law Systems', in JAR Nafziger and SC Symeonides (eds.), *Law and Justice in a Multistate World. Essays in Honour of Arthur T. von Mehren* (Transnational Publishers, 2002), 533.

[3] See, for instance, RL Henry, 'Jurisprudence Constante and *Stare Decisis*' (1929) 15 *ABAJ* 11; AL Goodhart, 'Precedent in English and Continental Law' (1934) 50 *LQR* 40; M Ancel, 'Case Law in France' (1934) 16.3 *J of Comp Legislation and Intl L* 16–7.

[4] F Deak, 'The Place of the "Case" in the Common and the Civil Law' [1934] *Tulane LR* 341; J Blondeel, 'La common law et le droit civil' [1951] *Revue internationale de droit comparé*, 597; R Cross and JW Harris, *Precedent in English Law* (4th edn., Clarendon Press, 1991), 14; Z Bankowski, DN MacCormick, L Morawski and AR Miguel, 'Rationales for Precedent', in DN MacCormick and RS Summers (eds.), *Interpreting Precedents: a Comparative Study* (Dartmouth Publishing Co Ltd, Ashgate Publishing Ltd, 1997), 482; K Zweigert and H Kötz, *Introduction to Comparative Law* (3rd edn., Clarendon Press, 1998), 71.

[5] C Périphanakis, *Les sources du droit en science comparative et notions de droit civil comparé* (AE, 1964), 35; R David and C. Jauffret-Spinosi, *Les grands systèmes de droit contemporain* (9th edn., Dalloz, 1988), n° 99, 143; Poirier, n. 2 above, ii, 101; M Adams, 'The Rhetoric of Precedent and Comparative Legal Research' (1999) 62 *MLR* 464.

(ii) Status of Precedent in Belgium

The function conferred on judges in the classical civil law model is strictly limited. Stemming from the 1789 French Revolution, this model is chiefly characterized by the primacy of the legislature, a hierarchical organization of legal norms, and a rigid conception of the principle of the separation of powers. In this picture, the moment of the legislative creation of the rule is clearly distinct from that of its judicial application. In brief, this implies that the judge is confined to an application of statutory law bound by the letter of the text or the will—supposed unique and unequivocal—of the legislature.[6] Apart from where enactments are exceptionally 'silent, obscure or insufficient',[7] the judge must reason according to the syllogistic model. Robespierre's declaration that 'there is no case law'[8] constitutes a particularly radical statement of this view. This perfectly matches Bonaparte's assertion before the French *Conseil d'Etat* that judges should only be 'physical machines through whom statutes are enforced as time is marked by the hand of a watch'.[9]

Even though this picture quickly came to be seen as too restrictive,[10] the rejection of it has hardened in the last decades. Numerous studies have insisted on the normative power of case law. Some have applied to the legal field the hermeneutic insight that interpretation is potential creation. They have shown that formal logic, and in particular syllogism, cannot account for judicial reasoning because the application of any legal text presupposes its prior construction.[11] Other studies have described the tremendous creative function in practice fulfilled by case law.[12] The divergent solutions given by French and Belgian decisions,

[6] J-L Halpérin, 'Le juge et le jugement en France à l'époque révolutionnaire', in R Jacob (ed.), *Le juge et le jugement dans les traditions juridiques européennes* (LGDJ, 1996), 238.

[7] *Code civil*, art. 4, currently embodied in *Code judiciaire*, art. 5. For a useful commentary on the scope of this provision, see A Bayart, 'L'article 4 du Code civil et la mission de la Cour de cassation' [1956] *Journal des tribunaux*, 353; C Perelman (ed.), *Le problème des lacunes en droit* (Bruylant, 1968).

[8] Quotation from P Raynaud, 'La loi et la jurisprudence des Lumières à la Révolution française' [1985] *Archives de philosophie du droit*, 61.

[9] In subsequent statements, Bonaparte qualified his opinion given on 7th May 1806. See WJ Ganshof van der Meersch, 'Réflexions sur la révision de la Constitution' [1972] *Journal des tribunaux*, 478, col. 2.

[10] F Gény, *Méthode d'interprétation et sources en droit privé positif* (1st edn., LGDJ, 1899).

[11] See the numerous publications of Chäim Perelman, esp. 'L'interprétation juridique'[1972] *Archives de philosophie du droit*, 29–39; *Logique juridique. Nouvelle rhétorique* (2nd edn., Dalloz, 1979). See also M Van Quickenborne, 'La logique juridique et l'activité judiciaire. La portée logique de l'obligation de motiver', in *Rapports belges au XIème Congrès de l'Académie internationale de droit comparé* (Bruylant, 1982), 158 and 192; F Ost and M Van de Kerchove, *Le droit ou les paradoxes du jeu* (PUF., 1992). In favour of elaborating a dialectic between construction and argumentation, see P Ricoeur, *Le Juste* (Seuil, 1995), 163–83.

[12] M Waline, 'Le pouvoir normatif de la jurisprudence', in *Etudes en l'honneur de Georges Scelle. La technique et les principes de droit public* (LGDJ, 1950), ii, 613–32; J Boulanger, 'Notations sur le pouvoir créateur de la jurisprudence civile' [1961] *Revue trimestrielle de droit civil*, 417–441; WJ Ganshof van der Meersch, 'Propos sur le texte de la loi et les principes généraux du droit' [1970] *Journal des tribunaux*, 558; J Deprez, 'A propos du rapport annuel de la Cour de cassation. "Sois juge

while applying the same enactments, confirm this observation. An outstanding example is provided by the well-known decision of the Belgian *Cour de cassation* of 9 October 1980.[13] Reversing its previous position, the Court held that, when applying foreign law, judges must adhere to the interpretation received in the case law of the relevant country. Consequently, when applying article 1645 of the French *Code civil*—which is still identically worded in the Belgian *Code civil*—the lower court had to observe the construction implemented by the French *Cour de cassation* and not that given by the Belgian equivalent court.[14] This expressly recognizes that the same words may have legal meanings which are dependent upon the local case law.

These various studies asserting that the law cannot be reduced to enacted law have shaken the traditional representation of the sources of law, according to which statute law is unequivocal and supreme. While some French academic writers still discuss the equation 'case law equals source of law',[15] this debate is outmoded in Belgium. Currently, jurisprudential scholars attempt to replace the orthodox academic model with other representations, better able to account for the concept of legal rule and the assumptions which have led to it. They put into

et tais-toi" '[1978] *Revue trimestrielle de droit civil*, 509; X Dieux, 'Vers un droit "post-moderne"?—Quelques impressions sceptiques', in *Mélanges offerts à Jacques Velu. Présence du droit public et des droits de l'homme* (Bruylant, 1992), i, 42–3; P Jestaz, 'Source délicieuse... (Remarques en cascade sur les sources du droit)' [1993] *Revue trimestrielle de droit civil*, 81–2 and the reply of J Vanderlinden, 'Contribution en forme de mascaret à une théorie des sources du droit au départ d'une source délicieuse' [1995] *Revue trimestrielle de droit civil*, 80.

[13] [1981] I *Pasicrisie*, 159.

[14] The different scopes sometimes prescribed by the *Cour de cassation*, the *Conseil d'Etat* or the *Cour d'arbitrage* (Belgian constitutional court) to identical statutory provisions proceed from a similar reflection. On this topic, see, for instance, F Dumon, *La mission des cours et tribunaux. Quelques réflexions* (Bruylant, 1975), 42, n. 138; J Velu, 'Contrôle de constitutionnalité et contrôle de compatibilité avec les traités' [1992] *Journal des tribunaux*, 730, n° 7; P Martens, 'La Cour de cassation et la Cour d'arbitrage', in *Imperat Lex. Liber amicorum Pierre Marchal* (Larcier, 2003), 97.

[15] As studies discussing the status of case law in France, see, among others P Hébraud, 'Le juge et la jurisprudence', in *Mélanges offerts à Paul Couzinet* (Université des sciences sociales de Toulouse, 1974), 329–371; C Atias, 'L'ambiguïté des arrêts dits de principe en droit privé' [1984] I *Semaine juridique*, 3145, n° 1; P Raynaud, 'La loi et la jurisprudence des Lumières à la Révolution française' [1985] *Archives de philosophie du droit*, 61; J-D Bredin, 'La loi du juge', in *Etudes offertes à Berthold Goldman. Le droit des relations économiques internationales* (Litec, 1987), 19, n° 10; J Hilaire and C Bloch, 'Connaissance des décisions de justice et origine de la jurisprudence', in JH Baker (ed.), *Judicial Records, Law Reports and the Growth of Case Law* (Duncker & Humblot, 1989), v 48; F Zénati, *La jurisprudence* (Dalloz, 1991), 116; See also the exchange of views on the status of case law 'La jurisprudence aujourd'hui. Libres propos sur une institution controversée' [1992] *Revue trimestrielle de droit civil*, 338–361, esp. J Carbonnier, 342, G Cornu, 344, M Gobert, 345, F Terré, 355, F Zénati, 359; 'D'autres propos sur la jurisprudence' [1993] *Revue trimestrielle de droit civil*, 87, esp. M-C Rondeau-Rivier, 90; J Héron, 'L'infériorité technique de la norme jurisprudentielle' [1993] *Revue de la recherche juridique Droit prospectif*, 1083; P Jestaz, 'Source délicieuse... (Remarques en cascade sur les sources du droit)' [1993] *Revue trimestrielle de droit civil*, 81–2 and the reply by J Vanderlinden, 'Contribution en forme de mascaret à une théorie des sources du droit au départ d'une source délicieuse' [1995] *Revue trimestrielle de droit civil*, esp. 80; J Ghestin and G Goubeaux, *Traité de droit civil. Introduction générale* (4th edn., LGDJ, 1994), 432 ff, n° 465 ff; J Hilaire, 'Jugement et jurisprudence' [1994] *Archives de philosophie du droit*, 181; H Le Berre, 'La jurisprudence et le temps' [2000] *Droits (Revue Française de Théorie Juridique)*, 71; P Morvan, 'En droit, la jurisprudence est source de droit' [2001] *Revue de la recherche juridique—Droit prospectif*, 94.

question the very notion of source of law, speaking instead of 'strange loops and entangled hierarchies' (*boucles étranges et hiérarchies enchevêtrées*),[16] 'archipelagos of the legal norm' (*archipels de la norme*),[17] and even 'clouds' (*nuages*).[18]

The present difficulty in comprehending the true status of case law also stems from the paradoxical discourses that have surrounded the organization of the judiciary. In the days following the French Revolution, the legislature reconciled, although not without ambiguity, the pervading distrust towards judges with the creation of a *Tribunal de cassation*. It combined a strict principle of separation of powers with the establishment of the *Tribunal de cassation* 'by the side of the legislative power'[19] to which it has to refer in certain circumstances. The *Discours Préliminaire du Code civil* deemed case law to be a genuine source of law,[20] whereas the code itself established a framework designed to prevent judicial rulings from ever becoming legal rules. Article 5[21] forbidding judges to lay down general rules of conduct was further strengthened by article 1351 which, in the context of the law of obligations, laid down the *res judicata* principle[22] (*autorité relative de la chose jugée*). In contrast, the effect of article 4[23] is to underline the persuasive value of case law. In providing that a judge may be prosecuted for denial of justice if he fails to reach a decision on the grounds of silence, lack of clarity, or insufficiency of the written law, this provision virtually impels the judiciary to seek guidance and inspiration from precedents in such situations.[24] In order to show its confidence in the judiciary, the Belgian Constituent Assembly of 1830–1 (*Congrès National*) raised it to the status of a separate power.[25] Nevertheless, the procedure of legislative reference (*référé législatif*) was not abolished before 1865.[26] Comparable ambivalence may be found in the fact that, whereas its

16 F Ost and M Van de Kerchove, *Jalons pour une théorie critique du droit* (FUSL, 1987), 205.

17 G Timsit, *Archipel de la norme* (PUF, 1997).

18 M Delmas-Marty, *Pour un droit commun* (Seuil, 1994), 283–4.

19 *Décret-loi des 27 novembre–1er décembre 1790 organisant le Tribunal de cassation*, art. 1.

20 Portalis, 'Discours préliminaire du Code civil', in JG Locré de Roissy (ed.), *La législation civile, commerciale et criminelle de la France, ou Commentaire et complément des codes français* (Treuttle et Würtz, 1836), 157–8, n° 12–13.

21 Currently embodied in *Code judiciaire*, art. 6. The change of attitude towards judges in civil law countries is well illustrated by comparing s. 5 of the 1804 French *Code civil* with s. 1 of the 1907 Swiss *Code civil.* The latter directs the judge facing an absence of statutory provisions or customary law to decide in accordance with rules which he would lay down 'if he had himself to act as legislator'. In doing so, he must search for assistance in 'approved legal doctrine and case law'. See G Terlinden, 'Une actualité juridique. Le nouveau Code civil suisse' [1912] I *Pasicrisie*, 10.

22 Currently embodied in *Code judiciaire*, art. 23. This provision prescribes that 'the authority of *res judicata* extends only to the subject matter of the judgment. The claim must be for the same thing, it must be based on the same cause of action, it must be between the same parties, and brought by and against them in the same qualities'.

23 Currently embodied in *Code judiciaire*, art. 5.

24 A West, Y Desdevises, A Fenet, D Gaurier and M-C Heussaff, *The French Legal System. An Introduction* (Fourmat Publishing, 1992), 58.

25 Constitution, art. 40; B Jottrand, *Les juges d'un peuple libre* (Bruylant, 1932), 4; J-P Nandrin, 'Le judiciaire et le politique. Approche historicienne de la fondation du pouvoir judiciaire de la Belgique contemporaine (1831–1848)' [1995] *Revue interdisciplinaire d'études juridiques*, 187–88.

26 *Loi du 7 juillet 1865 qui abroge les art. 23, 24 et 25 de la loi du 4 août 1832, sur l'organisation judiciaire, et les remplace par des dispositions nouvelles, Moniteur belge*, 11 July 1865.

first *Procureurs généraux*[27] portrayed the *Cour de cassation* as the guardian of uniformity in case law,[28] as late as 1925 Paul Leclercq still described it as the 'legislature's agent'.[29]

As a matter of statutory provision, a Belgian court is never bound to follow a precedent, apart from the very specific and limited exception of a second reference back on the same grounds (*deuxième cassation pour mêmes motifs*).[30] Yet, owing to its essentially normative nature, case law is fundamental to ascertaining what the law is. It represents the law in action. In this respect, the decisions of the *Cour de cassation* are of tremendous significance.

The idea that a single decision of the *Cour de cassation* has no binding force whatsoever may, strictly speaking, be true. Undeniably a petition for review based on the violation of the case law of the *Cour de cassation* is inadmissible.[31] Consistent with this view, no Belgian court may give as the sole reason for reaching its decision the fact that it followed an earlier authority.[32] The *Cour de cassation* itself, however, pays great heed to its precedents. When a decision of a lower court is quashed for violation of enacted law (*violation de la loi*), this violation most often lies in not construing the statute as the *Cour de cassation* has done. The assertion that the case law of the *Cour de cassation* forms 'a whole' with enacted law, is 'a supplement to the written law' or is of a 'quasi-normative' nature speaks for itself.[33] The annotation of the private codes[34] with rulings of the *Cour de cassation* offers further evidence of how far this approach is entrenched in daily

[27] The *Procureur général près la Cour de cassation* is the head of the *Parquet général près la Cour de cassation*. The main function of each member of the *Parquet général* is to give advice (*conclusions*) on the legality of the judgment attacked through a petition for review before the *Cour de cassation*. As such, he/she acts as an *amicus curiae* of the *Cour de cassation*. See J du Jardin, 'Le ministère public dans ses fonctions non pénales', *Discours prononcé à l'audience solennelle de rentrée*, Sept. 2004, 31–7 (available online: www.cass.be).

[28] See, for instance, M Leclerq, 'Examen des arrêts rendus chambres réunies en matière civile, depuis l'installation de la Cour' [1870] I *Pasicrisie*, (i)–(ii).

[29] P Leclercq, 'De la Cour de cassation (1925)', in *La pensée juridique du procureur général Paul Leclercq* (Bruylant, 1953), 67; *contra* L Cornil, 'La Cour de cassation' [1948] *Journal des tribunaux*, 454, col. 3.

[30] When the remanding court (*cour de renvoi*) decides in the same way as the court whose decision was quashed, and its judgment, in turn, being the object of a further hearing, is annulled on the same grounds by the *plenum* of the *Cour de cassation* (*chambres réunies*), this last finding binds the third lower court to whom the case is subsequently referred for implementation (*Code judiciaire*, arts. 1119–1120).

[31] Cass., 25 Nov. 1975 [1976] I *Pasicrisie*, 385; Cass., 4 Apr. 1989 [1989] I *Pasicrisie*, 778.

[32] Cass., 13 Feb. 1984 [1984] I *Pasicrisie*, 660; see also the examples given by WJ Ganshof van der Meersch, 'Propos sur le texte de la loi et les principes généraux du droit' [1970] *Journal des tribunaux*, 559, nn. 40 and 41; P Foriers, 'Les relations des sources écrites et non écrites du Droit (1970)', in *La pensée juridique de Paul Foriers* (Bruylant, 1982), ii, 685–7.

[33] Leclercq, n. 29 above, 74; L Cornil, 'La Cour de cassation. Considérations sur sa mission' [1950] *Journal des tribuanux*, 492, col. 3; WJ Ganshof van der Meersch, 'Propos sur le texte de la loi et les principes généraux du droit' [1970] *Journal des tribunaux*, 559; J Velu, 'Représentation et pouvoir judiciaire' [1996] *Journal des tribunaux*, 633, n° 13–14, 33; J du Jardin, 'Le ministère public dans ses fonctions non pénales', *Discours prononcé à l'audience solennelle de rentrée*, Sept. 2004, 33.

[34] Here, *codes* refers to the private publications of enacted law such as *Les Codes Larcier* or *Bruylant*.

practice. The fact that a decision of the *Cour de cassation* is an 'addition to enacted law' has even been ratified by the legislature when it provided that, just like a statute, every published judgment of the court must be translated into both national languages (Dutch and French).[35] There are also cases where the legislature expressly refers to established case law to fill lacunae in enacted law or in regulations putting into effect enacted law.[36]

As a result, the lower courts are urged to consider decisions of the *Cour de cassation* to avoid a reversal of their judgments. This practice is well-illustrated by the decision of the *Cour d'appel de Liège* on 23 April 1987[37] when construing the term *maison de débauche ou de prostitution* contained in the *Code penal*.[38] The *Cour d'appel de Liège* explicitly referred to a precedent of the *Cour de cassation*[39] as providing the true meaning of the provision, despite the fact that an analysis of the *travaux préparatoires* undoubtedly would have led to a different interpretation as pleaded by the appellant.[40]

(iii) Overruling Principles in the *Cour de cassation*

One could think, at first sight, that genuine overruling cases do not exist in Belgium, given the role formally assigned to the *Cour de cassation*. As the guardian of the true authority of statutory law, the *Cour de cassation* will only depart from one of its precedents when the latter is incorrect in this sense. Furthermore, one can argue that the formally non-binding character of Belgian case law makes the concept of overruling unnecessary, given that the court may simply ignore a single decision of its own of which it now disapproves.

However, such an intuitive assessment is unconvincing in the light of the practice of the *Cour de cassation*. The *Cour de cassation*'s great concern to ensure uniformity in case law and, especially, continuity within its own decisions[41] shows that departures are not self-evident. This makes sense if one takes into account the role fulfilled in practice by the *Cour de cassation*. Since the nineteenth century,

[35] *Loi du 15 juin 1935 concernant l'emploi des langues en matière judiciaire*, Moniteur belge, 22 June 1935, art. 28 and the *Exposé des motifs* in [1935] *Pasinomie*, 409, esp. 410.

[36] See, for instance, *Arrêté royal n° 78 du 10 novembre 1967 relatif à l'art de guérir, à l'exercice des professions qui s'y rattachent et aux commissions médicales*, art. 50, *Moniteur belge*, 14 Nov. 1967.

[37] [1987] *Journal des tribunaux*, 575.

[38] Art. 380 *bis*, 2.

[39] Cass., 30 Apr. 1985 [1986] *Journal des tribunaux*, 89.

[40] An analysis of the *travaux préparatoires* of art. 380*bis*, 2° of the *Code pénal* reveals that the terms *maison de débauche ou de prostitution* were treated as equivalent by the Commission of Justice (*Commission de la Justice*), whereas the *Cour de cassation* ruled that the former was broader than the latter (*Proposition de loi supprimant la réglementation officielle de la prostitution, Documents parlementaires—Chambre des Représentants*, 1946–1947, n° 421). See M Vincineau, *La débauche en droit et le droit à la débauche* (Université Libre de Bruxelles, 1985), 150–5 and 228–31.

[41] This concern has been manifest since the creation of the *Cour de cassation*. See, for instance, I Plaisant, 'Discours du 19 décembre 1833' [1834] I *Pasicrisie*, 8; H Lenaerts, 'Dire le droit en cassation aujourd'hui' [1991] *Journal des tribunaux*, 534, n° 10.

the *Cour de cassation* has considered that, besides being the guardian of statutory law, it also has to maintain uniformity within Belgian case law as a whole. And, in order to achieve such a task, it sometimes has to act as a regulating court and to adapt the law to the need of a society in constant evolution.[42] The function, so understood, of the *Cour de cassation* leads to the emergence of a jurisprudence of overruling which allows a dialectic between stability and change, both of which are encompassed in the *Cour de cassation*'s role.

Furthermore, if the concept of overruling has no place in the Belgian system, we might ask why the *Parquet général près la Cour de cassation*[43] is so concerned to discuss the reasons justifying a reversal in the *Cour de cassation*'s case law. Originally, such a discussion essentially took place extra-judicially, in the yearly *mercuriale* of the *Procureur général*, i.e. the formal speech on 'a subject suitable for the occasion' that the head of the *Parquet général* has to give at the time of the return of the judiciary after the annual holiday.[44]

Procureur général Faider had already emphasized in the 1880s the 'progressive' nature of case law. Some variations among the precedents of the *Cour de cassation* were still explained by virtue of continuous modifications of enacted law, judges' personalities, or misconstructions of statutes, while others were already depicted as the result of the changing nature of society.[45]

A real articulation of the reasons which legitimate a departure by the *Cour de cassation* from one of its previous decisions was first developed in 1928 by *Procureur général* Paul Leclercq.[46] As a matter of principle, he stressed that the *Cour de cassation* is bound by its precedents because of its role to maintain uniform construction of enacted law to guarantee 'social peace' and ensure 'legal certainty'. This mission implies that 'a wrong but permanent interpretation is preferable to successive and contradictory ones'. He emphasized that the *Cour de cassation* is not 'a learned society where the best solution to a legal problem is indefinitely discussed'.[47] From this perspective, the erroneous character of a decision of the *Cour de cassation* is irrelevant, provided that the lower courts do not 'rebel' against it.[48] For Leclercq, the crucial justification for reversal in case law is a 'breakdown in *paix judiciaire*',[49] said to be a 'new fact' arisen after the

[42] See the annual reports the *Cour de cassation* has been delivering since 1998.

[43] On the functions of the *Parquet general près la Cour decassation*, see n. 27 above.

[44] Such annual speeches have been compulsory since 1869. See the *Loi du 18 juin 1869 sur l'organisation judiciaire*, art. 222, *Moniteur belge*, 26 June 1869, currently embodied in *Code judiciaire*, art. 351.

[45] C Faider, 'La première année de la Cour de cassation' [1884] *Belgique judiciaire*, cols. 73–74; 'Discours du 15 octobre 1886' [1887] I *Pasicrisie*, v.

[46] *Conclusions* before Cass., 26 Jan. 1928 [1928] I *Pasicrisie*, 63–7.

[47] Leclercq, n. 29 above, 74–75; *conclusions* before Cass., 26 Jan. 1928 [1928] I *Pasicrisie*, 64.

[48] [1928] I *Pasicrisie*, 67, n. 1.

[49] I shall call *paix judiciaire* the situation where lower courts are following the position advocated by the *Cour de cassation* on the legal issue under consideration. This phrase may be translated as 'judicial accord'. However, I shall keep the French expression given that no conceptual equivalent exists in English law where lower courts are forbidden to disobey House of Lords' rulings.

precedent at issue was handed down.[50] He listed three situations in which this might occur.[51] First, there is the rare circumstance where a decision of the *Cour de cassation*, instead of ending the controversies, has multiplied them, either because of its equivocal character or because it has not been understood by the legal profession. Secondly, the solution advocated by the *Cour de cassation* may be the object of an immediate adverse reaction from the lower courts. Thirdly, due to social, intellectual, or technical changes, it may be opportune either to reconsider solutions which seem too severe in the light of changed opinion, or to lay down the scope of particular rules regarding situations which did not exist at the time they were originally laid down. When he referred to the second cause of breakdown in *paix judiciaire* (immediate resistance from lower courts), Leclercq urged the *Cour de cassation* to ensure that the rejected precedent had not been too hastily formulated and that important aspects had not been overlooked either by counsel or by the member of the *Parquet général* concerned in the case.

In 1950, *Procureur général* Cornil endorsed the doctrine of his predecessor, but he made two principal developments.[52] First, he enlarged the concept of *paix judiciaire*: the *Cour de cassation* should consider the reactions to the previous decision, not only of the lower courts, but also of academic writers, public opinion, and speeches in the legislative Chambers. Secondly, he considered that, even when such *paix judiciaire* (in the extended sense) exists, a departure in the case law of the *Cour de cassation* is legitimate in the two following situations: the precedent at issue is manifestly erroneous, or it is outdated because the will of the Nation has significantly evolved. In these two situations, as Cornil acknowledged, it would generally be the case that the *paix judiciaire*, even taken in a narrow sense, would have been disturbed. Indeed, when a precedent is clearly mistaken or provides an interpretation of a statute which is outmoded by virtue of intellectual, social, or technical changes, it will usually be disregarded by lower courts before the *Cour de cassation* has had a chance to intervene. In substance, the theories of Leclercq and Cornil are closely akin to each other: the *Cour de cassation* has to follow its precedents, except when they are widely disputed. In such situations, this court has failed its mission of ensuring uniformity in case law. It has therefore to propound new solutions to bring back certainty in the law.

In the 1960s, *Procureur général* Hayoit de Termicourt stressed that the need for stability and certainty in the case law of the *Cour de cassation* stems from its mission of ensuring that lower courts comply with enacted law. He distinguished stability from stagnation, the latter producing 'ossification of the law'. In contrast, he defined stability in case law to be 'interpreting statutes with constancy in a given social state'. In his view, reversals in the case law of the *Cour de cassation* are

[50] P Leclercq, *conclusions* before Cass., 26 Jan. 1928 [1928] I *Pasicrisie*, 64, n. 2; comment under Cass., 23 Mar. 1933 [1933] I *Pasicrisie*, 177.

[51] *Conclusions* before Cass., 26 Jan. 1928 [1928] I *Pasicrisie*, 64–5; comment under Cass., 31 Jan. 1935 [1935] I *Pasicrisie*, 135–6.

[52] L Cornil, 'La Cour de cassation' [1948] *Journal des tribunaux*, 493.

'justified and even compelled' when an old statute is out of line with 'moral evolution, social or technical progress' provided that 'the terms of the statute do not forbid judges to soften, restrict or enlarge its scope'.[53]

Procureur général Ganshof van der Meersch continued in this line. While underlying the essential creative nature of the process of adjudication, he emphasized the importance of 'searching for an adequate balance between stability and evolution'.[54] Accordingly, he asserted that a reversal in the *Cour de cassation*'s case law must remain exceptional to comply with 'legitimate expectations' of individuals. Yet, he considered that a reversal is warranted in situations where there is no such reliance. This arises when the precedent is systematically disregarded by a significant number of lower courts (no *paix judiciaire*) or when 'the legal rule becomes unacceptable owing to exceptional changes in social structured relationships'.[55] In particular, he made the point that, because of the passivity of the legislature, an intervention of the *Cour de cassation* is often necessary.[56]

By contrast, the next *Procureur général*, Frederic Dumon, was much more conventional. He seemed to favour stability and certainty to conscious judicial evolution of the law and defined restrictively the situations where a modification in the case law of the *Cour de cassation* is acceptable.[57] Reacting against his predecessors, he made three observations. He first denied the need for the courts to develop the law because vague concepts evolve naturally without judicial intervention. Secondly, he stressed that changes might be brought about because of legislation in related areas. Thirdly, while acknowledging that the *Cour de cassation* is entitled to reverse a precedent when the *paix judiciaire* is impaired, he emphasized that such a departure is only conceivable if the court truly believes that it was mistaken. If not, an insurrection from lower courts could not lead the *Cour de cassation* to interpret a norm in a way of which it disapproves. In such a situation, the *Procureur général* must suggest to the competent public authorities a modification of the legislation or an interpretative statute.

At the end of the 1980s, *Procureur général* Krings continued, to some extent, with the cautious attitude displayed by Dumon. He reiterated that the Belgian Constitution did entrust the *Cour de cassation* with the task of sustaining 'stability in case law' and that this aim could only be achieved providing that this court ensures 'stability in its own case law'.[58] He nevertheless noted the important

[53] R Hayoit de Termicourt, 'Les audiences plénières à la Cour de cassation' [1967] *Journal des tribunaux*, 477, col. 1.

[54] WJ Ganshof van der Meersch, *Réflexions sur l'art de juger et l'exercice de la fonction judiciaire* (Bruylant, 1973), 5 and 7.

[55] WJ Ganshof van der Meersch, 'Propos sur le texte de la loi et les principes généraux du droit', [1970] *Journal des tribunaux*, 558 and n. 35.

[56] WJ Ganshof van der Meersch, 'Réflexions sur le droit international et la révision de la Constitution' [1968] *Journal des tribunaux*, 496, col. 3.

[57] F Dumon, *La mission des cours et tribunaux. Quelques réflexions* (Bruylant, 1975), 9–10; 'De l'Etat de droit' [1979] *Journal des tribunaux*, 478, nn. 28–29.

[58] E Krings, *Aspects de la contribution de la Cour de cassation à l'édification du droit* (Bruylant, 1990), 7, n° 4, and 81, n° 78.

evolutions which had occurred in the decisions of the *Cour de cassation* since 1950 and, therefore, its contribution to 'the edification of the law'. Yet, he underlined the different roles fulfilled by the legislature and the *Cour de cassation.* Primarily, he asserted that although this court has always tried to preserve a fair balance between the interests at stake, it is not entitled to make choices which, in the end, could have a political impact. Such choices belong to the legislature.[59] More generally, he stated that any judge is forbidden 'to decide *contra legem*' even if he is of the opinion that the statute under consideration is out of date. Secondly, he stressed that, as a matter of principle, the legislature provides for the future whereas the *Cour de cassation* settles past situations. Because the *Cour de cassation* decides on existing rights, it has to manifest 'a total independence and an objectivity without any flaws'.[60] However, with regard to the procedural rules which govern an appeal against a decision where a litigant failed to appear, Krings criticized the too formalistic attitude of the *Cour de cassation.* He recommended a reversal in case law on this point rather than a legislative modification in order to have 'immediate effects'.[61]

In 1994, *Avocat général* Piret asserted that the *Cour de cassation* has always been astute in respecting the legislature's will without substituting its own views. He emphasized that such an attitude 'prevents it neither from filling legal lacunae nor from modernising rules of law'.[62] When examining the reasons behind the reversal of the European Court of Human Rights in the *Borgers* case,[63] he referred to Professor Silvio Marcus Helmons' study and his observations on the phenomenon of departure in case law.[64] This study suggests that any final court has to be allowed to change its precedents. Yet, if a reversal is so fundamental that the new solution diametrically contradicts the previous one, it has to be justified by 'detailed and convincing reasons'.[65]

At the beginning of the twenty-first century, *Procureur général* du Jardin considered the mission of the *Cour de cassation* through what he calls 'the triad' which characterizes it, i.e. 'unity in case law, certainty and development of the law'. In this scheme, 'departures from precedents should remain exceptional'. They are, however, necessary when the law is unsatisfactory and leads to unpredictable results.[66]

[59] E. Krings, *Considérations sur l'Etat de droit, la séparation des pouvoirs et le pouvoir judiciaire* (Bruylant, 1989), n° 19, 26; *Aspects de la contribution de la Cour de cassation à l'édification du droit* (Bruylant, 1990), 80, n° 78.

[60] Ibid., 80, n° 78.

[61] E Krings, 'Considérations critiques pour un anniversaire' [1987] *Journal des tribunaux*, 551, n° 23.

[62] J-M Piret, 'Le parquet de cassation' [1994] *Journal des tribunaux*, 623, n° 7.

[63] *Borgers v Belgium*, 15 EHRR 92 (30 Oct. 1991) A240-B.

[64] J-M Piret, 'Le parquet de cassation' [1994] *Journal des tribunaux*, 628, n° 23.

[65] S Marcus Helmons, 'La présence du ministère public aux délibérations de la Cour de cassation ou l'affaire Borgers', in *Mélanges offerts à Jacques Velu. Présence du droit public et des droits de l'homme* (Bruylant, 1992), iii, 1380.

[66] J du Jardin, 'Audience plénière et unité d'interprétation du droit' [2001] *Journal des tribunaux*, 642.

In sum, one can say that most *Procureurs généraux* share the view that the *Cour de cassation* is generally bound by its precedents. However, to varying degrees, they all give, as reasons for reversals, the fact that the *paix judiciaire* is impaired and the character of a precedent has become outmoded by changes in society. Of course, these two situations are largely indeterminate and the *Procureurs généraux* define them with reference to their own perceptions of the respective roles of the *Cour de cassation* and Parliament. With regard to the legal force of the decisions of the *Cour de cassation*, it is striking to note that the mission of this Court shifted quickly from ensuring respect for enacted law by lower courts to sustaining uniformity in case law 'of which modernization of law and legal certainty are the corollaries'.[67]

The annual *mercuriale* is not the only occasion where the *Parquet général* discusses the circumstances in which the *Cour de cassation* is entitled to depart from an earlier position. Such considerations are also developed in the extensive advice (*conclusions*) on the legality of the judgment attacked the member of the *Parquet général* gives to the *Cour de cassation*. In a very large number of cases, the *Cour de cassation* follows such an advice (*arrêt rendu sur conclusions conformes*). According to the Belgian Supreme Court itself, its decisions have to be understood in the light of its *Parquet général*'s opinions.[68] This is especially true with respect to the decisions given by an enlarged bench of nine judges (*audience plénière*). The system of *audiences plénières* was established in 1954,[69] specifically to avoid conflicting decisions between the French and Dutch sections of a *Cour de cassation*'s chamber. But such a procedure is also considered suitable when the precedent at stake requires a new examination on the part of the *Cour de cassation* 'either given social or legislative evolutions, resistance from lower courts, academic controversies, or seeing its lack of internal consistency'.[70]

In reality, from the combination of more than a century of *mercuriales* and nearly fifty years of *conclusions* given in cases decided by an enlarged bench (*audience plénière*) springs up a genuine jurisprudence of overruling in the *Cour de cassation*.[71] The latter can be summarized as follows:

(1) As a matter of principle, the *Cour de cassation* strictly follows its previous decisions.

(2) The erroneous character of a decision of the *Cour de cassation* is neither a sufficient ground to depart from it nor a necessary prerequisite.

[67] H Lenaerts, 'Dire le droit en cassation aujourd'hui' [1991] *Journal des tribunaux*, 534, n° 10.

[68] *Rapport annuel de la Cour de cassation de Belgique (1997–1998)* (presses du Moniteur belge, 1998), 80. This annual report states that 'the *conclusions* of the *Parquet général* do clarify the short reasoning of the Court'.

[69] *Loi du 25 février 1954 relative à l'organisation de la Cour de cassation*, art. 134, *Moniteur belge*, 5 Mar. 1954; currently embodied in *Code judiciaire*, art. 131.

[70] R Hayoit de Termicourt, 'Les audiences plénières à la Cour de cassation' [1967] *Journal des tribunaux*, 477, col.1. See also J du Jardin, 'Audience plénière et unité d'interprétation du droit' [2001] *Journal des tribunaux*, 643 ff.

[71] For further developments, see I Rorive, *Le revirement de jurisprudence. Etude de droit anglais et de droit belge* (Bruylant, 2003). For a discussion of recent cases, see also the annual reports of the *Cour de cassation*.

(3) A departure in the case law of the *Cour de cassation* requires *prima facie* a 'new fact' which can either be a lack of *paix judiciaire* understood in a broad sense (adverse reactions towards the previous decision from lower courts, academic writers, or parliamentarians) or some material change in circumstances or in values.

(4) Such a lack of *paix judiciaire* is, however, an insufficient ground to justify a departure in case law. There must be additional 'good reasons' for legitimizing the change, such as compelling considerations of consistency, justice, and certainty or a misreading of the legislature's intention.

(5) Even where there are good reasons, a change through case law may be rejected either because the legitimate expectations of individuals are at stake or the reform in question will be better dealt with in Parliament.

(iv) Overruling Principles in the House of Lords

The jurisprudence of overruling of the *Cour de cassation* is very close to the overruling principles developed in the House of Lords after the 1966 Practice Statement, where the Law Lords decided 'while treating former decision of this House as normally binding, to depart from a previous decision when it appears right to do so'.[72] Since then, several authors have discussed the existence of a jurisprudence of overruling in the decisions of the House of Lords.[73] In Professor Harris's view 'a settled jurisprudence would require two things: first, that it be possible to articulate principles which would support the exercise of the power in those cases in which it has been used and also the refusal to exercise it in other cases; and secondly, evidence that such putative principles had the support of the bulk of judicial *dicta* on the subject'.[74] He considers that the first requirement is fulfilled, namely principles bearing out the exercise of the Practice Statement, whereas the second requirement, namely an explicit articulation of these principles, is largely lacking.

What seems certain is that the declarations of the Law Lords on the appropriate criteria to look at when considering the issue of overruling have developed to a

[72] *Practice Statement (Judicial Precedent)* [1966] 1 WLR 1234.

[73] See, for instance. R Brazier, 'Overruling House of Lords Criminal Cases' [1973] *CLR* 98; L V Prott, 'When Will a Superior Court Overrule Its Own Decision?' (1978) 52 *ALJ* 304; G Maher, 'Statutory Interpretation and Overruling in the House of Lords' [1981] *Scottish LR* 85 A Paterson, *The Law Lords* (Macmillan Press, 1982), 156; J Stone, 'The Lords at the Crossroads—When to 'Depart' and How!' (1972) 46 *ALJ* 483; J Stone, 'On the Liberation of Appellate Judges. How Not to Do It!' (1972) 35 *MLR* 469; J Stone, *Precedent and Law: Dynamics of Common Law Growth* (Butterworths, 1985), 172–85; I McLeod, *Legal Method* (Macmillan Press, 1993), 140–53; and the studies of JW Harris mentioned in the following footnote.

[74] J W Harris, 'Towards Principles of Overruling—When Should a Final Court of Appeal Second Guess?' (1990) 10 *OJLS* 135, esp. 136; see also JW Harris, 'Murphy Makes it Eight—Overruling Comes to Negligence' (1991) 11 *OJLS* 417; JW Harris, *Legal Philosophies* (2nd edn., Butterworths, 1997), ch. 13.

certain extent 'the status of case law in the sense of being cited in argument by counsel and developed in later cases'.[75] These overruling standards exceed the Practice Statement's guidelines. They are difficult to articulate for several reasons. First, their Lordships are reluctant to classify the instances where a departure is required or is undesirable. In this vein, Lord Reid stated: 'I would not seek to categorise cases in which [the Practice Statement] should or cases in which it should not be used. As time passes experience will supply some guide'.[76] Secondly, the overruling principles themselves are evolving. Lord Wilberforce emphasized this feature when pleading for overruling *Congreve*[77] on a point of statutory interpretation. He said, 'the discretion conferred by the Practice Statement... is a general one. We should exercise it sparingly and try to keep it governed by stated principles. But the fact that the circumstances of one particular case cannot be brought precisely within the formulae used in others, of a different character, should not be fatal to its exercise—or the discretion would become ossified.'[78]

As a matter of fact, there are principles which not merely explain, but also actually justify, the exercise of (or the refusal to exercise) the Practice Statement power. Such a jurisprudence of overruling emerges from the cases where the House of Lords explicitly departed from one of its precedents or refused to do so by virtue of the Practice Statement power.[79] Before departing from an earlier decision, the House of Lords must be satisfied that the present law will be altogether improved. Furthermore, this *prima facie* requirement is subject to constraining principles.[80]

As to the *improvement of the law requirement*, the fact that a precedent of the House of Lords is obviously wrong does not constitute sufficient grounds for overruling it. Lord Reid's much-quoted statement in *Knuller* offers a striking piece of evidence that incorrectness is not a sufficient ground to justify overruling a precedent of the House of Lords. Although he dissented in *Shaw*,[81] the case under review, and stressed in *Knuller* that he was still of the opinion that *Shaw* was wrong, he said, 'our change of practice in no longer regarding previous decisions

[75] G Maher, 'Statutory Interpretation and Overruling in the House of Lords' [1981] *Scottish LR* 87.

[76] *R* v *National Insurance Commissioner, ex p. Hudson* [1972] 1 AC 944, 966.

[77] *Congreve* v *Inland Revenue Commissioners* [1948] 1 All ER 948.

[78] *Vestey* v *Inland Revenue Commissioners* [1980] AC 1148, 1178.

[79] Since the 1966 Practice Statement, the House of Lords expressly departed from a precedent in at least 10 cases: *EL Oldendorff and Co GmbH* v *Tradax Export SA, The Johanna Oldendorff* [1974] AC 479; *Miliangos* v *George Frank (Textiles) Ltd* [1976] AC 443; *Dick* v *Burgh of Falkirk* [1976] SLT 21, 1976 SC (HL) 1, HL(Sc); *Vestey* v *Inland Revenue Commissioners* [1980] AC 1148; *R* v *Secretary of State for the Home Department, ex p. Khawaja* [1984] AC 74; *R* v *Shivpuri* [1987] AC 1; *R* v *Howe* [1987] AC 417; *Murphy* v *Brentwood District Council* [1991] 1 AC 398; *Westdeutsche Landesbank Girozentrale* v *Islington London Borough Council* [1996] AC 669; *R* v *G and another* [2004] 1 AC 1034.

[80] This presentation is primarily based on Professor Harris's research which I further developed in *Le revirement de jurisprudence. Etude de droit anglais et de droit belge* (Bruylant, 2003). Among the studies currently available, JW Harris's analysis provides the finest synthesis of these overruling principles. By contrast with other academic writers, he not only itemises the criteria taken into account in particular instances, but he outlines a model which is able to articulate them. In addition, he focuses on what the House of Lords is actually saying and doing, rather than what it could or should be doing.

[81] *Shaw* v *DPP* [1962] AC 220.

of this House as absolutely binding does not mean that whenever we think that a previous decision was wrong we should reverse it. In the general interest of certainty in the law we must be sure that there is some very good reason before we so act'.[82] In addition, to justify an overruling there is no need to assert that the House of Lords was mistaken when it decided the impugned precedent. Emphasis may be put on the fact that the circumstances had evolved tremendously from those prevailing in the earlier case.[83]

In order to determine whether an overruling will improve the law in general, the House of Lords takes into account considerations such as justice, certainty, and coherence.[84] As a matter of fact, a 'high threshold requirement' should be satisfied.[85] Their Lordships define the requirement of *justice* not in the light of the unjust results in the particular instance, but in view of the consequences that a universalized application of the impugned ruling had on an assignable class of persons.[86] The *certainty* consideration provides that the law may need to be changed because the current rule leads to unpredictable results or does not meet the 'bright' lines requirement.[87] The certainty that the content of legal rules demands is often linked with *consistency* considerations such as avoiding over-subtle distinctions that a precedent may induce in later cases.[88] Considerations of coherence can be more broadly referred to as the need for the law to be consistent in the area under consideration.[89]

Besides the improvement of the law requirement, there are four constraining principles which underlie the terms of the Practice Statement and the overruling cases. They import considerations of finality, reliance, comity with the legislature, and mootness.

82 [1973] AC 435, 455. In the same line, see *R* v *National Insurance Commissioner, ex p. Hudson* [1972] 1 AC 944, 966 *per* Lord Reid, 973 *per* Lord Morris, 996 *per* Lord Pearson, 1023 *per* Lord Simon of Glaisdale. More recently, see, for instance, *R* v *Kansal* [2002] 2 AC 69, para [27] *per* Lord Steyn; *Rees* v *Darlington Memorial Hospital NHS Trust* [2004] 1 AC 309, para [86] *per* Lord Hutton, para [102] *per* Lord Millett.

83 In *Miliangos*, the majority of the Law Lords did not conclude that the *Havana* decision was erroneous at the time at which it was pronounced ([1976] AC 443, 460 *per* Lord Wilberforce, 497 *per* Lord Cross of Chelsea, 501 *per* Lord Edmund-Davies). The departure was justified both in the light of commercial transformations which had occurred since *Havana* had been decided and in view of the fact that 'a new and more satisfactory rule [was] capable of being stated' without 'undue practical difficulties' (ibid., 467 *per* Lord Wilberforce). See also *Knuller (Publishing, Printing and Promotions) Ltd* v *DPP* [1973] AC 435, 484 *per* Lord Simon of Glaisdale.

84 JW Harris, 'Towards Principles of Overruling—When Should a Final Court of Appeal Second Guess?' (1990) 10 *OJLS* 135, 152–6.

85 *Jindal Iron and Steel Co Ltd* v *Islamic Solidarity Shipping Company Jordan Inc* [2005] 1 WLR 1363, 1370 para [16] *per* Lord Steyn.

86 *Vestey* v *Inland Revenue Commissioners* [1980] AC 1148, 1197 *per* Lord Edmund-Davies; *R* v *G and another* [2004] 1 AC 1034, 1955 para [33] *per* Lord Bingham, 1058–9 para [45] *per* Lord Steyn.

87 *EL Oldendorff and Co GmbH* v *Tradax Export SA, The Johanna Oldendorff* [1974] AC 479, 533 *per* Lord Reid, 555 and 561 *per* Lord Diplock; *Knuller (Publishing, Printing and Promotions) Ltd* v *DPP* [1973] AC 435, 480 *per* Lord Diplock; *Murphy* v *Brentwood District Council* [1991] 1 AC 398, 456 *per* Lord Mackay, 465 *per* Lord Keith, 481 *per* Lord Bridge, 487 *per* Lord Oliver, 497 *per* Lord Jauncey.

88 *EL Oldendorff and Co GmbH* v *Tradax Export SA, The Johanna Oldendorff* [1974] AC 479, 535 *per* Lord Reid; *R v Howe* [1987] AC 417, 437 *per* Lord Bridge, 438 *per* Lord Brandon.

89 *Westdeutsche Landesbank Girozentrale* v *Islington London Borough Council* [1996] AC 669, 710 and 713–14 *per* Lord Browne-Wilkinson.

(1) The '*no-new reason principle*' prevents an overruling 'where the contentions for or against the question of law in issue fail to introduce new reasons—that is, reasons not taken into account in the earlier case'.[90] By extension, the House of Lords does not feel confident in overruling one of its precedents in cases where neither party was prepared to advance reasons for declining to follow it.[91] The concept of new reasons is broad. For instance, the arguments in the precedent may have overlooked some important principles,[92] or evidence of legislative intention,[93] or have failed to advert to undesirable consequences which subsequent experience has brought to light.[94] There may have been some material change in circumstances, such as to require a new legal outcome to the issue in question.[95] And the law may have developed in a direction away from the doctrine of the precedent under review.[96] The justification for this constraining principle is to preclude the possibility for the House of Lords of third-guessing.[97]

(2) Considerations of *reliance* restrain the use of the Practice Statement 'if it can be shown that citizens who have relied upon the old ruling would thereby be prejudiced'.[98] As a matter of fact, an overruling has a retrospective effect and the House of Lords has not yet acknowledged the technique of prospective overruling, except incidentally, through individual statements of a few Law Lords.[99] However, the justified reliance principle is not an absolute one. First, the argument of

[90] JW Harris, 'Towards Principles of Overruling—When Should a Final Court of Appeal Second Guess?' (1990) 10 *OJLS* 135, 157–69, 196. See, for instance, *Fitzleet Estates Ltd* v *Cherry (Inspector of Taxes)* [1977] 3 All ER 996, 999 *per* Lord Wilberforce, 1000 *per* Viscount Dilhorne, 1002–3 *per* Lord Edmund-Davies; *Paal Wilson and Co AS* v *Partenreederei Hannah Blumenthal* [1982] 3 WLR 1149, 1162–3 *per* Lord Brandon; *Knuller (Publishing, Printing and Promotions) Ltd* v *DPP* [1973] AC 435, 463 *per* Lord Morris; *Gregg* v *Scott* [2005] UKHL 2, para [85] *per* Lord Hoffmann.

[91] *Kuddus (AP)* v *Chief Constable of Leicestershire Constabulary* [2002] 2 AC 122, 137, para [36] *per* Lord Mackay. Note that in *Westdeutsche Landesbank* (n. 89, above) the House of Lords invited counsel to discuss the overruling of a precedent heavily criticised by academics.

[92] See, for instance, *R* v *Secretary of State for the Home Department, ex p. Khawaja* [1984] AC 74, 109 *per* Lord Scarman, 125 *per* Lord Bridge; *R* v *G and another* [2004] 1 AC 1034, 1055, para [32] *per* Lord Bingham.

[93] See, for instance, *R* v *Shivpuri* [1987] AC 1, 21 *per* Lord Bridge; *R* v *G and another* [2004] 1 AC 1034, 1056, para [35] *per* Lord Bingham, 1058–9 para [45] *per* Lord Steyn, 1065–6 para [70] *per* Lord Rodger.

[94] See, for instance, *Vestey* v *Inland Revenue Commissioners* [1980] AC 1148, 1176 *per* Lord Wilberforce, 1187 *per* Viscount Dilhorne, 1196 *per* Lord Edmund-Davies.

[95] See, for instance, *Miliangos* v *George Frank (Textiles) Ltd* [1976] AC 443, 462 *per* Lord Wilberforce, 497 *per* Lord Cross of Chelsea, 501 *per* Lord Edmund-Davies.

[96] See, for instance, *Dick* v *Burgh of Falkirk* [1976] SLT 21at 29 *per* Lord Kilbrandon.

[97] See, for instance, *R* v *National Insurance Commissioner, ex p. Hudson* [1972] 1 AC 944, 996–7 *per* Lord Pearson; *R* v *Kansal* [2002] 2 AC 69, para [110] *per* Lord Hutton; *Rees* v *Darlington Memorial Hospital NHS Trust* [2004] 1 AC 309, para [31] *per* Lord Steyn.

[98] JW Harris, 'Towards Principles of Overruling—When Should a Final Court of Appeal Second Guess?' (1990) 10 *OJLS* 135, 169–77, 196. See, for instance, *Westdeutsche Landesbank Girozentrale* v *Islington London Borough Council* [1996] AC 669, 714 *per* Lord Browne-Wilkinson; *Jindal Iron and Steel Co Ltd* v *Islamic Solidarity Shipping Company Jordan Inc* [2005] 1 WLR 1363, 1369–70, paras. [15]–[16] *per* Lord Steyn.

[99] In favour of prospective overruling in the House of Lords, see Lord Simon of Glaisdale in *R* v *National Insurance Commissioner, ex p. Hudson* [1972] 1 AC 944, 1026 (Lord Diplock concurring on that point at 1015) and in *Miliangos* v *George Frank (Textiles) Ltd* [1976] AC 443, 490; Lord Hope in *Arthur*

reliance has little weight in cases where the ruling at issue has led to over-subtle distinctions in subsequent instances.[100] Secondly, upsetting individuals' legitimate expectations does not make any sense in some class of cases where such prejudicial reliance is not plausible.[101]

(3) The '*comity with the legislature*' principle implies that 'the House of Lords ought not to overrule a prior decision of its own where, subsequent to the decision, parliament has acted on the assumption that the ruling in the earlier case represents the law'.[102] Nevertheless, such a principle must be accepted with considerable circumspection. Inferring any legislative intention from the fact that Parliament has enacted legislation in the general area of the impugned decision would always be problematic. In this respect, Lord Reid said: 'I am not greatly impressed by the argument that Parliament must be held to have approved that decision because in recent years there have been several occasions when parliament could appropriately have dealt with it if it had disapproved of the decision.'[103]

(4) The '*mootness doctrine*' implies that 'courts should not undertake review and development of the law where to do so would have no bearing on any litigated dispute'.[104] In civil litigation, where the public interest in certainty is not as paramount as it is in criminal cases, their Lordships seem to be of the opinion that an overruling is not justified if, on the facts, it makes no difference to the outcome of the appeal. This concern is reflected in their insistence in many positive overruling cases on showing that distinguishing the contested precedent is not sound and that exercising the Practice Statement power is the only appropriate path. However, the mootness principle is far from being conclusive,[105] and this doctrine does not always provide a satisfactory explanation why, in any particular case, the House of Lords resorts to its overruling power rather than employing the distinguishing technique.[106]

JS Hall & Co v *Simons* [2002] 1 AC 615 and in *R* v *Governor of Her Majesty's Prison Brockhill, Ex p. Evans (no. 2)* [2001] 2 AC 19. See JW Harris, 'Retrospective Overruling and the Declaratory Theory in the United Kingdom—Three Recent Decisions' [2002] *Revue de droit de l'U.L.B*, 153.

[100] See, for instance, Lord Reid's considerations in *EL Oldendorff and Co GmbH* v *Tradax Export SA, The Johanna Oldendorff* [1974] AC 479, 535.

[101] *Dick* v *Burgh of Falkirk* [1976] SLT 21, 28–29 *per* Lord Kilbrandon; *R* v *Shivpuri* [1987] AC 1, 11 *per* Lord Hailsham, 23 *per* Lord Bridge; *Murphy* v *Brentwood District Council* [1991] 1 AC 398, 472 *per* Lord Keith.

[102] JW Harris, 'Towards Principles of Overruling—When Should a Final Court of Appeal Second Guess?' (1990) 10 *OJLS* 135, 177. See, for instance, *Knuller (Publishing, Printing and Promotions) Ltd* v *DPP* [1973] AC 435, 466 *per* Lord Morris, 489 *per* Lord Simon of Glaisdale, 496 *per* Lord Kilbrandon. See also *R* v *National Insurance Commissioner, ex p. Hudson* [1972] 1 AC 944, 1025 *per* Lord Simon of Glaisdale.

[103] *Knuller* [1973] AC 435, 455.

[104] JW Harris, 'Towards Principles of Overruling—When Should a Final Court of Appeal Second Guess?' (1990) 10 *OJLS* 135, 180.

[105] See, for instance, Lord Keith's and Lord Oliver's attitude in *Murphy* v *Brentwood District Council* [1991] 1 AC 398.

[106] Compare, for instance, the House of Lords' position towards *Anns* v *Merton London Borough Council* [1978] AC 728 in *D & F Estates Ltd* v *Church Commissioners for England* [1989] 1 AC 177 and in *Murphy* v *Brentwood District Council* [1991] 1 AC 398.

The Practice Statement of 1966 marks a turning point in the way the House of Lords conceives its role as a superior court. Although its primary function remains the resolution of disputed claims, it acknowledges fulfilling a second function which is, in substance, quasi-legislative. In view of Parliament's supremacy, this secondary function cannot overtake the first one and, therefore, the overruling power is exercised with due restraint, and is controlled by constraining principles. One has, however, to keep in mind that overruling is only one of the techniques used by the House of Lords to induce a significant change in its previous decisions. It sometimes outflanks a precedent without recourse to the Practice Statement. And it may neutralize decisions which it dislikes by confining them to their own facts. There have been comparatively few attempts in the speeches of their Lordships to explain why, in any particular case, the House resorts to the Practice Statement power rather than employing the traditional techniques of development of the law. This is owing to the fact that the reasoning in the overruling cases is primarily directed towards the substantive question of law under review.

(v) Conclusion

A comparative approach of the revealed motivations behind the phenomenon of departure as practised by the *Cour de cassation* and the House of Lords challenges the appearance that formal definitions provide for the difference in attitude towards precedents between the two countries and, more broadly, between common law and civil law systems, without denying the existence of a distinctive legal culture.

An analysis of how reversals proceed in the case law of the *Cour de cassation* reveals that a single decision of this Court may be the sole source for a legal rule. Similar to the House of Lords, when a reversal occurs in the case law of the *Cour de cassation*, it operates retrospectively and has an immediate impact in the future on members of the community who were not parties to the litigation. The view that Belgian cases are only interpretative of enacted law, rather than a formal source of law, also does not stand up to analysis when confronted with the grounds justifying a reversal in the *Cour de cassation*'s case law. The *Procureurs généraux* emphasize that the primary mission of the Court is to sustain uniformity in its decisions, so as to provide reliable guidance for lower courts. From this perspective, they usually contend that a wrong but permanent interpretation of statute is preferable to successive and contradictory ones. This implies that a misconstruction of enacted law by the *Cour de cassation* becomes authoritative through its acceptance by the judiciary.

It is striking to note how similar are the responses that the Belgian and English systems give to the phenomenon of departure in case law, as practised at the highest level in the judiciary. While the *Cour de cassation* and the House of Lords consider themselves as generally bound by their precedents, they acknowledge that a departure from a previous position may be needed. As a matter of principle, both Courts stress the respect of past decisions. The erroneous character of a precedent is neither a sufficient condition nor a necessary one to justify a departure. In Belgium, the catalyst of the change is often worded in terms of a lack of *paix judiciaire*. Such an argument is also referred to by the Law Lords. For instance, in *R* v *G* Lord Bingham states:

> I do not think the criticism of *R.* v *Cadwell* expressed by academics, judges and practitioners should be ignored. A decision is not, of course, to be overruled or departed from simply because it meets with disfavour in the learned journals. But a decision which attracts reasoned and outspoken criticism by the leading scholars of the day, respected as authorities in the field, must command attention.[107]

To depart from a previous position, the Belgian *Parquet général* also stresses that a lack of *paix judiciaire* is not enough. There should be 'good reasons' linked to values of justice, consistency, and certainty. In addition, such reasons have to be counterbalanced by considerations of reliance and of the proper scope of judicial intervention.

In both countries, the construction of overruling principles emphasizes the inherent law-making power of judges which clashes with the notions of parliamentary sovereignty and democratic accountability. Their Lordships and the *Procureurs généraux* have been concerned to work out standards regulating overruling in the House of Lords and the *Cour de cassation*. They seem anxious to show that departures from precedents are not exercised in an arbitrary way.

There is, however, a different way 'to do things' in the two Courts, which accounts for a distinctive legal culture. Whereas the overruling principles are overtly discussed in the Law Lords' opinions, the decisions of the *Cour de cassation* are generally silent on this point. Although Belgian decisions of the *Cour de cassation* are more dialectic than their French counterparts, they still have the appearance of decree rather than opinion. This succinct style is consistent with the original task of the *Cour de cassation* to ensure that enacted law is properly construed by lower courts. Accordingly, it formulates clear-cut rulings in the form of a single majority decision. This feature accounts for the fact that the *contours* of the decisions of the *Cour de cassation* are broader than the decisions themselves, as acknowledged by the *Cour de cassation* itself.[108]

When searching for the circumstances which entitle the *Cour de cassation* to depart from one of its precedents, and for those which constrain it from doing so, the opinions of the members of its *Parquet général* are the primary material for consideration. The only explicit source for putative principles is, indeed, the *mercuriales* and the *conclusions* of the members of the *Parquet général près la Cour*

107 [2004] 1 AC 1034, 1055–6 para [34]. Other instances are developed in I Rorive, *Le revirement de jurisprudence. Etude de droit anglais et de droit belge* (Bruylant, 2003), 307.

108 See *Rapport de la Cour de cassation (1997–1998)* (presses du Moniteur belge, 1998), 80.

de cassation. Only on one occasion has the court itself expressed its opinion on the matter.[109] In this case, the State conceded that it was liable to relatives for the death of a soldier, but it disputed the way damages were calculated by the Brussels *Cour d'appel*. The *Cour de cassation* rejected the claim and referred to an earlier decision made in 1937. It stressed that 'this was the case law of the court' to be upheld unless a party puts forward 'a new reason' which 'would oblige' it to review its prior position.

In the 1920s and 1930s, when Paul Leclercq was *Procureur général*, several abstracts in the *Pasicrisie*, highlighting the doctrine of the *Cour de cassation*, seem to suggest that this Court had developed a theory articulating the circumstances which entitled it to modify its precedents.[110] In reality, a close analysis of these opinions shows that the *Cour de cassation* did not actually tackle this issue. The abstracts were written by the *Parquet général* under the supervision of Leclercq. They actually embody the ideas developed by Leclercq in his *conclusions* and in the footnotes which he personally enclosed in the *Pasicrisie*, rather than expressing the conception of the *Cour de cassation*.[111]

Such a methodological difference of practice between the House of Lords and the *Cour de cassation* does not undermine the fact that both Courts justify reversals in their case law, so as to participate in the modernization of the law. In their own formal way, they both take responsibility for shaping, restating, and ordering the doctrine that they themselves produce.

[109] Cass., 3 Feb. 1938 [1938] I *Pasicrisie*, 33, esp. 34.

[110] Cass., 26 Jan. 1928 [1928] I *Pasicrisie*, 63, 5 with the mention '*examiné par le ministère public*'; Cass., 21 June 1928 [1928] I *Pasicrisie*, 200, 2 with the mention of '*solution implicite*'; Cass., 27 Sept. 1928 [1928] I *Pasicrisie*, 235, 3 with the mention of '*solution implicite*'; Cass., 23 Mar. 1933 [1933] I *Pasicrisie*, 176, 4 with the mention of '*solution implicite*'; Cass., 31 Jan. 1935 [1935] I *Pasicrisie*, 133, 8 with the mention of '*solution implicite*'; Cass., 28 May 1936 [1936] I *Pasicrisie*, 273, 6 with no special mention but with reference to Cass., 23 Mar. 1933.

[111] This has been misconstrued by some academics as instances where the *Cour de cassation* formulated rules about the binding force of its precedents. See, for instance R Walormont, 'L'autorité du précédent judiciaire dans la jurisprudence de la Cour de cassation en Belgique et en France' [1951] *Annales de droit et de sciences politiques*, 77.

14

The Rationality of Tradition

*Lionel Smith**

This Chapter is concerned with the binding power of precedent. It argues that the commitment to a particular outcome, which is represented by an official decision on the issue, rightly provides a rational basis for dispensing with any re-examination of the same issue. This rational basis is independent from, and incommensurable with, the rationality (the set of substantive reasons) underlying the original decision. The irreconcilable tension between the two modes of rationality is resolved differently in different legal systems; the common law solution is that in some situations, the rationality that favours consistency is privileged as a mandatory rule of law (*stare decisis*) that disallows access to the rationality based on substantive reasons. Even in these systems, however, rationality based on reasons must sometimes prevail, so that a prior decision now thought to be incorrect can be abandoned. Paradoxically, the rationality based on consistency is both the source of, and the greatest hindrance to, the judicial power to develop the law.

(i) Introduction

The binding power of precedent was a subject of enduring concern for Jim Harris.[1] This Chapter attempts to shed new light on the ways in which precedent binds by reference to recent developments in thinking about rational decision-making. The argument will be that the way in which precedent binds is rational, but that the rationality in question is incommensurable with the rationality based on the substantive reasons that come into play when a decision must be made as a

* James McGill Professor of Law, Faculty of Law and Institute of Comparative Law, McGill University. I am grateful to Bruce Chapman and Robert H. Stevens for their helpful comments, although any faults in the analysis are mine alone.

[1] R Cross and JW Harris, *Precedent in English Law* (4th edn., Clarendon Press, 1991); JW Harris, 'The Privy Council and the Common Law' (1990) 106 *LQR* 574; JW Harris, 'Towards Principles of Overruling—When Should a Final Court of Appeal Second Guess?' (1990) 10 *OJLS* 135; JW Harris, '*Murphy* Makes it Eight—Overruling Comes to Negligence' (1991) 11 *OJLS* 416; JW Harris, 'Retrospective Overruling and the Declaratory Theory in the United Kingdom: Three Recent Decisions' (2002) 26 *Revue de droit de l'Université libre de Bruxelles* 153.

matter of first impression. This incommensurability is a notorious source of tension for judges. At the same time, an understanding of the rationality of consistency will allow us to generate a typology of situations in which judges can rationally and properly refuse to follow a precedent.

(ii) Modes of Rationality in Decision-Making

Law aspires to be rational, and so too does judicial decision-making. Rationality is usually understood to mean action or decision according to reasons. In the absence of any precedent, a judge addresses a point directly and is able to evaluate the reasons for deciding either way. In the words of Morden JA, which deserve to be immortal, '[i]n the absence of binding authority clearly on point it may reasonably be said that the law is what it ought to be'.[2] The difficult question, of course, arises where there is authority that has some binding force, and that authority points to a result that is different from what the particular judge thinks the law ought to be. Assume that the judge thinks that, according to her evaluation of all the relevant reasons for deciding, the plaintiff should win; but some authority indicates that the defendant should win. If the judge follows the authority, is she acting irrationally?

Chapman has evaluated reasons for acting in the context of prior commitments, such as promises or threats.[3] Assume that I have made a promise or a threat to you that, under certain conditions, I will perform some action. When the conditions are fulfilled, I find that all the reasons that operate on me, when taken together and weighed up, point in the direction of not performing the action. In that situation, it seems, it would be irrational of me to perform the action.[4] Chapman shows that this is not necessarily the case. There is more to rationality than reasons for acting. There are also normative requirements of rationality. Chapman illustrates this by an example drawn from theoretical reasoning.

[2] *Ontario (Securities Commission) v Greymac Credit Corp.* (1986) 30 DLR (4th) 1 at 24 (Ont. CA); in dismissing an appeal, the Sup Ct of Canada adopted in full the judgment of Morden JA: [1988] 2 SCR 172. Compare Willes J in *Millar v Taylor* (1769) 4 Burr 2303, 2312: '[P]rivate justice, moral fitness and public convenience, when applied to a new subject, make common law without precedent, much more when received and approved by usage'.

[3] B Chapman, 'Legal Analysis of Economics: Solving the Problem of Rational Commitment' (2004) 79 *Chicago–Kent L Rev* 471.

[4] Obviously, if I am concerned about my reputation as one who keeps promises or threats, this will be one of the reasons to be considered, which points in favour of performing the action. But this factor does not complicate the analysis, because I am assuming that when all the reasons (including that one, if applicable) are considered, the balance is against performing the action. Similarly, the problem addressed by Chapman is not resolved by positing that I have a moral commitment to keep my promises or threats. That would be another reason for performing the action, and we have assumed that the reasons in play point away from performing the action. In other words, the problem might never arise in the case of a person who always kept promises or threats as a matter of principle; but the question remains to be answered whether, in the case of a person who does *not* now have good reasons to perform the action, it is nonetheless rational to perform it because of the prior commitment.

Suppose that a person believes the proposition TG: 'Toronto is in Germany', and the proposition GE: 'Germany is in Europe'. Such a person would presumably conclude by believing proposition TE: 'Toronto is in Europe'.[5] Chapman argues that in a case like this, what makes the person believe TE is not a reason, so much as the simple requirement of internal consistency:

[Y]ou have no reason, based on these beliefs, to believe TE. Indeed, you have many other reasons, independent of these beliefs, *not* to believe TE. And it is not that these other reasons, based on independent beliefs, simply prevail over, or outweigh, the reason you have to believe TE based on your beliefs in TG and GE. Rather, it is that there simply is no such reason to believe TE at all. *Any* independent reason not to believe TE would be enough to provide an all-things-considered reason not to believe TE, at least if the only 'reason' that you claimed for believing TE was the fact that you believed TG and GE. This suggests that the weighing of conflicting reasons simply has no application here. The beliefs in TG and GE add nothing into the balance of reasons for believing TE.

Building on work by Broome,[6] Chapman argues that in this case the person is normatively required to believe TE, given his other beliefs TG and GE. It would be irrational to believe TG and GE and not to believe TE. This is so even though the person has no reason that directly points to a belief in TE. This kind of normative requirement is not subject to any process of comparison or weighing, as may occur when reasons are being evaluated. So long as one believes TG and GE, a failure to believe TE would be irrational.

Reasons, as such, point directly to the issue to be resolved, and may be weighed against one another. If the person has seen a globe, or more than one, showing that TE is false, that is a reason to disbelieve TE. If the person is told, by someone whose opinion he respects, that TE is true, that is a reason to believe TE. If the person were required to decide whether or not he believed TE, these reasons would have to be weighed against one another.

Applying this analysis to commitments like threats and promises, Chapman argues that an earlier commitment to a course of action (threat or promise) provides a normative imperative to carry out that course of action, which operates independently of the reasons for and against carrying it out that are in play when the time comes. In other words, it is *not* the case that the prior commitment is just one reason among many. Rather, the relationship between the prior commitment and its fulfilment is like the relationship between TG+GE and TE. A failure to carry out the commitment would be a kind of internal inconsistency, which is *prima facie* irrational. Of course, this *prima facie* irrationality can, in some situations, be addressed and removed. A person who is confronted with *reasons* for disbelieving TE might re-visit his belief in TG and GE and in this way be led to abandon his (false) belief in TG. Once that is done, there is nothing irrational in

5 Chapman, n. 3 above, 483.

6 Especially J Broome, 'Normative Requirements' (1999) 12 *Ratio* 398; J Broome, 'Are Intentions Reasons? And How Should We Cope With Incommensurable Values?' in CW Morris and A Ripstein (eds.), *Practical Rationality and Preference: Essays for David Gauthier* (CUP, 2001), 98.

this person disbelieving TE. In a similar way, a person may rationally repudiate a prior commitment. Chapman argues that it would be irrational to repudiate a commitment 'where the reason for repudiation was anticipated and accounted for when the prior intention was adopted'.[7] On the other hand, if the reason for repudiation was not so anticipated at that time, it could be quite rational to repudiate. The new reason must be taken into account, and it has not yet been.

So, there are two different modes of rationality for deciding whether to act in accordance with a prior commitment when the time comes. One mode of rationality is action for reasons: all of the reasons then in force must be weighed and considered. These reasons may relate to reputational effects or other future events that will be brought about by failing to fulfil the commitment. They may also consist of reasons that were not considered at the time the commitment was made. The other mode of rationality is action according to the normative requirements of practical rationality, which requires internal consistency. The prior commitment must be respected, unless its basis has failed in the sense that some factor has intervened which was not considered when the commitment was made. The difficulty, of course, is that the two modes of rationality are independent and incommensurable, so if they point in different directions, the actor has a very difficult decision to make.

Chapman concludes by noting the relevance of his analysis to common law judicial decision-making. His analysis supports the idea that law can be seen as a system of defeasible rules and, in particular, it shows how 'particular cases can, apparently simultaneously, both determine legal rules (as a matter of independent reason) and be determined by them (as a matter of normative requirement)'.[8] Law aspires to be rational, but if rationality were simply action or decision according to reasons, this would suggest that every judge needs to address his or her mind freshly in every case to the reasons for deciding one way or the other. In fact there is more to rationality than action or decision according to reasons. There are also the normative requirements of rationality, which demand consistency. Like cases must be treated alike; this is a fundamental tenet of the rule of law.[9] It is fundamental because it is a requirement of rationality, not in the sense of reasons for decision, but in the sense of consistency. A doctrine of precedent promotes treating like cases alike, over the plane of time.[10]

[7] Chapman, n. 3 above, 487–8.

[8] Chapman, n. 3 above, 494.

[9] On the independence of this formal standard of the alikeness of cases from the results dictated by the application of substantive reasons to the cases, see also B Chapman, 'Chance, Reason and the Rule of Law' (2000) 50 *UTLJ* 469, 477–89.

[10] Cross and Harris, n. 1 above, 3; RM Dworkin, *Taking Rights Seriously* (Duckworth, 1977), 113. TM Benditt, 'The Rule of Precedent', in L Goldstein (ed.), *Precedent in Law* (Clarendon Press, 1987) 89, 90 argues that the principle that like cases must be treated alike has nothing to do with the idea of binding precedent, because, given two cases which are alike but decided differently, it implies that (at least) one of them is wrong, but does not imply that the second, rather than the first, is wrong. But if the principle that like cases must be treated alike is understood as operating in the plane of time, then it privileges the earlier decision. Time's arrow points in one direction only. That the later decision should accord with the earlier is precisely what is exacted by the normative requirements of rationality.

Consider the two different modes of rationality as they apply to judicial decision-making. If a judge is faced with a question that has never arisen before, he or she is free to decide the question according to his or her evaluation of the reasons that point in each direction. This is rationality according to reasons, which we can call R1. On the other hand, we can picture a judge who has to make a decision that is clearly governed by a binding precedent. Here we can return to the problem posed at the beginning of this section. Assume that the binding authority indicates that the defendant should win; the judge, on the other hand, thinks that according to her evaluation of all the relevant reasons for deciding, the plaintiff should win. If the judge follows the authority, is she acting rationally? She is. She is deciding according to the normative requirements of rationality, which we may call R2. The legal system of her jurisdiction has already made a commitment to a resolution of the particular problem before her.

It is rationality of the mode R2 that ensures that like cases are treated alike over time. It is the basis of the doctrine of precedent, which, where it operates, denies decision-makers access to the mode of rationality R1. Even in systems that do not have a formal doctrine of precedent or *stare decisis*, however, the mode R2 remains important. It effectively underpins the notion of a legal tradition.[11] A legal tradition is a way of understanding and solving legal problems. The same legal problem may be approached in different ways by different legal traditions, even if ultimately they arrive at the same solution. They may use different terminology, and they may employ different legal abstractions as tools in the reasoning process. In the civil law tradition, for example, gifts are contracts, and in this way there is a legal basis for a transfer of property that would otherwise be legally untenable and, hence, reversible.[12] Legal traditions embody a kind of path-dependency that grows out of rationality in the mode R2. Once a legal system has decided to resolve issues in certain ways, there is a rational basis for continuing to do so.[13]

But it is in systems where decided cases are formally a source of law that R2 is especially important, because inconsistency among cases becomes inconsistency among the body of norms which govern citizens' conduct. This may be one way of understanding the rule of precedent or *stare decisis*: it is a legal norm that formally privileges R2 over R1. Let us return to the case of the judge who would decide one

11 HP Glenn, *Legal Traditions of the World* (2nd edn., OUP, 2004).

12 For example, Civil Code of Québec, arts. 1494 *in fine*, 1554, 1806.

13 Most civil law systems are codified, and so the legislative force of the codification might be thought to provide a sufficient explanation for the behaviour of judges in these systems. There are a number of responses to this. First, not every civil law system is codified; Scotland and South Africa are not, and in each of these cases we find a doctrine of *stare decisis*, albeit with different contours (see R Zimmermann, ' "Double Cross": Comparing Scots and South African Law', in R Zimmermann, D Visser, and K Reid (eds.), *Mixed Legal Systems in Comparative Perspective: Property and Obligations in Scotland and South Africa* (OUP, 2004) 1, 17). Secondly, even in codified systems we find some version of *stare decisis*, albeit not under that name: see n. 21 below, and the accompanying text. Finally, even in codified systems there are important extra-codal principles of substantive law, as well as extra-codal norms governing such things as acceptable modes of legal argumentation. These are carried forward in time, and are considered to have normative force, through rationality of the mode R2.

way according to reasons (R1), but is bound by precedent to decide the other way (R2). The rule of *stare decisis* obliges her to decide against the way that she would decide, if she could. In other words, whenever the two modes of rationality conflict, the rule of *stare decisis* says that R2 prevails over R1. We must acknowledge that this is one of the most difficult situations in which a judge can find himself or herself; and we must also acknowledge that, even in a system where such a rule applies, a judge who is apparently in that situation may struggle mightily to find a way to conclude that the precedent is not, after all, governing or binding.

(iii) Resolving Clashes Between Modes of Rationality

I feel myself bound to state that I must, when I decided that case, have seen it in a point of view, in which, after most laborious consideration, I cannot see it now.[14]
The matter does not appear to me now as it appears to have appeared to me then.[15]

These statements strike a chord with all of us. Once you have decided, it is hard to revisit the decision, and it is very hard to make a new decision that is inconsistent with a reasoned decision already reached. The difficulty can be understood as a clash between the two modes of rationality. Mode R2 suggests that today's decision should be consistent with the previous one, but mode R1 points in a different direction. Such a clash is perhaps particularly stressful where the previous decision was one's own.[16] The basis for the stress is that departing from the earlier decision is actually irrational, in one sense (R2), even while it is rational in another sense (R1).

In this section, I will attempt to provide a typology of solutions for situations where R1 clashes, or appears to clash, with R2. In other words, a judge is disposed to resolve a case in one way, based on the judge's own appreciation of the reasons which point in each direction; but there is, or appears to be, a precedent pointing in the opposite direction.

[14] Lord Eldon in *ex p Nolte* (1826) 2 Glynn & James 295, 308. I thank Jeffrey Hackney for his assistance with this reference, the series not being one which is reproduced in either the English Reports or the Revised Reports. This dictum is less well-known than that of Bramwell B that follows. See however *Longlitz v Matador Co-op Farm Assoc. Ltd.* (1970) 15 DLR (3d) 626 (Sask. QB); *S v K* (1995) 898 P2d 891 at 908 (Cal. SC).

[15] Bramwell B during argument in *Styrap v Edwards* (1872) 26 LT (NS) 704, 706, invoked in *McGrath v Kristensen* (1950) 340 US 162, 178; *Longlitz*, n. 14 above; *Cyprus Anvil Mining Corp. v Dickson* [1982] BCJ No 1801, [61] (SC); *Pawlowitsch v Pawlowitsch* (1982) 37 Nfld & PEIR 461, [30] (PEI SC); *S v K*, n. 14 above; *Truk Continental Hotel Inc. v State of Chuuk* (1995) 7 FSM Intrm 117, 120–1 (SC of the Federated States of Micronesia); *Wright v Morton* [1998] 3 VR 316 (CA).

[16] A more recent example: in *Anderton v Ryan* [1985] 1 AC 560 the House of Lords made a decision that a person could not be convicted of an 'impossible attempt'; it came to the opposite decision, overruling itself, just over a year later in *R v Shivpuri* [1987] 1 AC 1; Lord Bridge was in the majority in both decisions.

(a) Disqualifying the Precedent

The most obvious way to eliminate the apparent clash between R1 and R2 is to disqualify the precedent. If there is no prior decision on the issue before the judge, R2 does not apply at all, and the judge is free to decide the issue according to R1, the relevant reasons. 'In the absence of binding authority clearly on point it may reasonably be said that the law is what it ought to be.'[17] The important feature of this mode of reasoning is that it does not impinge on the logic or force of R2, but merely concludes that in the current situation, R2 plays no role.

1. Not Binding

I start with what might seem like a rather elementary way of disqualifying the precedent, but which turns out, on examination, to raise the most complex questions. If we leave judicial decision-making entirely aside, we can recall that R2 operates even in the absence of any rule along the lines of *stare decisis*. If I made a commitment to meet you for lunch, and nothing has happened which I did not already consider and take into account when I made that commitment, it is irrational of me (in the sense of R2) to breach the commitment and fail to appear. That is because the same person, or rational being, who made the commitment is now failing to fulfil it, without any good (in the sense of unaccounted for) reason. Of course, this irrationality does not breach any rule of law. On the other hand, if A makes a commitment to meet B for lunch, this has nothing to do with C. Perhaps C knows both of them and was made welcome to join them, but if C has not made a commitment, there is no irrationality in C's failure to appear at the agreed time and place. R2 exerts (non-legal) normative pressure on a decision maker based on a prior decision or course of action by *that* decision maker.

Now consider the case of a decision made by Judge A, without the benefit or burden of any prior decision on the point. The next week, the same point arises for decision before Judge C. If Judge A sits in the Ontario Supreme Court and Judge C sits in the New South Wales Supreme Court, then Judge C may be interested in the earlier decision, and may in particular be interested to read the reasons for judgment. But this is nothing to do with R2; rather, Judge C wishes to see *why* Judge A decided as he or she did. Judge C is interested in the reasons of Judge A, so that Judge C can weigh and consider these reasons; that is R1. But change the case again so that Judge A sits in the Chancery Division of the High Court in London, and Judge C also sits in the same division of the same court. Leaving aside for the moment the positive rule of *stare decisis*, there is every reason to suppose that the mode of rationality we have called R2 operates upon Judge C, in respect of the earlier decision by Judge A, even though Judge C is not the same person as Judge A. The force of R2 is that it requires rational decisions to be consistent. Judges in deciding cases do not act in a personal capacity, but exercise

[17] See n. 2 above.

powers entrusted to them for the administration of justice in a jurisdiction. So when Judge A decides, he or she decides not personally, but on behalf of the state or the system. Judge A's decision is a decision of the legal system of England and Wales, Judge A being an organ or agent of that system. To the extent that the decision exerts normative force, in the mode of R2, it does not operate merely on Judge A in his later decisions, but on all other judges in the same legal system.[18] In other words, if Judge C's decision were thought to be inconsistent with Judge A's, and a complaint was made that like cases were not being treated alike, we can think of any number of good responses which might be made by, or in defence of, Judge C or in defence of the coherence and rationality of the legal system of England and Wales; but among those good responses would not be the response, 'well, the earlier decision was by a different judge'.[19] In this way, official decisions (such as those of judges) are different from personal ones.

This allows us to address the role of a formal rule of *stare decisis*. Such a rule turns the normative force of R2 into a legally binding norm, which could, for example, be a ground of appeal that would allow the reversal of a judge's considered decision.[20] The translation of non-legal norms into legal norms is complex. We may think that all serious promises should be kept, but as that norm is translated into law, usually only some such promises are legally required to be kept. Reasons for this lack of fit may include the implementation of other, and inconsistent, norms governing conduct, or pragmatic matters such as concerns about evidence.

All systems implement R2 as a legal norm, to some extent. This is true even in civil law systems, where decided cases are not a formal source of law. In France, for example, it would surely be a reversible error for a trial judge to hold that there is no *actio de in rem verso* available to reverse unjust enrichment in the form of improvements to property, on the basis that no such action is described in the Civil Code. The availability of the action is established by a series of court decisions dating from the end of the nineteenth century.[21] In the common law tradition, where decided cases are a crucial formal source of law, it should be no surprise that R2 is more formalized. The manner in which it has been formalized is more or less what one

[18] Benditt, n. 10 above, 90 dismisses this far too readily. He says of judicial decision-making by different judges: 'If following precedent is required in such a context, it must be because institutional consistency is desirable, and not merely because one should not contradict oneself.' But this sentence seems to miss the point that in the institutional context, 'oneself' *is* the legal system as an institution, not the individual judge.

[19] If the mode R2 can operate on a person as a result of her own earlier personal decision, outside any official decision-making context, *and* it can operate on a person as a result of *someone else's* earlier decision, *within* an official decision-making context, then we can see that where the earlier decision *both* was made by the same person now deciding, *and* was made in an official decision-making context which continues to apply, the normative force of R2 might be especially strong. Hence the resonance of the plaintive utterances of Lord Eldon and Baron Bramwell cited earlier, nn. 14 and 15 above.

[20] See, e.g., *Davis v Johnson* [1979] AC 264.

[21] For a full discussion of the force of precedent in French law, and its relation to the principle that decided cases are not a formal source of law, see J Ghestin, G Goubeaux, and M Fabre-Magnan, '*Introduction générale*' in J Ghestin (ed.), *Traité de droit civil* 4th edn., LGDJ., 1994) 434–99. For Quebec, see JEC Brierley and RA Macdonald (eds.), *Quebec Civil Law* (Emond Montgomery, 1993),

would expect. Given the hierarchy of courts, which is a relatively recent creation of statute law,[22] inevitably a court higher in the hierarchy is not bound by a decision of a lower court. Within each level, however, the logic of R2 could be formalized as a rule of *stare decisis*, with every level of court bound by its own earlier decisions. If this were the case at all levels, though, change would be very difficult. Hence all common law jurisdictions have arrived at the position that the highest court in the hierarchy is not bound by its own decisions. That level can therefore be faced with the problem of resolving a clash between R1 and R2, because no precedent is ever binding, but some precedents are decisions of that court itself.[23] An earlier decision of the court itself brings to bear the normative force of R2, even if it is not raised to a mandatory rule of law; and if the later court thinks the earlier decision is wrong as a matter of R1, the clash arises.[24] At other levels, the existence of any binding precedent means that the case is resolved according to R2 and R1 drops out of the picture.

Of course, none of this means that decisions from other jurisdictions ought to be ignored. In the words of Peter Birks, 'Nationalism is always out of place in legal thought and argument. When it does push in, it always strikes a note which is either absurd or repulsive or both.'[25] The difference between binding and non-binding precedents is, however, the difference between R2 and R1, which are both modes of rationality. Non-binding precedents can be examined for their substance, in the sense of their reasoning; they do not, as a binding precedent does, prevent access to decision according to reasons.[26]

2. *Distinguishable*

Distinguishing an apparently relevant precedent is an obvious method for disapplying the logic of R2. If the earlier decision did not decide the point now in issue, then it does not have any normative force in the consistency-requiring sense that R2 embodies. Of course, the question whether a case is distinguishable inevitably

121–5 and A Mayrand, 'L'autorité du précédent au Québec' (1994) 28 *Revue juridique Thémis* 771. See also n. 13 above.

22 Dating, at least in the modern sense, from the mid-nineteenth century: JH Baker, *An Introduction to English Legal History* (4th edn., Butterworths, 2002) , 138–143.

23 In some jurisdictions, an intermediate appellate court may also not be bound by its own decisions, and so may also find itself in the same position; see e.g. *Nguyen v Nguyen* (1990) 169 CLR 245, 269–70; *Jones v Sky City Auckland Ltd.* [2004] NZLR 192 (CA). In England, the Divisional Court overruled itself in *R v Governor of Brockhill Prison* [1997] QB 443. Some Canadian trial-level courts have held that they are not bound by decisions of other judges of the same court, but these cases seem largely explicable as ones in which the earlier judgment was disqualified using one of the techniques here discussed. This is the approach, e.g., in *Re Hansard Spruce Mills Ltd.* [1954] 4 DLR 590 (BCSC), described as a 'revered authority' in *Spooner v Ridley Terminals Inc.* (1991) 62 BCLR (2d) 132.

24 This problem will be addressed below, in Part (iii) (b).

25 P Birks, *Unjust Enrichment* (2nd edn., OUP, 2005), 128.

26 JW Harris, 'The Privy Council and the Common Law' (1990) 106 *LQR* 574; *Invercargill City Council v Hamlin* [1996] AC 624, 639–44; R Bronaugh, 'Persuasive Precedent', in L Goldstein (ed.), *Precedent in Law* (Clarendon Press, 1987), 217. At 247, in conclusion, Bronaugh argues that non-binding precedents can help to construct an argument showing that an apparently binding precedent is distinguishable: 'persuasive precedents are powerful and fair instruments of invention because, when convincing, they will show ways in which—again rationally and in all fairness—the fetters of

creates a penumbra of uncertainty; we might even go further and suppose that not every example of distinguishing a case is intellectually honest. The fact remains that R2 (and hence the rule of *stare decisis)* has no application unless the point now in issue has earlier been decided.

3. Obiter Dictum *or Decided without Argument*

It is elementary that the rule of *stare decisis* is triggered by the *ratio decidendi* of a decision, the reason for the decision. It is not activated by mere *obiter dicta*, 'things said by the way'. Distinguishing between the two is not necessarily easy;[27] but the *ratio* is that part of the decision that is essential to the outcome. This is consistent with the logic of R2, because an *obiter dictum*, by its definition, is not a decision that a judge was required to make. A judge's institutional responsibility is confined to resolving *disputes* about the law.[28] In that sense, an *obiter dictum* is an opinion, no doubt a learned one, but it is not an institutional decision on a point of law. That status is confined to the *ratio*, which is therefore the only part that engages, institutionally, the logic of R2.

Slightly different, but related, is the principle that a statement of law by a judge in a judgment does not constitute a binding precedent if it was made without argument, even if it is part of the *ratio*.[29] These are points that were simply assumed to be the case by the judge, whether or not there was an express concession. Here again, we can say that there was no institutional decision. The matter was not submitted to the judge for resolution. Therefore, even though the judge was required to form an *opinion* on the point, the judge has not *decided* the point, in the sense that he or she has not applied the logic of R1 to reach a rational decision.

4. Per incuriam

An earlier decision, otherwise binding, need not be followed if it was *per incuriam*, which means that the earlier decision was made 'in ignorance or forgetfulness of some inconsistent statutory provision or of some authority binding on the

binding precedent can be slipped'. This must be correct, because just as no rule can determine the scope of its own application, so no precedent can itself decide what later cases it governs. In this I disagree with Benditt, n. 10 above, 90–1.

[27] Cross and Harris, n.1 above, ch. 2.

[28] And, in some cases, about facts, but that is not relevant here. Where courts are constitutionally restricted to the primary curial function of resolving disputes, they take the position that they have no jurisdiction to give advisory reference opinions. For the US, see *Muskrat v US* (1911) 219 US 346, but note *Re Extradition of Lang* (1995) 905 F Supp 1385, 1392–3 (CD Cal.). For Australia, see *Re Judiciary and Navigation Acts* (1921) 29 CLR 257; but note that judges in the majority in that case arguably contradicted their own principle when they issued, under the same style of cause and apparently of their own motion, a 'statement' as to the meaning of their earlier judgment: *Re Judiciary and Navigation Acts* (1923) 32 CLR 455. Even where a jurisdiction to give such opinions is specifically granted by the legislature, in theory the opinion has no status as a binding precedent, but is only persuasive: *A.-G. Ont. v A.-G. Canada* [1912] AC 571, 589. Moreover, the court retains a jurisdiction not to answer any question referred, which is clearly not the case in ordinary dispute resolution: *Reference Re Secession of Quebec* [1998] 2 SCR 217; *Reference Re Same-Sex Marriage* [2004] 3 SCR 698.

[29] Cross and Harris, n. 1 above,158–61.

court concerned'.[30] This begins to resemble a resolution not to follow the earlier decision simply because it was wrongly decided, in the sense of R1. That, however, is exactly the resolution that the later court cannot make, if the earlier decision is binding. *Stare decisis* subordinates any use of R1 where there is a binding precedent; in such a case, it is not possible to impugn the earlier decision on the basis of R1. The logic of *per incuriam* is therefore slightly different. It is procedural rather than substantive. It disqualifies the earlier decision from being a prior institutional decision that is effective, in the mode R2, to prevent any re-examination of the question decided; and it does this on the basis that the earlier court ignored a legal rule that was clearly binding on it. It failed to consider something that it was bound to consider. In this way, the earlier decision is disqualified while the logic of R2 and *stare decisis* are respected.

Of course, it may seem that they are respected only in a very formal way, but R2 is a formal mode of rationality.[31] There is a clear analogy here with the judicial review of administrative action, in which administrative decisions may often be reviewed not on their substance, but on procedural or jurisdictional grounds. This respects the logic that the substantive decision does not belong to the reviewing court; it only reviews the procedures that were followed by the administrative decision-maker. Just as in judicial review, of course, and just as in the ordinary inquiry into whether an earlier decision can be distinguished, the formal logic of *per incuriam* involves a difficult penumbra of uncertainty.

5. No Longer Sustainable

A final way of disqualifying a precedent might seem to come closest to substantively disagreeing with it, but I will argue that, as in the case of *per incuriam*, the logic of R2 is ultimately respected. A court may conclude that the earlier decision, which on its face is a binding precedent, was made in and for societal conditions that no longer exist. For this reason, it may conclude that the decision need not be followed. This does not correspond to disagreeing with the decision, substantively, as matter of R1. Recall Chapman's argument that a person may repudiate a prior commitment, while still maintaining rationality in the mode R2. This is the case if the reason for repudiation was not anticipated and accounted for at the time the commitment was made.[32] In these circumstances, the earlier commitment does not bind in the sense of R2, and the person is free to evaluate the new reason, as a matter of R1.

In the judicial context, the same reasoning could be applied to an otherwise binding precedent. The social conditions that underpinned it may have

[30] *Morrelle Ltd. v Wakeling* [1955] 2 QB 389, 406 *per* Lord Evershed MR. See generally Cross and Harris, n. 1 above, at 148–52.

[31] Inasmuch as it is concerned, not with the substantive reasons for acting (or deciding cases) one way or another, but with respect for internal consistency. See also n. 9 above.

[32] Chapman, n. 3 above, 487–8.

so changed that it is obsolete.[33] This conclusion does not mean that the decision must now be seen to have been wrong. It may well have been right at the time it was made. But the world has changed, in a way that was not considered and addressed by the judge who made the earlier decision. In this sense, this mode of disqualifying the precedent is consistent with the mode of rationality R2.[34]

One of the most famous examples of this kind of reasoning is *R v R*, in which the House of Lords overruled the idea, widely thought to be the law before then, that a man cannot rape his wife because marriage supposedly imported a kind of irrevocable consent to sexual activity.[35] In the words of Lord Keith of Kinkel, '[o]n grounds of principle there is no good reason why the whole proposition should not be held inapplicable in modern times.'[36] In *Canada Trust Co. v Ontario (Human Rights Commission)*,[37] a scholarship trust was created in 1923 by a man who believed that: 'the White Race is, as a whole, best qualified by nature to be entrusted with the development of civilization and the general progress of the World along the best lines', and who therefore restricted eligibility to those who could be described as 'a British Subject of the White Race and of the Christian Religion in its Protestant form'. In the words of the majority of the Ontario Court of Appeal:[38]

> It must not be forgotten that when the trust property initially vested in 1923 the terms of the indenture would have been held to be certain, valid and not contrary to any public policy which rendered the trust void or illegal or which detracted from the settlor's general intention to devote the property to charitable purposes. However, with changing social attitudes, public policy has changed. The public policy of the 1920s is not the public policy of the 1990s. As a result, it is no longer in the interest of the community to continue the trust on the basis predicated by the settlor. Put another way, while the trust was practicable when it was created, changing times have rendered the ideas promoted by it contrary to public policy and, hence, it has become impracticable to carry it on in the manner originally planned by the settlor.

[33] Compare Cross and Harris, n. 1, 162–3. This is a discussion of obsolescence of a precedent due to changes in the law.

[34] This is related to an understanding of judging which supposes that judges, in some sense, 'find' the law, but unlike the traditional 'declaratory theory' (criticized by Cross and Harris, n. 1 above, at 27–34), this understanding does not suppose that the law is unchanging. See Dworkin, n. 10 above, at 110–23; L Smith, 'Restitution for Mistake of Law: *Kleinwort Benson Ltd. v Lincoln City Council*' (1999) 7 *Restitution L Rev* 148.

[35] *R v R* [1992] 1 AC 599. The accused, convicted of attempted rape, brought proceedings against the UK in the European Court of Human Rights on the basis that the offence of which he was convicted was retroactively created after the conduct in question. This claim failed: *R. v UK* [1996] 1 FLR 434.

[36] Ibid. 621. The only other question was whether the immunity of the husband had been impliedly preserved by legislation, but it was held that it had not.

[37] (1990) 69 DLR (4th) 321 (Ont CA).

[38] Ibid., 335–6. For a full discussion of the case, see B Ziff, *Unforeseen Legacies* (University of Toronto Press, 2000).

Other examples could be cited.[39] These decisions did not specifically involve the departure from a court decision that would otherwise have been binding, but it seems clear enough that the reasoning would have applied in such a case. It is not that the later judge simply disagrees with the earlier one; rather, the conclusion is that the earlier judge would not have decided as he or she did, had he or she been operating in the conditions of today. In those circumstances, the precedent ceases to bind.

6. *Conclusion*

By any one of the routes described above, one can disqualify a precedent. In this way, one can decline to follow it, while still being respectful of the logic of R2, which demands institutional consistency. This allows the judge to apply R1; that is, to decide the case as he or she thinks, according to reasons, it should be decided. Of course, it is possible to invoke one of those routes in an intellectually dishonest way, so as to avoid either the rule of *stare decisis* or having to face the problem discussed in the next section, where R1 clashes with R2 in its non-legal, but still normatively potent, form.[40] That possibility does not detract from the legitimacy of those routes in other contexts.

(b) Overruling

If a precedent is disqualified, then the logic of R2 is inapplicable and the judge is free to decide according to R1. If the precedent cannot be disqualified, then, generally, the rule of *stare decisis* gives a legal effect to the logic of R2 which privileges it over R1, and requires the judge to follow the precedent. But sometimes there is a third possibility. If the earlier decision cannot be disqualified, but it is an earlier decision of the same tribunal that is now called to decide the same issue, it may well be that *stare decisis* does not apply. This is the case for the highest appellate court in a jurisdiction, and, in some jurisdictions, for intermediate appellate courts as well.[41] But R2 exerts a normative force in this situation, even though it is not made into a mandatory rule of law. A court that is not required to follow its

[39] In *Miliangos v George Frank (Textiles) Ltd.* [1976] AC 443, the House of Lords overruled its earlier holding in *Re United Railways of Havana and Regla Warehouses Ltd* [1961] AC 1007, that English courts could render money judgments only in sterling. Although the earlier decision was only 15 years old, the majority judges rested their decision primarily on the fact that the world had changed radically since then in terms of the stability of currencies (463, 501). In *Williams v Roffey Bros. & Nicholls (Contractors) Ltd.* [1991] 1 QB 1, one judge (Glidewell LJ) suggested (at 16) that the passage of time and changing conditions had rendered obsolete the precedent the Court was now declining to apply (*Stilk v Myrick* (1809) 2 Camp 317). In *Harrison v Carswell* [1976] 2 SCR 200, the issue was whether employees picketing in a shopping centre during a labour dispute were guilty of a petty trespass where the landowner had forbidden them access to the land. The dissenting judges would have said that they were not, on the basis that such land must now be understood to have a public character, even if privately owned.

[40] Lord Denning, *The Discipline of Law* (Butterworths, 1979), 297–8.

[41] See n. 23, above.

own earlier decisions is still faced with the fact that its own earlier decisions exist as sources of law for that court. To take one concrete example, the Supreme Court of Canada is not bound, as a matter of *stare decisis*, either by its own decisions or by the decisions of the House of Lords. However, a decision of the House of Lords does not exert normative force of the kind R2 on the Supreme Court of Canada; such a decision could be examined on its merits, in the mode of R1. But a previous decision of the Supreme Court of Canada, while not binding, still exerts some non-binding normative force of the kind R2. This creates the difficulty that a court must decide, without being bound by a rule on the matter, whether to apply the logic of R2 and maintain consistency with its earlier decision, or whether to re-examine the question according to R1. On its face, the latter course is irrational according to the mode R2, unless the earlier decision is disqualified in some way. At the institutional level, a court's decision to overrule itself amounts to more than merely expressing a view that the earlier case was badly decided. Such institutional inconsistency also threatens to undermine the authority of the current decision—and by extension all decisions—for why should it be thought any more secure than the decision now being overruled?

The two modes, R1 and R2, are incommensurable, and it is not surprising that the resolution of a tension between them effectively calls for meta-principles.[42] That is, one can seek reasons for departing from R2; these are not going to be reasons for deciding the case in any particular way (R1), but rather reasons about whether one is free to look to such reasons for deciding the case in a particular way. They could be understood as the mode of rationality R1′.[43] If overruling is done according to some such articulable reasons, then the court in question can continue to claim to act rationally, and so avoid charges of unjustifiable institutional inconsistency or, perhaps, politicization.

Looking at a set of decisions of the House of Lords in the period 1966–91, Jim Harris tried to formulate principles of overruling of this kind.[44] He found four constraining principles, one of them itself subject to a constraint. The

[42] For an analysis of how rational actors can and do address multiple incommensurable values in decision-making in general, see B Chapman, 'Law, Incommensurability, and Conceptually Sequenced Argument' (1998) 146 *U Pa L Rev* 1487. Within that framework of conceptually structured argument, it seems that R2, where it binds, is conceptually prior to R1; a court which wishes to decide according to R1 must therefore first decide, either by disqualifying the earlier decision or by overruling it, that R2 is not in play.

[43] And inevitably, there must be a mode of rationality R2′. That is, if a court chooses principles to govern when it should be free to overrule its own prior decisions (R1′), there will be a normative force which will constrain that court, in the name of consistency (R2′), from changing those principles. If it was thought that they were wrong and had to be changed, one could appeal to principles of the order R1″, and so on. But there is no reason to think that the principles of R1″ would differ from those of R1′.

[44] 1966 is the date of the Practice Statement by which the House of Lords declared itself free to depart from its own decisions: *Practice Statement (Judicial Precedent)* [1966] 1 WLR 1234. See JW Harris, 'Towards Principles of Overruling—When Should a Final Court of Appeal Second Guess?' (1990) 10 *OJLS* 135 which identifies seven such decisions, and the later article, JW Harris, '*Murphy* Makes it Eight—Overruling Comes to Negligence' (1991) 11 *OJLS* 416 which added

constraining principles were that the earlier decision should not be overruled where: (i) no new reasons or arguments have been presented; (ii) there has been some justified reliance by citizens (not the executive) on the earlier ruling; (iii) overruling would be inconsistent with comity with the legislature;[45] (iv) the point is moot to the current dispute, at least in private law litigation. I make some observations on only the first two of these.

The second principle protects the reliance of citizens. This is a factor that is frequently mentioned by judges in considering whether an earlier decision should be followed or not. The importance of reliance, however, seems difficult to assess. The concern, presumably, is not with actual or proven reliance; in the nature of our litigation process, that would be generally impossible to assess, because the reliance in question is not that of the parties but of other members of society. Rather, it is a question of speculation as to whether there has been extensive reliance on the decision now being reconsidered.[46] Even if the speculation is accurate, however, reliance on its own can hardly *prevent* legal change, not even judicial change that keeps within the limits being discussed here. This is because wherever plans or transactions are formulated, by at least some citizens, with an eye on the law—and that potentially implicates most fields of law—we can plausibly suppose that almost every rule that might come to be reconsidered has been relied upon by *someone*.[47] If reliance excluded change, there could almost never be change. But it may be that the extent of (presumed) reliance is a factor which can properly be considered, at the level of R1′, in deciding whether the decision can be revisited at the level of R1.[48]

Harris's first principle has some affinity with the idea, discussed earlier, of *per incuriam*.[49] The idea that an earlier decision does not count as a precedent because it is *per incuriam* depends on the finding that some binding rule of law was not considered by the court, and so this is a narrower principle than the one formulated by Harris. In other words, it is easier to show that some argument or reason (in the sense of R1) was not considered earlier than it is to show that the earlier

another case. For some reviews of the US practice, see *Planned Parenthood of Southeastern Pennsylvania v Casey* (1992) 505 US 833; EM Maltz, 'No Rules in a Knife Fight: Chief Justice Rehnquist and the Doctrine of Stare Decisis' (1994) 25 *Rutgers LJ* 669; TR Lee, 'Stare Decisis in Historical Perspective: From the Founding Era to the Rehnquist Court' (1999) 52 *Vand L Rev* 647.

[45] This principle would argue against overruling if, since the first decision, the legislature had acted in some way that indicates that it understood the first decision to be the law.

[46] See, e.g. *Friedmann Equity Developments Inc. v Final Note Ltd.* [2000] 1 SCR 842.

[47] There may be exceptions. In *R. v Shivpuri* [1987] 1 AC 1, Lord Hailsham of St. Marylebone LC (at 11) and Lord Bridge (at 23) thought that it was impossible that anyone had relied on the earlier holding in *Anderton v Ryan* [1985] 1 AC 560, since it dealt with cases in which the accused was acting under a mistake. Also in the field of criminal law, any reliance that may have occurred might well be considered unworthy of protection; presumably this would have been the case in *R. v R* [1992] 1 AC 599.

[48] See KN Llewellyn, *The Common Law Tradition: Deciding Appeals* (Little, Brown & Co., 1960), 303. More generally, at 299–309, Llewellyn suggested that judges should, where possible, overrule in two steps, the first step being a warning that the old rule or decision was likely to fall. This would reduce reasonable reliance on that rule in advance of its actual fall.

[49] Part (iii) (a) 4.

decision was *per incuriam*. But the requirement that the later court should find, at least, some such 'gap' in the reasoning of the earlier decision seems to be based on a similar idea. It allows the later court to say, with some plausibility, that even the earlier court would have decided differently, had it been presented with the same arguments and reasons that are now being presented. In other words, a court that makes this move is effectively disqualifying its own earlier decision as a matter of R2, although it is doing it in a way that is not permitted by the legal version of R2 known as *stare decisis*.[50]

Harris found evidence of a qualification of this principle, however: 'there are fundamental matters as to which it is enough that the present court is sure that the earlier decision was simply wrong'.[51] These may be fundamental principles of the common law (such as whether a person can escape a conviction for murder by pleading duress), or of the constitution.[52] It seems, however, to raise a very difficult point. This is not really a principle of R1′, but rather an application of R1. It amounts to saying that where a court is *sure* that the previous decision was wrong it should depart from it. In other words, in the final analysis, and except where R2 is privileged over R1 by the doctrine of *stare decisis*, the ordering goes the other way: R1 ultimately prevails over R2. But the implication of that is the abandonment of consistency over time, which, ultimately, will undermine the legitimacy of a court.[53] I think Harris's first principle should always apply, as a minimum condition for a court to overrule itself. If there is really nothing different between the first decision and the second decision, except a different judge or set of judges, then the court, seen as a single institution, is acting irrationally in overruling itself. The same institution is considering the same issue, with the same arguments before it, and is deciding differently.

(iv) Conclusion

It is not my intention to present an argument that amounts to a reactionary approach to the doctrine of precedent. Nor should injustice, in the sense of bad law, be perpetuated in the name of a foolish consistency.[54] But, on the other hand, a court must have a better reason for overruling itself than that the judge or judges have changed. The logic of R2 promotes consistency, not for its own sake, but in

50 Within the logic of *stare decisis*, the earlier decision must be followed or overruled.

51 JW Harris, 'Towards Principles of Overruling—When Should a Final Court of Appeal Second Guess?' (1990) 10 *OJLS* 135, 186.

52 Harris's proposition is supported by the recent decision of the Judicial Committee of the Privy Council to overrule itself regarding the procedural rights of convicted persons facing the death penalty: *Lewis v A.-G. Jamaica* [2001] 2 AC 50.

53 See the dissenting advice of Lord Hoffmann in *ibid.*

54 P. Wesley-Smith, 'Theories of Adjudication and the Status of *Stare Decisis*', in L Goldstein (ed.), *Precedent in Law* (Clarendon Press, 1987), 73, 87. My argument in favour of *stare decisis* is, however, different from both of those that Wesley-Smith rejects.

the name of rationality. If an earlier decision can be disqualified, in the sense discussed earlier in this Chapter, then the logic of R2 does not apply and the court is free to make what it believes to be the best decision. If that is not possible, then in some cases the court will be bound by *stare decisis*, a legally binding version of R2. The legally binding force of prior decisions can seem like the greatest hindrance to judges' ability to develop and improve the law; but, paradoxically, it is exactly because R2 is sometimes legally binding that judges have the power to make and develop law. It is the binding force of R2 that elevates judicial decisions into a source of law in the common law tradition; and it is because decisions are a source of law that judges, who are primarily resolvers of disputes, also have a law-making role.

Where a court is not bound by *stare decisis*, but is faced with its own earlier decision that it now wishes to repudiate, there is a difficult choice to be made between institutional consistency and what the current court sees as the requirements of justice. I would argue that it is not enough for the later court simply to say that it now disagrees with its earlier decision. That does not satisfy the requirements of R2, and that approach will ultimately threaten the integrity of the court as an institution. The later court may be able to disqualify the earlier decision, perhaps on the basis that the social context has changed in an important way. Even if that is not possible, at the very least the later court should be satisfied that some argument or reason was presented to it, which was not presented to the earlier court. If that is true, then the later court is faced with a decision that is different in at least one important way from the one faced by the earlier court. There is nothing irrational in changing one's mind when one is faced with a new set of arguments.

PART IV

HUMAN RIGHTS

15

Judging Rights in a Democratic South Africa

*Hugh Corder**

The most important issue subsumed within the question "Do and should judges legislate?" is political and constitutional. Members of any free society disagree about how governments should treat their citizens—about how resources should be allocated, about appropriate controls on the executive, about when state force should be applied.[1]

Jim Harris had many connections with South Africa. One of his earliest published articles, which appeared in the journal of the Faculty of Law at the University of Cape Town, explored the concept of sovereign will as a conceptual metaphor, and described briefly the principles comprising the logic of legal science.[2] The existence of legality or the rule of law in apartheid South Africa was questioned in *Legal Philosophies* when introducing the notion of the morality of law.[3] I had the enormous pleasure of hosting Jim and José during their brief, but happy, visit to Cape Town in the second half of 2002, as they were en route to Australia.

More significant, however, was Jim's mentorship of a number of South African law students who spent time at Keble. Edwin Cameron led the way in 1976, and his thoroughly positive experience reading law under Jim's guidance influenced at least Alastair Franklin (1979), Jonathan Watt-Pringle (1981), David Dyzenhaus (1983), Trevor Norwitz (1987), and me (1979), to seek admission to the College.[4] Jim's warm support, critical questioning, and robust engagement no doubt assisted each of us in coping with the vicissitudes we encountered, both at Oxford and afterwards. I am much in his debt.

I have chosen by way of appreciation to pursue the theme initiated in discussions in Jim's room some twenty-five years ago, that of the role of judges in

* I appreciate the comments of Anne Pope, the editors, and the anonymous reviewer, but am responsible for the shortcomings which remain.

1 JW Harris, *Legal Philosophies* (2nd edn., Butterworths, 1997), 209.

2 JW Harris, 'The Concept of Sovereign Will' [1977] *Acta Juridica* 1.

3 See Harris, n. 1 above, 144.

4 Jim's first question to me, at any rate, on a bleak mid-January day in 1979 was whether I knew Edwin Cameron. Franklin, Watt-Pringle, and Norwitz are today successful practitioners in Johannesburg, London, and New York, respectively. Dyzenhaus is a Professor of Philosophy and Law in the University of Toronto, and an internationally-respected writer on jurisprudence and the judicial process.

government.[5] The context, however, could not be more different: then, the focus was judicial authority in a thoroughly unjust legal regime; in what follows, I explore the way in which South African appellate judges are grappling with the meaning to be given to constitutional rights which allocate resources and regulate public power. I do so by discussing two recent judgments of the Supreme Court of Appeal: happily, Cameron JA was a concurring presence in each of them. Before doing so, it is important to note the essence of the constitutional and political context.

(i) Constitutional Rights and Judicial Authority

This is not the place for a detailed account of the formal transformation of South Africa's constitutional system from autocracy to democracy,[6] except for the following critical features. The Bill of Rights in the final Constitution[7] contains the usual list of civil and political rights to be expected in a late twentieth century constitution, with some unusual emphases and formulations. The presence of most of these novelties can be explained by the dreadfulness of the injustices before 1994, and the determination that such excesses should at least be unconstitutional in the future. So, we find that the protected rights are in principle applicable also 'horizontally';[8] that the equality clause outlaws unfair discrimination on a very large number of listed grounds;[9] and that the property clause is phrased negatively, providing protection against the unlawful deprivation of property and setting out the circumstances within which property may be expropriated, the factors influencing the amount of any compensation to be paid, and so on.[10] The section further reflects the urgent commitment to land reform, including

[5] The title of my DPhil thesis was *The Role and Attitudes of the South African Appellate Judiciary, 1910–50* (1982).

[6] An excellent account is to be found in R Spitz with M Chaskalson, *The Politics of Transition* (Witwatersrand UP, 2000). For a contemporary summary, see H Corder, 'Towards a South African Constitution' (1994) 57 *MLR* 491.

[7] Constitution of the Republic of South Africa, Act 108 of 1996.

[8] Ibid., s. 8.

[9] Ibid., s. 9.

[10] As the provisions of s. 25 are so relevant in what follows, I have included it in full. It reads:

(1) No one may be deprived of property except in terms of law of general application, and no law may permit arbitrary deprivation of property.

(2) Property may be expropriated only in terms of law of general application—
   (a) for a public purpose or in the public interest; and
   (b) subject to compensation, the amount of which and the time and manner of payment of which have either been agreed to by those affected or decided or approved by a court.

(3) The amount of the compensation and the time and manner of payment must be just and equitable, reflecting an equitable balance between the public interest and the interests of those affected, having regard to all relevant circumstances including—
   (a) the current use of the property;
   (b) the history of the acquisition and use of the property;
   (c) the market value of the property;

equitable access to land, legally secure tenure of land, and restitution of land to those from whom it was taken on the basis of race discrimination.

The second feature of the Bill of direct relevance to this discussion is the extensive, but qualified and nuanced, protection accorded to economic and social rights, including a right to an environment which is not harmful to health and well-being.[11] The rights to housing, health care, food, water, and social security[12] are cast as 'rights to have access to adequate/sufficient/appropriate' levels of service provision. A further qualification is to be seen in the obligation[13] on the state 'to take reasonable legislative and other measures within its available resources, to achieve the progressive realisation' of these rights. The flexibility of this formulation is emphasized by the significantly 'harder' language used when granting such rights to perhaps the most vulnerable group, children, for we read that:[14] '[e]very child has the right... to basic nutrition, shelter, basic health care services and social services'. While I am sure that the interpretive possibilities would have delighted Jim Harris, such formulations inevitably extend the scope of judicial authority in realizing such rights, for courts of law must ultimately assess the constitutionality of governmental compliance with the corresponding duties. The inclusion of these socio-economic interests as 'rights' emphasizes the non-absolute nature of the concept of a 'right' which is integral to an understanding of the South African Bill of Rights.[15]

Thirdly, the Bill of Rights contains what may be described as a charter of due process, being the rights of access to information,[16] of just administrative

(d) the extent of direct state investment and subsidy in the acquisition and beneficial capital improvement of the property; and

(e) the purpose of the expropriation.

(4) For the purposes of this section—

(a) the public interest includes the nation's commitment to land reform, and to reforms to bring about equitable access to all South Africa's natural resources; and

(b) property is not limited to land.

(5) The state must take reasonable legislative and other measures, within its available resources, to foster conditions which enable citizens to gain access to land on an equitable basis.

(6) A person or community whose tenure of land is legally insecure as a result of past racially discriminatory laws or practices is entitled, to the extent provided by an Act of Parliament, either to tenure which is legally secure or to comparable redress.

(7) A person or community dispossessed of property after 19 June 1913 as a result of past racially discriminatory laws or practices is entitled, to the extent provided by an Act of Parliament, either to restitution of that property or to equitable redress.

(8) No provision of this section may impede the state from taking legislative and other measures to achieve land, water and related reform, in order to redress the results of past racial discrimination, provided that any departure from the provisions of this section is in accordance with the provisions of section 36 (1).

(9) Parliament must enact the legislation referred to in subsection (6)

[11] See Constitution of the Republic of South Africa, Act 108 of 1996, s. 24.

[12] See ibid., ss. 26 and 27.

[13] Imposed in ibid., s. 26(2) and 27(2).

[14] See s. 28(1)(c).

[15] Again, Jim Harris would have been familiar with such an approach: see e.g., his discussion of 'Legal Concepts' in ch. 7 of *Legal Philosophies* (n. 1 above), particularly 86–93.

[16] Constitution of the Republic of South Africa, Act 108 of 1996, s. 32.

action,[17] of access to court,[18] and of arrested, detained, and accused persons.[19] While the last set of rights is to be found in most constitutions, the first three are highly unusual inclusions in lists of specially protected rights. Their presence once more attests to the drafters' and politicians' determination to ensure the maximum constitutional foundation to prevent a repetition of the executive lawlessness, obsessive secrecy, and privative clauses so characteristc of apartheid.

While this last group of rights was included in the transitional Constitution,[20] there was some controversy about the perpetuation of the rights of access to information and to administrative justice in the final Constitution, but in the end it was agreed to include them, tempered in scope by Parliamentary legislation.[21] The opposite approach was followed with regard to economic and social rights, as it had been seen as inappropriate to include their protection in an interim constitutional arrangement. In addition, there had been a healthy level of informed debate in the early 1990s about the wisdom of including such 'second generation' interests as enforceable rights, rather than as 'directive principles of State policy', following the Indian example.[22] The sub-text of much of this discussion was the political question of the relative scope of judicial, as opposed to legislative and executive, authority. There was a well-grounded apprehension that its elevation to the status of rights would subject the urgent socio-economic programme of the majority government unduly to the vagaries of an unreconstructed judiciary with a jurisprudential record manifestly unsympathetic to the needs of the poor and dispossessed. There was also much concern expressed about the judicial ability to perform the polycentric tasks that would be expected of them in this sphere. The outcome of these deliberations was the inclusion of the substantially qualified socio-economic rights set out above.

A further issue of general concern relates to the structure and scope of judicial authority since 1994. The main features are by now well known,[23] but what bears emphasis here is the express and generous grant of judicial independence in the Constitution,[24] and the obligation imposed[25] on 'organs of state' to 'assist and protect the courts to ensure [their] independence, impartiality, dignity, accessibility and effectiveness'. The judicial record since 1994 indicates that the worst fears of those who expected the courts to be a recalcitrant and obstructive force, in the way

[17] Constitution of the Republic of South Africa, s. 33. [18] Ibid., s. 34.

[19] ibid., s. 35, by far the most detailed and longest section in the Bill of Rights.

[20] Constitution of the Republic of South Africa Act, 200 of 1993.

[21] For an account of this series of events, see H Corder, 'Administrative Justice in the Final Constitution' (1997) 13 *SA Journal on Human Rights* 28.

[22] See, e.g., N Haysom, 'Constitutionalism, Majoritarianism, Democracy and Socio-Economic Rights'; E Mureinik, 'Beyond a Charter of Luxuries: Economic Rights in the Constitution'; and D Davis, The Case against the Inclusion of Socio-Economic Demands in a Bill of Rights except as Directive Principles', all of which appeared in (1992) 8 *SA Journal of Human Rights* at 451, 464, and 475, respectively.

[23] For a recent general account, see H Corder, 'Judicial Authority in a Changing South Africa' (2004) 24 *Legal Studies* 253 [24] Constitution, n. 7 above, s. 165(2).

[25] Ibid., s.165(4).

of implementing the substantial reforms and changes necessary to dismantle centuries of institutional racism, have not materialized. Indeed, many judges, led by the Constitutional Court, have displayed admirable adaptability to the foundational values and overall project represented in the Constitution, gaining much respect internationally, even in the sphere of realizing socio-economic rights.[26]

In some respects, the first decade of democracy has been less challenging than might have been expected, the constitutional system benefiting from the substantial measure of popular support for the relatively peaceful and reconciliatory transfer of political power. In addition, the courts found it a simple matter to set aside the most egregious remnants of legalized racism and autocracy. Much harder questions are currently reaching the appellate courts, however, and the outcomes of these disputes have thrown the relationship between the judiciary and the other two branches of government into sharp relief. It is clear, as is to be expected, that many questions remain unresolved, and this is particularly apparent in the socio-economic sphere, to which I now turn.

(ii) Socio-economic Issues in the Courts

The Constitutional Court, as the final authority on all constitutional questions, has delivered five major decisions dealing with socio-economic interests. They have dealt with the rights to health care (both acute[27] and medium-term[28]), to housing (both a positive claim to habitable shelter[29] and the 'negative' protection against eviction[30]) and to social assistance in the form of grants, in this case to permanent residents who are not citizens.[31] These judgments have generally been welcomed by critics, who have praised the Court for its creative yet pragmatic approach to the enforcement of these rights.[32] Some have criticized the courts generally for perceived shortcomings in their interpretive approaches and for being too slow to insist on the implementation of substantial programmes of socio-economic upliftment,[33] in particular, in not crafting remedies which would

26 See generally, MH Cheadle, DM Davis and NRL Haysom (eds.), *South African Constitutional Law: The Bill of Rights* (Butterworths, 2002).

27 *Soobramoney v Minister of Health, Kwa-Zulu Natal* 1998 (I) SA 765 (CC).

28 *Minister of Health and Others v Treatment Action Campaign and Others* 2002 (5) SA 721 (CC).

29 *Government of the Republic of South Africa v Grootboom and Others* 2001 (1) SA 46 (CC).

30 *Port Elizabeth Municipality v Various Occupiers* 2005 (1) SA 217 (CC).

31 *Khosa and Others v Minister of Social Development and Others* 2004 (6) SA 505 (CC).

32 See, e.g., J Sloth-Nielsen, 'Extending Access to Social Assistance to Permanent Residents' (2004) 5(3) *ESR Review* 9; K Pillay, 'Property *v* Housing: Balancing the Interests in Evictions Cases' (2004) 5(5) *ESR Review* 16; and CR Sunstein, 'Social and Economic Rights—Lessons from South Africa' (2000/01) 11 *Forum Constitutionnel* 123.

33 See, e.g., C Scott and P Alston, 'Adjudicating Constitutional Priorities in a Transitional Context: A Comment on *Soobramoney's* Legacy and *Grootboom's* Promise' (2000) 16 SA *Journal on Human Rights* 206; D Bilchitz, 'Towards a Reasonable Approach to the Minimum Care: Laying the Foundations for Future Socio-Economic Rights Jurisprudence' (2003) 19 *SA Journal on Human*

require the executive to report back on steps actually taken to meet the relief granted.[34] On the other hand, the ruling party has recently criticized the judiciary for being insufficiently in touch with the values, hopes, and needs of the people who struggled against past tyrannies.[35] This warning comes in the wake of a dispute about the legality of a government scheme to reduce the cost of medicines, which was initially upheld in the Cape High Court, but overturned unanimously on appeal to the Supreme Court of Appeal.[36]

As already indicated, access to property in the form of land is a highly significant and emotive political issue, especially in those countries in which invading forces took away such access by brutal means and retained ownership unjustifiably. The 'land question' is very much on the agenda in South Africa, the cynical manipulation of land ownership in Zimbabwe being very much in the media over the past few years.

It is in this context that the two cases under review must be seen. Both of them concern rights to property and executive action in relation to such rights, but in substantially contrasting circumstances. The judgments were delivered on consecutive days, and two judges of appeal heard both cases.[37] I will discuss them in the order in which judgment was delivered.

(iii) Informal Settlement on Private Property

Access to land and the return of land to those from whom it was removed for no reason other than their race raise urgent and emotional questions in South Africa. The state has had a national programme of land reform in place since 1994[38] which focuses on three aspects: the restitution of land rights, the redistribution of land, and improving the security of a wide range of forms of tenure of land.[39] The present Constitution requires[40] the state 'to foster conditions which enable citizens to gain access to land on an equitable basis', and provides, furthermore,

Rights 1; and DM Davis, 'Socio-Economic Rights in South Africa: The Record after Ten Years' (2004) 2 *New Zealand Journal of Public and International Law* 47.

[34] Several commentators have urged the Court to use 'structural interdicts' to this end. For a recent and comprehensive review of the socio-economic rights jurisprudence, and an argument for a substantial review of the courts' approach, see M Pieterse, 'Coming to Terms with Judicial Enforcement of Socio-Economic Rights' (2004) 20 *SA Journal on Human Rights* 383. Pieterse discusses remedies at 411–16.

[35] See the African National Congress, 'Anniversary Statement', 8 Jan. 2005.

[36] *Pharmaceutical Society of South Africa and Others v Tshabalala-Msimang and Another NNO, New Clicks South Africa (Pty) Ltd v Minister of Health and Another* 2005 (3) SA 238 (SCA).

[37] Judgments were handed down on 27 and 28 May 2004, and Cameron JA and Southwood AJA were on the Bench in both cases.

[38] As envisaged in the 1993 Constitution, s. 8(3)(b).

[39] Much legislation has been enacted to implement and regulate this programme. See, e.g., the Restitution of Land Rights Act, 22 of 1994; the Development Facilitation Act, 67 of 1995; the Communal Property Associations Act, 28 of 1996; the Extension of Security of Tenure Act, 62 of 1997; the Housing Act, 107 of 1997; and the Prevention of Illegal Eviction from and Unlawful Occupation of Land Act, 19 of 1998.

[40] 1996 Constitution, s.25(5).

that someone 'dispossessed of property after June 1913 as a result of racially discriminatory laws or practices is entitled . . . either to restitution of that property or to equitable redress'.[41] Due to rapid urbanization from the mid-1980s after the abolition of the system of influx control of black South Africans set in place and strictly policed under apartheid, large areas of 'informal settlement' have mushroomed in all large cities and many towns, and this pressure on land for urban residence gave rise to the Modderfontein Squatters cases.[42]

The factual situation which gave rise to this dispute was as follows.[43] Modderklip Boerdery[44] owned a farm close to the large formal township part of Benoni, a city east of Johannesburg. Due to overcrowding in the township, about 18,000 people, occupying about 4,000 residential units (shacks), moved onto a portion of the farm in a five-month period in 2000. Modderklip duly applied for the eviction of the occupiers, and this was granted by the High Court in April 2001, acting under the Prevention of Illegal Eviction from and Unlawful Occupation of Land Act[45] (known as PIE). The court order was duly served on the squatters, but they neither moved nor noted an appeal, and their number grew to about 40,000, with the settlement increasingly 'formalized'. The farm owner then applied to the Sheriff to execute the court order, but she was unwilling to do so without a substantial monetary deposit to cover the costs, to a value which exceeded that of the property concerned. In a parallel strategy, Modderklip laid criminal charges of trespassing against a number of squatters, but those tried and convicted merely returned to the settlement, and the head of the local prison asked Modderklip not to proceed with such charges, as this would have placed an impossible burden on the prison.[46]

Faced with this impasse, Modderklip informally sought assistance from a number of government authorities, without success. The attitude of the police was that it was not their responsibility to enforce the convictions for trespass or to execute judgment in a civil dispute. Modderklip thus returned to court to seek enforcement of its rights, from a number of government agencies.[47] Response from government can be summed up as follows: 'that the issue is not simply one relating to enforcement of a court order, but that it is intimately connected to the larger legal, social and political issue of access to land'.[48] It appeared that the occupied land was unsuitable

[41] Ibid., s.25(7). Claims for restitution of both urban and rural land had to be registered by the end of 1998; many such claims remained undetermined as of early 2005. For a general discussion of this part of the law, see G Budlender *et al., Juta's New Land Law* (Juta, 1998).

[42] The full citation is: *Modderfontein Squatters, Greater Benoni City Council v Modderklip Boerdery (Pty) Ltd (Agri SA and Legal Resources Centre, Amici Curiae) and President of the Republic of South Africa and Others v Modderklip Boerdery (Pty) Ltd (Agri SA and Legal Resources Centre, Amici Curiae)* 2004 (6) SA 40 (SCA) (hereafter *Modderfontein*).

[43] See ibid., para. 2.

[44] Literally, 'Mud-stone Farming', the respondent in each case.

[45] 19 of 1998.

[46] See *Modderfontein*, n. 42 above, paras. 3 to 6. These facts and incidents are not uncommon in South Africa, and give a clear sense of the magnitude of the problem facing the farmer, the authorities, the squatters, and the court. They inevitably lead to a necessity to balance rights and interests, which may well impact negatively on the customary enjoyment of rights to property.

[47] Ibid., paras. 7–12.

[48] Ibid., para. 13.

for housing, so that alternative land would have to be found in any event, but central government had, in several statements, indicated its strong opposition to 'land invasion' of this type, which, if tolerated in the sense of providing alternative accommodation for the squatters, would unfairly advantage them over those waiting patiently on the housing lists, thus amounting to 'queue-jumping'.[49]

In these circumstances, the farm owner sought, and obtained, an order[50] from the court confirming its rights to ownership of property and the government's constitutional obligation to provide some form of housing for the squatters, and reminding the 'organs of state' of their further obligations to assist the courts to ensure their independence and effectiveness.[51] In addition, the court ordered the government by a certain date to produce a comprehensive plan to restore the land to its owners and the provision of alternative shelter for the occupiers. The occupiers and various parts of government duly appealed against both the initial eviction order as well as this order of the Transvaal High Court.

Harms JA, for the unanimous Supreme Court of Appeal,[52] tackled this rather impenetrable situation with an argument from basic constitutional principles, tempered with a healthy dose of pragmatism. The court took as its point of departure the order made by the court *a quo* rather than the judgment appealed against, because the latter 'tend[ed] . . . to overstate matters, and be inappropriately critical of state organs',[53] particularly in its sweeping admonition of the state to assist the courts in order to ensure their effectiveness.[54] Having acknowledged[55] the breach of the constitutional rights against unlawful deprivation of property (Modderklip) and to housing (the occupiers), Harms JA approved the application of the right to equality by the Transvaal High Court, in the sense that Modderklip (as an 'individual') had to bear the burden of accommodating 40,000 people on its land. While acknowledging that the right of access to adequate housing could, conceivably, be invoked horizontally (against an individual, and not the state), this was not such a case.[56] The court then proceeded to determine whether, as the appellants alleged, Modderklip had in some way acquiesced in the occupation of their land and so was to blame for the predicament in which it found itself, concluding that the long-drawn-out negotiations which culminated in court proceedings and their aftermath were not culpable or unreasonable.[57]

This cleared the way for a consideration of the appropriate relief to be granted to Modderklip, a process which relied on a realistic balancing of the respective

[49] *Modderfontein*, paras. 14–18.

[50] The terms of the order are set out in para. 19 of the judgment of the SCA. The judgments *a quo* are unreported (Case Nos 187/03 and 213/03, Witwatersrand Local and Transvaal Provincial Divisions of the High Court).

[51] The constitutional provisions referred to by the court are, respectively, ss. 25(1), 26(1) and (2), and 165(4).

[52] Farlam JA, Cameron JA, Mthiyane JA, and Southwood AJA, concurring.

[53] See *Modderfontein*, n. 42 above, at para.20.

[54] Ibid., para. 29, in which the court stated that it could not 'fathom how the State should know' what it was meant to do in fulfilment of such obligations in the circumstances.

[55] Ibid., paras. 21–30.

[56] Ibid., para. 31.

[57] Ibid., para. 38 and the preceding paras.

rights and obligations of the land owner, the occupier, and the various agencies of the state involved. The Court first held that the declaratory order granted *a quo* had been 'too broadly formulated', and that the 'structural interdict' it had proposed had been insufficiently precise, had imposed an unrealistic time limit, and seemed to justify queue-jumping.[58] In doing so, Harms JA had the following to say[59] generally about structural interdicts:

Structural interdicts . . . have a tendency to blur the distinction between the Executive and the Judiciary and impact on the separation of powers. They tend to deal with policy matters and not with the enforcement of particular rights. Another aspect to take into account is the comity between the different arms of the State. Then there is the problem of sensible enforcement: the State must be able to comply with the order within the limits of its capabilities, financial or otherwise. Policies also change, as do requirements, and all this impacts on enforcement.

Such criticism of the approach taken *a quo* did not solve the problem, however. While the ideal solution might have been the expropriation of the occupied land by the state, 'it is questionable whether a court may order [the] State to expropriate property'. Nevertheless, Harms JA continued:[60]

Courts should not be overawed by practical problems. They should 'attempt to synchronise the real world with the ideal construct of a constitutional world' and they have a duty to mould an order that will provide effective relief to those affected. . . . What 'effective relief' entails will obviously differ from case to case.

As return of the land was not feasible, the only appropriate relief was the award of 'constitutional' damages.[61] The occupiers would thus be allowed to remain on the land, so avoiding the prospect of their jumping the queue for housing and upsetting the orderly process which the state had in place. The state could, naturally, expropriate the land, in which case compensation would cease, in the sense that Modderklip would no longer be suffering damage for breach of a constitutional right.[62] As to the measure of damages, the court discussed whether it should be based on market value or the value of the right of occupation and whether the land should be regarded as vacant or occupied illegally, and so on. As these issues had not been argued, Harms JA concluded that it was appropriate to order an inquiry into damages, thus obviating the need for Modderklip once more to institute proceedings.[63] The Court so ordered.

[58] Ibid., para. 40.

[59] Ibid., para. 39 (footnotes omitted).

[60] Ibid., paras. 42–43. The Court here referred with approval to the extensive discussion of remedial alternatives by the Constitutional Court in *Fose v Minister of Safety and Security* 1997 (3) SA 786 (CC).

[61] This is, to my knowledge, the first occasion on which 'constitutional damages' have been awarded. The Court describes them as 'damages due to the breach of a constitutional entrenched right'. In practical terms it seemed that the Court was effectively ordering the state to 'hire' or 'rent' the land concerned from Modderklip, for so long as it could not be used by the latter for 'cultivating hay'. *Modderfontein*, n. 42 above, para. 43.

[62] Ibid., para. 44.

[63] Ibid., paras. 51 and 52.

The judgment has been welcomed by those who are concerned with realizing economic and social rights, there being particular support for the Court's remarks about the necessity for evictions to be executed as humanely as possible.[64] The state, however, lodged an application for leave to appeal to the Constitutional Court, which was duly granted.[65] The Constitutional Court dismissed the appeal unanimously and sustained the views of the Supreme Court of Appeal in most respects. This endorsement has added further pressure on all levels of government to prioritize an urgent, orderly, and sustained plan to provide basic shelter and amenities for the homeless, so as not to be vulnerable to land invasions of the type which precipitated *Modderfontein*. I will return to some more general remarks about the judicial approach to rights in this case in the final section of this article, but the salient features of the other case under consideration provide a useful foil for such an assessment.

(iv) Administrative Justice, Town Planning, Respect for Religion, and Changing History

One of the reasons for the continuing attraction of the natural beauty of the city of Cape Town is that successive local authorities, of whatever political persuasion, have used their authority to regulate town planning to preserve substantial portions of the peninsular mountain range from residential development. On the western side of Table Mountain on the Atlantic seaboard, contiguous urban development ceases at a particular point, except for long-established smaller settlements further south, leaving the steeply-sloping mountainside in its natural state. While this land is held in both private and public hands, it is gradually being consolidated as a national park. The rights of the private owner of one such property to develop his land, which adjoins the last established suburb, gave rise to the case of *Oudekraal Estates (Pty) Ltd v City of Cape Town and Others*[66] (hereafter *Oudekraal*).

The factual basis of this dispute is relatively simple.[67] Oudekraal Estates, the appellant landowner, had purchased the substantial property in 1965, which had since 1962 been officially laid out and approved as a 'township'. It had taken no steps to develop the township, however, until 1996, when its application for

[64] See A Christmas, 'Case Review 2' (2004) 5(3) *ESR Review* 11, 12.

[65] *See President of the Republic of South African and Another v Modderklip Boerdery and Others* (Case No CCT 20/04, judgment delivered by Langa ACJ on 13 May 2005, unreported). Whereas the SCA had, in its order, declared that the state, by failing to provide land for the squatters, had infringed their rights to shelter and the property rights of Modderklip (see para. 52), the Constitutional Court (see para. 68) declared that the state's failure 'to provide an appropriate mechanism to give effect to the eviction order' had infringed Modderklip's right of access to Court in s. 34 of the Constitution. The emphasis thus shifts away from rights to property: it is too early to assess the significance of this move to the less controversial sphere of 'fair process'.

[66] 2004 (6) SA 222 (SCA).

[67] They are set out in paras. 1–6 of the judgment.

approval of an engineering services plan was refused by the local authority, claiming that the development rights had lapsed. This claim was based on the landowner's failure to comply timeously with two provisions of the relevant provincial planning ordinance, both of which required it to lodge a general plan of the township with appropriate government authorities within a certain period. Although such period had been extended several times, each extension was granted only after expiry of the previous period, and the planning ordinance provided that the permission to develop would be deemed to have lapsed in such circumstances. Thus, despite the existence of an approved general plan for a township having been lodged with the Registrar of Deeds, Oudekraal Estates could not proceed with development. After trying to gain such permission through political means, it turned to the courts for assistance some five years later, seeking declaratory relief to the effect that all administrative action connected to the application had been valid and that the permission to develop was of full force and effect.[68]

Three of the four state agencies which were cited as respondents[69] in the initial application and on appeal opposed the application, which was duly refused by the Cape High Court.[70] The court *a quo* based its judgment on the finding that the extensions of time granted were invalid, and that granting the relief sought would undermine the principle of legality. This fact, together with the fact that the existence of Muslim burial sites on the land had not been properly taken into account when the township plan had been approved almost forty years earlier, moved the court to allow the collateral challenge by the local authority to the validity of the decision of the provincial authority.[71]

The Supreme Court of Appeal[72] chose to focus its attention on the ultimate decision of the province (the appropriate planning authority) to approve and proclaim the township plan in 1962, thus rendering it unnecessary to determine the lawfulness of the extensions of time granted after that date.[73] In determining the lawfulness of the provincial decision, the judgment sets great store by the existence on the land of more than twenty graves, which have special religious and cultural significance for the Muslim community of Cape Town.[74] The evidence disclosed that such graves were visited by thousands of people each year, a practice which dated back at least 100 years. Furthermore, these burial sites, including that regarded as the holiest, fell within the space to be occupied by a proposed school

[68] *Oudekraal*, n. 66 above, at para 7.

[69] Being the local authority, the City of Cape Town, the provincial Minister of Local Government and Development Planning (who did not oppose), and two national agencies, the Parks Board (which owns adjoining land), and the Heritage Resources Agency (as it is concerned with sites of cultural and historical significance).

[70] Reported with the same citation in 2002 (6) SA 573 (C) per Davis and Veldhuizen JJ.

[71] *Oudekraal*, n.66 above, at para. 12.

[72] See n. 66 above. Judgment was given by Howie P and Nugent JA, with whom Cameron JA, Brand JA, and Southwood AJA concurred.

[73] *Oudekraal*, n. 66 above, at para. 13.

[74] See the evidence summarized, ibid., in paras. 14 and 15. Two of the graves were 'kramats', the burial place of Muslims who, 'through conspicuous piety', had attained 'an enlightened spiritual situation'.

and several private residences, and even in the path of a proposed public road.[75] After a review of the further evidence surrounding the approval process, the Court concluded that either the provincial officials who approved the general plan were ignorant of the existence of the graves or that they had chosen to ignore it—the Court preferred the former conclusion in the circumstances.[76] Whichever conclusion was reached, the judges held that the presence of the graves on the land was a factor that should have been considered, and that the failure to do so, for whatever reason, rendered the decision to approve the township invalid.[77]

What were the consequences of this initially unlawful decision, some forty years earlier? Howie P and Nugent JA were clear that such an error did not authorize the local authority, without more, to ignore the 'approval' granted. In their words:[78]

> [I]t exists in fact and it has legal consequences that cannot simply be overlooked. The proper functioning of the modern State would be considerably compromised if all administrative acts could be given effect to or ignored depending upon the view the subject takes of the validity of the act in question.

The rest of the judgment deals with these administrative law issues, in the course of which the Court engaged in an extensive review of the law relating to collateral challenge to the validity of an administrative act and its application to the facts under review. In essence, the Court adopted the English approach to such questions, relying on several decisions in the House of Lords[79] and the commentary of Forsyth on the matter.[80] In other words:[81]

> A collateral challenge to the validity of an administrative act will be available... only 'if the right remedy is sought by the right person in the right proceedings'.... [I]n those cases in which the validity of an administrative act may be challenged collaterally a court has no discretion to allow or disallow the raising of that defence... While the Legislature might often, in the interests of certainty, provide for consequences to follow merely from the fact of an administrative act, the rule of law dictates that the coercive power of the State cannot generally be used against the subject unless the initiating act is legally valid.

The case before the Court demonstrated 'a further aspect of the rule of law, which is that a public authority cannot justify a refusal on its part to perform a public duty by relying... on the invalidity of the originating administrative act'.[82] Applying these conclusions to the dispute before them, the judges were guided by

[75] *Oudekraal*, n. 66 above, para. 16. [76] Ibid., paras. 20–23.

[77] Ibid., paras. 24 and 25. Appellants may well feel aggrieved at the role which changing circumstances played in this judgment, yet they delayed development for some 30 years, and the ending of apartheid has made development a very attractive proposition. [78] Ibid., para. 26.

[79] Ibid., paras. 30–32, particularly *Boddington v British Transport Police* [1999] 2 AC 143 (HL).

[80] C Forsyth, ' "The Metaphysic of Nullity": Invalidity, Conceptual Reasoning and the Rule of Law', in C Forsyth and I Hare (eds.), *Essays on Public Law in Honour of Sir William Wade QC* (Clarendon Press, 1998), 141.

[81] *Oudekraal*, n. 66 above, at paras. 35–37, quoting Forsyth's formulation.

[82] Ibid., at 246 G–H.

the view that it would generally be inappropriate to declare on the validity of an administrative act in isolation of particular consequences.[83] In the circumstances, the Court held that the registration and gazetting of the township by the officials concerned were lawful, notwithstanding the invalidity of the provincial approval on which they were based.[84] This conclusion did not, however, mean that Oudekraal Estates was entitled to the declaratory relief which it sought, due to its 'all-embracing and undifferentiated' nature, irrespective of the consequences of the invalid administrative act which had been identified.[85] The appeal was accordingly dismissed, leaving the appellants holding property rights with severely restricted opportunities for use.

While this judgment is perhaps more relevant to the development and rejuvenation of post-apartheid administrative law and justice, it also demonstrates a judicial approach to property rights informed by a healthy awareness of the socio-political context in which they are sought to be expressed. I will take up this theme in the concluding section which follows.

(v) Making 'Rights' Real

Such extraordinary progress has been made over the past decade in a formal legislative manner to transform South African law into a system which conduces to justice that it is very easy to forget the dire straits in which it found itself in the late 1980s. This is a mistake, for the undeniable achievements of these years have been built on a constitutional practice and a respect for basic rights and fairness which is but fragile and of short duration. One of the key determinants of the successful consolidation of these formal gains is the confidence which the judiciary enjoys in the public mind, a quality which started with a considerable deficit in 1994 and which must be sensitively nurtured, within the constraints of the Constitution. The judiciary must be both sensitive and robust, accountable and independent, and the enforcement of socio-economic rights provides a key testing ground for the development of the courts' legitimacy.

The two judgments described above show, in my view, that the second-highest court in South Africa is prepared to meet the challenges presented to it in this area with an encouraging level of commitment to principle and creativity, blended with a flexibility informed by the human and financial constraints on the delivery of such rights. The Supreme Court of Appeal has been careful not to expect too much of the executive in this sphere, yet simultaneously has not shrunk from criticism of conduct which falls short of constitutional standards, and has crafted remedies which apply gentle yet sustained pressure on government to comply with its obligations to deliver socio-economic goods and services.

[83] Ibid., at para. 38. [84] Ibid., at para. 39. [85] Ibid., paras. 41–45.

The approach in *Modderfontein* will have an impact nationally, as such situations of desperate need, leading to self-help to obtain some form of shelter, exist throughout South Africa, and each level of government faces the problem of how to balance immediate crisis with orderly planning and fair development. The payment of constitutional damages allows a little time to be bought, while not unfairly depriving the landowner of its property rights. The judgment amply demonstrates a judicial policy which is thoroughly aware of the real pressures which are brought to bear on all the parties in such a situation, and the constitution and relevant law are so drafted as to accommodate such a realistic approach, without damaging the fabric of the enterprise.

Oudekraal represents a markedly different set of concerns at the other end of the socio-economic scale. Here the Court constructs an argument which is cast in the relatively traditional language of judicial review of administrative action, yet in substance the judgment relies on the heightened awareness of the value of diversity in culture, religion, and heritage which is such a central feature of the Constitution and much legislation adopted since 1994. At the same time the judgment relies on a principled reading of the rule of law in reminding government of the necessity to observe due process in dealing with the rights of an individual.

A conceptual link between the two cases is the willingness of the court to embrace the relative nature of the right to property, where the owner of property sought to insist on the usual expression of its rights to use and develop the land, but was faced with the competing demands of social justice. In *Modderklip*, the basic needs of the tens of thousands of squatters and the dilemma facing the local and provincial authorities provided the countervailing pressure; in *Oudekraal* it was the cultural and political significance of the burial sites, with an unexpressed sub-text of concern for the natural environment. In each set of circumstances, judicial attitudes just fifteen years earlier would in all likelihood have confirmed an absolute notion of the ownership of land, paying little heed to such concerns. Here the Court was prepared to take a more nuanced view of the bundle of entitlements that make up the 'right to property' and to admit that certain aspects of it may have to yield to the furtherance of the interests of social justice.

In real terms, Modderklip was unable to regain vacant possession of its land by persuading the Court to order the eviction of the squatters because the political ramifications of such a decision (as well as the logistical problems), allied with the competing constitutional rights of the squatters to basic shelter, made this an unsustainable course of action. Similarly, though less dramatically, Oudekraal Estates has had to accept that its rights to develop its property have been restrained (and in effect negated) by recently-recognized constitutional protection accorded to the religious and cultural rights of others. In each of these cases, as judges so often have to do, a balance has to be struck not only between the competing interests of the parties directly concerned, but also indirectly between the tensions inherent in the wider project, being the establishment and strengthening of the sort of democracy expressed in the Constitution and especially the Bill of Rights.

These interpretive tasks play themselves out in another context, which is the anxiety of the courts to establish their legitimacy, both with the public in general and Parliament and the executive in particular. There can be no doubt that the judicial process in South Africa is, for the present, more *overtly* sensitive to stresses and shifts in public policy, and that disputes over property rights in particular are fought out against the backdrop of the 'land question'. The Constitutional Court has recognized the 'public' aspect of property rights,[86] and its lead has been followed recently by the Supreme Court of Appeal.[87] This extract[88] exemplifies the judicial approach:

> At the same time one should never lose sight of the historical context in which the property clause came into existence. The background is one of conquest, as a consequence of which there was a taking of land in circumstances which, to this day, are a source of pain and tension . . . [T]he purpose of section 25 is not merely to protect private property but also to advance the public interest in relation to property.

Scholarly writing about constitutional property law in South Africa is abundant[89] and wrestles with the tensions between the public and private aspects and between the absolute and relative nature of the rights in question. Jim Harris's project in *Property and Justice*[90] adds considerably to an understanding of such tensions. As he wrote:[91]

> Political and legal decisions have to be made about questions of property distribution and property—institutional design. In reaching them, the claims of 'justice' cannot be ignored. Property has to be confronted with justice.

South African lawyers and judges would do well to mull over the many aspects of the necessary relationships between property and justice as they are set out in the pages of this book.

While the picture of the judicial record sketched in these judgments has not been invariably followed across all divisions of the superior courts of South Africa, there is to my mind no doubt that it is characteristic of the general approach of the two most influential courts, the Constitutional Court and the Supreme Court of Appeal. As has been noted, substantial challenges will continue to test the judiciary in all courts, but I would argue that a solid foundation has been laid for a measurable degree of public confidence in the courts to act as a significant watch-dog of government, in the public interest. My sense is that Jim Harris would have approved.

86 See *First National Bank of South Africa v Commissioner, SA Revenue Service and Another* 2002 (4) SA 768 (CC).

87 *Minister of Transport v Du Toit* 2005 (1) SA 16 (SCA), para. 8.

88 *First National Bank*, n. 86 above, para. 64.

89 See the considerable list of publications in *First National Bank*, n. 86 above, 792 in note 79 to the judgment of Ackermann J. Of particular significance are AJ van der Walt, *The Constitutional Property Clause* (Juta, 1997) and AJ van der Walt, *Constitutional Property Clauses: A Comparative Analysis* (Juta, 1999).

90 JW Harris, *Property and Justice* (Clarendon Press, 1996).

91 Ibid., p. vii.

16

Invoking Human Rights

*John Eekelaar**

(i) Introduction

Everyone who heard Jim Harris give the annual lecture to the Society of Legal Scholars in the summer of 2003 realized that something special was happening. With clinical precision, Harris cut through the tangles of scholarship and laid before the audience a taut and logical template for understanding human rights discourse.[1] One year earlier I had tried to persuade myself, and my audience, that human rights concepts could be applied within domestic contexts.[2] This required an attempt on my behalf to understand the general character of human rights discourse.[3] It was my misfortune that Jim Harris's analysis was not available to me when I wrote my essay. When I heard his exposition, I naturally worried about what I would have written had I been able to read it first, for although the analyses seemed to have different starting points, they also seemed to share a number of features. It then seemed to me to be worthwhile to revisit my effort, and re-present it in the manner I might have done had it been possible to pre-view his lecture. In doing this I have removed various sections of my original paper, which were more specifically directed at my immediate theme. If the result has any merit, it could be to strengthen the contributions which each analysis makes, though I have no doubt that Harris's text shows the master's hand.

(ii) The Central Case of Rights

On a visit in 1988 to a region of northern Uganda, the journalist Ryszard Kapuściński made the following remarkable observation:

> We set out for a walk, though I quickly found it a somewhat disconcerting experience. It is the local custom for women, when they see a man walking toward them, to move to the

* Pembroke College, Oxford.

[1] JW Harris, 'Human Rights and Mythical Beasts' (2004) 120 *LQR* 428.

[2] Address to 11th World Conference of the International Society of Family Law, Copenhagen, Aug. 2002.

[3] J Eekelaar, 'Personal Rights and Human Rights' (2002) 2 *Human Rights LR* 181.

side, kneel and wait on their knees until he approaches. He greets them, and in response to this they inquire whether there is anything they can do for him. If he answers 'nothing' they wait until he passes and only then rise and go their way. Similar scenes were repeated later, as I sat with Cuthbert on a bench in front of his house: passing women came up to us, knelt and silently waited. Sometimes my host, busy talking, failed to notice them. They would continue to wait, motionless, until he finally greeted them, wished them farewell, at which point they would get up and walk away.[4]

The idea of human rights is a central element in the development of an international morality. But can we have an international morality which extends to the private sphere? Can we even have rights in the private sphere? Think of the scene described by Kapuściński. It is not domestic, though if it has any accuracy, it is perhaps not difficult to imagine the implications for domestic life. To universalize the case, I will call the woman Eve, the man, Adam, and the location, Eden. It can stand as a paradigm for many human rights issues which arise in domestic settings. For what if Eve were to protest against this custom, or if others in the outside world were to do so, claiming it to be a violation of her human rights? Harris refers to this as an 'invocation' of human rights. He argues that an invoked human right is 'either (a) a supposedly universal strictly-correlative or domain right, or (b) a background right alleged to be common to all human beings living within political communities'; and, further, that 'to announce that *I* (an interest) founds a human right in the second sense is to affirm (1) that *I* is of value to all human beings; (2) that *I* warrants protection and promotion by community measures and (3) that each and every human being has standing, either himself or herself or through his or her representative, to insist that such measures be at least considered for adoption so far as that person's participation in *I* is concerned.' Following Harris's framework, Eve or her supporters might claim a strictly-correlative right: that members of communities have a duty to desist from enforcing compliance with a custom in which women manifest their subservience to all men. This would be part of a code of such precepts (like the duty not to torture), but a moral claim in its own right, without need of any 'meta-ethical scaffolding', which is 'universal and timeless'. Harris is content to sidestep philosophical doubts about objectivity of moral truth and to recognize the existence of such a code from the fact that, for people who (genuinely) assert such rights, that is their moral position.[5] That is enough to establish the existence of the right as a strictly-correlative right. In this case, it would not be open to characterize the claimed right in the alternative formulation as a 'background' right, because that would require its acceptance through community practice, which is patently not the case.

In what follows I will outline a somewhat different approach, which starts with a theory of rights generally and moves from there to one about human rights. In so

[4] R Kapuściński, *The Shadow of the Sun: My African Life* (Allen Lane, 2001), 150. I am grateful to Dr Fareda Banda for knowledge of this book.

[5] The position seems similar to that of Ronald Dworkin in 'Objectivity and Truth: You'd Better Believe It' (1996) 25 *Philosophy and Public Affairs* 87.

doing, I will refer to the points of contact between it and the views of Harris. The similarities are a comfort to me; the differences may not turn out as great as first sight suggests.

(a) 'Having' Rights: Two Levels of Meaning

To speak of 'having' rights is a strange usage, as if one could possess an abstraction.[6] The theory proposed here joins with Harris in rejecting the idea that rights represent certain predetermined categories which are given special protection. Such 'essentialist' theories have been expressed in different forms by theorists such as Shue, Rawls, Finnis, Okin, Habermas, and Gewirth.[7] Rights of these kinds are Harris's 'mythical beasts'. Instead the argument I elaborate later is that the central case of rights arises where an individual makes a claim that an end-state the individual identifies as being in his interests should be socially recognized as an entitlement for that individual *and that that claim is socially recognized.* It is necessary to distinguish between claims *to* a right and statements *about* rights. The latter operate at two levels, both of which are loosely covered by the expression 'having rights'. The first such statement is descriptive of the result where claims to rights (as outlined above) are socially recognized. I will call that 'having' rights in the strong sense. The second is a statement of abstract moral principle, such as that gay people have always and everywhere had the right to have their sexual relationships respected. Such statements have value as part of moral discourse, but if such respect is not shown as a matter of entitlement in social practice, the right 'exists' only in a weak sense. The claim gay persons would make must be to have rights in the strong sense; they are unlikely to be much concerned with how philosophers conceive their well-being. However, since a claim to a right is a demand for social recognition of an entitlement, such a claim can take the structure of a demand that an existing right should be socially recognized. In that case, the right would exist independently of its social recognition. But individuals or groups of individuals can demand all kinds of things as entitlements. Despite the rhetoric, they 'exist' as rights only in aspiration. It is only when the aspiration is matched by some degree of social recognition that the right exists in a strong sense, which is what those who claim rights seek. There is another context in which the distinction between having rights in a strong and weak sense must be made, which

[6] HLA Hart, 'Definition and Theory in Jurisprudence' (1954) 70 *LQR* 37.

[7] H Shue, *Basic Rights: Subsistence, Affluence and US Foreign Policy* (Princeton UP, 1980); J Rawls, *The Law of Peoples* (Harvard UP, 1999). See further J Tasioulas, 'From Utopia to Kazanistan: John Rawls and the Law of Peoples' (2002) 22 *OJLS* 367; J Finnis, *Natural Law and Natural Rights* (Clarendon Press, 1980); S Muller Okin, 'Liberty and Welfare: Some Issues in Human Rights Theory', in JR Pennock and JW Chapman (eds.), *Human Rights* (Nomos XXIII, NYUP, 1981), ch. 12; J Habermas, *Between Facts and Norms: Contributions to a Discourse Theory of Law and Democracy* (Polity Press, 1996); A Gewirth, *Human Rights: Essays on Justification and Applications* (U Chicago Press, 1982). These are discussed in more detailed in Eekelaar, n. 3 above.

will be described shortly. It will be seen later that the distinction between these two senses of 'having' rights is of great importance for understanding human rights.

(b) Nature of End-states

A core feature of rights-claims is the identification of end-states, whether they be such things as freedom from torture, or clean air, good public health, protection of privacy, or enhancement of respect, which some person or persons are seen as having a duty to provide. This focus upon end-states perhaps derives from the early idea of rights as referring to a relationship between a person and a 'thing'.[8] This is well captured by Harris's description of a rightholder as someone with standing to 'insist on something'. The end-state is that something. The nature of the duties needed to secure those end-states, on whom they fall, and their extent, needs to be worked out in the light of the nature of the end-state concerned. The duties need not fall on identified individuals. So one can imagine that certain end-states, such as being provided with sufficient means to support one's children, might be protected by duties on the community rather than on an individual.

There is an alternative formulation, which holds that people can have rights which protect end-states which the alleged right-holder does not believe to be in her interests, although others do. That would mean that people could have rights they do not want. There is again a sense in which this is true. Someone could be said to 'have' a right even if they did not wish to exercise it. But this is once more a weak sense of 'having' rights, even if socially recognized, and also a dangerous one. It is dangerous because, although it is not necessarily wrong to impose outcomes on people which they do not want, to do this under the guise of protecting their rights is to misuse the central feature of invoking rights, just described.[9] An attempt may be made to avoid this by holding that rights always imply choice,[10] and that therefore we can have rights we do not want, but will always be free to decline to *exercise* them. It is true that we can have rights, but decline to exercise them. But they will not be rights which we do not want. We must distinguish between voluntarily waiving a right, as where someone chooses not to enforce a right to be paid for working for someone too poor to pay, and situations where someone does not believe they have a right in the first instance. For example, if campaigners wished to persuade someone that they had a right to exact payment from their children for bringing them up, that person might reject such an end-state

[8] Finnis, n. 7 above, 201–2.

[9] See K Simmonds, 'The Modern Will Theory', in M Kramer, K Simmonds, and H Steiner (eds.), *A Debate over Rights* (OUP, 2000), 223–32; and H Steiner, 'Some Real Problems with the Interest Theory', in ibid., 298–301.

[10] As HLA Hart considered to be true of the paradigm case of civil legal rights: 'Bentham on Legal Rights' in AWB Simpson (ed.), *Oxford Essays in Jurisprudence (Second Series)* (Clarendon Press, 1973), ch. 7.

as being part of their conception of their well-being. They would not simply decline to exercise it.[11] They might be upset if social pressure were to be put on their children to make payments, or on others to bring about this result. They are likely to object even more strongly if this was put forward by way of protecting their rights. Some women might see the right to have an abortion in this way. Even if such a right were socially accepted, they would 'have' it, but only in the weak, and not the full-blooded sense.

It is thus better to say that rights invocations are always claims to choose outcomes, for favourable choice implies identification with the outcome, rather than pre-articulated outcomes which rightholders are free to exercise or not. If a right-holder is not allowed to decide against the exercise of a right, as when Diane Pretty[12] sought legal permission to be assisted in her suicide when her disease made her life unbearable, and was refused, it seems perverse to see this outcome as an enforcement of *her* right to life. The outcome must have *diminished* the total sum of her rights (that is, it removed her right to *choose* to live). To say that certain rights are inalienable[13] can only mean that they refer to end-states which it can be assumed people would normally identify as being part of their well-being and that, accordingly, apparent expressions of individuals' wishes to the contrary are to be treated with much caution. But to impose an outcome which is expressly rejected as a right violates the core idea of the right as recognition of an end-state with which the individual identifies his or her well-being. Having a right in this strong sense is akin to possessing or even owning[14] the right. Like other goods, such as aesthetic experience and friendship, we only truly possess rights by virtue of our participation in them. They are ours if, and only if, we embrace them. This is not surprising in view of the close relationship between rights and identification of our well-being. Sometimes, perhaps often, we may choose not to exercise a right, or even think that it is wrong to do so, just as we choose not to have friendships with everyone. But that does not mean that we value the right any the less. If it did, such as if our political apathy was so great that we cared not at all whether we could vote or not, then the right to vote would have lost all meaning for us.

Hence, the central case of rights to which I hold is premised on the capacity of the individual to have a genuine appreciation of his or her goals; that is, it is assumed the individual is fully competent and acting in conditions of freedom. Can the incompetent, and those too oppressed to make claims, then, have no rights? Surely they must have. But to what? If we believe in rights at all, we must

[11] The power to choose whether to exercise a right can be an important element of a right. For example, I may decide not to, or never to, write letters to the press, or even to vote, and still believe these are important rights to have. However, a person who was so contemptuous of democracy that he despised free expression or the electoral process might be reluctant to consider those rights as being of any significance, or even to be undesirable.

[12] See European Court of Human Rights, App. 2346/02 *Pretty v United Kingdom*.

[13] N MacCormick, 'Rights in Legislation' in PMS Hacker and J Raz (eds.), *Law, Morality and Society: Essays in Honour of H.L.A. Hart* (Clarendon Press, 1977), ch. 11.

[14] See Hart, n. 10 above, 193.

believe they have a right to be freed from oppression and to achieve competence as far as possible, so that they can exercise the requisite choices. That is consistent with what Hart appeared to argue when he stated that 'in the case of special rights as well as of general rights, recognition of them implies the recognition of the equal right of all men to be free'.[15] In so far as competence and freedom are always imperfectly achieved, rights are correspondingly less fully realized. But do the incompetent and unfree have rights other than to become competent and to be freed? We must be careful in ascribing specific rights in such circumstances. Too often, interests have been attributed to children and people of uncertain mental competence which are really the interests of adults, or those of sound mind. Sometimes, those attributed interests have carelessly been said to be rights (as when it was said that those children who were 'exported' to the colonies from England, with scant attention to their wishes, had a 'right' to be sent). But we can nevertheless talk of children and others having rights to end-states which they are not competent to identify, but only if we make real efforts to empathize with their own perception, conscious or unconscious, of their interests.[16] Where this cannot be done, it will be necessary to make an assumption about which viewpoint the child or incompetent adult would take about their interests, were they able to take it with full information. This concession has a fictitious quality to it, but is a small price to pay for maintaining coherence with the nature of the central case of rights expressed here, and has the virtue that it focuses the attention of people making decisions for children on the child's perspective as it grows up. In any case, even very young children do in fact demonstrate biological and psychological drives which identify many end-states as being in their interests, especially their nutrition, health, and protection.

(c) Grounds for Entitlement

Thus far, my account seems far from that of Harris. I have insisted on a social element, which Harris requires only for background rights, not strictly-correlative universal ones. And I have said nothing of morality. But our accounts begin to converge at the next stage of my analysis. For a claim to a right is a claim to an entitlement, and not simply a demand or assertion of power. The claim must therefore be capable of being supported by justificatory reasons. Like Harris, I make no claims about objective moral truth. I think my response is very similar to his, but I have broken it into three elements. The first consists in reference to moral values. Rights claims do not *constitute* morality, but they do *presuppose* a moral system in the same way as Hart showed that claims to legal rights presuppose the existence of a legal system.[17] The strength of rights claims is that, like legal cases in common

15 HLA Hart, 'Are there any Natural Rights' in J Waldron (ed.), *Theories of Rights* (OUP, 1984), 90.

16 I have written extensively about this elsewhere: most recently in 'Children between Cultures' (2004) 18 *Int'l J of Law, Policy and the Family* 178.

17 HLA Hart, 'Definition and Theory in Jurisprudence', in HLA Hart, *Essays in Jurisprudence and Philosophy* (OUP, 1983), ch. 1.

law systems, they focus on fact-situations which apply, interpret, and, often, extend the *application* of moral principles through the extension of duties. I take this to express the same idea as that described by Harris as 'the enforcement hinge', whereby background rights evolve over time. Suppose Eve claims to be free from the humiliation she feels to be caused to her by the custom. This builds on background notions of care and personal respect, which are likely to be present in other contexts in her society. The point of Eve's assertion of entitlement is to try to extend those general moral aspirations into a duty to bring about the specific end-state (freedom from the manifestation) which she identifies as being an important aspect of her well-being. Such accretions can be strongly contested, of course, as the history of rights claims shows. But the overall result is the expansion of the scope of obligations. For here the driver is the obligee rather than the obligor, and the engine is the assertion of autonomy.[18]

There is a second element to the issue of justification. Suppose Eve were to claim that she, but no other Edenite woman, should be free from the humiliating custom. This also raises moral issues. Why should those duties be owed to her alone? Moral principles are by their nature generalizable. Suppose Eve bases her claim on the fact that she is the daughter of a particular family. What moral reasons can she find to restrict her claim to such a narrow base? She may prefer to base it on the effects of the custom on her, but then why only the effects on her and not on other Edenite women? If she is married to Adam, she might extend the claim to women who are wives, perhaps basing it on the dignity of being a wife in that community, a conception of status. By identifying with other wives, she recognizes that others within the same class or category have the same entitlement. Even a king's assertion of the divine right to rule is rooted in the claimant's qualification for status, and implicitly extends to all monarchs. I will call this the *social base* for the right, because it refers to some social category, event, condition, or activity through which the claimant claims to be qualified for the entitlement. This important implication is much neglected in contemporary rights analyses. Indeed, the failure to recognize it accounts for the misleading picture of the nature of rights expressed by all those who seem to view rights discourse as nothing more than selfish assertion, such as in the American discourse of rights described by Glendon.[19] This has important consequences, for, in referring to the social base of Edenite wives, Eve is committed to believing that other Edenite wives should have this right as well. This is of great importance when we consider human rights.

[18] This explains why the rhetoric of rights appears to be most important in circumstances where the right is threatened or contested. See J Donnelly, *Universal Human Rights in Law and Practice* (Cornell UP, 1989).

[19] MA Glendon, *Rights Talk: The Impoverishment of Political Discourse* (The Free Press, 1991), ch. 3. See also Onora O'Neill, Second Reith Lecture, BBC Radio 4, 10 Apr. 2002, and Sir John Laws, 'Beyond Rights' (2003) 23 *OJLS* 265. The recognition of the social base also resolves the contradiction John Charvet alleged to exist in rights claims between assertions of self-determination and ideas of equality: 'A Critique of Human Rights' in Pennock and Chapman (eds.), n. 7 above.

The third element to be considered as a ground for entitlement is whether the claim is strong enough to impose an obligation. There may be nothing *immoral* in my claiming that all fathers have a right to be served breakfast in bed by their children, and my identification with the class of fathers provides a basis for an entitlement, but is it strong enough to give rise to a duty, especially when seen in the context of other claims on my children? The answer must relate to the weight of the interest with respect to which the claim is made.[20] The fathers' claim, at any rate as a claim to a moral right, would gain weight if confined to parents who were physically disabled. Conversely, imagine that the only way my well-being can be protected is if the person under a duty to protect it sacrifices his life. Thus the extent of the duty generated by the end-state in particular cases will depend on a weighing of the interests involved.

In assessing the weight of an interest, it is important to remember that the claim is to an end-state which the claimant perceives as an element of his or her well-being. Is it possible to evaluate the importance of various end-states to the well-being of different claimants? This might be difficult since aspects of our well-being may be incommensurable.[21] The concept of rights in itself cannot generate measures for assessing the relative weights of different interests. But that does not mean that there can be no standard against which rights claims can be measured. We could assess the impact they have on an individual's life. It is normally more important for someone to attend a job interview than that another should attend a sporting event, so if only one can be achieved, the former should be chosen. The decision about with whom a child should live is more important to the child than it is for either adult who disputes it, because of the potential long-term effects on the child's life. A woman's decision about whom she wishes to marry is more important to her than it is to any of her family members. Of course, such judgments raise normative issues. A person's well-being cannot be evaluated *solely* in terms of the strength of that individual's desires. It must include the value of integrating that individual within a community which demands respect for the rights, and therefore the well-being (in the sense explained here), of all others.[22]

Finally, the strength of the justification may be related to the extent to which the exercise of the right is bound up with responsibilities. Suppose it is the understanding in Eden that, while women offer service to men in the way described, every man is expected to provide protection to any woman in the community

[20] Raz says that this is not so, and that rights may apply disproportionately to the strength of the right-holder's interest. Yet his example of the right to an old shirt relies on a *legal* right surviving other (perhaps moral) claims, and that is something which must have much weight: J Raz, 'Rights and Individual Well-Being', in J Raz, *Ethics in the Public Domain* (OUP, 1994), ch. 3. His position would be harder to sustain were he to consider only competing moral rights, for example, if a person promises to give his only bottle of medicine to both A and B, but only A is really ill. In those circumstances A's claim to be entitled to the performance of the promise must be stronger than B's.

[21] See Raz, n. 20 above, ch. 13.

[22] See generally R Crisp and B Hooker (eds.), *Well-Being and Morality: Essays in Honour of James Griffin* (OUP, 2000).

should she confront any physical threat. For all I know, that could be the case in that area of Uganda described by Kapuściński. How does this affect the idea of the men's rights? The first point to make is that there is no *necessary* linkage between rights and responsibilities of this kind. It is conceptually quite possible to claim a right, and indeed to have one, without undertaking any corresponding responsibility (other than of the 'horizontal' kind mentioned). Rights to humane treatment are perhaps of this kind: claiming such rights necessarily implies recognizing the rights of others to humane treatment, but does not necessarily imply that you owe any other duties to those you expect to act humanely towards you. The right not to suffer violence, or to be afforded freedom of marriage, demands no payment in return. However, though there is no necessary linkage, such a linkage may be very important. Indeed, it may be common, especially in personal relationships. Such reciprocity may be imposed by social norms. One could characterize the duties of fidelity and domestic subservience, visited on women by traditional marriage law and custom throughout history, as being part of a compact under which husbands, in return, undertook to provide lifelong economic support to their wives. And if you think this is no longer acceptable, consider what the position would be if husbands undertook no such reciprocal responsibility. It is possible that such linkages still occur, though in post-modern society the reciprocal element may not be imposed, but individually negotiated. These linkages, then, may play an important part in the grounds for justification of rights. Indeed, by claiming to place a constraint upon others, through the duties which are implied in rights-claims, the claimant is committed to a moral dialogue, in which his or her own responsibility is in issue. Even such claims as those for economic well-being and good environmental standards raises issues of the responsibility of the claimant, among others, towards achieving those goals. This is, therefore, another way in which rights-discourse promotes community morality.

(iii) Human Rights

Human rights have the same structure as all rights. My thesis is that the only difference lies in the nature of the social base through which the entitlement is claimed. Claims to human rights are claims to social recognition of specific end-states (described and justified as explained above) *where the social base is the whole of humanity*. Human rights exist (in the strong sense) to the extent that such social recognition is won. Of course, such social recognition need not be absolute: socially recognized claims may conflict, and mechanisms may be necessary for deciding between them in that case. There is nothing startling in saying this. Perry has put it this way: 'any claim about what one is due as a human being in particular circumstances is essentially just a claim about the contextual implications or requirements . . . of a norm concerning what anyone and everyone is due simply as a human being. In this sense, human rights claims are invariably about what one is due as a human being.'[23] This opens up a conception of human rights which allows the content to be driven by claims made by individuals, or groups of individuals, or their representatives on their behalf. It thus becomes unnecessary to attempt to identify *a priori* what kinds of matters are of 'special' importance for humans or to specific constitutional arrangements. However, its implications need to be spelled out in the light of other features of rights described earlier.

(a) The Nature and Role of the Social Base in Human Rights Claims

First, we need to look more closely at the *nature* of the social base. To claim qualification for an entitlement through my humanity requires some elucidation. Sometimes it might be quite straightforward: I should be protected against torture simply because no one should torture a human being. But it extends to claims arising out of experiences or conditions common to all humans. Suppose someone claimed that all humans are entitled to know whether the other partner in a sexual relationship is suffering from AIDS. The social base covers only those people engaged in sexual activity. But it can be seen as a claim to a human right because sexual activity is a universal human activity. The same is true for the right to respect for family life, proclaimed as a human right under the European Convention. This only arises where a person has a family life to be respected. But participation in family life is also a standard human condition. The same reasoning holds for claims of rights by the poor, sick, or disabled.

Secondly, we must be careful to understand the correct relationship between the end-state claimed and the social base. For example, the claim that the right to marry is a human right implies a certain conception of marriage. At its most fundamental, if that conception is confined to heterosexual unions, proclaiming it a universal right does not imply accepting a right to same-sex marriage. However, if the end-state claimed is more broadly drawn, for example, as the legal and public recognition of an intimate relationship between adults of full competence (of which marriage is but one example), then resting the claim on a universal basis would imply recognition of same-sex unions. Similarly, the claim of a right to marry includes a conception of rights which *should* constitute that institution. If these include the right to equal treatment within marriage, then claims to equality of treatment within marriage will normally be framed as human rights. The claimants see this as an end-state which should form part of the constitutive elements of an institution which is, or should be, open to all humans. The same might be said of some other rights claims, such as to the peaceful enjoyment of property and protection against unreasonable deprivation of property rights. Clearly these rights are confined to property holders. Yet some form of property holding can be claimed as a human right, and is almost universal. Children's rights are even more easily thought of as being 'human' rights because all humans are, at

[23] M Perry, *The Idea of Human Rights: Four Inquiries* (OUP, 1998), 47.

one time, children, so their rights are the rights of all humans who, at the relevant time, just happen to be children.

Thirdly, a distinction must be made between factors which are *constitutive of* an end-state to which a right is claimed, and factors which serve only as a *qualification* for the right claimed. So the claim of a right to marry includes a conception of rights which *should* constitute that institution. If these include the right to equal treatment within marriage, then claims to equality of treatment within marriage will normally be framed as claims to human rights. The claimants see this as an end-state which should form part of the constitutive elements of an institution which is, or should be, open to all humans. Compare the following: suppose a Muslim were to claim the right to wear a headscarf at school. If wearing a headscarf were a *constitutive element* of education, and one could plausibly claim education as a human right, then the claim to wear a headscarf would be a claim to a human right. But it is not a constitutive element of education, such as access to books may be. The claim would be a claim to a right, to be sure, but would not be to claim the right as a human right, only of a schoolchild's right. This is because being at school would only be a *qualification* for the right claimed. However, the claim could be put (more effectively) as a claim that *Muslims* should have the right to have their religious practices respected, and wearing a headscarf could be seen as one of the constitutive features of practising Islam. Is *this* a claim to a human right? Not in that form, since it is confined to Muslims. It is a claim for the rights of Muslims. If, however, the claim were grounded in the right of everyone to choose (or not) his or her religion, and to be able to perform a constitutive feature of a chosen religion, then it has a universalist base, and can be said to be a claim to a human right. Like other human rights, though, its social recognition may require compromise in cases of conflict with other rights.

The fourth point to emphasize is the *role* of the social base. By grounding the entitlement claim in the class of humanity, the claimant accepts the extension of the entitlement to everyone. This is not only a powerful expression of solidarity with others: it implies a commitment to realizing similar claims made by anyone else, wherever they be. The significance of this can be illustrated by comparing it to a situation where a human right is *overridden* by some other right. For example, the right to respect for family life is a qualified right, and therefore can be overridden, such as where this is necessary to protect a child's welfare.[24] But if it were overridden by some characteristic of a claimant to the right, for example, his sexual orientation,[25] then the right would not be viewed as a human right (or at least be less of one). Hence, if it is a human right, the right to respect for family life must apply to non-nationals as well as to nationals,[26] although, if the right is overridden (for example, by reason of commission of offences, provided the override is

[24] *Olsson v Sweden* (1989) 11 EHRR 259.
[25] See *Salgueiro da Silva Mouta v Portugal* [2001] 1 FCR 653.
[26] *Berrehab v The Netherlands* (1989) 11 EHRR 322.

proportionate) then a non-national may be subjected to the severer penalty of deportation, for the immunity against deportation applies only to nationals, and is not therefore a human right.

(b) Three Objections

I will consider three objections which may be levelled against this position. The first would query the capacity of some claims thought to be to human rights to rest on a universalist social base. Cranston, for example, has indeed argued that economic and social rights lack the universality to be considered truly as human rights.[27] One might indeed, when conceptualizing such claims, see them entirely as limited to restricted classes of people, and therefore not as human rights. Suppose someone were to claim the right to be compensated for environmentally caused illness. This is a condition to which any human being is open. But the claim *might* simply be grounded in the claimant's citizenship, because the argument might depend on analogous cases where compensation has been given within the legal system to which the claimant belongs, and be dependent on the economic conditions prevailing in that country. The claim would not then be for a human right, but a citizenship right. But on another level (which would become clearer if the legal system rejected the claim), the claim *could* be grounded on the fact of the claimant's humanity. If so, the claimant would be committed to believing that, for people in poorer countries whose societies are less easily able to protect them, the international community (comprising multi-national corporations; the richer economies, amongst others) has duties to ensure they are compensated. This would then be seen as a human right. The same could also be said of the right to work, or to a fair wage, or, within the family context, to adequate recognition of contributions to the household.[28]

The second objection is that the analysis would allow trivial matters to be included as human rights, for example, a claim to be allowed to wear one's hair in a certain style. But some apparently trivial matters can assume a greater significance in certain contexts.[29] Harris explains this by drawing attention to domain rights, which include all kinds of activities, many of which might themselves be inconsequential, but which are protected by 'fencing duties', such as duties not to

[27] M Cranston, *What are Human Rights?* (Bodley Head, 1973).

[28] Nelson observes that the duty to protect human rights is normally ascribed to nation-states: W Nelson, 'Human Rights and Human Obligations', in Pennock and Chapman (eds.), n. 7 above, ch. 14. This is largely true in view of state monopolies over enforcement mechanisms. But people believing their rights-claims to rest on a universal social base can assert that the duties to observe such rights extend much wider than that.

[29] It was reported during 2001 that the Taliban government in Afghanistan banned the wearing of hair styled in the fashion of the film actor, Leonardo di Caprio. Donnelly, n. 18 above, 14, has pointed out that *claims* to human rights are characteristically made by people whose legal rights are denied: 'when human rights are made effectively justiciable, those whose rights are violated will usually *claim* legal, not human, rights (although they continue to *have* all the same human rights)'.

invade privacy or restrict free speech. Thus, the claim to wear a certain hairstyle may indirectly assert a claim to freedom of expression. Harris regards fencing duties as expressive of 'a timeless, universal and culture-transcending moral code'.

The third objection is the most important. It is that this position is imperialistic. On what grounds can a claimant put forward a claim on behalf of the whole world? This raises the issue of relativism. On this, my position seems contradictory. On the one hand, I have said that for a right to exist the end-state must be identified by the right-holder as being an important aspect of her well-being. On the other hand, I have said that the right-holder is committed to believing that anyone in the same position has the same right, whether they make the same identification or not. The apparent contradiction is resolved by distinguishing between having a right either in the weak sense or in the strong sense, described earlier. So, if Eve, using justificatory arguments of the kinds described earlier, convinces large numbers of the international community to recognize that she, as an Edenite woman, is entitled to be free of the custom (and therefore has a right in the strong sense), it would be natural for the community to think that *all* Edenite women had the same right. But many of those women might not believe they have the right at all. They might think that the custom supports a respectful society and promotes trust and stability, and might not welcome people saying they have a right to be free of it. In such circumstances, their right to be freed from it is a right only in the weak sense. We should recognize that we cannot claim rights in the strong sense for people who do not identify their well-being in the same way as we do ours. To do so is both insulting and destructive of the force of rights claims. But claiming them in the weak sense is not without importance as long as we recognize the limitations, and risks, of such a claim. It implies that the culture of Eden should be open to the possibility that its women might make the claim to be free of the custom. This involves what Sampford has called a 'fourth' dimension to human rights: the necessity for social arrangements to avoid pressures which impede the making of such choices.[30] This simply underlines the importance, frequently asserted, of dialogue, at both the national and international level.[31] But it arises from the point already made, that the rhetoric of rights is deeply associated with assumptions about freedom. Those who see freedom as threatening will also be wary of that rhetoric. *In this respect only* the idea of rights applies to people irrespective of how they define their well-being.

Suppose, however, that the matter is freely discussed within Eden but the rights, though now asserted by a number of Edenite women, are denied because they are deemed inconsistent with other values of Edenite society? It seems clear from my analysis that, if people outside Eden believe *they* have a human right to certain end-states and if *some* Edenite women claim the same end-states, then the

[30] C Sampford, 'The Four Dimensions of Rights', in B Galligan and C Sampford (eds.), Rethinking *Human Rights* (The Federation Press, 1997), ch. 4.

[31] For an example, see A An Nai'im, 'Cultural Transformation and Normative Consensus on the Best Interests of the Child', in P Alston (ed.), *The Best Interests of the Child: Reconciling Culture and Human Rights* (Clarendon Press, 1994), 62–81.

outsiders must think that those women have that right in the strong sense. It is possible, though, that cultural variables may raise matters which affect the *exercise* or *mode of enforcement* of the right. In particular, the impact its exercise may have on the well-being of others could be an important restraint. This could vary in different cultural contexts. But this is not surprising. All rights must be exercised in social contexts which include the rights of others, and there may be good reasons for modifying their impact. But that does not deny their existence or the importance of openly and genuinely assessing their weight.

(iv) To Conclude

(a) Comparing the Analyses

It may seem that I have conflated the two types of human right which Harris went to great pains to distinguish. For I have maintained that the extent of existence of rights (and therefore of human rights), in a strong and important sense, is directly related to the degree of social recognition given to the claim; and I have suggested that the ethical element is provided by a combination of (i) appeals to background principles of a moral kind; (ii) identification of others as co-claimants (the social base); and (iii) a weighing of the importance of the interest to the claimants as against the importance of competing interests to competing claimants. This is almost identical to Harris's description of background rights. Yet Harris's strictly-correlative and domain rights appear to occupy a pre-eminent place in his analysis, by virtue of their timelessness, universality, and absolute character, while I have perceived such socially unsupported rights as but shadowy spectres, rights in a weak sense. Does it matter? In fact, it can be safely assumed that the types of rights which Harris classes as strictly correlative, such as those against torture, or rape, are invoked by everyone. Who would not claim these for themselves? Even tyrants today claim to be innocent of the vilest abuses. So in practice the categories will merge. But there are grey areas. Some domain rights might be less clear-cut. Ideas of privacy and freedom of expression may vary significantly between cultures. The Ugandan custom may be one, and here it might be well to recognize that, in the absence of support within the women of the community, the discourse about the rights of its members by those beyond the culture assumes a weaker, more aspirational, form.

So can my analysis of human rights fit completely within Harris's class of background rights? The fit is close, but not exact. For Harris, the conventional right acquires its moral status and universality as a human right by virtue of the relationship between the background right itself (that is, the conventional, or social, recognition of the relevant duty) and a universally recognized human interest.[32] I prefer a slightly different formulation. The end-state towards which the invocation

[32] 'The ethical dimension is founded on the ethical arguments that establish the truth of assertions about the equivalent inter-personal universal moral rights ("human rights" in the other sense).'

of a right insists that measures must be taken, must indeed be supported by reference to moral principles, and usually moral principles have a universalist character. But to make the invocation one of a human right requires, I have argued, that the claimant grounds his assertion of entitlement in the fact of his humanity. Thus on the one hand, a wounded member of an army might appeal to the ethical principle of compassion in insisting on help from his fellow-countrymen, but he may not think that a wounded enemy has a similar entitlement. He calls upon compassion as a basis for action, but a partial compassion due to him in his capacity as a fighter for his country. He is not claiming a human right. On the other hand, if someone appeals for the relief of his poverty, without thought for anything other than his humanity as being the ground of entitlement, then a human right is invoked.

(b) In Summary

In rejecting essentialist theories—Harris's 'mythical beasts'—I have made the idea of human rights dependent on claims we make ourselves. They must be claims for social action, not philosophical analyses about the nature of the good life. We have to start with ourselves. We could recognize that others have rights which we do not claim for ourselves, for example, that shareholders have rights when we do not own shares, or acknowledge the rights of French people when we are British. But then we could not be referring to their human rights, only to their rights as shareholders or as citizens. We could hardly claim that other people should have rights arising solely from their humanity, which we do not think we ourselves should have. And if we make a claim to an entitlement by reference to our status as human beings, we are committed to believing that it holds for all other human beings. This is indeed what Harris calls a 'breath-takingly bold ethical claim'.

Taking the actual invocation of rights as the starting (but by no means the finishing) point lays the ground for an expansive concept of human rights, generating the dynamism Harris describes background rights as having. If some people claim damages for, say, harm to their reputation, and ground it in their concept of human self-worth, then this, and many other claims, could become human rights. And why not? Some might think that this would undermine the force of the constitutional protection of human rights, such as in the Canadian Charter of Rights or the European Convention on Human Rights and Fundamental Freedoms. For these, in different ways, give certain identified rights special constitutional protection. Surely, it might be said, this should not extend to rights such as those just mentioned, for that would severely disable legislative competence. But recognition of rights does not necessarily imply that they should have special legal or constitutional protection. Social or political processes may be sufficient. Yet suppose a legislature were to prohibit claims for defamation (by private persons). It would surely be at least arguable that such acts breached the broad principles (in Harris's terms, 'fencing duties'—whether expressed in terms of due process, privacy, property, family life, or something else) set out in those and other constitutional documents or, if they did not, that the principles *should* encompass them.

So where does this leave human rights principles set out in such instruments and developed in jurisprudence? It seems that rights proclaimed in human rights instruments contribute significantly to the background morality against which rights claims are made. But they can be instantiated only through specific end-states. Take equality norms. Few people would want to be treated on an equal footing with the oppressed or deprived. As Harris puts it, '[e]quality as such is not, in my view, a measure-warranting issue'. But equality adds weight to a claim to an end-state someone desires, but which is denied, while others enjoy it. So, equality claims allow rights claimants to maintain that specific end-states previously denied to them should extend to them, or that newly proclaimed end-states should attract certain duties which they did not do before. The development of this universality in jurisprudence is an important part of the social acceptance of the claim necessary for it to exist as a right in the strong sense.

But recognition of rights as human rights recognizes equality in a far deeper sense, for the nature of the social base through which the claim is made identifies the claimant with the whole of humanity. There may be no conclusive argument that compels us to use humanity as our social base, any more than there is (or may be) an argument to treat human beings as sacred. But someone who confines the social base to his co-religionists, co-citizens, or his gender might have an uncomfortable time explaining why the social base is *not* extended to all human beings. That is why it is a mistake to see rights claims as fundamentally, or even largely, self-interested. For those who believe all human beings are entitled to an end-state they are claiming, and who can make good justificatory arguments for the claim, then, to the extent that others are denied that outcome, they must surely believe, in Harris's words, that they 'have standing to insist' that something should be done about it.

17

The Infant in the Snow

*Timothy Endicott**

In order to work out which claims to human rights are sound (if any), you need to work out what sense they can be given (if any). Jim Harris set about that job in 'Human Rights and Mythical Beasts', a lecture that he gave to the Society of Legal Scholars in the last year of his life.[1] The lecture was part of a larger project, on which Jim had been working for two years. That larger project resulted in a substantial manuscript, bearing the provisional title, 'Resources and Human Rights: Moral Foundations of Human Rights, Property Rights, and Resource-depleting Rights'.[2] The project built on the serious attention he had given (over a period of years) to justice in the use of resources—a problem that turns out to be central to an understanding of many human rights claims. His work is refreshing to read because it is careful and consistent. He was passionately concerned for people, and dispassionately concerned to tell the truth. I wish I could talk to him about it; having lost him, I will try to follow the example he set in his careful and critical response to other writers. My purpose is partly to show what I think is true and important in what he says, but since he has already said it, I will focus on the points at which I think that I disagree. If you don't mind, I'll talk about 'Harris' and what he says, to give myself the detachment I need.

Harris offered his work as 'an analytical sketch for a complete overview of human rights invocations' (428). I will argue that the sketch can be simplified and clarified, because human discourse (sections (ii), (iii)) and human conventions (sections (iv), (v)) play no role in human rights. That discussion will lead us to the foundations of human rights, which Harris found partly in what he called 'natural equality', and partly in the practices of particular communities. But community practices play no role in human rights. And I will argue that natural equality, while a genuine characteristic of all human beings, is not necessary for and

* Balliol College, Oxford. For valuable comments on an earlier version of this Chapter I am grateful to John Finnis, Aileen Kavanagh, and an anonymous reviewer for this book.

[1] Since published under the same title, (2004) 120 *LQR* 428. References in the text by page numbers in round brackets are to this article in the *Law Quarterly Review*, which I will call 'Mythical Beasts'.

[2] I will refer to it as 'the Manuscript', with references in the text in square brackets.

does not explain human rights (section (v)). Human rights are explained by considerations of justice that Harris himself had identified in his book, *Property and Justice*.

So the gist of my argument is that human discourse and human conventions do not have the importance for human rights that Harris ascribes to them. Suppose that you are wandering across the tundra, and you find an infant, all alone, in the snow. An infant is incapable of discourse. And there is no one to conduct discourse for her. And yet, she has the same human rights as anyone who is capable of discourse. There in the snow, whether she is in Canada in 2006 or Antarctica in 2000 BC, the infant has all the human rights that anyone has in any community with any social conventions. These claims run contrary to much rights talk. They also run contrary to certain features of Harris's analysis of rights. Perhaps that is partly because, as we will see, he presents his analysis as an analysis *of* rights talk.

(i) A Sketch of the Sketch

Harris's analytical sketch supports six propositions which I will copy down here (with added emphasis) and refer to below.[3] I offer a necessarily condensed explanation of the terms of these propositions below, but I rely on the further explanation in 'Mythical Beasts' itself.

1. A person, group, corporation, people, or state is said to have a right when he, she, or it is supposed to have standing (either as principal or through a representative) to insist on something.
2. The assertion of a *strictly-correlative right* expresses the content of a duty from the point of view of the subject to whom the duty is owed.
3. The assertion of a *domain right* refers to a liberty to act or not to act, or a power to control or not to control acts of others, within a protected sphere of action.
4. The assertion of a *background right* conjoins the interest of a subject with measures that are taken to be warranted as ways of protecting or promoting that interest.
5. A '*human right*' is either (a) a supposedly universal strictly-correlative or domain right, or (b) a background right alleged to be common to all human beings living within political communities.
6. To announce that *I* (an interest) founds a human right in the second sense is to affirm (1) that *I* is of value to all human beings; (2) that *I* warrants

[3] But please note that there are no wasted words in Harris's formulation of these propositions, and I won't pretend that it is possible to understand them simply by reading the explanation that follows; it may be necessary to read 'Mythical Beasts', n. 2 above, in order to follow the discussion.

> protection and promotion by community measures; and (3) that each and every human being has standing, either himself or herself or through his or her representative, to insist that such measures be at least considered for adoption so far as that person's participation in *I* is concerned.

So three kinds of rights (strictly-correlative,[4] domain, and background rights) can count as human rights. A strictly-correlative right is a right to a specific 'action or abstention', which is a duty of the person(s) against whom the right is held. A domain right is, roughly, a freedom: an 'open-ended, unlistable domain of action reserved to one by fencing duties' (434). Strictly-correlative rights and domain rights are human rights when they are universal. Background rights, which protect interests, are human rights when the three tests in proposition 6 are met: the interest is of value to all human beings and warrants community measures, and every human being has 'standing to insist' that measures be considered.[5]

An example of a strictly-correlative right is your right not to be tortured; an example of a domain right is your right to freedom of movement; an example of a background right is your right to investigation of a criminal offence against you. Although we should avoid 'the superstition of conceptual univocalism' (430), and some theorists have made the mistake of trying to reduce all rights to one form (440), it is true that all three are related: no one can torture you without infringing your freedom of movement. And by what Harris called the 'enforcement hinge', people may acquire a background right against their government to protection from violations of their strictly-correlative and domain rights. The enforcement hinge is, as I understand it, a connection between your (strictly-correlative and domain) rights, and the responsibility of state (and perhaps other) authorities to take measures to protect those rights.[6] Other background rights, such as welfare rights, may arise from other interests.

But background rights are human rights only when there is support for them in the practices of a community. Harris called strictly-correlative and domain human rights 'universal moral rights', and he argued that background human rights are different. They have a 'historical timeframe', and do not exist 'in communities which lack conventional support' for the view that they exist; they have 'two dimensions, one conventional and one ethical' (453). Harris endorsed an ethical

[4] Harris says 'strictly' because of the resourceful tenacity with which some rights theorists hold onto the idea that rights correlate to duties (interpreting what Harris calls 'domain rights' as correlative to 'fencing duties', and what Harris calls 'background rights' as correlative to duties to promote an interest). See (432).

[5] In Harris's account, 'standing to insist' is a requirement for all rights. It is restated in the analysis of background human rights in proposition 6. I take it that Harris restates it at that point because 'standing to insist' follows from the duty to which a strictly-correlative right correlates, and it follows from the liberty to which the assertion of a domain right 'refers'. But in proposition 6, standing to insist needs to be stated independently in order to distinguish interests from rights.

[6] But I should note that Harris describes the enforcement hinge somewhat differently, as 'an evolutionary process whereby it comes to be accepted that the political community must not merely enforce but also foster the interests protected by some correlative rights' (447). So it is linked, in Harris's essay, to the conventional dimension of background rights, discussed below.

theory that he called 'natural equality', and hinted that it provided the ethical dimension for background human rights (as well as supporting strictly-correlative and domain human rights). He concluded that 'there can be universal background rights to dignity, autonomy and equality' (453); their conventional dimension consists in 'lip-service acceptance of natural equality and responsibility for the enforcement hinge' (453); there is much room for disagreement over their implications.

(ii) Rights in the Linguistic Mode

In outlining his sketch in this way, perhaps you will say that I have altered Harris's views. I have translated much of what he said into statements about human rights. He actually gave an overview not of human rights, but of 'human rights *invocations*' (428). Each of his six propositions is in the linguistic mode (by which I mean that it says something about the language of rights), rather than the material mode (saying something about rights). Proposition 1 explains when someone 'is said to have a right', and propositions 2–4 and 6 explain what is done by an assertion or announcement [2–4, 6]. The crucial Proposition 5 puts 'human right' in quotation marks, and identifies it as something supposed or alleged.

Why didn't Harris simply give an overview of human rights? Why did he write about communicative acts (invocations, assertions, announcements, allegations) and linguistic expressions, rather than about human rights? Why not simply state the conditions under which someone has a human right (thereby, incidentally, furnishing a test for the truth or falsity of human rights invocations, assertions, and so on, and for the true application of the expression 'human right')?

It may seem that he did so because, like Jeremy Bentham, he thought that there is really no such thing as human rights, but merely a lot of talk (talk that is neither true nor false, but is used as a rhetorical device free of meaningful content). But no. Harris gently derides Bentham (435–6; his gentleness is a mark of progress from Bentham's violence).[7] To Bentham, the language of rights was of serious philosophical interest, because his scepticism about rights led to the view that rights talk was 'unmeaning' (unless it could be translated into statements concerning threats of coercion[8]).

To Harris, it is clear, human rights exist. He was sometimes oblique in saying so. I think that it is implied overall by his project of making sense of invocations of human rights.[9] In any case, he came out and said that there are universal

[7] See e.g., Bentham's account of the language of rights in *Pannomial Fragments*, in *The Works of Jeremy Bentham* (J ed. Bowring, Wm. Tait, 1843), ii. II, 501. That and other features of Bentham's approach are discussed in TAO Endicott, 'Law and Language', in JL Coleman and S Shapiro (eds.), *Oxford Handbook of Jurisprudence* (OUP, 2002), 935, 939–45.

[8] So Bentham thought that the phrase 'legal rights' made sense (unlike 'human rights'), because he thought he could explain law as an expression of will backed by inducements of pleasure or pain.

[9] Cf. his discussion of 'existence conditions' for rights (456).

strictly-correlative human rights against 'gross invasions of bodily integrity' (452), corresponding domain human rights, and background human rights 'that have emerged via the enforcement hinge' (452).

I have the impression that there are at least two ways in which we could understand Harris's motivation in using the linguistic mode. First, he was genuinely fascinated by human rights talk; in one sense it *was* his research topic, and in another sense it offered a way into his *real* research topic, which (I think) was human rights. He wanted to work out how to make sense of claims people make. To Harris that did not mean (as it did to Bentham) working out what they are *really* up to when they *pretend* to assert a right. It meant trying to understand people on their own terms, if at all possible. Like H.L.A. Hart's interest in the language of *law*, Harris's interest in talk of *rights* was joined to a yen for clear thinking, and an open-minded attitude to the subject matter of the talk. While he really was interested in human rights, he set out on a research project that approached that subject matter by way of the things people say about it.

Secondly, the linguistic mode was a distancing device that enabled him to study what it would take to make a human rights claim true, without fear or favour, in a way that would make it possible to communicate both with human rights advocates and with scoffers. It was his way of being accessible to any audience.

But these are matters of motivation and tone. I propose that we can understand Harris's propositions as propositions *about rights*, and not only about rights invocations. So we can translate his propositions into the material mode. I think that Harris's argument supports these material propositions:

1. A person, group, corporation, people, or state has a right when he, she, or it has standing (either as principal or through a representative) to insist on something.
2. A strictly-correlative right reflects the content of a duty from the point of view of the subject to whom the duty is owed.
3. A domain right is a liberty to act or not to act, or a power to control or not to control acts of others, within a protected sphere of action.
4. A background right conjoins the interest of a subject with measures that are warranted as ways of protecting or promoting that interest.
5. A human right is either (a) a universal strictly-correlative or domain right, or (b) a background right common to all human beings living within political communities.
6. *I* (an interest) founds a human right in the second sense if and only if (1) *I* is of value to all human beings; (2) *I* warrants protection and promotion by community measures; and (3) each and every human being has standing, either himself or herself or through his or her representative, to insist that such measures be at least considered for adoption so far as that person's participation in *I* is concerned.

Finally, though, I should note the possibility that the linguistic mode in 'Mythical Beasts' reflects not merely the motivations I have suggested, but a genuine ambivalence about the relation between human rights and the facts of social behaviour and attitudes. Harris argues, with no ambivalence, that background human rights depend on convention (see below, section 4). But there are wider suggestions that human rights are based on social phenomena. It is hard to pin down the ambivalence that I have in mind. It is suggested in some of his statements, such as:

> If they [human rights] exist it is because there are agreed understandings of their functions and settled ontological conditions for their invocation. (431)

Doesn't the claim contradict his own view that 'universal moral rights' do not depend on agreed understandings? And how can a right be a human right if it depends on an agreed understanding or a settlement among some class of people? Ironically, here I think Harris *ought* to have spoken in the linguistic mode. The *meaning of words* (including the words 'human' and 'right') is determined by agreed understandings. If the phrase 'human rights' has a meaning, it is because there are agreed understandings as to how to use it. But the *existence of human rights* does not depend on agreed understandings.

You may disagree, and say:

1. Whether human rights exist depends *both* on the reference of the phrase 'human right', and on what exists in the world.
2. But the reference of the expression 'human right' depends on the shared understandings that determine its meaning.
3. Therefore, whether human rights exist depends on shared understandings, as well as on what exists in the world.

But this argument equivocates. It uses the word 'depends' in two different senses. Of course, whether (for example) unicorns exist does depend, in one sense, on what 'unicorns' means. But the question whether they exist can be restated without using the word 'unicorns', so in the important sense (the sense intended by someone who asks, 'do unicorns exist?') their existence does not at all depend on the meaning of the word 'unicorns'.

The suggestion of ambivalence also comes out in Harris's approach to moral scepticism. We have already seen that he argued that there are human rights. Far from being a sceptic himself, he offered the analytical groundwork for understanding claims of right, and that groundwork included a sustained defence of the idea that moral statements can be true. He defended 'Moral Truth', in a section of the same name, against John Mackie's critique of 'moral objectivity' (436). Perhaps, though, Harris was too gentle, with the result that his defence of human rights is equivocal.

Mackie thought that moral beliefs are false beliefs, but that a humane disposition 'naturally manifests itself in hostility to and disgust at cruelty and in sympathy with pain and suffering' (436–7). Harris wrote, 'I could, with Mackie, deny moral truth, but still claim that these rights ought to form part of any invented code.' (437) But he did not come out and say the obvious, which is that it would be incoherent to claim that those rights ought to form part of any invented code, and to deny moral truth at the same time. He only hinted that Mackie was clinging to a philosophical position that makes no real difference. Things are worse than that for Mackie. To make a true claim, as Aristotle said, is to claim of what is that it is.[10] If it is the case that certain rights ought to form part of any invented code, then it is true that they ought to. And if it is true, it is a moral truth. Harris would *agree* with all that, and it makes Mackie's views (as Harris presents them) incoherent.[11]

(iii) Standing to Insist

Harris borrowed the idea of 'standing to insist' (in propositions 1 and 6) 'from procedural and public law', but he used it 'in a much looser and broader sense' (431). Standing in his sense is broader because he does not mean to refer to standing to take part in legal proceedings.

But standing, in the legal sense or the loose sense, *is* a right. And in law (but elsewhere too, if we think of standing in the loose sense), a right may be *a ground for* standing to insist on something.[12] So how can the idea of standing be used to explain the nature of a right?

Moreover, standing presupposes some process. Whether in law or in the loose sense, it is a right to communicate with some decision maker (although the decision may not be judicial, or even juridical). And standing *to insist*, in particular, is an entitlement to communicate. But it makes sense to think that a person has a right, without conceiving him or her to have any entitlement to communicate. Imagine a warlord whose soldiers take hostages. He refuses to listen to representations from the hostages, and tells his soldiers to say to them, 'you have no standing to communicate with the Warlord in any way'. But he takes effective measures to see that his soldiers do not harm any of the hostages, purely because he ascribes a value to their lives that makes it unacceptable to slaughter them, no matter how convenient it would be. He respects their right to life, and his refusal to listen to them is consistent with that respect (even if he violates some other right by refusing to listen to them).

So in order to have a right, it is not essential to have standing to insist. Yet the device was so important to Harris's project that in his Manuscript he called it 'the core idiom of rights talk' [7]. How can we understand this role for 'standing'

10 Or to say of what is not, that it is not. *Metaphysics* Γ 7.27.

11 Although Mackie's 'error theory' was at least self-consistent, it is not consistent with his claim that anything 'ought' to form part of any invented morality. See JL Mackie, *Ethics: Inventing Right and Wrong* (Penguin, 1977).

12 At least, an allegation of entitlement to a remedy for infringement of a legal right (actual or threatened) gives standing in law. Of course, such a case is a trivial instance of standing. The interesting legal problems of standing arise when a party seeks standing without asserting any legal right.

in his work?[13] Perhaps it was simply an artefact of his attention to human rights *invocations*: any invocation presupposes a claim to standing in the loose sense. But Harris quite deliberately extended the idea from the conditions for a warranted invocation, to the conditions for the existence of a right. In the Manuscript, Harris began explaining the idea in this way:

> An invocation of 'rights' foregrounds the situation of someone within a normative or dialogic context. Many reasons may have a bearing on why something should be done or not done. S (the right-subject) is introduced as a focus for special attention. If he really has a 'right', then his insistence on something has some degree of peremptory force within all the flow of reasons that apply. [7]

An invocation of rights certainly does foreground the situation of the right-subject, but the force of that subject's insistence does not explain the nature of the rights. The force of the insistence depends on the force of the rights.

Imagine that as you wander across the tundra, you find the infant in the snow. I think (and aside from the idea of standing, everything in 'Mythical Beasts' suggests) that the infant has what Harris calls a strictly-correlative right corresponding to your duty not to kill her or enslave her (she has many other rights, too). But the infant is not insisting on anything. The idea of standing to insist cannot help to explain the rights of infants. What has peremptory force is not any communicative act of the infant, but the complex of moral principles and facts about the infant that would make it unjust to kill or enslave her. If the infant *were* capable of insisting, then the reasons why that complex of facts and principles has a peremptory call on you would *lend* force to her insistence. So the rights of adults (who very often are capable of insisting, and very often have standing in the loose sense to do so) are not well explained by pointing out their standing to insist; rights lend force to adults' insistence, if they do insist.

In the Manuscript, Harris offered a paradox to show that rights require standing to insist: suppose a reformer argues that education would be in the interest of women in a society, even if they do not want to be educated. To make the further claim that the women have a *right* to be educated whether they wish it or not 'would be paradoxical unless the reformer can identify some person, perhaps himself, as the true representative with standing to insist on behalf of the unwilling women' [10]. Even this conditional paradox disappears, if we think of the right of children to compulsory education. Their having such a right is consistent with their hostility to the idea. Can a reformer only claim that children have a right to it if some person has standing to insist on it as a representative? Representative standing is certainly possible, both in law[14] and in the loose sense. But people

[13] One way to understand it would be as reflecting the influence of other writers who tried to explain rights by focusing on the right-subject's claim (J Feinberg, 'The Nature and Value of Rights' (1970) 4 *J of Value Inquiry* 263–7) or choice (HLA Hart, 'Legal Rights', in HLA Hart, *Essays on Bentham* (OUP, 1982), 162–93).

[14] Examples include the standing of an advocate to address a court on behalf of a client.

(e.g. parents) who have standing in the loose sense to insist on education for children are not representatives (in the case of parents, their standing to insist in the loose sense derives from their presumptive authority over their children, which in turn derives from the children's interests and the relationship between parents and children).

Children may have a right to compulsory education even if they have no parents, or if their parents are insisting that the children go to work instead of to school. And note that, because there is no paradox in asserting that children have a right to something they despise, there is no paradox in asserting that women and men have such rights, either. Whether they have them is another question. In many cases, the claim that it is their right to have something imposed on them against their will would simply be defeated by the fact that imposing it on them would interfere unjustly with their autonomy. I think that this feature of adults' rights explains the air of paradox in Harris's scenario.

So I do not think that the idea of representative standing in proposition 6 can be extended to explain the rights of the infant in the snow. To do so, we would have to loosen the idea of representation to the point where anyone making a decision that affects a person could (should?) himself assume the role of 'representative' of that person. At that point, standing to insist has no role in explaining the nature of a right. When a reasonable person would insist on not killing the infant in the snow, we might say, the infant has a right. And then we would have to explain the right in terms of the considerations which would lead the reasonable person to insist, not in terms of any person's direct or representative standing to insist. Here, I think, is the best interpretation of Harris's use of standing: it is simply a way of indicating the peremptory force that a right lends to *anyone's* insistence on conduct in accord with the right.

I think that the idea of standing to insist is best understood as a metonymy (like saying 'the kettle is boiling', when it is really the water that is boiling). It is a metonymy for the peremptory force of the considerations that support conclusions that a person has a right. The danger of this figurative device is that it suggests that having a right involves participation in a discourse, however broad. It would be a mistake to think that. The peremptory force of the considerations that support arguments in favour of a right, along with the focus on the point of view of the right-holder toward a normative relation, is the common core of rights. Those two aspects of rights give rights talk all the sense that it has.

(iv) The Universality and the Content of Background Human Rights

In Harris's account of background human rights offered in propositions 5 and 6, I think that two important details ought to be modified. The first detail is the limitation to human beings 'living within political communities' in proposition 5; the second is the provision that a person with a background human right has standing to insist only 'that such measures be at least considered for adoption' in proposition 6.

(a) Universality and Convention

The first point arises from the special role that Harris gave to social facts in background rights. He wrote that 'human rights may derive universality either from moral truth or from convention' (453). The distinction Harris draws is between 'universal moral rights' (human strictly-correlative rights and human domain rights) on the one hand, and background rights on the other. He said that background rights have an 'historical timeframe'—that is, they depend on what is (or was) going on in a community at the time at which it is asserted that a right exists (or existed). The historical timeframe corresponds to a 'conventional dimension'[15] of community acceptance, which Harris calls 'a necessary condition for the existence of a background right' (443). Strictly-correlative and domain rights (when they are human rights) are universal, but a background right does not exist unless it is 'accepted within a community' (443).

If it is a moral truth that a right is universal, then the right is universal. But no right can gain universality from convention. There can be a convention of treating a right as universal, but that does not make the right universal. If the infant in the snow has any rights, they do not have a conventional dimension. Harris would presumably say that her right not to be killed is a 'universal moral right'. But it seems to me that she has what Harris called a background right to your help (if you are able to help). The reasons for which she has that right have nothing to do with any historical timeframe or convention. She has it, in fact, for the same reasons that give her the rights that Harris called 'universal moral rights'. If there are human rights that are background rights, it is because there are interests that are of value to all human beings.[16] And it seems to me obvious that there are such interests. Harris wrote, 'That is a breathtakingly bold ethical claim,' (444) yet, as he says:

> During the last 50 years, canonical proclamations have come into being, claiming that some background rights are enjoyed by all human beings simply by virtue of their humanity. For that reason 'human right' has the sense expounded in proposition 6, as well as standing for universal, inter-personal moral rights. (445)

Harris seems to have been saying that those proclamations supply the global community with the 'conventional dimension' for human rights claims. I think that it would be better to say that the reason that people have background human

[15] It might be called something like a 'social-fact dimension'. Harris explained that it might include authoritative proclamation in a community, and not only convention.

[16] At least, that is part of the reason; it also depends on whether those interests can ground duties in others.

rights has nothing to do with any proclamation: if people have such rights they have them (as Harris reported the proclamations as claiming) simply by virtue of their humanity.

The infant in the snow has a background right to receive help. It really is a human right: the infant has it just by virtue of being human, and not by virtue of the fact that any community accepts it. It *is* conditional on the capacity of some person or institution to assist. But if you come along in your parka, with your sled piled with the equipment to keep people safe and well in the wild, then simply in virtue of her humanity, there is peremptory reason to help her. That reason to help her can well be described as a right of the infant. It has no conventional dimension.

(b) A Right to Consideration?

A background human right is extremely weak in Harris's account, since it is only a right to *consideration* of the right holder's interest (see proposition 6).[17] But I think that human rights advocates claim more than that. People who 'announce that *I* founds a human right' typically mean to assert that (some) measures must be taken, at least in some circumstances. So there is a rare dissonance between human rights talk and Harris's conclusion. Perhaps Harris had in mind the fact that public provision of certain goods is simply inappropriate or even impossible in some social circumstances. Then, you might say, people have no general right to such provision, but only a right that, as Harris said, 'measures at least be considered'—considered, that is, in light of the facts that determine whether it is feasible to deliver the measures, and in light of the value in making other use of the resources that the measures would require.

Remember the infant in the snow, who has a background right to assistance. The duties correlative to that right are conditional on people's capacity and circumstances. You have no duty to provide (and she has no right to) assistance that you cannot give. One way of expressing the conditional nature of the right to assistance would be to say that the infant has a right that measures should be considered. But to express it in that way would be misleading, because she has more than that: not just a right that you should consider carrying her to safety, but that you should do so if you can.

Public lawyers are familiar with the way in which a duty to consider can be transmuted into a duty to do the right thing (start by saying that the consideration has to be in good faith, then add that it must exclude irrelevant considerations and be reasonable, then say that is not reasonable if it exaggerates the importance of some consideration...). Harris did not explain whether background human rights include standing to insist on the *appropriate emphasis* being put on the relevant considerations. That is what I think it would take to make sense of

[17] Although there are suggestions elsewhere that to have a background right is to have standing to insist on *measures* (440).

background human rights claims: no one claiming such a right would be happy to say that the right has been observed if a decision maker considered measures and decided to take none because he misjudged their feasibility.

If we revise the right to consideration of measures so as to add a right to *due* consideration, as I think we must, then a background human right entails a right to the taking of particular measures in the right circumstances. When the conditions are met, the right is not satisfied by mere consideration.

These points concerning background rights raise a more general puzzle: if, in Harris's view, those rights are based on *convention*, and the subject only has standing to insist on *consideration* of measures, why does Harris think that some of them are worth calling 'human rights'? Moreover, he explains that the outcome of a successful invocation of a background right is 'an all-things-considered judgement in which the cited right may be weighed against... considerations having nothing to do with rights' (440). At this point, perhaps Harris really is saying something about human rights discourse, and not about rights at all. No decision of right weighs the right against open-ended considerations having nothing to do with rights. So perhaps Harris's discussion of background human rights is best understood as an argument that they are not human rights at all, but that the discourse can be understood as a metaphorical extension of the language of human rights, which applies non-figuratively only to what he calls 'universal moral rights'. I will argue in section (vi) that some human rights talk is metaphorical; but also that some background rights are human rights in a focal, non-figurative sense.

(v) Natural Equality and its Pragmatic Foundation

Natural equality, Harris says, is:

> the ethical theory that, whatever treatment is due to *X*, nothing less is due to *Y* on the ground that *Y* is a different kind of human being from *X*. Its pragmatic foundation derives from the technology of modern worldwide communication. (438)

There is a great deal packed into the phrase 'different kind'. Unpacking it would mean dealing with the old problem of anti-discrimination law: 'different kind' needs to be understood not to apply where, for example, you are deciding whom to hire for a job and *X* is the kind of human being who is good at the job, and *Y* is the kind of human being who is not. But the idea is still clear: equality among human persons is the basis of strictly-correlative and domain human rights ('universal moral rights'), and provides the 'ethical dimension' for background human rights.

Two objections can be made to Harris's use of this idea. One is that, although he suggests that it is part of the basis of human rights, he does not need it for his conclusions, and it does not help to support them. The other is that it does not have (and does not need) the 'pragmatic foundation' that he says it has.

(a) The Role of Natural Equality

Natural equality was an element in the 'minimalist conception of justice' that Harris developed in his book *Property and Justice*.[18] The *other* elements in that conception were 'the value of autonomous choice' and 'the banning of unprovoked invasions of bodily integrity'. Consider that those other elements provide grounds for the universal strictly-correlative and domain rights that Harris asserted in 'Mythical Beasts'. And consider that those values can generate background rights by way of the 'enforcement hinge' that Harris explained in 'Mythical Beasts'. Consider also that a less minimalist account of human interests would form the basis for a richer understanding of rights that might have attracted Harris himself, if he had not been engaged in mediating between human rights advocates and scoffers.

Once we consider all that, it seems to me that no task remains for natural equality to perform. Natural equality itself remains, of course: every human being is naturally equal to every other human being in respect of being human. But that tautology is not needed to support any claim of right. It could, you might say, support a claim of right in the following way: 'since Alvin has right *a* just because of his humanity, and Susan is naturally equal in that respect, Susan has right *a*'. But it is not needed to support the claim that Susan has right *a*, precisely because the reasons for saying that Alvin has right *a* are also reasons for saying that Susan has right *a*. Those reasons can be offered (with no mention of Alvin, or of equality between Alvin and Susan) in support of the claim that Susan has right *a*. Any sound claim of right would be supported by the elements in a conception of justice that Harris offered as separate elements in *Property and Justice*.

(b) Its 'Pragmatic Foundation'

Why did Harris say of natural equality that 'its pragmatic foundation derives from the technology of modern worldwide communication' (438)? It seems to me that if you and your family are nomads travelling the tundra and you come across another family of nomads, you are capable of seeing their natural equality to you, and you are responsible for seeing it (and refraining from torturing or enslaving them . . .). If natural equality has a pragmatic foundation, isn't it simply the human capacity to understand that other people are human too, and have the needs and interests that human beings have? Perhaps modern technology makes it less convenient (far from impossible, as Harris points out) to pretend that things are otherwise.

So we might say that the human capacity to recognize other human beings as human is a pragmatic foundation (and it can be pragmatically shored up by social and cultural and technological conditions that make it embarrassing or inconvenient to

[18] JW Harris, *Property and Justice* (Clarendon Press, 1996), 171.

pretend that other human beings are less than human). But a foundation for what? It is not a foundation for natural equality, or for rights. The people coming toward you across the tundra have interests, as a result of which it would be wrong to torture or to enslave them (interests in autonomy and in bodily integrity, to use only the abstemious elements of Harris's minimal conception of justice). That is the case because they are human beings, and it needs no pragmatic foundation in order for it to be the case. Natural equality (and human rights) need no pragmatic foundation, but *respect for* natural equality and the *observance* of human rights do need such a foundation. Without the foundation of recognition, it is observance of human rights that will tumble down (and not their existence). If the people coming across the tundra are to get past you without being tortured or enslaved, they may need to trust either to your capacity to see them as human beings or to their superior firepower. But their rights do not depend on your capacity, any more than they depend on relative firepower.

Perhaps we can say that the pragmatic foundation Harris has in mind is a foundation not merely for human rights observance, but also for human rights *discourse*? Invoking human rights loses its communicative point, you might say, if the conditions for effective communication are absent; and those conditions include what it takes for people to grasp what you are saying when you invoke a human right. That explains Harris's emphasis on the technology of modern worldwide communication (but he could have added all sorts of other features of culture in this century), which may give invocations of human rights a communicative potential that they would not have had in, say, ninth-century Europe. If that is the case (but I do not know that it is), then the technology is not a pragmatic foundation for natural equality, but a pragmatic foundation for success in communicating about it.

(vi) In What Sense Are Human Rights *Human*?

The following question really is a question of social convention: what does the phrase 'a human right' mean? By ordinary rules of English phrase construction, it refers to a right that can be qualified as human. And to qualify a right as human is presumably, at least, to qualify it as a right of (that is, held by) humans. But that is all that the language gives us, and it is unspecific. The rules of the English language do not specify the relationship between a human right and humanity. If we want to make something of the phrase, we need to assert our ancient liberties as English speakers, and specify the qualification in a way that will make it into a useful tool for practical discourse (and for reasoning with ourselves). Should we say that a right is a human right if it is held by a human? Then your right to be paid your salary is a human right, and that would not give the phrase any distinctive value for our purposes. It would not be much more useful to say that a human right is one that you hold *because* you are human. We would still find a very difficult problem in distinguishing human rights from other rights: any good explanation of your right to your salary will either include the premise that you are a human being, or presuppose it.

Harris can help us here: we can use the term for a right 'enjoyed by all human beings simply by virtue of their humanity' (445). There are two ways I can think of in which we could unpack the word 'simply'. The first is to abstract from all the particular *facts about you* that give you rights that other human beings do not have, and to say that human rights are those that all human beings share in virtue of their humanity. The second is to abstract from all the particular *facts about a social or political situation* that give you the rights that you have, and to say that human rights are those that you have not as a result of any human artifice, or custom, or attitude, or declaration, or any other contingency, but because of some feature of your nature as a human being that ground duties on the part of others. I think either form of abstraction is a fair way of using the phrase 'human right'. Either way, your right to your salary is not a human right, although it may be grounded on certain human rights. On the second form of abstraction, human rights are natural rights (they are rights that you and I have because of our human nature, and not because of any human action or disposition). On the first form of abstraction, they are general enough to be held by all human beings.

Harris was comfortable with the idea of natural rights: considering arguments that we should avoid the term 'natural right' because it carries weird metaphysical baggage, he said, 'I cannot see what the fuss is about' (435):

> for someone who has overcome any philosophical queaziness about the idea of moral truth and of a universal and timeless code that confers rights, there ought to be no further ontological problems. (436)

So with a light touch he set aside the fear and loathing of metaphysics that both energized and disfigured twentieth-century moral philosophy: '[u]niversal strictly-correlative and domain rights "exist" because, supposedly, we have sound ethical arguments to back them up' (436).

If a human right is a natural right, then 'Human Rights Act 1998' and 'European Convention on Human Rights' are misnomers, because most of the rights in the Convention are civil rights—moral rights that you and I have in a particular form of civil society (and which the law ought to protect in such a society). The infant in the snow is human, but she does not have a right to freedom of speech unless she is part of a society in which free speech has some meaning and some value. And the family you meet on the tundra have no right to a trial before an independent and impartial tribunal: if you think that they have stolen your food, then you ought to treat them fairly (by listening to anything they may have to say about it, if it is feasible to communicate with them) before you exact a remedy for the putative wrong. But they have no right to a hearing before an independent tribunal, even if one should come over the horizon. The rights protected by the European Convention on Human Rights are (by and large) moral rights that correspond to the ways in which public authorities in communities, such as the member states of the Council of Europe, ought to treat people today. They are not rights that people have simply by virtue of their humanity. We cannot even say that they are rights that all civil societies ought to respect: the particular ways in which a community ought to protect free speech vary from one community to another quite dramatically, and perhaps there have been decent communities, which show appropriate respect for their members, but which allow nothing recognizable as freedom of speech.

But in my view, the background right that the infant in the snow has to your assistance is a central case of a human right. Conditional as it is on your capacities and her need, it is a right that she has simply because she is a human being. Just for that reason, her need will pre-empt other considerations in your thinking, if you are reasonable. So it is simply irrelevant whether the tundra where you meet her is in Canada in 2006, or Antarctica in 2000 BC; her background right (contrary to Harris's argument) has no conventional element at all.

I do not think that this view is more faithful to human rights discourse than Harris's. It leads to the conclusion that some welfare rights are paradigms of human rights, while rights of freedom of expression, privacy, and assembly, and rights to vote, and rights to independent tribunals are not human rights at all, except in a distantly metaphorical sense. Moreover, in this way of understanding human rights, they can be explained with no reference at all to state authorities (though state authorities may have various special roles in observing and promoting some of them). In the modern discourse, human rights are often characterized as being held against state and quasi-state authorities. Human rights talk these days starts from the supposition that freedoms and process rights and political rights are paradigms of human rights, and that it is deeply problematic whether any welfare rights are human rights.

Perhaps the controversies over welfare rights in states arise not from the fact that there are no human rights to welfare, but from the conditional nature of those rights. Go back to the tundra; now instead of you, your sled, the infant, and snow reaching to the horizon, imagine that the infant's parents are there too (but they are in some sort of difficulty) and her big sisters, and representatives of the Red Cross and other voluntary organizations are nearby, and a United Nations outpost, and your own cold and hungry children, and other people like you who want your help to build shelters because a storm is coming. And timber wolves are attacking the Red Cross representatives, and the UN outpost is on fire. Now the situation is complicated (but I think that it is not nearly as complicated as the situation faced by political authorities in any state). It may become obvious that the infant has no right to your assistance—or it may become a very complex and difficult question. Her conditional right to assistance, and your correlative hypothetical duty, may or may not ground any actual duties on your part.

This view of rights has important implications for understanding relations among the rights that Harris identified. His analysis has the virtue of showing that strictly-correlative and domain rights are connected to background rights; he suggested that background rights arise out of strictly-correlative and domain rights by way of the 'enforcement hinge'. But there is another connection: strictly-correlative rights and domain rights themselves arise in the same way as background rights, out of background interests. A person's special interest in bodily integrity is the ground of the strictly-correlative right that Harris identifies, not to be subject to violent infringements of that integrity. Background rights are based on interests of people and, whenever they are human rights, they have no conventional aspect, for the same reason that (as Harris says) strictly-correlative and domain human rights have no conventional aspect. While it is true that people have many different interests in different cultures, the rights that they have simply because they are human arise out of the interests that they share because they are human.

(vii) Conclusion

In this chapter I have only been trying to test Harris's inventive techniques, and a small group of his provocative conclusions. For the reasons I have tried to explain, I think that the six propositions can be reshaped as follows (taking them out of the linguistic mode, replacing the idea of standing with a direct reference to peremptory force, and reformulating background rights to remove the 'conventional dimension'):

1. A person, group, corporation, people, or state (the subject) has a right when an interest of the subject is a reason for action in favour of the subject regardless (to some extent) of (some[19]) other considerations.
2. A strictly-correlative right reflects the content of a duty from the point of view of the subject to whom the duty is owed.
3. A domain right is a liberty to act or not to act,[20] within a protected sphere of action.
4. A background right conjoins the interest of a subject with measures that must be taken to protect or promote that interest regardless (to some extent) of (some[21]other) considerations.

[19] Here is why these disappointingly open-ended parentheses are needed: you have a right to my turning up at the pub when I promised to do so; it is (normally) a reason for me to turn up regardless of the fact that, as I discover, *The Simpsons* is on TV just then. Your right is *not* a reason for me to turn up regardless of the fact that I discover that I need an operation this very afternoon for appendicitis. In that case, I can leave you sitting at the pub looking at your watch without infringing your right. I think we have to read a qualification of that kind to the phrase 'standing to insist' into Harris's own formulation: you do not have standing to insist that I come to the pub in an emergency.

[20] I have removed 'or a power to control or not to control acts of others' from Harris's formulation, because it seems to me that not all such powers are rights (and to the extent that such powers are entailed by the liberty, they go without saying).

[21] See n. 19 above.

5. A human right is either (a) a universal strictly-correlative or domain right, or (b) a background right common to all human beings.
6. *I* (an interest) founds a human right in the second sense if (1) *I* is of value to all human beings; (2) *I* warrants protection and promotion; and (3) there is reason to take measures to enhance every human being's participation in *I* regardless (to some extent) of (some[22]) other considerations.

Harris is a model of care and seriousness in his approach to making sense of human rights claims. He is also optimistic about that task. The core meaning of 'human right' lies in its use to refer to rights that persons have simply because they are human. Except as a metaphor, I cannot make sense out of claiming a right, as a human right, when the claim depends not simply on your being human, but on attitudes in the culture in which you are making the claim—on whether the people of the community accept the claim. Though, of course, language is flexible enough that the phrase can be used to mean 'rights of great importance to humans in some situation', or 'rights that are specially endangered by oppressors who are not merely selfish, but inhumane', or even 'rights considered to be important to human beings'. Using the phrase in such ways may be rhetorically effective for some purpose (or it may backfire). It carries with it the virtue and the danger of metaphors. The virtue is to highlight a likeness. And the attitude of a torturer bears a certain likeness, in its disregard of human interests, to the attitude of a government that allows wire-tapping in fraud investigations when it is not necessary, or fails to provide good procedure in coroners' inquiries into deaths, or levies retroactive taxes. The danger is that the metaphor is indiscriminate. It masks differences.

Early in his paper, Harris suggested that 'practising lawyers' need to solve the problems of the existence of human rights that he addresses. He rejected the idea that 'opinions can be written and advice given without troubling ourselves with such deeper questions' (429). But, fortunately for their clients, I think that lawyers can give good advice on the effect of the Human Rights Act and the European Convention for the Protection of Human Rights without having done the remarkable things that Harris did in 'Mythical Beasts', and even while having no view whatsoever on whether human rights exist, or while taking the view that it is all malarkey. Even the latter sort of lawyer will merely think of those instruments as misnamed—not as being senseless or as having no effect.[23]

So I am not as concerned about the need to make sense of human rights discourse as Jim was (I think that legal and political practice can carry on with a considerable amount of extravagantly metaphorical or even false or even meaningless discourse). And I am not as optimistic about the prospects. But you may

[22] See n. 19 above.

[23] Harris added that '[i]nternational agencies are committed to projects which would be senseless if there were no such thing as human rights' (428). I think that those projects are not at all senseless—only radically misnamed in a way that may or may not be important.

prefer Jim's optimism, and I find it attractive. It fits his approach to his life and to his work. If you have seen him lecture, or present papers at conferences, you will know that he did so with a bright smile on his face. The smile would evolve through varieties of enjoyment of this irony or that, through wry amusement at the views of this author or that, to transparent pleasure at the understanding that he found it possible to reach. At that point he would be gleeful. The evolutions of his physiognomy reflected a generosity to the audience, and to people whose ideas he was dismantling. I think that explains his conclusions in 'Mythical Beasts', and in the manuscript: Jim was able to make sense of what people say because he was so generous. He lost none of that generosity in the ordeal he went through when he was ill. His work in writing 'Mythical Beasts' for us was, I think, an instance of it.

18

Matter Matters

*Bernard Rudden**

(i) Introduction

I used to live in North Oxford and liked to walk home by paths which avoid the stench of traffic on the main road. Frequently, at the end of a working day, I would meet Jim Harris as he left his college and set out on the same peaceful route; he would put his arm through mine and we would stroll home together. One of the many things we had in common was that we had both been solicitors and so, naturally enough, we would swap stories of our most memorable moments in practice, and brood over the fact that, so far as our clients were concerned, much of the advice we handed out was both entirely correct and—in Jim's words—'mumbo-jumbo'. We would wonder why some institutions took so long to change, why, when they did so, they were so complex, and, for ourselves, why we thought they should, or should not, be so reformed.

In these discussions we each seemed to assign the other a role: Jim was the one who was well read in philosophy and ethics, while I was supposed to know bits and pieces of the law of other countries. He would cite J.S. Mill to the effect that 'the only purpose for which power can be rightfully exercised over any member of a civilized community, against his will, is to prevent harm to others. His own good, either physical or moral, is not a sufficient warrant.'[1] I would point out that a precisely similar proposition was enacted as law in eighteenth-century Prussia.[2] So our conversations were sometimes fanciful: that is to say we felt under no obligation to be punctiliously accurate, but instead were free to speculate and, above all, to discover that we knew very little and understood much less. In memory of a dear friend and fine scholar, I try now to recall the kind of things we used to say.

* Professor of Comparative Law, Emeritus, in the University of Oxford, and a Fellow of Brasenose College.

[1] JS Mill, *On Liberty* (1859) (ed. M Warnock, Fontana, 1962), 135.

[2] Allgemeines Landrecht für die Preussischen Staaten 1794, I 3 27: *Niemand darf den Andern, etwas zu unterlassen, blos aus dem Grunde zwingen, weil der Handelnde dadurch sich selbst schaden würde.* (No one may compel another to refrain from something solely on the grounds that, by acting, he may harm himself.) From Prussia the provision finds its way into Dalmacio Veléz Sársfield's 1871 Argentine Civil Code (Art.911).

In the late 1950s I was a solicitor in an English county town, and well remember many of my clients. With the young couple who had just married and bought their first house, I conscientiously went through the deeds, explaining that they now held their home 'on trust to sell the same' and meanwhile had just leased it to the local Building Society for three thousand years. I then consoled them with the news that the conveyance expressly confirmed their full power to mortgage, charge, or otherwise dispose of the house during the lifetime of the descendants then living of Her Majesty Queen Victoria and a period of twenty-one years thereafter.

Even more memorable was the advice I had to give the young woman who came to consult me, her jaw all swollen. 'My husband kicked my teeth in', she mumbled. I was obliged to tell her that she could not claim compensation from him for her injuries unless her teeth were false, in which case she could, of course, recover their value by an action under the Married Women's Property Act of 1882. In England this situation lasted until the Law Reform (Husband and Wife) Act 1962, and most women throughout Europe and the Americas would have found themselves constrained by similar, if not identical, attitudes, customs, and laws. The supremacy of the male as husband and father was embedded in the legal system and was justified by philosophers and priests. In Rousseau's *Social Contract*, women are mentioned only in passing, twice to consider their fecundity, once to exclude them, along with children and slaves, from the census of citizens.[3] In his *Metaphysics of Morals*, Kant explains why women, like servants and children, lack civil personality.[4]

The listing of women alongside these other categories was repeated in a lawsuit which Jim Harris and I, both members of the Law Society, knew well. At the beginning of the last century the profession set its face adamantly against women solicitors. This was not easy because the Solicitors Act 1843 required the admission of 'any person' who satisfied certain conditions, and furthermore the wretched statute's interpretation clause stipulated that 'every word importing the masculine gender shall extend and be applied to a female'. When Ms Bebb—an Oxford graduate—was forbidden to sit the professional examinations, her action for a declaration and mandamus was decisively defeated by the Law Society's three silks, who had little difficulty in persuading both Joyce J and a unanimous Court of Appeal to rely on Coke's citation from the Mirror of Justices: '*fems ne poient estre attorneyes, ne enfans, ne serfs*'.[5]

This linking of women with children and serfs prompted us to attempt a rough list of the groups which seem to have attracted the most law reform. Many of the

[3] J-J Rousseau, *The Social Contract* (Wordsworth Classics, 1998), 49, 50, 91.

[4] I Kant, *Metaphysics of Morals* (trans. Mary Gregor, CUP, 1996), 92.

[5] *Bebb* v *Law Society* [1914] 1 Ch 286 (Cozens-Hardy, Swinfen-Eady, Phillimore LJJ affirming Joyce J). Co.Litt 128a: 'women cannot be attorneys; neither can children nor serfs'. The Society admitted women in 1919, possibly in return for its acquisition of disciplinary powers previously exercised by the High Court.

reform movements overlapped but, adopting a very rough chronological order for initial developments in this country, the categories affected seem to be: slaves, children, animals, women, and homosexuals. Broadly speaking, similar legal changes in all these fields have taken place in the richer countries of the world during the last couple of centuries. Most of these movements involved considerable dispute, and in all of them, much of the impetus for legal reform stemmed from ethical and moral propositions which were advanced in, and have gained ground since, the late eighteenth century.

(ii) Law and Ethics

(a) Slaves

The nineteenth-century abolition of slavery is something of which we readily approve, although from Aristotle to Grotius slavery was accepted as 'natural'.[6] Indeed, in the year after the US Thirteenth Amendment (1865) the Holy Office in Rome published a statement claiming that, under proper conditions, the practice was not 'against the natural and divine law' and, so fortified, the large Catholic country of Brazil maintained the institution of slavery until 1888.[7] Nowadays, however, it is universally condemned by international and constitutional law and, though said to be still practised in some poor countries, is nowhere lawful.[8]

(b) Children

While slavery was dwindling in the developing economies of the West, children were still working up chimneys, down mines, and in factories, or were contributing to the family income on the farm. Here is Rousseau: '*Je vois dans vos campagnes de grands garçons labourer, biner, tenir la charrue, charger un tonneau de vin, mener la voiture tout comme leur père; on les prendroit pour des hommes, si le son de leur voix ne les trahissoit pas.*'[9] Their economic importance to the American family was noted by Adam Smith: 'a numerous family of children, instead of being a burthen, is a source of opulence and prosperity to the parents. The labour of each child, before it can leave the house, is computed to be worth a hundred pounds clear gain to them. A young widow with four or five young children . . . is there

6 Aristotle, *Politics* (trans. TA Sinclair, Penguin, 1964), 34 (Book I chap. 5); Grotius, *de Jure Belli ac Pacis* (1625) 'that slavery should have its origin in human act, i.e. contract or tort, is not repugnant to natural justice' (trans. F W Kelsey, Bobbs-Merrill, 1925), 3.7.1, and cf. 2.5.27.

7 G O'Collins SJ and M Farrugia SJ, *Catholicism* (OUP, 2003), 342.

8 Universal Declaration of Human Rights 1948, Art.4; European Convention on Human Rights 1950, Art.4(1).

9 JJ Rousseau, *Emile* (1762) (Collection Complète des Oeuvres de Jean-Jacques Rousseau, Geneva 1782), viii 3–4: '[i]n your countryside I see big boys digging, hoeing, ploughing, loading a barrel of wine, driving the cart just like their father. You would take them for men if the sound of their voices did not give them away.'

frequently courted as a sort of fortune.... The value of children is the greatest of all encouragements to marriage.'[10] For the community as a whole, children were an economically important source of future labour-power and parental support, so, given the high rates of infant mortality, society had, for centuries, responded by encouraging their birth. The point was made explicitly in 1923 by the Soviet feminist, Alexandra Kollontai: '[t]he woman must observe all the requirements of hygiene during pregnancy, remembering that during those months she does not belong to herself, that she is working for the collective, that from her own flesh and blood she is producing *a new unit of labour*'.[11]

The birth of children was encouraged by a variety of means: religion, ethics, custom, convention, and law. Thus the Code of Canon Law of the Roman Catholic Church of 1983 adverts to 'the fact that marriage is a permanent partnership between a man and a woman, *ordered to the procreation of children* through some form of sexual co-operation'.[12] In his book on Aquinas, John Finnis states that

> the intrinsic point of marriage includes procreation, which is primary at least in the sense that without procreation (and the complex and ambitious project of raising of children which is procreation's completion) the other aspects of marriage's points and marriage's other benefits, would provide no sufficient ground for marriage's characteristic unity, exclusiveness, and permanence. So their sexual acts will not allow spouses to experience and actualize their *marriage* unless they are acts of the procreative type.[13]

For the same reason, some religions set their face against contraception and, even more adamantly, against abortion. In the USA, Utah—where 69 per cent of all residents are Mormons—produces 90 children annually for every 1,000 women of childbearing age, whereas Vermont—the first state to embrace same-sex marriage—produces 49.[14] In 2002, shortly before becoming Turkey's Prime Minister, Recep Tayyip Erdogan railed against contraception as 'straight-out treason to the state'. 'Have babies', he told a cheering crowd. 'Allah wants it.'[15]

The importance of children to the economy was, of course, reflected in the law. On the negative side, contraception, abortion, and homosexual acts were forbidden in many countries, while social and legal barriers kept women out of the professions. On the positive side, several systems provided that the income of a child's property flowed upwards to the parents during their lifetime, and this was balanced by reserving to the children an indefeasible right to a portion of the parents' capital on their death.[16] In this country, from 1602 to 1949, the Poor

[10] A Smith, *The Wealth of Nations* (1776) (Everyman's Library, 1991), 62.

[11] A Kollontai, *Women's Labour in Economic Development* (Pamphlet, 1921) (emphasis added); extracted at RA Schlesinger, *The Family in the USSR* (Routledge Kogan Paul, 1949), 54.

[12] Art. 1096(1), emphasis added.

[13] J Finnis, *Aquinas: Moral, Political, and Legal Theory* (OUP, 1998), 150.

[14] P Longman, *The Empty Cradle* (Basic Books, 2004), 34.

[15] Ibid., 39.

[16] For instance, French *Code civil*, arts. 382 (formerly 384), 913; California Civil Code art.197. See also BGB, arts.1601, 1619, 2303 ff.

Law made it 'the duty of the . . . child of a poor, old, blind, lame or impotent person, or other poor person not able to work, if possessed of sufficient means, to relieve and maintain that person'.[17]

In England, Peel's Act of 1802 begins the slow process of limiting children's hours of work. The reform movement is expressed, no doubt quite sincerely, as stemming from a concern for child welfare. Peel's statute is called 'The Health and Morals of Apprentices Act', and it is followed by a score of later measures which both extend protection and provide for some form of education.[18] Some time after developments in France and Germany, our 1870 Education Act introduces the notion of compulsory schooling and the leaving age is gradually raised from 12 to 14 to 16. The process is fortified by criminalizing parents whose children regularly play truant.[19] School teachers cannot use corporal punishment, and at the time of writing Parliament is debating whether to forbid parents to smack their offspring.[20] Meanwhile, children are already protected from glue, tobacco, harmful publications, tattooing, being hypnotized in public, and riding a horse, pony, mule, or donkey on a road without protective headgear.

(c) Animals

The development of the rich countries' attitudes to, and laws on, animals is extremely complex, since their ethical, social, and legal attitudes have seen great changes and bitter conflicts in the last couple of hundred years. True, from early times, an important role has been played in the visual and mythical world of a people by the image of a particular beast—Rome's wolf, Russia's bear, China's dragon, our own Lion and Unicorn (they are always picturesque, if rarely edible), while, from Aesop onward, animals have enlivened many a moral tale. Actual living specimens, however, were rarely accorded much sympathy. So 1800 saw the failure of even a modest Parliamentary attempt to ban bull-baiting, and the same is true of Thomas Erskine's Cruelty to Animals Bill of 1809 (whose promoter kept two pet leeches, named after famous surgeons of the day). But cattle were given some statutory protection in 1822, and two years later the Society for the Prevention of Cruelty to Animals was founded, a Society whose growing public approbation was signalled by Royal patronage in 1840. Since then, as we all know, general sentiment has changed profoundly, from the first Cat Show of 1871 to the recent declarations of 'animal rights' and even, in their defence, to violence by some humans against others.[21]

[17] Poor Relief Acts 1601 s.7 to 1930 s 14(1). Repealed by the National Assistance Act 1948, s.42 of which makes the parents liable to maintain each other and the children.

[18] For a superb account, see Part IV of S Cretney's *Family Law in the Twentieth Century: a History* (OUP, 2003).

[19] Education Act 1996 s.444.

[20] Education Act 1996 s.548; Children Bill 2004 cl. 49. The notion would have astonished the jurist who wrote the leading treatise on 'The Slap': S Stryk *Tractatio juridica de alapa* (Halle, 1735).

[21] The history is well summarized in M Radford, *Animal Welfare Law in Britain: Regulation and Responsibility* (OUP, 2001), ch. 3.

If we attempt a general glance at the law on all this, we see a number of features. First of all, in legal (as opposed to scientific) discourse, humans are not animals; or rather, the category of animals is defined—or deemed—to exclude us. It is true that Ulpian seems to have begun his Institutes by reminding the reader that we and the other species are subject to the same law—we are born, we breed, we die—and this finds its way into Justinian.[22] But the rest of the basic text is resolutely anthropocentric, and we are soon told that law exists 'for the sake of persons'.[23]

The word 'persons' leads to a second feature of the modern law of animals, namely, that it betrays a certain hesitation about assigning them to an appropriate meta-category within the legal order. The dilemma does not, of course, greatly trouble most common lawyers, by whom it is hardly perceived as a problem, but it does seem to exercise those of a more orderly cast of mind, above all where their private law is codified. We should first of all recall that for centuries in medieval Europe, non-human living creatures, including insects, were treated as property until they misbehaved, whereupon they could be regarded as 'persons' in the eyes of the penal law, subjected to formal trial, given counsel to act in their defence, and, if found guilty, punished by banishment or execution. To modern eyes this looks both preposterous and cruel, yet their treatment was similar to that of human miscreants: they were equal before the law.[24]

This practice had withered before the age of codification and, dating from 1804, we find that the French Civil Code classifies animals as property (*biens*). They can therefore be treated as well or as badly as any other of our belongings and are also 'things' (*choses*) whose custodian must answer for any damage they cause.[25] They can be 'property' for the purposes of our Theft Act 1968[26] and our Criminal Damage Act 1971[27], and are 'agricultural products' for that of the European Community's Common Agricultural Policy.[28] The most systematic of civil codes, the German, treated them as things until its enigmatic amendment of 1990 which declares that '[a]nimals are not things. They are protected by special laws. The current provisions on things apply to them unless otherwise declared'.[29] The new Russian Civil Code of 1996 classifies animals (*zhivotnye*) as 'objects' (*ob'ekty*), states that the general law of property applies unless specifically excluded, but forbids the cruel or inhumane exercise of one's rights over them.[30]

[22] D 1 1 3, J Inst. 1 2 pr.

[23] Justinian Inst. 1 2 12. Gaius, Inst. 1 1 starts straightaway with humans—'*omnes populi*'.

[24] See JEP Evans, *The Criminal Prosecution and Capital Punishment of Animals* (Faber & Faber, 1987).

[25] *Code civil*, arts. 524, 1384.1, 1385. In the Swiss Civil Code they are also treated as *choses* (Art. 719.3).

[26] S.4(4).

[27] S.10(1).

[28] EC Treaty Art 32(1); in 1997, however, 'animal welfare' was added to the list of Community concerns: Protocol No. 33 annexed by the Treaty of Amsterdam to the EC Treaty.

[29] Art. 90a.

[30] Art. 137.

These last two, very general and recent, provisions may be evidence of a movement in the more orderly systems towards the creation, as part of their normative default structure, of a separate category for animals, outside the traditional trio of persons, things, and (trans)actions. In the American context, the desirability of such a reform has been most tenaciously argued by Gary L Francione,[31] although the standard commentary on the German text cited above describes it as mere 'sentimental rhetoric'.[32]

Meanwhile, the ordinary citizen might think this all very well, but would want to see specific and detailed rules to protect animals from humans in a whole range of activities, scientific, agricultural, sporting, and domestic. There are such safeguards in the other legal systems, but we need turn only to a common law country where there is nothing but specific and detailed regulation: it is estimated that currently in the UK there are some three and a half thousand such provisions in force. Each deals with a particular area of activity and so most of them have to define the word 'animal' differently. 'Animal' may mean any living vertebrate other than Man; it may mean any kind of mammal other than Man; it may include birds and reptiles but not fish. The details will readily and readably be found in specialized works, but my favourite definition is that of the Animals Boarding Establishment Act 1963. This takes several pages to tell us we have to get a licence to run such an establishment and ends by saying that 'in this statute "animal" means any dog or cat'.[33]

Not only is the category of 'animal' defined in dense and differing detail, but human conduct towards them is also subjected to scrupulous distinctions. Rarely are we forbidden to kill them, at least if they are not uncommon, they are ours, and we do not hurt them. But as our attitudes change, perhaps our statutory provisions may become more general. The first sentence of the Protection of Animals Act 1911 (which will not be repeated here) is, at 330 words, much longer than the Gettysburg Address. That of the Wild Mammals Protection Act 1996 is almost as dogged: '[i]f, save as permitted by this Act, any person mutilates, kicks, beats, nails or otherwise impales, stabs, burns, stones, crushes, drowns, drags or asphyxiates any wild mammal with intent to inflict unnecessary suffering he shall be guilty of an offence'. The latest Amendment Bill will replace it by the following: '[a]ny person who intentionally causes undue suffering to any wild mammal shall be guilty of an offence'.

Behind these legal provisions, general and particular, lies a whole host of human attitudes, movements, groupings, programmes, and disputes. Some are on the higher plane of 'rights theory', including Francione's agile arguments that animals should not be classified as things.[34] Others are subject to political

[31] See n.34 below.

[32] '*Eine gefühlige Deklamation*'. O Palandt, *Bürgerliches Gesetzbuch* (57th edn., Munich, 1998), ad 90a.

[33] S.5(2).

[34] GL Francione, *Rain without Thunder: the Ideology of the Animal Rights Movement* (Temple UP, 1996).

practicalities, such as the notion that we can ban the minority pastime of fox-hunting because it hurts the fox, but not the much more popular sport of coarse fishing, on the overt grounds that we do not know that the (inedible) roach suffers pain.

(d) Women

The legal status of women has changed only in the last century and a half. They have gained access to universities and the professions (except, in some religions, the priesthood or the higher clerical offices). French women got the vote in 1944, Argentinian women in 1947, Chilean women in 1949, Greek women in 1952, and the Swiss had to wait until 1971.[35] Over much the same period, most wives acquired the freedom to choose their surnames and their professions, the entitlement to a greater share of their husband's property on his death or on divorce, and (at least in theory) the right to equal pay and equal treatment in employment. Divorce has been made easier and the unmarriage recognized by such devices as the 'civil solidarity pact' of the French.

Particularly striking has been women's gain of control over their reproductive process: abortion, once a wrong, is now their right, and in the USA it is their constitutional right not to tell their husbands about it.[36] The Supreme Court has found this in the due process clause of the Fourteenth Amendment to the Constitution, while European countries have, on the whole, worked through the legislator. Nonetheless, in interpreting the French legislation, the Conseil d'Etat has held that, during the first ten weeks of pregnancy, it is for the woman, and for her alone *'d'apprécier elle-même si sa situation justifie l'interruption de la grossesse'*.[37]

(e) Homosexuals

Of the categories under discussion, this has seen the most recent, and rapid, changes: in linguistic sensitivity, in media treatment, and in law. The word itself—appearing for the first time in the English version of Krafft-Ebing's *Psychopathia Sexualis* (1892)—is becoming distasteful, while the older slang is even less acceptable. Most important in legal terms has been the removal of any criminal stigma. This occurred in 1967 in England, and later in other parts of the UK and the British Isles (under pressure from the European Court of Human Rights).[38]

[35] See J-J Halpérin, *Histoire des droits en Europe de 1750 à nos jours* (Flammarion, 2004), 209–10.

[36] Justice Sandra Day O'Connor, writing for the Court, in *Planned Parenthood of Southeastern Pennsylvania* v *Casey* 505 US 833 (1992).

[37] 'to decide for herself whether her situation justifies the termination of pregnancy'. CE, 31 Oct. 1980, rec. 403, l'arrêt *Lahache*; D 1981 38, concl. Genevois; Loi 75–17 du 17 janvier 1975 relative à l'interruption volontaire de la grossesse.

[38] Sexual Offences Act 1967 s.1 *Dudgeon* v *UK* (1981) 4 EHRR 149; *Norris* v *Ireland* (1988) 13 EHRR 186.

But in the USA, it was not until 2003 that the Supreme Court struck down a state law making it an offence to 'engage in deviate sexual intercourse with another person of the same sex'. This provision was held to be an undue restriction on the exercise of liberty under the due process clause of the Fourteenth Amendment, whose drafters, according to Justice Kennedy, 'knew that times can blind us to certain truths, and later generations can see that laws once thought necessary and proper in fact serve only to oppress'.[39]

On the positive side, the principle of non-discrimination on the grounds of sexual orientation (absent from the European Convention on Human Rights) is enjoined by Article 21 of the European Charter of Human Rights. It has also been put into practice by a number of decisions both of the European Court of Human Rights and of national courts. For instance, in England, partners of the same sex can benefit from the Rent Act protection originally designed to cover spouses, and the refusal of a Chief Constable to appoint as a woman police officer a transsexual who had undergone gender reassignment has been held a breach of the Sex Discrimination Act 1975.[40] The issue of gay marriage, however, remains highly contentious, being described in 1998 by a Lord Justice of Appeal as 'fundamentally abhorrent' to the common law.[41] It is permitted in Canada, about to be introduced in Spain, and some US officials have performed same-sex marriage ceremonies, though (at the time of writing) their validity is being litigated. Meanwhile, some of the states have already amended their constitutions in an attempt to make such marriages impossible.[42] New South Wales, by the way, has made it a crime to subject homosexuals to public ridicule or to express in public serious contempt for their lifestyle.[43]

(iii) Matter and Muscle

In greater or lesser degree the law reforms affecting the five categories discussed above have a number of features in common. First, they have been, and some still are, deeply contentious. Secondly, they have provoked cascades of litigation, legislation, and executive action. Thirdly, the reform movements and the surrounding public debates have been largely conducted in terms of ethics, morality, philosophies, in short of *ideas*. If we take animals as an example, we find many thinkers concentrating on the mental, not the physical, abilities of other species. For Thomas Hobbes it is important that 'they have little or no foresight of time to

39 *Lawrence* v *Texas* 123 S Ct 2472 (2003), 2484.

40 *Ghaidan* v *Godin-Mendoza* [2004] UKHL 30; *A (Respondent) v Chief Constable of West Yorkshire Police (Appellant)* [2004] UKHL 21.

41 *S-T (formerly J)* v *J* [1998] Fam. 103, *per* Ward LJ at 141.

42 Alaska Const. Art I sec. 25 (1998); Nebraska Const. Art I sec 29 (2000); Hawaii Const. Art I sec 23 (2000) now authorizes the legislature to reserve marriage to opposite-sex couples.

43 NSW Anti-Discrimination (Homosexual Vilification) Amendment Act no. 97 1993, Sched. 1 49ZT, 49ZS.

come'.[44] John Locke points out that they 'have no power of abstracting', and 'no use of words or other general signs'.[45] Schopenhauer avers that they 'lack conceptions, that is abstract ideas', Hegel that they 'cannot think'.[46] As to reform movements, Alan Watson, in his foreword to a book on animal rights, says that 'social revulsion to oppression . . . may be swift and driven by an *intellectual idea*'.[47]

It is, of course, both true and obvious that argued ideas are the proximate cause of much law reform. But what provokes the birth of these ideas? Has no part been played by innovations in our technology, in our mastery of matter? Is it not possible that Marx was basically right, and that developments in our ethical and legal perceptions are, in the end, intuitive, if complex, responses to changes in the relations of production in our society? Not in the neat rhythms of commanding classes that he envisaged, but in a more profound though less articulate way, with all the lags and conflicts that beset the attempt to live solely in the world of ideas.

One of the main tenets of that raw and fleering work on *German Ideology* is that:

> the production of ideas, of conceptions, of consciousness is at first directly interwoven with the material activities and the material intercourse of men, the language of real life. Conceiving, thinking, the mental intercourse of men appear at this stage as the direct efflux of their material behaviour. The same applies to mental production as expressed in the language of politics, laws, morality, religion, metaphysics etc. of a people. Morality, religion, metaphysics, all the rest of ideology and their corresponding forms of consciousness . . . have no history, no development; but men, developing their material production and their material intercourse, alter, along with this their real existence, their thinking and the products of their thinking. Life is not determined by consciousness but consciousness by life . . . . It must not be forgotten that law has just as little an independent history as religion.[48]

Treated with the intellectual rigour of a Jim Harris, Marx's proposition is open to at least two objections. First, it does not attempt to explain the causal process by which material change leads to a different mental, ethical, and legal outlook. Secondly, the whole thesis itself, being part of human consciousness, must ultimately be determined by the underlying mode of production: the thesis itself is thus a member of the set which it is seeking to delineate. Confronted with these

[44] T Hobbes, *Leviathan* Part 1, sec. 12, in Sir William Molesworth (ed.) *Collected English Works of Thomas Hobbes of Malmesbury*, (John Bohn, 1839), iii, 94.

[45] J Locke, *Essay concerning Human Understanding* (1689), *Works of John Locke* (Printed for W Otridge *et al.*, 1812), i, 139.

[46] A Schopenhauer, *The World as Will and as Idea* (1819) (trans. RB Haldane and J Kemp, Kegan Pual, Trench, Trübner, 1896), ii, 228. GWF Hegel, *Lectures on the Philosophy of History* (1840) (trans. J Sibree, HG Bohn, 1857), 73.

[47] G L Francione, *Introduction to Animal Rights: your child or the dog?* (Temple University Press, 2000), p. ix (emphasis added).

[48] K Marx and F Engels, *The German Ideology* (Laurence & Wishart, 1965), 37–8, 90. Written in 1845–6, the full text was not published until 1932 (German), 1933 (Russian).

difficulties, one can either grapple with the problems or ignore them. The latter plainly being the coward's way, I shall continue to take it, and shall simply state the obvious.[49]

In order for humans to survive they must always have food, and must usually have clothing and shelter. Providing these invariably and incessantly requires that we move matter (including ourselves) from one place to another. The most immediate, and accessible, way of doing this is to use muscle-power, whether our own or that of others. The obvious others are slaves, servants, family, and animals. There have then occurred changes in the means of production (natural resources, sources of energy, the technology available, and so on). These alter the way in which human beings direct the movement of matter from one location to another, whether it be earth in the cornfield, bricks to a kiln, buttons on a shirt, or ourselves from suburb to city. Having, in the 1760s, invented (or at least greatly improved) the steam-engine, James Watt needed a way to rate its capacities and, by observing horses at work in the mines and mills, first defined 'horse-power' as the amount of matter, by weight, moved a given distance in a given time (33,000 foot-pounds per minute). About a century later his steam-engine was followed by that other great matter-mover, the motor vehicle's internal combustion engine, whose performance was still measured in horse-power. At about the same time came overhead electricity conductors, and every light-bulb to this day recalls the name of Watt.

These discoveries wrought enormous changes in our everyday life, so it seems quite possible that they also provoked developments in our perceptions of right and wrong. Further, that these responses may not be clearly and consciously perceived as such; that is to say, we may take for, and compliment ourselves on, greater understanding or greater virtue, what are in fact just intuitive reactions to changes in the way we move matter around. The intellectual processes involved may well be slow and uneven so that some of our attitudes, or the views of some of us, may be, as it were, the deposits of earlier stages of production. In short, it may be worth asking whether the rapid and profound changes in our treatment of the categories outlined above are not, in the end, the result of developments in technology. Marx himself points the way when he remarks that 'slavery cannot be abolished without the steam-engine and the mule and spinning jenny'.[50] Indeed, long before him, Aristotle had reached a similar conclusion: '[s]uppose that every

[49] In his *Grundrisse*, Marx acknowledges that 'the really difficult point . . . is how the relations of production develop unequally as legal relations. Thus, for example, the relation of Roman private law to modern production': *K. Marx, Grundrisse der Kritik der Politischen Ökonomie (Rohentwurf)* (trans. M Nicolaus, Pelican, 1973), 109. The point is further developed by Engels in his letter to J Bloch of 1890 (Marx and Engels, *Selected Works*, (Foreign Languages Publishing House, 1950), ii, 488. Later stalwarts of Marxism repeat the materialist doctrine but tend to assert, rather than explain, the causal process: see for instance VI Lenin *The Three Sources and Three Component Parts of Marxism* (*Selected Works* (Progress Publishers, 1963, revised 1976), 45; JV Stalin, *Marxism and Problems of Linguistics* (Foreign Language Press, 1972), 8–9; H Marcuse, *Soviet Marxism: A Critical Analysis* (Pelican Books, 1971), 39.

[50] *German Ideology*, n. 48, above, 56.

tool we had could perform its function either at our bidding, or itself perceiving the need. Then . . . masters would have no need of slaves'.[51]

Before the arrival of the steam-engine most matter was moved by muscle, and that of slaves, serfs, servants, and domestic animals was most completely at their masters' disposal. So it is not surprising to find Aristotle describing 'slaves by nature' and observing that 'the use of slaves hardly differs at all from that of domestic animals; from both we derive what is essential for our bodily needs'.[52] Children are the next most likely source of muscle-power; as soon as they can walk they can look after the barnyard fowl, can then progress to heavier tasks, and the poor man who is without slaves, or is even a slave himself, can always produce them. Provided, that is, that he has the services (willing or not) of a woman.

The importance of children as an energy supply, coupled with the high rate of infant mortality, means that the fertile woman's main task is to bear them. It thus seemed 'natural' and right, on the one hand, to deny her access to the distractions of other activities and, on the other, to believe in the wickedness of, and to make unlawful, contraception, abortion, and homosexuality. Malthus, for instance, was deeply (and, it turns out, unnecessarily) concerned about the growth in population, and brooded on possible ways of restraining it. But the methods just mentioned were dismissed with the comment: 'as to unnatural passions and improper arts to prevent the consequences of irregular connections—these evidently come under the head of vice'.[53]

Since then, while there are still ethical, and above all religious, disagreements about these practices, on the whole the law has removed all sanction. The story can be seen most clearly in the decisions of the US Supreme Court, which has held invalid and unconstitutional state laws banning contraception (1965), abortion (1973), and homosexual activity (2003). Interestingly enough, this last case supports the view advanced here. Justice Kennedy, writing the opinion of the Court, states that 'early American sodomy laws were not directed at homosexuals as such but instead sought to prohibit *non-procreative* sexual activity more generally'.[54]

What the United States has done by judicial fiat, other industrialized countries have achieved by legislation, executive action, and economic pressures. Modern capitalism may be efficient, but it erodes individual incentives to invest in children by offering competing and more lucrative uses of time and money and by appropriating most of the human capital produced by parents. One legal response has been to remove or limit the child's automatic entitlement to a share of their deceased parents' estate, as has happened, for instance, in Mexico, Panama, and Nicaragua.[55] The human response is not to have children, and the

[51] *Politics*, above, n.6, Book I, ch. 4, 31. [52] Ibid., 34.

[53] T Malthus, *A Summary View of the Principle of Population* (1824) (Mentor Books, 1960), 38.

[54] *Griswold* v *Connecticut* 381 US 479 (1965) and *Eisenstadt* v *Baird* 405 US 438 (1972); *Roe* v *Wade* 410 US 113 (1973); *Lawrence* v *Texas* 123 S.Ct 2472 (2003), 2479.

[55] MC Mirow, *Latin American Law* (U Texas Press, 2004), 208.

instruments of their unbirth—contraception and abortion—are now blessed by the law. The use of contraceptives, once a sin and in some countries a crime, is nowadays a good thing. The termination of pregnancy is not a wrong but a right. In Romania, in 2003, 162,000 babies were born; there were 170,000 abortions.

In the developed countries nowadays, successful men seem to have more sex and more sexual partners than their less successful peers, but produce fewer offspring. Those who devote themselves full-time to raising children get no wages and must forego the chance to earn elsewhere, while much of their children's future income will, through tax and national insurance levies, be spent on others who are not parents. As Phillip Longman puts it, 'we are headed for a future in which only rich people will be able to afford to raise and educate a child and rich people, generally, are not much interested in the work. If they were they would not be rich.'[56]

Of course there are undoubted satisfactions in having children. They are a source of pride, they provide affection, companionship, and an entry to similar social groups. But so also do pets. Developed societies no longer use animals to move people and things from one place to another. No longer are the ploughs pulled by oxen, the loads carried and commuters transported by beasts of burden. The replacement of horse power by other forms of energy means that the only live animals that most of us encounter are our own, or our friends', pets. In his remarkable study of *Man and the Natural World*, Keith Thomas points out that 'the triumph of the new attitude was closely linked to the growth of towns and the emergence of an industrial order in which animals became increasingly marginal to the processes of production'.[57]

We could say the same of children, and the Office of National Statistics tells us that, in 2003, the common names for human babies—things like Molly, Chloe, Ben, and George—are also among the top fifteen names for cats, and the top thirteen for dogs. Our pets now have their own toys, their own Christmas presents, we have bereavement counsellors to comfort us in their loss, and some courts will award monetary compensation for the grief we suffer if they are injured by another's fault.[58] I sometimes suspect that nowadays, children, pets, and endangered species have all come to be treated in much the same way. Californian law permits twenty or more citizens or residents to 'form a corporation for the prevention of cruelty to children or animals or both'.[59] I have a T-shirt inscribed 'Save the Badgers'. My oven-glove says 'Save the Children'.

56 *The Empty Cradle* (Basic Books, 2004), 145.

57 K Thomas, *Man and the Natural World: Changing Attitudes in England 1500–1800* (Penguin Books, 1983), 181.

58 For instance, Tr. Gr. Inst. Caen, 30 Oct. 1962, D 1963 J 92; *Campbell* v *Animal Quarantine Station* 63 Haw. 587, 632 P 2d. 1066 (1981).

59 California Corporations Code s.10400.

James W. Harris 1940–2004

The eldest of three children, Jim Harris was born in Southwark during the first months of the Second World War. He lost his sight at the age of four, which led to him receiving his education first at Linton Lodge School and then The Royal Worcester College. He always spoke in high regard of the inspirational teaching from which he benefited, particularly at the former. In 1959 he went up to Oxford to study at Wadham College. Despite his blindness, he both rowed in a Gentleman's VIII and rode in a riding club based on the Port Meadow. He soon won a reputation for brilliance across the University and took a First in Finals, but did not head straight into academia. He first qualified as a solicitor before returning to Oxford to read for the B.C.L., and his practical experience of lawyering added an earthy dimension to his refined scholarly work. His first academic position at the London School of Economics led to him teaching, among others, Cherie Booth. While at the L.S.E. he pursued the Ph.D, which was later to become *Law and Legal Science*. For a short time, he found himself in the unusual position of acting as his own supervisor when a colleague left, transferring all his graduate students to Harris, including Harris himself.

In 1968 Jim Harris married José (née Chambers), a distinguished Oxford historian. This was a marriage of great hearts and minds. Their son Hugh became an officer in the Royal Navy. In 1973, Jim was appointed to a Fellowship at Keble College, Oxford, where he was to remain for the rest of his career. As a young Fellow in the mid-1970s he caused consternation in the Senior Common Room with a proposal that women should be allowed to dine in college without restriction, but the proposal was carried by the casting vote of the Warden, Denis Nineham. He was later a strong supporter of the decision to admit women students in 1979. As a keen traveller, Jim had no hesitation in accepting invitations to teach and research in Sydney, Hong Kong and Princeton. Possessed of a strong Christian faith throughout his life, he remained an active member of the Anglican church right up until his death in March 2004.

Jim Harris published across a formidable array of subjects. His first book, on *Variation of Trusts* (1975), was followed by the monograph *Law and Legal Science* (1979). In the latter book, he voted with Kelsen for a concept of legal science based on a hierarchy of duties, with powers characterized as conditional duties. He was even more insistent than Kelsen on the splitting of legal and moral categories of obligation. If this put up a wall against natural right theories of law, it also left open a path to conventionalist justifications of obligation that Jim would explore in his later work. Jim Harris's jurisprudence added to the imposing body of theoretical inquiry animating the Oxford Law Faculty. It was, however, his next three books that captured his unique style of reasoning and exposition best, and which won him international fame. *Legal Philosophies* (1980) was a textbook in legal theory comprising short polished essays on leading figures and schools of thought. The reader quickly perceived that the author was in complete mastery of a vast and intricate literature of law, philosophy, and politics, and many of the essays are original contributions to the subject. The style itself was a delight; Jim made the austere thoughts of his subjects, from Aquinas to Weber, live as if the ideas themselves were actors on a stage, vociferously arguing and gesturing. Jim had been a keen actor in his youth and, had it not been for the loss of his sight at an early age, he might have pursued the stage as an alternative career.

In 1991 Jim took on the fourth edition of Sir Rupert Cross's classical text on precedent, and made it even better. *Cross and Harris On Precedent in English Law* is regularly cited by the courts, perhaps unaware of the precipitous philosophical issues raised by seemingly simple questions of why, how, and when one court ought to obey the authority of another.

Property and Justice, published in 1996, may be counted as Jim Harris's masterpiece. It established him as the most distinguished theorist of property of our time. Jim's deep knowledge of the fine details of property law allowed him confidently to transcend the technicalities so beloved of lawyers and yet harness the creativity of the common law tradition in order to drive the inquiry further than any property theorist before him. No one else could have blended so many strands of learning so elegantly and so productively.

Jim's answer to the analytical question, 'What is property?', consciously departed from Hohfeld's celebrated correlative rights scheme, which disintegrated property into a series of personal rights and duties; and also differed from Honoré's influential approach, which was to isolate and list 'standard incidents' of property, being largely the interlocking indicia of control. These two approaches align with realist and civilian modes of analysis, modes that Jim, with his roots in the English common law, appreciated but did not follow. Instead Jim identified two core qualities of property, being a spectrum of control powers over a resource, whether tangible or not; and trespassory rules identifying the right to exclude others from use and control. He did not argue that his method of analysis falsified past theories, but he did suggest that his approach avoided some circularities, and, though simple, still managed to capture most of what was interesting and unique about property rights as they appear in juristic and common practice.

How, then, could the institution of property be justified? Jim's book assayed the classical justificatory theories from Locke and Hegel through to modern-day libertarian and utilitarian approaches, and after just appraisal he rejected monochromatic theories as either wrong, exaggerated, or incomplete. His destruction of Lockean theories of property as based on labour, desert, or creation without wrong to others was particularly powerful and convincing. Instead of postulating his own coercively deductive theory, he used a series of imagined utopias to show how one might choose various internal or external perspectives on how to allocate resources. Ultimately Jim defended a liberal theory of justice that prized and protected freedom and individuality, and, given what we know of human psychology, history, and convention, he argued that robust property institutions served the goal of promoting a just society. His employment of social convention to ground theoretical claims was subtle and original. He concluded that one could demand as a requirement of justice that a society should afford and protect property rights, always remembering that such rights were no absolutes. As he wrote, 'Property is just, to a degree, sometimes'. He concluded that the ability to command property rights was an essential attribute of any decent liberal society, though he was deeply aware of the imperfections and injustices of property-holding societies.

Jim's attainments were recognized by his election as a Fellow of the British Academy and his award of the Oxford Doctorate of Civil Law. But these formal recognitions do not begin to capture the impact he had. His scholarly imagination and flair were critical to the intellectual flourishing of his colleagues and students in Oxford and beyond. By 2000 his graduate class in property theory had emerged as one of the most exciting places to learn in Oxford or anywhere, and his unrivalled qualities as a teacher and mentor became legendary. All who knew him prized his intellectual and emotional honesty, his lively company, and his unquenchable reserves of kindness.

His first phase of property analysis was summed up in his British Academy Maccabean Lecture of 2001, but it soon transpired that he had conceived a new horizon—to investigate how property rights and other conventional legal rights coalesced with the new discourse of human rights in Britain and indeed all over the world. His disciplined curiosity remained unabated throughout his final illness. He delivered a fascinating lecture to the Society of Legal Scholars in Oxford in September 2003 on how 'human rights' might avoid becoming noisy 'mythical beasts' signifying nothing. He came from the hospital bed to meet that particular lecturing commitment, and the brilliance of the lecture transfixed his large audience. He was able to develop his lecture into a major article in the *Law Quarterly Review* that was published shortly after his death. This last contribution now evokes not only admiration but also a sense of wonder at the thought of what Jim was set to achieve in his last great project.

Bibliography of the works of James W. Harris

BOOKS

Variation of Trusts (Sweet & Maxwell, London, 1975)

Law and Legal Science (Clarendon Press, Oxford, 1979)

Legal Philosophies (Butterworths, London, 1980, 2nd edn., 1997)

Cross and Harris: Precedent in English Law (4th edn., Clarendon Press, Oxford, 1991)

Property and Justice (Clarendon Press, Oxford, 1996)

(Edited) *Property Problems: From Genes to Pension Funds* (Kluwer Law International, London, 1997)

PRINCIPAL ARTICLES

Ten Years of 'Variation of Trusts' (1969) 33 *The Conveyancer and Property Lawyer (NS)* 113–134, 183–202

'Trust, Power and Duty' (1971) 87 *Law Quarterly Review* (*LQR*) 31–65

'When and Why Does the Grundnorm Change?' (1971) 29 *Cambridge Law Journal* (*CLJ*) 103–133

'Kelsen's Concept of Authority' (1977) 36 *CLJ* 353–363

'The Concept of Sovereign Will' [1977] *Acta Juridica* 1–15

'A Structuralist Theory of Law, an Agnostic View', in A. Podgorecki and C.J. Whelan (eds.), *Sociological Approaches to Law* (Croom Helm, London, 1981), 33–43

'Olivecrona on Law and Language—The Search for Legal Culture' (1981) 94 *Tidsskrift for Rettsvitenskap* 625–646

'Can You Believe in Natural Law?' (1981) 44 *Modern Law Review* (*MLR*) 729–735

'Ownership of Land in English Law', in N. MacCormick and P. Birks (eds.), *The Legal Mind: Essays for Tony Honoré* (Clarendon Press, Oxford, 1986), 143–161

'Kelsen and Normative Consistency', in R. Tur and W. Twining (eds.), *Essays on Kelsen* (Clarendon Press, Oxford, 1986), 201–228

'Legal Doctrine and Interests in Land', in J. Eekelaar and J. Bell (eds.), *Oxford Essays in Jurisprudence* 3rd series (Clarendon Press, Oxford, 1987), 167–197

'Connaissance Juridique (Theorie de la)', in A.J. Arnaud (ed.), *Dictionnaire Encyclopedique de Theorie et de Sociologie du Droit* (Libraire Générale de Droit et de Jurisprudence, Paris, 1988), 60–64

'Unger's Critique of Formalism in Legal Reasoning: Hero, Hercules and Humdrum' (1989) 52 *MLR* 42–63

'Kelsen, Revolutions and Normativity', in E. Attwooll (ed.), *Shaping Revolution* (Aberdeen University Press, Aberdeen, 1991), 1–16

'Towards Principles of Overruling—When Should a Final Court of Appeal Second Guess?' (1990) 10 *Oxford Journal of Legal Studies* (*OJLS*) 135–199

'The Privy Council and the Common Law' (1990) 106 *LQR* 574–600

'Murphy Makes it Eight—Overruling Comes to Negligence' (1991) 11 *OJLS* 416–430

'The Basic Norm and the Basic Law' (1994) 24 *Hong Kong Law Journal* 207–230
'Private and Non-Private Property: What is the Difference?' (1995) 111 *LQR* 421–444
'Who Owns my Body?' (1996) 16 *OJLS* 55–84
'Kelsen's Pallid Normativity' (1996) 9 *Ratio Juris* 94–117
'Overruling Constitutional Interpretations', in C. Sampford and K. Preston (eds.), *Interpreting Constitutions: Theories, Principles and Institutions* (Federation Press, Sydney, 1996), 231–247
'China, Hong Kong and Divided Sovereignty after 1997', in W. Krawietz, E. Pattaro, and A.E.-S. Tay (eds.), *Rule of Law: Political and Legal Systems in Transition* (Duncker & Humblot, Berlin, 1997), 325–333
'Is Self-Ownership a Human Right?', in B. Galligan and C. Sampford (eds.), *Rethinking Human Rights* (Federation Press, Sydney, 1997), 172–188
'What is Non-Private Property?', in J.W. Harris (ed.), *Property Problems: From Genes to Pension Funds* (Kluwer Law International, London, 1997), 175–189
'Legal Positivism', in P. Newman (ed.), *New Palgrave Dictionary of Economics and Law* (Macmillan, Basingstoke, 1998), ii, 545–548
'Justice, Informality and Home-Sharing', in P. Jackson and D. Wilde (eds.), *Contemporary Property Law* (Ashgate, Aldershot, 1999), 96–119
'Is Property a Human Right?', in J. McLean (ed.), *Property and the Constitution* (Hart Publishing, Oxford, 1999), 64–87
'Doctrine, Justice, and Home-sharing' (1999) 19 *OJLS* 421–452
'Inheritance and the Justice Tribunal', in S. Munzer (ed.), *New Essays in the Legal and Political Theory of Property* (Cambridge University Press, Cambridge, 2001), 106–137
'Rights and Resources—Libertarians and the Right to Life' (2002) 15 *Ratio Juris* 109–21, and in A. Soetman (ed.), *Pluralism and Law* (Kluwer, Stuttgart, 2003), i, 76–85
'Property—Rights in Rem or Wealth?', in P. Birks and A. Pretto (eds.), *Themes in Comparative Law: In Honour of Bernard Rudden* (Oxford University Press, Oxford, 2002), 51–63
'Reason or Mumbo Jumbo: The Common Law's Approach to Property' (2002) 117 *Proceedings of the British Academy* (The Maccabaean Lecture 2001), 445–475
'Retrospective Overruling and the Declaratory Theory in the United Kingdom: Three Recent Decisions' (2002) 26 *Revue de Droit de l'Université Libre de Bruxelles* 153–181
'Human Rights and Mythical Beasts' (2004) 120 *LQR* 428–456

Index of Names